The I-Series **SECOND EDITION**

Computing Concepts

Complete Edition

The I-Series

SECOND EDITION

Computing Concepts

Complete Edition

Stephen Haag

Daniels College of Business
University of Denver

Maeve Cummings

Kelce College of Business
Pittsburg State University

Alan I Rea, Jr.

Haworth College of Business
Western Michigan University

Boston Burr Ridge, IL Dubuque, IA Madison, WI New York San Francisco St. Louis
Bangkok Bogotá Caracas Kuala Lumpur Lisbon London Madrid Mexico City
Milan Montreal New Delhi Santiago Seoul Singapore Sydney Taipei Toronto

THE I-SERIES: COMPUTING CONCEPTS, COMPLETE EDITION

Published by McGraw-Hill/Irwin, a business unit of The McGraw-Hill Companies, Inc., 1221 Avenue of the Americas, New York, NY, 10020.

This book is printed on acid-free paper.

domestic 1 2 3 4 5 6 7 8 9 0 QPD/QPD 0 9 8 7 6 5 4 3
international 1 2 3 4 5 6 7 8 9 0 QPD/QPD 0 9 8 7 6 5 4 3

ISBN 0-07-283411-0

Editor-in-chief: *Bob Woodbury*
Senior sponsoring editor: *Donald J. Hull*
Associate sponsoring editor: *Craig S. Leonard*
Developmental editor: *Gina M. Huck*
Manager, Marketing and Sales *Paul Murphy*
Senior producer, Media technology: *David Barrick*
Lead project manager: *Mary Conzachi*
Manager, New book production: *Heather D. Burbridge*
Photo research coordinator: *Jeremy Cheshareck*
Photo researcher: *Jennifer Blankenship*
Senior supplement producer: *Rose M. Range*
Senior digital content specialist: *Brian Nacik*
Cover design: *Asylum Studios*
Interior design: *Mary L. Christianson*
Typeface: *10/12 New Aster*
Compositor: *ElectraGraphics, Inc.*
Printer: *Quebecor World Dubuque Inc.*

Library of Congress Cataloging-in-Publication Data

Haag, Stephen.
Computing concepts : complete edition / Stephen Haag, Maeve Cummings, Alan I. Rea, Jr.—2nd ed.
p. cm. — (The I series)
ISBN 0-07-283411-0 (alk. paper) — ISBN 0-07-121467-4 (international : alk. paper)
1. Electronic data processing. I. Cummings, Maeve. II. Rea, Alan I. III. Title. IV. Series.
QA76.H215 2004
004—dc21

2003054084

INTERNATIONAL EDITION ISBN 0-07-121467-4

www.mhhe.com

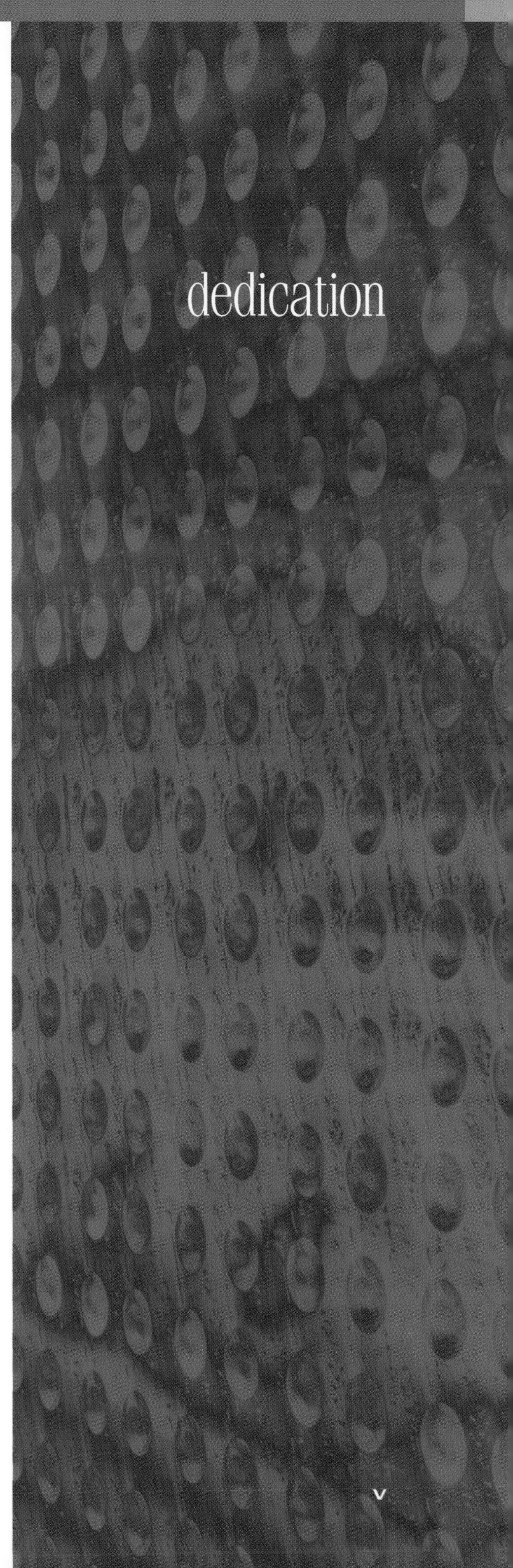

dedication

For Pam, my companion and soul mate.

STEPHEN HAAG

To Elizabeth Dolores: In the successes of your life may you find joy and fulfillment; in your failures, humor and wisdom.

MAEVE CUMMINGS

For my wife, Lynda. You are phenomenal.

ALAN I REA, JR.

THE I-SERIES: IT'S ALL ABOUT PRODUCTIVITY

The I-Series is a collection of more than 20 books designed to help you deliver exceptional quality in the classroom as you teach technology concepts and personal productivity skills. If you choose to cover just personal productivity skills, you can select from among numerous titles within *The I-Series* on Microsoft Word, Excel, PowerPoint, Access, Outlook, Windows XP, and Windows 2000. You can also choose from among two different volumes of Microsoft Office 2003 that include several of the software tools listed above.

If you integrate the teaching of technology concepts with your personal productivity skills, then you'll want to evaluate our two editions of *The I-Series: Computing Concepts*. The first (Introductory Edition) is 11 chapters and takes your students from personal technologies up through databases and database management system software and finally emerging technologies. The second (Complete Edition) is 15 chapters and includes additional chapters on systems development, programming, organizational information systems, and decision support systems and artificial intelligence.

Regardless of which you choose, both contain an appendix on the history of computing, an appendix on building a Web site with HTML, and an introduction to our *Life-Long Learning Modules,* which appear on the Web site for this text at www.mhhe.com/i-series.

The I-Series: Computing Concepts is built entirely around one theme—**productivity.** While providing your students with the most current and relevant information technology content, *The I-Series: Computing Concepts* couches every single topic within the context of your students' productivity.

But what is productivity? How can you ensure that your students are learning more than just definitions and lists of advantages and disadvantages?

Within the context of productivity, we believe your students should learn about technology and then be able to answer one or more of the following questions.

1. **What can I now do with technology that will make me more efficient and effective?** This will make your students productive users of technology.
2. **How am I better prepared now to make a purchasing decision?** This will make your students productive consumers of technology.
3. **How much more do I now understand about the role of technology with respect to ethics, security, and privacy?** This will encourage your students to use technology in an ethical way.
4. **What can I now envision of future uses of technology?** This will enable your students to become productive managers of technology as it changes on a daily basis.
5. **How can I continue to learn about technology once my class ends?** This will transform your students into life-long learners.

Throughout this text, your students will indeed learn important definitions related to technology concepts, and they will learn lists of advantages and disadvantages related to those technologies. Even more important, with every major technology topic, your students will be able to answer one or more of the five questions in a very positive way.

To help you foster this productivity theme, we've included several key pedagogical elements, including:

- *New!* **I-Can** boxed elements
- *New!* **Student Learning Outcomes**
- **Practically Speaking** boxed elements
- **I-Series Insights: Ethics, Security & Privacy** boxed elements
- **Life-Long Learning Modules**
- **End-of-Chapter Activities**
  - **Level 1 Multiple Choice and True/False Questions**
  - **Level 2 Questions and Exercises**
  - **Level 3 Hands-On Projects**
    - **E-commerce**
    - **Ethics, Security & Privacy**
    - **On the Web**
    - **Group Activities**

POWERFUL PEDAGOGY REINFORCES STUDENT PRODUCTIVITY

To support the productivity theme within *The I-Series: Computing Concepts,* your students will encounter and—we believe—enjoy a number of pedagogical elements.

New! I-Can Boxed Elements

The I-Can boxed elements directly address your students' productivity. In these, your students will learn about vitally important topics such as:

- Organizing files
- E-resumes
- Ergonomics
- Firewalls

New! Student Learning Outcomes

To provide a "road map" that your students can use as they read through and learn the material, we've provided a set of Student Learning Outcomes at the beginning of each chapter. These are very student-centric. They do not represent your teaching goals or the goals of the chapter; rather they clearly identify what your students should know and/or be able to do.

Practically Speaking Boxed Elements

The Practically Speaking boxed elements take a pragmatic approach to the discussion of technology. Some of these include:

- Selecting a cell phone
- Computer forensics
- Internet addiction
- Virtual reality applications

I-Series Insights: Ethics, Security & Privacy Boxed Elements

Reviewers have consistently told us that ethics, security, and privacy are key concerns. So, we've woven discussions of these important topics into each chapter as well as included a complete chapter on ethics, security, and privacy. Within the I-Series Insights: Ethics, Security & Privacy boxed elements, your students can learn more about such topics as:

- Dot-cons
- Implant chips
- E-commerce trust
- Offensive e-mail

Life-Long Learning Modules

Just because your students complete your course doesn't mean that they stop learning. That's why we created (and will provide continuous updates to) five *Life-Long Learning Modules* (LLLs) on the Web (www.mhhe.com/i-series). These include:

- LLL/a Enhanced Web Development
- LLL/b Care and Feeding of Your Computer
- LLL/c Careers in Information Technology
- LLL/d New Technologies Impacting Your Life
- LLL/e Computers in Your Life Tomorrow

End-of-Chapter Activities

Reading is seldom enough for your students to actually learn and synthesize key terms and concepts. In addition to a chapter-opening crossword puzzle and a page of Level 1 multiple choice and true/false questions, we've created six pages of activities at the end of each chapter.

Level 2: Review of Concepts

The Level 2 questions and exercises focus on getting your students to practically apply what they've learned in a chapter. There are two pages of these questions and exercises at the end of each chapter. Some of these include:

- Understanding ethics
- Spreadsheet formulas and functions
- File storage
- Organizing information with XML

Level 3: Hands-On Projects

We also ask your students to roll up their sleeves and apply their newly gained knowledge or perhaps even find new information. Each of these hands-on project sets is a full page and includes the following categories:

1. **1.** E-Commerce
2. **2.** Ethics, Security & Privacy
3. **3.** On the Web
4. **4.** Group Activities

THE I-SERIES: INTERACTIVE . . .

Learning is an active participation process, not a passive one. Encourage your students to take advantage of the many interactive features in *The I-Series: Computing Concepts.*

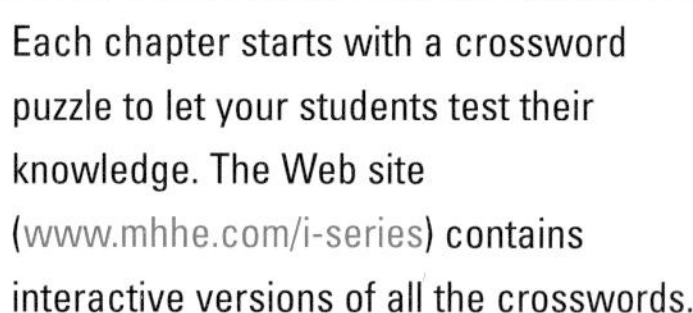

Each chapter starts with a crossword puzzle to let your students test their knowledge. The Web site (www.mhhe.com/i-series) contains interactive versions of all the crosswords.

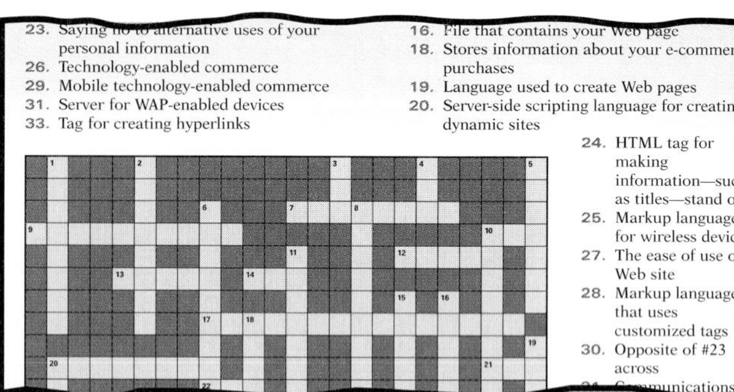

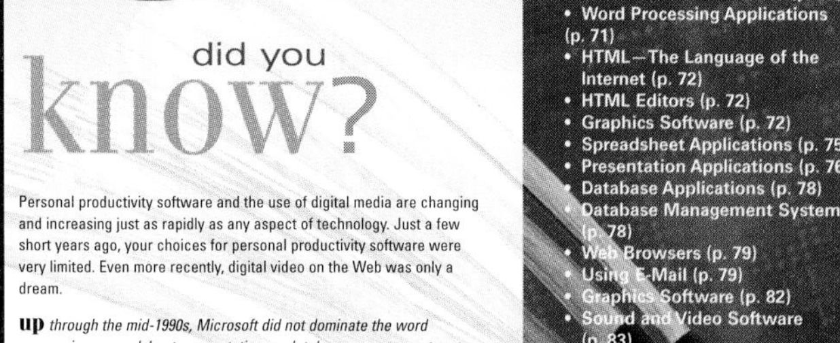

Did You Know?

Interesting facts and statistics appear at the beginning of the chapter and are integrated throughout each chapter. One at the beginning is always left blank—encourage your students to visit the Web site to find the answer.

Your students can prepare for exams by taking multiple choice and true/false exams on the Web. These provide instant feedback to help your students learn.

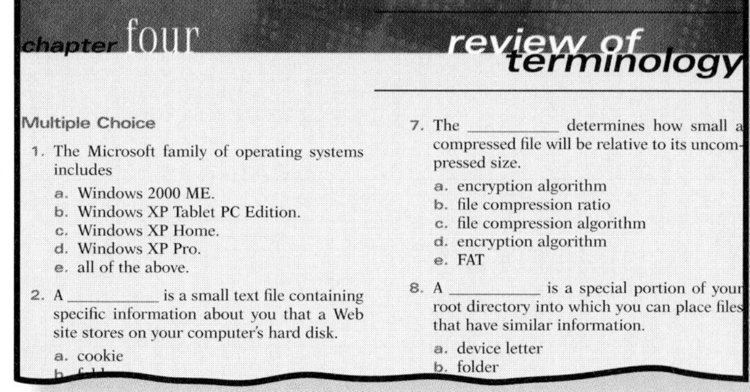

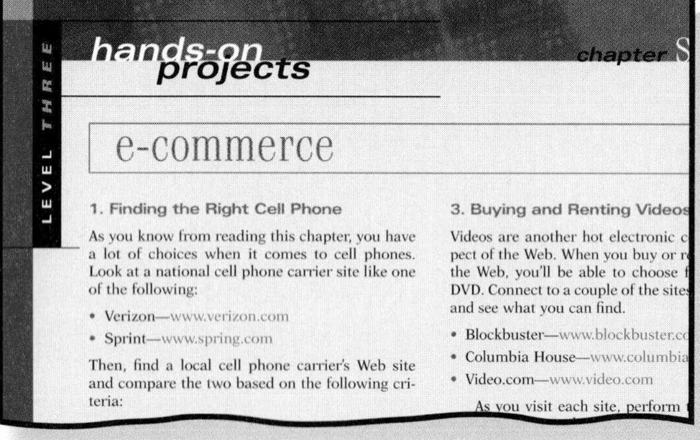

The **Level 2** and **Level 3** end-of-chapter activities contain a wealth of hands-on projects that help your students synthesize key concepts and learn even more about technology. The Level 3 projects include **E-Commerce, Ethics, Security & Privacy, On the Web,** and **Group Activities.**

THE I-SERIES: USER-FOCUSED . . .

As your students read *The I-Series: Computing Concepts,* they will be focusing on answering the following question: **What can I now do with technology that will make me more efficient and effective?**

practically speaking

Are You Addicted to the Internet?

Do you glance at the clock and realize that you've spent more time than you wanted to surfing the Web? Do you find yourself checking e-mail throughout the day and being disappointed when you don't have any? Do you find yourself looking forward to more time on the Internet? If you answered yes to any one of these questions, you may be addicted to the Internet. You just can't seem to get enough of it, and, when you try to quit, you can't.

Dr. Kimberly Young is one of the first "cyber-psychologists." She is a professor at the University of Pennsylvania and author of articles and books on cyber-addictions. On her Web site (www.netaddiction.com), Dr. Young notes that cyber-addiction takes many forms—cyber-relationships, online gambling, and excessive chat room use. Over 60 percent of the surfing for information. Dr. Young suggests answering certain questions to determine if you're addicted:

- How often do your grades or schoolwork suffer because of the amount of time you spend online?
- How often do you check your e-mail before something else that you need to do?
- How often do you find yourself anticipating when you will go online again?
- How often do you lose sleep because of late-night log-ins?

Internet addiction is serious. Although it's very different from being addicted to a substance (a chemical or physical dependence), psychological addiction can be very powerful

Many of the **Practically Speaking** boxes help you and your students maintain a "user" focus.

Snooping by Others

If you're on the receiving end of snoopware and want to disable activity-monitoring programs like Spector Pro, you can get a free program from www.idcide.com called the *Privacy Companion* or one called *Who's Watching Me* from www.trapware.com.

E-Mail Is Never Private

Since e-mail is so insecure, some people like to encrypt their e-mail, and there are many products on the market that will do the job. ZixMail is an example. Others are CertifiedMail, PrivacyX, and SafeMessage. Disappearing Email gives you a slightly different type of e-mail protection. This software is free and sends a self-destructing message with the e-mail so that the e-mail deletes itself after the period of time you specify. Before the recipient opens the e-mail the Disappearing Email software checks with the Disappearing server that the e-mail hasn't passed its expiration date. However, you can defeat this feature by copying the text out of the e-mail and pasting it somewhere else.

We never introduce an important technology topic within the text without "bringing it home" to your students and their personal lives.

Resolution

The ***resolution of a screen*** is the number of pixels it has. ***Pixels (picture elements)*** are the dots that make up the image on your screen. The *larger-number-is-better* philosophy that applied to cameras and scanners applies to monitors as well (see Figure 5.10). Of course, your resolution depends not only on the monitor but also on the graphics or video card you have. This is the hardware inside the system unit that sends the image to your monitor based on instructions from the CPU.

FIGURE 5.10

The resolution of monitors is expressed in pixels and tells you the number of dots across and down that a monitor has.

	Resolution	
Type	Horizontal	Vertical
VGA	640	480
SVGA	800	600
XGA	1,024	768
SXGA	1,280	1,024
UXGA	1,600	1,200
HDTV	1,920	1,080
QXGA	2,048	1,536

five white slots and the blue slot that you can see on the motherboard in Figure 6.3, #5, are called PCI slots. A ***PCI (peripheral component interconnect) slot*** is a type of expansion slot which you'd use to plug in video cards, sound cards, or network cards. Expansion cards, such as video and sound cards, have ports that are accessible on the back of your computer when you replace the cover of the system unit. This is where you would plug in your monitor or speakers. The ***AGP slot*** is an expansion slot reserved exclusively for an AGP video card. It's the brown slot in Figure 6.3, #6.

If you're interested in computer system hardware, either designing it or trouble-shooting it, you have a lot of good career choices, everything from electronic engineering, designing chips and other computer components, to running a help desk or a computer store. To learn more about expansion cards and slots, complete the "Expansion Cards and Slots" tutorial on your SimNet Concepts Support CD.

BUSES

How Does Information Move around the Motherboard?

Buses, or ***data buses,*** carry information in the form of bits around the motherboard in your computer. As you've already seen, the pathway that

Throughout the text, your students will find a **Careers Icon** that identifies significant opportunities for employment in the field of information technology.

THE I-SERIES: CONSUMER-FOCUSED . . .

As your students learn important technology concepts that relate to them personally, they will be focusing on answering the following question: **How am I better prepared now to make a purchasing decision?**

i·can

Understand the Choices I Need to Make to Connect to the Internet and Use the Web

You now know the choices you're faced with when you decide you want to become a Web surfer. Let's review them.

First, you need some sort of computer. Your primary options here are a traditional notebook or desktop computer, a PDA, a tablet PC, or a smart phone. If you choose a PDA or smart phone, they will come equipped with the necessary wireless modem, Web browser software, and connectivity software. Smart phones usually require you to use your phone service as the ISP. Some PDAs offer you various ISP options. If you choose a notebook, desktop, or tablet PC, you have numerous options for both a modem and an ISP.

Modem choices include a telephone modem (the slowest), cable and DSL modems (both much faster than a telephone modem), and a satellite modem (probably the fastest of the four). You may or may not have the option of choosing a cable, DSL, or satellite modem depending on where you live and the types of services your local telephone company and cable TV company provide.

When faced with the choice of a Web browser, you can use either Internet Explorer or Netscape Communicator. Both are freely available on the Web. Some commercial ISPs, such as AOL, provide their own unique Web browser software for you to use.

Connectivity software is not a major consideration. If you're using a telephone modem, you'll use the connectivity software that comes standard with your computer. If you're using a DSL, cable, or satellite modem, the service provider will provide you with the necessary connectivity software.

Many of the **I-Can** boxes help make your students intelligent and effective consumers of technology.

Student Learning Outcomes

After reading this chapter, you should be able to:

1. List and describe the ways in which B2C e-commerce businesses personalize your shopping experience on the Web.
2. Define how B2C e-commerce businesses create Web sites that are "sticky."
3. Describe the various marketing and advertising strategies B2C e-commerce businesses use to reach you.
4. Discuss your payment options for making e-commerce purchases and the methods e-commerce businesses use to ensure the security of those transactions.
5. Describe how to publish and maintain a Web site.
6. Discuss how Web developers use XHTML, XML, CSS, and other Web technologies to make e-commerce and m-commerce Web sites.
7. Compare and contrast client-side Web programming languages with server-side Web programming languages.

In Chapter 2, we briefly touched on electronic commerce when we introduced you to the Web and the Internet. In this chapter, we will further explore the world of e-commerce by addressing two major topics: (1) business to consumer e-commerce activities and (2) Web site authoring and management. Let's remind you of the following definitions:

Some of the **Student Learning Outcomes,** which drive the contents of each chapter, reinforce for your students the notion that making a purchasing decision is also an important task.

5.4 CONSUMER Q&A

1. How Can I Tell How Many Megapixels My Camera Should Have to Print Good 8 × 10 Photos?

A rule of thumb that photographers use is to divide the pixel dimensions of the camera by 200 to get the maximum size that will still be a good picture. For example, say you have a 3-megapixel camera with 1,500 pixels across and 2,000 down, dividing by 200 would give you 7.5 × 10, so an 8 × 10 print is as large as you could go and still have a good quality picture.

2. What Type of Mouse Should I Get for Gaming?

You can get a mouse that plugs in with a PS/2 port or one that uses a USB port. A USB mouse is continuously receptive to mouse movement, whereas a PS/2 mouse checks for movement intermittently. Admittedly, this happens many, many times per second, but in games, where timing is everything, you'll get better performance with a USB mouse.

3. Are Flat Panels and Flat Screens the Same Thing?

While they sound similar, these terms are actually not the same thing at all. A flat *panel* refers to an LCD or gas plasma flat-panel display, whereas a flat *screen* means a television-like monitor with a flat rather than a curved screen. A CRT (or a traditional television) started out with a curved screen because the way it works is that electrons are sprayed from the back of the device onto the inside of the viewable screen, which is coated with phosphor. As the electrons hit the phosphor, the phosphor glows. To ensure that all the electrons hit the screen when they should, the screen has traditionally been curved, but this distorts the image somewhat. Lately, CRT manufacturers have found a way to make the screen of a CRT flat, improving the quality of the image.

4. What Should I Look for in a Scanner?

When you're choosing a scanner, its resolution is a strong determining factor in the quality of the electronic image you get. In the case of scanners, resolution is measured in dots p[illegible]

Where applicable, we provide numerous in-text discussions focused on giving your students the ability to make an informed purchasing decision.

THE I-SERIES: ETHICS-FOCUSED . . .

Technology is indeed important, but even more important is how your students choose to use technology. By reading *The I-Series: Computing Concepts,* they will be focusing on answering the following question: **How much more do I now understand about the role of technology with respect to ethics, security, and privacy?**

Chapter 9 is completely devoted to the vitally important topics of ethics, security, and privacy.

FIGURE 9.5

The Federal Trade Commission (FTC) is on the trail of Internet criminals and publishes a list of the Top 10 Online Frauds (www.ftc.gov).

Dot-Con Scams

- **Travel/vacation fraud:** You're offered a luxury trip with all sorts of "extras" at very low prices. Then you find that what you get is much lower quality than was promised. Or, you're hit with hidden charges after you've paid.
  FTC says: Make sure you have all promises in writing, including the cancellation policy, before you sign up.
- **Bogus business opportunities:** You see an offer to stay at home, be your own boss, and earn big bucks. But then you find that the scheme is a bust and you're probably worse off than before.
  FTC says: Check with others who have started businesses with the company. Get all promises in writing and get an attorney or accountant to check the contract.
- **Online auction fraud:** In this case you get something less valuable than what you paid for, or you might even get nothing at all.
  FTC says: Always use a credit card or an escrow service.
- **Internet service provider scams:** You get a check for a small amount ($3 or $4) in the mail and cash it. Then you find you're trapped into long-term contracts with ISPs that exact huge penalties if you cancel.
  FTC says: Read ALL the information about the check before you cash it and watch for unexpected charges.
- **Credit card fraud:** You get an offer which says you can view adult-oriented Web sites for free if you provide a credit card number—just to prove you're over 18. Then your credit card bill has charges for goods and

ethics, security & privacy

THREE

1. Finding Social Security Numbers of Deceased People

Social security numbers are very private and personal information. As a rule, you should never give out your social security number unless you are required to do so by law.

However, when you die, your social security number actually begins to appear in a lot of places, some of which are on the Web. For example, at RootsWeb.com (http://ssdi.genealogy.rootsweb.com/cgi-bin/ssdi.cgi), you can simply type in the name of a deceased person and obtain his or her social security number.

Connect to that particular site and type in the

- Yahoo! PeopleSearch—www.people.yahoo.com

a. How easy was it to find someone?
b. What information were you able to find?
c. Do you like the fact that you can look up people on the Web?
d. Do you like the fact that people can look you up on the Web?
e. Young children today are growing up with the Web. In 10 years, will these people have any problems with their information being so easily available?

One chapter isn't enough. So, each chapter contains a full page of **Level 3 Ethics, Security & Privacy** projects.

i-series insights *Ethics, Security & Privacy*

Do You Really Want a Chip in Your Body?

Implant chips are the central issue of much debate, mainly in the area of privacy. On an implant chip, you can store a wealth of information about yourself, including your medical history and other forms of personal information. Then, if you ever need that information, it can easily be scanned.

Most people are in favor of that use of the technology. But many want it to stop there, while others see more applications. For example, that same implant chip could be used (in conjunction with satellites) to track the movements of people. So, we could easily find lost skiers and children tall who burglar-napped child. Those sound like good uses of technology.

If we can track anyone anywhere, however, what's to stop certain people or organizations from tracking others for the wrong reasons? Couldn't the government easily follow you wherever you go? Couldn't your school easily track you to see where you are when you're supposed to be in class? Couldn't the ATF (Bureau of Alcohol, Tobacco, and Firearms) use those implant chips to determine who should be able to drink alcohol or own a gun?

What do you think? Is this a technology that we should repress

be used in a bad way? Or should we move forward with its use while enacting

I-Series Insights: Ethics, Security & Privacy boxes also appear in each chapter to reinforce that your students need to focus on the ethical use of technology.

you over the Web, you need to think about security and privacy.

Security

Most businesses work hard to protect information about you. They use the data administration subsystem within a DBMS to specify who can access your information and what they can do with it. Nonetheless, hackers can break into Web databases containing credit card numbers from e-commerce sites, Internet banking sites, and online medical records. As an individual you can't do much to stop hackers. However, we would encourage you to closely monitor your checking account balances and your credit card statements.

Privacy

More businesses are compiling information about you in their databases as it becomes easier to do so. As businesses merge, so do their databases. The legal system has ruled that information (including customer information) is a business asset. So, when one business acquires another, it also

We've also integrated discussions of ethics, security, and privacy throughout the text.

THE I-SERIES: MANAGER-FOCUSED . . .

Your students may start in the business world primarily as users of technology. But soon, they will take on the role of managing people and technology. *The I-Series: Computing Concepts* helps your students answer the following question: **What can I now envision of future uses of technology?**

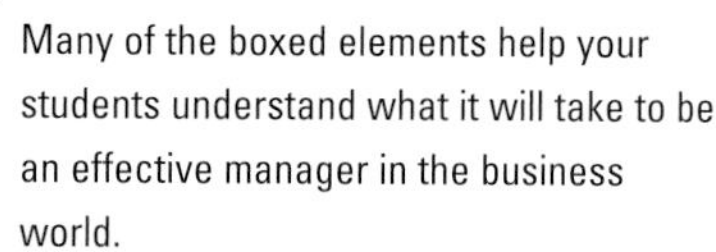

i-series insights — *Ethics, Security & Privacy*

Is Someone Monitoring Your Keystrokes?

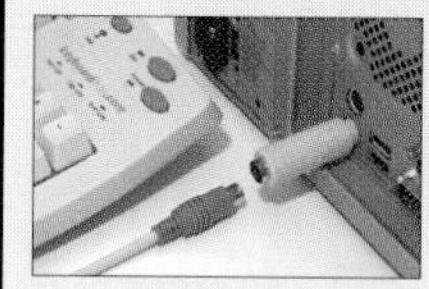

The cable from your computer may plug into the PS/2 port on the back of your computer. But, there may also be a little lipstick-sized device back there too. Someone can spy on you by inserting a hardware key logger between the PS/2 port and the PS2/connector on your keyboard cable. A ***hardware key logger*** is a hardware device that captures keystrokes on their journey from the keyboard to the motherboard. It captures and records every keystroke. However, since it catches every delete, backspace, and enter, it may be a bit bothersome to review the information stored there.

If your employer does this, you'll find little sympathy from the legal system. Employers have the legal right to monitor the use of their resources and that includes the time they're paying you for and the computer systems you're using. Remember, too, that employers are liable for the actions of employees.

Maybe you should check the back of your computer every now and then? Although, that wouldn't necessarily protect you since there are also hardware key loggers that can be installed inside the keyboard.

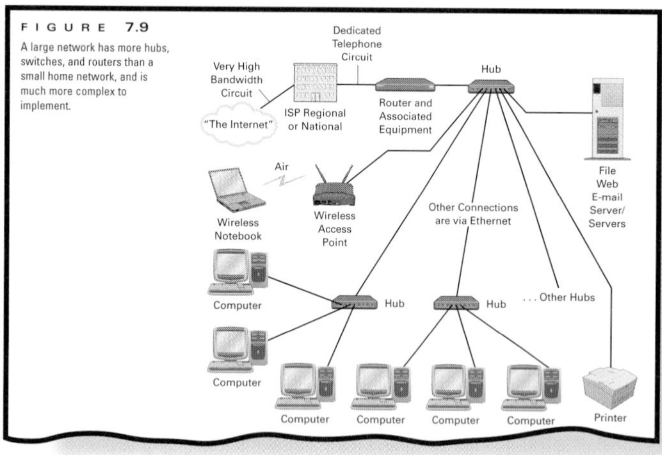

FIGURE 7.9
A large network has more hubs, switches, and routers than a small home network, and is much more complex to implement.

Throughout the text, your students will find integrated discussions of key management issues, of both people and technology.

FIGURE 10.19
From a central data warehouse, an organization can create numerous data marts, each with a special focus.

Merchandising
Advertising
Distribution
Sales
Organizationwide Data Warehouse
Marketing
Production
Service
Accounts

The **Careers Icon** identifies employment opportunities in IT. Your students may someday manage IT people. So, they need to know what skills they have.

search term. We found over 450 job listings requiring expertise in Microsoft Access. In Figure 1.18, we've listed several of the job titles we found and their descriptions. Notice that not a single job title is IT-specific. Rather, they represent job openings in such areas as guest satisfaction, project management, finance, merchandising, product marketing, medicine, and transportation.

Don't sell yourself short in the job market by not learning all you can about technology! Then, having acquired IT knowledge, be sure to include a section on your resume that details what technology skills you have.

Using Technology to Find a Job

As you prepare your resume and begin your job search, we recommend that you use technology by exploring the electronic job market. The ***electronic job market*** makes use of the Internet to recruit employees and is growing by leaps and bounds. According to the *Industrial Standard* (www.thestandard.com), a leading magazine on the Internet economy, the average cost of online recruiting is $152 per hire while the cost of more traditional methods is $1,381. So, many organizations now post jobs and recruit potential employees via the Internet. The most

THE I-SERIES: FUTURE-FOCUSED . . .

Technology will always change—that means your students must be life-long learners if they are to be successful in the business world. *The I-Series: Computing Concepts* helps your students answer the following question: **How can I continue to learn about technology once my class ends?**

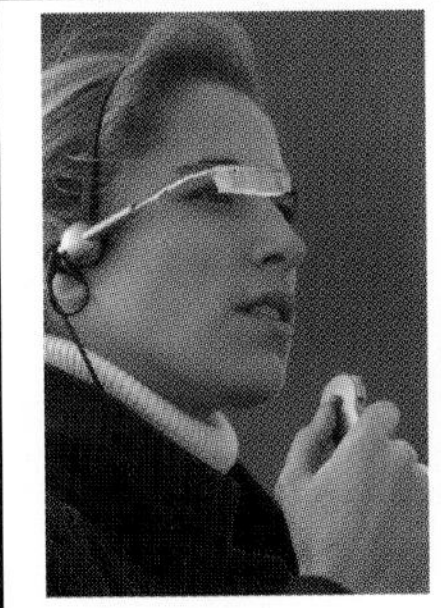

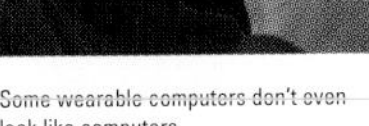

Some wearable computers don't even look like computers.

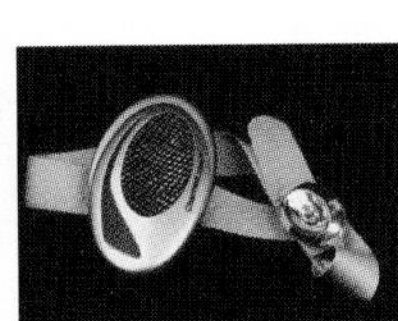

Charmed Technology wants you to wear your CPU on your belt.

Xybernaut's wearable poma clips onto your belt and includes a small screen that covers one of your eyes.

Chapter 11 is devoted entirely to introducing your students to emerging technologies including e-cash, CAVEs, biometrics, biochips, and membrane-based technologies.

Right from the beginning in Chapter 1 your students will learn about emerging technologies such as tablet PCs, smart phones, and WiFi.

FIGURE 1.14

You have many personal technology alternatives to PDAs, notebook computers, and desktop computers.

Slate tablet PCs have their storage devices, CPU, and RAM integrated into the screen.

Some watches now include PDA capabilities.

Smart phones, such as the Motorola T720, are sophisticated cell phones.

COMPUTERS IN YOUR LIFE TOMORROW

Well, if you do have a crystal ball, we'd certainly like to borrow it sometime. The simple fact of the matter is that no one can predict the future with any real consistency, especially with respect to technology.

However, we can make some statements regarding the future of technology in general. For example, we know that future technologies will begin to incorporate more of your senses (speech for example), just as we discussed in Chapter 11. We also know that complete and high-speed wireless communications are just around the corner. But how those will come about and exactly when is a mystery.

This *Life-Long Learning Module* will take you on a whirlwind tour of what we think the future holds for technology. More important, we want to alert you to how the future of technology will impact your personal life, business life in general, and your own career.

We call these *Life-Long Learning Modules* because we want you to visit them long after you've completed your computer class. The content in this particular module will change frequently and perhaps dramatically. Bookmark it (www.mhhe.com/i-series) and drop back in for a visit from time to time.

Big Today—How Small Tomorrow?

Technology today is still relatively "big." Although you may think that a PDA that weighs

The five **Life-Long Learning Modules** (LLLs) will keep your students up-to-date on technology even after they've finished your class.

For your students, the future is all about getting a well-paying and fulfilling job. The **Careers Icon,** integrated throughout the text, points out many opportunities in the field of IT.

For that reason, you probably won't find it on very many personal computers in a home or workplace environment. If your computer is for personal use such as surfing the Web, typing documents, sending e-mail, and the like, Linux is probably not the operating system for you. Linux can be either a personal operating system or a network operating system.

Although Linux may not be a good personal operating system for you right now, it does represent some substantial career opportunities. We believe Linux will play prominently in the future of technology. If you're interested in learning how to write operating system software, we definitely recommend that you focus some of your efforts on Linux.

To learn more about Mac OS, Linux, and other operating systems, complete the "Other Operating Systems" and "The World of Macintosh" tutorials on your SimNet Concepts Support CD.

Stephen Haag is a professor in and Chair of the Department of Information Technology and Electronic Commerce in the Daniels College of Business at the University of Denver. He is also the Director of the Masters of Science in Information Technology program. Stephen holds a B.B.A. and M.B.A. from West Texas State University and a Ph.D. from the University of Texas at Arlington. Stephen has been teaching in the classroom since 1982 and publishing textbooks since 1984. He has also written numerous articles appearing in such journals as *Communications of the ACM,* the *International Journal of Systems Science, Socio-Economic Planning Sciences,* and the *Australian Journal of Management.*

Stephen is the author of over 40 books including *Management Information Systems for the Information Age* (now in its fourth edition), *Interactions: Teaching English as a Second Language* (with his mother and father), *Information Technology: Tomorrow's Advantage Today* (with Peter Keen), *Excelling in Finance,* and 18 other books within *The I-Series.*

Stephen lives with his wife, Pam, and their three sons—Indiana, Darian, and Trevor—in Highlands Ranch, Colorado. When not teaching and writing, Stephen is a trainer for the federal government teaching managers how to effectively develop and assess technology metrics.

Maeve Cummings is a professor of Information Systems at Pittsburg State University. She holds a B.S. in Mathematics and Computer Science; an M.S. in Mathematics; an M.B.A. from Pittsburg State University; and a Ph.D. in Information Systems from the University of Texas at Arlington. She has published in various journals, is on the editorial boards of several journals, and is a co-author of *Management Information Systems for the Information Age,* now in its fourth edition.

Maeve has been teaching for almost 20 years and lives in Pittsburg, Kansas, with her husband, Slim.

Alan I Rea, Jr. is an associate professor of Computer Information Systems at Western Michigan University's Haworth College of Business. Alan holds a B.A. from Pennsylvania State University, an M.A. from Youngstown State University, and a Ph.D. from Bowling Green State University. He has published in various journals, including the *Mid-American Journal of Business* and *Computers and Composition,* and regularly serves as a reviewer for journals such as the *Journal of Information Systems Education.* Alan is a member of various professional committees concerned with teaching technology.

When not teaching or writing, Alan spends time programming open-source software, computer gaming, or hanging out with his family. Alan lives in Kalamazoo, Michigan, with his wife, Lynda, son, Aidan, two cats, and various forms of wildlife.

FROM STEPHEN HAAG

We would be nowhere without the insight, patience, and guidance of Dan Silverburg and Gina Huck. Dan is our former sponsoring editor, our rock of Gibraltar, and my close personal friend. Gina is our developmental editor—her contributions are so great that she should be listed as an author, most probably even first.

Maeve and Alan always inspire me to be better than ever before. In the process of writing this book, they often made me laugh, even when the completed manuscript seemed years away.

When Darian was born in August 1999, my mother and father moved to Colorado. I'm truly blessed to be so near my parents. My mother and I tell stories and laugh; my father and I search for rare coins, solve the world's problems, and drink a lot of coffee together.

But first and foremost are my wife, Pam, and my sons, Darian and Trevor. For all the work that Pam has done on this project, she should be listed as an author alongside Gina. Darian was born in the twentieth century, and Trevor followed shortly in the twenty-first. The most special times of my life are taking a bath with my boys and grocery shopping while Darian and Trevor run through the aisles. My life would not be a complete journey without my children.

FROM MAEVE CUMMINGS

My sincere thanks goes to the many people who helped directly and indirectly with this project. Dan Silverburg and Gina Huck guided us through the writing process with their considerable experience and their motivational and organizational abilities. Many thanks to Alan, whose creativity and insight are great assets to our team, and of course to Steve, who is indisputably our tireless and fearless leader. Without Jenny Cantu and Barbara Clutter, the road to completion of this book would have been a lot more rocky.

I am blessed to be the recipient of a continuous flow of support from my family and friends, and from my husband, who makes possible everything I do. In this regard, I am wealthy beyond measure.

I continue to learn daily in the classroom. Indeed, I learn as much or more with my back to the chalkboard than I ever did facing it. And this I owe to my students—this continuous process of exploring and learning that I am so fortunate and privileged to experience.

FROM ALAN REA

I'm impressed with the professionalism and hard work of the project team for the second edition. There's no way we could deliver such a high-quality product unless everyone worked together to make it happen. I can't name everyone, but I'd like to thank Dan for his lucid observations and Gina for her impressive skills.

I'd also like especially to thank Stephen and Maeve. They never cease to amaze me with their passion for writing and drive to create an outstanding textbook. I've learned much from them in our few years together as co-authors and friends.

Of course, thanks go out to my colleagues and the administration at Western Michigan University. They've created an environment that encourages a student-centered approach to teaching that allows me to embark on adventures such as writing this textbook.

Finally, I'd like to give my greatest thanks to my wife, Lynda. She has been my supporter, critic, and front-line editor. Her contributions to this textbook are too numerous to list. Without her, I never would have made it this far.

FROM THE AUTHOR TEAM

Writing textbooks is a wonderful endeavor; writing textbooks for the best publisher is a dream come true. To the people at McGraw-Hill we offer our heartfelt gratitude. We can't name them all, but there are some who have been "in the trenches" with us. They include Mary Conzachi, Mary Christianson, Jeremy Cheshareck, Greg Bates, and Rose Range. Paul Murphy, our marketing manager, has also worked diligently to carry our story into the field of education.

We wish to acknowledge the reviewers of *The I-Series*. You will never know of the unbelievable wealth of insight and guidance you have provided. We will forever be in your debt.

We welcome any and all feedback from you, our valued customers. Please e-mail us at i-series@mcgraw-hill.com with any suggestions, corrections, or noteworthy additions you want to pass along. Our names appear on the cover of this project, but it really belongs to you. You make it come to life in the classroom. We hope your school recognizes your worth and is paying you appropriately.

We understand that, in today's teaching environment, offering a textbook alone is seldom sufficient to meet the needs of the many instructors who use our books. To teach effectively, you must have a full complement of supplemental resources to assist you in every facet of teaching, from preparing for class to conducting a lecture to assessing your students' comprehension. *The I-Series* offers a complete supplements package and Web site.

INSTRUCTOR RESOURCES

Instructor's Resource Kit

The Instructor's Resource Kit is a CD-ROM containing the Instructor's Manual in both MS Word and .pdf formats, PowerPoint slides with Presentation Software, Brownstone test generating software, accompanying test item files in both MS Word and .pdf formats, and an important document titled "Creating Your IT Course." The CD also contains figure files from the text. Please feel free to use these as they best suit your purposes. The features of each of the four main components of the Instructor's Resource Kit are highlighted on this page.

Instructor's Manual

- Chapter outline with teaching tips.
- Lecture notes illustrating key concepts and ideas.
- Instructor Excellence boxes that include Presentation Tips, Break Outs, To the Web, SimNet, and suggestions for integrating the teaching of applications.
- Answers to all Making the Grade and end-of-chapter questions and exercises.

PowerPoint Presentation

Prepared by Margaret Trenholm-Edmunds
Mount Allison University

The PowerPoint presentation is designed to provide you with comprehensive lecture and teaching resources, including:

- Chapter Student Learning Outcomes followed by source content that illustrates key terms and key facts per chapter.
- FAQ's (Frequently Asked Questions) to show key concepts through the chapter. Also, lecture notes to illustrate these key concepts and ideas.
- End-of-chapter exercises and activities per chapter as taken from the end-of-chapter materials in the text.
- Speaker's notes are incorporated through the slides per chapter.
- Figures/screen shots are incorporated throughout the slides per chapter.

PowerPoint includes presentation software for you to design your own presentations for your courses.

Test Bank

Prepared by Margaret Trenholm-Edmunds
Mount Allison University

The I-Series test bank, using Diploma Network Testing Software by Brownstone, contains over 2,000 questions categorized by topic, page reference to the text, and difficulty level of learning. Each question is assigned a learning category:

- Level 1: Key Terms and Facts
- Level 2: Key Concepts
- Level 3: Application and Problem-Solving

The types of questions consist of 40 percent multiple choice, 40 percent true/false, and 20 percent fill-in/short-answer questions.

Creating Your IT Course

This particular document was developed by the authors of the text. It includes:

- Explanations of the key pedagogical elements and how to use them.
- Annotated syllabi, using multiple term formats and two exam formats—(1) a midterm and final exam and (2) two exams and a final exam.
- Comprehensive projects that incorporate key concepts across multiple chapters.

DIGITAL SOLUTIONS FOR INSTRUCTORS AND STUDENTS

Online Learning Center/Web Site

The Online Learning Center (OLC) that accompanies *The I-Series* is accessible through our Information Technology Supersite at www.mhhe.com/catalogs/irwin/it/. This site provides additional review and learning tools developed using the same three-level approach found in the text and supplements. To locate *The I-Series* OLC/Web site directly, go to www.mhhe.com/i-series. The site is divided into three key areas:

- **Information Center** contains core information about the text, the authors, and a guide to our additional features and benefits of the series, including the supplements.
- **Instructor Center** offers instructional materials, downloads, additional activities and answers to additional projects, relevant links for professors, solution files, the PowerPoint slide presentations, the Instructor's Manual, and more.
- **Student Center** contains chapter learning outcomes and outlines, interactive self-quizzes, additional projects, student data files, Web links, the crossword puzzle for each chapter in an interactive format, the multiple choice and true/false questions for each chapter in an interactive format, and more.

As teachers, we realize that no printed text can be completely up-to-date. *The I-Series: Computing Concepts* Web site augments the printed texts by providing the most up-to-date reviews of technology and much more. Below is just a partial list of exciting topics you'll find on the Web site.

- Personal Digital Assistants
- Virus Resources
- CPUs and RAM
- Wireless Devices
- Wireless Home Networks
- Groupware Suites
- Emerging Technologies
- Privacy
- Hackers
- E-commerce Web Technologies

Online Courses Available—OLCs are your perfect solutions for Internet-based content. Simply put, these centers are "digital cartridges" that contain a book's pedagogy and supplements. As students read the books, they can go online and take self-grading quizzes or work through interactive exercises.

PageOut

As our Course Web Site Development Center, PageOut offers a syllabus page, URL, McGraw-Hill Online Learning Center content, online exercises and quizzes, gradebook, discussion board, and an area for student Web pages. For more information, visit the PageOut Web site at www.pageout.net.

PowerWeb

PowerWeb for Information Technology is an exciting online product available for *The I-Series.* Features include an interactive glossary; current events with quizzing, assessment, and measurement options; Web survey; links to related text content; and WWW searching capability via Northern Lights, an academic search engine.

SimNet Concepts Support CD

SimNet Concepts is a simulated assessment and learning tool. It comes on the CD accompanying each student text. It contains a rich variety of over 70 tutorials covering such topics as digital cameras, data representation using binary codes, the world of Windows, project management applications, multimedia development, wireless communications, Web utilities, network configurations, B2B and e-commerce, ergonomics, and careers.

For more information on the extensive *I-Series* supplements package, contact your local McGraw-Hill/Irwin representative or visit our Web site at www.mhhe.com/i-series.

brief contents

END-OF-BOOK

table of contents

CHAPTER 3
APPLICATION SOFTWARE AND DIGITAL MEDIA: What Can Your Computer Do for You? 66

CHAPTER 4
SYSTEM SOFTWARE, VIRUS PROTECTION, AND FILE MANAGEMENT: What Software Runs Your Hardware? 96

15

CHAPTER 15

COMPUTER BRAINPOWER: How Can You Use Your Computer to Help You Think? 454

END-OF-BOOK

I-CAN

PRACTICALLY SPEAKING

I-SERIES INSIGHTS: ETHICS, SECURITY & PRIVACY

CAREERS COVERAGE

The I-Series

SECOND EDITION

Computing Concepts

Complete Edition

crossword puzzle

Across

1. "Permanent" devices
4. Devices for capturing information and commands
5. For sending text messages, usually from cell phone to cell phone
7. Set of tools
8. #5 across including sound, images, and video
10. Large, organizational computer
12. Faster than "snail mail"
13. Short-distance wireless technology
14. Brains of your computer
16. Software that enables you to be productive in your tasks
17. Slates and convertibles are types of these new computers
18. Virtual meeting place
19. You double-click on this
21. Physical devices of your computer
23. Devices for seeing and hearing information
24. Small, hand-held computer
25. User interface with buttons and icons
26. Technical term is hyperlink
27. Internal memory

Down

1. Opposite of #21 across
2. Opposite of #16 across
3. What guides your behavior
6. Biggest and fastest computer
9. Can be deadly to your computer
11. Most popular type of personal computer
13. You click once on this
15. Also known as a laptop
20. Place you visit on the Web
21. People who use their knowledge in the wrong way
22. Technology with better distance than #13 across

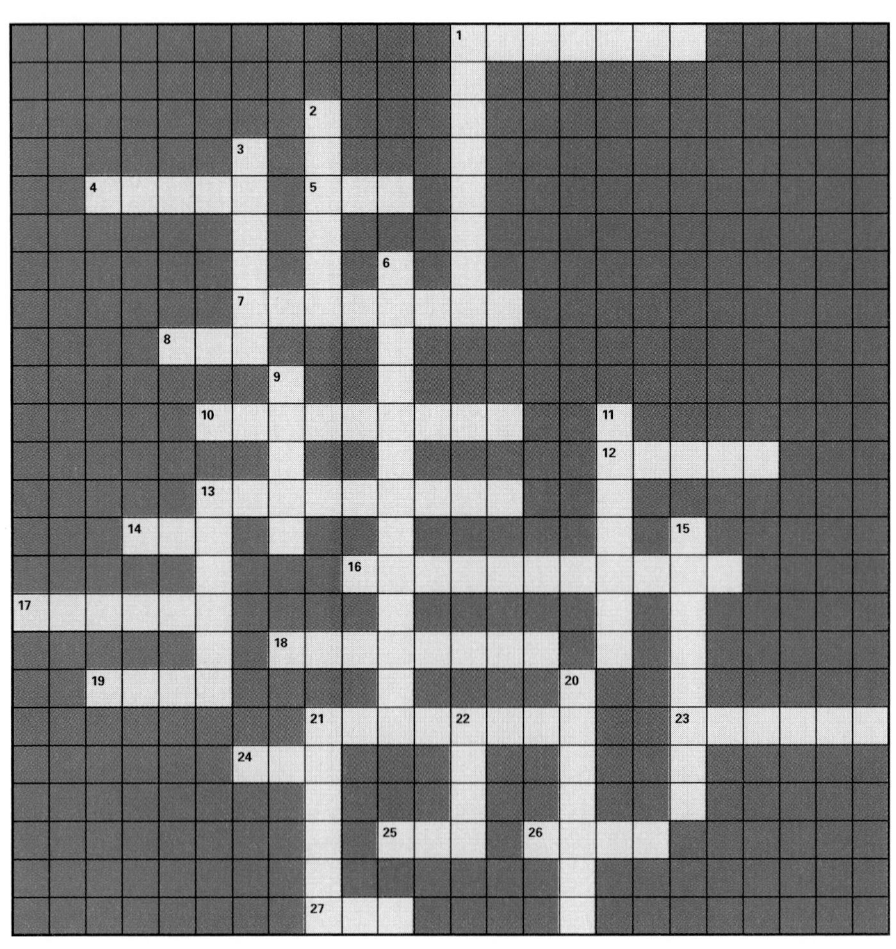

CHAPTER one 1

Computers in Your Life Today

Are You Ready to Become Wired and Unwired?

SIMNET CONCEPTS SUPPORT

did you know?

People throughout history have always tried to predict the future. Some have been surprisingly successful while others haven't. Let's hear what some people have had to say.

"**everything** *that can be invented has been invented," according to Charles H. Duell, Office of Patents in 1899.*

"**there** *is no reason anyone would want a computer in their home," according to Ken Olson, president, chair, and founder of Digital Equipment Corporation, in 1977.*

"**i** *think there is a world market for maybe __??__ computers," according to Thomas Watson, IBM Chair, in 1943.*

To find out just how many computers Thomas Watson of IBM thought there might be a world market for, visit www.mhhe.com/i-series.

Student Learning Outcomes

After reading this chapter, you should be able to:

1. Define a computer and describe the two major components of hardware and software.
2. Describe the two categories within computer software.
3. Describe the six categories within computer hardware.
4. Describe various personal technology alternatives to notebook and desktop computers.
5. Discuss your ethical role while using technology.

Few things in your life are as dynamic and everchanging as the world of technology (of which computers are a part). Today, there are millions of computers in people's homes all over the world. You simply won't believe how small the world market for them Thomas Watson, chair of IBM, in 1943 thought there would be. As you see, we open each chapter with some interesting facts, statistics, and quotes, but always leave one blank and encourage you to visit the Web site for this text (www.mhhe.com/i-series) to find the answer and fill in the blank. While you're at our Web site, check out the other great support we've provided for you there.

Of course, just because technology is dynamic and always changing doesn't automatically mean that you're better off because of it. The key lies in your being able to use the technology to be productive. That is the focus of this text—to help you be as productive as possible with technology. So, before we even begin with definitions of and concepts about computers, let's talk about productivity.

What is productivity? Perhaps the best way for us to answer that is to offer you five questions that you should be able to answer as you read along in this text.

1. What can I now do with technology that will make me more efficient and effective in work and life?
2. How am I better prepared now to make a computer purchasing decision?
3. How much more do I now understand about aspects of technology respecting ethics, security, and privacy?
4. What can I now envision of the future uses of technology?
5. How can I continue to learn about technology once my class ends?

It is our goal that you'll have positive answers to the above questions after you've read each chapter in this text. If you do, then you'll be productive.

Let's begin by seeing how technology can help you start a presentation in class in an effective and attention-grabbing way.

1.1 THE PRODUCTIVITY OF TECHNOLOGY

When you make a presentation, you want to grab the attention of your audience immediately. One good way to do so is to start your presentation with music (or other audio) playing. Of course, you can bring in a CD player and use a projector to show transparencies. On the other hand, if you choose to use a computer you can also build a presentation of slides

did you know?

"Who wants to hear actors talk?" asked H. M. Warner of Warner Brothers in 1927. (This is actually a paraphrase as Mr. Warner used an expletive.)

with music incorporated into one or more of the slides. If you embed the music into the first slide, that music will begin playing when you start your slide presentation. Sound difficult to do? Think again. Using presentation software—such as Microsoft PowerPoint which we'll be showing you—you can create an electronic slide presentation that includes music.

To start PowerPoint, you need to understand something about your computer's interfaces. In Figure 1.1, you can see a screen capture of Windows XP's desktop, which is a graphical user interface. A ***graphical user interface (GUI)*** is a graphic or icon-driven interface on which you use your mouse (or some other input device) to start software, use that software, and initiate various other functions. When you start your computer, this is the type of interface you'll first encounter. It may look slightly different from the screen in Figure 1.1, but it will include the same functionality. To learn more about your Windows desktop, complete "The World of Windows" tutorial on your SimNet Concepts Support CD.

Any GUI typically contains buttons and icons. A ***button*** is a graphic representation of something that you click on once with the left mouse button (the **Start** button in the lower left corner is an example). An ***icon*** is a graphic representation of something you click on twice or double-click.

In Figure 1.1, you can start Microsoft PowerPoint by either double-clicking on its icon or by clicking once on the **Start** button and continually highlighting elements within the menu until you see Microsoft PowerPoint, which you then click on once. In performing the latter, we clicked once on the **Start** button, highlighted **All Programs**, and then clicked

FIGURE 1.1

Your Windows desktop is a graphical user interface (GUI) with buttons and icons.

This is an icon. You can double-click on it to start PowerPoint.

Click on the **Start** button to view your available programs and options.

FIGURE 1.2

When you start PowerPoint, you can immediately begin typing in the content of your title slide.

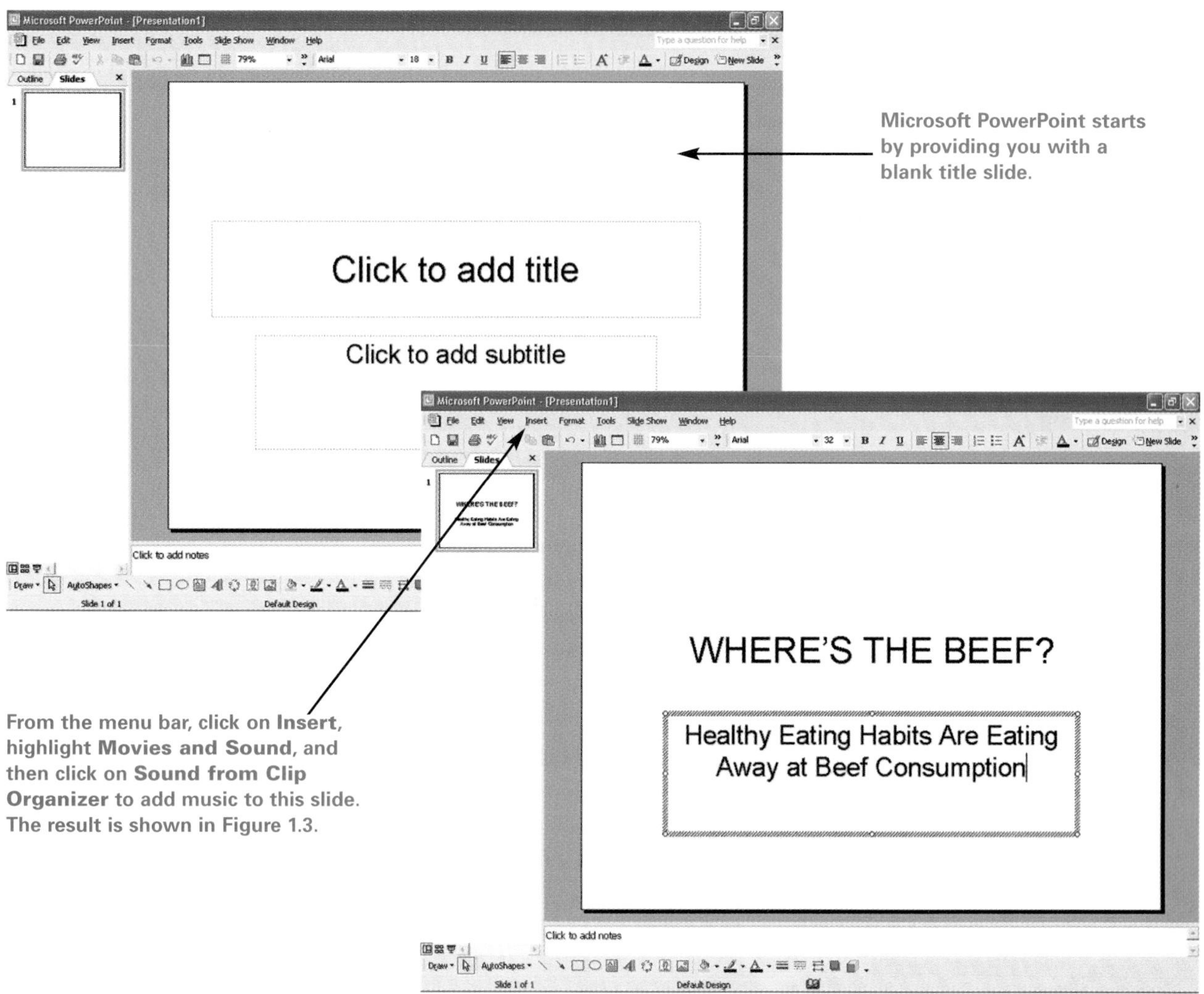
Microsoft PowerPoint - [Presentation1]
Click to add title
Click to add subtitle
Click to add notes
Microsoft PowerPoint starts by providing you with a blank title slide.
WHERE'S THE BEEF?
Healthy Eating Habits Are Eating Away at Beef Consumption
From the menu bar, click on Insert, highlight Movies and Sound, and then click on Sound from Clip Organizer to add music to this slide. The result is shown in Figure 1.3.

once on **Microsoft PowerPoint**. The result is the background screen you see in Figure 1.2.

PowerPoint is very easy to use in building a slide presentation. In the foreground screen in Figure 1.2, we entered some text for the title and subtitle. As you can probably guess, we're building slides for a presentation concerning the decline in the sales of beef over the past few years. When we show this first slide, we want music to start also. So, we need to add music to this slide.

That's a simple process. From the menu bar, we clicked once on **Insert**, highlighted **Movies and Sounds**, and clicked once on **Sound from Clip Organizer**. (The menu bar, located across the top of most software, typically includes such functions as **File, Edit, Help,** and others.) Microsoft then displayed a list of available sounds on the right side of the screen (see Figure 1.3 on the opposite page). We scrolled down through that list and selected the **Mystery Score** clip. (It seemed to go with the title of our presentation which is in the form of a question.) PowerPoint then asked us if we wanted the music to start when the slide was shown and we answered yes. Now, all we have to do is click once on the **Slide Show** button in the lower left corner. PowerPoint will show the first slide and also start the music.

You can imagine how much more dramatic and effective it is to start a presentation like this than to just stand up and start talking! It is quite impressive, demonstrates your ability to use your computer in a productive way, and instantly seizes your audience's attention. We would encourage you to take a couple of moments and perform the steps above. You can be creating great slide presentations with music in just a few short minutes. To learn more about PowerPoint, complete the "Presentation Applications" tutorial on your SimNet Concepts Support CD.

There is a downside to watch out for (as there almost always is). Too much music or other audio can be overpowering and distracting. So you need to learn guidelines for developing a good presentation. You should never add audio to a slide presentation just for its own sake or because you can.

Let's stop and talk about what we just did for a moment as you begin to create an intellectual map for what you want to learn in this course. To insert audio into our PowerPoint presentation, we used the mouse and clicked only three times, used the scroll bar and found what we wanted, and then answered one simple question concerning how the music should start. All that was very easy. The most challenging aspect is determining when and when *not* to have audio in a presentation.

The truth be told, it's far easier to learn how to use technology than it is to learn how to use technology correctly, ethically (we'll discuss the concept of ethics in an upcoming section), and productively. Think about driving a car. Learning to drive a car is easy. Learning how to deal with challenging or ambiguous traffic situations or to avoid road rage is far more difficult.

FIGURE 1.3

PowerPoint comes with a library of prerecorded sounds.

The challenge ahead of you is twofold. First, you need to learn how to use the technology, starting with understanding key terms and concepts and progressing from there. But you can't just stop with that knowledge. You need to develop your judgment, your ability to use your new knowledge in the best ways—to buy the right personal computer and software programs and devices, to take advantage of application software and use it creatively, to send e-mails that do not offend anyone, to protect your computer from hackers, to help your organization achieve the greatest advantage through the use of technology—the list is endless.

Some people focus only on the first task—learning how to use technology and understanding key terms and concepts. We challenge you to learn how to use technology correctly, ethically, and productively. Are you ready?

SECTION 1.1

making the grade

1. A(n) ___________ is a graphic representation of something that you click on once with your left mouse button.
2. A(n) ___________ is a graphic representation of something you click on twice or double-click.
3. A(n) ___________ is a graphic or icon-driven interface on which you use your mouse (or some other input device) to start software, use that software, and initiate various other functions.

1.2 COMPUTING BASICS

In the previous section, we began to discuss the true productivity of technology. Technology is a broad term that includes all electronic devices—cell phones, VCRs, ATMs, the electronic ignition system in a car, and, of course, computers. A ***computer*** (or ***computer system***) is a set of tools that helps you perform information-processing tasks. Your computer can help you surf the Web and order concert tickets, view your local weather forecast, and find money to help you pay for college. Each of those is an information-processing task. Even playing a video game is an information-processing task. The animated figures on your screen are simply representations of information—their location, their direction of movement, what activities they can perform, and so on. You control those figures, and thus their information, with devices such as a joystick or gamepad. To learn more about a computer system, complete the "Introduction to a Personal Computer System" tutorial on your SimNet Concepts Support CD.

did you know?

"We don't like their sound and guitar music is on the way out," according to Decca Recording executives in 1962 while rejecting the opportunity to sign the Beatles to a recording contract.

YOUR COMPUTER HARDWARE AND SOFTWARE

What Are the Major Components of My Computer?

Stated simply, everything in your computer falls into one of two categories—software or hardware.

- ***Software*** is the set of instructions that your computer hardware executes to process information for you.
- ***Hardware*** consists of the physical devices that make up your computer system.

FIGURE 1.4

A typical computer ad will tell you everything that comes with the "system."

Do you need both? Yes, absolutely. In our previous example of adding music to a slide presentation, the software we used was Microsoft PowerPoint (presentation software), and we used such hardware devices as a mouse and keyboard (to enter information and commands) and a monitor (to view the presentation).

In Figure 1.4, you'll find a typical ad for a computer system. It contains both hardware (for example, monitor, CD-RW drive, and speakers) and software (for example, Windows Office 2003 Suite and Windows 2000 ME Home operating system).

CATEGORIES OF COMPUTER SOFTWARE
What Can My Software Help Me Do?

You can think of software as your intellectual interface to your computer. That is, software is the set of instructions that you would process with your mind if you didn't use a computer. There are two major categories of software:

- ***System software***—the software that determines how your computer carries out technology-specific and essential tasks such as writing to a disk, starting your Web browser software so you can surf the Web, and sending a document to your printer.
- ***Application software***—the software that allows you to perform specific information-processing tasks such as managing inventory, paying accounts payable, handling payroll, writing a term paper, or creating slides for a presentation.

System software is the software that your computer uses to run itself, regardless of what type of task you're performing. So, when you turn on your computer, your system software takes over and performs a variety of tasks—checking to see what devices you have connected such as a printer and mouse, potentially verifying your connection to a network so you can use the Internet, and even asking for and verifying your password.

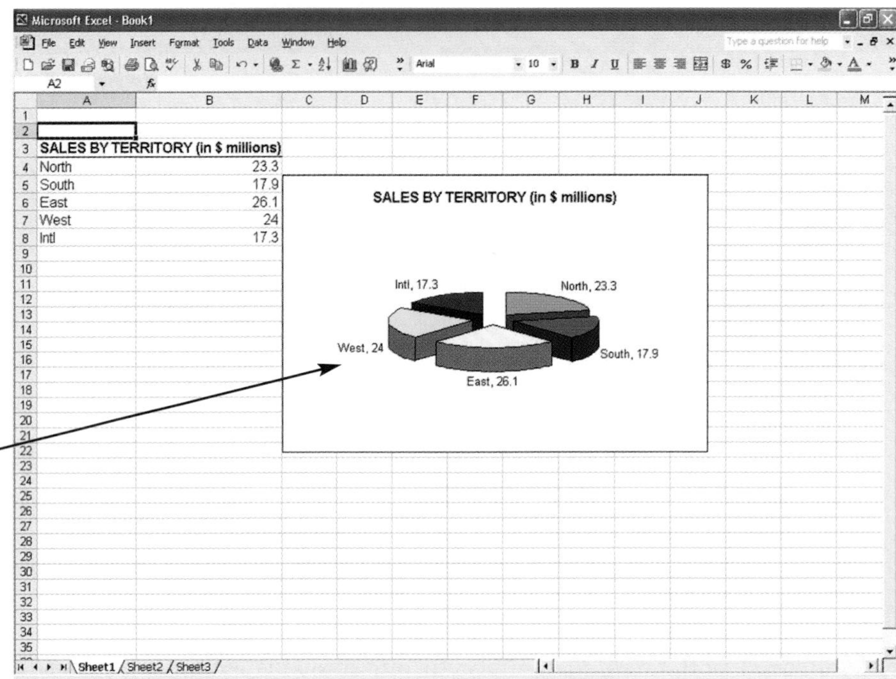

FIGURE 1.5

Excel spreadsheet software is a type of application software that can help you easily build graphs from a table of numbers.

We created this graph with only seven clicks of the mouse.

On the other hand, application software is the software you use to perform tasks specific to your needs. For example, you can use Excel—spreadsheet software—to enter information in the form of a table and then create a high-quality, colorful graph. In Figure 1.5, you can see a table of sales information we entered. With seven clicks of the mouse we created the graph. Microsoft PowerPoint is another type of application software called presentation software. We used it in the previous section to illustrate how to incorporate music into a presentation. To learn more about the capabilities of your software, complete the "Introduction to Software" tutorial on your SimNet Concepts Support CD.

CATEGORIES OF COMPUTER HARDWARE
What Can My Hardware Help Me Do?

Although software may be the most important component in your computer, you must also have hardware. Essentially, hardware includes all of those devices that you can touch—your monitor, your keyboard, a floppy disk, and numerous pieces contained within your system box, just to name a few.

The six categories of computer hardware are (see Figure 1.6 on the opposite page):

1. Input devices for capturing information.
2. Output devices for presenting information.
3. CPU and RAM for creating new information.
4. Storage devices for storing information.
5. Telecommunications devices for communicating information.
6. Connecting devices for moving information to and from your various hardware.

did you know?

"Denial *ain't just a river in Egypt," stated Mark Twain.*

FIGURE 1.6

Different components of your computer hardware help you perform different tasks.

A keyboard is an input device for capturing information.

A monitor is an output device for presenting information.

Intel's Xeon is a CPU chip that creates new information.

Floppy disks are storage devices that store information.

A DSL modem is a telecommunications device that communicates information.

A parallel connector is a connecting device commonly used for a printer.

FIGURE 1.7

A joystick is an example of an input device.

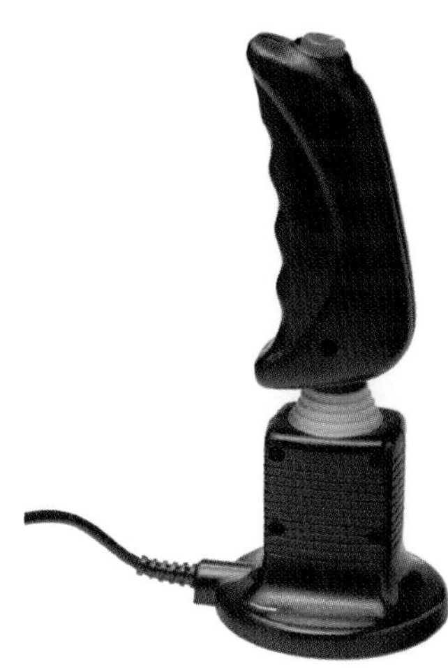

Input Devices for Capturing Information

An ***input device*** captures information and translates it into a form that can be processed and used by other parts of your computer. Input devices play a vitally important role in a computer system by helping you enter information. For example, you can use a scanner to capture images and photos that exist on paper and an Internet video camera to capture your likeness in the form of a video. In our computer ad (see Figure 1.4 again), you can find input devices such as a keyboard, mouse, and Internet video camera.

Output Devices for Presenting Information

An ***output device*** takes information within your computer and presents it to you in a form that you can understand. Output devices are the complement to input devices. While input devices help you enter information into a computer system, output devices help you see, hear, or otherwise receive information stored within your computer system. For example, you can

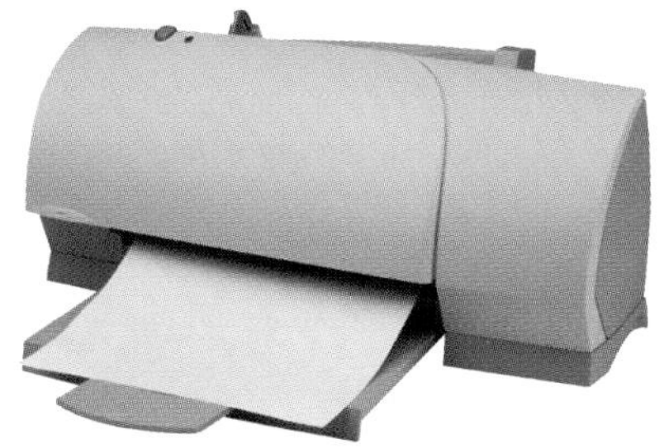

FIGURE 1.8

A printer is an example of an output device.

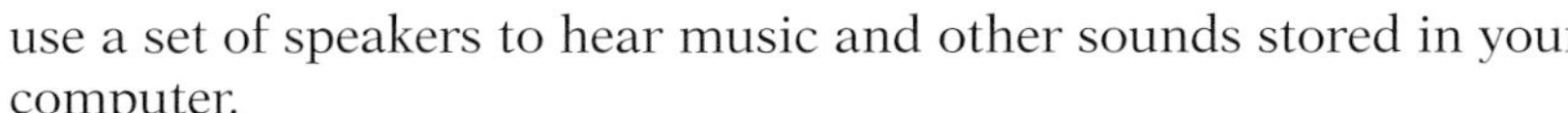

use a set of speakers to hear music and other sounds stored in your computer.

In our computer ad (Figure 1.4), the output devices include a 17" monitor, JBL platinum speakers, and a bubble jet color printer. In Chapter 5, we'll delve more into various types of input and output devices and what you need to know to make an informed purchasing decision.

CPU and RAM for Creating New Information

The most important components of your hardware are the CPU and RAM, which together make up the real brains of your computer. The ***central processing unit*** (***CPU*** or ***processor***) is the chip that carries out instructions it receives from your software (see Figure 1.9). The computer in our ad includes the Pentium 4 processor as its CPU. Other CPUs include the Apple PowerPC, AMD Athlon, and Intel Celeron.

RAM (random access memory) is temporary memory that holds software instructions and information for the CPU. RAM is rather like your short-term memory. When you turn off your computer, all information in RAM is gone. In our computer ad, RAM is listed as 256MB shared SyncDRAM memory, which is roughly 256 million characters. In Chapter 6, we'll explore the CPU and RAM, including what speed you need (for your CPU) and how much RAM you need.

FIGURE 1.9

Your CPU carries out instructions it receives from your software.

Storage Devices for Storing Information

Temporary information storage in RAM is not enough, of course. You need a means to more permanently store information so you can recall and use it at a later time. This is the role of storage devices. A ***storage device*** stores information so you can recall and use that information at a later time.

The computer in our ad comes with a variety of storage devices (most do) including a 3.5" disk drive, 100 gigabyte hard drive, DVD-RW drive, and 40X max CD-ROM drive. We'll talk more about your storage device needs in Chapter 5.

Telecommunications Devices for Communicating Information

In today's world, communication is vital. Cell phones, e-mail, and digital pagers are an important part of most all our lives. These are all computer-based tools that help you communicate information to people in other locations. Those people may be next door or somewhere around the world—the distance doesn't really matter.

A ***telecommunications device*** helps you communicate information to people in other locations. The computer in our ad includes a v.90 56Kbps high-speed modem and a 10/100 network card as telecommunications devices. Don't let all that computer jargon scare you. Once you've read Chapter 7, you'll be well equipped to make an informed decision regarding what telecommunications devices you need to buy.

FIGURE 1.10

CDs and DVDs are popular storage devices. DVDs are slightly smaller than CDs.

Connecting Devices for Moving Information to and from Your Various Hardware

Finally, your computer contains a variety of connecting devices so that information can move around all your hardware. For example, you need some sort of connection between your computer and a printer. At a minimum, this includes a port and a connecter (provided that it's not a wireless printer, which we'll discuss in Chapter 5). Ports are usually located on the back of your computer, while connectors are located on the end of a cable or wire. When you add your monitor to your desktop computer, you plug its cable into your computer by inserting the connector into the appropriate port. You perform a similar task for a mouse, a keyboard, a modem, a scanner, and other devices.

We'll talk more about your connecting device needs and the roles they play in Chapters 5, 6, and 7.

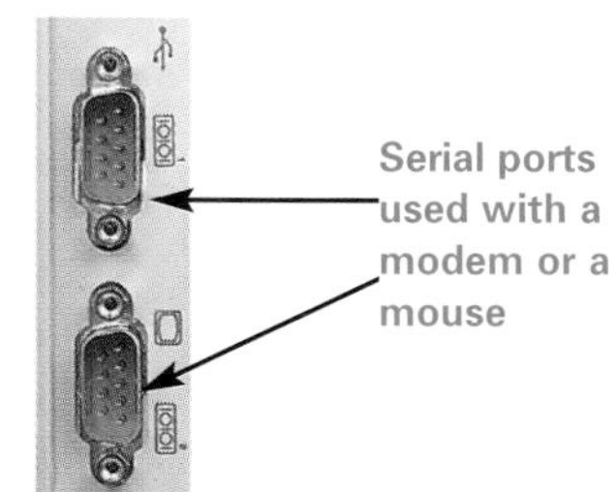

FIGURE 1.11

Connecting devices include a port (located on the back of your computer) and a connector (located on the end of your cable).

COMPUTERS FOR PERSONAL USE
What Do People Use for Personal Computing?

Computers come in different sizes, shapes, and forms. Some are extremely small and lightweight, while others are almost the size of a telephone booth. Size in some way equates to a computer's power, speed, and price. To handle your personal needs, you'll most often be considering personal digital assistants, notebook computers, and/or desktop computers (see Figure 1.12).

Personal digital assistants (PDAs) are small hand-held computers that help you perform simple tasks such as note taking, maintaining a calendar and appointment book, maintaining an address book, and perhaps even surfing the Web. PDAs have a small screen that acts as both an input and output device. On the screen, you can see information and you can also use a special writing stylus or pen to write directly on the screen, with the screen capturing what you're writing. On the Web site for this text at www.mhhe.com/i-series, you'll find a great review of some of the better PDAs available today.

A ***notebook computer*** (sometimes called a ***laptop computer***) is a small, portable, fully functional battery-powered computer designed for you to carry around with you. Notebooks, some weighing as little as four pounds, come completely equipped with all the hardware and software you need. If you need portability, then a notebook computer is probably your answer.

Desktop computers are the most popular choice for personal computing needs, with prices ranging from about $500 to several thousand dollars. Dollar for dollar, you

FIGURE 1.12

Common computers for personal use include PDAs, notebook computers, and desktop computers.

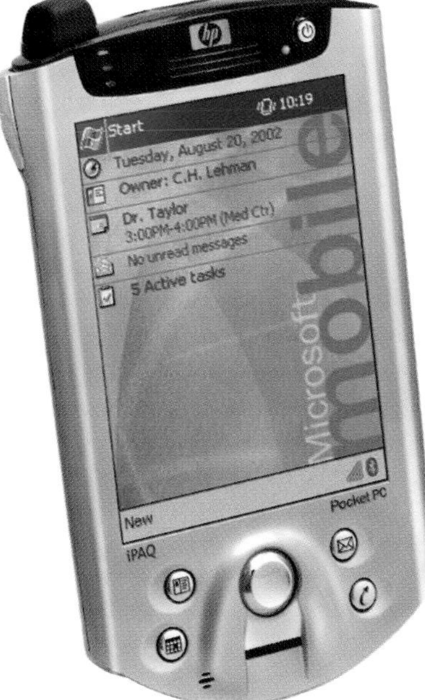

A personal digital assistant (PDA) is a small hand-held computer.

Notebooks are fully functional battery-powered computers you can easily carry.

Desktop computers come in a variety of shapes and sizes.

can buy more computing power with a desktop than with a notebook (or a PDA). Of course, PDAs and notebooks offer you great portability, while desktops offer none.

COMPUTERS THAT SUPPORT ORGANIZATIONS

What Computers Do Organizations Use to Support Their Processes?

Within any organization, people use PDAs, notebooks, and desktop computers for their personal needs. While doing so, they also need access to larger computers that store software and information that everyone can use. These larger computers are minicomputers, mainframe computers, and supercomputers (see Figure 1.13).

A ***minicomputer*** (sometimes called a ***mid-range computer***) is designed to meet the computing needs of several people simultaneously in a small to medium-size business environment. Minicomputers are more powerful and faster than desktop computers but also cost more, ranging from $5,000 to several hundred thousand dollars. Minicomputers are well suited for small to medium-size business environments in which people need to share common information, processing power, and/or certain peripheral devices such as high-quality color printers. Many organizations also use minicomputers for Web server computers (which we'll discuss in the next chapter).

A mainframe computer is a step up in size, power, capability, and cost from a minicomputer. A ***mainframe computer*** (sometimes just called a ***mainframe***) is a computer designed to meet the computing needs of hundreds of people in a large business environment. Mainframes can easily cost in excess of $1 million. With processing speeds greater than 1 trillion instructions per second, mainframes can handle the processing needs of hundreds of people simultaneously.

FIGURE 1.13

Minicomputers, mainframe computers, and supercomputers can simultaneously process transactions for many people.

A minicomputer is well suited for small to medium-size business environments.

Mainframe computers meet the computing needs of hundreds of users in large business environments.

Supercomputers are extremely fast "number crunchers."

Supercomputers are the fastest, most powerful, and most expensive type of computer. Organizations such as NASA that are heavily involved in research and "number crunching" employ supercomputers because of the speed with which they can process information. Other very large, customer-oriented businesses, such as General Motors and AT&T, employ supercomputers to handle their customer information and transaction processing.

That ends our very basic and quick tour of technology. Throughout the remainder of this chapter and all the other chapters, we'll further explore these and related topics. Along the way, we'll also focus on helping you make the best possible decisions regarding what technology to buy and how to use that technology.

making the grade

SECTION 1.2

1. Everything in your computer falls into one of two categories—____________ or ____________.
2. A 3.5" disk drive, a hard drive, and a CD-RW drive are examples of ____________ devices.
3. A(n) ____________ takes information within your computer and presents it to you in a form that you can understand.
4. A(n) ____________ is a small, portable, fully functional battery-powered computer designed for you to carry around.
5. ____________ are the fastest, most powerful, and most expensive type of computer.

1.3 COMPUTING PRODUCTIVITY WITH AND WITHOUT . . .

Throughout this text, we'll stress how rapidly and explosively technology is changing—especially computers. In this context of dynamic and ever-changing technology, let's consider some key issues.

COMPUTING WITHOUT A PC

Do I Need a Traditional Notebook or Desktop Computer in Order to Be Productive?

Just a few short years ago, people met their personal computing needs by buying either a desktop or a notebook computer. Then along came another alternative, PDAs. Today, you have many more choices—all of which can help you be productive depending on your particular needs. Here, we alert you to tablet PCs, smart phones, and wrist watches that act as PDAs.

A ***tablet PC*** is a pen-based computer that provides the screen capabilities of a PDA with the functional capabilities of a notebook or desktop computer. Similar to PDAs, tablet PCs allow you to use a writing pen or stylus to write notes on the screen and touch the screen to perform functions such as clicking on a link while visiting a Web site. Tablet PCs come in two designs—convertibles and slates. Convertible tablet PCs look much like a notebook computer, including a screen that you lift up and set in position with a full keyboard and touch pad underneath. Using a convertible tablet PC, you can swivel the screen and even lay it flat on the keyboard,

FIGURE 1.14

You have many personal technology alternatives to PDAs, notebook computers, and desktop computers.

Slate tablet PCs have their storage devices, CPU, and RAM integrated into the screen.

Some watches now include PDA capabilities.

Smart phones, such as the Motorola T720, are sophisticated cell phones.

making it a "convertible" notebook computer with no top. Toshiba's Portege 3500 is a convertible tablet PC.

Slate tablet PCs come with no integrated physical keyboard. (So, the tablet is the entire computer.) You can buy a docking station for a slate tablet PC, however, giving you the ability to connect a keyboard and mouse. Slate tablet PCs have their storage devices, CPU, and RAM integrated into the screen. The Fujitsu Stylistic ST4000 is a slate tablet PC (see Figure 1.14).

Smart phones are cell phones that include such capabilities as surfing the Web and sending and receiving e-mail (see the right photo in Figure 1.14). Smart phones today have high-quality screens capable of supporting up to 4,000 colors on which you can view Web sites and play games. Some even offer you the capability of sending and receiving color photos.

The center photo in Figure 1.14 shows Fossil's new wrist watch that acts as a PDA. You can synchronize the information on your PDA wrist watch with your more traditional PDA. In doing so, your PDA wrist watch can store thousands of addresses, years of appointments, hundreds of to-do items, and notes. You can even use infrared technology to send and receive business card information to and from other wrist watch PDAs and traditional PDAs. By the way, your PDA wrist watch can also tell you the time of day.

These are just three of the many alternative personal technologies that offer you productivity. Which you choose is a function of what you need. Notice that all offer you great portability and mobility, even beyond some of today's lightest and best notebook computers. So, you may not need a desktop or notebook computer to be productive.

did you know?

"In America, anybody can be president. That's one of the risks you take," said Adlai Stevenson.

COMPUTING WITH THE WORLD
How Can the Web Help Me Be Productive?

Perhaps the most visible and explosive technology is the Web (supported by the Internet, both of which we'll discuss at length in the next chapter).

On the Web, you visit places called Web sites. A ***Web site*** is a specific location on the Web that you can visit electronically to gather information and perhaps order products and request services. In Figure 1.15, we've provided two screen captures of FinAid! (its Web site address is www.finaid.com), one of the most well-known sites for finding financial assistance while going to school.

In the background screen, we simply clicked once on the **Scholarships** link. FinAid! then moved us to the new page you see in the foreground. From there, we could click on other links (for example, **Loans** or **Military Aid**) to find more information and eventually get to a list of financial assistance.

While traversing through FinAid!, we were clicking on links. A ***link*** (the technical term is ***hyperlink***) is clickable text or an image that allows you to move from one Web site to another or move to a different place within the same Web site. In our case, we were staying within the same Web site. (Notice that the Web site address in the background screen is www.finaid.com while the Web site address in the foreground screen is www.finaid.com/scholarships.) To learn more about the productivity of the Web, complete the "Introduction to the Internet and the World Wide Web" tutorial on your SimNet Concepts Support CD.

Could you be more productive if you could find financial assistance so you wouldn't have to work while going to school? Could you be more productive by searching library Web sites to find information you need for a

FIGURE 1.15

FinAid! is a popular stop on the Web for finding financial aid while going to school.

practically speaking

The Travels of Information throughout History

Today, many people use their personal digital assistants to connect to the Web and obtain up-to-the-minute forecasts, stock market quotes, and other useful information. It's how they get their information. If we traverse back through the past, an interesting story unfolds concerning how people have communicated information to each other.

- **3500 B.C. Ancient Rome**—you would write a letter in the form of a pictograph on clay. A messenger service could deliver your clay tablet a distance of 10 miles in about a week.
- **900 B.C. China**—the Chinese developed a postal system, but it could be used only for government purposes.
- **100 B.C. Rome**—the Romans developed their postal system for delivering correspondences on papyrus, animal skins, or bones.
- **1400 B.C.**—handwritten books and manuscripts were common among the aristocracy. Chances are that you were not one of the lucky ones who had books or could read.
- **1661**—American colonies developed a postal system, but you would have had to wait until 1673 to send mail from Boston to New York.
- **1785**—stagecoaches began delivering mail. By 1800, it took only 20 days to deliver mail from Georgia to Maine.
- **1837**—Samuel Morse invented the telegraph.
- **1876**—the telephone was invented.
- **1900**—most people could afford a camera.
- **Early 1900s**—radio became commonplace.
- **1921**—Western Union could send photos via a wire system.
- **1928**—the first televisions were introduced into U.S. homes (three of them, to be exact).
- **1944**—the first digital computer was invented.
- **1975**—you could buy a kit and build your own computer.
- **1982**—IBM introduced its IBM PC.

Since then, we've made quantum leaps in technology and how we deliver information. If you're interested in a detailed and informative presentation on the history of technology, visit Appendix A.

term paper instead of going to the library? We believe the answer is yes to both questions.

COMPUTING WITHOUT E-MAIL

Can I Use the Web to Talk to People Live?

The Web certainly can help you be more productive, especially in communicating with other people via e-mail. ***E-mail*** (short for ***electronic mail***) is software you use to electronically communicate with other people. E-mail works much the way you send and receive mail through the postal service. You have an e-mail box in which your messages reside until you open it and read them. When you send a message, it sits in the recipient's e-mail box until he or she opens it.

E-mail has certainly enabled people all over the world to communicate. But most e-mail isn't real time. That is, e-mail is asynchronous in that it doesn't instantly get to you when it's sent. Rather, it goes to your e-mail box and waits there until you open it.

There are alternatives that are instantaneous. Four such alternatives include chat rooms, instant messaging, Short Messaging Service, and Multimedia Messaging Service. A ***chat room*** is a virtual meeting place on the Web in which you can communicate live with people who happen to be on

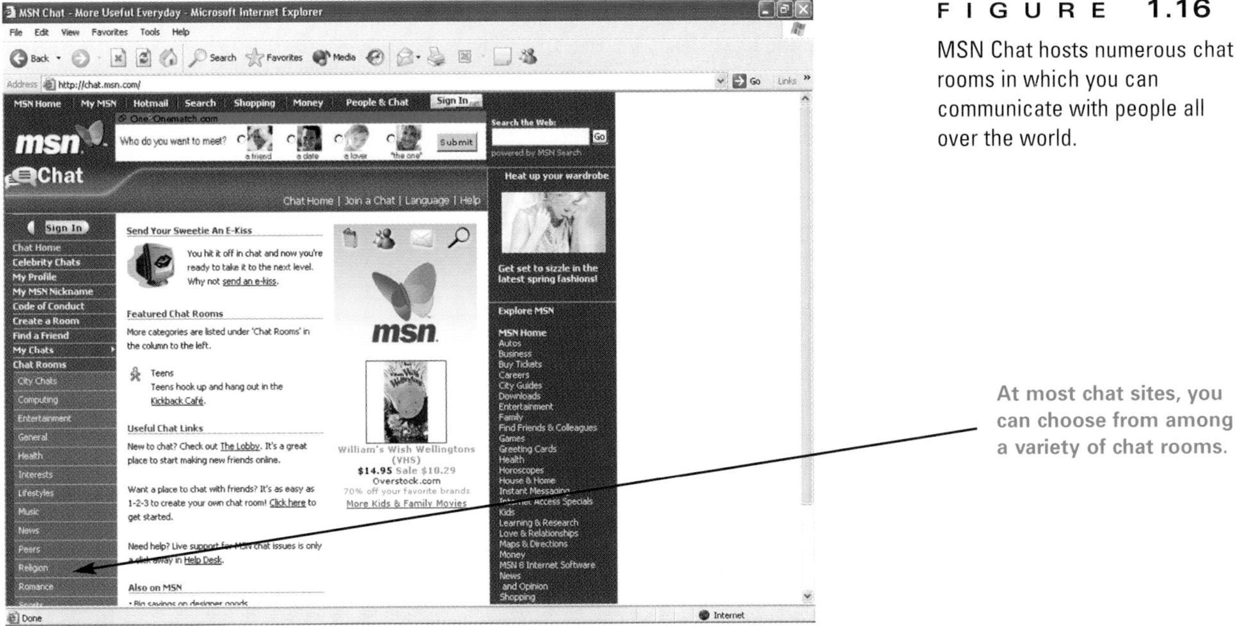

FIGURE 1.16

MSN Chat hosts numerous chat rooms in which you can communicate with people all over the world.

At most chat sites, you can choose from among a variety of chat rooms.

the Web and in the same chat room at the same time. Figure 1.16 shows a list of chat rooms provided by MSN Chat (chat.msn.com). All you have to do is pick a chat room or topic and click on it, and you'll be placed in a virtual room. As other chatters type in their comments, those comments instantly appear on your screen. You can join in the conversation at any time by typing in your own comments.

Instant messaging is a bit different. ***Instant messaging*** is a private version of a chat room in which you communicate only with people you choose. For example, AOL's Instant Messenger allows you to direct your comments to a specific person (via his or her e-mail address). In turn, he or she can respond to your comments. Instant messaging is rather like having a telephone conversation through your computer while chat rooms are open to most anyone. AOL's Instant Messenger now supports full voice communication. So, you don't even have to type your comments—instead, you speak them.

Short Messaging Service (SMS) is a technology that enables you to send a text message, usually from your cell phone to the cell phone of another person. Basically, SMS is a form of instantaneous e-mail via cell phone or instant messaging via cell phone. ***Multimedia Messaging Service (MMS)*** is a technology upgrade to SMS, giving you the ability to send messages containing not only text but also sounds, images, and video, usually from your cell phone to the cell phone of another person. Right now, almost all cell phone services support SMS and many are quickly moving to support MMS.

To learn more about communicating with the Internet, complete the "Using the Internet to Communicate" tutorial on your SimNet Concepts Support CD.

COMPUTING WITHOUT WIRES

Can I Be Productive Wirelessly, instead of Wired?

To communicate with other people via e-mail or instant messaging, retrieve stock quotes, find financial assistance, and perform a variety of other tasks, you need to connect your computer to the Web. To do that today, most people use some sort of land-based line such as a telephone line, but that, along with most other aspects of technology, is changing on a daily basis. As we've already discussed, you can wirelessly access the Web using such devices as a PDA, a smart phone, and a combined smart phone/PDA. But what if you have a desktop or notebook computer and want wireless access to the Web (and peripheral devices such as a printer)?

One alternative (there are many) for wirelessly connecting to the Web is WiFi. ***WiFi*** is a standard for transmitting information in the form of radio waves over distances of up to 300 feet, often used for wireless access to networks. In your home or dorm room, for example, you could connect a wireless access point device that provides wireless access to your phone line. You would then install a wireless adapter in your desktop computer or a wireless PC Card in your notebook computer. You could then be anywhere in your home or dorm room and wirelessly connect via WiFi to the wireless access point device, which would allow you to connect to the Web.

FIGURE 1.17

A Bluetooth PC Card adapter provides you with a variety of wireless connectivity options.

You can also wirelessly connect your computer to peripheral devices such as a printer or to other appliances in your home such as a refrigerator using Bluetooth. ***Bluetooth*** is a standard for transmitting information in the form of short-range radio waves over distances of up to 30 feet, and is used for purposes such as wirelessly connecting a cell phone to a computer. So you could use Bluetooth to connect your PDA, notebook computer, or desktop computer to a printer. You could also connect to your TV set (provided it had Bluetooth technology). If so, you could control the volume and change the TV channels from your PDA, notebook computer, or desktop computer.

The possibilities surrounding wireless productivity are enormous, to say the least. Today, some home builders aren't even installing land-based phone lines in many new homes. Those home builders understand that many people want completely wireless access running throughout their homes. To learn more about the productivity of wireless technologies, complete the "Wireless Communications" tutorial on your SimNet Concepts Support CD.

COMPUTING WITH YOUR CAREER IN MIND

How Can Technology Help Me in My Career?

No matter which career you choose, you'll undoubtedly be required to use technology in your daily work. It has become a simple fact of life. Learning about information technology (IT) can help you in your career by (1) making you valuable in many non-IT fields, (2) helping you advertise yourself to potential employers, and (3) offering you a wide variety of careers in the IT field itself.

did you know?

"Every day I get up and look through the *Forbes* list of the richest people in America. If I'm not there, I go to work," stated Robert Orben.

Computing for Any Career

If you choose a career that is not in information technology, you still need information technology skills. Those skills definitely include the basics of using word processing software, spreadsheet software, presentation software, e-mail software, and others we'll talk about in Chapter 3. You should also hone your skills in working with databases—large organizations of customer information, supplier information, inventory information, and so on. Microsoft Access is the most popular personal productivity database management system (the software for working with a database).

Job Title	Description
Guest Satisfaction Analyst	Receives and/or places high volume telephone calls or e-mails in a call center environment for account inquiries, disputes, and conflict resolution.
Project Analyst	Leads special projects as identified in annual objectives as well as other special projects identified during the year. These projects include further migration of accounting functions to Business Services.
Senior Financial Analyst	Provides analytical support to the WW FPA Manager and WW Ops Finance Management with a high degree of professionalism and confidentiality with minimal supervision.
Merchandise Planner/Analyst	Responsible for engaging the buying, allocations, logistics, and systems teams with the goal of ensuring that an appropriate flow and mix of merchandise are supplied to the stores.
Product Marketing Analyst	Competitive intelligence and research; analyze product features for improvements; customer needs analysis and market research.
Medical Economics Consultant	Develop detailed analytical models which will identify and quantify the immediate/long-term drivers of medical cost trends.
Transportation Supervisor	Responsible for several aspects of regional transportation and logistics, including the areas of carrier management, financial analysis and service.

FIGURE 1.18

Many different careers require technology expertise such as the ability to use Microsoft Access, a popular software tool for working with databases.

We performed a search on Monster.com using "Microsoft Access" as a search term. We found over 450 job listings requiring expertise in Microsoft Access. In Figure 1.18, we've listed several of the job titles we found and their descriptions. Notice that not a single job title is IT-specific. Rather, they represent job openings in such areas as guest satisfaction, project management, finance, merchandising, product marketing, medicine, and transportation.

Don't sell yourself short in the job market by not learning all you can about technology! Then, having acquired IT knowledge, be sure to include a section on your resume that details what technology skills you have.

Using Technology to Find a Job

As you prepare your resume and begin your job search, we recommend that you use technology by exploring the electronic job market. The ***electronic job market*** makes use of the Internet to recruit employees and is growing by leaps and bounds. According to the *Industrial Standard* (www.thestandard.com), a leading magazine on the Internet economy, the average cost of online recruiting is $152 per hire while the cost of more traditional methods is $1,381. So, many organizations now post jobs and recruit potential employees via the Internet. The most popular

Web site that organizations use for posting job openings is Monster.com (www.monster.com, see Figure 1.19).

In preparation for entering the electronic job market, you need to create an ***e-portfolio***—a personal Web site that contains your e-resume and a gallery of important projects you've completed, papers you've written, presentations you've made, references, and other types of valuable information. When talking to recruiters, you should give them your e-portfolio address and encourage them to review your work. This method of providing information is often much more effective than simply distributing a paper resume.

Choosing a Technology Career

Of course, you may choose a career in the technology field. If so, you have many, many choices. Throughout this text, you'll frequently see a Careers icon (shown to the left) in the side margin. We've placed it beside important text that discusses a career in the technology field. Below, we've described just a few of many options you have. You can also complete the "Careers" tutorial on your SimNet Concepts Support CD to learn more about employment opportunities in IT.

- Database analyst/programmer—analyzes business environments and designs, develops, and implements database solutions to support various processes.
- Database administrator (DBA)—management position overseeing the database activities within an organization.
- Web-gineer—designs, develops, and implements solutions for Web-based activities such as electronic functions.
- Programmer—takes user requirements and writes software to match those requirements.
- Analyst—works with users to develop a list of requirements and the design of a computer solution to support those requirements.

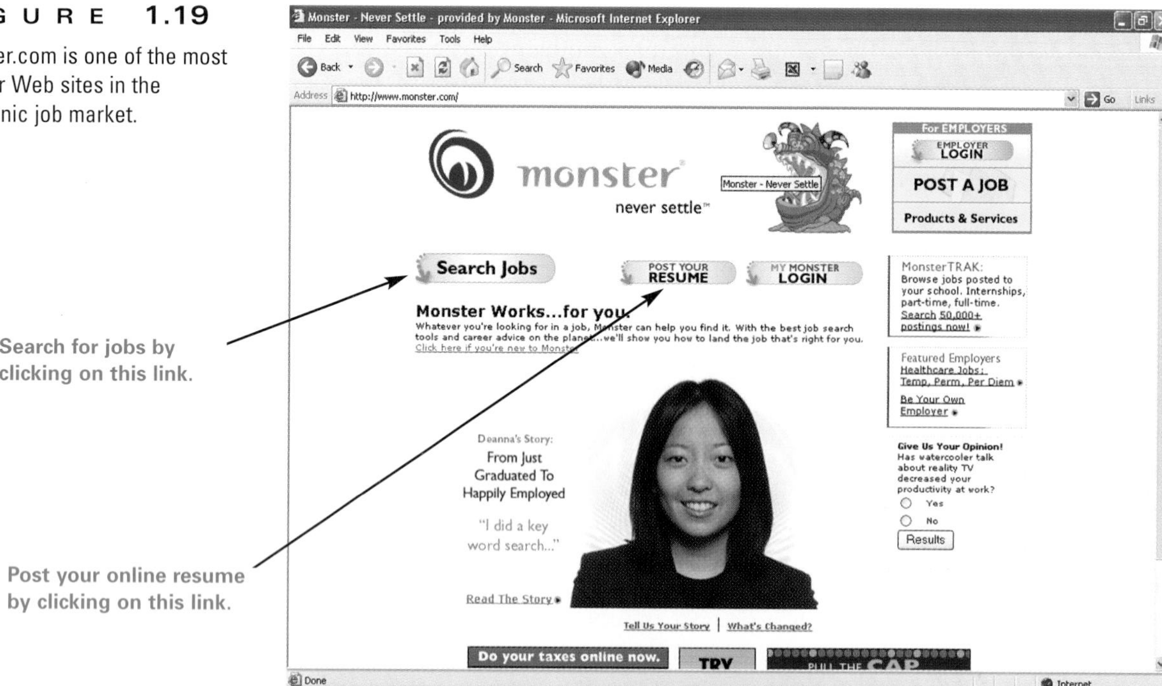

FIGURE 1.19

Monster.com is one of the most popular Web sites in the electronic job market.

i•series insights — Ethics, Security & Privacy

Are Transactions on the Internet Really Safe?

Many people enjoy surfing the Web, reading interesting material, and e-mailing friends and family. When it comes to ordering products, however, they have a different view. The most common reason people don't order products on the Web is that they believe they're providing their credit card and personal information for everyone to see. Is that true?

The answer is really no. It's just as safe as using your credit card in a restaurant. Think about using your credit card to pay for a meal. You give your card to the waitstaff to take to a back room to process the transaction. What sort of guarantee

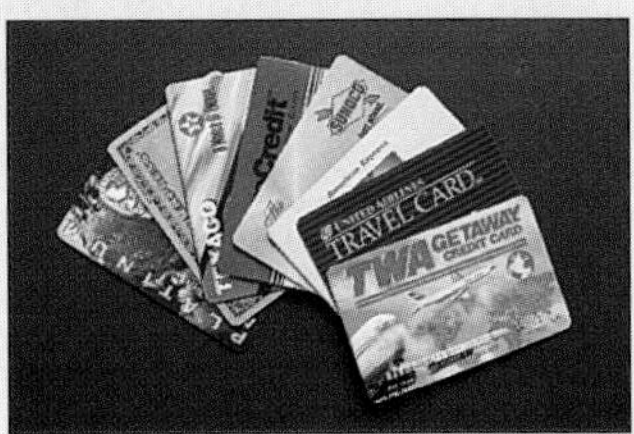

do you have that your credit card information isn't being recorded by the wrong person for the wrong reason? Couldn't the waitstaff record your card information and then use it later for a telephone order or perhaps even an order on the Web?

On the Web, you still have your card in your possession, but it's true that your credit card information is traveling over a vast network of computers. However, most Web sites that require credit card information provide some security while your information is traveling. In this instance, the Web site may "scramble" your card information at your computer when you enter it, send it through the Web, and then "unscramble" it when it reaches the Web site.

The process is just as safe as using your credit card in a restaurant. Currently, credit card fraud on the Web is estimated at less than 1 percent of all transaction fraud in terms of dollars.

- Chief information officer (CIO)—management position overseeing the use of information as a resource in an organization.
- Network administrator—designs, implements, and maintains the technical hardware and software necessary to run a network.
- Chief privacy officer (CPO)—management position focusing on the ethical use of information with respect to the issue of privacy.

COMPUTING WITH SOCIETY

Do I Need to Consider Other People while Using My Computer?

With your computer you can perform many tasks much faster than without a computer. You can talk live with people all over the world. You can apply for credit cards on the Web. You don't ever need to visit a library again to find materials for a term paper. However, for every good and productive use of a computer, someone has found a bad use.

The real "wrong" way to use a computer is to do so for unethical reasons. ***Ethics*** is the set of principles and standards we use in deciding what to do in situations that affect other people. Ethics differ from laws. Laws require or prohibit certain actions on your part. Ethics, on the other hand, involve how you personally view the rightness or wrongness of your actions. Unethical behaviors are a detriment to society and are often against the law. Consider these three terms that you've probably heard of.

- ***Hacker***—a very knowledgeable computer user who uses his or her knowledge to invade other people's computers. There are many types of hackers—black-hat hackers, crackers, hacktivists, cyber terrorists, script bunnies, and white-hat hackers (also called ethical hackers), with only the latter being a "good" kind of hacker.
- ***Computer virus (virus)***—software that is designed intentionally to cause annoyance or damage. A malignant virus, the worst kind, can destroy information on your computer, completely wipe out

your hard disk, and use your e-mail address book to send itself to your friends and family.

- ***Identity theft***—the impersonation by a thief of someone with good credit. The Web and the Internet have made it much easier for someone to find and use your most personal information such as your social security number and your credit card numbers.

Throughout this text (especially in Chapters 4 and 9) we'll alert you to these types of dangers and how you can protect yourself against them.

As a seemingly minor ethical dilemma, consider the issue of gossiping. Sharing gossip is not against the law (unless you say or publish something legally defined as harmful or slanderous), but many people consider gossiping unethical. That is, they refuse to pass along demeaning information until they have all the facts, and maybe not even then. Thus, ethics is a matter of personal interpretation. To you, gossiping may be unethical, while others may consider it okay. What do you think about it?

As another example, consider forwarding e-mail. E-mail is a simple, but powerful, tool for communicating electronically and all e-mail software allows you to forward messages. But is it right or wrong to do so? Some people would say that you shouldn't forward an e-mail message (no matter how trivial) unless you obtain the permission of the person who originally wrote the e-mail and sent it to you.

Ethical behavior is essential in our society and to your well-being. Computers have added greatly to ethical dilemmas concerning sharing all types of information. It's far easier to share information through computers than it ever has been. As you use your computer, you must consider the ethics of all people and the ethical standards of society in addition to your own ethics. To learn more about computing in society, complete the "Privacy Issues" and "Security Issues" tutorials on your SimNet Concepts Support CD.

SECTION 1.3

making the grade

1. A(n) ___________ is a pen-based computer that provides the screen capabilities of a PDA with the functional capabilities of a notebook or desktop computer.
2. A(n) ___________ is a specific location on the Web where you can visit, gather information, and perhaps order products and request services.
3. ___________ is a private version of a chat room in which you communicate only with people you choose.
4. ___________ is a standard for connecting devices wirelessly over short distances, usually not exceeding 30 feet.
5. ___________ is the set of principles and standards we use in deciding what to do in situations that affect other people.

did you know?

A statement once made by Elvis Presley—"I don't know anything about music. In my line you don't have to."

1.4 CONSUMER Q&A

At the close of each of the first seven chapters of this text, we've included a consumer Q&A section. In these sections, you'll find a list of questions (and our answers to them) that we frequently hear from students in the classroom.

1. Should I Buy a Desktop or a Notebook Computer?

This is a common question. It really boils down to two issues—price and portability. Dollar for dollar, you can buy more power and capability with a desktop computer than with a notebook computer. As for portability, if you need to be mobile with your technology, then you probably need a notebook computer. But don't kid yourself into believing that you need a notebook computer because you'll be able to take it on vacation with you. Do you really want to lie by the pool or on the beach and use your computer? It's definitely a personal choice.

2. Won't My Computer Be Obsolete Just as Soon as I Buy It?

The answer here is both yes and no. New, more powerful computers are becoming available every day. What you buy may be the best today—it won't be tomorrow. Don't let that stop you from buying a computer if you need one. Think of a car—today's best models are quickly replaced by next year's better models. But that doesn't stop people from buying cars.

3. Should I Consider Mail Order or Purchasing Locally?

Depending on the brand of computer, you can get equal quality from either mail order or a local purchase. Many people like to purchase locally because the service center is also local. At the same time, many mail-order computer companies do have "on site" repair and maintenance for a given period of time after you make the purchase. Sometimes though, if you buy through mail order and have a problem, you have to pack up your computer and send it off for servicing. Mail order sometimes provides better flexibility in customizing your computer.

4. Can I Expand My Computer after I Buy It?

The answer here is definitely yes. You can perhaps add more memory (RAM), upgrade your CPU to a faster speed, and easily add peripheral devices such as a CD burner or a scanner. Many people specifically plan to expand their computers a few months down the road. This gives you the ability to purchase a basic system now and add more functionality as you have the money.

1.5 SUMMARY AND KEY TERMS

You've been through a very fast but we hope great introduction to computers and what they can do for you. A ***computer*** (or ***computer system***) is a set of tools that helps you perform information-processing tasks. You need to use all the tools in your computer to be productive. Your computer tools are either hardware or software.

Software

- ***System software*** for technology-specific and essential tasks.
- ***Application software*** for specific tasks such as writing a term paper or managing inventory.

Hardware

- ***Input devices*** such as a mouse for capturing information.
- ***Output devices*** such as a printer for presenting information.
- ***CPU*** and ***RAM*** (your computer's brain) for creating new information.
- ***Storage devices*** such as a disk for storing information.
- ***Telecommunications devices*** such as a modem for communicating information to other people.
- ***Connecting devices*** such as a port for moving information around all your hardware.

You also learned about the categories of computers by size—***personal digital assistants (PDAs), notebook computers, desktop computers, minicomputers, mainframe computers,*** and ***supercomputers.*** For your personal technology needs, you'll primarily be using PDAs, notebook computers, and desktop computers.

You also learned about many key technologies and technology issues that make this field very dynamic and exciting, including:

- Computing with a PC—***tablet PCs, smart phones,*** and PDA wrist watches.
- Computing with the world—through the Web.
- Computing without e-mail—***chat rooms, instant messaging, SMS,*** and ***MMS.***
- Computing without wires—***WiFi*** and ***Bluetooth.***
- Computing with your career in mind—using technology to prepare yourself for the workplace.
- Computing with society—most notably, ***ethics.***

Finally, you should visit the Web site for this text at www.mhhe.com/i-series to learn more about PDAs.

KEY TERMS

application software (p. 9)
Bluetooth (p. 20)
button (p. 5)
central processing unit (CPU or processor) (p. 12)
chat room (p. 18)
computer (computer system) (p. 8)
computer virus (virus) (p. 23)
desktop computer (p. 13)
e-mail (electronic mail) (p. 18)
e-portfolio (p. 22)
electronic job market (p. 21)
ethics (p. 23)
graphical user interface (GUI) (p. 5)
hacker (p. 23)
hardware (p. 8)
icon (p. 5)
identity theft (p. 24)
input device (p. 11)
instant messaging (p. 19)
link (hyperlink) (p. 17)
mainframe computer (mainframe) (p. 14)
minicomputer (mid-range computer) (p. 14)
Multimedia Messaging Service (MMS) (p. 19)
notebook computer (laptop computer) (p. 13)
output device (p. 11)
personal digital assistant (PDA) (p. 13)
RAM (random access memory) (p. 12)
Short Messaging Service (SMS) (p. 19)
smart phone (p. 16)
software (p. 8)
storage device (p. 12)
supercomputer (p. 15)
system software (p. 9)
tablet PC (p. 15)
telecommunications device (p. 12)
Web site (p. 17)
WiFi (p. 20)

review of terminology

Multiple Choice

1. The real brains of your computer are the
   a. storage devices.
   b. CPU and RAM.
   c. CPU, RAM, and storage devices.
   d. telecommunications devices.
   e. input and output devices.

2. A personal Web site that contains your e-resume and a gallery of your important projects and other types of valuable information is a(n)
   a. chat room.
   b. job Web site.
   c. e-portfolio.
   d. example of system software.
   e. hardware device.

3. A device that captures information and translates it into a form that can be processed and used by other parts of your computer is a(n)
   a. input device.
   b. output device.
   c. storage device.
   d. telecommunications device.
   e. connector.

4. Smart phones allow you to
   a. send and receive phone calls.
   b. send and receive e-mail messages.
   c. surf the Web.
   d. perform all of the above.
   e. perform none of the above.

5. The technology that allows you to send only text messages, usually from your cell phone to another cell phone, is
   a. MMS.
   b. a chat room.
   c. SMS.
   d. a Web site.
   e. SMSM.

6. The technology that allows you to send messages that can contain a variety of media such as text, images, and video—usually from your cell phone to another cell phone—is
   a. MMS.
   b. a chat room.
   c. SMS.
   d. a Web site.
   e. SMSM.

7. The ____________ makes use of the Internet to recruit employees and is growing by leaps and bounds.
   a. tablet PC
   b. X generation
   c. MMS technology
   d. SMS technology
   e. electronic job market

8. A very knowledgeable computer user who uses his or her knowledge to invade other people's computers is a(n)
   a. database administrator.
   b. chief information officer.
   c. hacker.
   d. chief privacy officer.
   e. XML specialist.

9. Short-term memory that your computer uses as it processes information is
   a. a smart phone.
   b. a CD.
   c. a DVD.
   d. RAM.
   e. CPU.

10. All software is either
    a. application or utility software.
    b. application or system software.
    c. system or utility software.
    d. anti-virus or spreadsheet software.
    e. anti-virus or application software.

True/False

11. ____ The most popular choice for personal computing needs is a tablet PC.
12. ____ Many organizations use minicomputers for Web server computers.
13. ____ Links on the Web can be any amount of text but cannot be images.
14. ____ WiFi is a standard for transmitting information using infrared technologies over very short distances.
15. ____ All computer viruses are destructive.

Take this quiz online at www.mhhe.com/i-series and get instant feedback.

review of concepts

QUESTIONS AND EXERCISES

1. Creating a Hierarchy of Computer Components

Fill in the boxes below to complete the categories of the components of your computer.

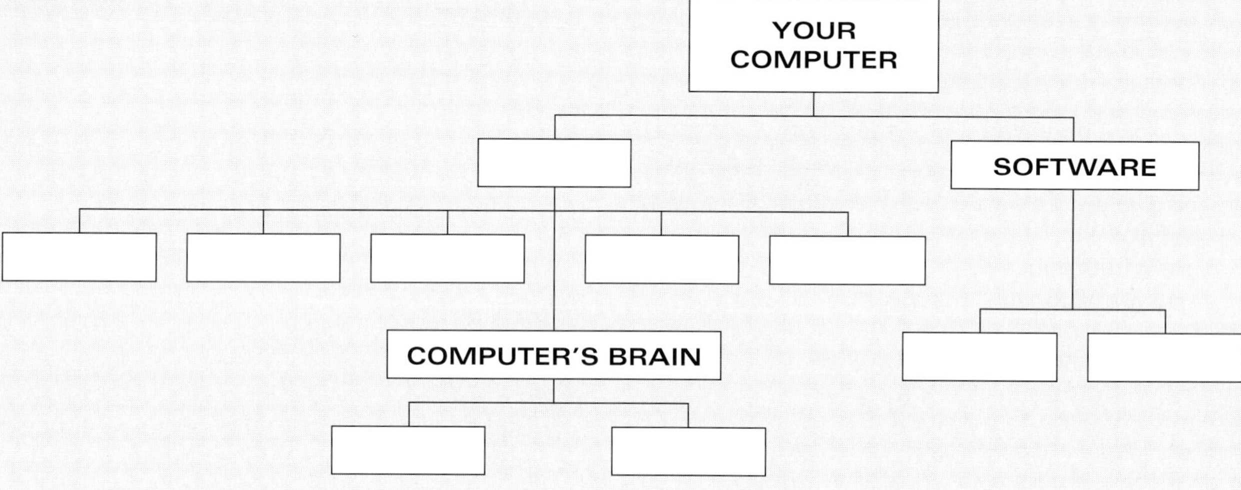

2. Comparing Types of Computers and Modes of Transportation

Consider the following terms in a related group. For each, place beside it its equivalent computer by size. Limit computers by size to PDAs, notebooks, desktops, minicomputers, mainframes, and supercomputers. We've provided one to get you started.

Cruise ship ____________________

50-passenger bus ____________________

Roller blades ____________________

Airplane seat ____________________

Minivan ____________________

Motorcycle ______desktop______

3. Reading Forward

Textbooks are not like novels in that you can easily skip forward to certain chapters in a textbook and read what they have to say without ruining the "story." In this chapter, we provided you with several glimpses of what you'll find in future chapters. In the section entitled "Computing Productivity With and Without . . ." we discussed some key technologies as categorized in the table below. Your task is to find out more about those categories by briefly reading ahead through some of the future chapters. As you do, write down some key terms and concepts that interest you.

Categories	Chapters	Key Terms and Concepts
Computing without a PC	11	
Computing with the World	2, 8	
Computing without Wires	7	
Computing with Your Career in Mind	All	
Computing with Society	9	

4. Comparing Computer Components and the Human Anatomy

In many ways, the components of your computer are similar in functionality to parts of the human anatomy. For example, your vocal cords are similar to a set of computer speakers in that your vocal cords produce output in the form of sound just as computer speakers do. For each of the following parts of the human anatomy, identify which computer component is most similar in terms of functionality. You may determine that a given human anatomy part is similar to several components of a computer. If so, list them all.

Hands and fingers ______________________

Feet and legs ______________________

Mouth ______________________

Ears ______________________

Eyes ______________________

Nose ______________________

Brain ______________________

Central nervous system ______________________

Stomach ______________________

Blood vessels ______________________

5. Understanding Your Ethics

Ethics and laws are often very different. Laws explicitly require or prohibit action on your part. Ethics, however, are greatly a matter of personal interpretation. What may be right to you may not be to someone else. For each of the situations below, write down what action you would take based on your ethical perspective. Then, determine if your actions are against the law.

Situation	Your Action	Against the Law?
A. Leaving school one night, you find a money clip (with no markings) with $10.	______________	______
B. Leaving school one night, you find a money clip (with no markings) with $1,000.	______________	______
C. You find a quarter in a pay phone booth. You did not see the person who previously used the phone.	______________	______
D. You find a quarter in a pay phone booth. The previous person using the phone booth is walking a few paces down the street.	______________	______
E. You notice two people in class cheating on an exam. You know them both and don't like either of them.	______________	______
F. You notice two people in class cheating on an exam. You know them both and like them very well.	______________	______
G. Someone asks you for a copy of some software you recently purchased.	______________	______
H. Someone asks you to make a copy of a chapter in one of your textbooks.	______________	______
I. You find a photo on ESPN's Web site that you want to place on your personal Web site.	______________	______

e-commerce

1. Participating in a Chat Room

As we discussed in the chapter, you can communicate with people through technology in a variety of ways—e-mail, instant messaging, SMS, MMS, and chat rooms. Connect to MSN Chat at chat.msn.com and see what it takes to participate in a chat room. Choose any chat room that interests you. As you do, answer the following questions:

a. What is a .Net Passport?
b. Why must you provide your birth date?
c. What is the role of a nickname in a chat session?
d. What sort of software do you have to download?
e. Which chat room did you choose? Why?

Why do you believe chat rooms are so popular on the Internet? Do they appeal to you? Why or why not? Is it possible that people are becoming less adept at personal face-to-face communications because they spend so much time in chat rooms?

2. Finding an Internship

Sometime in your college career you'll probably take an internship to learn more about the field you're working in. Connect to the following Web sites and search for internships in a career field that interests you.

- Internships.com—www.internships.com
- InternshipPrograms.com—internships.wetfeet.com
- InternJob.com—www.internjobs.com
- InternWeb.com—www.internweb.com

Now, answer the following questions:

a. Which internships did you find interesting?
b. Which features helped you find the types of internships you wanted?

3. Finding a Job

To help you learn how to search electronic job ads, we'd like you to get on the Web and connect to two of the following job database sites:

- Monster.com at www.monster.com
- America's Job Bank at www.ajb.dni.us
- CareerNet at www.careernet.com
- CareerBuilder at www.careerbuilder.com

While you're at each site, do some looking around and perform the following tasks:

a. Perform a job search by job title such as "accountant" or "physical therapist."
b. Perform a job search by location such as "Massachusetts" or "International."
c. Perform a job search by company name such as "Microsoft" or "United Airlines."

How many jobs did you find in each instance? Which job database site was easiest to use? Why?

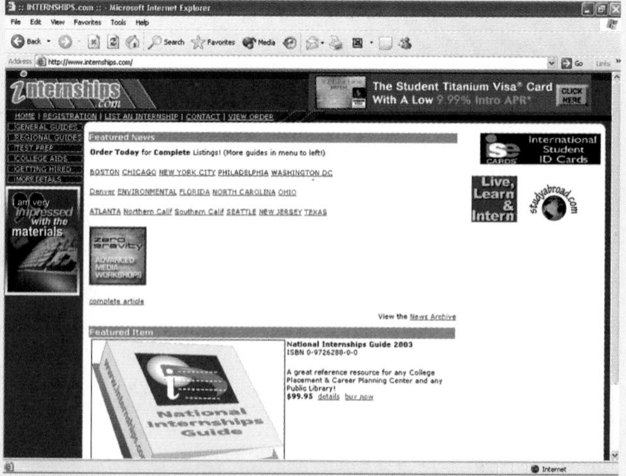

ethics, security & privacy

1. Proposed Laws Concerning Cell Phone Use

Currently, there is much legislation pending that would prohibit the use of cell phones while driving and make it a moving violation (with a stiff penalty) if you were caught in the act. Further, some legislation proposes that, if you were involved in an accident while using a cell phone, the fault of the accident would be assigned to you.

Of course, you can extend that legislation to other technology devices. Many people use their PDAs while driving down the road to check e-mail and even obtain a weather report. Others might use a PDA wrist watch to check their daily calendar of appointments. In reference to using technology while driving, answer the following questions:

a. Do you use some form of technology, such as a cell phone, while driving?
b. Do you believe people should be prohibited from using technology while driving? Why or why not?
c. Given that accidents do occur because people were paying more attention to their technology than their driving, should insurance carriers be allowed to raise your rates if you own a cell phone or other technology device? Why or why not?
d. Should insurance carriers be able to obtain lists of all cell phone users and raise their rates? Why or why not?

2. Ethical E-Mail

Several years ago (true story), a man working at Chevron distributed what he thought was a funny joke through Chevron's e-mail system. A woman who received the joke was offended by it and sued Chevron to take action against the other employee. After a lot of legal mumbo-jumbo, Chevron paid the woman $2 million to settle out of court. Answer the two sets of questions below:

Question Set #1

a. Who was paying the male employee while he was working?
b. Who owned and maintained the e-mail system he used to distribute the offensive joke?
c. Because he was on company time and using company facilities, was Chevron responsible for his actions?

Question Set #2

a. If you believe Chevron was responsible for his actions, would you mind if your school constantly monitored your e-mail to determine what you're distributing? Why or why not?
b. If you believe Chevron was not responsible for his actions, are you prepared to periodically receive "garbage" e-mail at school and not sue your school if some of it offends you? Why or why not?

3. Your Personal Ethics

Consider the following situation and then answer the questions below and justify your answers. You work at a local flower shop. You also have a great female friend who believes she has met the man of her dreams. At work one day, you see the man ordering flowers for another woman.

a. Do you tell your female friend?
b. Do you tell your female friend if she just got engaged to the man?
c. Do you tell your female friend if you can't confirm that the man wasn't ordering flowers for his mother or sister?
d. Do you tell your female friend if you know she's also seeing another man "on the side"?

on the web

1. Finding Information on the Web with Google

If you don't know exactly which Web site to visit to find information that you may need, you can use a search engine. Search engines are facilities on the Web that allow you to type in key words and sometimes questions. In turn, search engines will provide you with a list of relevant Web sites. One of the more popular search engines is Google (www.google.com). Connect to the Web, visit Google's site, and perform some searches for information that interests you, such as African safaris or perhaps a favorite sports team. As you do, answer the following questions:

a. What is the purpose of the **I'm Feeling Lucky** button?
b. Do you use Google by entering key words or questions?
c. How do you establish a preference for finding Web sites only in certain languages?
d. How do you limit a search so that only Web sites with both words "African" and "Safari" are presented to you?

2. Consumer Rights on the Web

For many people, shopping on the Web is a "click in the dark" because they know little about the products they're buying. To avoid clicking in the dark, you need to be an informed consumer. Luckily, many Web sites can help, including:

- Consumer Reports—www.consumerreports.org
- Consumer World—www.consumerworld.org
- The Better Business Bureau—www.bbb.org

Connect to at least one of the sites above and see what information is offered. If you were considering purchasing a product, would you visit any of these sites to find out more information? Why or why not? Now, pick a particular product such as a home stereo system and search the Web for other sites that provide product comparisons. What sites did you find? Was the information helpful? Why or why not?

3. Listening to Radio Stations

There are radio stations online for every listener's taste. You can listen to radio stations that feature music from a particular decade or that play only rock, jazz, country, or classical. Or you can listen to talk radio. You can even listen to radio broadcasts from another country, which might be helpful if you're studying a foreign language—you can practice your comprehension skills. Whatever your needs or taste, you'll probably find a radio station on MIT's list of radio stations that appeals to you. The address is www.radio-locator.com.

Visit MIT's radio locator site and answer the following questions:

a. Can you search for a radio station by geographic location such as state or zip code?
b. Can you search for a radio station by its call letters?
c. Can your search for a radio station by format (e.g., music type)?
d. How do you search for a radio station in a country other than the United States?

4. Finding Friends and Family

On the Web, you can easily find addresses, phone numbers, and e-mail addresses for family and friends. Connect to the Web and then go to a search engine site such as HotBot (www.hotbot.com), AltaVista (www.altavista.com), or WebCrawler (www.webcrawler.com). At those sites, you'll find a feature for searching for people. Try to find several friends, family members, or perhaps even yourself. What information did you have to provide? Was your search successful? How do you personally feel about this type of information being available on the Web?

5. Exploring Yahoo!

Connect to Yahoo! at www.yahoo.com. Then select any one of the many links you see such as "Entertainment" or "Social Science." What did you find? Are there other categories within those categories to choose from? Once you went to the new link, what was the new Web site address? Did you really leave Yahoo! or did you just go to another part of the Yahoo! Web site? Don't links take you to a "new" site? How can it be that you're still in Yahoo!?

group activities

1. Evaluating Tablet PCs

Tablet PCs are among the newest innovations in personal computing technologies that offer a wide range of functionality and capabilities. Released in late 2002, tablet PCs are being embraced quickly by people who need mobility and portability. The leading manufacturers of tablet PCs include:

- Motion Computing
- ViewSonic
- Toshiba
- Fujitsu
- Acer
- Compaq

As a group, you are to pick one model from each manufacturer and create a comparison of features and prices. Be sure to include the type—convertible or slate. Based on your analysis, which manufacturer and model would you choose and why?

2. Researching PDA/Cell Phones

Among the many new personal technology alternatives is a device that is a combination of both a PDA and a cell phone. One of the more popular such devices is T-Mobile's Sidekick. Do some research and determine the functional characteristics of T-Mobile's Sidekick. As you do, also determine its price and weight. Now, find another PDA/cell phone. Compare the two. If you were to buy one which would it be and why?

3. Reviewing Computer Systems

Visit a local computer store and obtain a list of specifications for a computer system being sold there (or perhaps find a computer ad in a newspaper). Now, answer the following questions:

a. Who is the manufacturer?

b. What is the model number?

c. What is the CPU speed?

d. How much RAM does it have?

e. How many storage devices are present?

f. How much information can the hard disk hold?

g. Does it come with a printer? If so, what is the printer type?

h. What is the viewable image size of the screen?

i. Does it come with wireless capabilities?

Now, connect to the Web and find the same system. You can visit the Web site of the manufacturer or a site such as Buy.com (www.buy.com). Compare the price of the local system and the price of the system on the Web. Which is cheaper? Why do you believe the price difference exists?

4. Desktops and Notebooks

Find two computer systems—one notebook and one desktop—for sale that have similar features (for example, CPU speed). What's the difference in price? How can people justify the higher price for a notebook computer? Do you believe that the prices of similar notebooks and desktops will be more or less comparable over time? Justify your answer.

5. Starting Your Career Search

Gather a few classmates who are interested in the same field of study as you. Perhaps it's computing, but it could also be accounting, marketing, forestry management, cosmetology, or any other field. Now, find someone in your local business community with a career in that field. Interview that person concerning your field of interest and obtain answers to the following questions:

a. What general skills are necessary?

b. What field-specific skills are necessary?

c. What technology skills are necessary?

d. What certifications—if any—are particularly helpful?

Now, determine which classes your school offers that provide you with those computing skills. Report your findings to the class.

crossword puzzle

Across

4. Part of a Web site
7. Collection of computers
8. Point on the Internet where several connections converge
9. Type of wireless modem
11. What makes the Web possible
12. Protocol for moving information among computers
13. Mobile e-commerce
17. The "C" in B2C e-commerce
19. Technical term for Web site address
20. Standard
21. Search engine that creates hierarchical lists
22. Where you keep your Web site
24. Supports e-mail
27. Three-character domain extension
28. Supports chat rooms
30. Technical term for a Web page address
31. Software that works outside your browser to play multimedia
32. Modem that uses your cable TV connection

Down

1. Software for creating Web sites with significant interactivity
2. Major set of connections in the Internet
3. Software for Web surfing
5. The "B" in B2B e-commerce
6. Software that works inside your browser to play multimedia
9. Media that plays while still downloading
10. Business that provides you a connection to the Internet
14. Brick-and-______ —performs no e-commerce
15. Commerce facilitated by technology
16. World Wide ______
18. Software you use to connect your computer to another computer or network
21. High-speed modem
23. Click-and-______—also known as a pure play
25. Software that helps you create animated and interactive Web pages
26. Communications protocol for the Web
27. Search engine that lets you ask questions
29. Creates a virtual world of Web multimedia

CHAPTER two

2

The World Wide Web and the Internet

How Vast Is Your Virtual Imagination?

SIMNET CONCEPTS SUPPORT

did you know?

The Web is exploding all around you. Never before has the world seen such a dynamic and exciting technology become a major part of our lives so quickly. Important to think about, the Web is radically changing how we live our lives and raising serious issues society must address.

in *mid-2002, it was reported that 63 percent of children in homes with an annual income exceeding $75,000 had access to the Internet, compared to only 14 percent of children in homes with an annual income less than $15,000.*[1]

the *fastest growing part of the U.S. Internet audience by age is now people over age 50.*[2]

according *to BIGresearch, __??__ percent of men and __??__ percent of women surf the Web while simultaneously watching television.*[3]

To find out the percentages of men and women who simultaneously surf the Web and watch television, visit www.mhhe.com/i-series.

Student Learning Outcomes

After reading this chapter, you should be able to:

1. Define electronic commerce, the two primary types of e-commerce businesses, and the three primary e-commerce activities.
2. Describe the relationships between Web terms, including Web site, Web page, Web site address (domain name), Web page address (URL), and top-level domain.
3. Contrast the use of directory search engines and true search engines.
4. Describe the various types of Web multimedia formats and the software you need to enjoy Web multimedia.
5. Identify your four main options for an Internet service provider and your four choices for a modem.

At the end of each chapter, we provide several e-commerce projects, and we hope you completed one or more of them for Chapter 1. We haven't yet formally defined electronic commerce. ***Electronic commerce (e-commerce)*** is really just commerce—but it's commerce that technology facilitates and enhances. The technology aspect of e-commerce allows you to reach more customers, distribute information quickly, establish strong and lasting relationships, and be innovative in how you perform all types of commerce functions.

Of course, we can't speak of e-commerce without talking about the World Wide Web and the Internet. So let's briefly discuss some key aspects of e-commerce and then we'll talk about the World Wide Web and the Internet, including what you need to know to get connected. To learn even more about the Web and the Internet, complete the "Introduction to the Internet and the World Wide Web" tutorial on your SimNet Concepts Support CD.

2.1 ELECTRONIC COMMERCE

Electronic commerce (and business technology in general) is a broad topic and a wide field. It's a hot topic in business and an expanding field. E-commerce is not the "fad of the month"—it's here to stay. Here, we briefly introduce you to the fascinating world of electronic commerce. To learn more, read Chapter 8 and complete the "B2B and E-Commerce" tutorial on your SimNet Concepts Support CD.

did you know?

Children *and teenagers, ages 2 (yes, 2) to 17, account for 25 percent of all the users of instant messaging on the Internet.*[4]

TYPES OF E-COMMERCE BUSINESSES

Can Businesses Exist in Cyberspace and the Physical World?

You can categorize a business in different ways—whether it's product or service oriented, whether it sells primarily to individual consumers or to other businesses, or by its industry (food, manufacturing, health care). You can also categorize a business according to how or whether you can interact with it through e-commerce. Some, but not many, businesses are wholly ***brick-and-mortar businesses;*** they exist only in the physical world and perform no e-commerce functions. Most businesses today, however, do perform some type of e-commerce. The two primary models of e-commerce businesses include click-and-mortar and click-and-order.

Click-and-mortar businesses have both a presence in the physical world (such as a store in a shopping mall) and a Web site that supports some type of e-commerce. JCPenney, for example, has physical stores and also a Web site with its catalog so you can buy items with your credit card and have them delivered to your home.

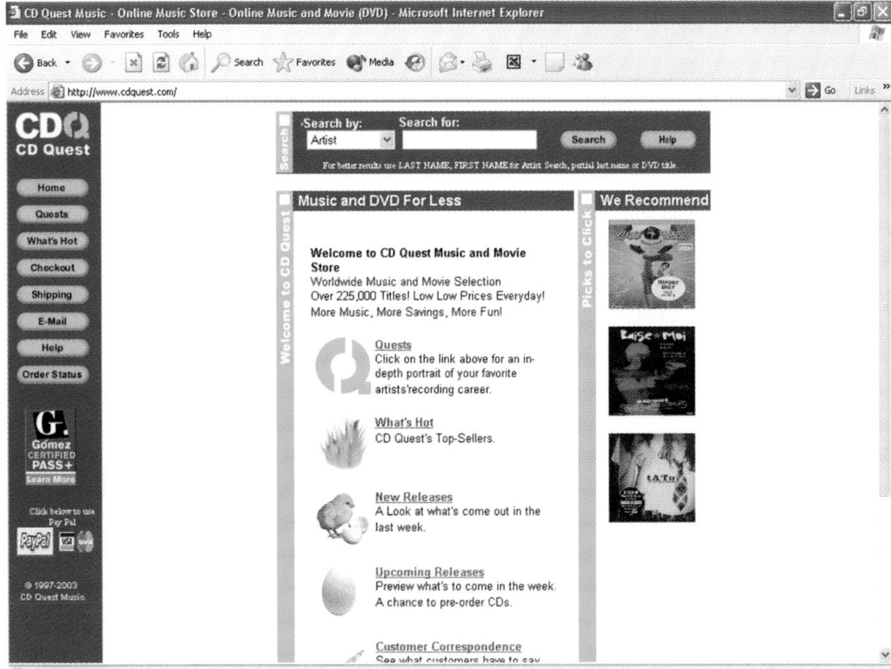

FIGURE 2.1

CD Quest sells you music on the Web but not in stores. Therefore, it's a click-and-order business.

Click-and-order businesses (also called ***pure plays*** or ***e-tailers***) exist solely on the Web with no physical presence that you can visit to buy products and services. Amazon.com and CD Quest are click-and-order businesses (see Figure 2.1).

TYPES OF E-COMMERCE ACTIVITIES

How Do Businesses and Customers Interact through E-Commerce?

Different e-commerce activities have different purposes. Is the business targeting individual customers like you or does it cater to other businesses? Maybe the e-commerce isn't even a company, but someone trying to sell something to another individual on the Web. There are many different types of e-commerce activities with the three primary ones being B2C e-commerce, B2B e-commerce, and C2C e-commerce.

Business to consumer electronic commerce (B2C e-commerce) occurs when a business sells products and services through e-commerce to customers who are primarily individuals. Thousands of B2C e-commerce businesses exist on the Web. Although B2C e-commerce has been the most visible, only about 3 percent of all e-commerce revenues are in the B2C space. Most of the revenues are in the B2B space. To learn more about B2C e-commerce, complete the "E-Commerce and Shopping Online" tutorial on your SimNet Concepts Support CD.

Business to business electronic commerce (B2B e-commerce) occurs when a business sells products and services through e-commerce to customers who are primarily other businesses. Gates Rubber Company, for example, makes rubber- and synthetic-based products such as belts

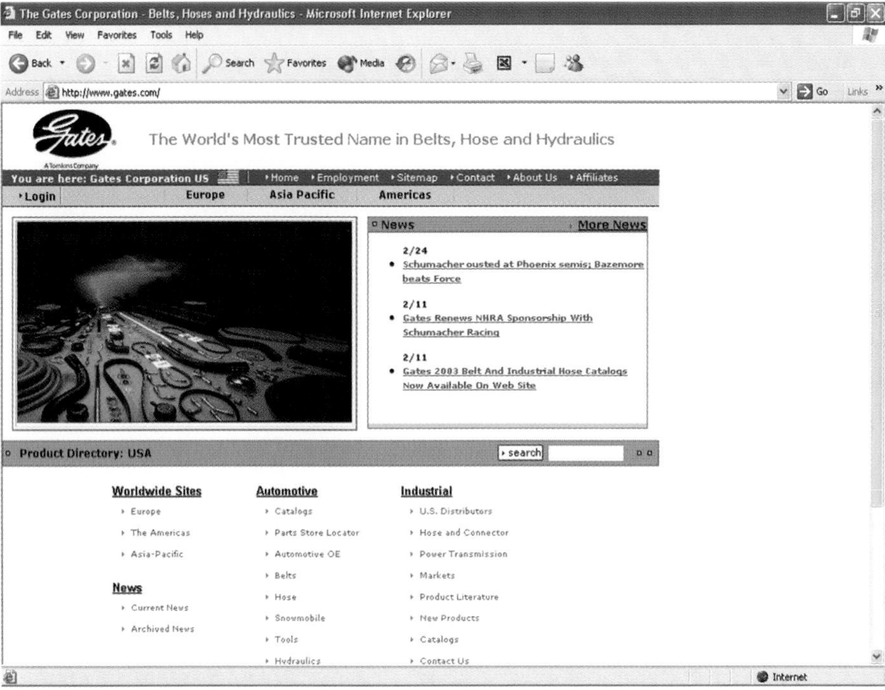

FIGURE 2.2

If you were an automaker, you could buy hoses and belts from the Gates Rubber Company over the Web. This is business to business (B2B) e-commerce.

and hoses for cars. But Gates doesn't sell directly to you. Instead, parts stores and automakers buy its products (see Figure 2.2).

Consumer to consumer electronic commerce (C2C e-commerce) occurs when a person sells products and services to another person through e-commerce. The most well-known site that supports C2C e-commerce is eBay (www.ebay.com). EBay is a form of a click-and-order business, but it does no more than provide an electronic marketplace where you can buy and sell products from and to other people.

As we've stated, e-commerce is here—and here to stay. Your productivity will grow along with your judgment in determining how best to interact with various e-commerce businesses and their e-commerce activities. To do that, you need to understand the World Wide Web and the Internet.

SECTION 2.1

making the grade

1. ___________ is really just commerce, but it's commerce that technology facilitates and enhances.
2. ___________ businesses exist only in the physical world and perform no e-commerce functions.
3. Click-and-order businesses are also known as ___________ or ___________.
4. B2C e-commerce occurs when a business sells products and services through e-commerce to customers who are primarily ___________.
5. ___________ e-commerce occurs when a person sells products and services to another person through e-commerce.

2.2 THE WORLD WIDE WEB

As we begin our exploration, let's first define two terms—the *Internet* and the *World Wide Web*. The ***Internet*** is a vast network of networked computers (hardware and software) that connects millions of people all over the world. The ***World Wide Web (Web)*** is a multimedia-based collection of information, services, and Web sites supported by the Internet. So, the Internet is the technology infrastructure that makes the Web possible, and the Web is what you use to have fun, to work, and to be productive with.

WEB SITES, PAGES, AND ADDRESSES

How Do I Know where I Am on the Web?

As you begin to surf the Web, you'll encounter Web sites and pages, each with a unique address. As formal definitions, we would offer you the following.

- ***Web browser software*** (or a ***Web browser***)—the software that allows you to surf the Web. The most popular are Internet Explorer and Netscape Communicator.
- ***Web site***—a specific location on the Web that you can visit electronically to gather information and perhaps order products and request services.
- ***Web page***—a specific portion of a Web site that deals with a certain topic.
- ***Web site address***—a unique name for an entire Web site. The technical term for a Web site address is a ***domain name.***
- ***Web page address***—a unique name for a Web page within a Web site. The technical term for a Web page address is a ***URL (uniform resource locator).***

For example, the *USA Today* is a Web site, and its Web site address (domain name) is www.usatoday.com (see Figure 2.3). Like most Web sites, *USA Today* contains numerous Web pages. For example, you can

FIGURE 2.3

Most Web sites include many Web pages. At the *USA Today* site, for example, you can click on **Sports** to go to a Web page devoted to that topic.

FIGURE 2.4

Top-level domains and country extensions can tell you a lot about a Web site.

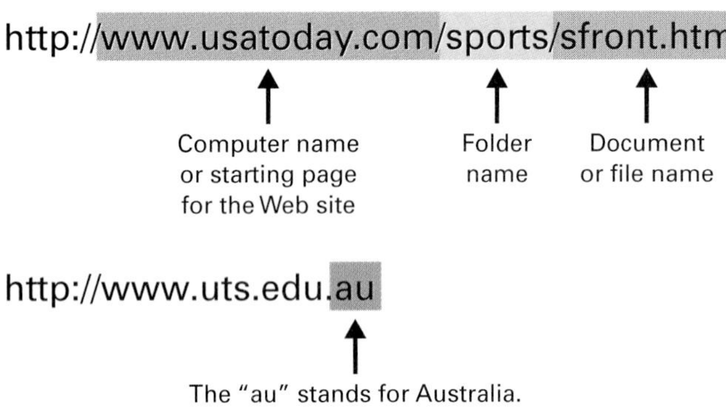

Top-Level Domain	Description
com	Commercial or for-profit business
coop	Cooperative
edu	Educational institution
gov	U.S. government agency
mil	U.S. military organization
net	Internet administrative organization
org	Professional or nonprofit organization
int	International treaties organization
info	General information
biz	Business
museum	Accredited museum
name	Personal
pro	Accountants, doctors, lawyers, etc.

click on the **Sports** link in the *USA Today* Web site and be taken to a Web page that deals with only the topic of sports. The Web page address (URL) for sports within the *USA Today* Web site is www.usatoday.com/sports/sfront.html.

The Web site address or domain name tells you a lot about the site you're visiting, most notably the type of organization and the country of origin of the Web site. Most Web site addresses end with a three-character extension such as "com" which stands for a commercial or for-profit organization (as in www.usatoday.com, for example) or "edu" which stands for an educational institution (as in www.ucla.edu, for example). This three-character extension can take on many other forms and is referred to as the ***top-level domain*** (see Figure 2.4). Thus, www.ucla.edu is the Web site address for UCLA, an educational institution.

Some Web site addresses also contain another two-character extension, such as "au," after the top-level domain. If so, that extension denotes the country of origin. For example, www.uts.edu.au is the Web site address for the University of Technology in Sydney, Australia. The two-character extension (au) following the top-level domain identifies that the country of origin is Australia.

To learn more about the Web and Web browser software, complete the "Web Browsers" and "Web Pages" tutorials on your SimNet Concepts Support CD.

did you know? Approximately *one in every three girls has reported being sexually harassed in a chat room.*[5]

USING A SEARCH ENGINE
What if I Don't Know Which Site I Should Be Visiting?

Finding information on the Web is easy; finding the right information isn't always. What if you need information, but don't know exactly where to find it? Fortunately, you can find your information (and probably more than you want) by using a search engine. A ***search engine*** is a facility on the Web that allows you to find Web sites by providing key words or questions.

There are many types of search engines, with the two most popular being *directory* and *true* search engines. A ***directory search engine*** organizes listings of Web sites into hierarchical lists. Yahoo! is the most popular directory search engine. A ***true search engine,*** on the other hand, organizes Web sites in such a way that it can provide you with a list of Web sites based on a question you ask. Ask Jeeves is the most popular true search engine.

Suppose, for example, that you wanted to find out who won the Academy Awards in the year 2002. Using Ask Jeeves (see Figure 2.5), you would simply enter the question, **Who won the Academy Awards in 2002?** and click on the **Ask** button. As you can see in the second screen in Figure 2.5, Ask Jeeves would then provide a list of Web sites with the information you wanted.

Using a directory search engine is a bit different (see Figure 2.6 on the following page). For example, to find out who won the Academy Awards in 2002 using Yahoo!, you would click on **Arts & Humanities, Awards, Movies and Film@, Academy Awards,** and finally **74th Annual Academy Awards (2002).** You could then select whichever Web site seemed to offer the information you wanted.

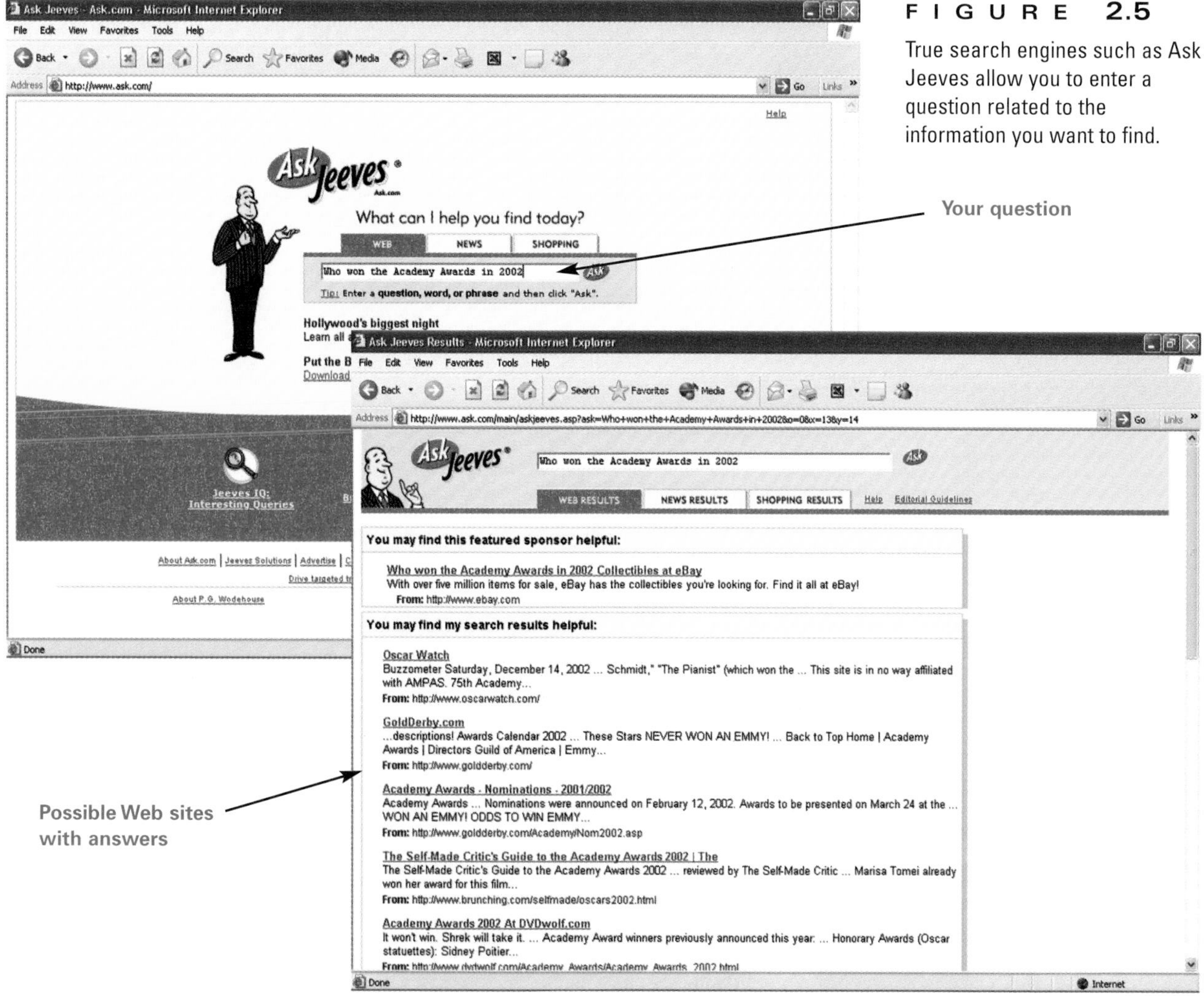

FIGURE 2.5

True search engines such as Ask Jeeves allow you to enter a question related to the information you want to find.

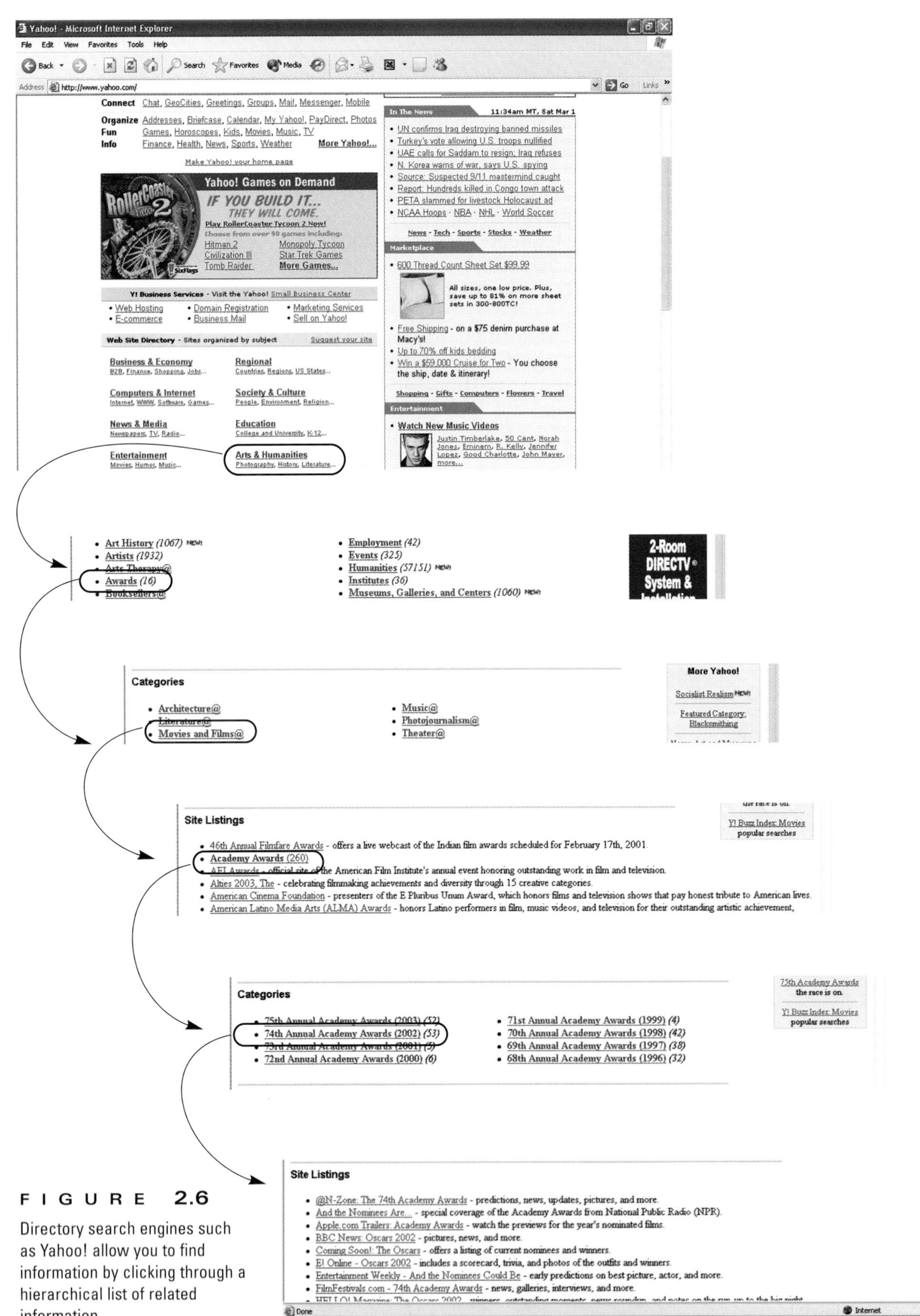

FIGURE 2.6

Directory search engines such as Yahoo! allow you to find information by clicking through a hierarchical list of related information.

You can also use directory search engines in a different fashion. For example, in any of the screens in Figure 2.6, we could have entered **academy +awards +2002** in the field immediately to the left of the **Search** button and then clicked on the **Search** button. This particular search would yield a list of Web sites similar to the list we received by continually choosing categories within categories.

You might notice that we entered the plus sign (+) in a couple of different places in our key terms list. By doing so, we limited the search to finding just sites that included all three words. Likewise, if you want to limit a search so that it won't show Web sites that contain certain key words, you use a minus sign (–). For example, if you wanted to find Web sites that contained information about the Miami Dolphins NFL team, you could enter **Miami +Dolphins.** That would probably yield a list of suitable sites, but it might also include sites with information about watching dolphins (the aquatic version) in Miami. You could further refine your search by entering something like **Miami +Dolphins –aquatic –mammal.** That search would yield a list of Web sites that have the terms *Miami* and *Dolphins* but would eliminate any sites that have the term *aquatic* or *mammal.* We refer to plus and minus signs in searching as *Boolean operators.*

Both types of search engines are easy to use. Your productivity lies in determining which type of search engine best matches how you think. Some people think in terms of categories and subcategories, in which case directory search engines are best. Other people think in terms of asking questions, in which case true search engines are best.

To learn more about using search engines, complete the "Searching for Information on the Internet" tutorial on your SimNet Concepts Support CD.

ENJOYING WEB MULTIMEDIA
Does the Web Have Only Text, Photos, and Art?

If you recall, the Web is a *multimedia-based* collection of information, services, and Web sites. That simply means that on the Web you can enjoy rich forms of media beyond simple text, photos, and art. You can listen to audio, watch videos, play interactive games, and even virtually experience physical places all over the world. All of this is possible using Web multimedia (and we definitely recommend that you experience it). Using Web browsers such as Internet Explorer and Netscape Communicator, you can easily hear some audio and watch various types of animation. But when you get into watching videos and playing interactive games online, you might need to install some extra software. To learn more about this type of software, complete the "Web Utilities: Plug-Ins and Helper Applications" tutorial on your SimNet Concepts Support CD.

Plug-Ins and Players

To enjoy certain types of Web multimedia, you may need to install either a plug-in or a player (or perhaps both). A ***plug-in*** is software that works within your Web browser to play Web multimedia. For example, if you want to play most interactive multimedia-based games on the Web, you may need a Shockwave plug-in. Getting and installing a plug-in is a very simple process. Many Web sites such as Plugins.com (www.plugins.com,

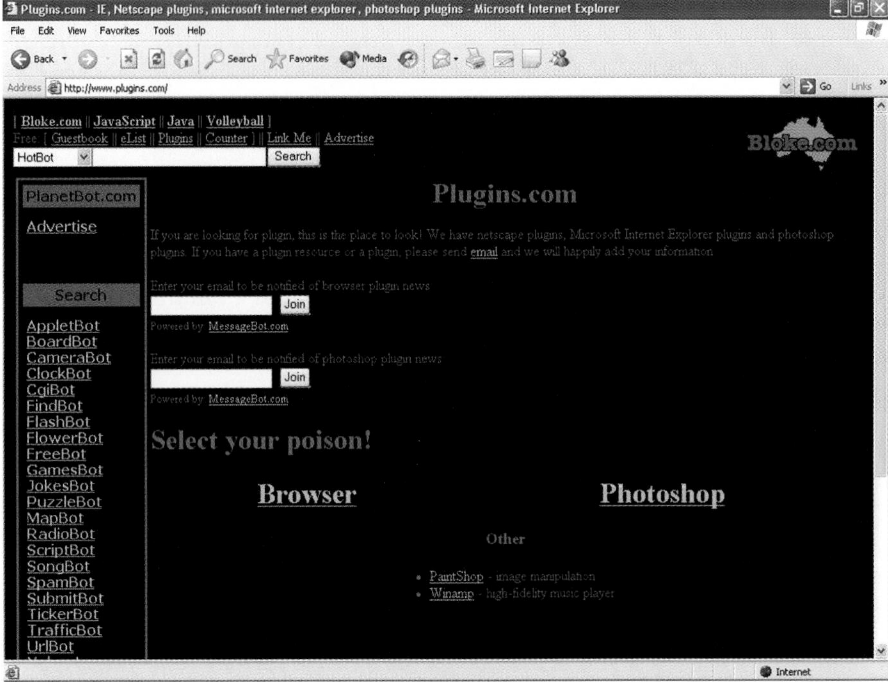

F I G U R E 2.7

Sites such as Plugins.com provide plug-ins that you can easily download and install.

see Figure 2.7) provide a variety of plug-ins for both Internet Explorer and Netscape Communicator.

A plug-in works in your Web browser. A ***player,*** on the other hand, is software that works outside your Web browser to play all forms of multimedia (not just Web-based). The most popular players are Windows Media Player (which comes installed on computers with Windows as the operating system, see Figure 2.8), RealNetworks RealOne Player, and QuickTime Player. Macromedia also has a Shockwave player for interactive games and animation.

F I G U R E 2.8

The Windows Media Player lets you enjoy music and video without having to wait until your browser downloads the entire file.

The difference between plug-ins and players really depends on when you want to enjoy Web multimedia. If you have the right plug-in, you can download and watch a video with your Web browser. Alternatively, you can download and save the video to your computer. Then later, without being connected to the Web, you can start a player (Windows Media Player, for example) and watch the video.

Again, most Web browsers today come with many plug-ins already installed and most computer systems come equipped with one or more players already installed. If you need additional plug-ins or players, visit the Web site that supports this text at www.mhhe.com/i-series for a list of sites that provide plug-ins and players.

MULTIMEDIA FORMATS
So, What Multimedia Can I Access?

With the right plug-ins and players, you can enjoy all types of Web multimedia, including audio, video, and streaming video.

Web Audio

Web audio is all of the sounds and music on the Web. Most Web audio is stored in files that have the extension .wav (wave) or .au (audio). Today's newest versions of Web browsers come equipped with the necessary plug-ins allowing you to listen to Web audio.

Web Video

Web video is all of the video footage (full-length movies, video clips, trailers, and the like) on the Web. Video files come in many formats, with QuickTime and Windows AVI being the most common. Because there are so many different Web video formats, you may have to install several different plug-ins and/or players to view all the different Web videos.

Streaming Media

Because of their size, some Web videos and audio can take a long time to download. To get around this, many Web multimedia publishers provide the files as streaming media. ***Streaming media*** continually sends small parts of a large file to your Web browser as you watch and listen to what you've already downloaded. In doing so, you don't have to wait for the entire Web multimedia file to download before enjoying it.

INTERACTIVE WEB MULTIMEDIA
What's the Best of All Web Multimedia?

Many people believe that the best Web multimedia is interactive. This would include Web multimedia with significant interactive animations, games, video, and three-dimensional (3-D) elements. The best example of interactive Web multimedia is SimCity Online, a Web-interactive, multiplayer game based on the popular Electronic Arts (EA) SimCity game.

To take advantage of Web multimedia with significant interactivity, you'll probably need either a Flash plug-in or a Shockwave player. ***Flash*** is software that helps you create animated and interactive Web pages. So, a ***Flash plug-in*** enables you to view and interact with Flash-based Web pages. ***Shockwave,*** published by Macromedia, is software that helps you create Web pages with significant interactivity through Web multimedia. So, a ***Shockwave player*** enables you to view and interact with Shockwave-based Web pages (these are often called *shocked pages*).

FIGURE 2.9

You can interact with a virtual world at this Web site, thanks to Virtual Reality Modeling Language (VRML) and the Cortona player.

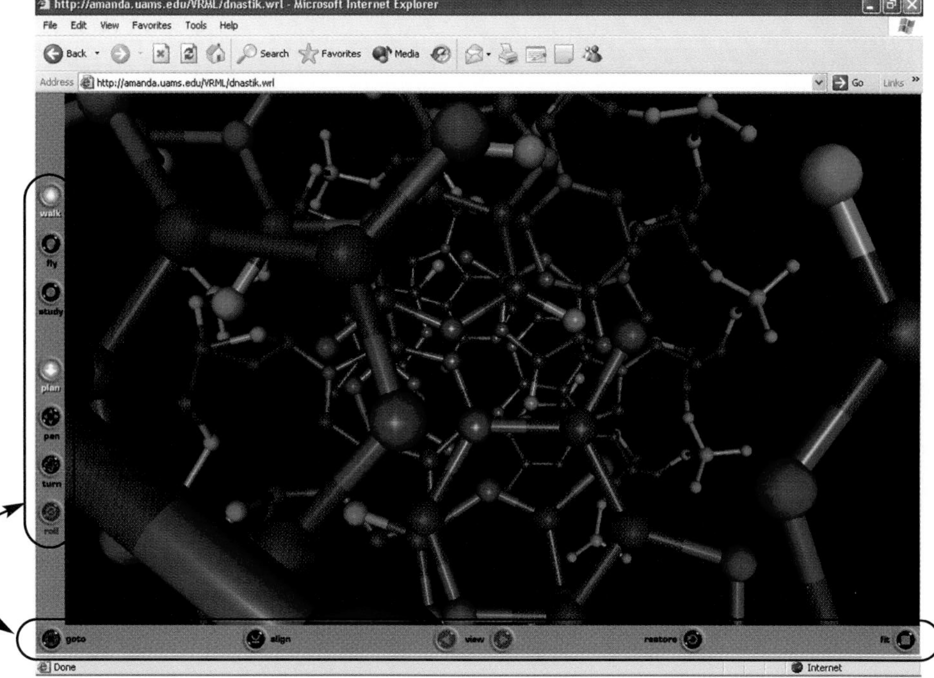

Finally, you might want to take advantage of VRML technology. ***VRML,*** or ***Virtual Reality Modeling Language,*** creates a virtual world in which you have the illusion that you are physically participating in the presentation of the Web multimedia. VRML displays three-dimensional images, and a VRML player, such as Cortona (see Figure 2.9), provides you with controls that allow you to turn those 3-D images and view them from different perspectives.

If you're interested in developing Web sites and software using such tools as Flash, Shockwave, and/or VRML, you have some substantial career opportunities. We performed a search of job openings on Monster (www.monster.com) using Flash, Shockwave, and VRML as key terms and found almost 1,000 postings. Think about it. To learn more about virtual reality, complete the "Virtual Reality and Artificial Intelligence" tutorial on your SimNet Concepts Support CD.

SECTION 2.2

making the grade

1. A(n) ___________ is software that works within your Web browser to play Web multimedia.
2. A(n) ___________ is software that works outside your Web browser to play all forms of multimedia (not just Web-based).
3. ___________ is all of the sounds and music on the Web.
4. ___________ continually sends small parts of a large file to your Web browser as you watch and listen to what you've already downloaded.
5. ___________ creates a virtual world in which you have the illusion that you are physically participating in the presentation of the Web multimedia.

2.3 THE INTERNET BEHIND THE WEB

The Web is easy to learn and use and most people agree that it's even fun to surf, especially when you can take advantage of Web multimedia. Underneath or behind the Web are the Internet and all its technologies. Let's pop the hood and see what it looks like.

THE STRUCTURE OF THE INTERNET

What Exactly Is the Internet?

The Internet (the vast network of computers that connects millions of people all over the world) is what makes the Web possible. The Internet is a collection of hardware and software in the form of a worldwide network. A ***network*** is simply a collection of computers that support the sharing of information, software, and hardware devices. The ***Internet backbone*** is the major set of connections for computers on the Internet (see Figure 2.10). A ***network access point (NAP)*** is a point on the Internet where several connections converge. At each NAP is at least one computer that simply routes Internet traffic from one place to the next. In Figure 2.10 you can see that Dallas is an NAP, with lines converging from Atlanta, Los Angeles, Kansas City, Houston, Austin, and several other places. To learn more about the Internet, complete the "Introduction to the Internet and World Wide Web" tutorial on your SimNet Concepts Support CD.

At any given NAP, an Internet service provider such as AOL may connect its computers to the Internet. An ***Internet service provider (ISP)*** is a company that provides individuals, organizations, and businesses access to the Internet. To use the Web, you connect your computer to an ISP (more technically, to one of your ISP's computers). So, your ISP provides you access to the Web by allowing you to connect your computer to the Internet through its computer. We'll talk more about choosing an ISP in the next section.

COMPUTERS ON THE INTERNET

Do Different Computers on the Internet Perform Different Functions?

There are two basic types of computers on the Internet—servers and clients. An ***Internet server computer*** (also called an ***Internet host computer***) is a computer on the Internet that provides information and services

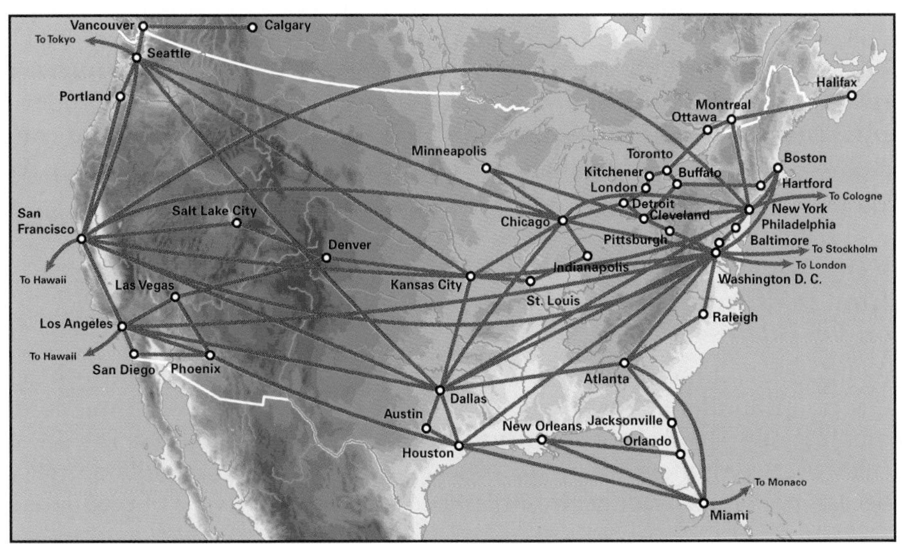

FIGURE 2.10

The Internet backbone is the major set of connections for computers that make up the Internet.

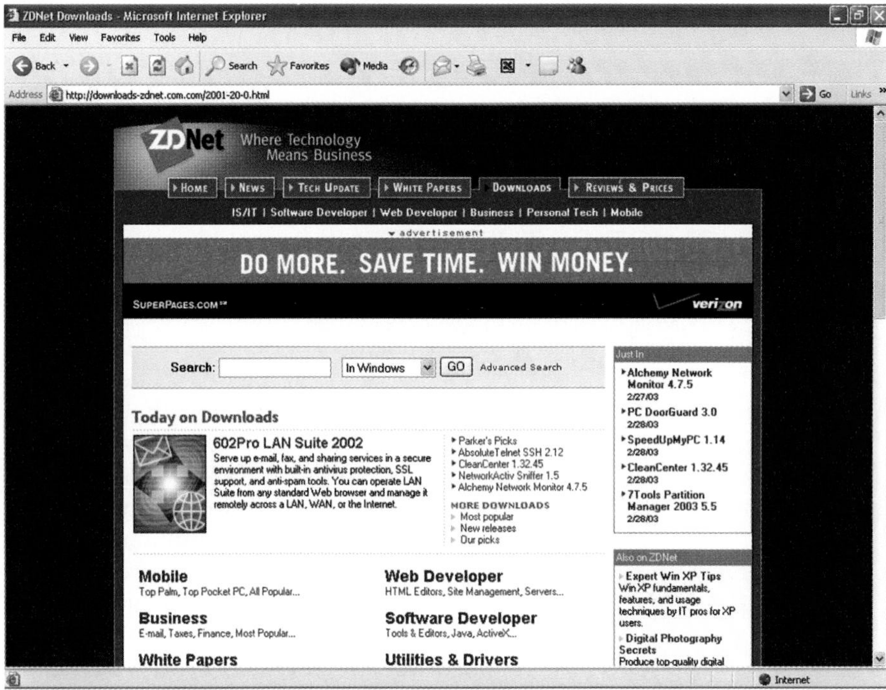

FIGURE 2.11
FTP servers such as Zdnet.com/downloads maintain many files that you can download to your computer.

to other computers and Internet users such as you. These Internet server computers are often minicomputers or mid-range computers we discussed in Chapter 1, but they can also be high-end workstations or even mainframe computers. A ***Web client*** is essentially the computer you use to move around the Internet and access the information and services on a server computer. So, a client computer can be your desktop or notebook, your smart phone, your PDA, or even your tablet PC. To learn more about using different types of devices to access the Internet, complete the "Internet Appliances" tutorial on your SimNet Concepts Support CD.

There are many types of server computers on the Internet. The ones we've been visiting as we introduced you to the Web are called Web servers. A ***Web server*** provides information and services to Web surfers. So, when you access www.census.gov to obtain government census data, you're accessing a Web server with your Web client.

Other servers on the Internet include mail servers, FTP servers, and IRC servers. A ***mail server*** provides e-mail services and accounts. An ***FTP server*** maintains a collection of files you can download (see Figure 2.11). These files can include software, music files, and games. An ***IRC (Internet relay chat) server*** supports your use of discussion groups and chat rooms. IRC servers are popular hosting computers for sites such as Epinions.com (www.epinions.com). At Epinions.com you can earn money by writing reviews of various products.

did you know?

It is predicted that teenagers in Europe and the United States will spend $10.6 billion online in 2005, up from $1.3 billion in 2001.[6]

INFORMATION ON THE INTERNET

How Does Information Move from Computer to Computer on the Internet?

As information moves around the Internet, bouncing among network access points until it finally reaches you, it does so according to various communications protocols. A ***communications protocol (protocol)*** is a set of rules that computers follow to transfer information. Protocols are very necessary in a network environment because different types of computers

i•series insights *Ethics, Security & Privacy*

Getting Conned by Dot-Cons

The "brick-and-mortar" business world has its shady deals and scams. So does the "click-and-order" business world of the Web. And it's even harder to pursue and prosecute criminals in the virtual world of the Web. Hiding behind Web site addresses may be an effective mechanism to swindle you. Here's just a sampling of shady deals that have gone down on the Web.

- One-time auction houses that advertised an upcoming auction—when the auction was over and money was collected, no goods were shipped.
- Typical credit card fraud in which card numbers were used to illegally order other products.
- "All expenses paid" vacations that ended up including a hotel that wasn't free.
- A variety of health care products that turned out to be snake oil (a big scam on the Web).

One Web site offered free access to adult-oriented material, which turned out to be far from free. Once someone went there, the site disconnected their phone call through their modem, kept their line active, and used it to call a long-distance number to another service provider outside the United States.

Be careful when you're ordering products and services on the Web. As always—deals that seem to be too good to be true probably are. If you feel you've been scammed on the Web, immediately contact the Federal Trade Commission at www.ftc.gov.

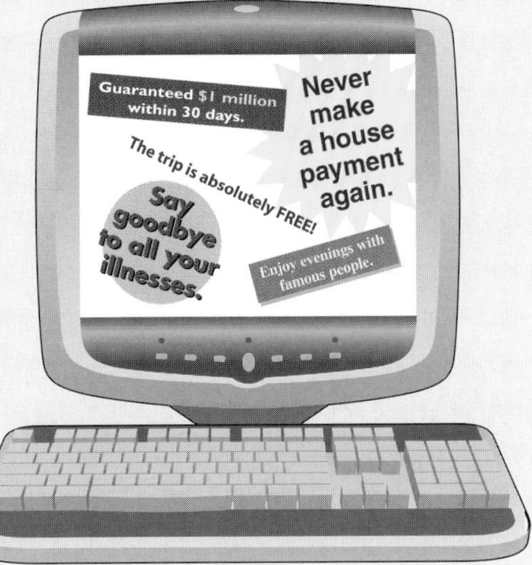

handle information internally in different forms, and there are many types of computers on the Internet—server computers that can be minicomputers, hand-held devices such as your smart phone, desktop and notebook computers. If we want them all to communicate effectively, computers must have common protocols for moving information among themselves on the Internet.

TCP/IP

TCP/IP (Transport Control Protocol/Internet Protocol) is the basic communications protocol that makes the Internet work. It defines the rules that allow various computers to communicate across the Internet. It doesn't matter if you're viewing streaming video from a Web server, transferring a file from an FTP server, or chatting across an IRC server, TCP/IP is the foundation for the movement of information.

Hypertext Transfer Protocol (http)

Hypertext transfer protocol (http) is the communications protocol that supports the movement of information over the Web, essentially from a Web server to you. That's why Web site addresses start with "http://." That beginning portion of the address informs all the Internet technologies that you want to access something on the Web. For example, it tells your Web browser software that you want to access a Web site. Most browser software today assumes that you want to access a Web site on the Internet. So, you don't even have to type in the http:// if you don't want to. Essentially, http://www.whitehouse.gov is the same thing as www.whitehouse.gov.

Since the Internet is the infrastructure supporting your use of the Web, when you access a Web site, your computer is using both TCP/IP (to transfer any type of information over the Internet) and http (because the information you want is Web-based).

File Transfer Protocol (FTP)

File transfer protocol (FTP) is the communications protocol that allows you to transfer files of information from one computer to another. FTP servers are popular stops for Web surfers who want to download a variety of different types of files—software such as games and music are the most common. When you download a file from an FTP site, you're using both TCP/IP (the basic Internet protocol) and FTP (the protocol that allows you to download the file).

If you'd like to read more about the technical Internet, we've provided a list of books and resources for you on the Web site for this text at www.mhhe.com/i-series.

SECTION 2.3

making the grade

1. The ___________ is the major set of connections for computers on the Internet.
2. A(n) ___________ is a company that provides individuals, organizations, and businesses access to the Internet.
3. A(n) ___________ maintains a collection of files you can download.
4. ___________ is the basic communications protocol that makes the Internet work.
5. ___________ is the communications protocol that supports the movement of information over the Web, essentially from a Web server to you.

did you know?

In 2002, over 50 million Americans used the Internet in the hope of finding a job.

2.4 GETTING CONNECTED

So, what does it take to get connected to the Internet from your home or your dorm? You need four things—a computer, an ISP, a modem, and communications software. You're already familiar with many computer options, such as notebooks, desktops, and tablet PCs, so let's focus on choosing an ISP, identifying the right kind of modem, and ensuring that you have the necessary communications software.

INTERNET SERVICE PROVIDERS

What Options Do I Have for an ISP?

Your choice for an ISP (Internet service provider) includes commercial ISPs, free ISPs, your school, and perhaps your place of work.

FIGURE 2.12

AT&T WorldNet is a popular commercial ISP.

Commercial ISPs charge you a monthly fee, just as your telephone company charges you a monthly fee for phone service. This ISP fee can range from just a few dollars to about $20 per month. Popular worldwide commercial ISPs include Microsoft (MSN), AOL, and AT&T WorldNet, just to name a few (see Figure 2.12). Most commercial ISPs provide you with Web space, which may be very important to you. ***Web space*** is a storage area where you keep your Web site. You can't actually keep your Web site on your home computer and have people access it.

Free ISPs are absolutely free, as their names suggest. But there are some catches. Depending on which free ISP you choose, you may or may not get 24×7 technical support or a toll-free number to call. And some free ISPs do not offer you Web space. Popular free ISPs include FreeLane (www.freelane.excite.com), FreeInternet.com (www.freei.com), and Juno (www.juno.com).

Your third and fourth options are your school and place of employment. You typically don't have to pay for these options. However, many employers and schools that act as ISPs for employees and students monitor their movements on the Web. Some even restrict where you can go on the Web. That's definitely a downside. To learn more about ISPs, complete the "Internet Service Providers" tutorial on your SimNet Concepts Support CD.

MODEMS AND THEIR CAPABILITIES

Do Different Types of Modems Offer Differing Speeds and Advantages?

To connect your computer to the Internet you need some sort of modem, with the four primary alternatives being a telephone modem, DSL modem, cable modem, and satellite modem. Each of these is a telecommunications device that allows you to connect your computer to another computer or to a network of other computers. For surfing the Web, this "network of other computers" is in fact the Internet. To learn more about

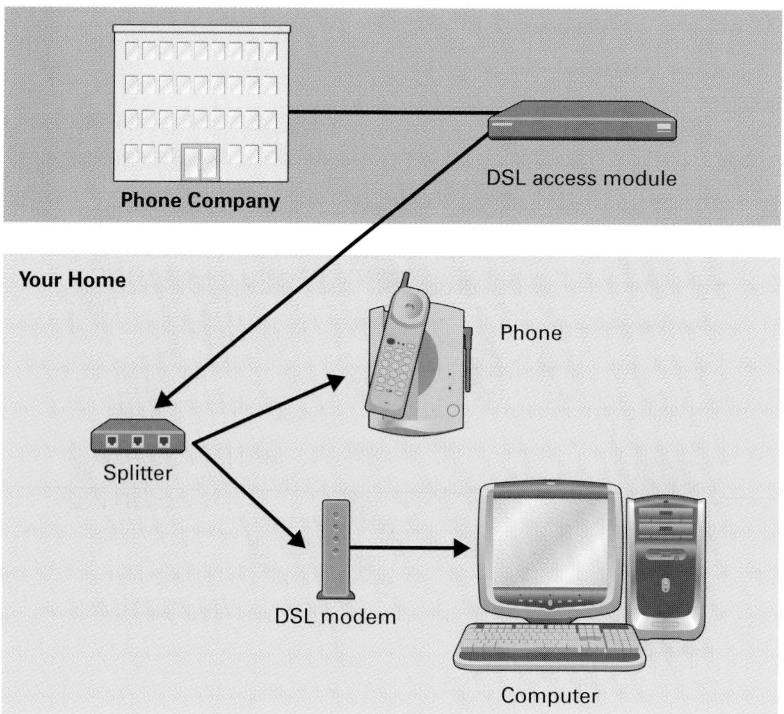

FIGURE 2.13

A DSL modem brings you Internet access through your phone line, while giving you the ability to use that phone line to make and receive calls at the same time.

connecting to the Internet, complete the "Connecting to the Internet" tutorial on your SimNet Concepts Support CD.

A ***telephone modem*** is a telecommunications device that connects your computer through a phone line to a network of other computers. A telephone modem is the slowest type of modem, with speeds up to 56 Kbps (56 thousand bits per second). Telephone modems also tie up the use of your telephone line. So, for example, you can't receive incoming phone calls if you're surfing the Web. You can, of course, get a second telephone line, but that creates additional cost. Telephone modems come standard on all desktop and notebook computers.

A ***DSL (Digital Subscriber Line) modem*** is a high-speed telecommunications device using a phone line, which allows you to use your phone line for voice communication at the same time (see Figure 2.13). With speeds up to 100 times faster than a telephone modem, a DSL modem provides you with an "always-on" Internet connection giving you instant access without having to dial in. Whether or not you can use a DSL modem is determined by the ability of your phone company to provide such a service. Certain phone companies don't provide DSL capabilities in some areas of the country.

A ***cable modem*** is a telecommunications device that uses your TV cable to produce an Internet connection (see Figure 2.14 on the opposite page). The speed of transmission with a cable modem is between 20 and 100 times faster than a telephone modem. A cable modem has similar advantages to a DSL modem: increased speed, an always-on connection, and the ability to surf the Web and watch cable TV simultaneously. But as with a DSL modem, whether or not you can actually use a cable modem is determined by whether your cable TV service can provide such a service.

did you know?

Almost *70 percent of U.S. consumers are fearful that their privacy is at risk online.*[8]

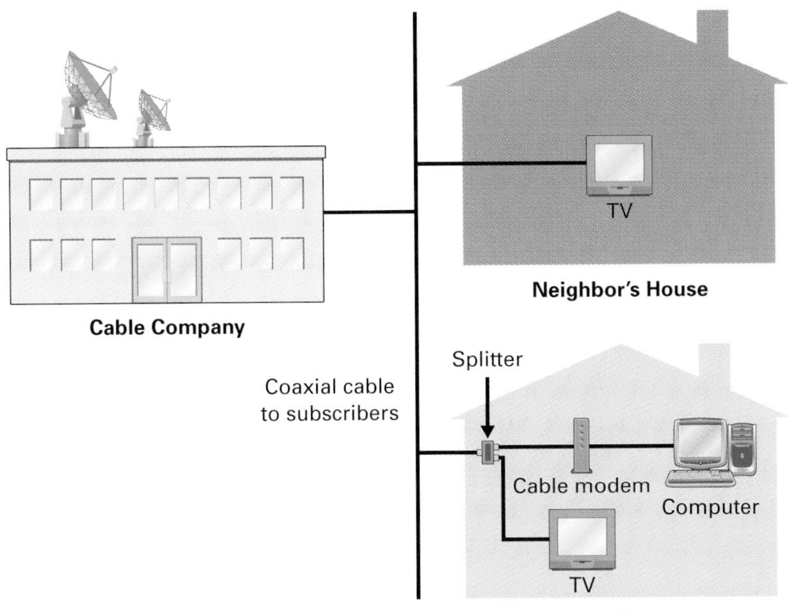

FIGURE 2.14
A cable modem gives you Internet access using the same wiring that brings you cable TV.

Finally, a ***satellite modem*** is a telecommunications device that allows you to get Internet access using a satellite dish. For this, you'll need the right type of antenna (i.e., satellite dish). Some cable TV providers now offer you a satellite dish that you can use both for receiving cable TV and accessing the Internet. Like DSL and cable modems, satellite modems are much faster than telephone modems and offer an always-on Internet connection.

So, which type of modem should you use? That depends on cost and availability. In general, we would encourage you to use the fastest type of modem you can, depending on how much you can afford and whether or not the necessary service is available. DSL, cable, and satellite modems are the most expensive (some of these services cost about $50 per month) but also offer the greatest speed, enabling you to enjoy all forms of Web multimedia which may simply not be possible with a telephone modem.

SOFTWARE FOR WEB SURFING

What Software Do I Need to Access the Internet?

To access the Internet and surf the Web you need only two basic types of software: Web browser software (or a Web browser) and connectivity software.

For the Web sites we've been showing you in the illustrations throughout this chapter, we've been using Internet Explorer as our Web browser. It comes standard on all Windows-based computers. Another popular alternative is Netscape Communicator, which offers a slightly different-looking interface than Internet Explorer but has the same functionality. If your computer doesn't have Netscape Communicator on it, you can download it free from Netscape's Web site (www.netscape.com).

To surf the Web you also need connectivity software. ***Connectivity software*** allows you to use your computer to connect to another computer or a network. If you're using a standard telephone modem, you'll be using

i•can

Understand the Choices I Need to Make to Connect to the Internet and Use the Web

You now know the choices you're faced with when you decide you want to become a Web surfer. Let's review them.

First, you need some sort of computer. Your primary options here are a traditional notebook or desktop computer, a PDA, a tablet PC, or a smart phone. If you choose a PDA or smart phone, they will come equipped with the necessary wireless modem, Web browser software, and connectivity software. Smart phones usually require you to use your phone service as the ISP. Some PDAs offer you various ISP options. If you choose a notebook, desktop, or tablet PC, you have numerous options for both a modem and an ISP.

Modem choices include a telephone modem (the slowest), cable and DSL modems (both much faster than a telephone modem), and a satellite modem (probably the fastest of the four). You may or may not have the option of choosing a cable, DSL, or satellite modem depending on where you live and the types of services your local telephone company and cable TV company provide.

When faced with the choice of a Web browser, you can use either Internet Explorer or Netscape Communicator. Both are freely available on the Web. Some commercial ISPs, such as AOL, provide their own unique Web browser software for you to use.

Connectivity software is not a major consideration. If you're using a telephone modem, you'll use the connectivity software that comes standard with your computer. If you're using a DSL, cable, or satellite modem, the service provider will provide you with the necessary connectivity software.

connectivity software to dial up and connect to another computer. Figure 2.15 shows this type of connectivity software that comes standard on Windows-based machines. Notice that you have to provide your user name and password as well as the phone number you need to call to connect to your ISP.

FIGURE 2.15

Basic connectivity software allows you to dial up and connect to another computer while using a telephone modem.

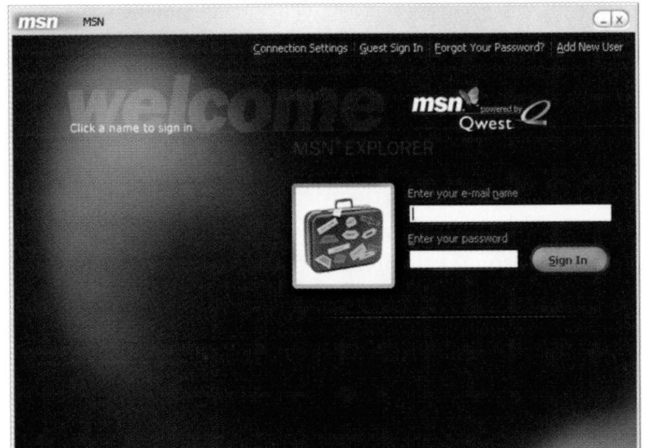

FIGURE 2.16

MSN will provide you with the necessary connectivity software if you use its DSL service.

If you're using a DSL, cable, or satellite modem, you don't really "make a call" to connect to your ISP. Instead, you initiate the connectivity software provided to you by your ISP, which in essence makes the connection for you. In Figure 2.16, you can see the connectivity software that MSN provides for DSL modem access.

making the grade

SECTION 2.4

1. ____________ ISPs charge you a monthly fee, just as your telephone company charges you a monthly fee for phone service.
2. A(n) ____________ modem is a high-speed telecommunications device using a phone line, which allows you to use your phone line for voice communication at the same time.
3. A(n) ________________________ is a telecommunications device that uses your cable TV to produce an Internet connection.
4. A(n) ____________ is a telecommunications device that allows you to get Internet access using a satellite dish.
5. ____________ software allows you to use your computer to connect to another computer or a network.

2.5 CONSUMER Q&A

1. What Is the Format of an E-mail Address?

E-mail addresses are similar to Web site and page addresses in that they must be unique. The typical format of an e-mail address is username@orgname.orgtype. For example, Stephen Green, a student at UCLA, might have sgreen@ucla.edu as an e-mail address or Stephen.green@ucla.edu, depending on how UCLA assigns user names. And people can have several e-mail addresses. For example, if Stephen was also using Yahoo! for e-mail, his address might be StephenGreen@yahoo.com. To learn more about e-mail, complete the "Using E-Mail" tutorial on your SimNet Concepts Support CD.

2. How Fast Can I Surf the Web?

Speed, as far as surfing the Web is concerned, means how fast you can access and load Web sites into your Web browser for you to see and use. Of course, this is largely determined by what type of modem access you use—telephone modems are the slowest while satellite modems may be the fastest. More generally, what determines speed is bandwidth. Bandwidth is the amount of information that can travel from one place to another in a given amount of time. We typically measure bandwidth in bits per second. So, a 56k (or kbps) modem can transmit and receive information at a maximum speed of 56 kilobits (thousand characters) per second.

3. Can I Spend Too Much Time Surfing the Web?

Yes, you can, and many people do. This is a real problem and this problem is a mental health issue. Many insurance providers today even cover Web addiction as a treatable and insurance-covered health problem. Web interactive role-playing games, real-time strategies games, and chat rooms are where most Web addicts spend too much time. If you find yourself missing class too often because you're on the Web, staying up too late at night surfing the Web, or needing to check your e-mail every 30 minutes, you need some time away from the Web.

4. How Can I Get My Business Online?

The easiest way to get your business online is to use the services of a Web hosting service such as Yahoo! Stores (www.stores.yahoo.com) or zShops at Amazon (www.amazon.com). These types of hosting sites will help you build an electronic catalog, set up processing for credit card orders, and even advertise your site. Don't expect to make much money quickly, as the dot-coms—turned dot-bombs—of the late 20th century quickly found out. Before starting any business, you must define a clear path-to-profitability (P2P). Otherwise, you're just wasting your time (and money). To learn more, complete the "Web Hosting" tutorial on your SimNet Concepts Support CD.

5. Can I Take Advantage of Web E-commerce Using a PDA or Smart Phone?

M-commerce, or ***mobile e-commerce,*** allows you to use wireless devices such as smart phones or PDAs to buy and sell products and services through Web e-commerce. Many Web sites are developing their content just so that it can be displayed on the relatively small screens of a smart phone or PDA.

2.6 SUMMARY AND KEY TERMS

The ***World Wide Web (Web)*** is a multimedia-based collection of information, services, and Web sites supported by the Internet. The Web supports ***electronic commerce***—just commerce, but commerce that technology facilities and enhances. Within e-commerce, there are ***click-and-mortar businesses*** (having both a physical and Web presence) and ***click-and-order businesses*** (having only a Web presence). These e-commerce businesses perform three types of e-commerce activities: (1) ***B2C e-commerce*** (business to consumer), (2) ***B2B e-commerce*** (business to business), and (3) ***C2C e-commerce*** (consumer to consumer).

As you surf the Web, you'll be using ***Web browser software*** to access ***Web sites,*** locations you visit electronically to gather information and perhaps order products and request services. Each ***Web site address*** or ***domain name*** is unique. Web sites often have many ***Web pages,*** each dealing with a specific topic. ***Web site addresses*** or ***URLs*** are also unique.

To find information on the Web you can use a ***search engine***—a facility that allows you to find Web sites by providing key words or questions. The two most popular types of search engines are ***directory search engines*** (that create hierarchical listings of Web sites) and ***true search engines*** (that provide a list of Web sites in response to a question you pose).

To enjoy Web multimedia—which can include ***Web audio, Web video, Flash*** pages, ***Shockwave*** pages, and even ***VRML*** (much of it in ***streaming media*** form)—you need either a ***plug-in*** (software that works in your Web browser) or a ***player*** (software that works outside your Web browser).

The Internet is what makes the Web possible. The ***Internet*** is a vast network of computers that connects millions of people and organizations all over the world. The technical infrastructure of the Internet includes server computers (***Internet server computers, Web servers, mail servers, FTP servers,*** and ***IRC servers***) and communications protocols (***TCP/IP, http,*** and ***FTP***).

To get connected you need four things:

1. Computer—such as a tablet PC or smart phone.
2. ***ISP***—a company that provides individuals, organizations, and businesses access to the Internet.
3. Modem—***telephone modem, DSL modem, cable modem,*** or ***satellite modem.***
4. ***Connectivity software***—that allows you to use your computer to connect to another computer or network.

To learn even more about the topics covered in this chapter, including popular sites for downloading plug-ins and players and technical Internet resources, visit the Web site for this text at www.mhhe.com/i-series.

KEY TERMS

brick-and-mortar business (p. 36)
business to business electronic commerce (B2B e-commerce) (p. 37)
business to consumer electronic commerce (B2C e-commerce) (p. 37)
cable modem (p. 52)
click-and-mortar business (p. 36)
click-and-order business (pure play, e-tailer) (p. 37)
communications protocol (protocol) (p. 48)
connectivity software (p. 53)
consumer to consumer electronic commerce (C2C e-commerce) (p. 38)
directory search engine (p. 41)
domain name (p. 39)
DSL (Digital Subscriber Line) modem (p. 52)
electronic commerce (e-commerce) (p. 36)
file transfer protocol (FTP) (p. 50)
Flash (p. 45)
Flash plug-in (p. 45)
FTP server (p. 48)
hypertext transfer protocol (http) (p. 49)
Internet (p. 39)
Internet backbone (p. 47)
Internet server computer (Internet host computer) (p. 47)

Internet service provider (ISP) (p. 47)
IRC (Internet relay chat) server (p. 48)
m-commerce (mobile e-commerce) (p. 56)
mail server (p. 48)
network (p. 47)
network access point (NAP) (p. 47)
player (p. 44)
plug-in (p. 43)
satellite modem (p. 53)
search engine (p. 40)
Shockwave (p. 45)
Shockwave player (p. 45)
streaming media (p. 45)
TCP/IP (Transport Control Protocol/Internet Protocol) (p. 49)
telephone modem (p. 52)
top-level domain (p. 40)
true search engine (p. 41)
URL (uniform resource locator) (p. 39)
VRML (Virtual Reality Modeling Language) (p. 46)
Web audio (p. 45)
Web browser software (Web browser) (p. 39)
Web client (p. 48)
Web page (p. 39)
Web page address (p. 39)
Web server (p. 48)
Web site (p. 39)
Web site address (p. 39)
Web space (p. 51)
Web video (p. 45)
World Wide Web (Web) (p. 39)

review of terminology

Multiple Choice

1. The technical term for a Web page address is a(n)
   a. domain name.
   b. top-level domain.
   c. URL.
   d. NRL.
   e. protocol.
2. A ___________ provides a list of Web sites in response to a question you ask.
   a. true search engine
   b. directory search engine
   c. player
   d. plug-in
   e. protocol
3. Com, edu, and mil are all examples of
   a. communications protocols.
   b. top-level domains.
   c. ISPs.
   d. Web browser software.
   e. URLs.
4. Your choices for modems include
   a. telephone modems.
   b. cable modems.
   c. DSL modems.
   d. satellite modems.
   e. all of the above.
5. The type of server that supports your use of a chat room is specifically called a(n)
   a. FTP server.
   b. mail server.
   c. IRC server.
   d. Internet host server.
   e. Web server.
6. The type of server that maintains a collection of files that you can download is specifically called a(n)
   a. FTP server.
   b. mail server.
   c. IRC server.
   d. Internet host server.
   e. Web server.
7. Web pages that include significant interactivity are often created in
   a. Flash.
   b. Shockwave.
   c. either Flash or Shockwave.
   d. FTP.
   e. either Flash, Shockwave, or FTP.
8. Yahoo! is an example of a(n)
   a. network access point (NAP).
   b. click-and-mortar business.
   c. brick-and-mortar business.
   d. directory search engine.
   e. true search engine.
9. The type of server that supports e-mail services and accounts is specifically called a(n)
   a. FTP server.
   b. mail server.
   c. IRC server.
   d. Internet host server.
   e. Web server.
10. Web multimedia includes
    a. Web audio.
    b. Web video.
    c. VRML.
    d. streaming media.
    e. all of the above.

True/False

11. ____ The Web is the technical infrastructure that supports the Internet.
12. ____ It is not possible to participate in e-commerce using such devices as a smart phone or PDA.
13. ____ The technical term for a Web site address is a domain name.
14. ____ Web space is a place where you keep your Web site.
15. ____ When accessing the Web, the technology you use such as a tablet PC is called a Web server.

Take this quiz online at www.mhhe.com/i-series and get instant feedback.

review of concepts

QUESTIONS AND EXERCISES

1. Identifying Servers on a Web Page

In this chapter, we discussed different types of servers including mail servers, IRC servers, and FTP servers. Many sites actually provide you with access to all these types of servers in a seamless fashion such that you may not even be aware that you are connecting to or using a different server. MSN is one such site. We've provided a screen capture of that site below. Your task is to identify on it links to (1) a mail server, (2) an IRC server, and (3) an FTP server. Simply circle the links and provide a call-out box.

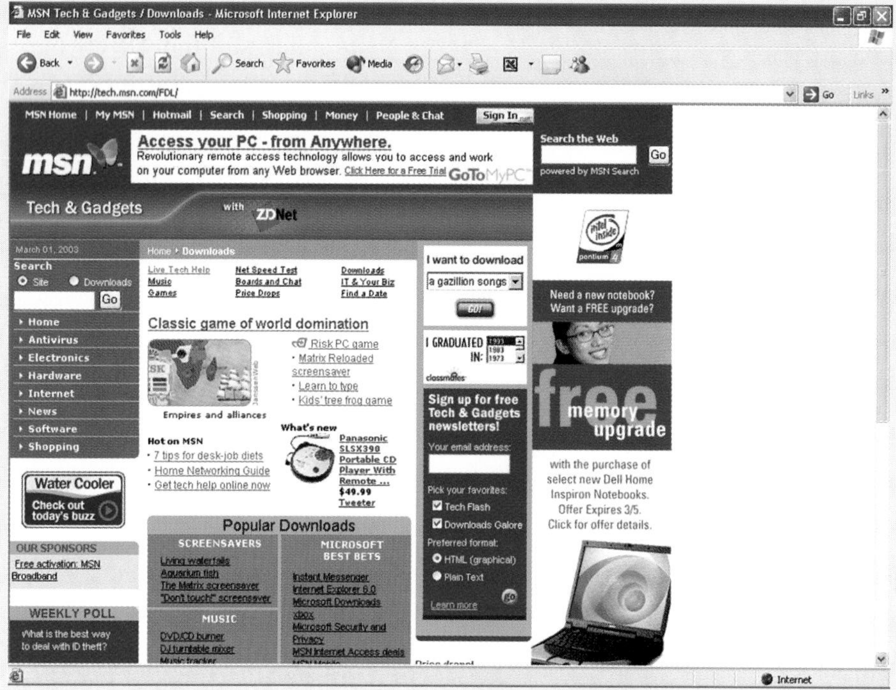

2. Matching Technical Terms

In the right column below, we've provided a list of technical terms that support or are equivalent to the terms in the left column. Your task is to match the appropriate technical term in the right column with its associated term in the left column. Some terms in each column may not have an equivalent term in the other column.

A. Plus sign and/or minus sign	_______	http
B. FTP server	_______	Web client
C. Web page address	_______	Internet
D. Educational institution	_______	IRC server
E. Internet server	_______	TCP/IP
F. Web site address	_______	FTP
G. Web	_______	Boolean operator
H. Web server	_______	Domain name
I. Chat room	_______	URL
J. Notebook computer	_______	edu

3. Comparing the Real World to the Web & Internet

In the real world, you can find many equivalents to the Web, the Internet, and all the Internet technologies. For each real world concept below, provide the Web or Internet equivalent.

A. 1234 Main Street ________________

B. 1234 Main Street Apt #12A ________________

C. Stop light ________________

D. Interstate ________________

E. Yellow pages ________________

F. Telephone company ________________

G. 1-800 number ________________

H. Motorcycle ________________

I. Post office box ________________

J. State, such as Maine ________________

K. Handshake ________________

L. Water hose ________________

M. Strictly mail-order business ________________

4. Dissecting a Web Page Address

Wayne Herndon Rare Coins is a site on the Web where you can find most any coin that you'd like to add to your collection (that is, if you're a numismatist, or coin collector). One of Wayne's Web pages is devoted to allowing you to order brilliant uncirculated rolls of quarters in the 50 States Quarter program. The address for that Web page is given below.

www.wayneherndon.com/comfiles/pages/category81.shtml

Your task is to dissect the above Web page address or URL and identify the (1) name for the entire site, (2) names of the various folders and their hierarchy, and (3) Web page file name. Provide this information in the diagram below.

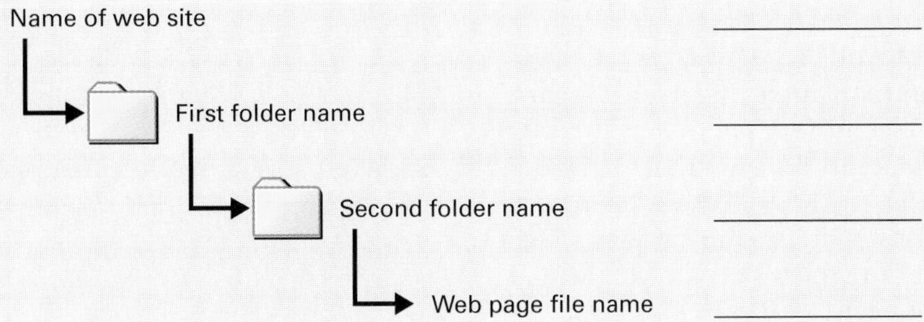

hands-on projects

e-commerce

1. Setting Up a Business on the Web

You may be like many people—you may want to set up your own business on the Web. If so, it's actually not that difficult a process if you use the services of Web hosts. Web hosts can be places such as Yahoo! Stores (www.stores.yahoo.com) or zShops at Amazon (www.amazon.com), both of which we mentioned earlier in this chapter. Other Web hosts are:

- FreeMerchant—www.freemerchant.com
- MonsterCommerce—www.monstercommerce.com
- ShopSite—www.shopsite.com

Connect to one of these Web hosts and explore what it takes to set up your business on the Internet. As you do, answer the following questions:

a. What packages can you subscribe to and what are their price levels?

b. How does the Web host advertise your business?

c. Will the Web host submit your site to various search engines?

d. What must you do to be able to accept and process credit card orders?

e. Does the Web host make any guarantee concerning the amount of traffic that will visit your site?

2. Participating in E-Commerce Auctions

One of the truly great things about the Web is that it has brought together people from all over the world with common interests. You can discuss issues in chat rooms, join fan clubs, and buy and sell items in auction houses. If you have a particular hobby or enjoy collecting memorabilia, auction houses will probably be a place you'll want to visit. The most popular is eBay at www.ebay.com. Connect to eBay and answer the following questions:

a. What process do you go through to register as a buyer or seller?

b. Can you search for items without registering first?

c. Does eBay guarantee the quality and authenticity of items being sold?

d. What sort of mechanism is used to rank the quality of buyers and sellers?

e. What search capabilities can you use to find items that might interest you?

f. How does eBay make money by simply letting other people buy and sell products?

3. Finding an ISP

Finding an ISP is certainly not a difficult task. There are many to choose from and most have similar fees and features. The two major categories of ISPs are free and commercial, with commercial ISPs charging fees but offering more features and services.

Below, we've provided four Web sites that will help you find the right ISP. Visit a couple of these and find at least two ISPs that might interest you.

- Internet.com—thelist.internet.com
- FindAnISP—www.findanisp.com
- ISP Finder—www.ispfinder.com
- ISP.com—www.isp.com

For the two ISPs you're interested in, answer the following questions:

a. What is the monthly subscription rate?

b. For how long must you sign an agreement?

c. Is an e-mail service provided?

d. Is Web space provided?

e. How fast can you surf the Web? That is, what's the bandwidth speed?

f. Do you have to download and install any software?

g. What sort of technical support is provided?

h. Based on your answers to the questions above, which ISP would you choose? Why?

ethics, security & privacy

1. Finding Social Security Numbers of Deceased People

Social security numbers are very private and personal information. As a rule, you should never give out your social security number unless you are required to do so by law.

However, when you die, your social security number actually begins to appear in a lot of places, some of which are on the Web. For example, at RootsWeb.com (http://ssdi.genealogy.rootsweb.com/cgi-bin/ssdi.cgi), you can simply type in the name of a deceased person and obtain his or her social security number.

Connect to that particular site and type in the name of a deceased relative or friend and answer the following questions:

a. Were you able to find information on that person?
b. Did it include his or her birth date and date of death?
c. What other information did you find?
d. Does it bother you that this type of information is so freely available on the Web?
e. Isn't it possible that a criminal could search this site for a social security number and use it illegally?
f. In your view, should this type of information be available on the Web or should the government enact legislation to prevent this type of information from being published on the Web? Justify your position.

2. Finding Personal Information on the Web

Information about you is all over the Web. You may not have even given your permission, but it's there for everyone to see. Most commonly, you can find information about people by using people searches. We've listed a few below—access these and try to find yourself, a friend, or a family member and then answer the questions below.

- WhoWhere?—www.whowhere.lycos.com
- Netscape PeopleFinder—http://wp.netscape.com/netcenter/whitepages.html
- Yahoo! PeopleSearch—www.people.yahoo.com

a. How easy was it to find someone?
b. What information were you able to find?
c. Do you like the fact that you can look up people on the Web?
d. Do you like the fact that people can look you up on the Web?
e. Young children today are growing up with the Web. In 10 years, will these people have any problems with their information being so easily available?

3. Finding E-Mail Addresses on the Web

At many schools (and yours may be one), you can easily look up people to find their e-mail addresses. All you have to do is type in a first name or last name. You don't even need to know the correct spelling. The school will tell you if that person is a registered student (or faculty member) and how to contact them by e-mail.

a. Does your school actually provide this type of service?
b. Is this good or bad? Why?
c. Did you know that your school might offer this type of service?
d. Should your school get your permission before making this type of information available to anyone who has access to the Web?

on the web

1. Registering a Domain Name

In the e-commerce projects section, we discussed what it takes to get your business on the Web. Another important task you may need to complete is that of registering your domain name or Web site address. As you can probably guess, it's a formal process in which you submit a domain name and then that domain name is verified to ensure that no one else is using it.

Many Web sites offer you assistance in registering a domain name, including:

- Verio—http://hosting.verio.com/
- Web.com—www.web.com
- Register.com—www.register.com
- SiteLeader.com—http://worldwidedomains.com/
- DomainMart—www.domainmart.com

Visit a few of the above sites, attempt to find an unused domain name, and answer the following questions:

a. How do you submit a domain name for verification?
b. How long does the verification process take?
c. What is the fee for registering a domain name?
d. How do you pay the fee?
e. Can you request to buy a domain name that already exists?
f. How easily did you find a domain name that was not currently used?

2. Finding Maps and Directions

You need never be lost again in a city or traveling across the country. Why? Because the Web is full of sites that can offer you driving directions. At many of these sites, you simply type in where you are and where you want to go. The site will then give you a detailed map along with specific driving directions, often telling you exactly how far to travel on each leg of your journey.

Let's visit a few of these sites and see what they have to offer. Below is a list of four Web sites that offer maps and directions. Connect to a couple of them.

- www.maps.expedia.com
- www.mapquest.com
- www.maps.com
- www.maps.yahoo.com

At each site you choose, pick a starting point and a destination for your journey. Now, try to enter that information to receive driving instructions. As you do, answer the following questions.

a. How easy is it to specify your starting point and destination?
b. Do you have to know exact addresses or can you pick a location by something such as a business or hotel name?
c. Does the site give you both a map and driving instructions or a combination of the two?

As you travel, would you prefer to have directions from a Web site or use a "fold-up" map? Can the information on a Web site be as reliable as a fold-up map? Or, in reverse, can a fold-up map that was probably printed some time ago be as up-to-date as the information on a Web site?

3. Your School's Web Site Structure

At the beginning of this chapter, we took a brief look at the *USA Today* Web site and how it creates a well-organized hierarchy of Web pages. This is key to developing a good Web site. Visit your school's Web site (its address is probably www.schoolname.edu where *schoolname* is your school's actual name or abbreviation). As you click on various links, create a diagram of the hierarchy of Web pages within your school's Web site. Is your school's Web site well organized and easy to follow? How easily can you find a list of classes for the upcoming term? A list of faculty members by department? A list of majors and minors? How would you reorganize your school's Web site from a student point of view?

group activities

1. Learning about Web Space at Your School

Many schools offer students Web space for creating and storing personal Web sites and e-portfolios. Do some checking around at your school and see what it offers with respect to Web space. As you do, answer the following questions:

a. Does your school provide you with Web space?

b. How much Web space is each individual student allocated?

c. What types of activities and/or information does your school prohibit (e.g., can you start a business?)?

d. For how long after you leave school does your Web space remain active?

e. If you create a Web site within your Web space, what is the Web site address?

2. Managing Your Cookies

As you surf the Web, many Web sites will store cookies on your hard disk. These cookies are small text files that contain information about your surfing habits while at a specific site. You can set up your Web browser so that it will accept all cookies, accept no cookies, or something in between.

Start your preferred Web browser and peruse through the menu to find how to adjust the settings for handling cookies. (In Internet Explorer, click on **Tools** and **Internet Options** and then select the **Privacy** tab.) As you do, answer the following questions:

a. What are the various levels or options you can choose from for handling cookies?

b. What is the current level of your Web browser for handling cookies?

c. After reviewing the various options, did you choose to change your browser's level? Why or why not?

3. Finding a Regional ISP

In the e-commerce projects earlier, you explored finding an Internet service provider (ISP) through several Web sites. Now, let's focus on finding a regional ISP by using a phone book and phone. Flip back to the yellow pages of your phone book and find ISPs. Make a phone call to a couple of listed ISPs and determine their monthly fees and features. Did any seem to be better or cheaper than the ISPs you found while completing the e-commerce projects? Are the regional ISPs really located in your town or perhaps a town close by? Would you rather use a well-known commercial ISP such as AOL or a regional ISP you've never heard of?

4. Connecting to the Web through Your School

Contact your school's technical support group that can tell you how to use your school to connect to the Web. Answer the following questions:

a. What connectivity software must you have?

b. Is that connectivity software already on your own computer or do you have to download it?

c. What is the phone number you call to make a connection between your computer and your school's computer?

d. Is there a time limitation for staying connected to the Web through your school?

e. Does your school provide FTP software so you can download files from the Web?

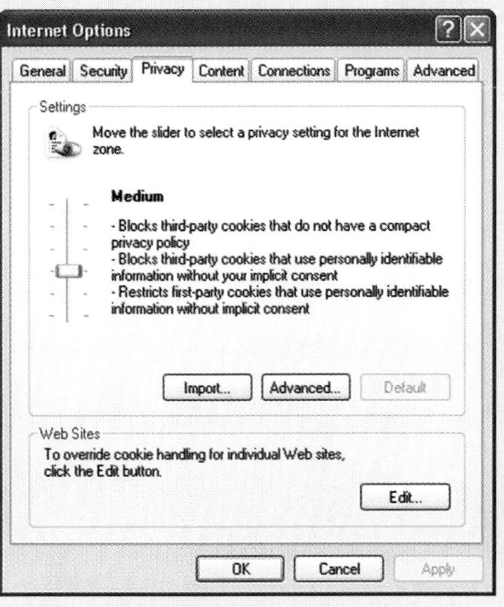

crossword puzzle

Across

1. ______ publishing—extended word processing software
5. Graphics that store instructions for creating images
7. Electronic banking
8. Software iteration
11. Software for working with logically related information
13. Resolution measurement for digital cameras
16. RealAudio file format
17. Skeletal structure of a 3-D graphic image
18. Native file format for Windows environments
21. Rate at which video frames are captured
23. High-resolution file format used in print publishing
26. Software for working with information in cells
28. Software for video compression and decompression
29. Bundle of software
31. Software for creating basic text documents
33. Public domain alternative to #20 down
34. Color palette without "color"
35. "Try before you buy" software
36. Composing two or more colors to create another color

Down

2. Rate at which audio is captured
3. Palette that takes advantage of 16.7 million colors
4. Document that states your rights to software
6. Opposite of #15 down
9. Personal information management software
10. Software for working with images and photos
12. Also called a raster graphic or a bitmap
14. Software for creating electronic slides
15. Opposite of #6 down
16. Adding shades and shadows based on a light source
19. Any information stored in digital form
20. Graphics file format used primarily for Web sites
22. Standard for storing audio information for electronic instruments
24. Software with no cost
25. Selection of colors for a bitmap graphic
27. Process of covering a wireframe with colors and textures
30. Graphics file format for Web sites with good compression
32. File format for audio

C H A P T E R three 3

Application Software and Digital Media

What Can Your Computer Do for You?

SIMNET CONCEPTS SUPPORT

did you know?

Personal productivity software and the use of digital media are changing and increasing just as rapidly as any aspect of technology. Just a few short years ago, your choices for personal productivity software were very limited. Even more recently, digital video on the Web was only a dream.

up *through the mid-1990s, Microsoft did not dominate the word processing, spreadsheet, presentation, or database management system software markets.*

a *movie theater-quality 10-minute video in digital form requires almost 34 gigabytes (billion) characters of storage. How much hard disk space does your computer have?*

a *typical floppy disk, which has a storage capacity of 1.44 megabytes (or characters), can hold only about __??__ seconds of CD-quality music.*

To find out how many seconds of CD-quality music a floppy disk can hold, visit www.mhhe.com/i-series.

Student Learning Outcomes

After reading this chapter, you should be able to:

1. Describe the difference between application software and system software.
2. Define key concepts in application software including personal productivity software, versions, and suites.
3. List and describe the eight major categories of personal productivity software tools.
4. Describe digital media and why knowing something about digital media is important.
5. Define the concepts related to two-dimensional images and photos, 3-D graphics, audio, and video.

There are two major categories of software—system software and application software. ***System software*** is the software that determines how your computer carries out technology-specific and essential tasks such as writing to a disk, starting your Web browser software so you can surf the Web, and sending a document to your printer. ***Application software*** is the software that allows you to perform specific information-processing tasks such as managing inventory, paying accounts payable, handling payroll, writing a term paper, or creating slides for a presentation.

Both system and application software are vitally important to your productivity. In this chapter, we'll focus on application software, and in Chapter 4 we'll focus on system software. For a review of all types of software, complete the "Introduction to Software" tutorial on your SimNet Concepts Support CD.

3.1 THE APPLICATION SOFTWARE YOU NEED

As a personal computer user (and buyer), you'll most often be interested in a subset of application software called personal productivity software. ***Personal productivity software*** is application software that is designed to help you be more productive in performing personal tasks such as writing letters, managing your checkbook, and creating electronic slides.

LET YOUR NEEDS DRIVE YOUR PURCHASE

If I Know What I Want to Do, Can I Decide What Software to Buy?

We can tell you this: First determine what you need (or want) to do and then let that drive what software you buy. In the area of personal productivity software, your needs will generally fall into some mix of eight categories (see Figure 3.1 on the opposite page). Of course, once you determine a specific need, you'll be faced with many choices of specific software. For example, if you need word processing software, you must decide from among several major word processing software packages.

SOFTWARE PUBLISHERS, NAMES, AND VERSIONS

What's in a Software Title?

Let's consider a software package such as Corel Paradox 10. Without even knowing what that software can help you do, you can identify three of its characteristics. First, Corel is the software publisher. Second, the name of the software is Paradox. And third, its version number is 10.

did you know?

In *1972, there were just barely over 600,000 businesses owned by women. By 1992, that number had grown to over 6.4 million.*[1]

What You Want to Do	What Software You Need
Create mainly text (letters, term papers, flyers, etc.)	• Word processing software or • Desktop publishing software
Build Web sites	• Web authoring software
Work with photos and art	• Graphics software
Work with numbers, calculations, and graphs	• Spreadsheet software
Build a slide presentation	• Presentation software
Manage personal information	• Personal information management software and/or • Personal finance software
Organize and access large amounts of information	• Database management system software
Communicate with other people	• E-mail software and/or • Web browser software

FIGURE 3.1

Always buy software according to what you want or need to do.

A ***software version (version)*** tells you which iteration of the software you're using. For Paradox, it's version 10. Version 10 is newer than all other versions of Paradox with lower numbers. Some publishers use years instead of version numbers. So, Microsoft Excel 2003 came out in 2003 and is newer than Excel 2002, Excel 98, or Excel 95. Whatever the case, you should always buy the newest software possible. It will include the greatest number of productivity features.

As publishers release new versions of their software, they usually provide you with the ability to upgrade your existing software. Upgrading your software from a previous version to a newer version typically costs less than if you purchase the newer version. Keep this in mind when a software publisher comes out with a new version of software you're currently using.

If you frequently connect your computer to a network of other computers at school or at work, your technology support department may provide these software updates to you. You should contact the appropriate department to determine if this is available to you. If it is, we recommend that you take advantage of it.

APPLICATION SOFTWARE SUITES

Can I Buy Software in Bundles or Just Specific Packages?

Most computer users have some common fundamental personal productivity software needs—some combination of the eight categories we listed in Figure 3.1. You can buy individual software to meet any or all of these needs if you want to, or you can buy a software suite.

FIGURE 3.2

Personal productivity software suites include a variety of different software packages.

	Microsoft Office 2003 Pro	Microsoft Office 2003 Premium	WordPerfect Office 2002 Standard	WordPerfect Office 2002 Pro
Word processing	Word	Word	WordPerfect	WordPerfect
Spreadsheet	Excel	Excel	Quattro Pro	Quattro Pro
Presentation	PowerPoint	PowerPoint	Presentations	Presentations
Desktop publishing	Publisher	Publisher	Trellix	Trellix
Personal finance	Money	Money		
Personal information management	*Comes as a part of Outlook	*Comes as a part of Outlook	CorelCentral	CorelCentral
Web authoring	FrontPage	FrontPage	Trellix	Trellix
Graphics		PhotoDraw		

Software suites are "bundles" of related software packages that are sold together. In Figure 3.2, we've listed some major personal productivity software suites and which specific software tools they include. There are four major software suites listed in Figure 3.2—Microsoft Office 2003 Pro, Microsoft Office 2003 Premium, WordPerfect Office 2002 Standard, and WordPerfect Office 2002 Pro. As you can see, each provides some combination of personal productivity software. Purchasing all the software individually in any suite will cost you two to three times as much as the suite. So, even if you don't need everything in a suite, it's still cheaper to purchase the suite than the exact software you need.

To decide which suite to buy, you should consider what everyone around you is using. For example, if your school recommends and supports Microsoft Office 2003 (either Pro or Premium), you should definitely consider one of those two suites. If your employer uses WordPerfect Office 2002 (either Standard or Pro), then one of those two might be the way to go. Microsoft dominates the personal productivity market, controlling about 80 percent of it.

SECTION 3.1

making the grade

1. ___________ is the software that determines how your computer carries out technology-specific and essential tasks such as writing to a disk and sending a document to your printer.
2. ___________ is the software that allows you to perform specific information-processing tasks such as managing inventory and creating slides for a presentation.
3. ___________ software is software that is designed to help you be more productive in performing personal tasks such as writing letters, managing your checkbook, and creating electronic slides.
4. A(n) ___________ tells you which iteration of the software you're using.
5. Software ___________ are "bundles" of related software packages that are sold together.

3.2 PERSONAL PRODUCTIVITY SOFTWARE TOOLS

Within the category of personal productivity software, you'll find a variety of tools that can definitely help you be more productive. Your goal is to determine which to buy in light of the tasks you need to perform.

WORD PROCESSING AND DESKTOP PUBLISHING SOFTWARE

What Software Do I Need for Creating Term Papers, Letters, Advertising Flyers, and the Like?

If you need to create documents that consist primarily of text, you need word processing or desktop publishing software. ***Word processing software*** is application software that helps you create papers, letters, memos, and other basic documents. ***Desktop publishing software*** is application software that extends word processing software by including design and formatting techniques to enhance the layout and appearance of a document.

This book is a good example. As authors, we created this textbook using Microsoft Word (word processing software). We then gave it to a book production expert who imported our Word documents into QuarkXPress, one of the leading desktop publishing software tools. The book production expert created the various formatting you see, the applications of color, the "did you know?" sidebar features and other features, the art and photos and special headings, and all the backgrounds. We simply couldn't perform some of those tasks with only word processing software.

You definitely need word processing software for creating term papers, writing letters, and other tasks. As for desktop publishing software, you may or may not need it. Word processing software now includes many desktop publishing features such as creating multiple columns of text, wrapping text around photos and art, and other tasks. To learn more about the capabilities of word processing software, complete the "Word Processing Applications" tutorial on your SimNet Concepts Support CD.

WEB AUTHORING SOFTWARE

What if I Want to Build My Own Web Site?

To create a basic Web page you use Hypertext Markup Language, or HTML. HTML allows you to specify (1) the content to appear on your Web site and (2) the formatting of that content. For example, if you wanted the text "Awards & Honors" to appear bolded and underlined in your Web e-portfolio, you would write the following:

<strong><u>Awards & Honors</u></strong>

So Awards & Honors is the content and the notations between the less than and greater than signs are the HTML formatting. In this instance, **<strong>** starts bold formatting, **<u>** starts underline formatting, **</strong>** ends bold formatting, and **</u>** ends underline formatting. Notations, such as **<strong>,** are called *HTML tags.* We'll talk more about HTML in Chapter 8 and in Appendix B.

HTML is actually quite simple to learn. However, there are about 1,000 different HTML tags. So, many people have opted to learn Web authoring software to create Web sites and pages. ***Web authoring software*** is application software that helps you design and develop Web sites and pages that you can publish on the Web.

When using Web authoring software, you create a document much like a word processing document. And instead of providing the necessary

FIGURE 3.3

Web authoring software helps you design and create Web sites and pages that you can publish on the Web.

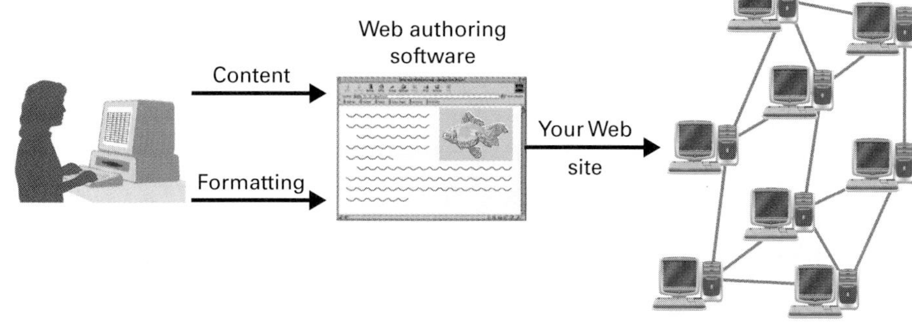

tags for formatting, you use GUI buttons and menu options just as you would with word processing software. When you've finished creating your Web site or page, your Web authoring software will automatically generate the HTML tags necessary to create the formatting you've specified (see Figure 3.3). You can then post your Web site or page to your Web space using FTP software. We discussed both Web space and FTP in Chapter 2.

Good developers of Web sites and Web pages are in high demand. We performed a simple search on Monster.com for Web developers and found over 1,000 job openings. In Appendix B of this text, we've provided a great introduction to creating a Web site or page with HTML. To learn more about Web authoring software and building a Web site, complete the "HTML—The Language of the Internet" and "HTML Editors" tutorials on your SimNet Concepts Support CD.

GRAPHICS SOFTWARE

What if I Need to Work with Photos and Images?

If you really want to work productively and effectively with photos and images, you need graphics software. ***Graphics software*** is application software that helps you create and edit photos and images. Using graphics software you can easily

- Crop (adjust) photos to an appropriate size.
- Add captions.
- Change and transpose colors.
- Combine photos to create a photo collage.
- Work freehand to create drawings.
- Create and manipulate 3-D images.
- Add animation features.

These are just a few of the many wonderful tasks you can perform with graphics software, and some graphics software is quite easy to learn. If your computer's operating system is Microsoft Windows, for example, you already own a couple of basic graphics software packages—Kodak Imaging for Windows (for photo editing) and Microsoft Paint (for art)—both easy to learn and use, although both somewhat limited. To learn more about graphics software, complete the "Graphics Software" tutorial on your SimNet Concepts Support CD.

If you want to really become proficient, then you'll want to learn a graphics package like PhotoShop, Illustrator, FireWorks, or FreeHand. We'll talk more about the issues involved in creating and editing photos and images (including video) in the next section of this chapter on digital media.

did you know?

In 1999, Fortune 1000 companies estimated over $45 billion in losses from theft of their proprietary information.[2]

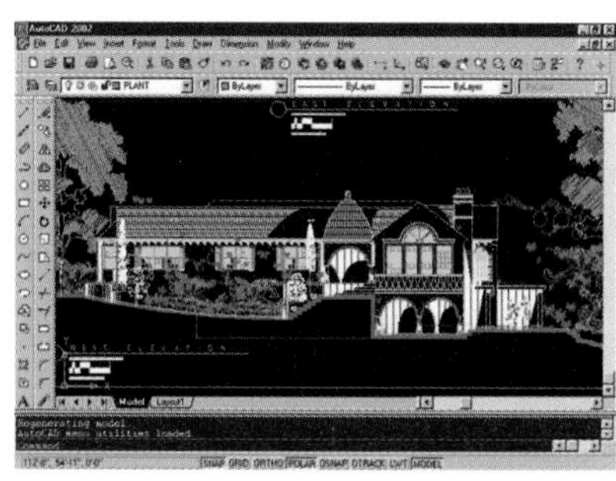

FIGURE 3.4

Graphics software helps you create and edit photos and art, including 3-D images.

SPREADSHEET SOFTWARE

What if I Need to Work with Numbers, Calculations, and Graphs?

Spreadsheet software is application software that helps you work with numbers, performing calculations and creating graphs. With spreadsheet software, you enter each piece of information in a *cell* (a cell is the intersection of a row and column), and then use the cells' identifiers or addresses in formulas and functions to create new information. If you change the information in a cell, your spreadsheet software will automatically recalculate all the formulas and functions.

In Figure 3.5, you can see a simple workbook in Excel for an income statement. In cell B3 we entered $100,000 for gross sales, and in cell B4 we

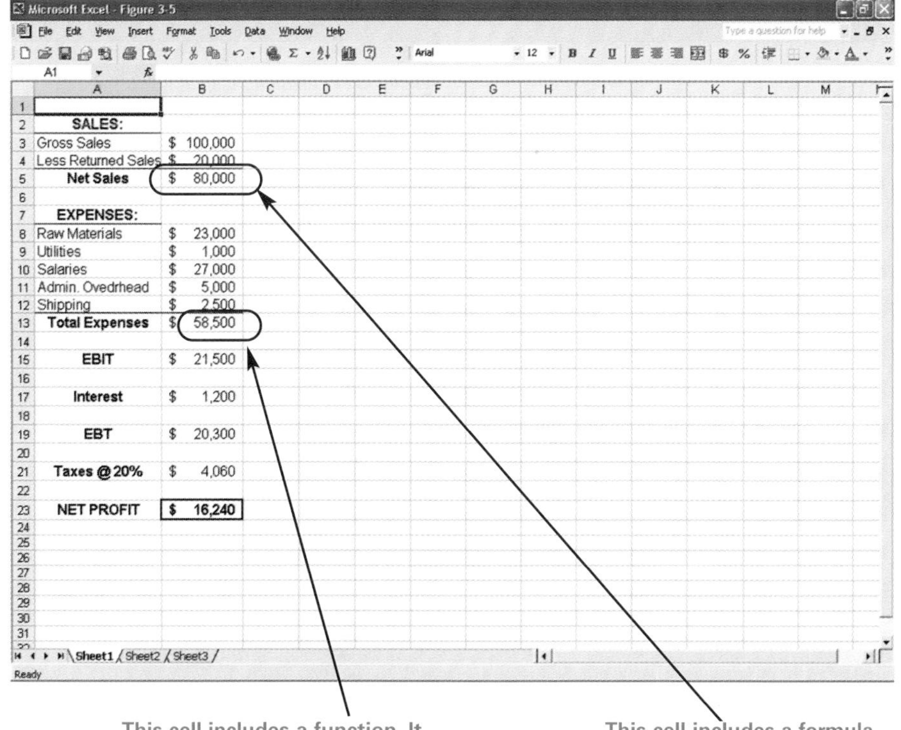

	A	B
1		
2	**SALES:**	
3	Gross Sales	$ 100,000
4	Less Returned Sales	$ 20,000
5	**Net Sales**	$ 80,000
6		
7	**EXPENSES:**	
8	Raw Materials	$ 23,000
9	Utilities	$ 1,000
10	Salaries	$ 27,000
11	Admin. Ovedrhead	$ 5,000
12	Shipping	$ 2,500
13	**Total Expenses**	$ 58,500
14		
15	**EBIT**	$ 21,500
16		
17	**Interest**	$ 1,200
18		
19	**EBT**	$ 20,300
20		
21	**Taxes @ 20%**	$ 4,060
22		
23	**NET PROFIT**	**$ 16,240**

Microsoft Excel - Figure 3-5
This cell includes a function. It is =SUM(B8:B12).
This cell includes a formula. It is =B3-B4.

FIGURE 3.5

With spreadsheet software, you enter information in cells (the intersections of a row and column), and then use the cells' identifiers in formulas and functions.

FIGURE 3.6

Spreadsheet software allows you to manipulate information with functions and create high-quality, revealing graphs.

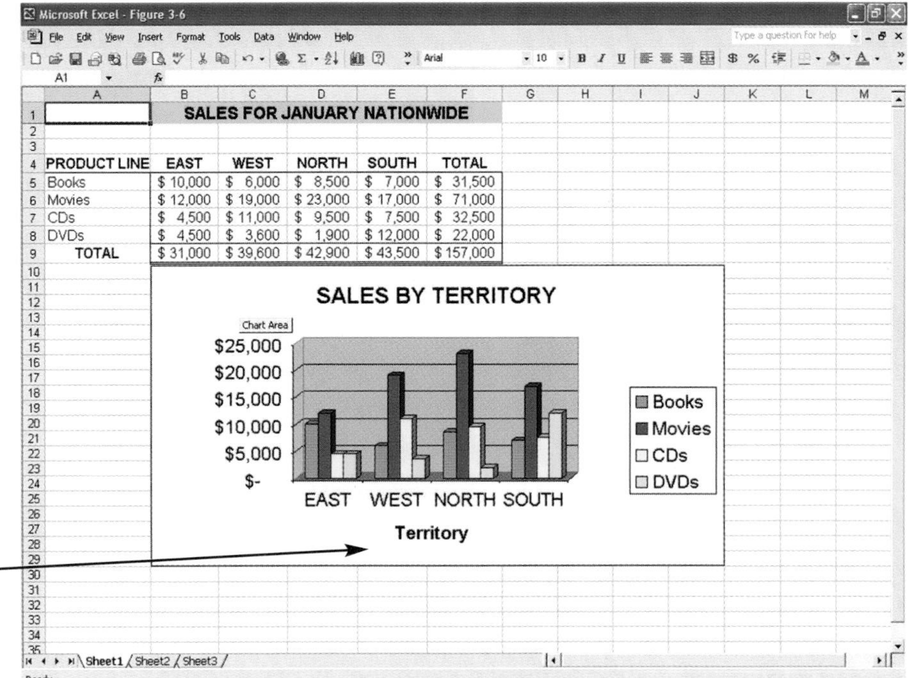

SALES FOR JANUARY NATIONWIDE

PRODUCT LINE	EAST	WEST	NORTH	SOUTH	TOTAL
Books	$ 10,000	$ 6,000	$ 8,500	$ 7,000	$ 31,500
Movies	$ 12,000	$ 19,000	$ 23,000	$ 17,000	$ 71,000
CDs	$ 4,500	$ 11,000	$ 9,500	$ 7,500	$ 32,500
DVDs	$ 4,500	$ 3,600	$ 1,900	$ 12,000	$ 22,000
TOTAL	$ 31,000	$ 39,600	$ 42,900	$ 43,500	$ 157,000

We easily created this graph using the table of numbers, column headings, and row labels (product lines).

entered $20,000 for returns. In cell B5, however, we did not enter $80,000 for net sales. Instead, we entered the formula **=B3–B4.** Excel used that formula to derive the actual value for net sales. Now, if we ever type in new information for gross sales (cell B3) or returns (cell B4), Excel will automatically recalculate the formula in cell B5 and derive a new net sales figure.

Spreadsheet software is a powerful tool (and an easy one to learn) for manipulating numerical information that is in some way related. Throughout the workbook in Figure 3.5 we used formulas and functions for such items as total expenses, EBIT (earnings before interest and taxes), EBT (earnings before taxes), and net profit. That way, for example, if we do change our gross sales figure in cell B3, Excel will automatically recalculate every formula and derive a new net profit figure (cell B23).

As you see, you can immediately be productive with spreadsheet software in a matter of minutes. You can easily create a budget, develop a payment table for buying a car, create an electronic checking account balance ledger, and perform many other tasks. But you don't have to stop there with spreadsheet software. You can also very quickly create high-quality and revealing graphs.

In Figure 3.6, we created another workbook, this one containing sales information for January, broken down by product line and territory. In creating this workbook, we took advantage of two spreadsheet software features—functions and graphing.

In cell F5, we wanted a total sales figure across all territories for our book product line. So, we could have entered the formula **=B5+C5+D5+E5.** However, that's rather long, and would become even longer if we had 20 territories. Instead, we entered the function **=SUM(B5:E5).** Excel used that function to sum the contents of cells B5 through E5. As with formulas, if we ever change any of the values in cells B5, C5, D5, and/or E5, Excel will automatically recalculate the function and derive a new total sales figure across all territories for our book product line.

i•can

Integrate the Capabilities of My Personal Productivity Software

If you thoroughly explore all the features of personal productivity software such as word processing and presentation software, you'll find that most of them give you the ability to create a graph from a table of numbers just as we did with spreadsheet software. Spreadsheet software, however, offers you the best capabilities in creating and manipulating a graph.

So, if you need to include a graph in a term paper you're writing using word processing software, we would recommend that you write your term paper using word processing software and use spreadsheet software to create the graph. You can then easily copy the graph from your spreadsheet software workbook and paste it into your word processing document.

What's even more important is that you can copy the graph in such a way that, if you ever make changes to the graph in your workbook, the graph will automatically change in your term paper that you created with word processing software.

The process is quite simple. First, create your term paper using word processing software. Second, create the graph using spreadsheet software. Third, while in your spreadsheet software, copy the graph. To do this, highlight the graph, hold down the **Ctrl** key, and press the **C** key (often shown as **Ctrl+C**). Or, from the menu bar, click on **Edit** and then **Copy.**

Now, go to your term paper in your word processing software and place the cursor where you want the graph to appear. Then, from the menu bar, click on **Edit** and **Paste Special.** Then, choose **Paste link** and click on **OK.** Your graph will appear in your word processing document and change if you ever change the original graph in your spreadsheet software.

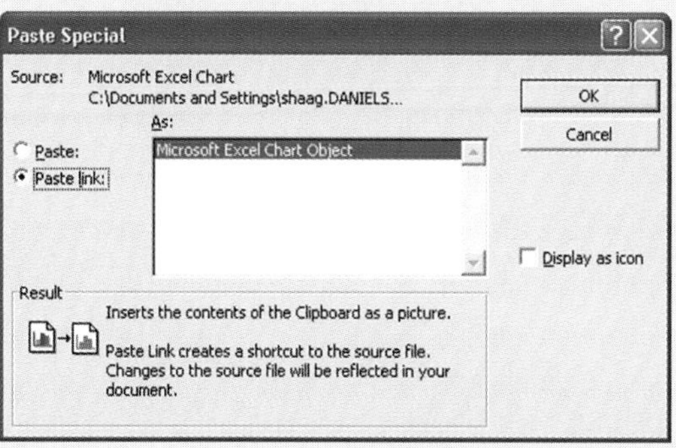

By choosing **Paste link,** you told your word processing software that it should always look in your spreadsheet workbook and present the most up-to-date copy of the graph. You can perform this special type of copying and pasting across all your personal productivity software tools. This enables you to take advantage of the best features of each.

Finally, we created the graph (Excel refers to graphs as charts) you see in Figure 3.6 with just seven clicks on the mouse. First we highlighted cells B4 through E8. We then clicked on the **Chart Wizard** button in the menu bar and provided a few simple instructions and pieces of information including the chart type (clustered column with a 3-D visual effect) and the chart title (SALES BY TERRITORY). That's all.

One of the productivity benefits of using spreadsheet software to create a graph is that Excel will automatically redraw the graph should we ever change any of the sales information. You cannot afford to ignore spreadsheet software as a valuable personal productivity software tool.

To learn more about the capabilities of your spreadsheet software, complete the "Spreadsheet Applications" tutorial on your SimNet Concepts Support CD.

PRESENTATION SOFTWARE

What if I Need to Create Slides for a Presentation?

In Chapter 1, we introduced you to the productivity of technology by showing you how to easily insert music into an electronic slide presentation. You are more productive through the use of technology to the extent that it helps you become a more effective and dramatic presenter in front of a group of people. Of course this means you must refine your judgment as to when and why to use such sound effects.

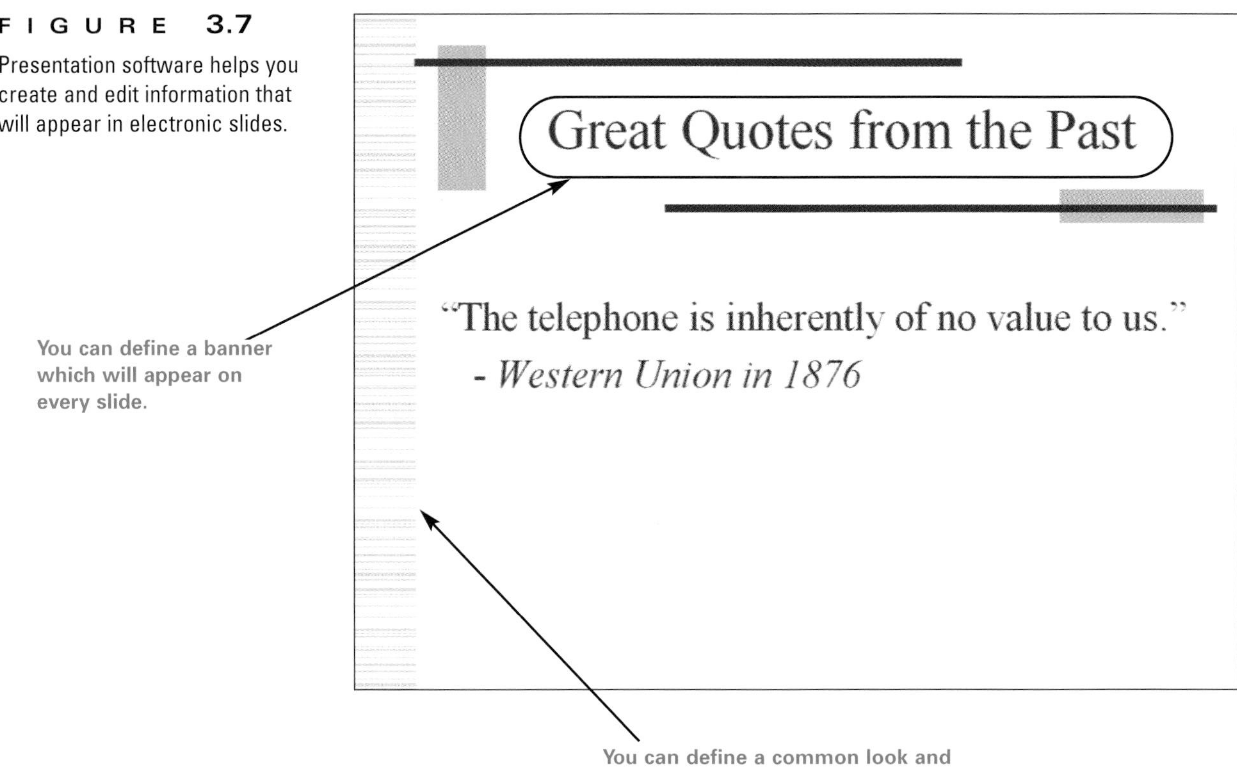
Great Quotes from the Past
"The telephone is inherently of no value to us."
- Western Union in 1876
You can define a banner which will appear on every slide.
You can define a common look and feel which appears on every slide.

FIGURE 3.7

Presentation software helps you create and edit information that will appear in electronic slides.

The software we used to create the slide presentation was Microsoft PowerPoint presentation software. ***Presentation software*** is application software that helps you create and edit information that will appear in electronic slides (see Figure 3.7). The information you include can be text, photos, art, tables, graphs, sound, animation, and even videos.

To be truly productive with presentation software, we recommend that you learn how to perform the following tasks:

- Add audio and video.
- Insert images, photos, and art.
- Incorporate links to Web sites.
- Use slide transitions to move from one slide to the next.
- Time the changing of the slides so you don't have to manually move from one slide to the next.
- Apply design templates to create a consistent look and feel for all your slides.
- Insert common header and footer information on all your slides.
- Print handout pages (with multiple slides per page) for your audience.

We certainly also recommend that you take a class on public speaking—technology can only help so much. By developing your public speaking skills, you will better understand when and how to put your knowledge of technology to its most productive use.

To learn more about presentation software, complete the "Presentation Applications" tutorial on your SimNet Concepts Support CD.

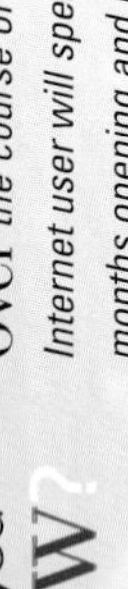

did you know?

Over *the course of a lifetime, the average Internet user will spend two years and four months opening and responding to e-mail.*[3]

PERSONAL INFORMATION MANAGEMENT AND PERSONAL FINANCE SOFTWARE

What if I Need to Manage My Personal Information and Finances?

Personal information management (PIM) software is application software that helps you create and maintain (1) to-do lists, (2) appointments and calendars, and (3) points of contact. PIM software is the primary software for personal digital assistants or PDAs, which we introduced you to in Chapter 1. If you don't have a PDA, you can still purchase PIM software for your notebook or desktop computer. If you use Microsoft Outlook as your e-mail software, then you already have PIM software. It's just a simple process of learning how to use it.

Using PIM software, you can easily track your appointments and scheduled activities by the day, week, or month. You can enter your class schedule, for example, and have your PIM software show those class times for the rest of the semester or quarter. You can ask your PIM software to remind you of important dates or events. So, your PIM software can remind you of an upcoming exam.

Also in the area of managing your personal information, ***personal finance software*** is application software that offers you capabilities for maintaining your checkbook, preparing a budget, tracking investments, monitoring your credit card balances, and even paying bills electronically (see Figure 3.8). If you can pay bills with your personal finance software, then it supports what we call online banking. ***Online banking*** is the use of your computer system to interact electronically with your bank, including writing checks, transferring funds, and obtaining a list of your account transactions.

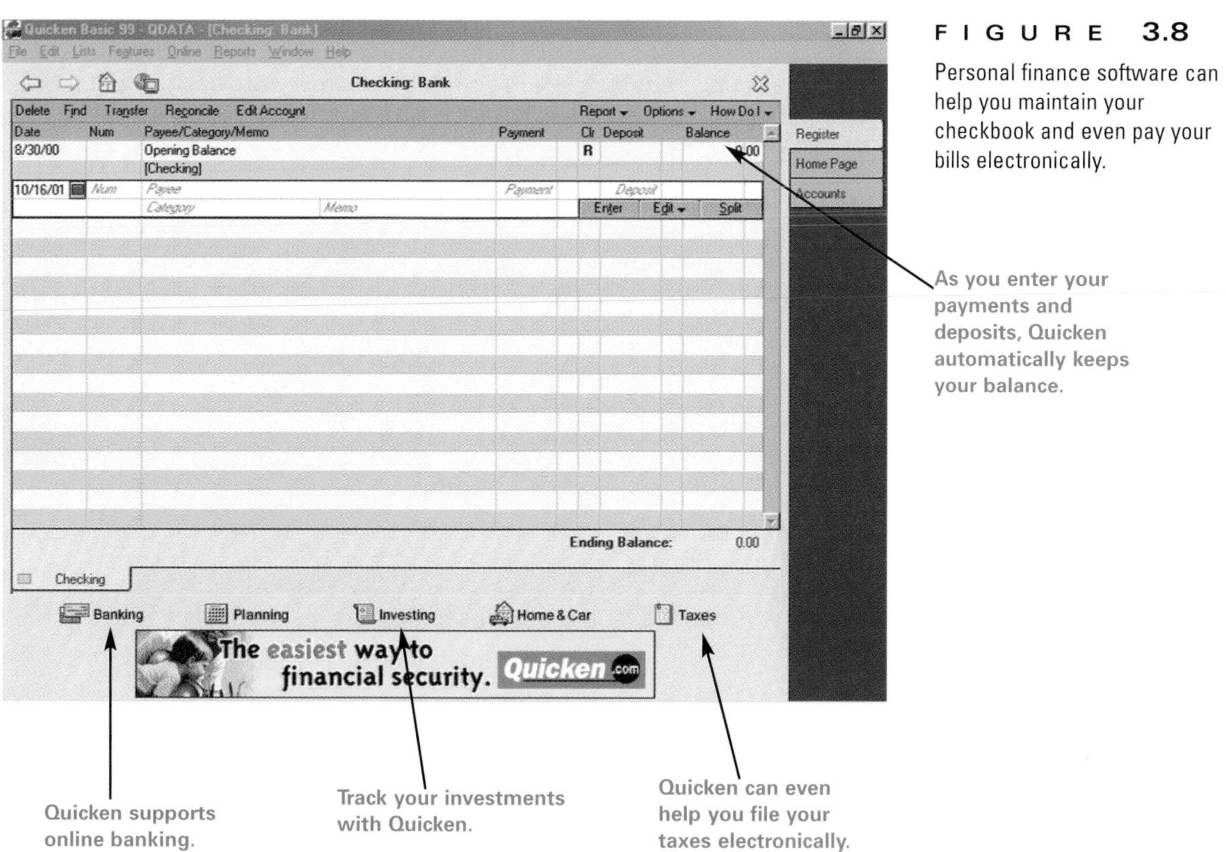

FIGURE 3.8

Personal finance software can help you maintain your checkbook and even pay your bills electronically.

DATABASE MANAGEMENT SYSTEM SOFTWARE

What if I Need to Logically Organize and Access Large Amounts of Information?

In today's information-based environment, it may be important for you to manage large amounts of information. For example, if you have a click-and-order business on the Web that sells rollerblades and related products, you'll need some way to logically organize and access information about your customers, suppliers, inventory, and sales. If so, you need to use database management system software.

Database management system (DBMS) software is application software that allows you to arrange, modify, and extract information from a database. We've devoted most of Chapter 10 to the topics of DBMS software and databases, so we won't go into great detail here. When creating a database, you create common groups of information, such as **Customer, Supplier, Inventory,** and **Sales,** and store them in different tables inside a database. In Figure 3.9 we've provided a glimpse of the database that would contain that information, showing only **Inventory** and **Supplier.** Tables in a database look similar to spreadsheets except that the rows are not numbered and the columns have field names for titles instead of characters.

Most important, there is a logical relationship between **Inventory** and **Supplier.** That is, each inventory item includes which supplier from which we order it. (Notice that **Supplier ID** exists in both tables.) By doing so, we can always determine from whom we purchased an inventory item. As well, our DBMS software will not allow us to enter a new item in inventory if we do not identify for it a supplier that exists in the **Supplier** table. This is called *referential integrity* and is a key feature of DBMS software.

Again, we'll talk more about DBMS software and databases in Chapter 10. To learn more about DBMS software, complete the "Database Applications" and "Database Management Systems" tutorials on your SimNet Concepts Support CD.

FIGURE 3.9

DBMS software features include referential integrity, which ensures that logical relationships are established among tables of information.

Inventory : Table

Product #	Product Name	Cost	Quantity on Hand	Supplier ID
1234	Plyers	$10.50	17	23
3456	Hammer	$4.85	37	11
4908	U.S. Socket Set	$22.75	14	17
5409	Metric Socket Set	$21.50	6	17
5983	Brake Fluid (12 oz.)	$2.95	26	23
		$0.00	0	0

Supplier : Table

Supplier ID	Supplier Name	Supplier Phone
11	ABC Wholesale	3035551111
17	Trutonics	6074341111
22	Fabrication Systems	2182223400
23	ValuTime	2083451234

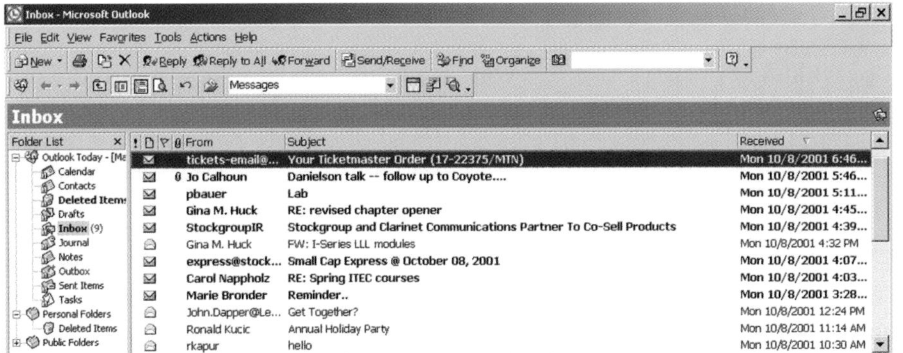

FIGURE 3.10

Microsoft Outlook provides folders, such as **Deleted Items, Inbox, Outbox, Sent Items,** and **Personal Folders,** to help you organize your e-mail.

E-MAIL AND WEB BROWSER SOFTWARE

What if Need to Electronically Communicate with Other People and Surf the Web?

In Chapters 1 and 2, we discussed the software you need to communicate with other people and to surf the Web. That software includes, at a minimum, e-mail software (for electronically communicating with other people) and Web browser software (for surfing the Web). If you want to communicate with people in a chat room or through instant messaging, you may have to download and install some other special software, including plug-ins, which we also discussed in Chapter 2.

Microsoft Outlook is the standard for e-mail software (see Figure 3.10). If you choose to use a free e-mail service (many people do) such as MSN's HotMail or Yahoo! Mail, you'll be using e-mail software specific to the service you choose. Regardless of the e-mail software you use, you can learn the basic functions on your own in about an hour or so. To learn about e-mail, complete the "Using E-mail" tutorial on your SimNet Concepts Support CD.

Internet Explorer and Netscape Communicator are the two most common Web browsers. With only what you've read about Web browsers in this text, you're probably well on your way to using Web browser software productively and efficiently. If you want to learn even more about the capabilities of your Web browser, complete the "Web Browsers" tutorial on your SimNet Concepts Support CD.

making the grade

SECTION 3.2

1. Desktop publishing software is an extension of __________ software.
2. __________ software is application software that helps you create and edit photos and images.
3. __________ software is application software that helps you create and edit information that will appear in electronic slides.
4. __________ is the use of your computer system to interact with your bank electronically.
5. __________ and __________ are the two most common Web browsers.

3.3 DIGITAL MEDIA

For whatever purpose you use your computer, you'll encounter and work with digital media. Broadly defined, ***digital media*** is any type of media or information that is represented and stored discretely as a series of 0s and 1s. Most people associate digital media with photos, images, art, animations, sounds, and video. If you scan in a photo for example, your scanner converts the photo into hundreds of thousands of individual 0s and 1s, each representing a specific color for a specific dot (or pixel) in the photo. If you want to view the photo on your screen, your computer sends all those 0s and 1s to your monitor, and then your monitor organizes all those (as dots) and presents the photo to you just as you scanned it.

Understanding the concepts behind digital media is important because they greatly affect your productivity and the productivity of others. For example, if you scan in a photo and include it on your Web site, the download time of your Web site is affected. Why? Because, depending on the image resolution (quality) at which you scanned your photo, the actual file size of the photo may be equivalent to anywhere from a couple of thousand characters to millions of characters. Obviously, if the file is small, it won't take long to download. If the file is large, the file may take a minute or more to download. You may have noticed that while trying to access a Web site with numerous images and photos.

So, while creating your Web site with media that is not text, for example, you need to walk a fine line between your desire for photos and images with a high quality of resolution and the issue of how long it will take somebody to download those photos and images. By the same token, if you create a word processing document with several photos and images, the document file will be much larger than a similar document with no photos and images.

In thinking of your career, you should be aware that people with technology skills in the area of creating and manipulating digital media are in high demand. People skilled in creating digital videos, building 3-D graphic images, and manipulating sounds are among the highest paid developers in the entire technology field.

FIGURE 3.11

Digital media includes photos, art, animations, sounds, and video.

TWO-DIMENSIONAL IMAGES AND PHOTOS

How Are Two-Dimensional Images and Photos Created and Edited?

Most two-dimensional images and photos are captured, created, and edited as either a bitmap graphic or a vector graphic. A ***bitmap graphic*** (also called a ***raster graphic*** or a ***bitmap***) is a grid of dots, with each dot representing a specific color, which makes up the entire image or photo. A ***vector graphic,*** on the other hand, creates and stores a set of instructions for re-creating the image or photo. The advantage of working with a vector graphic is that the image or photo does not become pixelated if you resize it. That is, if you create a bitmap graphic representation of a circle and then adjust its size, the circle may appear to have ragged edges. With a vector graphic–based circle, the circle will always appear smooth no matter what its size.

As you create or capture an image or a photo, you can adjust the quality of a bitmap graphic by adjusting its image resolution. ***Image resolution*** refers to the density of the grid used for the image. For example, the image resolution of a digital camera is expressed in ***megapixels***—the millions of pixels in a graphic (number of dots in a row times the number of columns). Monitor quality is also expressed in image resolution quality. This is called ***resolution of a screen***—the number of pixels that it has. Obviously, the greater the number of pixels, the higher the resolution will be.

You can also adjust the quality of a bitmap graphic by adjusting its color palette. A ***color palette*** is the selection of colors that will be used for each dot in the bitmap graphic grid. The smaller the selection of colors on the color palette the smaller the size of the bitmap graphic file. For example, some color palettes have only 256 possible colors—this is the case for ***grayscale palettes*** (a color palette which is used to produce images and photos in a black-and-white style using shades of gray). A ***true color***

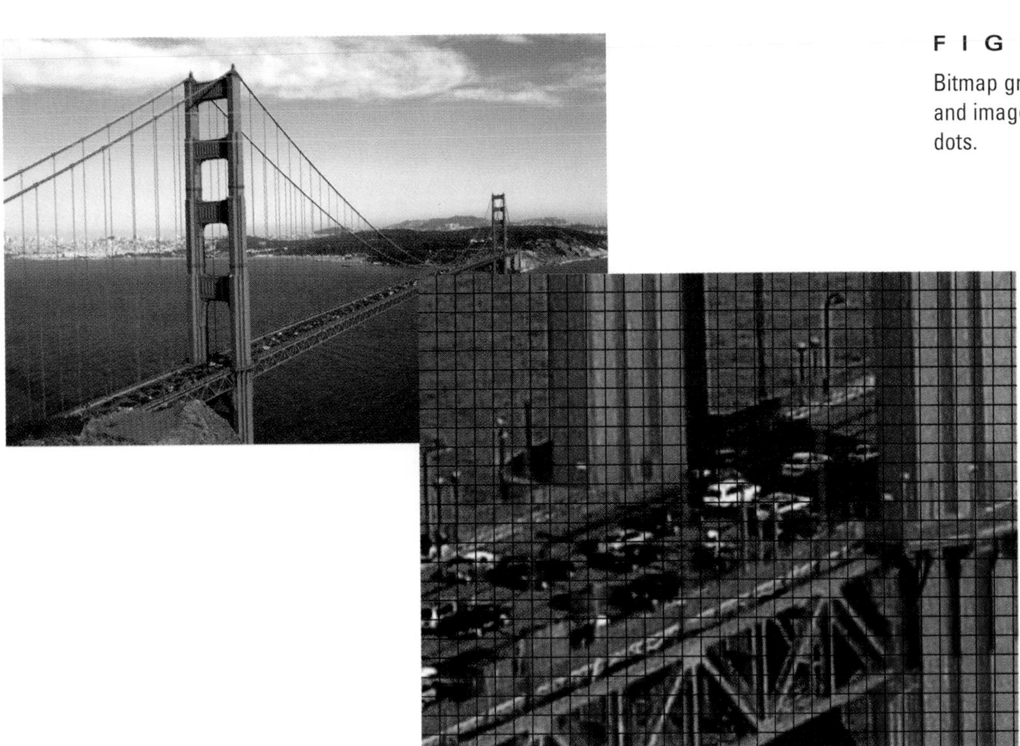

FIGURE 3.12

Bitmap graphics create photos and images by using a grid of dots.

FIGURE 3.13

A grayscale color palette produces images in a black-and-white style, while 24-bit and 32-bit color palettes produce images in color.

palette, or ***24-bit color palette,*** takes advantage of 16.7 million different colors. And a ***32-bit bitmap color palette*** takes advantage of 16.7 million colors as well as special effects such as transparency and dithering. ***Dithering*** is a process of composing two or more colors to produce the illusion of additional colors and shading.

As you save your images and photos, you can use a variety of graphics formats. We've listed just a few of the many.

- ***.bmp***—native bitmap graphic file format for Windows environments. Microsoft Paint creates .bmp file formats.
- ***.tiff,*** or ***.tif***—high-resolution bitmap graphics file format used in print publishing.
- ***.gif (Graphics Image Format)***—graphics file format used primarily for Web sites and pages and downloadable images on the Web.
- ***.jpeg,*** or ***.jpg***—graphics file format also used for Web sites, pages, and downloadable images on the Web as well as in digital photography. JPEG also supports good compression capabilities, making the overall size smaller.
- ***.png (Portable Network Graphic)***—public domain alternative to .gif that provides good compression capabilities.

Whatever the case, when you work with digital media—photos and images in this case—you need to consider overall size, image resolution, and color palette. If working with digital media is of particular interest to you, you'll have to learn how to use a digital camera, a digital video camera, and a scanner (all discussed in Chapter 5), as well as graphics software such as Illustrator, PhotoShop, FireWorks, or FreeHand. To learn more about graphics software, complete the "Graphics Software" tutorial on your SimNet Concepts Support CD.

3-D GRAPHICS

How Are 3-D Graphics Created and Edited?

3-D graphic images are similar to vector graphic images in that the actual image is stored as a set of instructions. For ***3-D graphics,*** however, the instructions include the length, width, locations, and drawing parameters

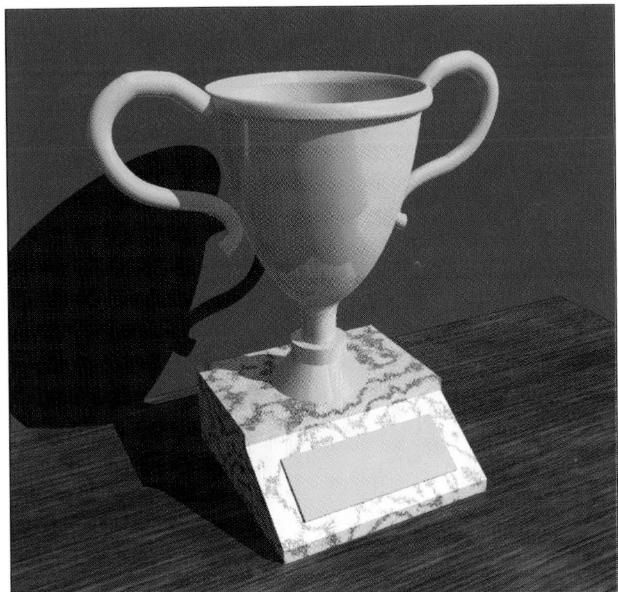

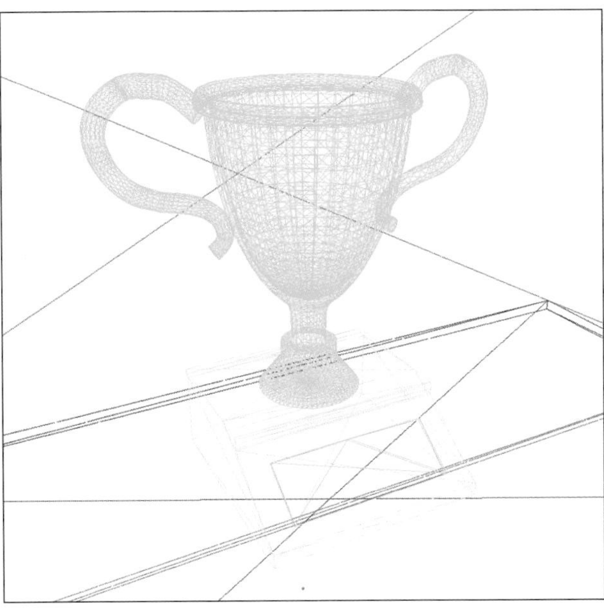

FIGURE 3.14

3-D graphic images are created by drawing a wireframe and then adding colors, textures, shades, and shadows through rendering and ray tracing.

for creating a wireframe of the image (see Figure 3.14). A ***wireframe*** is the complete skeletal structure of a 3-D graphic image, including its internal aspects that you cannot see once the surface colors, textures, and shades have been rendered. As you might well guess, ***rendering*** is the process of covering the wireframe with colors and textures.

Once you've completed the rendering of the 3-D graphic, you initiate the process of ray tracing. ***Ray tracing*** is a technique for adding shades and shadows to a 3-D graphic based on the location of a light source. Ray tracing is important because it makes 3-D graphics truly seem real because of the shadows cast and the shades illuminated on the image based on the location of a light source.

3-D graphic images, especially those that incorporate animation, movement, and sound, are most popular in gaming environments such as *The Age of Mythology, Quake, EverQuest*, and *The Sims*. If you want to create your own 3-D graphics you'll need 3-D graphics software, such as AutoCad or Caligari trueSpace. You'll also need an extremely powerful computer with a high-quality monitor and lots of CPU speed and RAM—and a lot of creativity and maybe some art training.

AUDIO

How Is Sound Recorded and Manipulated?

Although you may have been enjoying them for some time, audio and video are among the newest types of digital media appearing in technology. Here, we introduce you to the most important concepts for digital audio and video. To learn more about software for creating and editing audio and video, complete the "Sound and Video Software" tutorial on your SimNet Concepts Support CD.

Most sounds occur in waveform. To digitally record sound, you capture it in waveform audio. ***Waveform audio*** is a digital representation of sounds, in which samples of a sound are captured at periodic intervals

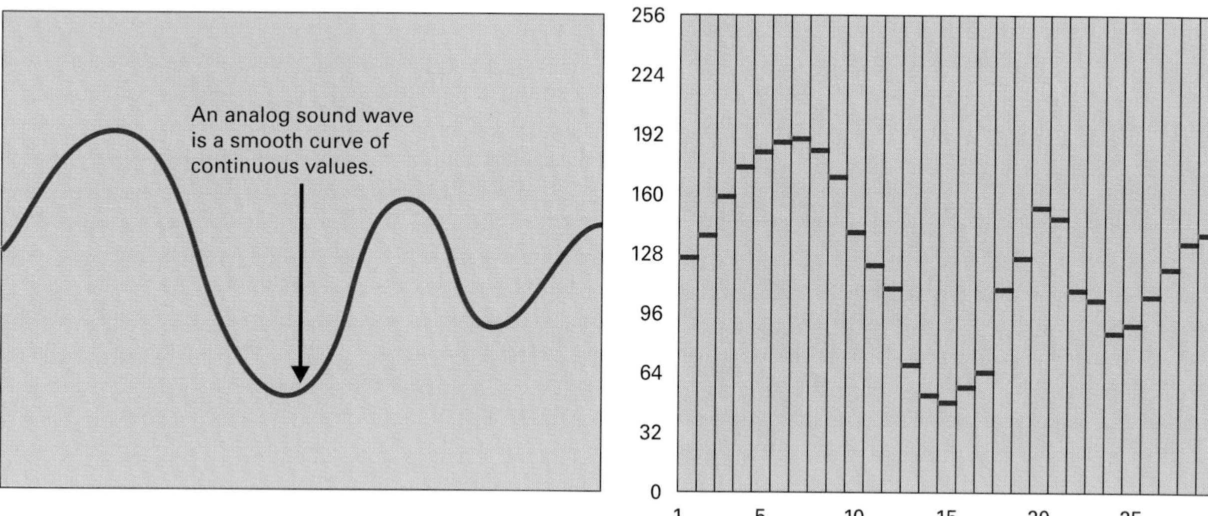

FIGURE 3.15

Waveform audio is captured by sampling sound at various intervals.

(called a sampling rate) and stored as unique sequences of 0s and 1s (see Figure 3.15). A ***sampling rate*** is the number of times per second that a sound is captured during the recording process. Sampling rates are most often expressed in hertz (hz). For example, 1,000 samples per second is 1,000 hz or 1KHz (kilohertz). Obviously, if you want high-quality sound, you'll want to capture it at a high sampling rate. As you do this though, the size of the file becomes increasingly larger.

Waveform audio is stored in a variety of file formats, including

- ***.wav (Wave)***—stores good quality sound that can be listened to within a browser without a plug-in but in a large, uncompressed format.
- ***.aif (Audio Interchange Format)***—stores good quality sound that can be listened to within a browser without a plug-in but in a large, uncompressed format.
- ***.mp3 (MP3)***—stores good quality sound in a compressed file format but requires the use of a player or a plug-in within a browser.
- ***.ra (RealAudio)***—stores good quality sound (although not as good as MP3) in a compressed file format but requires the use of a player or a plug-in within a browser.

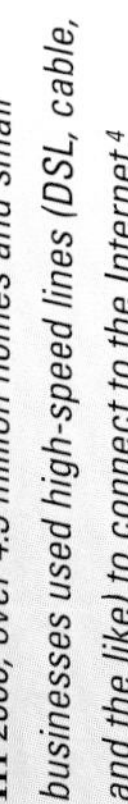

In 2000, over 4.3 million homes and small
businesses used high-speed lines (DSL, cable,
and the like) to connect to the Internet.4

An alternative to waveform audio is MIDI (its file extension is *mid*). ***MIDI (Musical Instrument Digital Interface)*** is a standard for storing audio information for computers, electronic MIDI instruments, and synthesizers. MIDI is simply a set of instructions for creating the volume, pitch, duration of notes, and other qualities of the sounds of various musical instruments. You might think of MIDI in this way: Waveform audio is to bitmap graphics just as MIDI is to vector graphics.

All Windows-based machines come with Microsoft's Sound Recorder that you can use to record audio. Microsoft's Media Player will play .wav, .aif, and .MP3 formats. Of course, many people buy MP3 players (similar to Walkmans) just so they can be portable with their music.

i•series insights — *Ethics, Security & Privacy*

Software That Kills

Software is available today that can actually help you make decisions, especially in the business world. For example, some software can help you determine how much inventory to carry, how to price rooms in a hotel based on seasonal travel, how your customer demographics seem to be changing, and which investment strategies will yield the highest returns. There's even software to help diagnose medical diseases and prescribe treatments.

Software, however, is only as good as the people who develop it. If software has a problem and doesn't produce the correct results, we say that it contains a "bug."

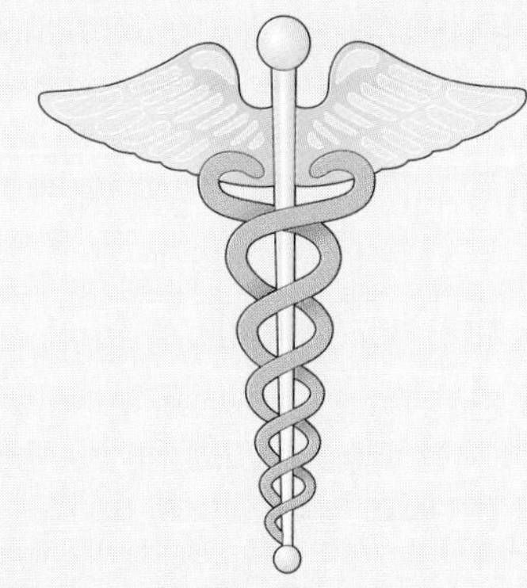

Some bugs may not be all that bad (calculating the wrong pay, for example), because their errors can be corrected. However, a bug in a medical program can do permanent damage.

Some years ago in the medical industry, software was developed to help determine how to treat cancer patients. It made a mistake and delivered 130 to 250 times the amount of radiation that patients needed. Four of those patients, unfortunately, died.

Software can help people automate tasks. But those tasks must be described in great detail by an expert. Then, the expert must validate that the software works perfectly. We may have some degree of tolerance for variation in personal productivity software but certainly not for software in the medical field that determines radiation levels.

VIDEO

What Are the Issues Concerning Video as Digital Media?

To capture and work with video, you need a digital video camera and video editing software. Once you've captured your video, your video editing software will allow you to manipulate it. You need to understand that video files are extremely large, mainly because of their video window size, frame rate, and the fact that they contain multiple tracks.

Video window size refers to how large the window is on your screen as it displays a video. If you make the window size smaller, the file also becomes smaller but it does reduce the quality of the video (probably making it seem blurry). ***Video frame rate*** is the number of frames per second (fps) used for a video. Most desktop video systems use 24 as the fps. However, this can still result in an extremely large file. So you can reduce the rate to 15 fps, making the file size smaller but also making the video seem a bit choppy.

Tracks in a video refer to the number of various forms of media in the video. If you have a video segment that includes voice and music, then you have three tracks—one for the voice, one for the music, and one for the video image itself. So, if you want to capture a video of a person speaking and then use your video editing software to add music in the background, your video file size will definitely increase.

To get around these sorts of issues, you can compress your video. A ***codec (compressor/decompressor)*** is software that enables you to compress a video file as you create and edit it and then decompresses the file when the video is displayed. On the Web, many video producers use streaming media (video in this case) as we discussed in Chapter 2. This allows viewers to start watching the video before the entire video has been downloaded.

To actually watch video on your computer, you'll most likely need a plug-in or player such as Windows Media Player, RealNetworks RealPlayer, or QuickTime Player.

SECTION 3.3

making the grade

1. A(n) __________ creates and stores a set of instructions for re-creating an image or photo.
2. A(n) __________ is the selection of colors that will be used for each dot in a bitmap graphic grid.
3. A(n) __________ is the complete skeletal structure of a 3-D graphic image, including its internal aspects that you cannot see once the surface colors, textures, and shades have been rendered.
4. __________ is a digital representation of sounds, in which samples of a sound are captured at periodic intervals.
5. __________ is the number of frames per second (fps) used for a video.

3.4 CONSUMER Q&A

1. When I Buy Software, Do I Really Own It?

When you buy software, you've only purchased the right to use that software. Software you purchase comes with a ***software license,*** which defines the way in which you can use the software. There are many types of software licenses. The most common for personal productivity software is a shrink-wrap license. A ***shrink-wrap license*** is a document that is shrink-wrapped to the outside of the software box.

2. Is There Software I Can Try Out before I Buy It?

Shareware is software that you can "test drive" or "try before you buy." With shareware, you usually receive a license that gives you the right to use the software for a trial period. The license will state that after the trial period is over you must pay a fee for continued use.

An alternative is ***freeware,*** which is public domain software—meaning that you can use it any way you wish free of charge. Be careful here: Some freeware is actually shareware in disguise. For a list of Web sites that offer shareware and freeware, visit the site for this text at www.mhhe.com/i-series.

3. Is Installing Software a Difficult Task?

No, installing most software is not difficult. Software usually comes with a short set of instructions that tells you how to perform the installation process. Most often, an ".exe" file accompanies the software, and all you have to do is execute that file and answer a few questions.

4. How Can I Add Video to My Web Site?

You can add video to your Web site in one of two ways. For either way, you must have your video stored in a file in your Web space. The first alternative is to create a link to a video file, using a statement such as **<a href="CarRace.avi">Car Race AVI Video</a>,** given that your video is stored in the file **CarRace.avi.** When someone clicks on the link (Car Race AVI Video), your video will be downloaded and a video player will be opened and will display the video in a window outside the browser. This is called an external video, because it plays outside a browser. This assumes, of course, that the person wishing to view your video has the right player installed.

The second alternative is to create an internal video using a different statement. That statement would be **<embed src="CarRace.avi">Car Race AVI Video</a>.** Instead of opening a separate window for the player, an internal video like this would play on your Web page when the link is clicked on by someone.

For either alternative, we suggest you include in the link the video type (for example, avi as we did above) and the size of the file. The latter will help people viewing your Web site determine whether or not the download process will take too much time.

3.5 SUMMARY AND KEY TERMS

There are two major categories of software:

- ***System software***—that determines how your computer carries out technology-specific and essential tasks such as writing to a disk, starting your Web browser, and sending a document to your printer.
- ***Application software***—that allows you to perform specific information-processing tasks such as managing inventory and writing a term paper.

A type of application software, ***personal productivity software*** helps you be more productive in performing personal tasks such as writing letters and managing your checkbook.

There are eight major categories of personal productivity software:

- ***Word processing*** and ***desktop publishing software***—both of which help you create text-based documents.
- ***Web authoring software***—helps you create Web sites and pages.
- ***Graphics software***—helps you work with photos and images.
- ***Spreadsheet software***—helps you work with numbers, calculations, and graphs.
- ***Presentation software***—helps you create electronic slide presentations.
- ***Personal information management*** and ***personal finance software***—both of which help you manage your personal information.
- ***Database management system (DBMS) software***—helps you organize and access large amounts of information.
- E-mail and Web browser software—both of which help you communicate with other people and surf the Web.

As you use your computer, you'll be working with digital media—any type of media or information that is represented and stored discretely as a series of 0s and 1s. Digital media includes:

- Two-dimensional images and photos—stored and manipulated as ***bitmap graphics*** or ***vector graphics;*** key considerations include ***image resolution, color palette,*** and image file format such as ***.bmp, .tiff, .gif, .jpeg,*** and ***.png.***
- ***3-D graphics***—stored as a set of drawing instructions for a ***wireframe;*** key considerations include ***rendering*** (covering the wireframe with colors and textures) and ***ray tracing*** (adding shades and shadows based on the location of a light source).
- Sound—stored and manipulated as ***waveform audio;*** key considerations include ***sampling rate*** (the number of times per second that a sound is captured during the recording process) and file format such as ***.wav, .aif, .ra,*** and ***.mp3.***
- Video—key consideration is ***video frame rate,*** the number of frames per second (fps) used.

To learn more about application software and digital media including popular shareware and freeware sites, visit the Web site for this text at www.mhhe.com/i-series.

KEY TERMS

.aif (Audio Interchange Format) (p. 84)
.bmp (p. 82)
.gif (Graphics Image Format) (p. 82)
.jpeg (.jpg) (p. 82)
.mp3 (MP3) (p. 84)
.png (Portable Network Graphic) (p. 82)
.ra (RealAudio) (p. 84)
.tiff (.tif) (p. 82)
.wav (Wave) (p. 84)
3-D graphics (p. 82)
32-bit bitmap color palette (p. 82)
application software (p. 68)
bitmap graphic (raster graphic, bitmap) (p. 81)
codec (compressor/decompressor) (p. 85)
color palette (p. 81)
database management system (DBMS) software (p. 78)
desktop publishing software (p. 71)
digital media (p. 80)
dithering (p. 82)
freeware (p. 86)
graphics software (p. 72)
grayscale palette (p. 81)
image resolution (p. 81)
megapixel (p. 81)
MIDI (Musical Instrument Digital Interface) (p. 84)
online banking (p. 77)
personal finance software (p. 77)
personal information management (PIM) software (p. 77)
personal productivity software (p. 68)
presentation software (p. 76)
ray tracing (p. 83)
rendering (p. 83)
resolution of a screen (p. 81)
sampling rate (p. 84)
shareware (p. 86)
shrink-wrap license (p. 86)
software license (p. 86)
software suite (p. 70)
software version (version) (p. 69)
spreadsheet software (p. 73)
system software (p. 68)
true color palette (24-bit color palette) (p. 81)
vector graphic (p. 81)
video frame rate (p. 85)
waveform audio (p. 83)
web authoring software (p. 71)
wireframe (p. 83)
word processing software (p. 71)

review of terminology

Multiple Choice

1. Digital media can include
   a. audio.
   b. video.
   c. two-dimensional images.
   d. 3-D graphics.
   e. all of the above.
2. The type of software that helps you create Web sites and Web pages is
   a. Web authoring software.
   b. personal information management software.
   c. personal finance software.
   d. spreadsheet software.
   e. DBMS software.
3. The software that helps you organize and access large amounts of information is
   a. Web authoring software.
   b. personal information management software.
   c. personal finance software.
   d. spreadsheet software.
   e. DBMS software.
4. The type of software that helps you manage information such as to-do lists and a calendar is
   a. Web authoring software.
   b. personal information management software.
   c. personal finance software.
   d. spreadsheet software.
   e. DBMS software.
5. The type of software that supports online banking is
   a. Web authoring software.
   b. personal information management software.
   c. personal finance software.
   d. spreadsheet software.
   e. DBMS software.
6. The palette used to produce images and photos in a black-and-white style is
   a. 32-bit bitmap color palette.
   b. true color palette.
   c. grayscale color palette.
   d. black-and-white color palette.
   e. none of the above.
7. The palette that enables you to take advantage of special effects such as transparency and dithering is
   a. 32-bit bitmap color palette.
   b. true color palette.
   c. grayscale color palette.
   d. black-and-white color palette.
   e. none of the above.
8. All of the following are file formats for graphics and images except
   a. .bmp.
   b. .jpeg.
   c. .png.
   d. .ra.
   e. .gif.
9. The process of composing two or more colors to produce the illusion of additional colors and shading is
   a. dithering.
   b. rendering.
   c. ray tracing.
   d. composition coloring.
   e. master coloring.
10. The process of covering the wireframe of a 3-D graphic with colors and textures is
    a. dithering.
    b. rendering.
    c. ray tracing.
    d. composition coloring.
    e. master coloring.

True/False

11. ____ Rendering is the process of adding shades and shadows to a 3-D graphic based on the location of a light source.
12. ____ Shareware is public domain software that you can use in any way you wish including "sharing" it with other people.
13. ____ The number of times per second that a sound is captured during the recording process is called a sampling rate.
14. ____ Spreadsheet software helps you work with numbers, performing calculations and creating graphs.
15. ____ .mp3 is a file format for storing audio.

Take this quiz online at www.mhhe.com/i-series and get instant feedback.

QUESTIONS AND EXERCISES

1. Identifying Personal Productivity Software Tools

Below, we've provided a list of personal productivity software tools in the left column. However, from their names you may not be able to immediately determine their software types (e.g., presentation, Web authoring, and so on). Your task is to determine in which category each tool belongs. You may have to do some research on the Web or at a local computer store. Be careful—some personal productivity software tools in the left column may belong in more than one category.

PERSONAL PRODUCTIVITY SOFTWARE TOOL	CATEGORY
A. Cool 3-D	
B. Publisher	
C. StoreFront	
D. PageMaker	
E. QuickBooks	
F. FileMaker	
G. Canvas	
H. Commotion Pro	
I. FrameMaker	

2. Matching Careers to Personal Productivity Software Tools

In the business world, depending on their careers, people focus more on the use of some personal productivity tools than others. In the table below, we've listed in the left column various functional areas within business. To the right are a series of columns for some of the personal productivity tools we introduced in this chapter. Your task is to determine which functional area would use a given personal productivity tool the most. For example, which functional area would use spreadsheet software more than any other functional area? Place an X in the appropriate box. You can pick only one functional area for each personal productivity tool. After you complete your analysis, be prepared to justify your answers.

	Desktop Publishing	Graphics	Spreadsheet	Presentation	DBMS
Accounting					
Finance					
Marketing					
Real Estate					
Construction Management					
Management					
Operations Management					

3. Understanding Formulas and Functions

Perhaps the most productive personal productivity tool you will ever use is spreadsheet software. (Some people would argue that the most productive is word processing software, but we won't debate that here.) Spreadsheet software is simple to use and easy to learn. Concepts such as functions and formulas are very familiar. It's usually just a matter of learning syntax. For example, the function to average a list of numbers is **=AVERAGE(first cell:second cell).**

Below, we've provided a screen capture of a workbook in Excel. Many of the cells make use of formulas and functions. Your task is to provide the formula or function used for the list of cells provided below the screen capture. Don't worry about exact syntax—simply determine which cells would use formulas or functions and what those formulas and functions would entail.

Microsoft Excel - Home Investment

File Edit View Insert Format Tools Data Window Help — Type a question for help

Arial 12

A2 THE ASSUMPTIONS

	A	B	C	D	E	F
2	**THE ASSUMPTIONS**			**CASH FLOW BEFORE TAXES**		
3	Home Price	$ 250,000.00		Gross Scheduled Income	$ 18,000.00	
4	Down Payment (20%)	$ 50,000.00		LESS: Vacancy Allowance	$ 1,500.00	
5	Loan Value	$ 200,000.00		GROSS OPERATING PROFIT	$ 16,500.00	
6	Loan Rate (30 YR Lock)	6.125%		LESS: Annual Operating Expense	$ 6,600.00	
7	Monthly PI Payment	($1,215.22)		NET OPERATING INCOME	$ 9,900.00	
8	Total Annual PI Payment	$14,582.65		LESS: Annual PI Payment	$14,582.65	
9				CASH FLOW BEFORE TAXES	$ (4,682.65)	
10	Down Payment	$ 50,000.00		Monthly Cash Flow	$ (390.22)	
11	Closing Costs	$ 3,500.00				
12	Initial Investment	$ 53,500.00		**CASH FLOW AFTER TAXES**		
13				NET OPERATING INCOME	$ 9,900.00	
14	Gross Monthly Income	$ 1,500.00		LESS: Annual PI Payment	$14,582.65	
15	Gross Annual Income	$ 18,000.00		**LESS: Cost Recovery (Depreciation)**		
16	Annual Vacancy Rate (1 month annualy)	8.33%		Improvement Value	$ 200,000.00	
17				Cost Recovery Period (in YRS)	27.5	
18	**Annual Operating Expenses**			Annual Cost Recovery	$ 7,272.73	
19	Property Taxes	$ 2,000.00		TAXABLE INCOME (LOSS)	$ (11,955.38)	
20	Insurance	$ 600.00		Investor Tax Bracket	35%	
21	Maintenance (10% of Rent - very high)	$ 1,800.00		TAX IMPACT (Savings)	$ (4,184.38)	
22	Management Fee (10%)	$ 1,800.00		CASH FLOW BEFORE TAXES	$ (4,682.65)	
23	Utilities	$ -		TAX IMPACT (Sign Inverted)	$ 4,184.38	
24	Home Owners Dues (HR)	$ 400.00		CASH FLOW AFTER TAXES	$ (498.27)	
25	**Total:**	$ 6,600.00		CASH FLOW MONTHLY	$ (41.52)	
26						
27						
28						
29						
30						
31						
32						
33						

Rent / Sale / Sheet3

Ready

B4: ____________________

B12: ____________________

B15: ____________________

B25: ____________________

E5: ____________________

E7: ____________________

E9: ____________________

E10: ____________________

E19: ____________________

e-commerce

1. Downloading Players and Plug-Ins

In Chapter 2 we introduced you to the necessity of plug-ins and players for viewing and listening to various types of digital media (which we discussed in this chapter). There are untold numbers of sites that provide you with downloadable players and plug-ins.

Connect to a couple of the following sites and do some research regarding players and plug-ins.

- www.plugins.com
- www.macromedia.com/software/shockwaveplayer/
- http://graphicssoft.about.com/cs/pluginsfilters/
- http://downloads-zdnet.com.com/

As you visit these sites, download a plug-in or player that interests you, and answer the following questions.

a. Which did you find—plug-ins, players, or both?
b. Is the site devoted to just a certain publisher of plug-ins and/or players? If so, which one?
c. What is the process for downloading a plug-in or player?
d. What is the installation process for a plug-in or player after downloading it?

2. Finding Freeware and Shareware

The computer field today is full of software, with literally thousands of packages for you to choose from. Some you have to pay for, but there are many more for free (or almost free). It's what we call freeware and shareware.

Connect to a couple of the following sites and do a little fact-finding concerning freeware and shareware.

- www.freeware-downloads.com
- www.freewareworld.com
- http://shareware.cnet.com
- www.jumbo.com

As you visit these sites, look around for some software that might interest you. As you visit each site, answer the following questions.

a. Who owns and maintains the site?
b. How does the site owner make money "giving away" software?
c. Can you search by category such as games or entertainment?
d. Is there any "free" software for which you must actually pay a fee?

3. Buying Software

There are two methods of buying software packages on the Web. The first is a conventional e-commerce transaction. You pay for it on the Web; then the company ships it to you.

The other method of purchase involves an electronic download. After you buy the software, you get an access code or small program that allows you to download the software package. Sometimes this download is available only for a limited time after the purchase date or for a limited number of downloads.

Check out these sites and search for a specific software package. Find at least one electronic download.

- Buy.com—www.buy.com
- Amazon.com—www.amazon.com
- Warehouse—www.warehouse.com

Answer the following questions:

a. Were you able to find your software package at all the sites?
b. Did you find an electronic download version? Was there a substantial price difference between it and the physical software package? (Remember, you don't have to pay shipping on an electronic download.)
c. Armed with a few price quotes on software packages (electronic download and physical delivery), go to a store that sells the software package. Which option saves you more money?

ethics, security & privacy

1. Software Piracy

The problem of software piracy grows larger every day. Software piracy is someone's illegally obtaining and using software. For example, you could make a copy of a game CD-ROM and give it to a friend. That's software piracy. Likewise, someone could post a copy of software on the Web for everyone to copy and use. If that software isn't public domain software, then it's software piracy.

Software piracy is a particular problem on a global scale. In some parts of the world, you can buy a copy of Microsoft Windows operating system software for just a few dollars. Two of the countries in which the practice of software piracy is the most rampant are Russia and China. The Software Publishers Association estimates that in those countries more software is pirated than obtained legally.

You should understand that the per capita gross domestic product of the people in Russia is about $5,000 per year; in China it's even less, about $2,500. In the United States on the other hand, the per capita gross domestic product is $27,000.

Consider the following questions in relation to software piracy.

a. Given that the path to economic prosperity in today's world involves having and knowing how to use information technology, what will happen to the relative economic position of poor countries if they can't get modern software?

b. Will increased poverty in a large part of the world adversely affect U.S. trade, and in turn the U.S. economy?

c. Is it okay for poor countries to acquire software illegally if they can't afford it, since without it they're heading for economic suicide?

d. If you answered no to the previous question, suggest what the United States should do about the problem. Should the government:
   - Clamp down very hard on the nations that pirate software?
   - Offer aid in the form of money or software to countries too poor to buy it legally?
   - Ignore the problem and take the heat from software publishers?

e. If you think it's okay for poorer countries to pirate software (you answered yes), answer the following questions:
   - Do the people who create software or music or who write books have a right to profit from their intellectual property?
   - Is there an upper dollar limit to that right?
   - If it's okay to pirate software, is it okay to steal other things, like computers or cars?
   - How poor do you have to be to have a right to steal?

All these issues and questions relate to what we call "the great digital divide"—the division between the "haves" and "have nots" of the world is now largely defined by technology, not money or even education. If you're interested, there's a lot of great reading in books and on the Web concerning the "digital divide." An excellent place to start is the Digital Divide Network at www.digitaldividenetwork.org/.

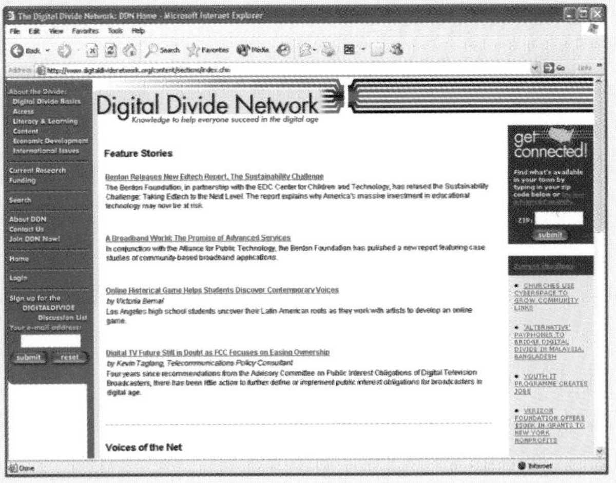

on the web

1. Storing Your Personal Files on the Web

As the use of personal technology alternatives with little storage capacity has increased, there are now an abundance of Web sites that allow you to store your personal files, many of which are free. For example, XDrive at www.xdrive.com offers in excess of 25 Mb (megabytes or characters) of free storage on the Internet. You can use one of these storage areas to back up your files. Connect to the Web and use your preferred search engine to find several sites that offer free storage. Peruse those sites and answer the following questions for each.

a. What sites did you find?
b. How much space are you allocated at each site?
c. Can you buy additional space?
d. Can you access the site and retrieve your files with a PDA or cell phone?

2. Learning More about Digital Media

In this chapter, we really just touched the "tip of the iceberg" in our presentation of digital media, including two-dimensional images, 3-D graphics, audio, and video. Indeed, you could spend a lifetime reading everything written about digital media. Below is a list of terms related to digital media that we did not discuss in this chapter. Your task is to do some research on the Web and define these terms.

a. Aliasing __________
b. Autotracing __________
c. Bitblt __________
d. Blue screen __________
e. CMYK __________
f. Favicon __________
g. Feathering __________
h. GPU __________
i. Jaggies __________
j. Morphing __________
k. PPI __________
l. Ripper __________
m. Sprite __________
n. Texel __________
o. Tweening __________
p. WBMP __________

3. Downloading Free Images, Photos, and Art

In the previous section of e-commerce projects, you visited some Web sites that offer freeware and shareware. And there's a lot more free stuff on the Web. For example, there are thousands of sites that provide free images, photos, and art. All you do is download them and use them as you wish. You can even change the way they look if you want. Start your favorite search engine and find sites that offer free images, photos, and art. Peruse those sites and answer the following questions for each.

a. What sites did you find?
b. Who owns and maintains the site?
c. How are the images, photos, and art categorized?
d. How do you download an image, photo, or art?
e. Does the site request that you give proper credit when using any of the free images, photos, or art?
f. In what way is the site making money by providing free images, photos, and art?

4. Finding Free Screen Savers

Another category of free stuff on the Web is screen savers. Perform another search on the Web and this time find free screen savers you can download. Download one of the screen savers and determine how to make it your screen saver of choice. Report back to your class the exact set of steps it takes to change a screen saver on your computer.

group activities

1. Building a Web Page with Microsoft Word

As we explained in this chapter, many of the personal productivity tools available to you can help you perform tasks at least in a basic way that really belong in a different category. For example, most word processing packages can help you build a graph, a typical function in spreadsheet software. Most word processing software allows you to build a Web page. All you have to do is create a document just the way you would want your Web page to appear and then save that document as a Web page. Start Word, create a simple document, and then save it as a Web page. As you do, answer the following questions.

a. How do you save a Word document as a Web page?
b. When your Web page is saved, what is the extension of the file name?
c. How do you view the actual HTML code that Word generated?
d. How do you change your Web page—can you change the Word document, can you change the HTML code, or can you do both?

2. Capturing Audio on Your Computer

All Windows-based machines come with Sound Recorder, software that allows you to capture and record sounds, such as your voice. To use Sound Recorder, click on **Start,** highlight **All Programs,** highlight **Accessories,** highlight **Entertainment,** and then click on **Sound Recorder.** What you'll then see is a small window with buttons (record is the button with the red dot) usually found on a CD or DVD player. Start recording and say a few words for about 10 seconds or so. Afterward, answer the following questions.

a. How do you stop recording?
b. How do you play back what you recorded?
c. What file format does Sound Recorder use when saving your recording?
d. How do you add an echo?
e. How do you "mix" your recording with another recording?

3. Games and Entertainment Software

Many people would also include "games and entertainment" as a category in personal productivity software. This particular set of software makes billions of dollars each year in revenue. You can probably find more public domain, shareware, and freeware games and entertainment software on the Web than you can for any other category of personal productivity software. Should "games and entertainment" be a category within personal productivity software? Suppose we asked you to join our author team on the next edition of this text and asked you to write a section on games and entertainment software. What would it look like? What specific software packages would you mention?

4. Using Microsoft Paint

Microsoft Paint is graphics software that comes with the Microsoft Windows operating system. To find it, click on the **Start** button, highlight **All Programs,** then **Accessories,** and click on **Paint.** Paint is quite easy to use—on the left you'll find your drawing tools (pencil, spray can, brush, and so on), and at the bottom you'll find your color palette. Choose a few drawing tools as well as some colors and create a free-hand drawing. What did you draw? How easy was it to learn the basic functions of Paint? Did you use the shapes such as rectangle and oval?

crossword puzzle

Across

3. Stores the physical location of files
9. Open source operating system
10. Upgrade to Windows 2000 ME
11. The ability to add devices without going through a manual installation of the device drivers
12. Unique identifier for each of your storage devices
14. Upgrade to Windows 2000 Pro
16. _______ file—smaller file in physical size
17. Software that can cause annoyance or damage
18. Operating system for a personal technology
19. The ability to work with more than one piece of software at a time
22. Software that controls your application software
26. Small text file that a Web site stores about you
27. Collection of information
28. Software and information for establishing communication to a new device
29. Opposite of application software
30. Named portion of a directory

Down

1. Device letter + folder + subfolder + filename + extension
2. Unplugging and plugging in different devices while your computer is running
4. Protects your computer or network from intruders
5. Unique name for a file
6. OS for today's Apple computers
7. Software that adds functionality to your operating system
8. Amount by which a file is made smaller
13. List of files on a storage device
15. Predecessor to Windows XP Home
20. Process of uncompressing a file
21. Software for protecting against viruses
23. File type
24. Operating system for networks
25. Single area on a storage device that holds a specific number of bytes
26. Collection of #25 down

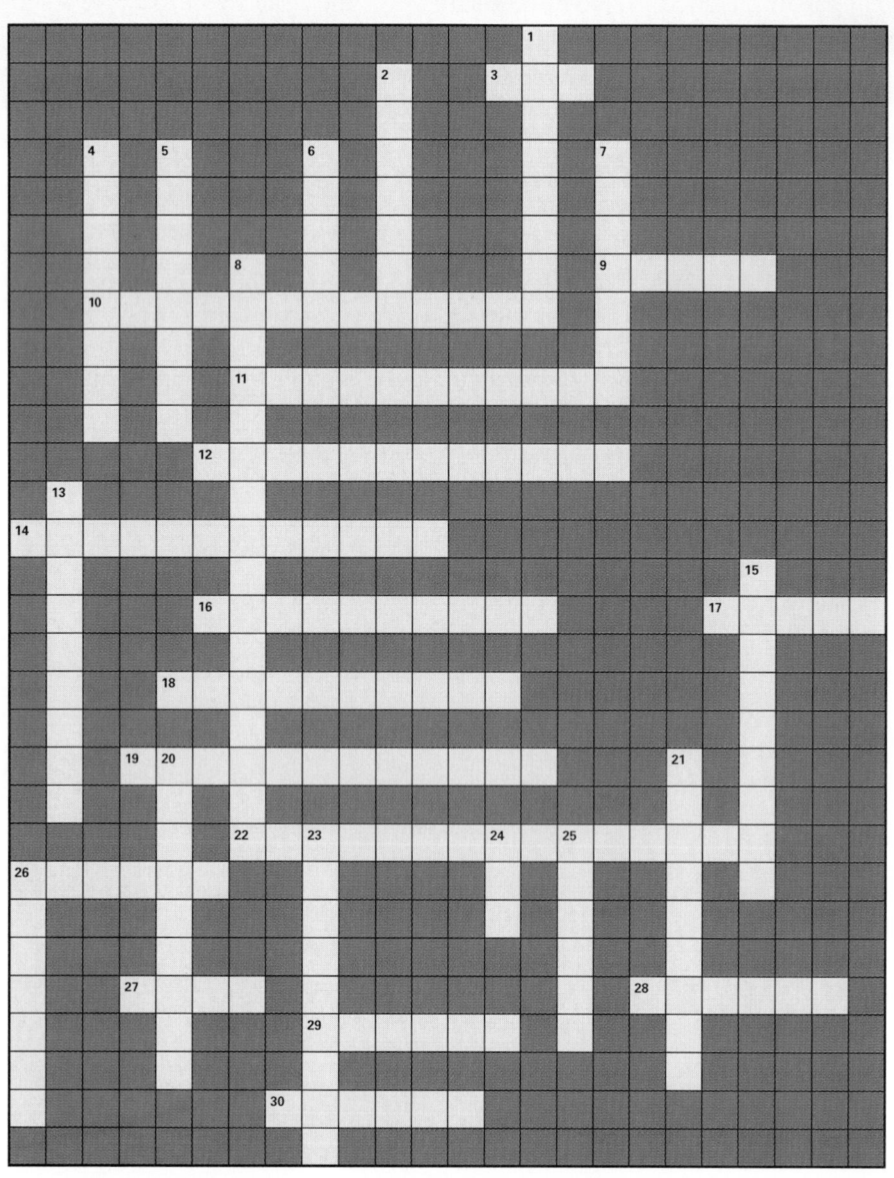

CHAPTER four

4

System Software, Virus Protection, and File Management

What Software Runs Your Hardware?

SIMNET CONCEPTS SUPPORT

did you know?

System software is vitally important to you as you use your computer and application software. Utility software (a subset of system software), such as anti-virus software, can protect your computer from deadly computer viruses. Other types of system software allow businesses to monitor the activity of their employees' Web surfing activities.

more *than 30,000 Web sites offer "hacking" tools that enable people to break into your computer. Many of these tools can be learned in less than an hour.*[1]

today, *33 percent of all businesses closely scrutinize their employees electronically, including their Web activities.*[2]

within *six hours of its being released, the notorious Love Letter virus infected __??__ personal computers.*[3]

To find out how many personal computers were infected by the Love Letter virus within six hours of its being released, visit www.mhhe.com/i-series.

Student Learning Outcomes

After reading this chapter, you should be able to:

1. Define the role of system software and the three main types of system software.
2. Describe the role of your operating system software as it manages peripheral devices and memory.
3. List and describe the different personal operating systems for notebook and desktop computers, PDAs, and tablet PCs.
4. Define the role of utility software as it relates to your operating system software.
5. Discuss why anti-virus software is so important.
6. Define the relationships among device letters, filenames, extensions, and folders in managing your information.
7. Describe the types of utilities you can use to compress and decompress files.

In the previous chapter, we covered application software, specifically focusing on personal productivity software. Application software helps you perform information-processing tasks such as inventory management and creating slides for a presentation. In this chapter, we cover the other major type of software—*system software.*

System software is software that determines how your computer carries out technology-specific and essential tasks such as writing to a disk, starting your Web browser software so you can surf the Web, and sending a document to your printer. System software is simply all the instructions that your computer processes regardless of what application software you're using. For example, when you start your computer, it will most probably ask you for a password. Verifying the password you enter is a responsibility of your system software. It doesn't matter what application software you choose to use after that—your system software must first verify that your password is correct. Other system software tasks include

- Removing software you no longer want from your hard disk.
- Allowing you to work with and across multiple pieces of application software at the same time.
- Compressing files to shrink their sizes and decompressing those same files.
- Configuring your modem to dial up and connect to your ISP.
- Setting the date and time when you change time zones (see Figure 4.1).
- Allowing you to change your screen saver and the default home page when you start your browser software.

As with all software, you need system software to run your computer efficiently and effectively. In fact, you can't even use your computer without system software.

There are three main types or categories of system software—operating system software, device drivers, and utility software.

FIGURE 4.1

Your system software allows you to change the date and time stored by your computer.

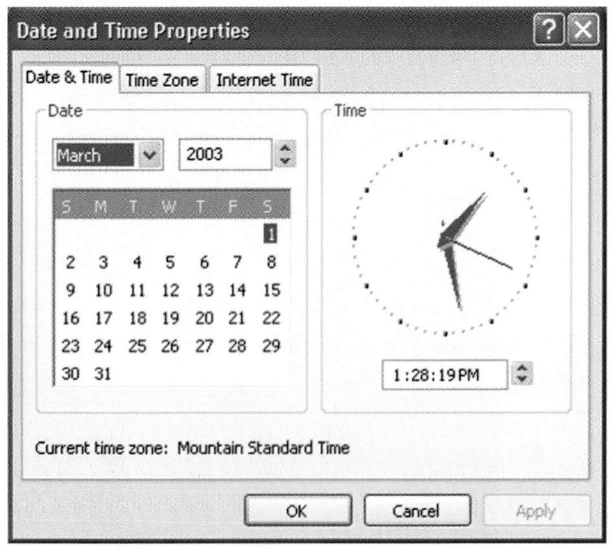

4.1 OPERATING SYSTEM SOFTWARE

Operating system software is system software that controls your application software and manages how your hardware devices work together. You've probably heard of several different types of operating system software including Microsoft Windows, Linux, UNIX, or Mac OS. Here, we introduce you to the various concepts you need to know to work effectively and productively with your operating system software. The best way, however, to learn about your operating system software is to see it in action. We definitely recommend that you complete the "What Is an Operating System?" tutorial on your SimNet Concepts Support CD to better understand the vitally important role of your operating system software.

TYPES OF OPERATING SYSTEM SOFTWARE

Do Operating Systems Differ for Different Technology Platforms?

As you know, there are numerous types of technology platforms—PDAs that you carry around; desktop computers that provide you a wide range of capabilities; minicomputers, mainframe computers, and supercomputers that support the information-processing needs of many people simultaneously. These different technology platforms require different operating system software, mainly either a personal operating system or a multi-user operating system.

Personal operating systems (personal OS) enable a single user to use a personal technology such as a PDA, smart phone, tablet PC, notebook computer, or desktop computer. Personal OSs are essentially operating systems designed for one person at a time using one computer. Later, we'll explore the more popular personal operating systems including the Microsoft family of operating systems, Linux, and Mac OS.

Multi-user operating systems (multi-user OS) enable many people simultaneously to use the resources of a central computer, which is usually a minicomputer, a mainframe computer, or a supercomputer. Multi-user OSs must process all those information-processing requests and determine, for example, the order in which documents will be printed on a printer, which task will receive priority for CPU processing, and so on. Network operating systems fall in this category. ***Network operating systems (network OS*** or ***NOS)*** run a network, steering information between computers, managing security and users, and enabling many people to work together across the network.

Network OSs and multi-user OSs may seem very similar, and they are. Network OSs don't necessarily have a central computer that performs information-processing tasks, however. In this chapter, we'll focus mostly on personal operating systems. In Chapter 7, you'll learn more about network operating systems and their capabilities.

OPERATING SYSTEM CHARACTERISTICS AND FUNCTIONALITY

What Tasks Does an Operating System Perform for Me?

Operating system software is fundamental to the working of your computer. While application software enables you to perform specific tasks such as surfing the Web or building a graph, your operating system software is always in the background orchestrating things.

FIGURE 4.2

Microsoft Windows XP Pro is a popular network operating system.

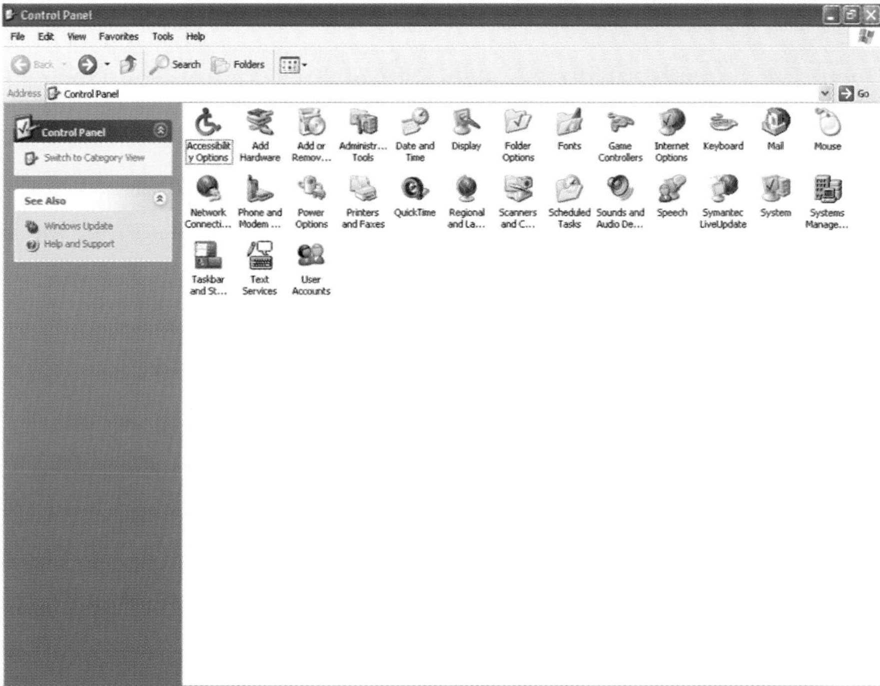

FIGURE 4.3
The Control Panel in Microsoft Windows lists many operating system tasks.

As you can see in Figure 4.3, a typical personal operating system supports many useful functions. You can change your password, configure your Internet display and connection settings, change your speech engine settings (for using speech recognition to enter information), set up your computer to send and receive faxes—but most important, while you use your computer and application software, your operating system handles the vital task of resource management. A *resource,* in this case, is any of your computer components.

Peripheral Management

For example, when you use your mouse to double-click on an icon to start a piece of software, your operating system must

- Determine the software you wish to use, by the location on the screen of the icon you double-clicked on.
- Find the software on your computer's hard disk.
- Tell your hard disk to transfer that software to your RAM so you can use it.
- Tell RAM and your CPU to start the execution of the software.

Your operating system coordinates and manages your computer resources —mouse, screen, hard disk, application software, RAM, and CPU—so they work together effectively to allow you to accomplish your immediate goal and be productive.

Memory Management

One of your most important resources that must be constantly managed by your operating system software is your internal memory, or RAM. While using your computer, your RAM temporarily stores your operating system, the application software you're using, and any information you're working with.

did you know?
22.2 *percent of computer users have lost information or software because of blackouts, electrical failures, viruses, or hackers.*[4]

Your operating system software	Word software	Excel software
	Your Word document	Your Excel workbook

FIGURE 4.4

Your operating system performs multitasking and memory management by allocating specific areas of RAM.

An important feature of effective memory management is your ability to perform multitasking. ***Multitasking*** allows you to work with more than one piece of software at a time. We illustrated the concept of multitasking in the previous chapter when we discussed how to integrate the capabilities of your personal productivity software. In that discussion, we helped you learn how to copy and paste a graph from Excel (spreadsheet software) to Word (word processing software).

To enable you to do that task from a memory management point of view, your operating system allocates areas within your RAM for five things (see Figure 4.4):

1. The operating system software itself
2. Word software
3. Excel software
4. Your Word document
5. Your Excel workbook

As you type in your Word document and its size increases, your operating system must allocate more RAM to it, while ensuring that the new allocation of space is not being used otherwise. Also, when you copy the workbook graph and then paste it into your word processing document, your operating system software must (1) determine the RAM location of the graph, (2) make a copy of it, (3) determine the RAM location of where you want the graph to appear in your word processing document, and (4) copy the graph from its original RAM position into the new position.

Likewise, if you change your graph, your operating system must be aware of the change, make another copy of the graph, and place the new copy of the graph in your word processing document.

As you can see, your operating system software is indeed vitally important.

making the grade

SECTION 4.1

1. A(n) ___________ enables a single user to use a personal technology such as a PDA, smart phone, tablet PC, notebook computer, or desktop computer.

2. A(n) ___________ enables many people to simultaneously use the resources of a central computer such as a mainframe.

3. A(n) ___________ enables many people to work together across a network of computers.

4. ___________ allows you to work with more than one piece of software at a time.

4.2 PERSONAL OPERATING SYSTEMS

There are various operating systems for the personal technologies available to you. Let's first take a look at operating systems for notebook and desktop computers (the Microsoft family of operating systems, Linux, and Mac OS), and then we'll discuss your operating system options for PDAs and tablet PCs.

THE MICROSOFT FAMILY OF OPERATING SYSTEMS

What Are the Most Popular Operating Systems?

Microsoft is the leading provider of operating systems for notebook and desktop computers. Microsoft has been making operating system software for personal computers since the early 1980s. Today, you'll mostly find four Microsoft personal operating systems in use.

Microsoft Windows 2000 Millennium (Windows 2000 ME or ***Windows ME)*** and ***Microsoft Windows XP Home (Windows XP Home)*** are both personal operating systems designed for a home computer user with utilities for setting up a small home network. Windows 2000 ME was released in 2000, and Windows XP Home was released in 2001. So, Windows XP Home is the newer of the two. It includes support for multiple people to use the same computer (although not at the same time), each with unique names and passwords. As you see in Figure 4.5, you can create different users. Windows XP Home also allows you to connect your computer (or home network of computers) to various intelligent appliances in your home.

We would characterize both of these versions of Microsoft Windows as personal operating systems as opposed to multi-user or network operating systems. If you buy a Windows-based computer today from a computer store or Web site such as Dell (www.dell.com), it will probably come with either Windows 2000 ME or Windows XP Home.

FIGURE 4.5

Microsoft's Windows XP Home helps you easily create different users for the same computer and create a home network of computers and intelligent home appliances such as a refrigerator.

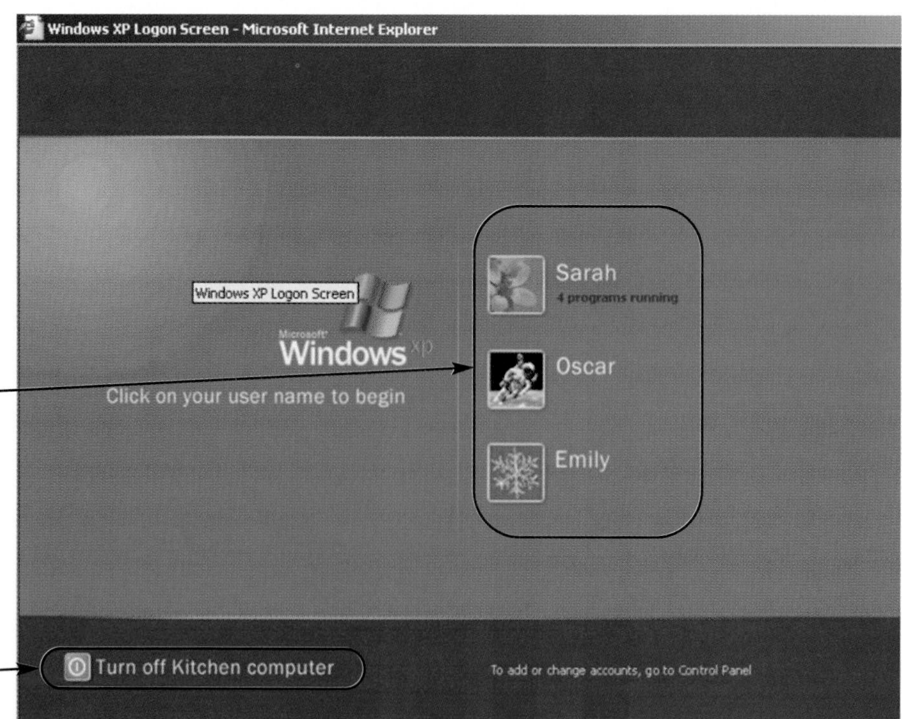

Microsoft Windows 2000 Professional (Windows 2000 Pro) and ***Microsoft Windows XP Professional (Windows XP Pro)*** are both personal operating systems for people who have a personal computer connected to a network of other computers at work or at school. Both of these operating systems offer increased security over Windows 2000 ME and Windows XP Home, making them more suitable for computers that run on a network. Windows XP Pro is the newer version, released in 2001 along with Windows XP Home.

Here, the distinctions between a personal operating system and a network operating system become a bit blurred. You can actually use Windows XP Pro to set up and run a fairly elaborate network with several servers (as such, using it as a network operating system). This may be the case in your school's computer lab. If so, your school may also recommend that you install and use Windows XP Pro on your personal computer. While connected at school, your personal computer Windows XP Pro can communicate seamlessly with the Windows XP Pro at your school acting as a network operating system. While you're at home, Windows XP Pro essentially operates as a personal operating system.

To learn more about the Microsoft family of operating systems, complete "The World of Windows" tutorial on your SimNet Concepts Support CD.

MAC OS AND LINUX

What Non-Microsoft Operating Systems Are Available?

Mac OS is the operating system for today's Apple computers. It supports a graphical user interface similar to Windows operating systems, although the look and feel is a little different (see Figure 4.6). With the newest release of Mac OS, you can enter your password by speaking it. So, you must not only remember your password, but also be able to speak it in a way that matches how you originally recorded it. If you buy an Apple computer, Mac OS is your choice of operating system software.

Linux is an open-source operating system that provides a rich operating environment for mostly high-end workstations and network servers.

FIGURE 4.6

Mac OS is the operating system for Apple computers and supports a graphical user interface similar to most Windows operating systems.

For that reason, you probably won't find it on very many personal computers in a home or workplace environment. If your computer is for personal use such as surfing the Web, typing documents, sending e-mail, and the like, Linux is probably not the operating system for you. Linux can be either a personal operating system or a network operating system.

Although Linux may not be a good personal operating system for you right now, it does represent some substantial career opportunities. We believe Linux will play prominently in the future of technology. If you're interested in learning how to write operating system software, we definitely recommend that you focus some of your efforts on Linux.

To learn more about Mac OS, Linux, and other operating systems, complete "The World of Macintosh" and "Other Operating Systems" tutorials on your SimNet Concepts Support CD.

CHOOSING THE RIGHT PERSONAL OPERATING SYSTEM

So, Which Personal Operating System Do I Need?

First, you need to decide if you want an Apple computer or an IBM/compatible computer. If Apple is your choice, then your operating system is Mac OS. If you go the other route, you need to consider how and where you'll use your computer. If you'll use your computer at home most of the time, get Windows 2000 ME or Windows XP Home. If your computer will be connected to a network at school or work much of the time, we recommend that you contact the appropriate technology support department at school or work. That department will help you determine which operating system is best.

OPERATING SYSTEMS FOR PDAS AND TABLET PCS

Do I Have Operating System Options for PDAs and Tablet PCs?

As we've stated, every technology platform must have an operating system of some kind—that includes PDAs and tablet PCs.

Operating Systems for PDAs

If you buy a PDA, you actually have numerous choices for an operating system. More practically, you choose from among different types of PDAs (by manufacturer), with your choice determining which PDA operating system you will have. The two most popular types of PDAs are: (1) ***Palm*** and ***Handspring*** and (2) ***PocketPCs.*** Both types offer similar functionality and capability—their only real difference is the operating system. The Palm/Handspring–type PDAs use the ***Palm Operating System (Palm OS),*** while PocketPCs run on ***Pocket PC OS.*** Manufacturers of Palm OS PDAs include Palm, Handspring, and Sony. Manufacturers of Pocket PC OS PDAs include HP (including Compaq) and Casio.

There are a few other manufacturers of PDAs that provide different operating systems, including Sharp (with its Zaurus PDA line, which uses a combination of Linux and a proprietary operating system) and Psion (with its Revo, Series 5MX, and Series 7 lines of PDAs, which use an operating system called EPOC).

FIGURE 4.7
Psion's Revo PDA uses an operating system called EPOC.

Operating Systems for Tablet PCs

If you buy a tablet PC (any brand), your primary choice for an operating system is ***Microsoft Windows XP Tablet PC Edition.*** This operating system is similar to Microsoft Windows XP Home, except that it includes special capabilities that enable a tablet PC to work effectively. When you buy a tablet PC, the operating system will come already installed.

making the grade

1. Microsoft Windows XP Pro is the newest version of Microsoft ___________.
2. Microsoft Windows ME and Microsoft ___________ are both personal operating systems designed for home computer users.
3. ___________ is the operating system for today's Apple computers.
4. PocketPC PDAs use ___________ as an operating system.
5. Palm and Handspring PDAs use ___________ as an operating system.

4.3 DEVICE DRIVERS, UTILITIES, AND VIRUS PROTECTION

Operating system software provides the basic instructions for your computer to work. But you really need more than just operating system software to work effectively and efficiently. You also need device drivers, utility software, and virus protection.

DEVICE DRIVERS

Do I Need Special Software when I Install Hardware Devices?

You can expand your computer capabilities in a variety of ways—add more RAM, perhaps add a new and faster CPU, and add any number of peripheral devices such as a scanner, a CD burner, a gamepad, or a printer.

When you add such devices, your operating system often needs some additional information about the device. If so, your operating system needs a device driver. A ***device driver*** is software and information that enables your operating system to establish the communications between your existing hardware and your new device. Typically, device drivers come on a CD or disk that accompanies your device. So, if you buy a new printer, it will come with a CD or disk that contains the appropriate device driver. To use your new printer, you must first install the device driver. If, for some reason, you need a device driver but don't have the disk, you can usually download the appropriate driver from the manufacturer's Web site.

When you add certain popular devices, your computer may have the necessary device drivers already installed. If so, you can take advantage of plug and play. With ***plug and play,*** you can add devices to your computer and your operating system will find and install the appropriate device driver without your having to go through a manual installation. If you don't already have the right device driver on your computer, your operating system will prompt you to insert the appropriate CD or disk.

Once you have the right drivers for all your devices, you can take advantage of hot swap. ***Hot swap*** is an operating system feature that allows you—while your computer is running—to unplug a given device and plug in a new one without first shutting down your computer. So, if you have both a laser printer and a high-quality color photo printer, you don't have to have both plugged into your computer at all times. By taking advantage of the hot swap feature, you can unplug and plug them in as you need to.

UTILITY SOFTWARE

What Additional Software Do I Need to Add to My Operating System Software?

Personal operating systems today come with just about everything you need to effectively use your computer—with some important exceptions. To accommodate these exceptions, you need utility software. ***Utility software*** provides additional functionality to your computer's operating system.

For example, you may want enhanced ***file security software,*** which is utility software that contains security features (mainly encryption) to protect your files and folders of information as well as to enable you to send secure e-mail messages. ArticSoft's FileAssurity software is a good example (see Figure 4.8). FileAssurity requires that you provide another password in addition to your own login password. Using the new password, FileAssurity will encrypt the files of your choice so that no one can use them. If someone were to steal your computer and copy your hard disk, that person would not be able to read the files that FileAssurity had encrypted. For information on other file security software, visit the Web site

FIGURE 4.8

ArticSoft's FileAssurity will encrypt and protect your most important files of information.

You can download a free trial version of FileAssurity here.

for this text at www.mhhe.com/i-series. Protecting your information is very important, and we'll discuss it further in Chapter 9 in the context of ethics, security, and privacy. To learn more about the role of your utility software, complete the "Utilities" tutorial on your SimNet Concepts Support CD.

UTILITY SOFTWARE SUITES

Can I Buy Utilities in Suites Just like Personal Productivity Software?

As with personal productivity software, you can buy utility software to meet your individual needs, or you can buy a utility software suite. A ***utility software suite*** is a "bundle" of utility software tools sold by the same manufacturer. As you can see in Figure 4.9, there are three popular utility software suites—McAfee Office, Norton SystemWorks, and Ontrack System Suite. As you read down through the list of utility tools included in these suites, you may not recognize some terms. For example, what is "Permanent delete"? When you delete a file from your hard disk, the file isn't *actually* erased. Rather, your operating system marks that area on your hard disk for available use. So, at some point in time when you create a new file of information, your operating system may overwrite the file you deleted (which was really only marked as not being used). If you want to really delete and remove a file from your hard disk, then any one of the three utility software suites in Figure 4.9 can enable you to do that.

Notice also that some of these suites support disk and/or file encryption. So, if you purchase McAfee Office (its price is about \$50 to \$70), you won't need to purchase other file security software such as ArticSoft's File-Assurity (its cost is about \$40).

Finally, notice that each of the three utility software suites includes virus protection, or anti-virus software. This is the most important utility software you need to acquire. Personal operating systems do not include anti-virus software.

Feature	McAfee Office 3.5	Norton SystemWorks 2001 Std.	Ontrack System Suite 3.0
Runs within Windows 95/98/ME	Yes	Yes	Yes
Runs within Windows NT/2000	No	Yes	Yes
Anti-virus software	Yes	Yes	Yes
Defragmentation tools	Yes	Yes	Yes
Crash protection	Yes	No	Yes
Undeletes file from recycle bin	Yes	Yes	Yes
File compression utility	No	Yes	No
Permanent delete	Yes	Yes	Yes
Disk encryption	Yes	No	Yes
File encryption	Yes	No	Yes
Hard drive failure early warning	Yes	Yes	Yes
Firewall	Yes	No	No
E-mail encryption	Yes	No	No
Cleans cookies	Yes	Yes	Yes

FIGURE 4.9

McAfee, Norton, and Ontrack provide the three most popular utility software suites.

FIGURE 4.10

Norton's LiveUpdate feature allows you to obtain new virus information for your anti-virus software on a weekly basis.

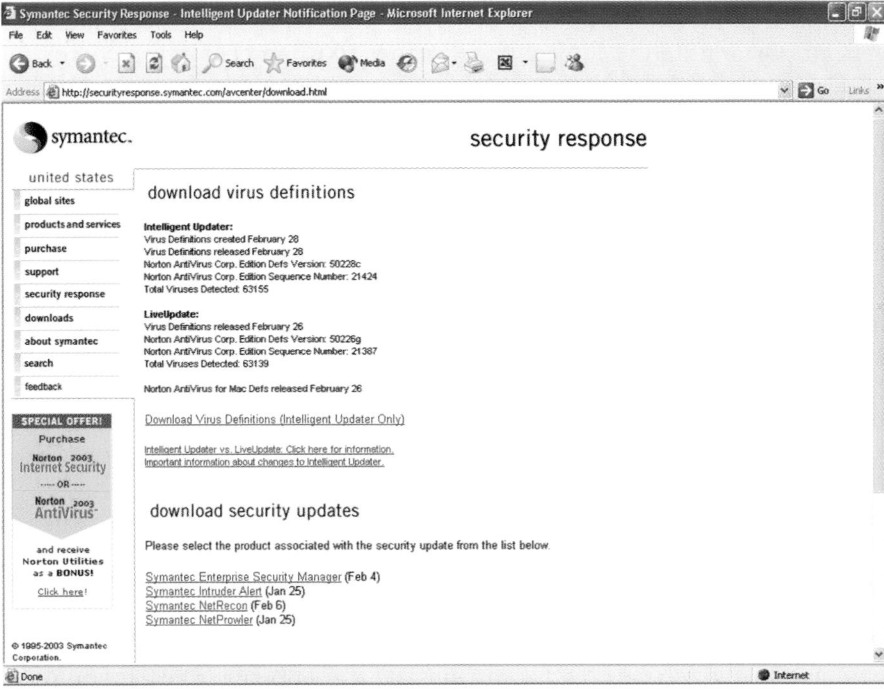

ANTI-VIRUS SOFTWARE

What Are Computer Viruses and How Do I Protect My Computer from Them?

A ***computer virus (virus)*** is software designed intentionally to cause annoyance or damage. Some viruses are relatively benign; they cause your screen to go blank (or something like that) but do not corrupt your information or software. Other viruses—called *malignant viruses*—damage your computer. Malignant viruses can scramble or delete your files, completely wipe out your hard disk, shut down your computer, alter your personal productivity software so that it doesn't work correctly, and even adversely affect some of your hardware such as a flash memory card in your digital camera so that you can't store photos any more.

With 200 to 300 new viruses surfacing each month, you need to protect your computer and your information with anti-virus software. ***Anti-virus software*** is utility software that continually scans your RAM, storage devices, and incoming files for viruses and removes the viruses. If you download a file from the Web, your anti-virus software will first check the file to see if it has a virus. If it does, your anti-virus software will alert you to the problem and remove the virus before allowing the downloading process to go ahead.

Once you install your anti-virus software, we recommend that you update it on a weekly basis. Norton provides weekly updates to its anti-virus software on its Web site (www.norton.com). All you have to do is download the updates (called LiveUpdate by Norton; see Figure 4.10) and your operating system software will automatically install the updates to your anti-virus software.

If you frequently connect your computer to a network of other computers at school or at work, your technology support department may provide these updates to you. You should contact the appropriate department to determine if this is available to you. If it is, we recommend that you take advantage of it.

did you know?

41 *percent of all computer users state that they do not personally back up their information.*[5]

i•series insights — *Ethics, Security & Privacy*

Firewalls for Protecting Your Computer and Information

Protection of all kinds is a necessity today for your computer and information. On the previous pages, you've read about some of the ways in which utility software provides protection, including file encryption and anti-virus software.

If you look back again at Figure 4.9, you'll find another important protection feature offered by McAfee Office. It's called a firewall. A ***firewall*** is hardware and/or software that protects a computer or network from intruders. In the case of McAfee Office, the firewall is strictly software for your personal computer.

For example, if you have an always-on Internet connection through a DSL, cable, or satellite modem (we discussed these options in Chapter 2), someone else on the Internet can actually gain access to your computer. So, while you're out for the evening, away for the weekend, or even asleep at night, an intruder can gain access to your computer, stealing your information and potentially causing all sorts of havoc.

To deter such actions, you need a firewall. Firewalls stop incoming access to your computer from the outside world. Would you leave your house or apartment unlocked? We think not, so why leave your computer vulnerable to outside attack?

We cannot stress enough how important it is to have and regularly update your anti-virus software. When you buy a new computer, it may or may not come with anti-virus software installed. If it does, update it on a weekly basis. If it doesn't, make it your first priority to buy and install anti-virus software. We'll certainly talk more about computer viruses in Chapter 9 on ethics, security, and privacy.

making the grade

SECTION 4.3

1. A(n) ___________ is software and information that enables your operating system to establish the communications between your existing hardware and your new device.
2. With ___________, you can add devices to your computer and because your operating system already has the appropriate device drivers, no manual installation process is necessary.
3. ___________ is an operating system feature that allows you—while your computer is running—to unplug a given device and plug in a new one without first shutting down your computer.
4. A(n) ___________ is a "bundle" of utility software tools sold by the same manufacturer.
5. ___________ is utility software that continually scans your RAM, storage devices, and incoming files for viruses and removes the viruses.

4.4 FILE MANAGEMENT

Your ability to create, store, and use files makes you more productive with your computer. Most of the information you work with is stored in files (and on storage devices such as your hard disk or CD). A ***file*** is a collection of information you need to use your computer effectively. While writing a term paper with word processing software, for example, you would create a file that contains the contents of your term paper. As you call up that file and refine and enhance your term paper, you make changes to the file and continually save those changes to your storage device.

The word processing software itself that you use to create and refine your term paper is stored in a file. The ID and password you use to log on to your computer are stored in a file. As you learned in Chapter 3, videos are each stored in a different file, as are audio clips, photos, and images. Thus, many different types of files are stored on your computer.

FILE NAMING CONVENTIONS
How Do I Specify a Filename?

When you create a file, you must give it a filename. A ***filename*** is a unique name that you give to a file of information. A filename is usually followed by a filename extension. A ***filename extension*** (most often just called an ***extension***) further identifies the contents of your file usually by specifying the file type. For example, you could create a file with the filename **Finance Term Paper 3-12-03.doc.** The portion appearing before the period or dot is the unique filename you provide (**Finance Term Paper 3-12-03**). The portion appearing after the period or dot is the extension. In this case, the extension is **doc,** which Microsoft Word automatically provides when you create a document using that software.

As you use most application software to create files, the application software will provide its recommended extension. Excel provides **xls,** Access provides **mdb,** and PowerPoint provides **ppt** (all Microsoft products and extensions).

When you provide a filename, it must adhere to the rules of your chosen operating system (called file naming conventions; see Figure 4.11). For the most part, you have a great deal of flexibility in choosing filenames. We certainly recommend that you use filenames that are as descriptive as possible to help you recall them. For example, because you have a date associated with it, **Finance Term Paper 3-12-03** is more descriptive than just **Finance Term Paper.**

FIGURE 4.11

File naming conventions are rules that you must follow in creating filenames and differ according to your operating system.

<table>
<tr><th></th><th>Linux</th><th>Mac OS</th><th>Windows 2000 & XP</th></tr>
<tr><td>Maximum filename length</td><td>256</td><td>31</td><td>255</td></tr>
<tr><td>Are spaces allowed?</td><td>No</td><td>Yes</td><td>Yes</td></tr>
<tr><td>Are numbers allowed?</td><td>Yes</td><td>Yes</td><td>Yes</td></tr>
<tr><td>Special characters not allowed</td><td>! @ # $ % ^ & * ( ) { } [ ] " \ ' ; < > ?</td><td>None</td><td>\ ? : " < > | * /</td></tr>
<tr><td>Is it case sensitive?</td><td>Yes</td><td>Yes</td><td>No</td></tr>
</table>

ORGANIZING YOUR FILES

With So Many Files, How Can I Organize Them Effectively?

To help you manage your files, your operating system includes utility software called file manager utility software. ***File manager utility software*** (or ***file management system software***) is utility software that helps you manage, organize, find, copy, move, rename, and delete files on your computer. To use your file manager utility software effectively, you need to know something about device letters, directories, folders, pathnames, and filenames (which we just discussed).

Identifying Your Storage Devices with Device Letters

As you probably already know, you can store and access files of information on different storage devices such as a floppy disk, hard disk, and CD (or DVD). Each of these devices has a device letter. A ***device letter*** is a unique identifier for each different storage device on your computer (see Figure 4.12). On almost all personal computer systems, the device letter for the floppy disk is A. So, we refer to it as Drive A. The hard disk is almost always Drive C. The drive letters for your other storage devices depend on the computer you have as well as your operating system.

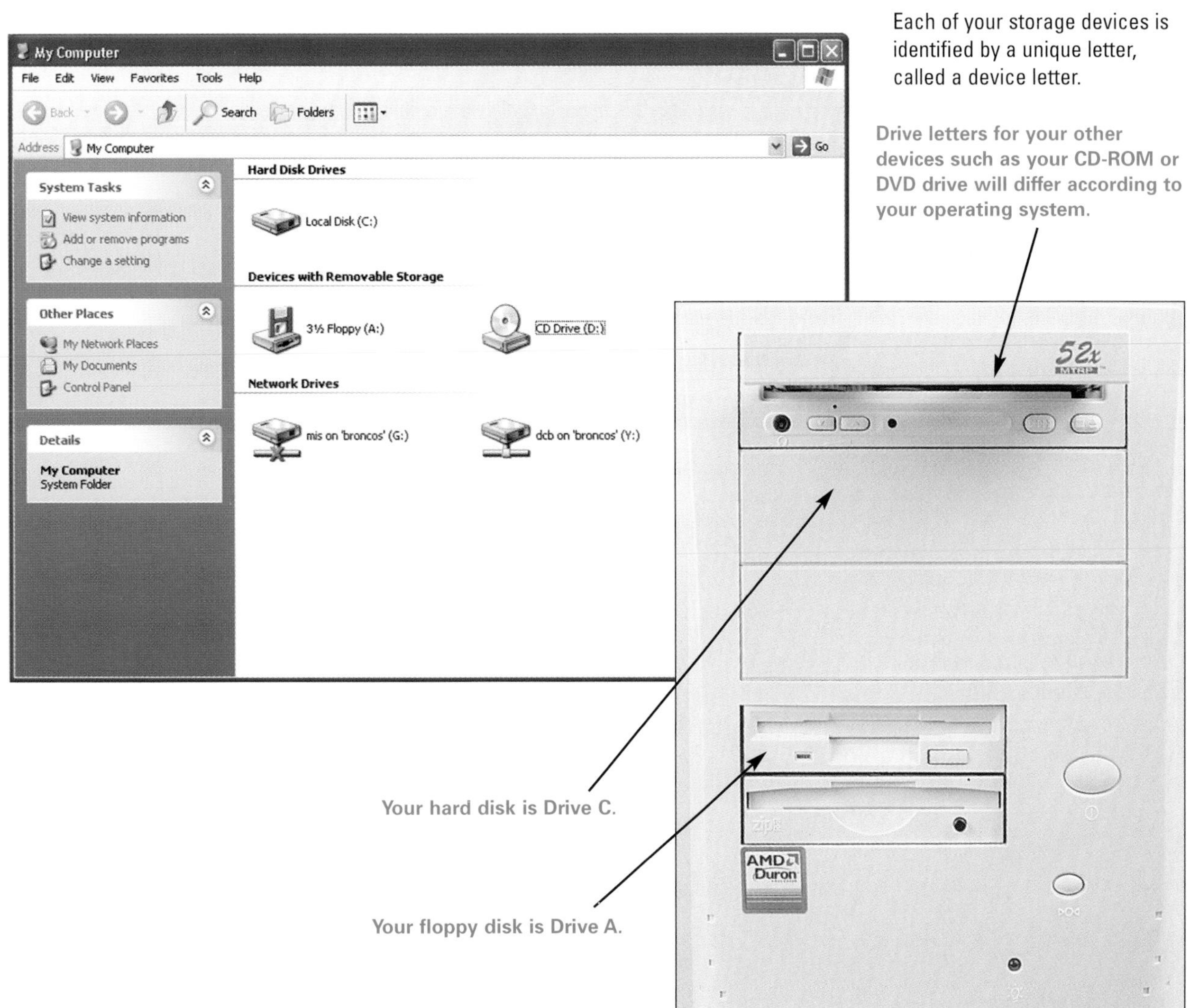

FIGURE 4.12

Each of your storage devices is identified by a unique letter, called a device letter.

Using Directories and Folders for Organizing Files

Each of your storage devices contains a directory. A ***directory*** is a list of the files (and *folders,* which we'll discuss next) on a particular storage device.

The main directory is often called the *root directory.* If you have many files, the root directory must contain them all, unless you create subdirectories, or folders. A ***folder*** (which your operating system will display as a manila folder icon) is a special portion of your root directory into which you can place files that have similar information. For example, you can create a folder called **Finance** and in it store all the files you create for your Finance class (see Figure 4.13).

You can also create folders within folders (these are called subfolders). So your **Finance** folder could contain the subfolders **Finance 3212** and **Finance 4032.** Your purpose in creating these would be to store all your files related to your Finance 3212 class in one subfolder and all your files related to your Finance 4032 class in another subfolder. In doing so, your filing system would begin to look like a pyramid (or hierarchical tree structure; see Figure 4.13), with the root directory at the top.

FIGURE 4.13

Your filing system should contain folders within folders to help you effectively organize your files.

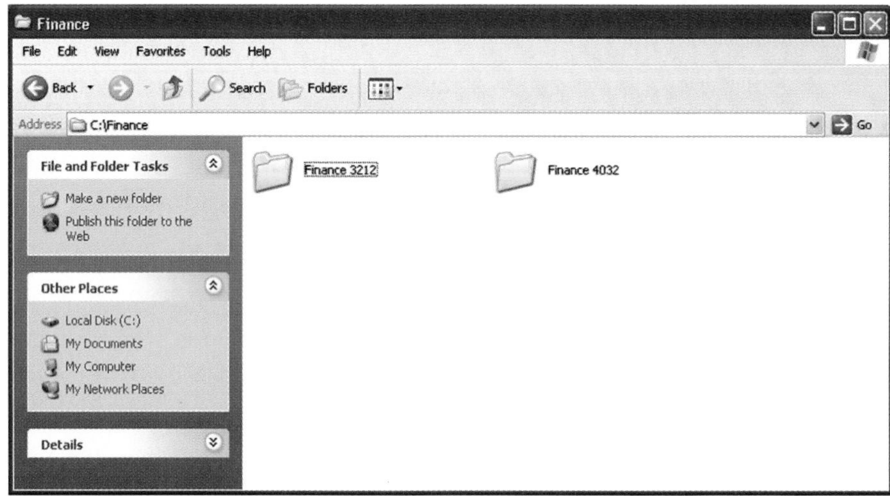

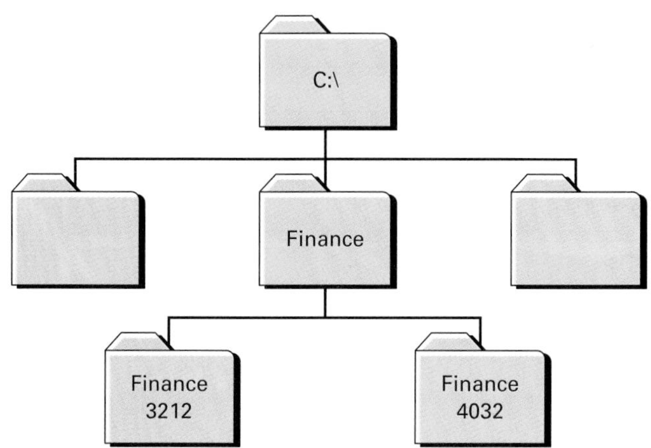

The **Finance** folder contains the subfolders of **Finance** 3212 and **Finance 4032.**

Using Pathnames to Identify File Locations

As you begin to organize your files by storage device and folders, you need to learn how to create and read a pathname. A ***pathname*** is the device letter, folder, subfolder (if present), filename, and extension that together describe a particular file and its location. In our previous example, there could be a file called **Finance Final Analysis.xls** stored in the **Finance 4032** subfolder within the **Finance** folder on Drive C. The pathname for that file is

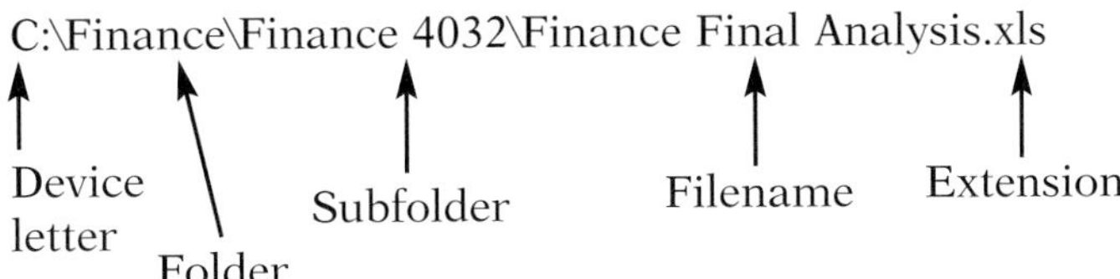

Why is this important? You may, from time to time, share a disk of information with friends or classmates. If you want to direct them to a particular file, you'll need to do so with the pathname. Of course, if you're passing around a disk, it's probably understood that the device letter is A.

Exactly how file manager utility software works and displays information and how it designates device letters is unique to your particular operating system. But the *concepts* of organizing files, folders, filenames, and extensions are the same regardless of your computing environment.

FILE ALLOCATION TABLES (FAT)

How Does My Computer Save and Find My Files?

As you save files to a hard disk (or perhaps a floppy disk or a rewritable CD or DVD), your computer finds the first available space. But your computer doesn't necessarily save a particular file all in the same place. Your computer allocates space on a storage device using sectors and clusters. A ***sector*** is a single area on a storage device that can hold a certain number of bytes of a file. (Usually this number is 512 bytes or characters.) Your computer groups sectors into clusters. A ***cluster*** is a collection of sectors on a storage device. A cluster can hold from 512 bytes to 256 kilobytes (256 Kb or 256,000 bytes), depending on your hard disk and your operating system.

So, if you have a 5 KB (5,000 character) file and your computer uses 4,086 byte clusters, your computer places the first 4,086 characters of your file in the first available cluster, and then finds another available cluster to store the remaining 914 bytes.

How does your computer keep track of where it places your files? Your computer uses its file allocation table. A ***file allocation table (FAT)*** is a file that stores information about the physical location of every file on your computer's hard disk. The FAT also tracks used areas on your disk so files don't overwrite each other.

Fragmentation

As you create, edit, and delete files on your hard disk, the contents of your clusters change and the FAT changes to keep track of where files are. As your computer moves, rewrites, and deletes files, your disk can fragment (see Figure 4.14). ***Fragmentation*** occurs when your computer places parts of files over many disk areas or clusters. Too much fragmentation reduces your drive's efficiency, especially for a hard disk. When this occurs, your computer must spend a lot of time moving across your disk to find all the pieces of a file. That can greatly slow your productivity.

As you allow your computer's hard drive to fragment, you increase the chance that your computer won't work as efficiently as it should. ***Access speed***—the time between when you ask for a file and when the computer delivers it to you—slows as your hard disk fragments. Increased fragmentation can lead to file and hard disk failures that can destroy your information.

To manage fragmentation, you need to run a defragmentation utility regularly. A ***defragmentation utility*** is utility software that reallocates file

FIGURE 4.14

As you store files on your hard disk, it can fragment. Periodically, you should run a defragmentation utility.

ASSUMPTION: Cluster size is 4,086 bytes.

Disk Clusters	1	2	3	4	5

ACTION #1: Create and save **ABC.doc** (size is 4,000 bytes).

Disk Clusters	1	2	3	4	5
	ABC.doc				

ACTION #2: Create and save **PET.xls** (size is 5,000 bytes). Because the size of **PET.xls** is greater than 4,086 bytes, it requires two clusters for storage.

Disk Clusters	1	2	3	4	5
	ABC.doc	PET.xls	PET.xls		

ACTION #3: Update **ABC.doc** and increase size to 8,000 bytes. The first 4,086 bytes will be stored in cluster #1 with the remaining bytes stored in cluster #4 (this is fragmentation).

Disk Clusters	1	2	3	4	5
	ABC.doc	PET.xls	PET.xls	ABC.doc	

ACTION #4: Update **PET.xls** and increase size to 10,000 bytes. This will require three clusters, causing more fragmentation.

Disk Clusters	1	2	3	4	5
	ABC.doc	PET.xls	PET.xls	ABC.doc	PET.xls

ACTION #5: Run a defragmentation utility to eliminate fragmentation. When complete, **ABC.doc** will be stored in contiguous clusters, and **PET.xls** will be stored in contiguous clusters.

Disk Clusters	1	2	3	4	5
	ABC.doc	ABC.doc	PET.xls	PET.xls	PET.xls

clusters and decreases fragmentation. Essentially, a defragmentation utility reorganizes your entire disk so that individual files are stored contiguously within clusters that are next to each other. Most operating systems come with a defragmentation utility. Many people believe that the defragmentation utilities in utility software suites such as Norton or Ontrack are much better than the standard operating system utilities.

FILE COMPRESSION

How Can My Computer Hold More Files?

When you compress something, you make it smaller. Using ***file compression,*** you can shrink a file into a smaller file. This smaller file is a ***compressed file.*** In order to use this compressed file, you need to ***decompress*** or "unshrink" it back to its original size. In Chapter 3, we discussed the use of codec—a utility for specifically compressing and decompressing video files. Not all personal operating systems come with utilities for file compression and decompression. If you need these types of utilities to save disk space, you'll have to buy the appropriate utility software. Most utility suites do include utilities for file compression and decompression.

You can control the file size by setting a file compression ratio. A ***file compression ratio*** determines how small you want the compressed file to be. If you set a file compression ratio of 30:1, the compressed file will be 30 times smaller than its original.

Compression Software

If you want to compress a file or files, you'll need file compression software (see Figure 4.15). ***File compression software*** is utility software that allows you to compress and/or decompress a file or files. PKZip, ZipIt, and

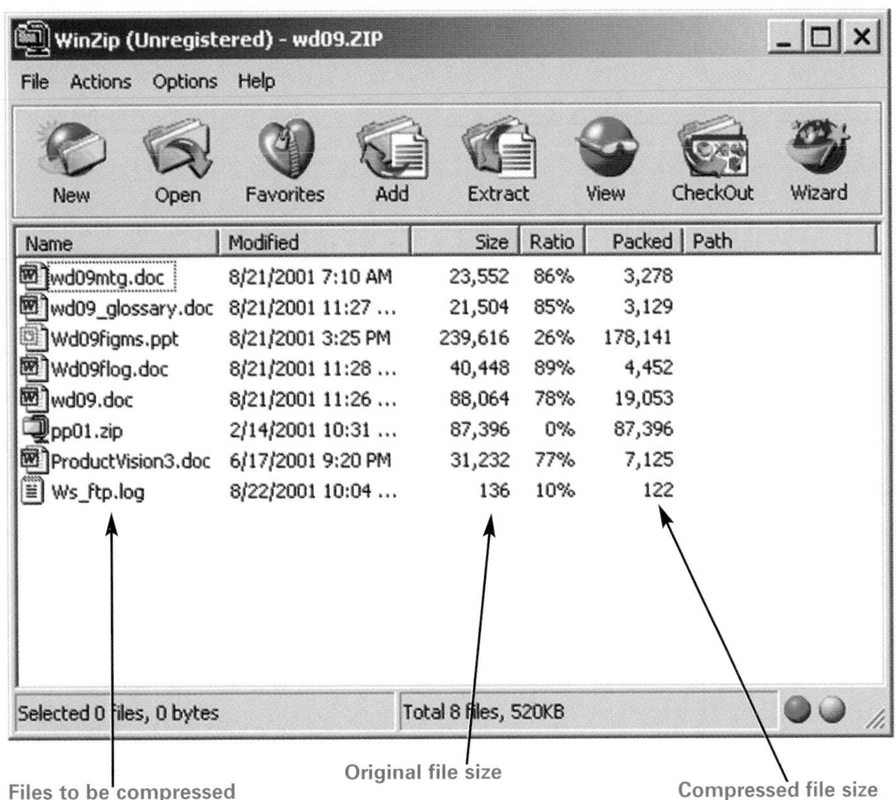

FIGURE 4.15

WinZip is compression and decompression utility software available to you.

i•can

Effectively Organize My Files for School

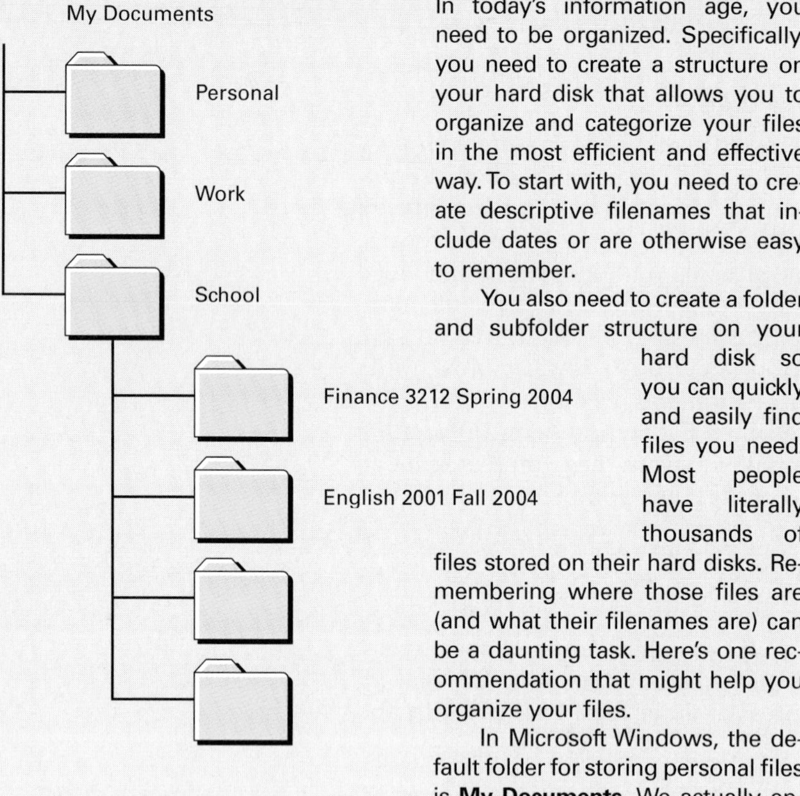

In today's information age, you need to be organized. Specifically, you need to create a structure on your hard disk that allows you to organize and categorize your files in the most efficient and effective way. To start with, you need to create descriptive filenames that include dates or are otherwise easy to remember.

You also need to create a folder and subfolder structure on your hard disk so you can quickly and easily find files you need. Most people have literally thousands of files stored on their hard disks. Remembering where those files are (and what their filenames are) can be a daunting task. Here's one recommendation that might help you organize your files.

In Microsoft Windows, the default folder for storing personal files is **My Documents.** We actually encourage you not to store any files there. Rather, you should create separate folders within **My Documents,** such as **Personal, Work,** and **School.** Within **School,** consider again not storing any files, but rather creating more subfolders including one for each of your classes. (Name them by class designation, number, term, and year such as **Finance 3212 Spring 2004.**)

Within each of those folders, you may even want to create another set of folders. For example, if one of your finance classes requires a lot of computer work and communication, you might want to create folders within it titled **E-mails, Homework, Assignments, Class Notes, Projects,** and **Exams.**

Whatever the case, your goal should be to store files only in the lowest level of folders. If you were to implement our suggestions above, you would store files only in the folders **E-mails, Homework, Assignments, Class Notes, Projects,** and **Exams.** You wouldn't store any files in **My Documents, School,** or **Finance 3212 Spring 2004.**

did you know? *27 percent of businesses have dismissed at least one of their employees for misuse of the Internet or e-mail.*[6]

WinZip are popular compression software programs. They've become so popular that most people refer to compressing a file as ***zipping*** and decompressing a file as ***unzipping.*** Zipped files have a .zip extension.

File compression software allows you to specify which files of information you want compressed. If your hard disk is already full and you want to compress all of your files of information, you can use a disk compression utility. A ***disk compression utility*** is utility software that (1) automatically compresses your files of information when you save them to your hard disk and (2) automatically decompresses your files when you access and use them with your application software. Using a disk compression utility slows down file access time, but it also allows you to save almost twice the information on your hard disk. If you want to use a disk compression utility, we definitely recommend that you purchase a good one such as those found in utility software suites.

making the grade

1. A(n) __________ is a unique identifier for each different storage device on your computer.
2. A(n) __________ is a list of the files and folders on a particular storage device.
3. A(n) __________ is a file that stores information about the physical location of every file on your computer's hard disk.
4. __________ occurs when your computer places parts of files over many disk areas (clusters).
5. A compressed file is commonly called a __________ file.

4.5 CONSUMER Q&A

We frequently get numerous questions about operating system software, virus protection, and file management from our students. Let's explore some of those questions and answers to them here.

1. How Can I Upgrade My Operating System Software when a New Version Is Available?

As with application software, publishers of operating system software provide upgrades and give you the ability to upgrade your existing operating system software at a price lower than if you actually purchased the new version. Most often, you'll be able to obtain the upgrade to your operating system software via CD or perhaps the Web. All you have to do is pay for the upgrade and follow the installation instructions.

We would provide a couple of important notes here. First, before upgrading your operating system software, we always recommend that you make copies of your files of information. That way, if something does go wrong during the installation process, you'll have backups. Second, you need to keep in mind that after upgrading your operating system software it's often impossible to uninstall the new version and go back to the previous version. If you have older application software, it may not work under the new version of your operating system software. But you can't go back—keep that in mind.

2. If I Receive a Zipped File as an E-mail Attachment, How Do I Decompress It?

Provided that you have file compression software like PKZip, ZipIt, or WinZip, you can easily unzip or decompress a file you receive via e-mail. All you have to do is start your file compression software, select the appropriate compressed file (you'll have to provide the path to it), and click on the **Extract** button (refer back to Figure 4.15 on page 115). Your software will then ask you to specify a location for storing the uncompressed file.

3. Which PDA Operating System Provides the Best Compatibility with My Computer's Operating System?

That will depend greatly on your computer's operating system. In general, Palm OS and Pocket PC OS PDAs are compatible with most—if not all—versions of the Microsoft family of Windows. Before you buy a PDA, we recommend that you read the specifications for the PDA. Those specifications will mention which personal operating systems the PDA is compatible with.

4. Figure 4.9 Mentions Cookies—What Are They?

A ***cookie*** is a small text file containing specific information about you that a Web site stores on your computer's hard disk. When you visit a given Web site, it may create a cookie that contains what pages you visited, what products you looked at, perhaps what products you purchased, and the types of searches you performed on the site. It will then store that cookie on your hard disk. When you visit again, the Web site can use the cookie information to better customize its offerings to you.

You can easily set your Web browser so that it won't accept cookies or so that it will ask you if you want a cookie from a given Web site stored on your hard disk. Utility software suites include tools for automatically deleting cookies when you end a browsing session or cookies belonging to Web sites that you haven't visited for a given period of time.

5. How Often Do I Need to Scan My Hard Disk for Viruses?

When you first install your anti-virus software, it will check all your storage devices (and your RAM) for viruses. After that, your anti-virus software will scan every incoming file (for example an e-mail attachment or a disk you insert into one of your drives). However, we don't believe that is enough. You should set your anti-virus software to scan all your storage devices on a daily basis. You can usually find this feature termed something like **Scan Schedule.**

6. Can I Compress Multiple Files into a Single Smaller File?

Often times, you may want to share several rather large files with someone. If so, you can compress or "zip" each of them individually and send them on their way. As an alternative, you can package all of the compressed or zipped files into a single file. You don't really save any additional space using this method but it does allow you to send a single file to another person. That person would then uncompress or unzip the package, which would result in the unzipping of each individual file.

7. What Happens if a Virus Attacks My File Allocation Table File?

Your file allocation table or FAT is probably the single most important file on your hard disk. It tracks the location of each file on your hard disk. Many viruses today just attack your file allocation table. All those viruses have to do is transpose a few numbers in your file allocation table and the result can be devastating. If your file allocation table does become corrupt (for whatever reason), you need to seek the assistance of a professional, and that may cost you a lot of money. Keep your eyes open for any news

did you know? More *than 77 percent of all businesses record and review employee electronic communications, including e-mail and phone calls.*[7]

of a virus that affects your file allocation table. If you hear of one, immediately update your anti-virus software. On the Web site that supports this text (www.mhhe.com/i-series), we've provided a list of resources that can alert you to new viruses.

4.6 SUMMARY AND KEY TERMS

System software is software that determines how your computer carries out technology-specific and essential tasks such as writing to a disk, starting your Web browser so you can surf the Web, and sending a document to your printer. You cannot use your computer without system software. System software includes operating system software, device drivers, and utility software.

Operating system software is system software that controls your application software and manages how your hardware devices work together. Types of operating system software include ***personal operating systems*** (for a single user using technology), ***multi-user operating systems*** (for many people simultaneously using the same technology), and ***network operating systems*** (for running and managing a network). All operating systems support such functions and tasks as peripheral management, memory management, and ***multitasking.*** Popular personal operating systems include:

- **Microsoft Windows 2000 Millennium**
- **Microsoft Windows XP Home**
- **Microsoft Windows 2000 Professional**
- **Microsoft Windows XP Professional**
- **Mac OS**
- **Linux**
- **Palm operating system and Pocket PC OS (for PDAs)**
- **Microsoft Windows XP Tablet PC Edition (for tablet PCs)**

A ***device driver*** is software and information that enables your operating system to establish the communications between your existing hardware and your new device. With the right device drivers installed you can take advantage of ***plug and play*** and ***hot swap.***

Utility software provides additional functionality to your computer's operating system. Examples include ***file security software*** (with encryption capabilities) and ***anti-virus software*** that continually scans your RAM, storage devices, and incoming files for viruses and removes the viruses. You can purchase ***utility software suite***s that contain a variety of tools.

When you store information on your storage devices you create ***files,*** collections of information you need to use your computer effectively. Key concepts of file management are

- ***Filenames*** and ***extensions*** that uniquely identify each file.
- ***File manager utility software*** for managing and organizing your files.
- ***Device letters*** for uniquely identifying each of your storage devices.
- ***Folders*** for creating special areas in which you store related files.
- ***Pathnames*** that describe a particular file and its location.

Utilities for effective file management include

- ***Defragmentation utility***—for decreasing disk fragmentation.
- ***File compression software***—for shrinking a file so it takes up less space on your hard disk.
- ***Disk compression utility***—for compressing files when you save them and decompressing them when you use them.

To learn more about virus resources and file security software, visit the Web site for this text at www.mhhe.com/i-series.

KEY TERMS

access speed (p. 114)
anti-virus software (p. 108)
cluster (p. 113)
compressed file (p. 115)
computer virus (virus) (p. 108)
cookie (p. 118)
decompress (p. 115)
defragmentation utility (p. 114)
device driver (p. 105)
device letter (p. 111)
directory (p. 112)
disk compression utility (p. 116)
file (p. 110)
file allocation table (FAT) (p. 113)
file compression (p. 115)
file compression software (p. 115)
file compression ratio (p. 115)
file manager utility software (file management system software) (p. 111)
file security software (p. 106)
filename (p. 110)
filename extension (extension) (p. 110)
firewall (p. 109)
folder (p. 112)
fragmentation (p. 114)
Handspring (p. 104)
hot swap (p. 106)
Linux (p. 103)
Mac OS (p. 103)
Microsoft Windows 2000 Millennium (Windows 2000 ME, Windows ME) (p. 102)
Microsoft Windows 2000 Professional (Windows 2000 Pro) (p. 103)
Microsoft Windows XP Home (Windows XP Home) (p. 102)
Microsoft Windows XP Professional (Windows XP Pro) (p. 103)
Microsoft Windows XP Tablet PC Edition (p. 105)
multi-user operating system (multi-user OS) (p. 99)
multitasking (p. 101)
network operating system (network OS, NOS) (p. 99)
operating system software (p. 99)
Palm (p. 104)
Palm Operating System (Palm OS) (p. 104)
pathname (p. 113)
personal operating system (personal OS) (p. 99)
plug and play (p. 105)
PocketPC (p. 104)
PocketPC OS (p. 104)
sector (p. 113)
system software (p. 98)
unzipping (p. 116)
utility software (p. 106)
utility software suite (p. 107)
zipping (p. 116)

Multiple Choice

1. The Microsoft family of operating systems includes
   a. Windows 2000 ME.
   b. Windows XP Tablet PC Edition.
   c. Windows XP Home.
   d. Windows XP Pro.
   e. all of the above.

2. A ___________ is a small text file containing specific information about you that a Web site stores on your computer's hard disk.
   a. cookie
   b. folder
   c. device letter
   d. compressed file
   e. filename

3. A ___________ further identifies the contents of a file usually by specifying the file type.
   a. filename
   b. filename extension
   c. device letter
   d. folder
   e. device driver

4. Compressed files are popularly called
   a. unzipped files.
   b. shrunken files.
   c. zipped files.
   d. encrypted files.
   e. none of the above.

5. Bundles of utility software tools are called
   a. disk compression utilities.
   b. operating system software.
   c. utility bundles.
   d. utility software suites.
   e. utility software versions.

6. A ___________ is software designed to intentionally cause annoyance or damage.
   a. personal operating system
   b. cookie
   c. FAT
   d. computer virus
   e. folder

7. The ___________ determines how small a compressed file will be relative to its uncompressed size.
   a. encryption algorithm
   b. file compression ratio
   c. file compression algorithm
   d. encryption algorithm
   e. FAT

8. A ___________ is a special portion of your root directory into which you can place files that have similar information.
   a. device letter
   b. folder
   c. filename
   d. filename extension
   e. compressed file

9. Your application software tools are each stored in a separate
   a. file.
   b. disk compression.
   c. cookie.
   d. utility software suite.
   e. firewall.

10. A pathname includes
    a. a device letter.
    b. a folder and subfolder (if present).
    c. a filename.
    d. a filename extension.
    e. all of the above.

True/False

11. ____ Access speed determines how fast your Web browser can load a Web page.

12. ____ A firewall can be either hardware or software.

13. ____ Linux is a popular operating system for most PDAs.

14. ____ A sector is a group of clusters.

15. ____ System software is a type of personal productivity software.

Take this quiz online at www.mhhe.com/i-series and get instant feedback.

QUESTIONS AND EXERCISES

1. Exploring Your Control Panel

Your computer's operating system comes with a variety of useful functions and tools that enable you to use your computer more effectively and efficiently. You can find most of these functions and tools in your **Control Panel.** Below, we've provided a list of things you can do in your **Control Panel.** For each, define where in the **Control Panel** you can perform it. You will need to specify the folder as well as any tabs within the folder.

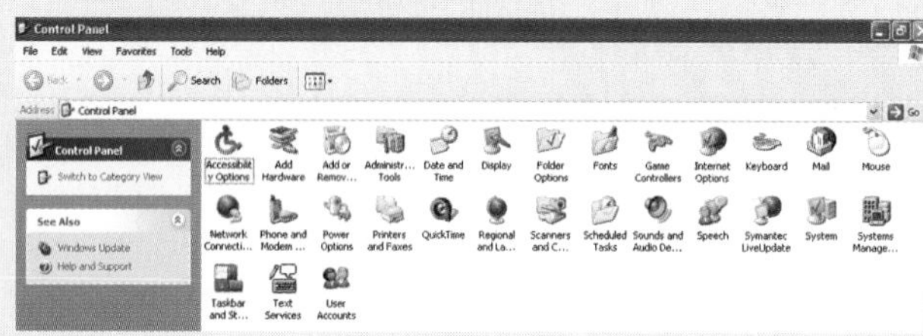

HELPFUL FUNCTIONS AND TOOLS	CONTROL PANEL LOCATION
A. Enable/disable hibernation	
B. Change the functionality of your right mouse button	
C. Change the time zone	
D. Change the resolution of your screen	
E. Turn off the playing of sound within Web pages	
F. Set the blinking rate of your cursor	
G. Change the wallpaper	
H. Set sound volume	
I. Add a regularly scheduled task	
J. Set a default printer	
K. Control your screen pointer with your numeric keypad	
L. Set your default home page for Web browsing	
M. Change the color palette of your screen	
N. Change your screen pointer design	
O. Delete cookies	
P. Set the double-click speed for your mouse	

2. Understanding File Storage

Refer back again to Figure 4.14 on page 114, where we illustrated how fragmentation occurs on a storage device as you save and update files. In this exercise, you'll be illustrating the same concepts and adding the functionality for handling the deletion of files. For each action, record the cluster location(s) of the appropriate files as they are manipulated. Assume that the cluster size is 4,086 bytes.

ACTION #1: Create and save **F1.html.** Size is 100 bytes.

1	2	3	4	5	6	7	8

ACTION #2: Create and save **FIN.xls.** Size is 12,000 bytes.

1	2	3	4	5	6	7	8

ACTION #3: Delete **F1.html.**

1	2	3	4	5	6	7	8

ACTION #4: Update **FIN.xls.** New size is 15,000 bytes.

1	2	3	4	5	6	7	8

ACTION #5: Create **MKT.doc.** Size is 9,000 bytes.

1	2	3	4	5	6	7	8

ACTION #6: Update **MKT.doc.** New size is 3,000 bytes.

1	2	3	4	5	6	7	8

ACTION #7: Update **FIN.xls.** New size is 20,000 bytes.

1	2	3	4	5	6	7	8

ACTION #8: Update **MKT.doc.** New size is 4,087 bytes.

1	2	3	4	5	6	7	8

e-commerce

1. Researching Anti-Virus Software

Anti-virus utility software is vitally important to your computer. Viruses can do deadly harm to your computer and information, not to mention costing you valuable time in recovering from contracting a virus. Below, we've listed some of the leading providers of anti-virus software.

- Command Software Systems—www.commandsoftware.com
- Network Associates (McAfee)—www.mcafee-at-home.com
- Symantec (Norton)—www.symantec.com
- Panda Software—www.pandasecurity.com

Connect to at least two of these sites and answer the following questions about the anti-virus software they each offer.

a. What is the price?
b. Can you scan zipped or compressed files?
c. Can you schedule automated scanning?
d. Does it scan for viruses in Java applets?
e. What is the annual price of virus definition updates?

Overall, which anti-virus software would you choose and why?

2. Finding Student Loans

You can find money all over the Web, for buying a house, for starting your own business (venture capital), and for going to school. That's right—there are a number of sites that offer services to help you find college funding. This funding can be in the form of scholarships, free money you don't have to pay back, and standard student loans.

There are a variety of student loan lenders, ranging from traditional banks and the government to private parties just wanting to give something back to society. For this exercise, connect to two of the following student funding sites:

- Student Loan Funding at www.studentloanfunding.com
- EStudentLoan at www.estudentloan.com
- Student Loan Marketing Association at www.salliemae.com
- Federal Student Guide at www.studentaid.ed.gov
- CSLF at www.cslf.com

At each, do some looking around and answer the following questions:

a. Can you find loans from the government, banks, private organizations, or some combination of all three?
b. Can you apply for a loan while at the site or must you request paper applications that you need to complete and return?
c. By what sort of categories of funding can you search?
d. Does the site seem sincere in offering funding to you?

3. Locating Games

Some of the most popular sites on the Web are those where you can buy, sell, and trade games and even play games online. Of course, many sites even offer free games (called freeware and shareware, which we discussed in the previous chapter).

Below, we've provided four sites where you can buy, sell, and trade games. Connect to a couple of these and let's see what's there.

- GamEscapes—www.gamelover.com
- GameSpot—gamespot.com
- GameStop.com—www.funcoland.com
- Blockbuster—www.blockbuster.com

For the two sites you visit, answer the following questions:

a. How can you search for games—by title, publisher, category, etc.?
b. Can you buy both new and used games?
c. Are chat rooms present so you can talk to other gamers?
d. Are product reviews provided?
e. Are tips provided concerning how to play certain games and achieve really high scores?
f. Can you demo video games or perhaps watch short clips of them on your screen?
g. What's the return policy for a game you buy but would rather not keep?

ethics, security & privacy

1. Content Filtering on the Internet

Every type of information imaginable is on the Web. That includes a lot of great and useful information and some not-so-great information such as pornography if you're a parent and have children at home who regularly surf the Web. To block access to certain types of content and Web sites you can use special utility software called *content filtering software.*

In the table below, we've listed the most popular content filtering software packages. Your first task is to complete the table, filling in any necessary information and identifying which content filtering software tools support which functions.

With respect to content filtering, address the following questions:

a. Do parents have the right to use content filtering software to protect their children? Why or why not?

b. If you answered yes to question *a,* at what age should a child not have content filtering by his/her parents?

c. Many students and employees spend time on the Web in places unrelated to school or work. Do schools have the right to use content filtering software to block access to certain sites? Why or why not?

d. If you answered *yes* to question *c,* what types of sites should be restricted? Pornography? Gambling? Sports? Witchcraft? Religious?

e. One of the features of most content filtering software packages is providing real-time alerts to a third party. If someone (such as a child) attempts to access a restricted site, the content filtering software will e-mail another person (such as a parent) of the activity. Isn't this some sort of invasion of privacy? Why or why not? What if your school sent an e-mail to your parents every time you visited an online gambling site?

f. Assume that you are married. Do you have the right to filter content for your spouse? Do you have the right to have an e-mail sent to you every time your spouse visits a certain site or type of site? Why or why not?

	Cyber Patrol 5.0	Cybersitter 2001	McAfee Internet Guard Dog 3.0	Net Nanny 4.1
Price				
Web site				
Filters hard drive for offensive content				
Supports multiple accounts				
Supports viewing and editing of restricted lists				
Blocks restricted Web content				
Blocks AOL Instant Messenger				
Provides logging and reports				
Allows limitation of online time				
E-mails reports				
Provides real-time alerts to third party				

on the web

1. Researching Disk Backup Utility Tools

Another vitally important utility software tool is disk backup. Disk backup utilities allow you to quickly and efficiently create backups of your hard disk by copying your information to a CD or DVD, creating a disk image, or a variety of other techniques. Below is a list of disk backup utilities, their manufacturers, and Web sites.

- Backup Exec Desktop 4.5 (Veritas Software)—www.veritas.com
- Backup NOW! Desktop Edition 2.2 (NewTech Infosystems)—www.ntibackupnow.com
- novaBackup 6.6 Workstation Edition (NovaStor)—www.novastor.com
- Retrospect Express 5.5 (Dantz Development)—www.retrospect.com

Do some research (perhaps by visiting the product Web sites) and answer the questions below for each disk backup utility.

a. What is the price?
b. From what Web sites can you order it?
c. What is the time to back up 50Mb of information?
d. Does the utility provide for password protection of the backup?
e. Does the utility compress information before creating a backup?
f. Does the utility back up information to CDs? Local area network drives? Internet drives? Tape drives? Zip drives?

2. Protecting Yourself with a Firewall

We discussed firewalls—software and/or hardware that protects your computer from an intruder—briefly in this chapter as we introduced you to utility software suites. If you don't want to purchase an entire utility software suite, you can certainly buy just a firewall. Below, we've listed some of the more popular firewall utilities, their manufacturers, and Web sites.

- BlackICE Defender 2.9 (Network ICE)—www.networkice.com
- eSafe Desktop (Aladdin Knowledge Systems)—www.ealaddin.com
- McAfee Internet Security 4.0 (Network Associates)—www.mcafee-at-home.com
- Norton Internet Security 2002 (Symantec)—www.symantec.com
- PC Viper 3.1 (Source Velocity)—www.pcviper.com
- Sygate Personal Firewall Pro 4.2 (Sygate Technologies)— www.sygate.com
- Tiny Personal Firewall 2.0 (Tiny Software)—www.tinysoftware.com

Visit at least two of the above sites and answer the following questions for each firewall.

a. Is there a free personal version?
b. Can the firewall operate in stealth mode? What is stealth mode?
c. Can the firewall halt all Internet traffic? Why is this important?
d. Does the firewall keep track of the number of hacking attempts?
e. Can the firewall trace back to find the origin of a hacker?
f. How many different security levels are available? What is the purpose of having various security levels?

Do you really believe you need firewall protection? Has anyone ever hacked into your computer?

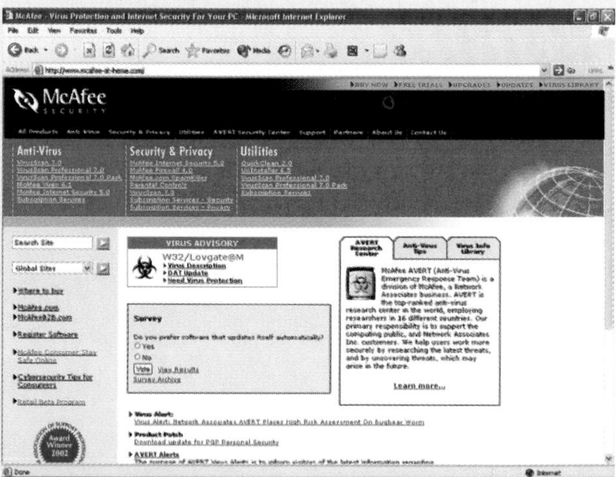

group activities

1. Building Your Own 3-D Screen Saver

In a previous chapter, you completed an exercise to learn how to download and install free screen savers to your computer. Most of the ones you found are probably fairly basic, including some limited movement and animation. However, there is utility software available that will allow you to build your own screen saver. One such piece of screen saver–generating software is CubeShow.

CubeShow allows you to create a 3-D cube, with each side of the cube containing some sort of personal photo. When in action, the 3-D cube will bounce and spin around your screen, showing different sides and photos. Your group's task is to download and install CubeShow and use it to build a customized screen saver. You'll find CubeShow at www.pcmag.com/utilities. As you build a customized screen saver with CubeShow, answer the following questions:

a. What is DirectX? Why must you install it on your computer to use CubeShow?
b. Which formats of photo files can you use?
c. How do you adjust the spin rate of the cube?
d. How do you adjust the speed with which the cube moves around your screen?
e. How can you get your cube to show more than six different photos?

2. Finding Out More about Tablet PC Operating Systems

In this chapter, we identified Microsoft Windows XP Tablet PC Edition as your main choice for a tablet PC operating system. It certainly is the most popular one, but there are others. Do some research and find out about other tablet PC operating systems. For each, answer the following questions:

a. What is the operating system name?
b. Who is the manufacturer of the operating system?
c. Is the operating system only for specific tablet PCs?
d. Is the operating system "proprietary"?

3. Finding Files on Your Hard Disk

Have you ever created a file and then couldn't remember what you named the file or in which folder you placed it? If so, don't feel embarrassed. Many people have, so many that your operating system software comes with a utility that allows you to find a file. You don't even have to know its name. For example, if the file contained a term paper on the pyramids in Egypt, you could search for the file just by knowing its content included key terms such as "pyramids" and "Egypt." Locate this utility within your operating system. How do you search for files if you know their filenames? How do you search for files if you don't know their filenames but do know their contents? How do you specify different drives on which the utility should look?

4. Your School's Operating System Software

Go on a fact-finding mission and visit your school's computer lab. If there are several, visit at least two of them. While you're there, determine which operating systems are on the various computers. Do some of the computers have different operating systems? If your school's computer lab is a network, inquire which operating system is used to run the network. Is it the same as the operating system on the individual computers? Also, inquire about the licensing agreement your school has to run a particular operating system on multiple computers. What sort of anti-virus software does your school use? Is it the same anti-virus software you have on your personal computer?

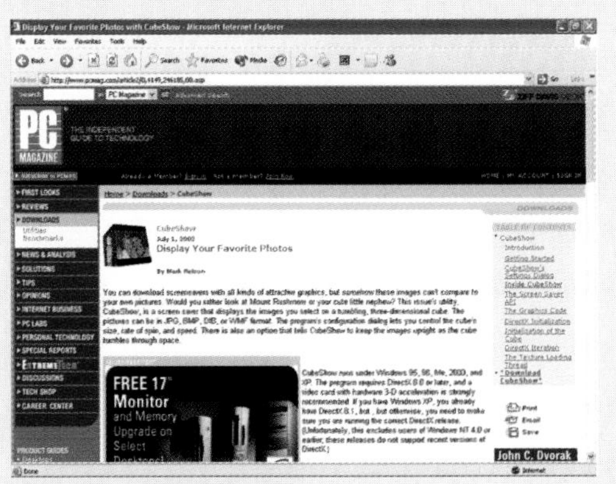

crossword puzzle

Across

2. A gaming _______ is good for racing games
8. Good quality flat-panel LCD
9. The usable part of the screen
10. This cam uploads to the Internet
11. You can write many times to this type of CD
12. You cannot change the information on this CD or DVD
14. Where the sound comes out
15. A special type of inkjet
17. A mouse with a ball underneath
18. Storage that has no spinning disk
20. Dots per inch
22. Type of flat-panel display
23. This printer will fax and copy too
24. A device that stores information long term
25. A type of flash memory card
26. Used with pressure-sensitive screens
28. A laser disc
29. Millions of pixels
32. It looks like a DVD
35. Flash memory card
37. It puts information onto a CD-RW
39. Safe number flash memory card
42. CDs and DVDs are based on this technology
44. _______ Picture Card
45. Storage for camera called flash _______
46. Pointing _______

Down

1. One thousand bytes
3. This type of hard disk drive plugs into a USB port
4. The rate at which the screen is refreshed
5. The technology on which hard disk drives are based
6. Feedback that your game controller gives you
7. One billion bytes
13. One million bytes
16. Device that lets you see the results of processing
17. MMC
19. Use it for gaming
21. A dot
27. Ball is on top
30. Flat-panel display on notebooks
31. Disk that is a magnetic storage medium
33. Cycles per second
34. You play games with this
36. Used for input on notebooks
38. "There are no strings on me"
39. Transfers printed information to RAM
40. Squirts ink from nozzles
41. Very common input device
43. Dot _______

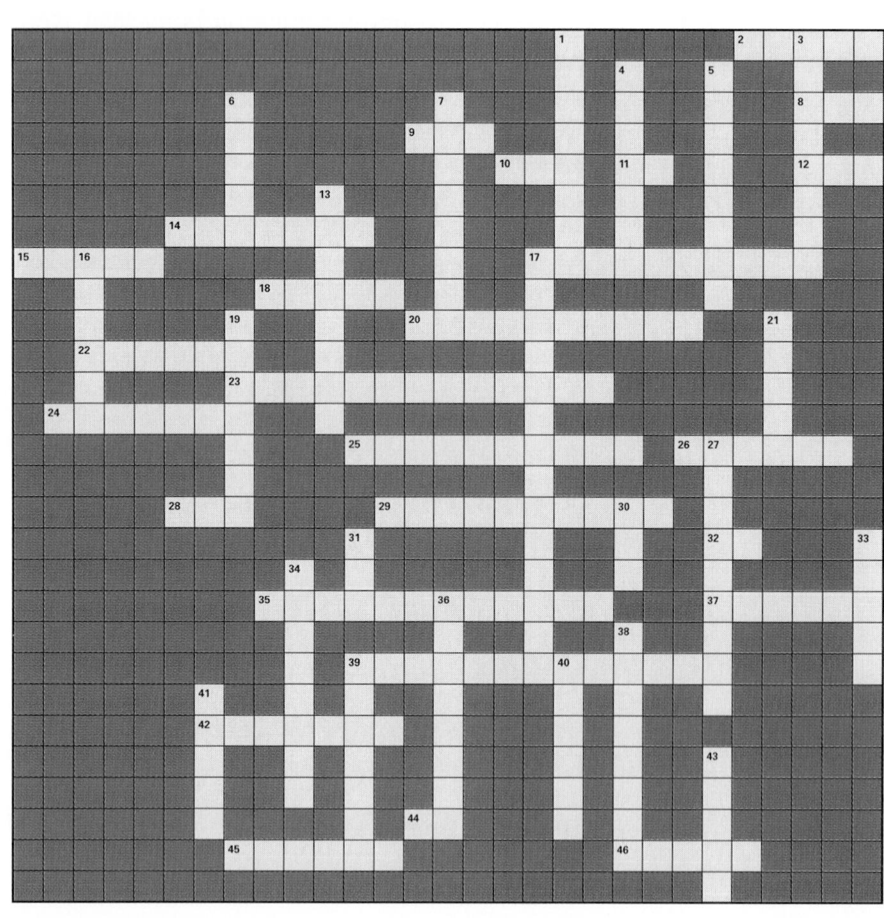

CHAPTER five

5

Input, Output, and Storage

What Kinds of Peripheral Devices Would Suit Your Needs?

did you know?

Computer peripherals have changed through the years. Input devices have gone from switches that you flipped up and down to keyboards to mice to speech recognition systems. Storage devices have changed drastically too. The beat goes on with new technologies and standards emerging all the time.

in *1980, Seagate Technology created the first hard disk drive for consumer computers. At the time, you could get a floppy disk that was 5 1/4" square with a storage capacity of 128 kilobytes. The new hard disk device, on the other hand, was so big it could store 5 megabytes (almost 40 times as much).*

a *movie DVD that you buy in the United States will not necessarily work in other parts of the world. Look at the fine print on a movie DVD, and you'll probably see something about its being viewable only on U.S. and Canadian DVD players.*

in *1956, IBM sold the RAMAC 305 computer, which stored a whopping 5 megabytes of information for the enticing price of $50,000. Today a gigabyte (200 times as much) of hard disk storage costs in the range of $_??_ to $_??_.*

To find out what a gigabyte of storage on a hard disk costs today, visit www.mhhe.com/i-series.

SIMNET CONCEPTS SUPPORT

Student Learning Outcomes

After reading this chapter, you should be able to:

1. List and compare eight input devices.
2. Define and describe four types of pointing devices.
3. Compare and contrast inkjet and laser printers.
4. Define the three major technologies on which computer storage is based.
5. Describe the three classes of CDs and the three classes of DVDs that are available.
6. List and describe five types of flash memory cards that are available for electronic devices such as computers and cameras.

Have you ever wondered why there are so many different automobiles and trucks out there? Probably not, because the answer is obvious. People have varied needs and lifestyles that are fulfilled by different combinations of features. Some people want a car that will hold up to seven people, others want a sports car. Some people want a vehicle that can go off road, so they buy an SUV, and others want to haul lumber, so they buy a truck. However, all vehicles do have certain basic features in common, such as engines and wheels. So it is with computers. They all have CPUs and RAM—the computer equivalent of an engine—and these we'll discuss in the next chapter.

FIGURE 5.1

There are many kinds of input, output, and storage devices.

A cordless mouse is an input device.
A digital camera is an input device.
A monitor is an output device.
A printer is an output device.
An external hard disk drive is a storage device.
A flash drive is a storage device.
Kodak
EasyShare
Iomega
Mini

In this chapter, we'll explore the many other features available in input, output, and storage devices so that you can make your computer as useful and productive as it possibly can be (see Figure 5.1 on the opposite page). You'll want to enhance your productivity whether you're into gaming, stock market day trading, or keeping the books for your lawn-care business.

5.1 INPUT DEVICES

Whether you're using your computer to prepare next year's budget in Excel, to write a term paper, or to play online games or the CD of your favorite band, you need a way to send information and commands (such as choosing a menu option or launching an application) to your computer. The hardware devices that you use to enter commands and send information to your computer are called input devices.

An ***input device*** captures information and translates it into a form that can be processed and used by other parts of your computer. So, what sort of input devices do you need? As always, that depends on what you want to use your computer system for. In this section, we'll discuss many types of input devices including keyboards, pointing devices, game controllers, scanners, styluses, microphones, digital cameras, and Web cams. To learn more about all different types of input devices, complete the "Overview of Input Devices" and "Other Everyday Input Devices" tutorials on your SimNet Concepts Support CD.

KEYBOARDS AND POINTING DEVICES

Are There Choices when It Comes to Keyboards and Mice?

Keyboards allow you to enter information and commands. They come in different types and styles. Some keyboards are wireless, so that you're not tied to the desk while you're surfing. Others have sets of special keys for multimedia that give you one-touch access to Web sites and e-mail, as well as controls to play CDs, MP3 files, and DVDs.

You can get portable keyboards for PDAs that give you a more normal keyboard to use with your PDA, but which fold up or roll up and can be tucked away in your backpack or pocket. These keyboards usually have a place to hold up the PDA while you're typing (see Figure 5.2). To learn more about keyboards, complete the "Keyboards" tutorial on your SimNet Concepts Support CD.

FIGURE 5.2

A portable keyboard allows you to enjoy the comfort of a full-sized keyboard when using your PDA, and it folds up for convenience.

FIGURE 5.3

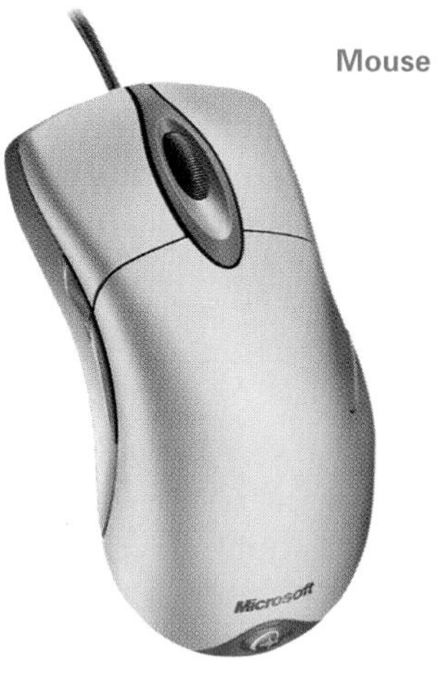

Newer mice and trackballs have extra programmable buttons for one-touch action to launch applications or files, cut or paste, enter keystrokes, and so on. For example, you could program a button to open your browser.

Pointing Devices

Today's software depends on point-and-click hardware, that is, pointing devices (see Figure 5.3). You use a pointing device mainly to choose and enter commands. Pointing devices and keyboards tend to have PS/2 connectors or USB connectors.

PS/2 and USB are different types of "plugs" for connecting devices to your computer. PS/2 has long been the type of connector used for keyboards and mice. A PS/2 connector fits into a PS/2 port, which is a small round socket with small holes that fit the pins on the connector.

USB is a newer way of connecting devices to a computer. USB connectors fit into USB ports, and these are small rectangular openings on the back or front of your computer, or even on your keyboard or monitor. You'll see much more about connectors, ports, and other hardware that allows you to connect devices to your computer system in Chapter 6. To learn more about connecting hardware, complete the "Ports and Cables" tutorial on your SimNet Concepts Support CD.

A ***mouse*** is a pointing device that you use to click on icons or buttons; select menu options; highlight text or images; and drag and drop images, text, files, and folders. Mice are the oldest form of pointing devices and are still the most widely used. There are many different types. There are also specialized mice. For example, there are mice designed for the small hands of children and mini-mice (wireless and wired) for use with notebook computers.

- A ***mechanical mouse*** is a pointing device that has a ball on the bottom that causes the cursor on the screen to move as the ball rolls. Most also have a scroll wheel that does the same job as the scroll bar on the right side of the screen.
- An ***optical mouse*** is a pointing device that senses movement with red light and moves the cursor accordingly. An optical mouse doesn't have to be on a flat surface, so you can move it along your arm or some other surface.
- A ***wireless mouse*** is a pointing device that sends signals about its movement to your computer by means of waves. It can be mechanical or optical. It's great for PowerPoint presentations, or any other situation where you don't want to be tied to your computer. A wireless mouse comes with a receiver that you plug into your computer. Make sure that the signal from the mouse has

did you know?

97 percent of the U.S. population lives in counties where cellular phone service is available.[1]

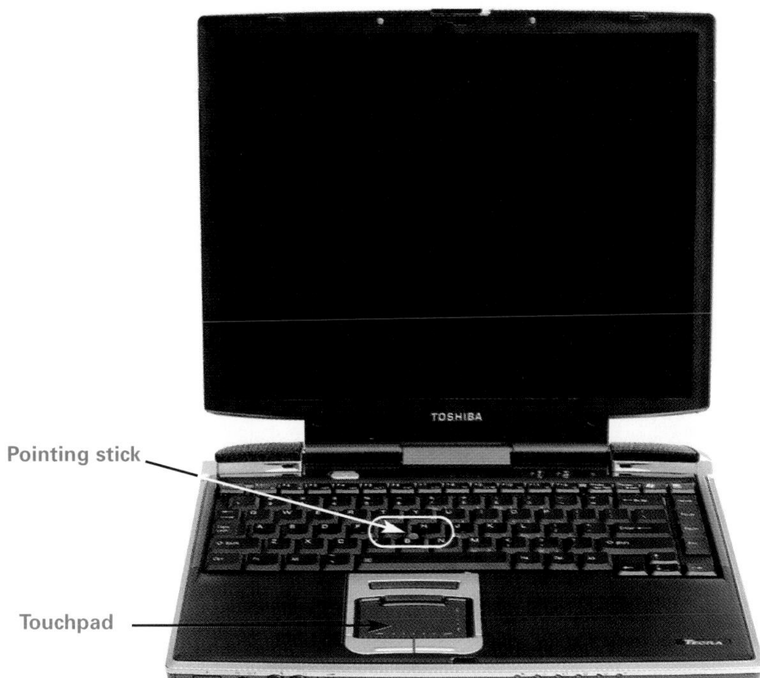

FIGURE 5.4

Notebooks have pointing sticks and touchpads as part of the keyboard for greater convenience.

an unobstructed path to the receiver. Also, remember to keep batteries on hand. To learn more about mice, complete the "Mice" tutorial on your SimNet Concepts Support CD.

A ***trackball*** is a pointing device that has a ball on the top, which you activate with a finger or thumb to move the cursor on the screen. It can be wireless and/or optical. A trackball has the advantage of staying stationary and so it doesn't need a lot of clear desk space.

A ***touchpad*** is a pointing device that consists of a little dark gray rectangle—as you move your finger around on it, the cursor on the screen moves accordingly. You often see touchpads on the base of notebook computers (see Figure 5.4).

A ***pointing stick*** is a pointing device that consists of a tiny rod that looks like a pencil-top eraser in the middle of a keyboard, and as you move the stick, the cursor on the screen moves correspondingly. The advantage of touchpads and pointing sticks is that they're built into the keyboard, which is great for portable devices like notebook computers.

GAME CONTROLLERS
What Input Devices Work Well with Games?

You can use your keyboard and mouse to play games, but most gamers prefer game controllers. You wouldn't use these devices to write a term paper, but if you need to race a car or frag an enemy these devices are a better choice. You can use many game controllers with gaming systems too, such as the Xbox, Playstation 2, and Gamecube.

Gamers usually have at least one gamepad. A ***gamepad*** is a multifunction input device that includes programmable buttons, thumb sticks, and a directional pad. You can program the buttons to correspond to certain actions, such as changing a weapon, opening a door, and so on. The directional pad and thumb sticks control movement. Thumb sticks are miniature joysticks.

FIGURE 5.5
Whichever controllers you choose to play your games with, they're all input devices.

For gamers who enjoy flight simulations, a joystick is a must. A ***joystick*** is an input device that controls movement on the screen with a vertical handle and programmable buttons. Joysticks have become more advanced in the last few years. Some of the latest joysticks, such as the Logitech Freedom 2.4, are wireless and feature completely programmable settings.

If you're into racing games, then a gaming wheel is for you. A ***gaming wheel*** is an input device that uses a steering wheel and a separate set of foot pedals to imitate real-world driving. Most gaming wheels incorporate programmable buttons as well.

For added realism, you can get force feedback on your game controller. ***Force feedback*** is a technology that sends electrical signals from the game to the game controller that cause it to shake and move. When you crash or fall, your game controller lets you know. Some gamers opt for even more realism with gaming gloves and virtual reality head-mounted displays. With these input devices, you don't look at the screen and press buttons. Rather, you stay immersed in the game itself, controlling your movements and interaction much as you would in the real world. Figure 5.5 shows some of the game controllers you can use.

did you know?

TV programs shown between 2 A.M. and 6 A.M. local time don't have to be closed captioned for the hearing impaired.[2]

SPECIALIZED INPUT DEVICES
What Other Types of Input Devices Can I Use?

In addition to keyboards, mice, and game controllers, you can use many others types of input devices. In this section, we'll discuss scanners, styluses, microphones, digital cameras, and Web cams.

Scanners

A ***scanner*** is an input device that creates an electronic image that your computer can use of text, images, maps, and so on. There are various kinds of scanners—you've seen barcode scanners in grocery stores. The type that you use with a home computer is an image scanner (often a flatbed type), which captures images from paper and transfers a copy to your computer. When scanning, a flatbed scanner looks very much like a miniature photocopier making copies.

You can even produce photos from negatives and slides with a special scanner feature called a *transparency adapter* that shines light through the film. Some scanners have this built in (see Figure 5.6). The connectors on scanners are usually USB but may be Firewire. Firewire is another type of connection system for getting information to and from your computer. (In Chapter 6 you'll find much more about hardware to connect devices to your computer system.)

FIGURE 5.6

Some scanners have transparency adapters for scanning negatives and slides.

The better the resolution of your scanner, the better the quality of the result. See the Consumer Q&A section at the end of this chapter for some pointers on how to choose a scanner.

If you need to be able to edit the text you scan, make sure that the scanner you're buying has optical character recognition software (most do). That means that you can scan text and edit it as though you had typed it in. The software that's included with a scanner is usually adequate, but if you want something better, you can buy more sophisticated optical character recognition software. To learn more about scanners, complete the "Scanners" tutorial on your SimNet Concepts Support CD.

Styluses

A ***stylus*** is an input device consisting of a thin stick that uses pressure to enter information or to click and point. You use a stylus with screens that are pressure-sensitive (see Figure 5.7). In fact, it's really the screen that's the input device. If you use a PDA or a tablet PC, even if you're using the keyboard that appears on the screen, you'd probably use a stylus or "pen," although your fingernail will often do the job too. You can also use a stylus with a graphics tablet, an input system ideal for graphics artists.

FIGURE 5.7

A stylus works with a tablet PC and any other device that has a pressure-sensitive screen.

Microphones

For audio input, you need a microphone. Many modern microphones come as part of a speech recognition system. Speech recognition, which requires microphones for input, is increasingly being included in application software. We'll talk more about this in Chapter 11. The three main types of microphones are desk microphones, headsets, and directional microphones.

Directional microphones are input devices that consist of a box or boxes, each containing one or more microphones. The advantage of directional microphones is that they pick up sound in their vicinity and you don't need to speak directly into them. The big problem with directional microphones is that they pick up background noise, too. The better, more expensive models control the extraneous noise to some degree.

Digital Cameras

With digital cameras you can produce and send photos to your computer and, often, small snippets of video (see Figure 5.8). As you learned in Chapter 3, the quality of a digital camera photo is largely determined by its image resolution. The more pixels (the dots that make up the picture on the screen) the better. Image resolution for digital cameras is measured in megapixels. ***Megapixels*** are the millions of pixels in a graphic (number of dots across by the number of dots down). One-megapixel cameras are fine for sending photos in e-mail, but for printing photos, you'll need at least two megapixels. Five-megapixel cameras are now available and produce excellent photos. See the Consumer Q&A section at the end of this chapter for information on how many megapixels you need for photos.

Depending on the type of digital camera, the pictures you take are usually stored on some type of flash memory card. CompactFlash, SecureDigital, and xD-Picture Cards are all examples of flash memory cards, and we'll discuss these and others later in this chapter along with how to transfer the pictures to other devices such as a printer or computer. To learn more about digital cameras, complete the "Digital Cameras" tutorial on your SimNet Concepts Support CD.

Web Cams

A ***Web cam*** is a video camera that you use to take images for uploading to the Web. Web cams have many different uses. You can take virtual trips to faraway places or use a Web cam on your own site for others to visit; you can use your Web cam as a security measure, or to check on your pets; and you can use a Web cam to send video e-mail.

There are many career opportunities today for people with an interest in digital photography and videos. Photographers and videographers at weddings, graduations, class reunions and other events mostly use digital photography these days, since it's easier and more efficient to work with. There are opportunities for you in promotional photography, sportscasting, television work, advertising, and so on. If behind-the-scenes technical work is more your speed, you can work in a popular new industry—converting old media to new—8 mm or reel-to-reel to DVD.

FIGURE 5.8
Some digital cameras let you capture video as well as photos.

making the grade

1. A(n) ___________ mouse sends signals about its movements to the computer by means of waves.
2. A(n) ___________ is an input device that controls movement on the screen with a vertical handle and programmable buttons.
3. A(n) ___________ is a pointing device that consists of a little dark gray rectangle—as you move your finger around on it, the cursor on the screen moves accordingly.
4. A device that allows you to convert text printed on a page to an electronic form that your computer can use is a(n) ___________.
5. ___________ is a technology that sends electrical signals from the game to the game controller that causes it to shake and move.

5.2 OUTPUT DEVICES

An ***output device*** takes information within your computer and presents it to you in a form that you can understand. The main output devices are monitors, printers, and speakers. You are no doubt familiar with these. When deciding what sort of monitor or printer you want, you face the same sorts of considerations we have mentioned before. Do you want an inexpensive monitor or one that doesn't take up much space on the desktop? Do you want to print good quality photos or just text? Your choice may hinge on which tasks you need to undertake, space considerations, or your budget. To learn more about all types of output devices, complete the "Overview of Output Devices" tutorial on your SimNet Concepts Support CD.

MONITORS

What Kind of Monitor Should I Get?

Monitors come in two basic varieties: CRTs and flat-panel displays (see Figure 5.9). CRTs are monitors that look like TV sets and are the most common type of monitor, although flat-panel displays are gaining market share at a rapid rate. ***Flat-panel displays*** are thin, lightweight monitors that are used in notebook computers, tablet PCs, PDAs, and cellular phones, and increasingly with desktop computers too. They take up much

Side view of flat-panel display

Front view of flat-panel display

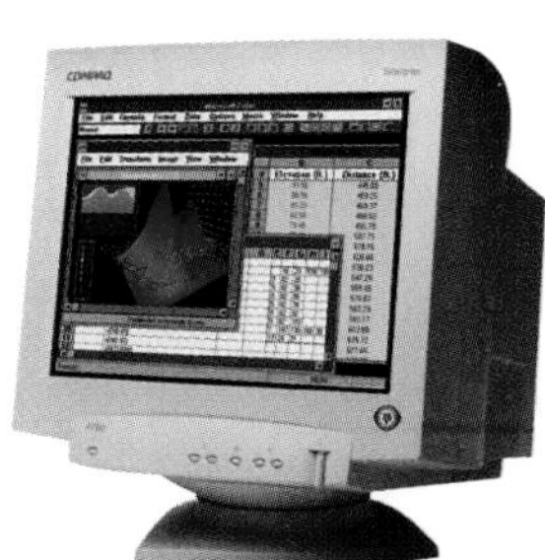

CRT

FIGURE 5.9

Monitors are either CRTs or flat-panel displays.

less space than CRTs. LCD monitors (a type of flat-panel display) are those little flat screens you see everywhere—hanging from the roof of a minivan or SUV behind the front seats, on the back of a car or airplane seat, or on the wall. Flat-panel displays use either LCD or gas plasma technology.

LCD (liquid crystal display) monitors shine light through a layer of crystalline liquid to make an image. LCD monitors are often advertised as TFT displays or monitors. ***TFT (thin film transistor) display monitors*** are flat-panel LCD displays that provide a high-quality, crisp image.

Many LCD monitors come with speakers, and may have USB ports built into the frame. Some LCD monitors allow you to pivot your screen 90 degrees; then you can rotate the image using your mouse. These screens are great for editing photos or reading pages of text.

Gas plasma display monitors shine light through gas to make an image. These are the large flat TVs or display screens that you hang on the wall. They tend to give you a better quality picture, but are more expensive.

Features you should watch for when evaluating monitors are screen size, resolution, dot pitch, and refresh rate.

Screen Size

The screen size of your monitor is measured from corner to opposite corner. CRTs are usually quoted with two numbers—the size of the screen itself and the size of the image seen. The picture on a CRT has a black border around the edge of the image. This is not true for LCDs. The ***VIS*** or ***visible image size*** is the size of the image on a screen and, for CRTs is smaller than the screen measurement, but is identical for LCDs. This is important if you're comparing, say, a 17" LCD and a 17" CRT monitor, which is often the size being offered with new computer systems.

LCDs are available in 15", 17", 19", and larger models. You might even consider buying two smaller monitors instead of one larger one. That gives you the option of separating your output. For example, you could have Word open on one monitor and a browser open on the other.

Resolution

The ***resolution of a screen*** is the number of pixels it has. ***Pixels (picture elements)*** are the dots that make up the image on your screen. The *larger-number-is-better* philosophy that applied to cameras and scanners applies to monitors as well (see Figure 5.10). Of course, your resolution depends not only on the monitor but also on the graphics or video card you have. This is the hardware inside the system unit that sends the image to your monitor based on instructions from the CPU.

FIGURE 5.10

The resolution of monitors is expressed in pixels and tells you the number of dots across and down that a monitor has.

	Resolution	
Type	**Horizontal**	**Vertical**
VGA	640	480
SVGA	800	600
XGA	1,024	768
SXGA	1,280	1,024
UXGA	1,600	1,200
HDTV	1,920	1,080
QXGA	2,048	1,536

Dot Pitch

Dot pitch is the distance between the centers of a pair of like-colored pixels. Color monitors make images with three pixel colors—red, green, and blue. A monitor with .24 mm dot pitch is better than one with .28 mm dot pitch because the dots are smaller and closer together giving you a better-quality image. So, when you choose a monitor, you want a larger number of dots (resolution) and a smaller size of dots (dot pitch). For more information on monitors, go to our Web site at www.mhhe.com/i-series.

Refresh Rate

The ***refresh rate*** or ***vertical scan rate*** is the speed with which a monitor redraws the image on the screen, and is measured in hertz. ***Hertz*** is a measure of cycles per second, and for monitors it means the number of times per second the screen is refreshed. Sixty hertz is all right for some people, but a good quality monitor will have a refresh rate of 70 hertz or more. Any less may cause fatigue and eye strain, since your eyes tend to detect the flicker of the refreshing process at 60 hertz or less. To learn more about monitors, complete the "Monitors" tutorial on your SimNet Concepts Support CD.

PRINTERS

Will I Get a Printer with My Computer System?

People buying printers for home or school usually buy either an inkjet or a laser printer (see Figure 5.11). Both types make images with dots. A printer's sharpness and clarity depend on its resolution. The ***resolution of a printer*** is the number of dots per inch (dpi) it produces. This is the same principle as the resolution in monitors, scanners, and cameras—the more dots, the better the image, and usually the more costly the printer. A printer may advertise a resolution of 2,400 × 2,400 dpi. Multiplying these numbers together gives you 5,760,000 dots per square inch. That resolution would yield a better quality image than a printer with 1,200 × 1,200 dpi (1,440,000 dots per square inch).

Laser printer

Inkjet printer

FIGURE 5.11

Laser and inkjet printers both make images with dots, but they use entirely different methods.

Inkjet Printers

Inkjet printers are the most popular type of printer. They're great for color as well as black-and-white printouts. ***Inkjet printers*** make images by forcing ink droplets through nozzles.

The two major categories of inkjet printers are general purpose and photo inkjet printers. General purpose inkjet printers have black, cyan (blue), magenta (purplish pink), and yellow ink (shortened to CMYK—the "K" is black), which comes in receptacles called tanks. You can buy inkjet printers that use separate tanks for all four colors or those that have just two, one for black and a larger one for the other three colors.

Separate cartridges cost $10 or so to replace, and the combination cartridges can cost up to $40. An inkjet printer with separate cartridges would make more sense if you use a lot of one color, for example, if you print a blue letterhead frequently. For normal use, you're likely to find that you need to replace inkjet cartridges five or six times a year.

Some inkjet printers are specially designed to produce high-quality photo images and are advertised as photo printers. A ***photo inkjet printer*** is an inkjet printer that can produce good quality photos as well as other documents. These have six colors (a second shade each of magenta and cyan) and so provide a better range of colors and shades, and some even have a seventh color—a lighter shade of black for better shades of gray.

FIGURE 5.12

This photo printer has slots into which you can slide flash memory cards and the printer will print the photos directly from there.

Many photo printers can print your photos directly from a camera or a flash memory card (see Figure 5.12). These printers contain specialized computers. Remember when using a photo printer that the smoother the surface the better the picture, so for good photos you'll be better off buying photo paper.

Laser Printers

Laser printers usually generate better-quality output than inkjets, but they're generally more expensive. A ***laser printer*** forms images using an electrostatic process, the same way a photocopier works. Laser printers print between 3 and 30 pages per minute depending on type. The color laser has two different speeds—the faster one for black only. It takes either three or four passes, depending on the type of printer, to print the color image, so color is slower. Color laser printers are much more expensive to maintain since you need to replace four cartridges instead of just one. Laser printer cartridges can cost $100 or more each, but you may find that you get a year or more out of one set of cartridges, depending on how much you print.

Multifunction Printers

A printer that will scan, copy, fax, and print is a ***multifunction printer (MFP).*** A multifunction printer can be either an inkjet or laser unit. You typically pay less for a multifunction printer than you would if you bought the devices separately. The multifunction printer will also take up less space on your desk, and an MFP is often offered as part of a complete computer system. For more information on printers, visit our Web site at www.mhhe.com/i-series. To learn more about printers, complete the "Printers" tutorial on your SimNet Concepts Support CD.

did you know?

More *people are killed every year by donkeys than by airplane crashes.*[3]

i•can

Use a Computer Without Neck and Shoulder Pain

Whether it's typing documents, memos, and letters or simply surfing the Web, you may sit for long periods using your keyboard and mouse, which can lead to physical problems. To avoid aches and pains, consider buying ergonomic computer devices.

Ergonomics deals with how you arrange and use your technology to reduce discomfort and avoid health problems. For example, there are many styles of keyboards and mice that are built to minimize strain on your neck, back, and arms. You should try several and find ones that suit you.

While using your computer, you need to sit correctly so you don't put undue strain on muscles and joints. Here are some guidelines to follow:

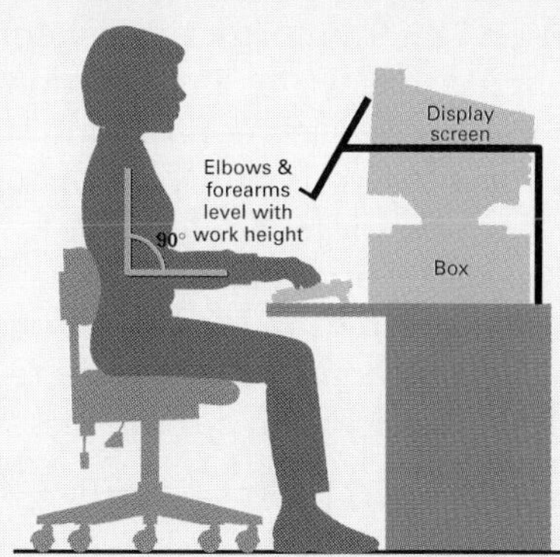

- Position your screen about the length of your arm away so that you look slightly down at it.
- Your feet should be flat on the floor.
- Your elbows, knees, and hips should form right angles.
- Your back should be at a right angle to the floor.
- Rest your eyes by looking away from the screen frequently.
- Stretch your shoulders, back, arms, and wrists at least every 30 minutes.
- Stretch your hands downward and backward frequently.

Most important, always listen to your body when it tells you that you're uncomfortable and *do something about it.*

To learn more about avoiding health problems, complete the "Ergonomics" tutorial on your SimNet Concepts Support CD.

SPEAKERS

What Are My Options for Speakers?

A ***speaker*** is a device that produces computer output as sound. Most computers come with a built-in speaker as standard equipment, but for many people the tinny quality of this speaker is insufficient. It's not hard to find better speakers. There are many different kinds on the market today. Some are the traditional two-device set, but if you want more you can get three, four, or five speakers for good surround sound. You can also get speaker sets with a separate subwoofer for low bass sounds.

making the grade

SECTION 5.2

1. A gas plasma screen is a type of ___________ display.
2. The quality of the image on a screen is determined by its VIS, resolution, dot pitch, and ___________.
3. A(n) ___________ printer is based on the same type of electrostatic process as a photocopier.
4. A(n) ___________ is an inkjet printer that can produce good quality photos as well as other documents.
5. A printer that will scan, copy, fax, and print is a(n) ___________.

5.3 STORAGE DEVICES

As you use your computer, you need to store information for future use. A ***storage device*** stores information so you can recall and use that information at a later time. A storage device consists of two parts: the ***storage medium*** on which information is stored such as a CD or floppy disk; the ***storage drive*** that writes information to the medium and reads information from it. To learn more about storage, complete the "Storage Concepts" tutorial on your SimNet Concepts Support CD.

The three major technology types that store information are magnetic, optical or laser, and flash memory. The space available on a storage medium is measured in *megabytes* or *gigabytes* for personal technologies. A byte is roughly equivalent to a character. When evaluating storage media and their capacities, you commonly see such terms as:

- ***Kilobyte (KB*** or ***K)***—exactly 1,024 bytes, but we round to 1,000 for the sake of simplicity.
- ***Megabyte (MB, M,*** or ***Meg)***—roughly 1 million bytes.
- ***Gigabyte (GB*** or ***Gig)***—roughly 1 billion bytes.

MAGNETIC STORAGE DEVICES
Do I Need Magnetic Storage Devices in My Computer?

Magnetic storage devices are the most common types of personal storage technologies, and you'll usually get at least one when you buy a computer (notebook, desktop, or tablet PC). Magnetic storage devices can be internal (built into the system unit) or external (connected from outside the system unit). In this section, we'll discuss hard disks, floppy disks, and Zip disks (see Figure 5.13).

Internal and External Magnetic Hard Disks

An ***internal magnetic hard disk*** is a magnetic hard disk that is contained in your system unit and is your primary storage device for both information and the software you use (including your operating system and application software). As a rule, you should always buy as much hard disk capacity as you can afford.

An internal hard disk is one kind of ***hard disk drive,*** which is a magnetic storage device with one or more thin metal platters (or disks) that store information sealed inside the disk drive. So, in the case of a magnetic hard disk drive, the read/write device and the medium are one unit.

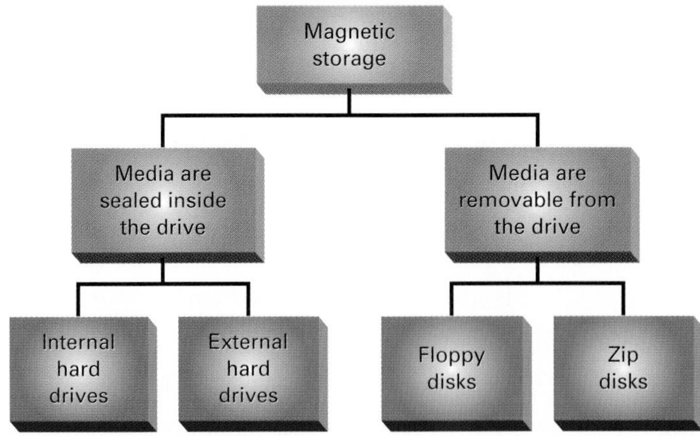

FIGURE 5.13

Magnetic storage media are either sealed inside the drive or removable from the drive.

i•series insights *Ethics, Security & Privacy*

Do You Know Where Your Deleted Files Are?

How "gone" a file is when you delete it depends on where it was stored in the first place—and how much trouble you're prepared to go to to get it back. Let's look at two separate cases: a file stored on a removable storage medium and on a hard disk.

Files on Removable Media

When you choose to delete a file, you'll get a message asking you whether you're sure you want to delete this file. If you answer yes, the name of the file will disappear from the directory or list of your folder or disk contents. That means that the name of the file has been marked in the directory as no longer needed, and the space is now available for saving new files. However, the file is not physically gone. It's still on the disk, and you can get it back with special utility software—it's often a lot of trouble, but you can do it. Note that even though you can't change the information on a CD-R, you can still delete a file. The delete process doesn't remove the file, it just makes it unavailable for normal access.

Files on the Hard Disk

When you delete a file that's on your hard disk, you get a slightly different message before the deed is done. The little window that pops up asks you whether you want the file to go to the recycle bin. If you answer no, the file stays where it is. If you answer yes, a copy of the file simply moves to another folder called the *recycle bin.* From there, you can undelete it by dragging it back to whatever folder you want it in. In other words, you have a backup copy until you empty the recycle bin.

You can also get an external magnetic hard disk drive, which is a hard disk drive that is outside your system. Note that there are also key-chain-sized external hard drives based on flash memory technology. We discuss these later in this chapter. ***External magnetic hard disk*** drives are portable storage units that you can connect to your computer as necessary. These are great for backup storage devices, and give you the ability to transport your hard disk from one computer to another. External magnetic hard drives require that you plug them into a USB or Firewire port or PC Card (see Figure 5.14). A PC Card is credit-card-sized device for connecting an external device to your notebook computer.

FIGURE 5.14

External magnetic hard disk drives often connect through the USB port on your computer.

When buying an external hard drive make sure that the model you're buying is designed for carrying around. The smaller type designed for notebook computers is very robust and ideal as a portable hard drive.

Typical sizes for internal magnetic hard disk drives run in the neighborhood of 100 gigabytes, while the capacity of external hard magnetic hard disk drives is less, usually in the neighborhood of 20 to 60 gigabytes. Again, buy all the capacity you can afford.

Floppy Disks and Zip Disks

Floppy and Zip disks, unlike hard disks, can be removed from their respective drives. These media are useful for storing files of information for backup or security purposes, or for transferring files from one computer to another.

Removable magnetic storage media come in two basic types: traditional floppy disks and Zip disks. Both store information on floppy Mylar disks housed inside plastic casing. Mylar disks are thin, flexible plastic disks. The Mylar disks inside a floppy and a Zip disk look the same, but the capacity of the Zip disk is a lot larger than that of the floppy disk.

FIGURE 5.15

A Zip disk is a removable magnetic medium. Zip disks come in capacities of 100 MB, 250 MB, and 750 MB.

A ***floppy disk*** is a removable magnetic storage medium that holds about 1.44 megabytes of information. Floppy disks are also called simply *floppies* or *diskettes*.

A ***Zip disk*** is a high capacity removable magnetic storage medium (see Figure 5.15). Zip disks come in three sizes: 100MB, 250MB, and 750MB. The drives for the higher capacity disks can read and write lower capacity disks, but not vice versa. You can't use the Zip drive to read from or write to floppies.

Floppy disk and Zip disk drives are also available as external drives, and are usually used with notebook computers. Floppy disks have very limited storage capacity by today's standards, and so they're likely to disappear within the next few years. Zip disks can store a lot more information, but they're very expensive, comparatively speaking. Therefore, it's not unlikely that they too will disappear, and the only magnetic storage device you'll be able to get for your computer system in the future will be a hard disk drive. To learn more about these types of storage devices, complete the "Removable Disks" tutorial on your SimNet Concepts Support CD.

OPTICAL STORAGE MEDIA
Should I Buy CD and/or DVD Drives?

CDs and DVDs are both examples of optical or laser discs and are great for storing large amounts of information on one removable disc. (Note that *magnetic disk* ends in "k" and *optical disc* in "c.") You'll need an appropriate drive to be able to use the CD or DVD. CD-ROMs, DVD-ROMs, CD-Rs, CD-RWs, DVD-Rs, and DVD-RWs are examples of different kinds of optical storage media. See Figure 5.16 for a graphical illustration of the various types of CD and DVD media.

The major difference between a CD and DVD, from a productivity point of view, is capacity. A CD is great for photos, music, graphics, and other "heavy" types of files. But a CD has only enough storage space for short videos—up to 20 minutes or so, depending on the quality and type of the video file. A DVD on the other hand, depending on its capacity and the type of video file, can store between 90 minutes and 8 hours of video.

FIGURE 5.16

A CD can store up to 700 megabytes and a DVD, depending on the way it's designed, generally stores from 4.7 to 17 gigabytes. This is why music comes on CDs and movies on DVDs—music takes a lot less space than video.

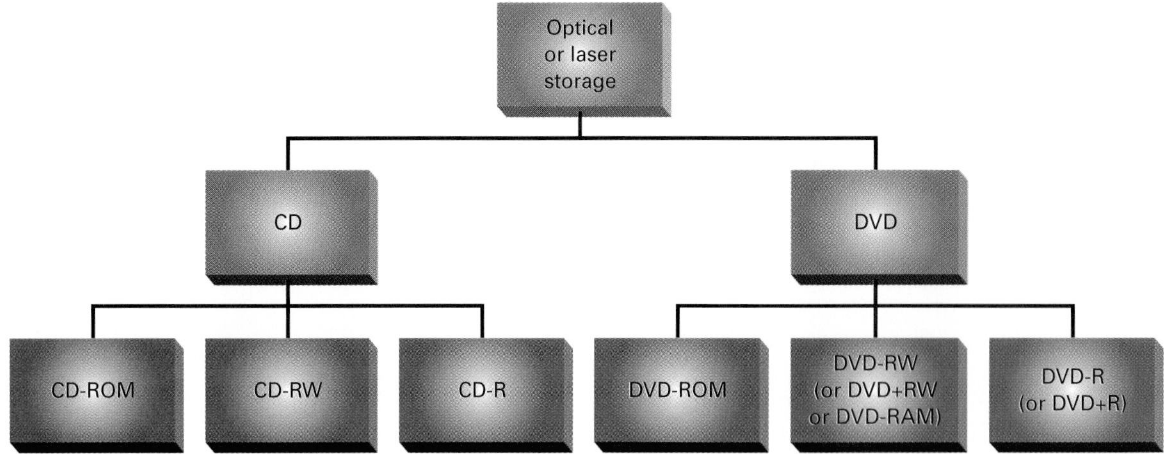

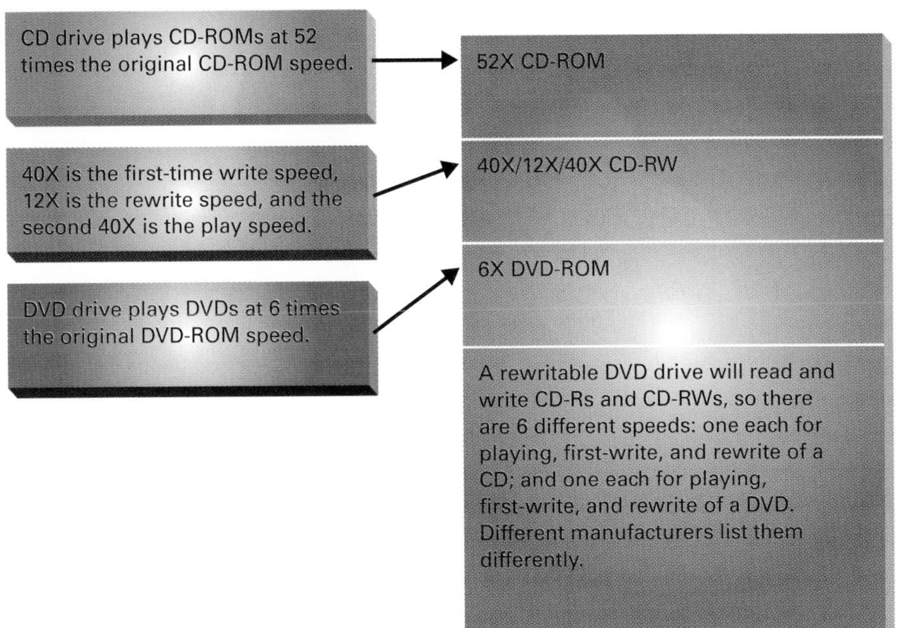

FIGURE 5.17

When describing optical media, manufacturers generally describe the access speed with "X" numbers.

Read-Only Optical Storage Media

When you see the term "ROM" after CD or DVD, you know that these are optical discs that come from the factory with information already on them that you can't change. A CD-ROM is the type of music CD you buy to play in your stereo and a DVD-ROM is the type of DVD that you buy or rent movies on.

A ***CD-ROM (compact disc read-only memory)*** is an optical or laser disc whose information cannot be changed. A ***CD-ROM drive*** is a device that lets you read (or play) a CD. You can store up to about 700 MB on a CD-ROM—about the same amount of information as 486 floppies would hold. That much information is equivalent to an entire set of encyclopedias.

The speed at which CD-ROM drives transfer information is usually shown as a number with an "X." The higher the number in front of the X the faster the transfer rate is. For example, 48X is faster than 12X. See Figure 5.17 for an illustration of optical storage transfer rates.

A ***DVD-ROM*** is a high-capacity optical or laser disc whose information can't be changed. This is the type you buy or rent movies on. (Note that there is disagreement as to what, if anything, DVD stands for.) The capacity of a DVD-ROM depends on whether information is stored on one side or two, and whether it's in one layer or two (see Figure 5.18 for different capacities). A ***DVD-ROM drive*** is a device that lets you read (or play) a DVD.

DVD Disc Type	1 side 1 layer	1 side 2 layers	2 sides 1 layer	2 sides 2 layers
Capacity	4.7 GB	8.5 GB	9.4 GB	17 GB
Hours of Video	2 hours	4 hours	4.5 hours	8 hours

FIGURE 5.18

The capacity of a DVD-ROM depends on the number of layers of information stored and whether both sides are used.

FIGURE 5.19

CDs and DVDs look a lot alike because they are—the major difference between them is capacity. Information is transferred onto both CDs and DVDs by a laser that burns tiny little grooves called "pits" into the surface of the CD or DVD.

One-Time Writable Optical Storage Media

When you see "-R" after the term "CD," you know that this is a CD you can write to *one* time only. With a DVD you may see "-R" or "+R" after "DVD" meaning that you can write to this DVD only once. You can go back and delete files on a CD-R, but you can't change the information already there, and you can't reuse the space of the deleted file (the file is actually still there, you just can't access it anymore).

A ***CD-R (compact disc—recordable)*** is an optical disc to which you can write one time only. You'd use CD-Rs for information you want to keep indefinitely, such as your photos, or backup copies of your hard disk. You can write information to a CD-R using any drive that lets you write to CDs (a CD or DVD burner). When you write standard music to your CD, you can usually play it in your stereo CD player if you've closed the CD. However, you can't add to or delete from the CD-R after you close it.

If you like to record music, you'll find you can get between 25 and 30 regular-length songs on a CD. That's if you don't use compression and the files are of the type .wav. If you use a file compression method like MP3, you can fit about 250 MP3 songs onto a CD. The number of songs you can fit even with compression depends on what sound quality you choose when compressing. Better sound quality means bigger files.

A ***DVD-R*** or ***DVD+R (DVD—recordable)*** is a high-capacity optical or laser disc to which you can write one time only. CDs that are of the write-once type always end in "-R," but DVDs are not as consistent. There are two types: DVD-R and DVD+R and they are not interchangeable.

If you're planning a presentation, a CD-R or DVD-R would be a good way to transport your presentation (see Figure 5.19). For many presentations, a CD-R will have enough capacity and you're more likely to find a CD drive than a DVD drive on most computers. Also, CD-Rs are very cheap, so you can afford to use them one time and throw them away. For more information on DVDs, visit the Web site for this text at www.mhhe.com/i-series.

did you know?

By *2004, 23.3 million households will have high-speed broadband Internet connections, up 38 percent from the 16.8 million in 2003.*[4]

Fully Read-and-Write Optical Storage Media

When you see the term "RW" after the term "CD" or "DVD" you can be sure that these are discs that you can write to multiple times, just like you do with a hard disk or a Zip disk. Again, the CDs always have "-RW," but DVDs can have "-RW," "+RW," or even "-RAM." And, again, these DVDs are different, and each must have its own drive or burner.

A ***CD-RW (compact disc—rewritable)*** is an optical or laser disc on which you can save, change, and delete files as often as you like. CD-RWs work in some CD-ROM drives. CD-RWs on which you record music will also play in some stereo systems.

Putting information onto an optical disc is called "burning" the CD or DVD. A ***CD burner*** is a drive that lets you read from and write information to a CD. A CD burner will record onto a CD-R or a CD-RW, but a CD burner will not write to a DVD.

A ***DVD-RW*** (***DVD-RAM,*** or ***DVD+RW*** depending on the manufacturer) is a very high-capacity optical or laser disc on which you can save, change, and delete files. The three types are battling it out in the marketplace and presumably, one will emerge as the standard. In the meantime, you have no guarantee of compatibility between DVD drives.

A ***DVD burner*** is a drive that lets you read from and write information to a DVD. This includes write-once DVDs and rewritable DVDs. DVD burners will read and burn CD-Rs and CD-RWs too. To learn more about CDs and DVDs, complete the "CD vs. DVD" tutorial on your SimNet Concepts Support CD.

FLASH MEMORY CARDS

Where Do Flash Memory Cards Fit in?

If you've seen the small memory cards that digital cameras use (there are various kinds) to store pictures, you already know what flash memory cards look like. ***Flash memory cards*** have high-capacity storage laminated inside a small piece of plastic. CompactFlash and xD-Picture Cards along with Memory Stick Media are all examples (see Figure 5.20). You can also use flash memory cards in any electronic device that has a flash memory slot, like a camera or PDA. You can also get flash memory devices that plug into the USB port on your computer.

The technology itself is not new—it's the principle on which CPU, RAM, and all other chips are built. A major visible difference between flash memory and magnetic or optical storage media is that flash memory cards don't need a drive with mechanical motors to spin disks nor heads moving in and out to grab the information off the disk.

Types of Flash Memory Cards

In general, different types of flash memory cards are not interchangeable. The digital camera you buy, for example, determines the type of flash memory card you'll use.

FIGURE 5.20

There are many types of flash memory cards and, in general, they're not interchangeable.

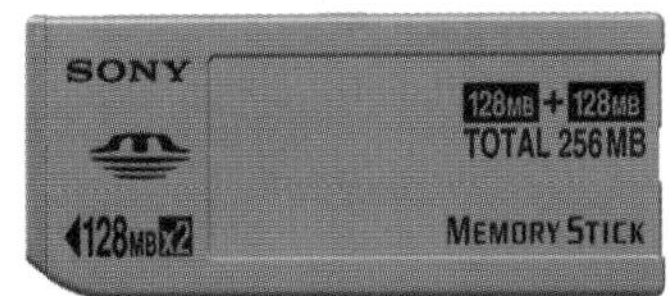

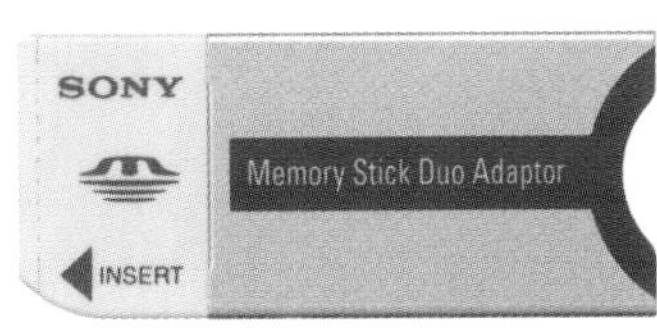

- A ***CompactFlash (CF) card*** is a flash memory card slightly larger than a half-dollar and about as thick as two quarters. It's about the size of a box, although not as deep, in which you might store a rare coin. CF cards come in various capacities; for example, you can get 384 megabyte, 512 megabyte, and 1 gigabyte CF cards.
- An ***xD-Picture Card (xD)*** is a flash memory card that looks like a rectangular piece of plastic slightly larger than a penny and about as thick, with one edge slightly curved. The capacity of xD ranges from 16 megabytes to an expected 8 gigabytes in the near future.
- A ***SmartMedia (SM) card*** is a flash memory card that is a little longer than a CF card with the thickness of a credit card.
- ***SecureDigital (SD) cards*** and ***MultiMediaCards (MMC)*** are flash memory cards that look identical (but SD cards have copy protection built-in), are a little larger than a quarter, and are slightly thicker than a credit card. They are used in cameras and often in MP3 players.
- ***Memory Stick Media*** is an elongated flash memory card about the width of a penny developed by Sony. Memory Stick Media comes in capacities from 4 megabytes to 1 gigabyte. Sony also sells a newer flash memory card called the *Memory Stick Duo,* about half as long as the original.

Flash Memory Card Readers

Some devices, such as PDAs and photos printers, have flash memory slots into which you can slide your flash memory card. Others, as on a desktop computer, use an *external flash memory card reader (external card reader* or *adapter).* This is a device that has one or more slots into which you slide the appropriate flash memory card so that you can transfer information between your computer and the flash memory card or between different types of flash memory cards (see Figure 5.21).

FIGURE 5.21

An external card reader has slots into which you plug flash memory cards to transfer information. The card reader attaches to your computer with a USB connector, as do flash memory drives.

This card reader reads CompactFlash, SmartMedia, and SecureDigital cards, along with MultiMediaCards and Memory Stick Media.

The USB connector on this flash memory drive retracts into the device when you're not using it.

The USB connector on this flash memory drive slides into the cover and disappears from view.

practically speaking

Storage that Combines Magnetic and Solid State Technology

A relatively new product from IBM is a Micro Drive, which is magnetic technology in the size and shape of a CompactFlash memory card. It's a magnetic hard disk drive with a rotating disk fixed inside a tiny magnetic drive, but which uses a CompactFlash adapter to read and write information. So, it's a regular magnetic hard disk, but

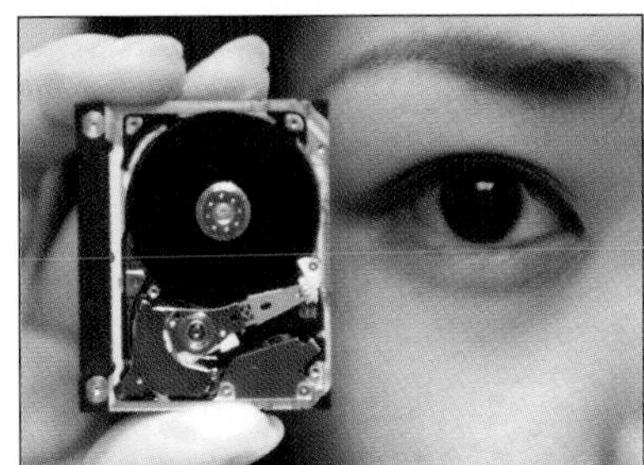

it's super tiny. What makes this little drive really different is that it plugs into a CompactFlash slot, or an adapter that you would then plug into a USB port. Or, you can use it with a camera, again by inserting it into a CompactFlash slot. You can use a micro drive with a desktop or notebook computer, or with a PDA or a digital camera.

Flash Memory Drives for Desktop and Notebook Computers

To get the convenience and security of high-capacity storage media that's small and robust for your desktop or notebook computer, you can use a flash memory drive. A ***flash memory drive*** is a flash memory storage device for a computer that is small enough to fit in your pocket and usually plugs directly into your USB port. There are several different kinds, two of which are shown in Figure 5.21 on the opposite page.

FIGURE 5.22

Some PDAs have slots for flash memory cards.

Flash Memory for PDAs

Newer i-Paqs and Palms have CompactFlash and/or SecureDigital slots built-in (see Figure 5.22). If yours doesn't, or if you need to use a different type of flash memory, you can use an expansion pack, which looks like a plastic case with the top part missing. You slide the PDA into this half-case and then slide the flash memory card into the back of the expansion pack. To learn more about flash memory, visit the Web site for this text at www.mhhe.com/i-series.

SECTION 5.3

making the grade

1. A(n) ___________ is a magnetic storage device with one or more thin metal platters (or disks) that store information sealed inside the disk drive.
2. You can write to a CD ___________ one time only.
3. A(n) ___________ is a drive that lets you read from and write information to a DVD.
4. A CompactFlash card is a type of ___________ storage.
5. A(n) ___________ is a flash memory storage medium for a computer that is small enough to fit in your pocket and usually plugs directly into your USB port.

5.4 CONSUMER Q&A

1. How Can I Tell How Many Megapixels My Camera Should Have to Print Good 8 × 10 Photos?

A rule of thumb that photographers use is to divide the pixel dimensions of the camera by 200 to get the maximum size that will still be a good picture. For example, say you have a 3-megapixel camera with 1,500 pixels across and 2,000 down, dividing by 200 would give you 7.5 × 10, so an 8 × 10 print is as large as you could go and still have a good quality picture.

2. What Type of Mouse Should I Get for Gaming?

You can get a mouse that plugs in with a PS/2 port or one that uses a USB port. A USB mouse is continuously receptive to mouse movement, whereas a PS/2 mouse checks for movement intermittently. Admittedly, this happens many, many times per second, but in games, where timing is everything, you'll get better performance with a USB mouse.

3. Are Flat Panels and Flat Screens the Same Thing?

While they sound similar, these terms are actually not the same thing at all. A flat *panel* refers to an LCD or gas plasma flat-panel display, whereas a flat *screen* means a television-like monitor with a flat rather than a curved screen. A CRT (or a traditional television) started out with a curved screen because the way it works is that electrons are sprayed from the back of the device onto the inside of the viewable screen, which is coated with phosphor. As the electrons hit the phosphor, the phosphor glows. To ensure that all the electrons hit the screen when they should, the screen has traditionally been curved, but this distorts the image somewhat. Lately, CRT manufacturers have found a way to make the screen of a CRT flat, improving the quality of the image.

4. What Should I Look for in a Scanner?

When you're choosing a scanner, its resolution is a strong determining factor in the quality of the electronic image you get. In the case of scanners, resolution is measured in dots per inch (dpi), like printers. To capture images to put on the Web, you'll be fine with 100 dots per inch, but if you want to capture text for optical character recognition, you'll need at least 300 dpi, and to be able to enlarge images and still have a good reproduction, you'll need a resolution of 1,200 or 2,400 dpi. But remember that high resolution takes up a lot of storage space, and the higher the resolution in the captured image, the longer the scanning process takes.

5.5 SUMMARY AND KEY TERMS

An ***input device*** captures information and translates it into a form that can be processed and used by other parts of your computer. Input devices include keyboards, pointing devices, game controllers, scanners, styluses, microphones, digital cameras, and Web cams. Pointing devices include ***mice, trackballs, touchpads,*** and ***pointing sticks.*** Game controllers include ***gamepads, joysticks,*** and ***gaming wheels.*** A ***scanner*** is an input device that creates an electronic image that your computer can use of text, images, maps, and so on. A ***stylus*** is an input device consisting of a thin stick that uses pressure to enter information or to click and point. A mi-

did you **know?**

Of *the people changing jobs in 2002, 59 percent wanted to move up, 58 percent wanted more money, 50 percent cited stress, and 38 percent were simply unhappy.*[5]

crophone lets you input sound. Digital cameras let you take pictures and transfer them to your computer. A ***Web cam*** is a video camera that you use to take images for uploading to the Web.

An ***output device*** takes information within your computer and presents it to you in a form you can understand. The principal output devices are monitors, printers, and speakers. Monitors come in two varieties: CRT and ***flat-panel displays.*** Flat-panel displays are either ***LCD*** (which are often advertised as ***TFT*** monitors) or ***gas plasma.*** When choosing a monitor, look for the ***VIS (visible image size), resolution of the screen, dot pitch,*** and ***refresh rate.***

Consumer printers also come in two types: inkjet and laser. ***Inkjet printers*** form images by forcing ink droplets through nozzles and come in two types: general purpose and ***photo inkjet printers.*** The photo type has more shades of colors. A ***laser printer*** forms images using an electrostatic process, the same way a photocopier works. A ***multifunction printer (MFP)*** will scan, copy, and fax, as well as print.

A ***storage device*** stores information so that you can recall and use that information at a later time. Storage is measured in ***kilobytes, megabytes,*** and ***gigabytes.*** The three technology types that store information are magnetic, optical or laser, and flash memory. There are three kinds of magnetic storage: hard disks, floppy disks and Zip disks. ***Floppy disks*** and ***Zip disks*** are removable storage media, and are similar, but Zip disks have greater capacity than floppies. ***Hard disk drives*** come in two types: internal and external. You usually connect the external type to your computer with a USB or Firewire connector.

There are two basic types of optical or laser storage (CDs and DVDs) and the major difference between them is capacity (DVDs store more). A CD or DVD with -ROM means that you can't change anything on the disc; -R or +R means that you can write to the disc one time only; and -RW or +RW or -RAM means that you can write, delete, and rewrite information.

Flash memory cards have high-capacity storage laminated inside a small piece of plastic. There are various types and they're not interchangeable. They include ***CompactFlash (CF) cards, xD-Picture Cards (xD), SmartMedia (SM) cards, SecureDigital (SD) cards, Memory Stick Media,*** and ***MultiMediaCards (MMC).***

To learn even more about the information in this chapter including sites on flash memory cards, printers, monitors, and the latest on DVD technology visit the Web site for this text at www.mhhe.com/i-series.

KEY TERMS

CD burner (p. 147)

CD-R (compact disc—recordable) (p. 146)

CD-ROM (compact disc read-only memory) (p. 145)

CD-ROM drive (p. 145)

CD-RW (compact disc—rewritable) (p. 147)

CompactFlash (CF) card (p. 148)

directional microphone (p. 136)

dot pitch (p. 139)

DVD burner (p. 147)

DVD-R or DVD+R (DVD—recordable) (p. 146)

DVD-ROM (p. 145)

DVD-ROM drive (p. 145)

DVD-RW (or DVD-RAM or DVD+RW) (p. 147)

external magnetic hard disk (p. 143)

flash memory card (p. 147)

flash memory drive (p. 149)

flat-panel display (p. 137)
floppy disk (p. 144)
force feedback (p. 134)
gamepad (p. 133)
gaming wheel (p. 134)
gas plasma display monitor (p. 138)
gigabyte (GB or Gig) (p. 142)
hard disk drive (p. 142)
hertz (p. 139)
inkjet printer (p. 140)
input device (p. 131)
internal magnetic hard disk (p. 142)
joystick (p. 134)
kilobyte (KB or K) (p. 142)
laser printer (p. 140)
LCD (liquid crystal display) monitor (p. 138)
mechanical mouse (p. 132)
megabyte (MB, M, or Meg) (p. 142)
megapixels (p. 136)
Memory Stick Media (p. 148)
mouse (p. 132)
multifunction printer (MFP) (p. 140)
MultiMediaCard (MMC) (p. 148)
optical mouse (p. 132)
output device (p. 137)
photo inkjet printer (p. 140)
pixel (picture element) (p. 138)
pointing stick (p. 133)
refresh rate or vertical scan rate (p. 139)
resolution of a printer (p. 139)
resolution of a screen (p. 138)
scanner (p. 135)
SecureDigital (SD) card (p. 148)
SmartMedia (SM) card (p. 148)
speaker (p. 141)
storage device (p. 142)
storage drive (p. 142)
storage medium (p. 142)
stylus (p. 135)
TFT (thin film transistor) display monitor (p. 138)
touchpad (p. 133)
trackball (p. 133)
VIS (visible image size) (p. 138)
Web cam (p. 136)
wireless mouse (p. 132)
xD-Picture Card (xD) (p. 148)
Zip disk (p. 144)

review of terminology

Multiple Choice

1. A mechanical mouse is
   a. an input device.
   b. an output device.
   c. a storage device.
   d. a flash memory device.
   e. none of the above.
2. An input device that is a thin stick to enter information using pressure on a screen is a
   a. pointing stick.
   b. stylus.
   c. microphone.
   d. speaker.
   e. joystick.
3. An optical mouse
   a. can be wired or wireless.
   b. uses red light to sense movement.
   c. is an input device.
   d. doesn't need a flat surface.
   e. is all of the above.
4. A TFT monitor is
   a. a flat-panel display monitor with a high-quality, crisp image.
   b. a CRT.
   c. an input device.
   d. a gas plasma display.
   e. none of the above.
5. The resolution of a monitor
   a. determines whether it's a CRT or a flat-panel display.
   b. is an unimportant factor in the quality of the image.
   c. is measured in pixels.
   d. is unaffected by the type of graphics card you have.
   e. is all of the above.
6. An inkjet printer
   a. can make multicolor output.
   b. is often used for photos.
   c. makes images by forcing ink droplets through nozzles.
   d. is relatively inexpensive compared to laser printers.
   e. is all of the above.
7. A megabyte is
   a. one thousand bytes.
   b. one million bytes.
   c. one billion bytes.
   d. one trillion bytes.
   e. none of the above.
8. A hard disk
   a. is an optical storage device.
   b. stores information by magnetizing the surface of thin platters.
   c. is removable from the drive.
   d. will soon be obsolete.
   e. is none of the above.
9. A ___________ is a high-capacity removable magnetic storage medium.
   a. Zip disk
   b. hard disk
   c. CD-ROM
   d. flash memory card
   e. controller
10. A ___________ is an optical storage medium with about three-quarters of a gigabyte of storage that you write to and change.
    a. DVD-ROM
    b. CD-ROM
    c. DVD-R
    d. CD-R
    e. CD-RW

True/False

11. ____ A directional microphone usually uses multiple microphones.
12. ____ A Web cam is a video camera that you use to record images for uploading to the Web.
13. ____ The term "MFP" refers to a printer that can print on either plain paper or photo paper.
14. ____ The refresh rate is the same as the vertical scan rate.
15. ____ SecureDigital (SD) cards and Memory Stick Media look identical.

Take this quiz online at www.mhhe.com/i-series and get instant feedback.

QUESTIONS AND EXERCISES

1. Stacking Bytes

In this chapter we saw a lot of material on storage devices. Anyone who talks about computers will use the terms "kilobyte," "megabyte," and "gigabyte." In the text, you learned that a byte is equivalent to one character, such as a "P" or "7" or "$." You also learned that we round off the storage capacity of kilobyte, megabyte, and gigabyte for the sake of convenience. Below are the exact numbers of bytes in each of these and several more storage capacity measures.

Your task is to figure out what this means in terms of typewritten sheets of paper and how high will they reach if you were to make a paper tower for each unit of capacity (kilobyte, megabyte, and so on).

Unit of Capacity	Exact Size in Bytes
Kilobyte (KB or K)	1,024
Megabyte (MB or M or Meg)	1,048,576
Gigabyte (GB or Gig)	1,073,741,824
Terabyte (TB)	1,099,511,627,776
Petabyte (PB)	1,125,899,906,843,624
Exabyte (EB)	1,152,921,504,607,870,976
Zettabyte (ZB)	1,180,591,620,718,458,879,424
Yottabyte (YB)	1,208,925,819,615,701,892,530,176

Unit of Capacity	Number of Sheets of Paper	Height of Paper Tower
Kilobyte (KB or K)		
Megabyte (MB or M or Meg)		
Gigabyte (GB or Gig)		
Terabyte (TB)		
Petabyte (PB)		
Exabyte (EB)		
Zettabyte (ZB)		
Yottabyte (YB)		

Some facts you should know before you embark on this task:

- If you type in 12 pt Courier font, double-spaced, and have 1" margins on a page, you can fit about 1,000 characters on the page, including periods, spaces, and such.
- You can round each unit as we normally do, i.e., consider a kilobyte to be about 1,000 characters, rather than 1,024 characters.
- A ream (or package) of paper that you buy for a printer contains 500 sheets and stands about 2" high.
- Twelve inches equals one foot, and 5,280 feet equals one mile.
- When working through this exercise you can ignore any reduction in the height of the paper tower caused by pressure on the lower sheets of paper from those on top.

Assignment:

A. Calculate the number of reams of paper it would take to fill sheets of paper with 12 pt Courier type if you used 1" margins for each unit of capacity.

B. Calculate how high each stack of paper would reach.

C. Make a graph of the results.

2. Organizing Input and Output Devices

Make a hierarchy chart of input and output devices. In this chapter you saw hierarchy charts for the different types of storage (see Figures 5.13 and 5.16). One for input and output devices would start out as follows (you will have to add more boxes vertically and horizontally):

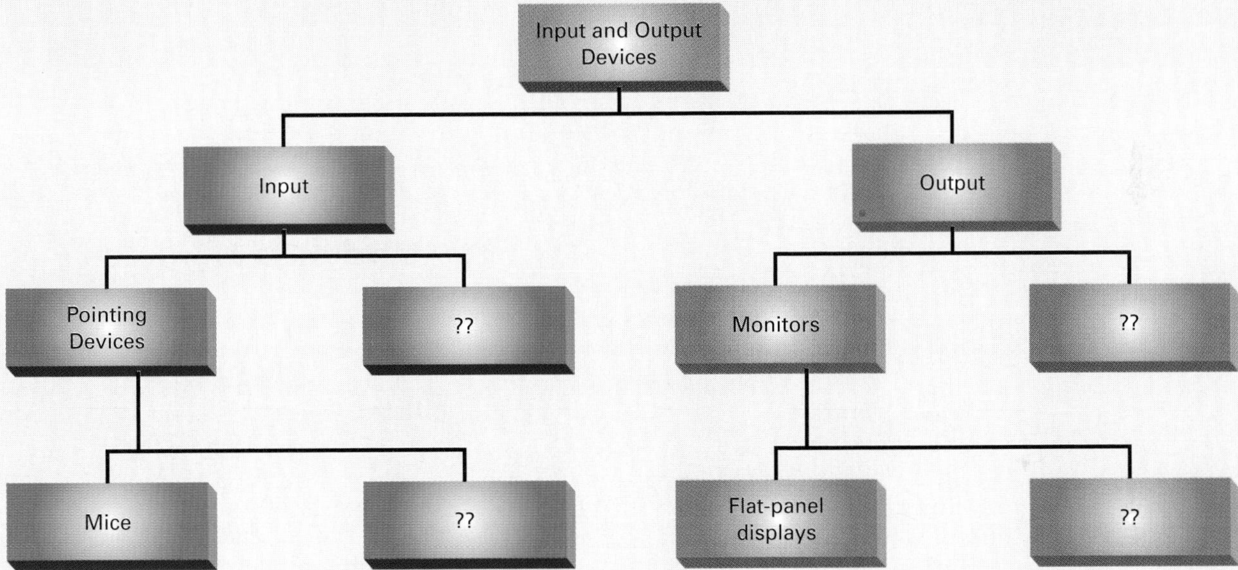

Assignment:

A. Make a hierarchy chart of all the input and output devices listed in this chapter, showing the category into which each device fits.

B. Find two input devices and two output devices not discussed in this chapter and put them in the appropriate places.

e-commerce

1. Choosing a Digital Camera

Like everything else, digital cameras range greatly in price, quality, and the number and type of features. Visit the following Web sites and make a table comparing digital cameras on the market. Here are some Web sites to try, or you can find others on your own.

- Canon—www.canon.com
- Kodak—www.kodak.com
- Sony—www.sony.com
- Olympus—www.olympus.com

Make a comparison of five different cameras and answer the following questions for each one:

a. How much does the camera cost?
b. What is the camera's highest resolution in megapixels?
c. What is the overall size and weight of the camera?
d. What sort of batteries does it use? Rechargeable? AA?
e. What is the optical zoom capability?
f. What sort of storage medium does the camera use? Is it CompactFlash or SecureDigital cards or something else?
g. Can this camera make video clips and record sound?

2. Buying Books

Buying books on the Web is a simple process. Just connect to any one of hundreds of sites selling books, find the ones you want, pay for them (usually by credit card), and wait for them to arrive in the mail. Let's see how this process works.

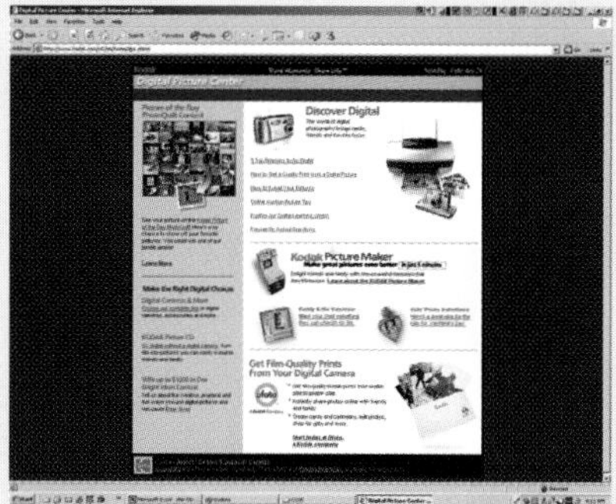

Below, we've provided four sites that sell books. Connect to two of them.

- Amazon—www.amazon.com
- Barnes & Noble—www.barnesandnoble.com
- Borders—www.borders.com
- Fat Brain—www.fatbrain.com

Now, think of a book that you'd like to buy (it can be one you already own or perhaps even a textbook like this one). For that book, answer the following questions:

a. How can you search for that book—by author, title, category, or perhaps some other way?
b. Does the site recommend other books you might be interested in based on the one you're looking for?
c. Is there a shipping fee? If so, what is it?
d. How can you pay for the book? Do you have to use a credit card?

3. Renting an Apartment

You'll probably need to look for an apartment some time if you haven't already. You could check classified ads or bulletin boards to find an apartment. But what if you need an apartment in another city? Let's check some Web sites that can help you find an apartment. As you use these sites, enter the same criteria to search for your apartment. For example, you might need a one-bedroom that allows cats for under $600 a month. Choose your own criteria and search the following Web sites:

- HomeStore.com—www.homestore.com
- ApartmentLinks—www.apartmentlinks.net
- Apartment Living/Rental—apartments.about.com

Now, answer the following questions:

a. Were you able to find an apartment using these sites? Was one site easier to use than another? Why or why not?
b. What if you wanted a roommate? Is it possible using these services? Would you use them to do this? Why or why not?

ethics, security & privacy

1. How's My Driving? Just Pop Out the Flash Memory Card!

Teens who feel safe from the watchful eyes of their parents while out driving with friends may not be for very much longer. A company called Road Safety International now makes a product called SafeForce™. It's a "black box" for an automobile. Black boxes in airplanes record everything that happens in the cockpit. Similarly, the SafeForce box records everything that happens and when. It even goes further than a cockpit black box would by issuing a warning to the driver about unsafe driving like speeding, hard braking, rapid acceleration, and hard cornering. If the driver ignores the first warning tone and continues to drive unsafely, the box emits a steady tone until the driver alters the offending behavior.

If parents want to know where the teen went and all the details of journey, all they have to do is pop the flash memory card out of the black box, plug it into their computer system, and download all the details. Isn't flash memory great?

What do you think about this new ability we now have to monitor each other's driving?

a. Should parents be able to check up on their children's driving?
b. What about someone driving your car? Should you be able to monitor that person?
c. Would you drive differently if someone in authority were able to check out the details of all your trips?
d. This SafeForce black box was first used to monitor emergency vehicles, which save countless lives, but are also somewhat of a danger on the road. Is this a good application of the box? Shouldn't emergency vehicles be made as safe as possible?
e. Should people who have a certain number or type of traffic citations have to have a black box in their cars at all times? Why or why not?

2. The All-Seeing Global Positioning System

A GPS (global positioning system) is a small device that can tell you where you are to within a few feet. You can buy a hand-held GPS or it can be part of another system. A GPS can tell you (or anyone else) what direction you're moving and at what speed. GPSs already have many applications, and have many more possibilities. Let's examine some of the implications of this technology.

a. Do you think that parents would want to put a chip into a baby's body at birth so that babies in the hospital could no longer be swapped by mistake?
b. Do you think that parents would like to know whether the baby-sitter took their baby out of the house and where they went?
c. If you think that identifying chips implanted in babies is a good idea, then at what age should we remove the chip? 10? 14? 18? 21? Never?
d. If you think that implanted chips are too much, how about something less intrusive? For example, you could put the tracking system in the book bags of school-age children. Such systems are now available. A good idea or not?

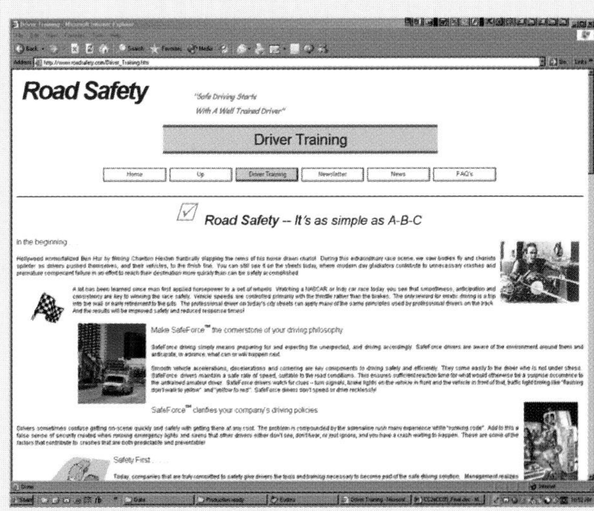

on the web

1. Comparing Printers

If you're considering buying a printer, you'll probably be choosing between inkjet and laser printers. Each has its strengths and weaknesses. Look at the following Web sites, or choose your own, and pick three inkjet and three laser printers.

- Epson—www.epson.com
- Hewlett Packard—www.hp.com
- Lexmark—www.lexmark.com
- Canon—www.canon.com

Compare the six printers and answer the following questions for each one.

a. What does the printer cost?
b. Does the printer have color? If so, what color cartridges/tanks does it have?
c. What does it cost to replace all the cartridges/tanks?
d. What is the speed of the printer measured in pages per minute (ppm)?
e. What is the resolution of the printer?
f. Does the printer promise good photos?
g. Does the printer take flash memory cards directly (i.e., can you print without a computer)?

2. Buying a Hard Drive

A hard drive has been a basic necessity on computer systems for a long time, and it looks as if that situation will continue into the foreseeable future. The biggest difference, from a consumer point of view, between one hard drive and another is its capacity. However, there are other features that may make a difference, depending on your productivity needs. Look at the following Web sites or others:

- Microwarehouse—www.microwarehouse.com
- Best Buy—www.bestbuy.com
- Circuit City—www.circuitcity.com
- Gateway—www.gateway.com

Choose five hard disk drives from five different manufacturers and answer the following questions about each one.

a. What is the capacity of the hard disk drive?
b. What is the cost of the drive?
c. What is the rotational speed (revolutions per minute or rpm) of the drive?
d. Is the drive internal or external?
e. Is the drive intended for a desktop or notebook or some other type of electronic gadget?

3. Ordering Photos Online

Most people love to have photos. Photos serve to remind us of people, places, and events that we want to remember. In this information age we have more choices than ever in photos we can have and how we display them. With digital photos you can even change the image easily.

You can get your film photos developed by processing businesses that are online. They will let you retrieve your photos from the Internet or put them onto a CD-ROM for you.

Here are some photo-related sites:

- Photo Works—www.photoworks.com
- Photo Alley—www.photoalley.com
- Shop@kodak—www.kodak.com
- Timeless Photo & Imaging—timelessphoto.com

Use the sites above, or find your own, and answer the following questions.

a. Does the site develop rolls of film?
b. Can you view your photos online?
c. Does the site offer a "smart" frame? (Hint: Try the Kodak site.)
d. Will the site make calendars for you?
e. Will the site make greeting cards out of your photos for you?

group activities

1. Exploring the Use of Web Cams

Web cams are everywhere. You may even have one trained on you as you read this. You can travel virtually to places all over the world by viewing Web cam images. Find Web cam pictures of at least four of the following:

a. Three capital cities in Europe.
b. Three capital cities in Asia.
c. Three capital cities in Africa.
d. Three capital cities in Australia.
e. The Sphinx in Egypt.
f. The Eiffel Tower in France.
g. The Taj Mahal in India.
h. The Sydney Opera House in Australia.
i. The Great Wall of China.

2. Researching DVD Recorders

In this chapter you read the discussion on DVD burners. There's another name for a DVD burner when it's used instead of a VCR to record television broadcasts. These DVD burners are marketed as "DVD recorders."

Find three DVD burners and three DVD recorders and compare them in relation to the following features.

a. Price.
b. Whether editing tools are available.
c. Type of DVD they use.
d. Connectors and ease of connectivity (may be a matter of opinion).

3. Multimedia Controller

People who do a lot of digital video editing often invest in a trackball-like device called a *multimedia controller* that's designed for multimedia development. One example of a multimedia controller is the ShuttlePro that has a knob capable of rotating 360 degrees, giving you better frame-by-frame control. It also has several speeds and programmable buttons for one-touch editing operations.

Find a comparable product and see how it stacks up to the ShuttlePro. Also find three different digital video editing software packages and compare them.

4. Protect Your Computer from Unauthorized Use

In an increasingly security-conscious world, pointing devices that won't click and point for just anyone are coming onto the market. One such device is a biometric mouse. It checks out the hand of the person moving it and verifies whether that person is authorized to do so or not. Another kind of biometric mouse reads your fingerprint, comparing it to its database of fingerprints and looking for a match. Another reads the veins in your hand. Look on the Web for the following information. Find:

a. A fingerprint mouse.
b. Another kind of fingerprint reader (that is not a mouse).
c. A signature identification device.
d. A voice authentication device.

crossword puzzle

Across

3. Radio frequency wireless standard
6. It carries information around the motherboard
8. Eight-bit coding system
10. It's within the CPU
12. Plug
13. A way of saving power in notebook CPUs
15. The _______ unit is where the motherboard is
16. Billions of cycles per second
17. Type of card that joins the device to the motherboard
20. Used by one manufacturer of mobile CPUs
21. _______ and play
22. A slot for an expansion card
25. Where a connector goes
26. Radio frequency
28. Is a type of connector
29. "Waiting room" memory for instructions
33. A special kind of notebook CPU
34. Coding system of large computers
37. A PC Card goes into a PC Card _______
38. Computer's brain
39. A 1 or 0
40. Type of connector

Down

1. Temporary storage for instructions and information
2. The type of bus that carries information to and from PCI slots
3. Two-valued system
4. A 16-bit coding system
5. Intel's new way to make CPUs run faster
6. Another name for a card
7. Expansion board for microphone and speakers
9. A character
11. Uses phone lines to connect computers
14. Expansion slot for video card
18. A key _______ traps every keystroke
19. Hot _______
22. A type of network
23. A connector for a printer
24. Wireless
27. Millions of cycles per second
29. An expansion _______
30. Keeps time for the CPU
31. Unit that retrieves instructions from RAM
32. The card that sends images to your monitor
35. CPU _______ has 4 steps
36. Type of port

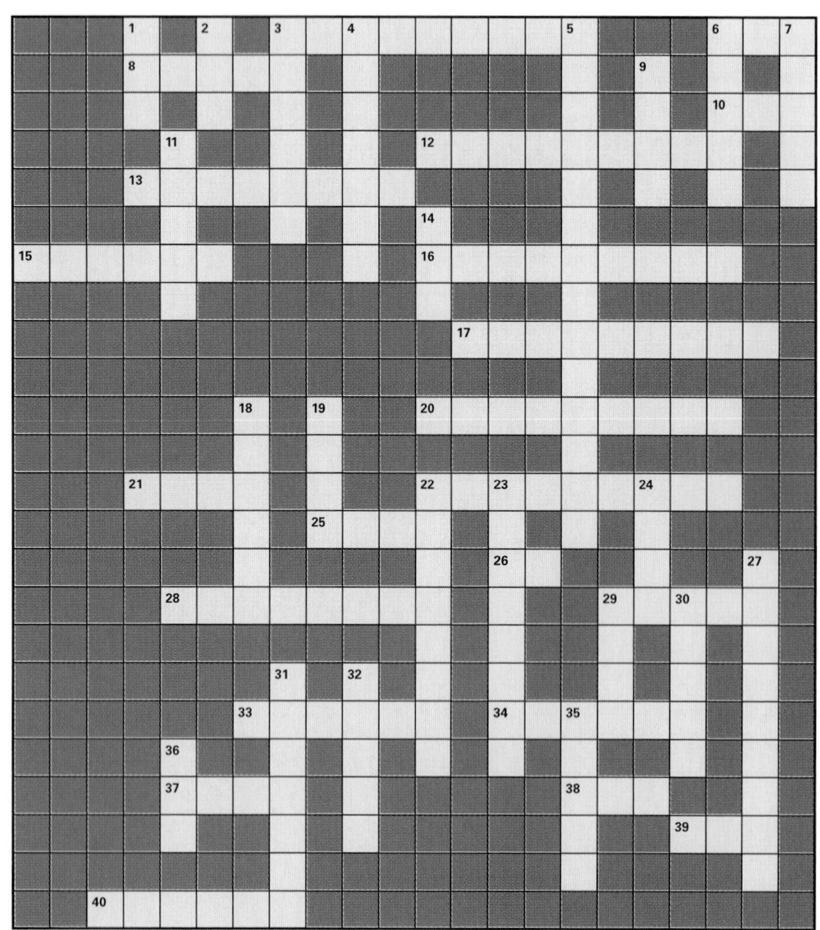

CHAPTER six

6

Computer Architecture

How Does a Computer Work?

SIMNET CONCEPTS SUPPORT

did you know?

Gordon Moore, co-founder of Intel, coined Moore's Law in 1965, which says that computing power doubles every 18 months. Below are some examples of CPU power.

the *Intel 8080 CPU, introduced in 1974, was one of the very early CPUs for consumer computers. It had 6,000 transistors and could manage a speed of up to 2 megahertz. Intel's contemporary Pentium 4 can run at a speed of 3.06 gigahertz (that's 1,530 times faster than the 8080) and has 55 million transistors (that's almost 10,000 times as many as the 8080).*

the *Cray X1, one of biggest, fastest computers in the world, is a supercomputer. Instead of one, or maybe two CPUs, it is scalable and can have up to 4,096 CPUs in 64 separate modules, called cabinets, that are tied together. The only catch is that it costs millions of dollars.*

the *chief technology officer at Intel says that Intel expects to be selling __??__-gigahertz CPUs for desktop computers (which is roughly 5 times the current speed) by 2010. PDAs should be running 5-gigahertz CPUs by that time.*

To find out how fast CPUs for desktop computers will be in 2010, visit our Web site at www.mhhe.com/i-series.

Student Learning Outcomes

After reading this chapter, you should be able to:

1. Identify the system unit as well as the motherboard with its components.
2. Define ASCII and describe how information is represented inside a computer.
3. Describe the role of the CPU, RAM, and CPU cycles in the functioning of a computer.
4. Define and explain the role of connectors, ports, expansion buses, expansion cards, and expansion slots.
5. Describe how you connect external devices to your computer.

At one end of the spectrum we have computers as big as a giant warehouse, such as the Cray X1 described on the opening page. The Cray comes in configurations of between 1 and 64 separate CPU cabinets, each of which has a footprint of about 3.5 feet by 7 feet. This doesn't even include storage modules. At the other end of the spectrum is a tiny computer the size of a credit card being developed by Sharp. The company, which makes computer monitors, expects that by 2005 it will be selling LCD screens that are 2 millimeters (1⁄12 inch) thick with a CPU built in, so that each little screen will, in fact, be a complete computer.

No matter how big or small computers are, they all have certain characteristics in common—for example they all have system units (see Figure 6.1). A ***system unit*** is what many people refer to as "the computer," that is, the case or box with the motherboard, internal storage units, and power supply. In this chapter we'll look at what's inside the system unit, because it's there that we can find the answers to questions like:

- "Why does my computer take longer to load a file with a lot of photos than my buddy's does?"
- "Why is it that when I have several applications open and then attempt to get on the Internet, I get a message saying something about insufficient memory?"
- "How come this Web cam I bought says on the box that it's 'USB 2.0 compatible,' but when I plug it into the USB port on my own computer it doesn't go as fast as it's supposed to?"

FIGURE 6.1

Desktop and notebook computers as well as tablet PCs all have system units that contain the computer "engine."

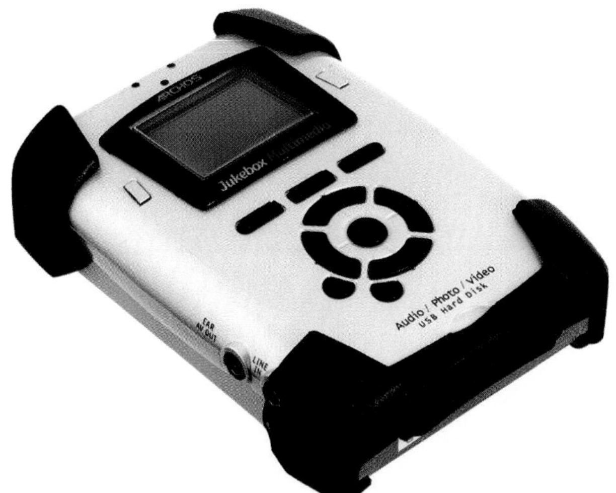

FIGURE 6.2

The Archos Jukebox can store the music of about 200 CDs (compressed in MP3 format), 200,000 photos, or 40 hours of video (compressed in MP4 format).

6.1 THE BIG PICTURE

To be able to answer these and other computer-related questions, you need to understand how things work inside the system unit and also how information goes from outside to inside the system unit, gets transformed, and comes out as something you can see or hear.

Let's work through an example. Say you have an Archos Jukebox 20 MP3 Player (see Figure 6.2). With 20 gigabytes of storage, it will store as much music for you as 200 CDs would. Of course, the music files are in a compressed MP3 format. When you get past the hype (Archos is marketed as a hand-held entertainment center), an Archos is a hard disk drive, although it's also a small, specialized computer that converts MP3 files into sound and, additionally, has a microphone for recording audio, and the multimedia model even has a little LCD screen on which you can view photos or video stored on the device. However, the Archos is primarily a hard disk, so you can store anything on it that you could store on any other hard disk.

When you want to play music, you have to attach the Archos to headphones or speakers. Let's assume you have a great sound system on your computer, and you'd like to play your Archos MP3 music files through your computer's speakers.

THE JOURNEY FROM AN EXTERNAL STORAGE DEVICE TO AN OUTPUT DEVICE

How Does Music Move from the Archos to the Speakers?

There are several steps involved in getting the music from the Archos hard drive to your computer's speakers so that you can hear the output. First, you have to connect the Archos to your computer to give the music data a pathway to travel on. Second, on your command, a copy of the directory, or a listing of available music data files, on the Archos device travels from the device into your computer. Third, again on your command, the music data you've chosen to play is brought into your computer and is processed to sound format. Last, the music moves to your speakers and is amplified so that you can hear it. Sounds simple enough, doesn't it? Actually, it's really not complicated.

FIGURE 6.3

The motherboard is the base that connects all computer components together so that information and instructions can move between them.

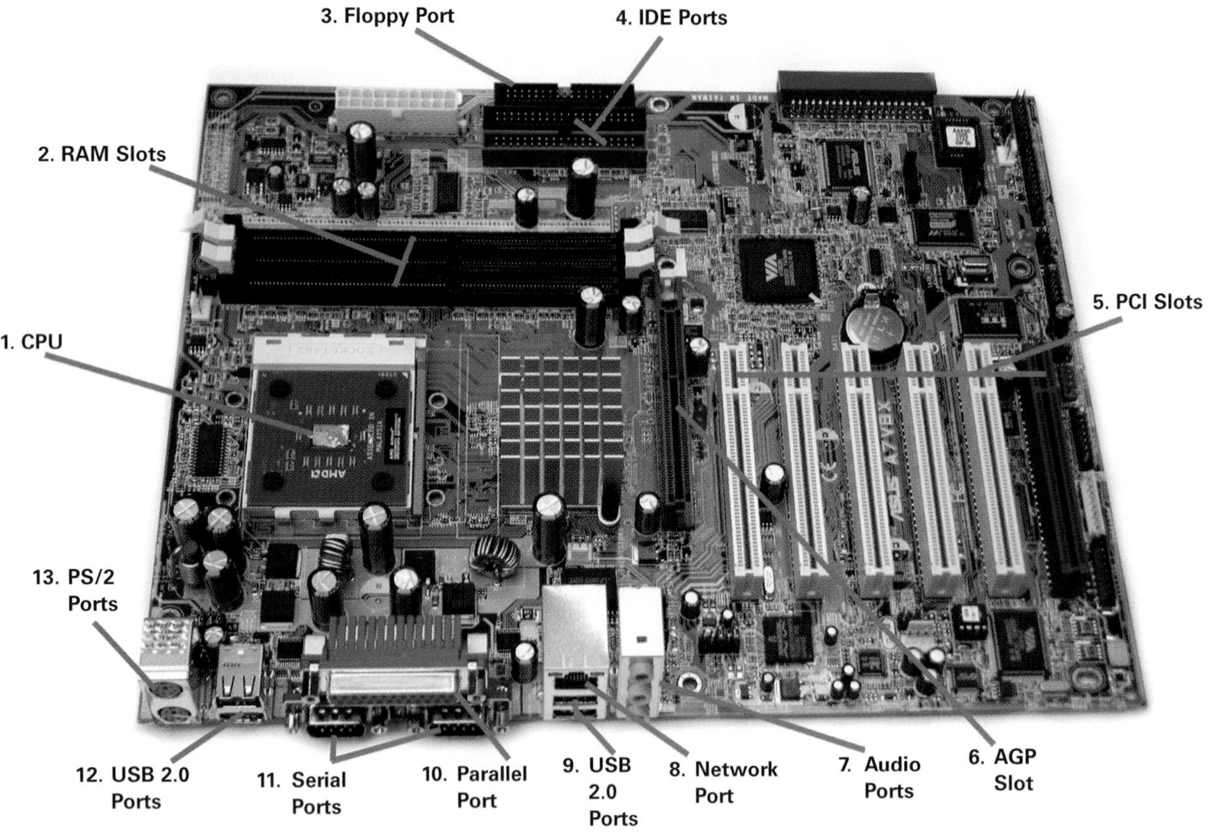

1. **CPU:** The central processing unit is the chip that carries out the instructions it receives from the software.
2. **RAM slots:** This is where the RAM modules go.
3. **Floppy port:** You'd plug an internal floppy drive in here.
4. **IDE ports (2):** Here you'd plug in internal storage devices like a hard disk drive or a CD-RW drive.
5. **PCI slots:** These slots are for expansion cards, sound cards, video cards, and modem cards.
6. **AGP slot:** This is a specialized slot for an AGP video card.
7. **Audio ports:** Here you'd plug in speakers and a microphone.
8. **Network port:** This is where a network connector, which looks like the connector on the end of a phone wire except that it's a little bigger, would go.
9. **USB 2.0 ports (2):** Here you'd plug in a scanner, digital camera, perhaps a printer, and an external hard drive.
10. **Parallel port:** Used almost exclusively for connecting printers.
11. **Serial ports (2):** Here you could plug in a mouse or a trackball.
12. **USB 2.0 ports (2):** Same as #9 in this list.
13. **PS/2 ports (2):** These ports are almost exclusively for keyboard and mouse connectors, although these devices are often USB 2.0 nowadays.

Let's look at each step in more detail. In doing so, we'll refer to Figure 6.3, which shows a motherboard. A ***motherboard*** is the major circuit board inside the system unit connecting all computer components together so that information and instructions can move between them. To learn more about motherboards, complete "The Motherboard" tutorial on your SimNet Concepts Support CD.

Step 1: Connecting to the Computer

One way to connect the Archos would be to use a cable with USB 2.0 connectors on each end. One end goes into your computer's USB 2.0 port and the other into the Archos USB 2.0 port.

A ***connector*** is the plug on the end of a wire from a device, like a printer, hard disk, or scanner, that you use to connect the device to the computer (see Figure 6.4). A ***port*** is the place on your system unit, monitor, or keyboard through which information and instructions flow to your computer system. For wired connections it's the place where you insert the connector, and for wireless devices a port is where the wave information goes in and out. Have a look at the USB 2.0 ports on the motherboard in Figure 6.3, #9 and #12.

The physical connection you establish with the cable gives the music a means of traveling from the device to the computer. That physical connection is detected by the operating system, which lists the device in the **My Computer** folder.

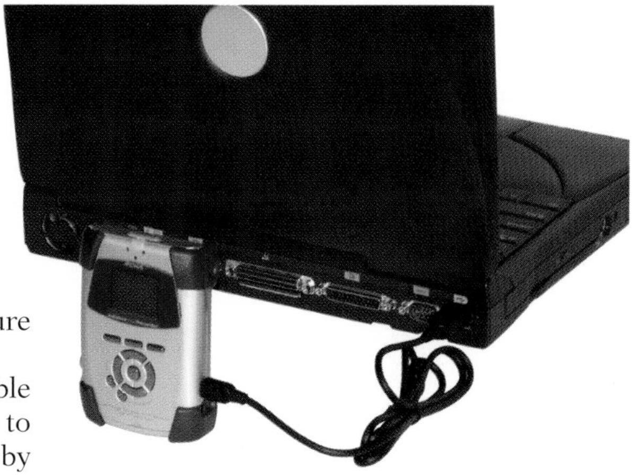

FIGURE 6.4

A USB 2.0 connector is a plug that you use to connect a device to your computer.

Step 2: Bringing the Music Inside

To get to the music files you would double-click on the folder that contains the Archos listing. The double-click action is your command to the CPU (see Figure 6.3, #1) to tell the operating system to open the folder and show you the files that are in the folder. The ***central processing unit (CPU*** or ***processor)*** is the chip that carries out instructions it receives from your software. The operating system software, or at least part of it, is always in RAM because that's the software that makes the computer work. In Figure 6.3, #2, you can see the slots where RAM modules go. ***RAM (random access memory)*** is temporary memory that holds software instructions and information for the CPU.

When you see the names of the music files, you would double-click on the name of the music file that you want played. That's your command to the operating system to load the application software (like WinAmp or MediaPlayer) that has the instructions that will retrieve the file from the Archos and process it into sound. Application software has to be loaded into RAM when needed, usually from your internal hard disk.

Step 3: Loading and Processing the Music Data

The CPU executes the MediaPlayer instructions to bring the music data into RAM. The music data then travels along the wire, in through the USB 2.0 port, and along the expansion bus to RAM. The ***expansion bus*** forms the highway system on the motherboard that moves information coming from and going to devices outside the motherboard. MediaPlayer also has instructions that the CPU uses to tell the sound card to convert the music data from its digital format (1s and 0s) to sound. Everything that's processed or stored on your computer is in the form of 1s and 0s.

FIGURE 6.5

A sound card is hardware that you would insert into an expansion slot, connecting the speakers and microphone to the ports so that you can hear audio. These days, sound cards are usually integrated into the motherboard, but you may want to use a different sound card.

Step 4: Music Comes out of the Speakers, Finally!

Next, the CPU executes the operating system instructions that send the music to a sound card. Your sound card is the hardware that delivers the sound out to the wires connected to the speakers. Our sound card, in this instance, is integrated into the motherboard in Figure 6.3 on page 164 (so you can't see it), but you can see the port (Figure 6.3, #7) that you would plug the speakers into using the audio connector.

Sometimes, a sound card is an expansion card (a circuit board) that plugs into an expansion slot (see Figure 6.5). An ***expansion slot*** is a long skinny socket on the motherboard into which you insert an expansion card. Figure 6.3, #5 shows six PCI expansion slots (five white and one blue), good for a variety of expansion cards. An ***expansion card (*** or ***board)*** is a circuit board that you insert into the expansion slot on the motherboard and to which you connect a peripheral device. To learn more about how your computer works internally, complete the "Inside the Computer" tutorial on your SimNet Concepts Support CD.

SECTION 6.1

making the grade

1. A(n) ___________ is the plug on the end of a wire from a device that you use to connect the device to the computer.
2. The place on your system unit through which information and instructions flow is called a ___________.
3. The ___________ is the chip that carries out instructions it receives from your software.
4. A(n) ___________ is a long skinny socket on the motherboard into which you insert an expansion card.
5. The ___________ forms the highway system on the motherboard that moves information coming from and going to devices outside the motherboard.

6.2 REPRESENTING INFORMATION INSIDE A COMPUTER

If you could peek inside RAM when the music arrives from the Archos, you'd see that the music data is all numbers, more specifically, all zeroes and ones—that is, digital. Computers use only these two digits to represent all information of every kind. How and why do they do this?

BINARY

What Is Binary?

In written English, our communication symbols include 56 alphabetic characters (A . . . Z and a . . . z); 10 numeric symbols (0 . . . 9); and many other miscellaneous characters such as the dash and dollar sign, for example. Other Western languages have similar symbol sets. Many Asian languages employ thousands of symbols.

The challenge, then, is to convert our complex natural language into something the computer can manipulate. So we use binary code, which consists of two digits, 0 and 1 (binary refers to any two-valued system). The 1 and 0 correspond to the computer's on-state and off-state, respectively. Computer components function on the basis of whether electricity is present or not. Thus they have two states—they understand two signals—on and off. Each 1 or 0 is called a ***bit.*** "Bit" is a contraction of the term binary digit. Everything is reduced to these bits or digits since that's the only form of information a CPU can process.

So, all our human communication symbols have to be converted into a code of 1s and 0s for processing and storage by computers, and then back again to human language for output. The obvious way to do that is to group the bits so that each unique pattern of 1s and 0s represents one natural language character.

By combining bits into groups of 8, we can make 256 (2^8) different patterns (see Figure 6.6). This is sufficient to represent the basic set of symbols we use in English and similar alphabets and therefore has become the standard over time. Each group of 8 bits is used to represent one natural language character and is called a ***byte.*** Each byte, hence each of 256 natural language characters, has a unique pattern of 1s and 0s. For example, if you were to type the word "COOL" on the keyboard, it would change into four bytes—one for each character—that would look like the following so it could be stored in RAM:

01000011	01001111	01001111	01001100
C	O	O	L

ASCII, EBCDIC, AND UNICODE

Does Every Computer Use the Same Coding System?

For software and information to be transferable from computer to computer, we need a standard for converting human communication symbols into binary code. The set of patterns, or coding system, that you saw used above for the characters in the word "COOL" is called ASCII.

0	1	1	0	0	0	1	0

FIGURE 6.6

A byte, 8 bits, is equivalent to one of our natural language characters. Each byte has a unique pattern of 1s and 0s. This one is a "b" in ASCII.

FIGURE 6.7

ASCII and EBCDIC are different ways of representing natural language characters in binary code.

Your Characters	ASCII	EBCDIC
(space)	00100000	01000000
!	00100001	01011010
#	00100011	01111011
0	00110000	11110000
1	00110001	11110001
2	00110010	11110010
3	00110011	11110011
A	01000001	11000001
B	01000010	11000010
a	01100001	10000001
b	01100010	10000010

ASCII (American Standard Code for Information Interchange), pronounced ASK-ee, is the eight-bit coding system that most personal computers use (see Figure 6.7). Large IBM computers use another set of patterns called ***EBCDIC.*** When information moves between ASCII and EBCDIC computers, the characters have to be converted into the appropriate coding system.

The 256 patterns that we get from the ASCII and EBCDIC encoding systems work well enough in languages that use alphabets similar to the English alphabet, but are inadequate for encoding languages that have many more symbols than English does. The solution to this problem is Unicode. ***Unicode*** is a coding system that uses 16 bits instead of 8, allowing for approximately 65,000 (2^{16}) different patterns. This is enough patterns to incorporate the characters required by the government standards of many Asian countries including Japan, Korea, China, and Taiwan. Additionally, Unicode also accommodates symbols used in the West that don't fit into the 256 patterns of ASCII such as various mathematical symbols, currency symbols, and miscellaneous other symbols such as the recycling symbol.

Because the first 256 patterns are the same as ASCII, Unicode is usable on ASCII computers too. The Windows NT operating systems (which include Windows 2000 and Windows XP) use Unicode. To learn more about binary, complete the "Data Representation Using Binary Codes" tutorial on your SimNet Concepts Support CD.

SECTION 6.2

making the grade

1. A 1 or a 0 is called a(n) __________, which stands for binary digit.
2. A group of 8 bits that represents a natural language character is called a(n) __________.
3. The 8-bit coding system that most personal computers use is called __________.
4. A coding system that uses 16 bits instead of 8 is called __________.
5. The term __________ stands for any two-valued system.

6.3 CPU, RAM, AND MACHINE CYCLES

The CPU is there to carry out software instructions. It does so in a very precise set of steps, called a machine or CPU cycle, that we'll discuss shortly. First, we'll examine the CPU itself.

THE CENTRAL PROCESSING UNIT (CPU)

What Does the CPU Do?

The CPU carries out both system software and application software instructions (see Figure 6.8). The CPU's role in your computer system is analogous to the role of your brain—which is your body's processor. Your brain performs two types of tasks. The first is to keep your body functioning; your brain controls your breathing, heartbeat, digestion, and so on. Your computer's equivalent is system software. Beyond these "housekeeping" tasks, your brain also has control over those jobs that your body performs because you want it to, like playing basketball or planting trees. Your computer's equivalent is application software.

It's obvious that, for your brain to process either system instructions (to keep your body going) or application instructions (to carry out particular tasks you direct your body to perform), it has to be connected to all your body parts so that messages can pass back and forth, and this is the role of your nervous system. Similarly, all computer components must be connected to the CPU. The motherboard provides the base for these connections. The CPU is seated into the motherboard and tiny wires radiate from it out to all computer components, which are either positioned on the motherboard (like RAM) or connected to the motherboard through special plugs or connectors (as your monitor is). To learn more about CPUs, complete "The CPU" tutorial on your SimNet Concepts Support CD.

RAM or memory is the workspace from which the CPU draws instructions and information when it needs them. It's also the place where the CPU puts processed information—the answers to calculations, the formatted document, the image you're editing. When you save a file, you're transferring the copy that's in RAM to a storage medium such as a CD or a Zip disk.

FIGURE 6.8

The CPU is the chip that carries out the instructions from the software.

RANDOM ACCESS MEMORY (RAM)

What Does RAM Do?

Along with your CPU, how much memory, or RAM, you have in your computer makes a big difference in what your computer can do and how fast it can do it. RAM holds:

- Operating system instructions that must be available to the CPU all the time the computer is on, since they are necessary to keep the computer functioning.
- The application software instructions you're using (such as Word or a Web browser).
- The document, picture, spreadsheet, Web page, etc., that you're working on.
- Your keyboard strokes and mouse movements.

To learn more about RAM, complete the "Memory" tutorial on your SimNet Concepts Support CD.

HOW INSTRUCTIONS ARE PROCESSED

What Happens to Make Software Work?

A ***machine cycle*** or a ***CPU cycle*** consists of retrieving, decoding, and executing the instruction, then returning the result to RAM, if necessary (see Figure 6.9). When you load (or open) a program, you're telling your computer to send a copy of the program from the storage device (hard disk or CD) into RAM. In carrying out the software instructions, the CPU repeatedly performs machine cycles as follows:

1. *Retrieve an instruction:* The ***control unit,*** which is the component of the CPU that directs what happens in your computer, sends a request to RAM for the next instruction and the information it needs. If the instruction says to add 4 and 6, the two numbers travel as information with the *add* instruction. The instruction travels from RAM on the system bus. The ***system bus*** consists of electrical pathways that move information between basic components of the motherboard, including between RAM and the CPU. When the instruction reaches the CPU it waits temporarily in ***CPU cache,*** which is a type of memory on the CPU where instructions called up by the CPU wait until the CPU is ready to use them. It takes much less time to get the instruction from cache to the control unit than from RAM, so cache speeds up processing.
2. *Decode the instruction:* The CPU gets the instruction out of cache, examines it to see what needs to be done, in this case, add 4 and 6.
3. *Execute the instruction:* The CPU then does what the instruction says to do. In our example, it sends the two numbers to the arithmetic logic unit to be added. The ***arithmetic logic unit (ALU)*** is a component of the CPU that performs arithmetic, as well as comparison and logic operations.
4. *Store the result in RAM:* The CPU then sends the result of the addition, 10, to RAM. There's not always a result to send back to RAM. Sometimes the CPU does intermediate calculations that don't get saved.

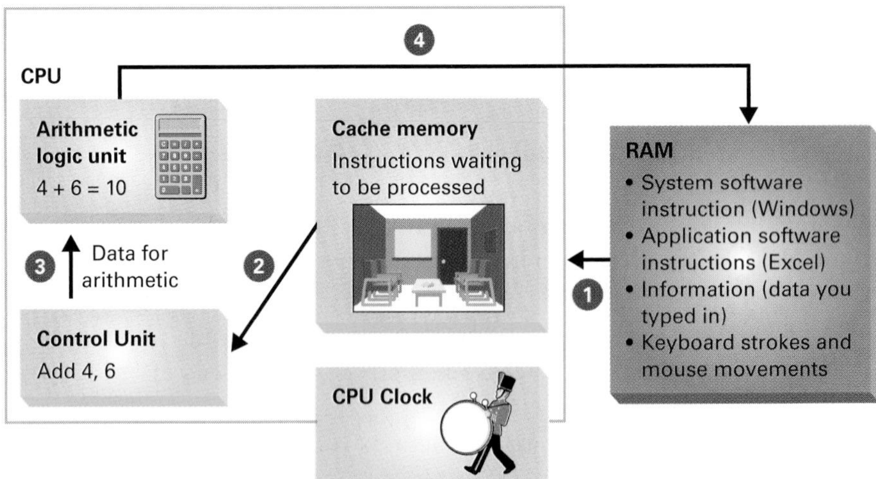

FIGURE 6.9

Instructions move from RAM into the CPU to be executed, and then the result is stored back in RAM, if necessary.

Step	Action
1	Get the instruction from RAM and put it into cache.
2	Decode the instruction.
3	Execute the instruction.
4	Store the result in RAM, if necessary.

FIGURE 6.10

A machine or CPU cycle has four steps.

You'll sometimes hear the CPU speed referred to as the "clock speed." This refers to the CPU clock. Every CPU has its own ***CPU clock,*** which is simply a sliver of quartz that beats at regular intervals in response to an electrical charge. The beat of the CPU clock is like the drummer in a marching band. Just as the drummer keeps everyone marching in time, the CPU clock keeps all your computer's operations synchronized. Each beat or tick of the CPU clock is called a clock cycle and is equivalent to a CPU cycle, also called a machine cycle. The CPU uses the CPU clock to keep instructions and information marching through your CPU at a fixed rate. To learn more about the role of your CPU clock, complete the "System Clock" tutorial on your SimNet Concepts Support CD.

The CPU completes one or more machine cycles for every tick of the CPU clock (see Figure 6.10). Nothing outside your CPU moves that fast. Some instructions are complex and take more than one machine cycle, and others are simpler and take less, so the number of instructions processed per second is not the same as the number of clock cycles. Some tasks require a lot more instructions than others. For example, putting graphics on the screen requires a lot more CPU time than text because it takes lots of calculations to get the color and intensity of each pixel just right. Lots of calculations means that lots of instructions are needed and, hence, lots of machine cycles. For more information on CPUs, visit the Web site for this text at www.mhhe.com/i-series.

CPU AND RAM PRODUCTIVITY ISSUES
How Fast Should My CPU Be and How Much Ram Do I Need?

The CPU and RAM are the two most important determinants of the power and speed of your computer. Other factors, like the type of system bus, are important, but the speed of the CPU and the amount of RAM you have make the biggest difference in performance.

CPU Speed

The type and speed of the CPU are generally the first things that computer ads tell you. The most helpful information for comparing CPUs is their relative speeds. CPU speed is usually quoted in megahertz or gigahertz. ***Megahertz (MHz) for a CPU*** is the number of millions of CPU cycles per second. ***Gigahertz (GHz) for a CPU*** is the number of billions of CPU cycles per second. A CPU cycle consists of the four steps just discussed. The number of CPU cycles per second determines how fast the CPU carries out the software instructions—more cycles per second means faster processing.

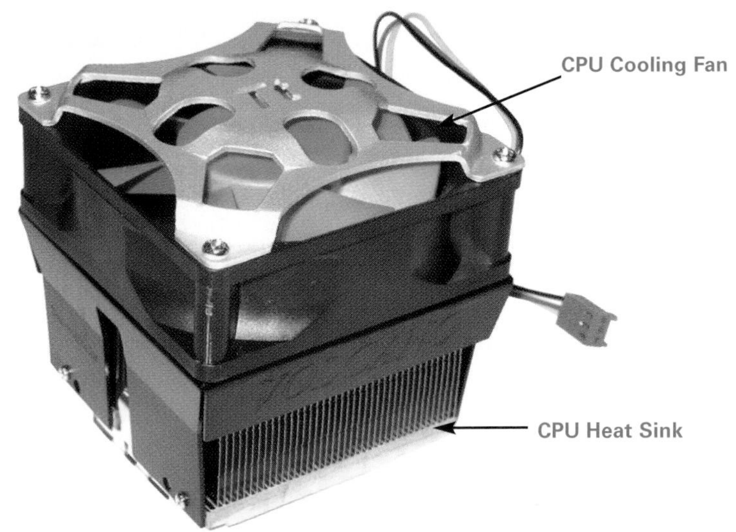

FIGURE 6.11

A CPU consists of tens of millions of transistors with electrons moving between them and generating as much heat as a 100-watt light bulb. So, a heat sink (a chunk of metal which conducts the heat away) and a fan are necessary to cool the CPU down.

Since the CPU carries out instructions from the software, it makes sense that the faster it does so the better. The faster a CPU is, however, the more heat it generates. It gets so hot it needs to be cooled constantly (see Figure 6.11).

You'll notice speed, or the lack of it, more in some applications than in others. While you're using your computer to create Word documents, for example, you might not see any great improvement with extra speed. If you routinely visit highly visual Web sites or work with video or complex graphics, which require many more calculations and hence many more instructions than a Word document does, you'll probably find that more CPU cycles per second make a big difference.

Classes of CPUs

The two major manufacturers of consumer computer CPUs are Intel and AMD (American Micro Devices) and their CPUs can be divided into two categories: desktop CPUs and mobile CPUs (which are for notebook computers and will be discussed later in this chapter). The speed range keeps shifting upward as CPUs get faster and more powerful (see Figure 6.12). High-performance CPUs are those that have the top speeds. These are the most expensive. The next layer down are the CPUs that run at less than the

FIGURE 6.12

CPUs generally have a range of speeds depending on how the computer system is configured.

Computer Type	Processor Name	Speed
Desktop	Intel Pentium 4	up to 3.06 GHz
	AMD Athlon	up to 2.2 GHz
	Intel Celeron	up to 2.0 GHz
	AMD Duron	up to 1.3 GHz
Notebook	Mobile Intel Pentium 4	up to 2.2 GHz
	Mobile AMD XP	up to 2.2 GHz
	Mobile AMD Athlon 4	up to 1.6 GHz
	Mobile Intel Pentium III	up to 1.3 GHz

practically speaking

Faster CPU Speed through Hyperthreading

Intel has recently developed a new way to make CPUs faster with a process called *hyperthreading.* This technology was first available on Intel's 3.06-gigahertz Pentium 4 CPU. Hyperthreading, according to Intel, is like one cook with two pans, reducing the total time needed to cook both dishes. Hyperthreading is an Intel CPU technology that allows one processor to work on two sets of software instructions simultaneously.

The 3.06 Pentium 4 with hyperthreading has been described as a physical processor and a virtual one in a single package. This may allow your software to run more efficiently and to multitask more effectively than ever before. For example, it makes it practical to edit digital video while encoding digital music, both of which are tasks that require a lot of work from the CPU.

A hyperthreading CPU will probably not make your Excel or Word go faster. However, it will help with software that needs hyperthreading for optimal performance like Adobe's Photoshop, software that often has multiple tasks under way simultaneously.

top speeds, and which were the high-performance processors up to the last round of speed increases. The price of these CPUs usually drops significantly when the new CPUs come onto the market, but a recently downgraded processor still does an excellent job handling the software currently on the market. Check out our Web site at www.mhhe.com/i-series for more information on CPUs.

RAM Capacity

Like almost everything else in your computer system, how much RAM you need depends on what you want to do with it. Recall that in Chapter 5 you learned about storage capacity, which is measured by the number of bytes it can hold. We measure memory with the same yardstick.

There is usually less capacity in memory than on hard disks, since RAM is just a workspace and not intended to store information long term. In Figure 6.13 you can see what RAM modules look like. So, how much should you get? A short, general answer would be "as much as you can afford."

About 256 megabytes may be adequate if you're planning on doing little more than using Word, Excel, e-mail, and minimal Web surfing. However, as soon as you start downloading shocked Web pages, or using graphics, or editing photos now and then, you're going to notice a severe reduction in performance. Usually, 512 megabytes of RAM, which is standard in most new computers, is pretty good for normal computer use, including Web surfing, some photo editing, and so on. If you do a lot of photo or video editing, or something else that needs really good performance, you'll need a gigabyte or more.

FIGURE 6.13

You buy RAM in the form of several chips seated into a little circuit board called a DIMM (dual inline memory module).

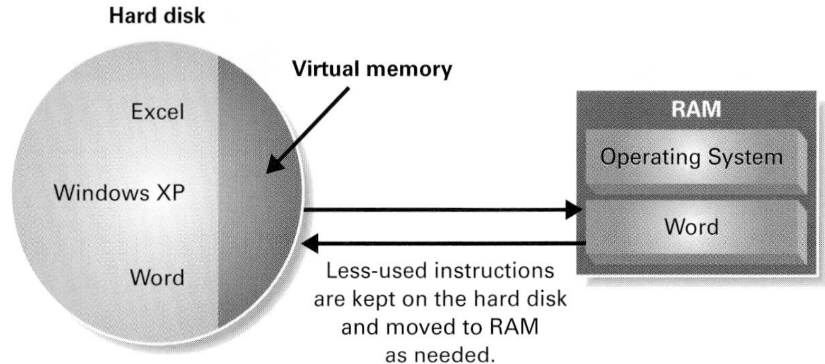

FIGURE 6.14

When there's not enough space in RAM for all the necessary instructions, some instructions are stored in virtual memory on the hard disk.

RAM and Virtual Memory

So can you still use your computer if you don't have enough RAM for the tasks you're working on? The answer is that you can, but everything slows down. And here's why. When your computer runs out of RAM space it uses hard disk space as temporary RAM, which is called *virtual memory.*

Let's say you're writing a report on the cost of computer systems. You'll need to have Word open. You'll need to consult the Web to get current prices, and you might want to use Excel to do the calculations. Also, while you're doing all this, you'd like your e-mail software to check for incoming mail every 10 minutes. Your CPU must process the instructions for all four applications as well as those of the operating system. All the instructions must be in RAM before the CPU can access them.

When the instructions don't all fit into memory at the same time, some are stored on the hard disk and then moved into RAM as needed (see Figure 6.14). ***Virtual memory*** is the space on your hard disk that holds software instructions for a program currently in use. If your RAM isn't large enough to hold all the instructions for all four applications along with everything else that has to be there, the most used instructions will be in RAM and the less used will be in virtual memory. Then, your CPU will swap out instructions between RAM and virtual memory as it needs them. This swapping back and forth slows down processing. It takes much longer to move instructions from the hard disk to RAM and then to the CPU than it does to move them directly from RAM, which is where they have to be before the CPU can access them. For more information on memory, visit our Web site at www.mhhe.com/i-series.

SECTION 6.3

making the grade

1. A(n) ___________ consists of retrieving, decoding, and executing an instruction, then returning the result to RAM, if necessary.
2. Temporary memory that holds instructions and information for the CPU is called ___________.
3. The ___________ consists of electrical pathways that move information between basic components of the motherboard, including between RAM and the CPU.
4. When there's not enough room in RAM for all the necessary instructions, the CPU uses hard disk space, called ___________.
5. The sliver of quartz within the CPU that beats at regular intervals in response to an electrical charge is a(n) ___________.

6.4 MAKING CONNECTIONS

All your computer devices, such as keyboards, mice, scanners, Web cams, and so on, have to connect to the CPU. For this to happen, you need connectors (plugs), ports (places to insert connectors), expansion cards (circuit boards with ports on them), and expansion slots (places on the motherboard where expansion cards go).

CONNECTORS AND PORTS

How Do I Know What to Connect Where?

Different devices have different types of connectors for plugging components into the computer. The connectors connect to ports. (See Figure 6.15 for different types of connectors and ports.) Common types of connectors are USB, Firewire, serial, PS/2, and parallel.

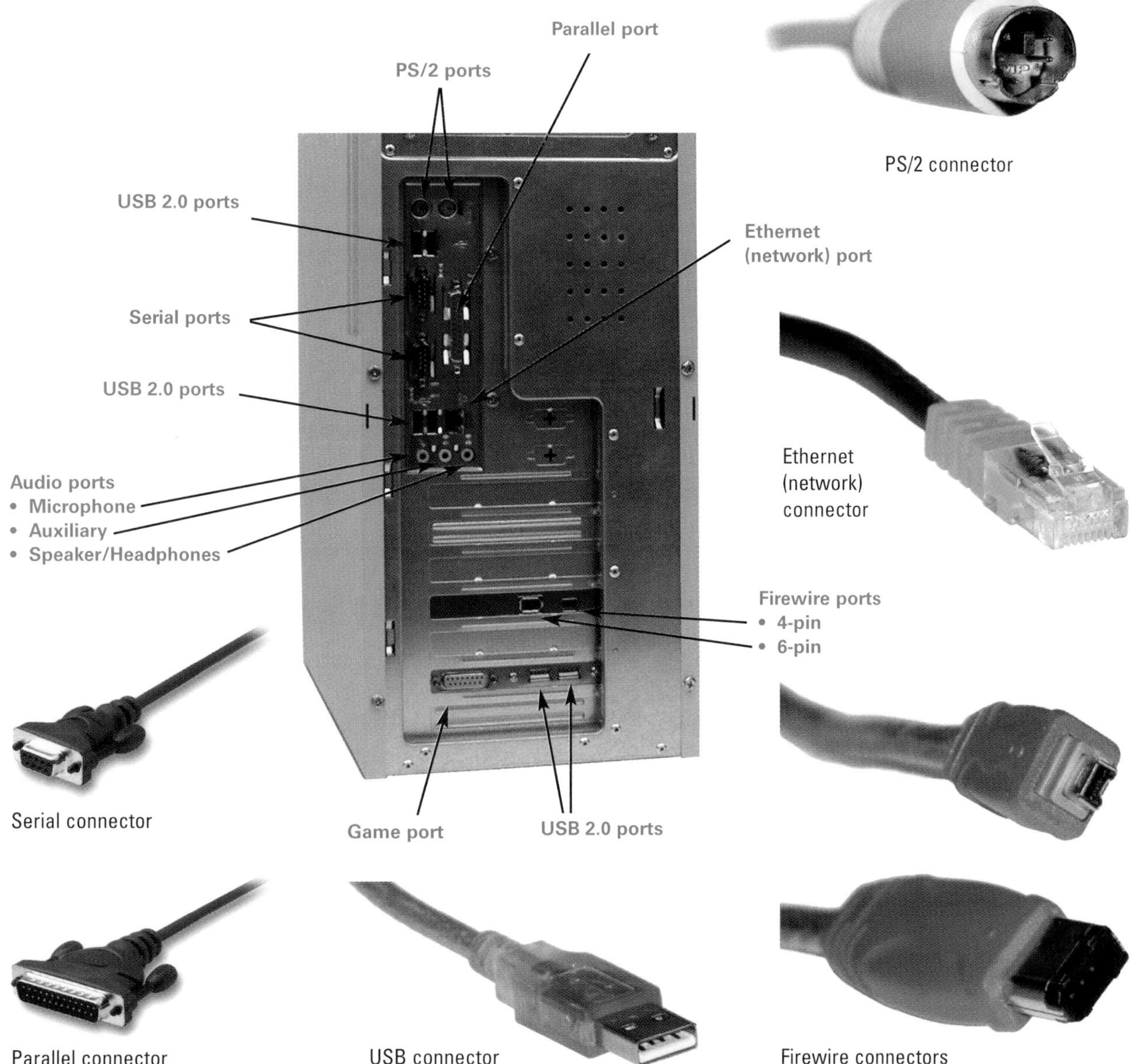

FIGURE 6.15

Computers have several different types of ports for different types of connectors on peripheral devices.

FIGURE 6.16

These ports and connectors are used to connect external devices.

Connector and Port	Used for
USB 2.0	Modems, keyboards, scanners, printers, hard disks, and many other devices
Firewire	Camcorders, scanners, hard disks, and many newer devices
Serial	Keyboards and mice
Parallel	Mostly printers
PS/2	Keyboards and mice

You'll see ports in various places on your computer. Some are inside the system unit for internal hard disk, CD, and DVD drives. Others are outside for external devices such as printers and scanners.

Many devices have two or more types of connectors. Newer printers, for instance, often have both parallel and USB connectors. Ports are often integrated into the motherboard, but may be on a separate circuit board—an expansion card—that you plug into the motherboard. See Figure 6.16 for a table of what devices the different ports are used for.

USB Connectors and Ports

USB (universal serial bus) connectors allow you to connect hot-swappable, plug and play devices to your computer. As you learned in Chapter 3, when you add devices to your computer with ***plug and play,*** your operating system will find and install the appropriate device driver without your having to go through a manual installation. If you don't already have the right device driver on your system, the operating system will prompt you to insert the appropriate disk or CD-ROM. In the opening example, we plugged the Archos into the USB port and the operating system detected it and listed it in the **My Computer** folder.

Hot swap is an operating system feature that allows you—while your computer is running—to unplug a given device and plug in a new one without first shutting down your computer. The device has to be hot swappable too, of course. When you connect devices that are both plug and play and hot swappable, it's sometimes called *hot plugging*.

A ***USB port*** is where you connect a USB device to your computer, and you can even connect multiple USB devices (up to 127) using a single USB port on your computer. There are usually at least two USB ports on desktop computers and at least one on notebooks. Today's USB ports are USB 2.0, which is also known in the consumer market as hi-speed USB. Earlier versions were USB 1.0 and USB 1.1. There are also two types of USB connectors/ports. There is an A type and a B type. The one shown in Figure 6.15 on the previous page is type A. The shape of type B is not as flat a rectangle as type A. To further complicate matters, there are different sizes of type B USB connectors. You'll find a very small one (called a mini-B connector) on one end of the cable that comes with your digital camera. The other end is usually type A. The type A connector goes into your computer, and the small type B goes into the camera, and then you can transfer photos. Mini-B connectors come in several sizes according to the manufacturer of the device.

did you know? 670 *million passengers a year take off and land in passenger airplanes.*[1]

i-series insights *Ethics, Security & Privacy*

Is Someone Monitoring Your Keystrokes?

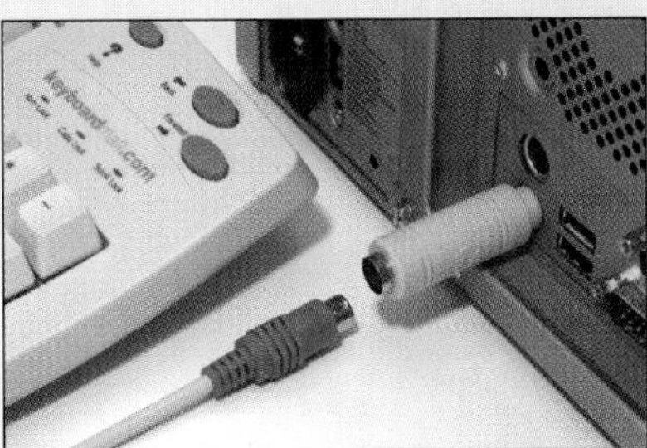

The cable from your computer may plug into the PS/2 port on the back of your computer. But, there may also be a little lipstick-sized device back there too. Someone can spy on you by inserting a hardware key logger between the PS/2 port and the PS/2 connector on your keyboard cable. A ***hardware key logger*** is a hardware device that captures keystrokes on their journey from the keyboard to the motherboard. It captures and records every keystroke. However, since it catches every delete, backspace, and enter, it may be a bit bothersome to review the information stored there.

If your employer does this on your computer at work, you'll find little sympathy from the legal system. Employers have the legal right to monitor the use of their resources and that includes the time they're paying you for and the computer systems you're using. Remember, too, that employers are liable for the actions of employees.

Maybe you should check the back of your computer every now and then? Although, that wouldn't necessarily protect you since there are also hardware key loggers that can be installed inside the keyboard.

Firewire Connectors and Ports

Firewire (also called ***IEEE 1394*** or ***I-link***) ***connectors,*** although different from USB, also allow you to connect hot-swap, plug and play devices to your computer. A ***Firewire port*** is where you connect a Firewire device and you can connect up to 63 devices using a single port. Firewire is used mostly for digital camcorders and high-capacity music players like the iPod, which was originally only available for use with a Macintosh computer, but which is now usable with PC compatibles too. Firewire also has two types that are different shapes. There's a 4-pin and a 6-pin type.

Serial Connectors and Ports

A ***serial connector,*** which plugs into a serial port, usually has 9 holes but may have 25, which fit the corresponding number of pins in the port. A ***serial port*** is where you connect a serial connector to your computer. Serial ports and connectors are usually used with mice and keyboards. A special type of serial connector is a ***PS/2 connector,*** which has pins that fit into a small round port (a ***PS/2 port***) in your computer and is used for keyboards and pointing devices like mice. Desktop computers usually have two PS/2 ports—and they are different—one is for the keyboard and the other is for a mouse. You need to plug the right device into the right port.

Parallel Connectors and Ports

A ***parallel connector,*** which plugs into a parallel port, has 25 pins, which fit into the holes that are in the port. A ***parallel port*** is where you plug a parallel connector into your computer. These days, parallel ports are used almost exclusively to connect printers, although most printers are also USB capable. To learn more about the different types of ports and connectors, complete the "Ports and Cables" tutorial on your SimNet Concepts Support CD.

The cordless mouse sends radio waves to the receiver, which is wired to the computer.

FIGURE 6.17

Some mice and remote control devices use an RF (radio frequency) technology, which is a different kind of radio wave (different frequency) from the Bluetooth standard. RF has the advantage that you don't need to point the device directly at the receiver (like you do with an infrared TV remote control).

Wireless Ports

With wireless devices, you don't need a wire with a connector—that's the big advantage of wireless devices. You have two major choices for wireless computer devices: IrDA (uses infrared light) and Bluetooth (uses radio waves). To use any wireless device with your computer, you must have one port on the device and another one on your computer (see Figure 6.17).

IrDA (infrared data association), also known as ***IR*** or simply ***infrared, ports*** use infrared light to send and receive information. Infrared light has a frequency that is below what's visible to the human eye. IrDA works the same way as your TV remote control and is useful for very short distances that are free of obstacles.

You can use an IrDA port, for example, to send information from your notebook to a wireless printer. PDAs also often have IrDA ports for sending information to a printer, a computer, or another PDA.

Bluetooth is a standard for transmitting information in the form of short-range radio waves over distances of up to 30 feet, and is used for purposes such as wirelessly connecting a cell phone to a computer. Bluetooth-enabled devices have a special chip that allows them to communicate with other Bluetooth devices. Virtually all digital devices, keyboards, joysticks, printers, headsets, tablet PCs, and so on, can be part of a Bluetooth system. Bluetooth is also adaptable to home appliances such as refrigerators, microwaves, and so on. Some day, your refrigerator might be Bluetooth-enabled and call the grocery store when it detects that you've run out of milk. IrDA and Bluetooth are not your only options for wireless devices over short distances. Some devices work on frequencies other than those used for Bluetooth. The cordless mouse shown in Figure 6.17 is an example. In general, a device that uses radio waves works better than one that uses IrDA. This is because an IrDA device has to point directly at the sensor while one that uses radio waves does not.

Bluetooth is especially good for portable devices since it requires little power to function, less for example, than WiFi, which has a longer reach and is a wireless standard usually used for wireless access to networks. You'll find more about wireless connections to networks, including WiFi, in Chapter 7.

did you know?

A Cray supercomputer can manage 52.4 teraflops—that's 52,400,000,000,000 operations per second, quite a bit faster than the 3 billion that a desktop computer can do.[2]

EXPANSION CARDS AND SLOTS FOR DESKTOP COMPUTERS

Where Does the Information Go When It Gets Past the Port?

Ports, where you connect devices to your computer, are part of your interface hardware. ***Interface hardware*** is the hardware that connects external devices to the motherboard. Information flows through the port to the interface hardware. Interface hardware can be either integrated into the motherboard or separate as an expansion card that plugs into an expansion slot.

The motherboard in Figure 6.3 on page 164 has an integrated sound card. You can't see the sound card, but you can see and access its ports. Most new computers today come with sound, video, telephone modem, Ethernet or network (for connecting to a network or a cable or DSL modem), and perhaps even wireless capabilities built in.

Expansion cards (see Figure 6.18) fit into the appropriate expansion slots—long skinny sockets on the motherboard. See Figure 6.3 again. The five white slots and the blue slot that you can see on the motherboard in Figure 6.3, #5, are called PCI slots. A ***PCI (peripheral component interconnect) slot*** is a type of expansion slot which you'd use to plug in video cards, sound cards, or network cards. Expansion cards, such as video and sound cards, have ports that are accessible on the back of your computer when you replace the cover of the system unit. This is where you would plug in your monitor or speakers. The ***AGP slot*** is an expansion slot reserved exclusively for an AGP video card. It's the brown slot in Figure 6.3, #6.

If you're interested in computer system hardware, either designing it or trouble-shooting it, you have a lot of good career choices, everything from electronic engineering, designing chips and other computer components, to running a help desk or a computer store. To learn more about expansion cards and slots, complete the "Expansion Cards and Slots" tutorial on your SimNet Concepts Support CD.

BUSES

How Does Information Move around the Motherboard?

Buses, or ***data buses,*** carry information in the form of bits around the motherboard in your computer. As you've already seen, the pathway that carries information between RAM and the CPU is part of the system bus. Much of the elaborate circuitry that you can see on the top and bottom of the motherboard is part of the expansion bus, which is another system of pathways along which information moves. The expansion bus forms the

FIGURE 6.18

You might want to install a new video card, perhaps one that has a TV tuner so that you can watch TV on your computer screen. Note that the video card has a heat sink and fan. Underneath the fan is a processor that helps the CPU with video processing tasks.

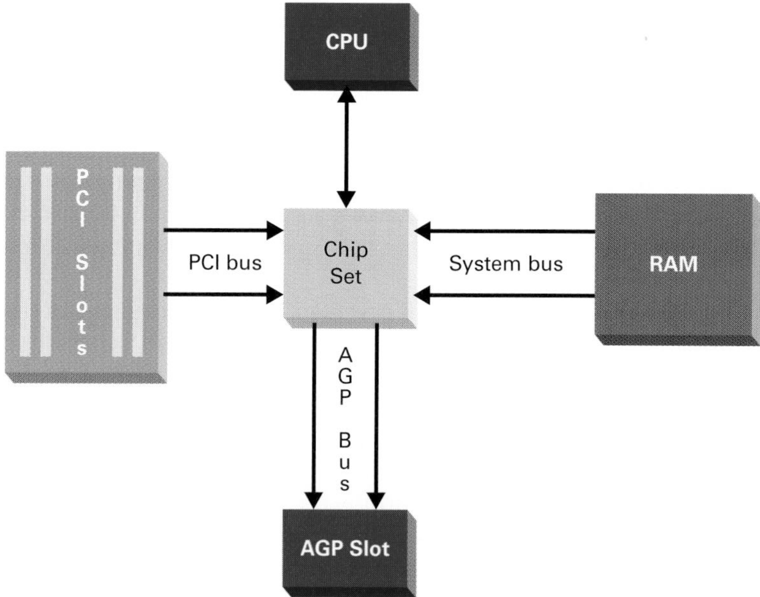

FIGURE 6.19

The PCI and AGP buses, which are part of the expansion bus, and the system bus, connecting the CPU and RAM, carry information around the motherboard. This information traffic is controlled by the chip set.

highway system on the motherboard that moves information coming from and going to devices outside the motherboard such as your microphone or printer (see Figure 6.19). The ***PCI bus*** is one part of the expansion bus, and ends in the PCI slots. The ***AGP bus*** is another part of the expansion bus, and ends in the AGP slot.

SECTION 6.4

making the grade

1. USB and ___________ connectors allow you to connect hot-swappable, plug and play devices to your computer.
2. A port that transmits and receives information in the form of infrared light and works like your TV remote control is called a(n) ___________ port.
3. The ___________ is part of the expansion bus and connects to the PCI slots.
4. The highway system on the motherboard that moves information coming from and going to devices outside the motherboard is called the ___________.
5. The port that is used almost exclusively for printers is a ___________ port.

did you know?

If you tried to count all the stars in our Milky Way galaxy at a rate of one every second, it would take about 3,000 years.[3]

6.5 NOTEBOOK COMPUTERS

A notebook computer is to a desktop computer as a recreational vehicle is to a home—everything is smaller and power to run devices is limited since you have to carry the power source with you. So electronic engineers work to reduce the power and size requirements of all parts of a notebook. Some components, like the keyboard, monitor, and ports, however, which could be made even smaller, lose their usefulness as they shrink.

Space and power are conserved where possible. For example, hard disks for notebook computers are physically smaller than those for a desktop and may slide into the side of the system unit or be installed into the bottom of the system unit. Similarly, the CPUs that are now being installed into notebook computers are no longer just low power versions of desktop CPUs, as was the case in the past.

NOTEBOOK CPUS AND RAM

How Are Notebook CPUs and RAM Different?

Today's notebook computer CPUs, called *mobile CPUs,* have special design features that distinguish them from traditional CPUs. A ***mobile CPU*** is a special type of CPU for a notebook computer that changes speed, and therefore power consumption, in response to fluctuations in demand. A desktop CPU, running at 1 GHz, uses between 75 and 100 watts of power. Contrast that with Intel's SpeedStep CPU, which runs at 34 watts, while the notebook computer is plugged into an electrical outlet, but reduces its power consumption even lower. This not only reduces the power that the CPU needs, it also generates less heat so that the fan uses less power. The CPU fan in a notebook computer doesn't run constantly. It comes on only when the CPU gets too hot.

AMD has a similar technology called PowerNow!, which changes the voltage of the CPU according to how busy the CPU is. That means that when the CPU is idle, between keystrokes or mouse movements, for example, the CPU reduces its speed.

Memory modules for notebook computers look a bit different from those for desktop computers (see Figure 6.20). To install or swap RAM in a notebook, you open up the small bay door on the system unit, and you'll see where the RAM modules go.

FIGURE 6.20

RAM for a notebook looks a little different from desktop RAM.

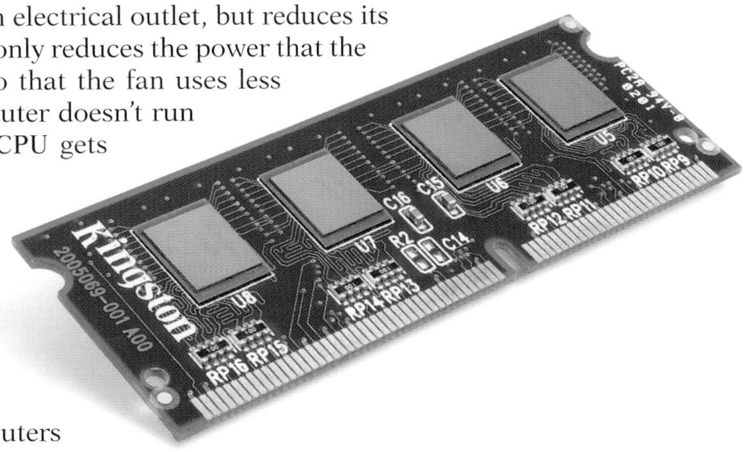

EXPANSION CARDS AND SLOTS FOR NOTEBOOK COMPUTERS

How Do I Add Devices to My Notebook Computer?

To add devices to your notebook, you would slide a PC Card into the PC Card slot on the notebook, and connect the device to the PC Card. A ***PC Card*** (which is an updated version of the traditional PCMCIA card) is the expansion card you use to add devices to your notebook computer. It looks like a modified credit card (see Figure 6.21). ***PC Card slots*** are the openings, one on top of the other, on the side or front of a notebook, where you connect external devices with PC Cards. For example, if you wanted to add a CD-ROM drive, you'd slide a PC Card into the slot and then connect the CD-ROM drive to the connector on the PC Card. One of the great things about PC Cards is that they allow you to hot-swap devices.

FIGURE 6.21

A PC Card provides expansion capabilities for a notebook computer. This one provides additional USB 2.0 and Firewire ports for external devices.

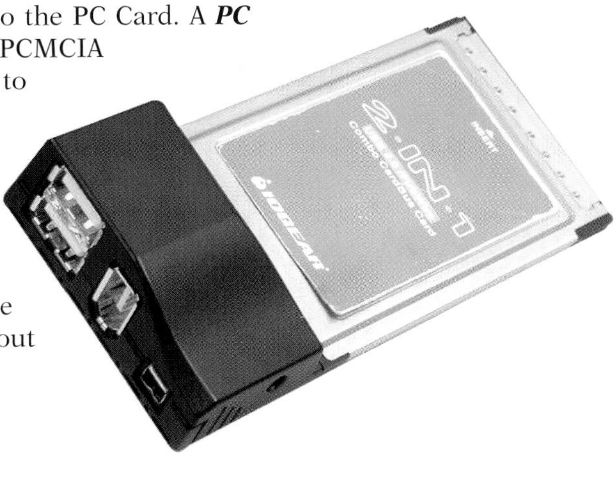

SECTION 6.5

making the grade

1. A(n) __________ is a special type of CPU for a notebook computer.
2. A(n) __________ is an expansion card that you use to add devices to your notebook computer.
3. A PC Card slot is found in __________ computers.
4. A notebook hard disk drive is usually physically __________ (larger/smaller) than one for a desktop computer.
5. AMD's PowerNow! and Intel's SpeedStep are technologies to lower the __________ that a mobile CPU uses.

6.6 CONSUMER Q&A

1. Why Does My USB Device Not Work Right in My USB Port?

The newer USB ports, connectors, and devices are USB 2.0. The earlier versions of USB (USB 1.0 and USB 1.1) were much slower than USB 2.0. If you don't have USB 2.0 ports on your computer and want to use a USB 2.0 device at full speed, you'll need an adapter. For a desktop you can buy a PCI expansion card that will provide you with USB 2.0 ports. For a notebook computer, you can get a PC Card USB 2.0 (like the one in Figure 6.21) and then your USB 2.0 device will run as fast as it's supposed to.

2. How Long Can I Expect My Notebook Battery to Last?

The length of time the battery power lasts in a notebook varies a great deal. The advertised length of time is usually a maximum. Under normal working conditions your battery will probably not last that long. It might be well worth the investment to buy a second battery so that you have a spare when the first one starts fading. If you're using your notebook somewhere you can plug it in, do so and save the battery. Also, it will make your mobile CPU go faster, since notebook CPUs are designed to slow down and use less power when running on the battery.

3. How Do I Connect Multiple Devices to a USB or Firewire Port?

USB: One of the convenient features of a USB connection is that you can connect so many devices to one port. If you want to plug in multiple devices, you'll need a USB hub. A USB hub is a sort of multiple outlet strip, like the one you use to plug several appliances into one electrical wall outlet. You plug the hub into your computer system and then plug the USB devices into that. The downside of plugging several devices into one USB port is that they have to share the port speed.

Firewire: You can also connect many devices into one Firewire port. In this case, you daisy-chain the devices together. The first device plugs into the Firewire port on the computer, the second device plugs into the first, and the third into the second, and so on. This daisy-chaining feature is why you'll see two Firewire ports on Firewire devices, one for the cable coming from the previous device and one for the cable going to the next device.

i•can

Expand the Expansion Capabilities of My Notebook

If you're buying a notebook, think carefully about what extras you might want, such as a modem or DVD drive, and try to choose a system which has devices built in since your expansion possibilities are limited unless you use a docking station. A docking station is a small platform into which you can plug your whole notebook computer. Docking stations have lots of ports. For example, a docking station might have a PS/2 or a USB port into which you could plug a regular keyboard and a parallel port for a printer. They also contain a connection for your power supply.

If you regularly use your notebook computer at home and your place of work, you might want two docking stations, one at home and one at work.

6.7 SUMMARY AND KEY TERMS

A ***bit*** is a 1 or a 0. Bits are grouped together into groups of eight called ***bytes.*** A byte represents a natural language or keyboard character. ASCII and EBCDIC are coding systems based on eight-bit bytes, giving 256 different and unique patterns representing characters. Unicode is a coding system based on 16 bits giving about 65,000 different combinations.

The ***central processing unit (CPU*** or ***processor)*** is the chip that carries out instructions it receives from your software. This applies to both system and application software instructions. ***RAM (random access memory)*** is temporary memory that holds software instructions and information for the CPU. Together, the CPU and RAM are the most important components in your computer system, because they execute the instructions from software in four steps called the ***CPU*** or ***machine cycle.*** The ***system bus*** carries instructions and information between the CPU and RAM. ***CPU cache*** is temporary memory in the CPU where instructions wait until the CPU needs them. The speed of a CPU, or how often it can execute the four steps of a CPU cycle in one second, is measured in ***megahertz*** or ***gigahertz.***

RAM capacity is important, because without enough memory, a computer slows down since it has to substitute hard disk space (called ***virtual memory***) for RAM. Moving information in and out of the hard disk takes a relatively long time.

The places in your computer system into which you plug devices, and through which information and instructions flow into your computer system, are called ***ports.*** You can find them on your system unit, monitor, or keyboard. Ports have corresponding ***connectors.*** Some of these are:

- USB 2.0 (earlier versions were USB 1.0 and 1.1)
- Firewire (also called IEEE 1394 or I-link)
- Serial
- PS/2
- Parallel

Wireless devices also use ports, but no wires. ***IrDA*** is infrared, like your TV remote control, and is used for sending information from notebook computers to printers or for exchanging information with a PDA. ***Bluetooth*** is a wireless technology that uses radio waves for distances up to 30 feet. Bluetooth-enabled devices can communicate with each other.

An ***expansion card*** (or ***board)*** is a circuit board that you insert into an ***expansion slot*** on the motherboard and to which you connect a peripheral device. You would do this if you don't have the expansion card integrated into your motherboard or want to use a different type of interface hardware from the one that came with the system. A ***PCI slot*** is a type of expansion slot into which you would plug an expansion card. An ***expansion bus*** carries information between the CPU and peripheral devices.

Since space is at a premium in notebook computers, everything is smaller and more compact than in a desktop. Notebook computers have ***mobile CPUs*** that reduce their power consumption and extend somewhat the battery life of the notebook. You would use a ***PC Card*** inserted into a ***PC Card slot*** to connect an external device to your notebook computer.

For more information on CPUs, RAM, and wireless devices, visit the Web site for this text at www.mhhe.com/i-series.

KEY TERMS

review of terminology

Multiple Choice

1. The pathway for information to travel from an external device to the motherboard is
   a. formed by connecting the cable from the device to the port.
   b. the expansion bus.
   c. system bus.
   d. internal bus.
   e. none of the above.
2. The CPU
   a. executes system software instructions.
   b. executes application software instructions.
   c. is not necessary for wireless devices.
   d. is both a and b.
   e. is both b and c.
3. Unicode is
   a. a group of 8 bits.
   b. a group of 16 bits.
   c. the coding system for ASCII characters.
   d. a 16-bit coding system.
   e. none of the above.
4. The system bus is
   a. the pathway that moves information from peripheral devices around the motherboard.
   b. the pathway that moves information between the CPU and RAM.
   c. the pathway between a connector and port.
   d. all of the above.
   e. none of the above.
5. Hard disk space that the CPU uses as RAM when there's not enough RAM is called
   a. virtual memory.
   b. flash memory.
   c. random access memory.
   d. electronic memory.
   e. none of the above.
6. IrDA and Bluetooth are
   a. types of connectors.
   b. types of data buses.
   c. wireless technologies.
   d. types of memory.
   e. none of the above.
7. Plug and play
   a. is the same as hot swap.
   b. is a type of operating system.
   c. means you can connect a device to your computer and the operating system will find it without further intervention from you.
   d. means you can disconnect a device from your computer and connect another without turning off the computer.
   e. is none of the above.
8. A parallel connector and port are
   a. plug and play and hot-swap capable.
   b. used for mice and trackballs.
   c. used mostly for printers.
   d. both a and b.
   e. both a and c.
9. Notebook computers
   a. have exactly the same type of CPUs as desktop computers.
   b. use PC Cards to add external devices.
   c. won't allow you to swap hard disk drives.
   d. won't allow you to add RAM.
   e. have none of the above characteristics.
10. Firewire is
    a. a type of cache.
    b. a type of CPU.
    c. a type of connector.
    d. a type of RAM.
    e. none of the above.

True/False

11. ____ Computers use only two digits to represent all information stored in and used by computer components.
12. ____ ASCII is a coding system that most personal computer systems use.
13. ____ The CPU and RAM are the two components that have the biggest impact on your computer's speed.
14. ____ PowerNow! is a technology that is used to speed up desktop CPUs.
15. ____ CPU cache is the memory that the CPU uses when there's not enough RAM.

Take this quiz online at www.mhhe.com/i-series and get instant feedback.

QUESTIONS AND EXERCISES

1. Working with Nibbles

Bits are 1s and 0s. When there are 8 places for bits, as in a byte, you get 2^8 or 256 different patterns; that is, you can represent 256 different keyboard characters. The formula is the base (2) raised to the power of the number of available places (8). So, with 16 places, like Unicode has, you get 2^{16} or about 65,000 (it's exactly 65,536) unique patterns of 1s and 0s.

Given "nibbles" of different sizes (2,3,4, and 5):

a. Figure out how many distinct patterns there would be (we've filled in one for you).

Nibble Size	Number of Patterns
2	
3	8
4	
5	

b. List all the patterns for each size nibble (we've done one for you).

With 3 places available, we have 8 (2^3) different patterns of 1s and 0s. Below is an exhaustive list—there are no other possibilities.

Patterns of 1s and 0s for a Nibble of 3 Bits
000
001
010
011
100
101
110
111

2. Comparing CPUs to the Human Body

In the text we compared CPUs to the human brain. They both process system instructions to keep the "machine" up and running, and application instructions to use the "machine" as a tool. Consider the following body parts and say what the equivalent computer component would be.

Human Body Feature	Computer Component
Nervous system	
Short-term memory	
Long-term memory	
Senses of sight or hearing	
Voice	
Hand signals	
Food intake	

3. Can You Identify Ports and Components?

a. On the motherboard photo below, label the appropriate ports for the following devices:

- IDE hard disk drive
- IDE CD burner
- Floppy disk drive
- Flash memory drive
- Keyboard
- Trackball
- Microphone
- Speakers

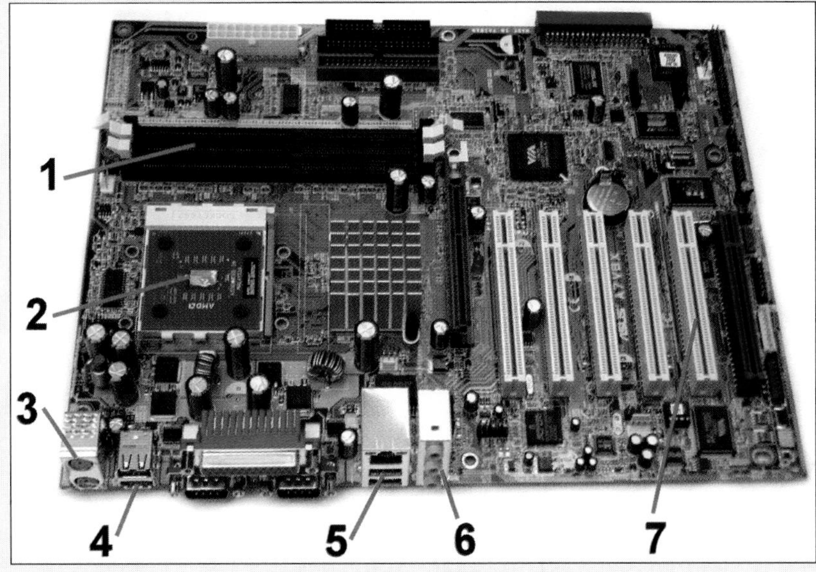

b. Match the motherboard components below to the numbered items in the motherboard photo above.

Component	Number(s) in Picture	Number of Instances
CPU		
RAM slot		
USB port		
PCI slot		
PS/2 port		
Audio port		

e-commerce

1. Buying RAM

RAM or memory modules come in many types as well as capacities. Three common types are SDRAM (Synchronous Dynamic Random Access Memory); DDR SDRAM (Double Data Rate SDRAM), referred to simply as DDR; and RDRAM or Rambus RAM. As the name implies, the DDR is twice as fast as plain SDRAM, and Rambus also runs at double the speed, meaning that information moves in and out faster. The speed is not necessarily noticeable to the average consumer, but DDR and Rambus may be more expensive. Here are some Web sites where you can find relevant information on RAM.

- Crucial—www.crucial.com. This site has a "memory selector" feature where you can find out what kind of RAM you need for your computer.
- MicroWarehouse—www.microwarehouse.com
- Memory Etc—www.memoryetc.com
- Kingston—www.shop.kingston.com

Make a comparison of the three different types of RAM for four different capacities (128, 256, and 512 megabytes, and 1 gigabyte), and answer the questions below for each type and each capacity.

a. Is it available for desktop computers? (You may not be able to find all capacities in all types of RAM.)
b. Is it available for notebook computers? (RAM modules for notebooks are a different shape.)
c. What is the price of the RAM module?
d. Does the site tell you the speed of the RAM module? If so, what is it?

2. Buying Devices with the Right Connectors

Newer devices tend to have USB 2.0 or Firewire connectors that plug into the corresponding ports on your computer system. Some devices have more than one way of connecting to your computer system. Here are some Web sites to look at to find devices.

- Price Watch—www.pricewatch.com
- MySimon—www.mysimon.com
- Dealspin—www.dealspin.com
- Deal Time—www.dealtime.com

Connect to three of these (or three of your own choosing) and answer the following questions for a CD-RW, hard disk, printer, and scanner.

a. What is the price of each at each site?
b. What connection type(s) does each have?
c. Is the device external or internal?

3. Buying Music

As a consumer, you can buy almost anything on the Web, from concert tickets to sports memorabilia. Here, we want to take a look at buying music. And we focus on buying traditional CDs in this project. To find music of interest to you and (potentially) buy it, connect to two of the following music sites:

- CDNow—www.cdnow.com
- Tower Records—www.towerrecords.com
- MSN eShop—eShop.msn.com
- Amazon—www.amazon.com
- Music Books Plus—www.musicbooksplus.com

Now, pick one CD you found that is of interest to you. What is the price? Is there a shipping charge? If so, what is it? How long will it take to have the CD delivered to you? Will the CD arrive by overnight service or parcel service?

Equipped with that information, go to a local music store and find the same CD. Is the price higher or lower on the Web? If there is a difference, speculate as to why the difference exists. Because you can purchase the CD right now in the store, why would people want to shop on the Web for music?

ethics, security & privacy

1. Business Computers Classify You as Profitable—or Not

Although companies have always offered preferential treatment to their more profitable customers, the speed and capacity of computers today are making the segmenting of customers possible to a degree unheard of just a few years ago. Businesses now have the ability to gauge whether individual customers are worth the trouble of making them happy. For example, if you called the bank that issued you your credit card and said that you didn't want to pay the annual fee any more, the bank could look at your previous account activity and decide whether your business is worth the cost of giving in on the annual fee issue.

The First Union Bank has software that categorizes people into red, green, and yellow depending on the customer's history and value to the bank. Customers who are "green" might get better credit card rates than customers who are "red" and are judged to add less to the bank's bottom line. Visa also uses this type of software as a way to help the company spot fraud and to determine which of their customers might default or go bankrupt.

Financial institutions are not the only ones, either. Catalina Supermarkets, for example, keeps track of which customers buy which products, how frequently, and what price they pay. The supermarket chain has increased its percentage of high-value customers by offering them services such as free home delivery.

The movie business is also getting in on the act. Twentieth Century Fox slices and dices the information in its databases to determine the most popular movies, actors, and plots to release in certain theaters, cities, and areas of the country. The result, however, may be that people in certain areas will not get the chance to see certain movies.

There was a time when certain neighborhoods or geographic regions were "redlined" by lending institutions and others. That meant that banks and other businesses wouldn't deal with anyone who lived in the redlined areas. Some people think that electronic market segmentation or customer categorization is a new form of redlining. Following are some questions for you to answer regarding this practice.

a. Do you think that the segmentation practices described above are fair?
b. Do you think you should get better treatment if you're a better customer?
c. How do you feel about being pigeonholed by computer software?
d. Would it help if you knew what the criteria were and how the determination was made?
e. Is it reasonable to predict future behavior of customers based on their previous actions?
f. Is this the same as redlining, or is it okay because it categorizes individuals by actual behavior rather than by assuming characteristics because of membership in a particular group?

on the web

1. Compare Computer Systems

Computers come in lots of different sizes and levels of power and performance. Use the Web to find out about computer system configurations. Do some comparison shopping for three types of computers: desktop, notebook, and tablet PCs. Here are some sites to look at.

- Dell—www.dell.com
- Gateway—www.gateway.com
- Hewlett-Packard—www.hp.com
- Acer—www.global.acer.com
- Toshiba—www.toshiba.com

From each of three of these or other sites, choose the most expensive and least expensive computer systems you can find for

- desktop computers
- notebook computers
- tablet PCs

Make up a table for each of the three types of computers and compare them based on the following criteria:

a. Type and speed of CPU
b. Type and speed of RAM
c. Amount of CPU cache
d. System bus speed
e. Hard disk capacity and speed (revolutions per minute or rpm)
f. Number and type of ports

2. Getting the Right Video Card

People who work extensively with images or engage in a lot of gaming often upgrade their video cards by buying a new video card that they plug into an expansion slot. This new one then takes the place of the video card if one came integrated into the motherboard. Many video cards today are AGP video cards. That means they don't go into one of the PCI slots on the motherboard, but instead they plug into the AGP slot (see Figure 6.3, #6, on page 164). This slot is exclusively for AGP video cards. The video card in Figure 6.18, page 179, is an AGP video card. Video cards usually have their own processors and memory. They're actually little, specialized computers in their own right. Since video is a heavy CPU-cycle user and takes up a lot of memory space, having a processor and memory on the video card takes some of the load off the CPU and RAM. In Figure 6.18 you'll notice a fan, which is there to cool off the video card processor.

Look at three sites and find out what's available in video cards. Below are some sites for you to try.

- Best Buy—www.bestbuy.com
- Circuit City—www.circuitcity.com
- PC Nation—www.pcnation.com

Find three video cards at each of three sites and answer the following questions:

a. Who is the manufacturer of the video card?
b. What sort of expansion slot (PCI or AGP) does the video card go into?
c. How much and what type of memory does the card have?
d. Does it support more than one monitor, i.e., can you divide up the output onto two or more monitors? If so, how many?
e. Is the video card plug and play?

3. Find Out about Wireless Devices

The types of wireless devices discussed in this chapter were IrDA and Bluetooth. Find five wireless or cordless devices (choose from mice, game controllers, keyboards, microphones, modems, PDAs, and so on) for sale at three Web sites:

- allNetDevices—www.allnetdevices.com
- Best Buy—www.bestbuy.com
- Deal Time—www.dealtime.com

Now answer these questions:

a. What devices did you choose?
b. What types of wireless devices are they (Bluetooth, IrDA, or RF)?
c. How much do they cost?
d. What wireless device would you especially like to have (may or may not be currently available) and why?

group activities

1. How Fast Is a Gigahertz?

Consumer computer CPUs can process at speeds above 3 gigahertz. That's actually quite fast. To see how fast it is, compare CPU speed to the blink of your eye. It takes you about one-tenth of a second to blink your eye. How long (in years) would it take you to blink enough times to match a second of CPU cycles in the table below, if you were to blink once per second? Do you think you'll live that long? How about if you blinked continuously—about 10 times per second?

CPU or Machine Cycles per Second	Time or "Blink Cycles"
1.8 GHz	
2.4 GHz	
3 GHz	
10 GHz	
15 GHz	

2. Visualize the Magnitude of Memory

In this exercise make some comparisons of area with amounts of memory. Let's say for argument's sake that 1 kilobyte of memory takes up 1 square inch of space. (You know that it's actually much, much smaller, or we couldn't fit so much RAM into such little chips.) How much memory would fit into the following areas?

Area	Amount of Memory
A 500-square-foot apartment. (Hint: 1 square foot is equal to 144 square inches.)	
A 3,000-square-foot house.	
A football field which is 120 yards by 53.33 yards. (Hint: 9 square feet make up 1 square yard.)	
A field that covers 1 acre.(Hint: An acre is 43,560 square feet.)	

3. Play CPU Cycle

As you now know, the CPU takes the instructions it gets from software and carries out those instructions. The CPU will do exactly what the instructions say to do—no more and no less. The CPU will assume absolutely nothing that the instructions don't tell it. To get some idea of how precise those instructions have to be, get different people in the group to play the various roles in the processing of software instructions. Play computer and make a peanut butter and jelly sandwich.

This is ideal for two-person teams. Let one person be the CPU and carry out the instructions that the other person gives—exactly. See how many ways there are to interpret any given instruction. For example, if the "instruction" person says, "put peanut butter on the knife," but hasn't yet instructed the "CPU" person to open the jar, the CPU person should say "ERROR."

4. What Type of Connectors Come on What Devices?

Some devices have USB connectors, others have Firewire, and still others use serial or parallel. Find five different models of each device below from different manufacturers, and note what type of connector or connectors are available with each one.

Device	Connector type(s)
External hard disk drive	
DVD burner	
CD burner	
Inkjet printer	
Laser printer	
Digital camera	
Digital camcorder	
Scanner	
Mouse	
Gamepad	

crossword puzzle

Across

1. It protects a network
3. Cat 5 provides a _______ for information
6. Joins computers together
9. Allowing file access from another computer on the network
11. Peer-to-_______
12. Network with wires
13. Joins computers together into a network
15. Wireless communication for medium distances
19. Two or more computers joined together
21. Mobile telephone switching office
23. Lets your customers have access to your internal Internet
26. Wireless standard
27. Internet for employees only
28. A system that helps people work together
29. Communications _______ facilitate the movement of information
30. Tells you where you are
32. A network that covers a small distance
34. Copy files on your computer to your PDA

Down

2. Strengthens a signal and passes it on
4. Wireless _______ point
5. Connects computers into a network
7. "There are no strings on me"
8. Provides services to client computers
10. Comes before 5
14. On the end of a wire
16. A device like a hub, switch, or router
17. The capacity of communications media
18. Fast Internet
20. Communication over great distances
22. _______ fiber
24. Local _______ network
25. A phone that you can use in the car
31. A unique number provided by the FCC
33. Network interface card

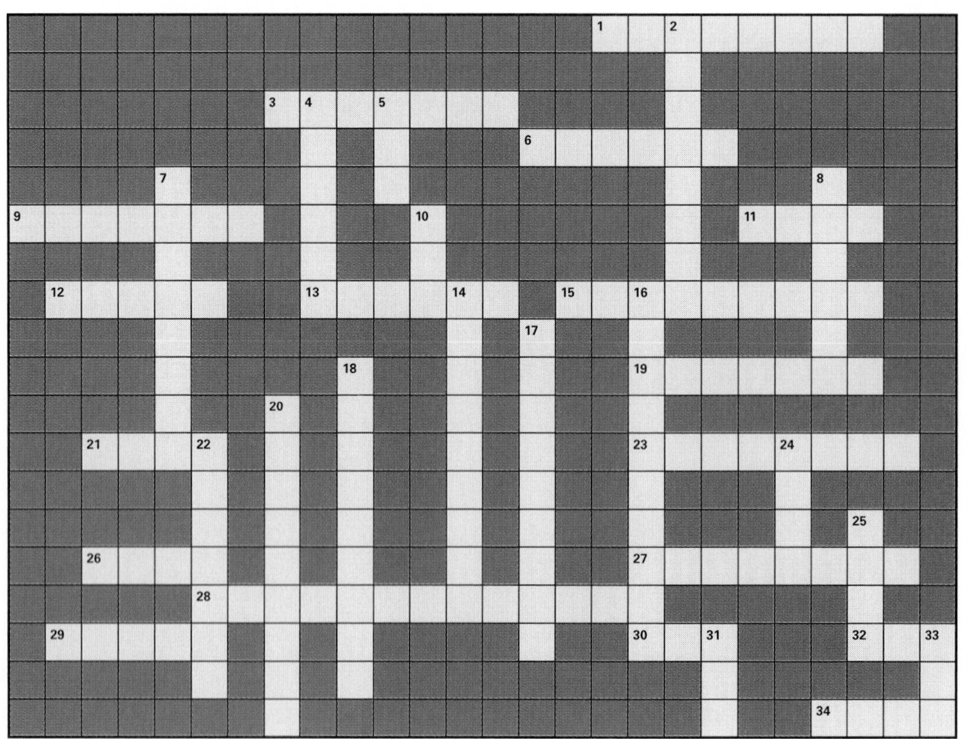

CHAPTER seven 7

The Nuts and Bolts of Networks

How Can You Use Networks to Your Advantage?

SIMNET CONCEPTS SUPPORT

did you know?

Networks are very much a part of modern life. They are used in many ways from file sharing at home and collaborating with people on different continents to finding your way in a blizzard and setting up your golf shot.

the *volunteers who searched for debris from the ill-fated space shuttle Columbia carried GPS receivers so that they could precisely determine the location of anything they found.*[1]

over *100 million Americans now use mobile phones, and tens of thousands of new customers join them every day. By 2005 the number of cell phone users will be about 1.6 billion worldwide.*[2]

each *GPS satellite (there are 24 of them) orbits the earth twice a day and, powered by the sun, travels at a speed of __??__ miles an hour.*

To find out how fast a GPS satellite travels, visit www.mhhe.com/i-series.

Student Learning Outcomes

After reading this chapter, you should be able to:

1. Identify and describe the four basic components of networks.
2. Describe what you need to set up a small peer-to-peer network at home.
3. Identify how you would wirelessly access a wired network.
4. Define client/server networks and what differentiates them from peer-to-peer.
5. Describe the three segments of a cellular phone system.
6. Explain the function of each of the three segments of a global positioning system.
7. Define the five types of communications media used in business networks.

Networks figure large in all of our lives. When you make a phone call, send an e-mail, engage in instant messaging, or do any other type of computer-based communication, you're using at least one network, and probably several. A ***computer network*** (which we simply refer to as a ***network***) is a collection of computers that support the sharing of information, software, and hardware devices. Computer technology and communications technology have merged to such an extraordinary degree that they're inseparable in some instances.

When you send an e-mail on your computer, you're actually using a lot of computers—not just one. The e-mail leaves your computer and travels across town, the nation, or the world, on its journey to the recipient. On the way, it stops briefly at many computers. So, in essence, you're using a number of computers to send e-mail. Actually, this works just like the snail mail you send, which goes from your local mail box to your local post office, then to another post office, and so on, until it reaches the recipient's local post office, from where it's delivered to the recipient's house. That is, it travels around the post office's mail network from you to the recipient.

When you rent a movie, a scanner reads the information on the video or DVD at the register. Then the register (which is actually a computer) goes to another computer (called a server) and gets the price and due date associated with that title. While consulting the server, the register also tells the server that the store's inventory has just been reduced temporarily by the title that you just rented. As the server gets the information about what has been rented and by whom, it can then tell the store assistant whether a particular title is in stock, and if not, when it's expected back, should a customer inquire.

If you order a pizza online, your order doesn't go directly to your local pizzeria. It first goes to your ISP's server, and from there zips from node to node on the Internet until it arrives at the pizza company's server, which finds the company's pizza parlor nearest to you and sends your order there. All this happens in a matter of seconds.

Networks make many of the conveniences of modern life possible—cellular phones, cars that can display maps of where you are, credit card authorization, online pizza ordering, and on and on.

did you know?

52 *percent of the foreign-born Americans are from Latin America, 26 percent from Asia, 16 percent from Europe, and 6 percent come from elsewhere.*[3]

7.1 NETWORKS: THE BIG PICTURE

The term "network" is a very elastic one. It can mean a few computers connected so that they can share a printer, or thousands of computers belonging to a large organization and tied together so that information can move between them. Undoubtedly, the largest network on the planet is the

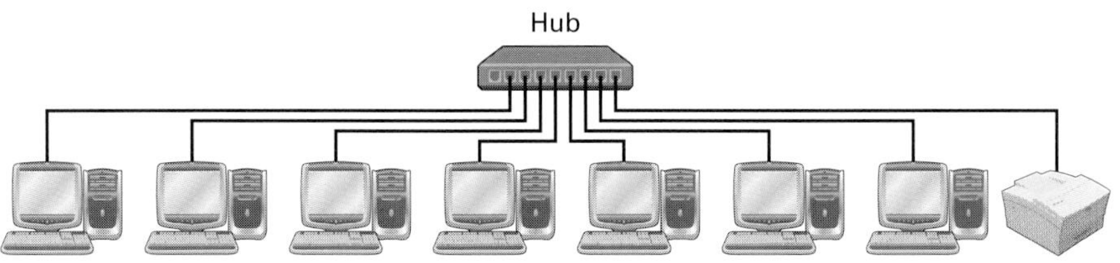

FIGURE 7.1

A hub is a device that ties together the computers in a network.

Internet with millions and millions of computers linking to and disengaging from that global network every minute of every day. But, no matter how large or small they are, all networks have certain characteristics in common. These are network cards, connecting devices, communications media, and network operating system software.

NETWORK CARDS
Do I Need Any Special Hardware in the Network Computers?

Each computer on the network must have a network interface card. A ***network interface card (NIC)*** is an expansion card or a PC Card (for a notebook computer) that connects your computer to a network and provides the doorway for information to flow in and out. Many people call an NIC a ***network card.***

CONNECTING DEVICES
What Directs the Information to the Right Network Recipient?

The whole point of a network is to connect computers so that information can flow between them. So, you need a way of connecting the computers. You do this with a connecting device—one type is called a hub (see Figure 7.1)—that ties the computers together and passes messages between them.

COMMUNICATIONS MEDIA
How Does Information Move between the Network Computers?

Information needs a pathway on which to move between the computers and the connecting device. In a wired network, information is converted into electrical or light pulses that run along the corresponding type of cable. In a wireless network, information in the form of waves is sent out through the air by one wireless device and captured by another.

NETWORK OPERATING SYSTEM SOFTWARE
Do I Need Any Special Software to Run Networked Computers?

As always, when you have hardware, you need software to make it work. The operating system in your computer moves information between components of the computer system. When you have a network, there's additional information movement required, that is, information has to move in and out of the computer itself. So you need a network operating system. A ***network operating system (network OS*** or ***NOS)*** runs a network, steering information between computers, managing security and users, and enabling many people to work together across the network (see Figure 7.2).

FIGURE 7.2

Each computer on a network needs network operating system software to facilitate information moving in and out of the computer.

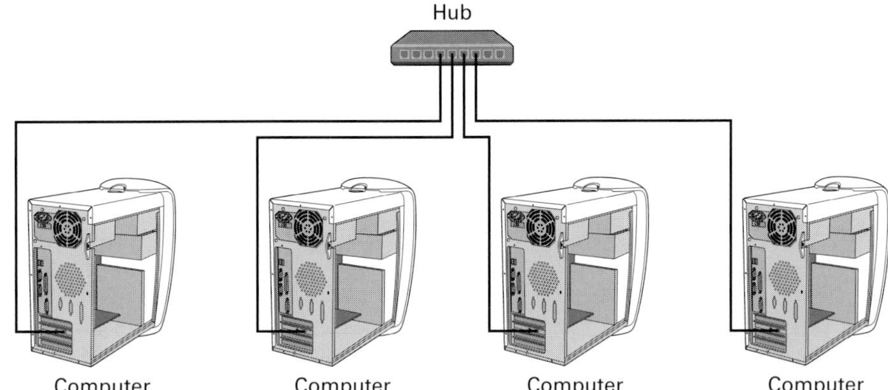

FIGURE 7.3

A network needs a hub, with cables connected to the network cards in the computers.

To recap, all networks have four basic components in common (see Figure 7.3). These are

1. A network card in each computer to act as a doorway for information to move in and out.
2. One or more connecting devices to connect the computers together and to pass messages between them.
3. Cable to provide a pathway for information to move around on or wireless devices that propel information through the air.
4. Software, in the form of a network operating system, that has the instructions that direct the movement of information.

To learn more about connectivity using networks, complete the "Connectivity Concepts" and "What Is a Network?" tutorials on your SimNet Concepts Support CD.

APPLYING NETWORK CONCEPTS
How Could I Use a Network of My Own?

In case you're wondering how this information on network components might be useful to you, think about the benefits of sharing. If you have roommates, you're sharing housing and thus benefiting from lower costs. Sharing your roommate's TV saves you from having to buy your own, and uses less energy. A computer network has some of the same advantages. With a network, you can share

- A printer (or other hardware) among several computers.
- Large (or small) files, so that you don't have to keep multiple copies on different computers.
- A broadband Internet connection among many computers.
- Online game playing with people in the same house (in a LAN party) or with others on the Internet.

A ***local area network (LAN)*** is a network in the same building, complex, or small geographic area. The term is used to describe a small network. So, when people get together, either physically or virtually, to play games online, it's called a LAN party.

In the next section you'll learn how to set up your own network at home so that you can benefit from the power of network computing. A lone computer brings you great benefits—by joining several computers into a network your advantages rise exponentially. And don't assume that the knowledge or skill you need to build a small network rises exponentially as well. Setting up a small network in your home or dorm is actually quite a simple task.

did you know?

75 percent of Americans had high school diplomas in 1990. That number went up 5 percent to 80 percent in 2000.[4]

making the grade

1. Two or more computers connected so that they can communicate with each other and share information is called a(n) __________.
2. A(n) __________ is an expansion card or a PC Card that connects your computer to a network, providing a doorway for information to flow in and out.
3. One type of network connecting device is called a(n) __________.
4. A small network in a building, or group of buildings, is called a(n) __________.
5. The software that runs a network, steering information between computers is called a(n) __________.

7.2 HOME NETWORKS

You can create a simple network at home that you could use to send information from your notebook computer to the printer attached to your desktop computer. You and your roommates could use your home network to access image, music, or data files on each other's computers, and of course, share hardware like a printer, as well as one Internet connection.

The simplest kind of network is a ***peer-to-peer network,*** in which all computers are equal, and each can have access to devices and files on the others. Each computer independently stores its own software and information, but can access the information on the other computers. All the computers on the network can access devices connected to any of the other computers. You can set up a small peer-to-peer network at home with some basic components that you can get at any store that sells computer hardware.

We discussed the general network components in the previous section. Now we'll look at the specific components you could use in a home network. You'll need (see Figure 7.4):

- *Network interface card:* An Ethernet network card (as the network interface card) for each computer in the network.

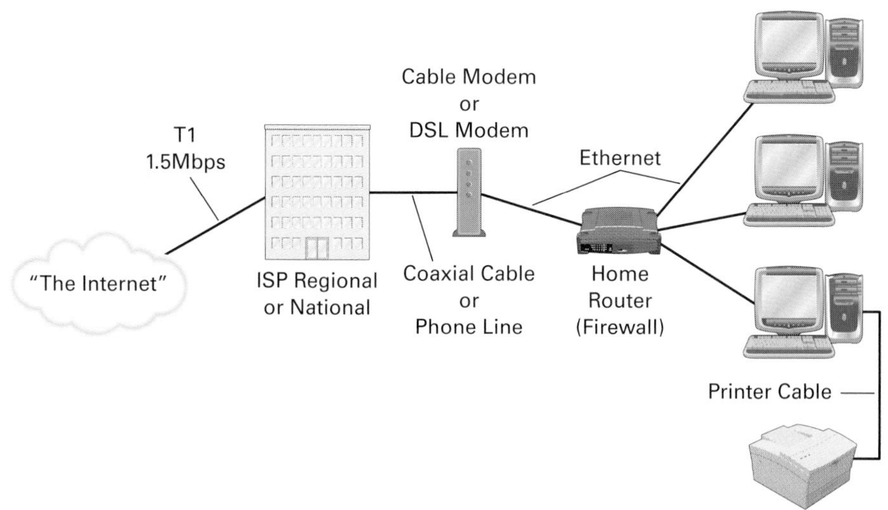

FIGURE 7.4

A wired home network could have a home router, cables, and Ethernet cards in each computer.

- *Connecting device:* A home router to act as a connecting device tying the computers together.
- *Pathways for information:* Cat 5 cables to provide a way to move information between the computers and the home router.
- *Network operating system:* Windows operating system software on each computer allows information to move in and out of that computer.

To learn more about peer-to-peer networks, complete the "Peer-to-Peer Systems" tutorial on your SimNet Concepts Support CD.

ETHERNET CARDS

What Is an Ethernet Card?

An ***Ethernet card*** is the most common type of network interface card. There are three forms of Ethernet cards. The first type is one that is integrated into the motherboard. You won't be able to visually examine the motherboard and pick it out—it's simply part of the circuitry, like printer and sound cards usually are. However, you will be able to see the Ethernet port and that's where you would plug in the cable.

The second type is an expansion card. If you don't have an Ethernet card integrated into your motherboard, or you want a different network card, you can buy an expansion card that goes into the PCI slot in your desktop computer. It has the same type of port for the cable as the integrated type. And, again, you can access it on the back panel of your computer.

The third type of Ethernet card is a PC Card that slides into the PC Card slot on your notebook computer. It, too, has a port for the cable.

The type of port that each of the Ethernet card types has is called an RJ-45 port that fits in an RJ-45 connector. An ***RJ-45 connector*** (also called an ***Ethernet connector***) is the same shape as the phone connectors on the ends of your telephone wire, but is wider. It's always accessible from outside your computer.

ROUTERS

What's the Difference between Hubs, Switches, and Home Routers?

Hubs, switches, and home routers are all connecting devices that pass messages between computers, but they have different features. A ***network hub*** or ***hub*** is a device that connects computers into a network, broadcasting all messages it gets to every computer on the network, although only the intended recipient computer takes the message. The computers that are not the recipients of the message simply ignore it. Also, a hub can handle only one-way information traffic at a time, like a narrow bridge that's only wide enough for one car.

A ***switch*** is a device that connects computers into a network and, unlike a hub, sends messages only to the computer that is the intended recipient. It can also handle multiple communications channels at the same time, like a multilane highway. Another feature of a switch is that it can temporarily segment parts of the network with high traffic from the rest of the network. For example, say you have computers in every room in your home connected into a network and people in three rooms are playing an online game. A switch on your network could separate these computers from the rest into a mini self-contained network, so that the heavy traffic among the three gamers does not disrupt the rest of the computer traffic. In effect, a switch is a hub with special features.

did you know?

On average, an American child spends 900 hours a year in school—and 1,500 hours a year watching television.[5]

i•can

Protect My Home Network from Intruders

With a broadband connection, you have an always-on Internet connection, meaning that unless your computer is off you're connected to the Internet. Remember that if you can get to the Internet, it can get to you, and it does so frequently in the form of cookies, e-mail delivery, and so on. Your network's router can help protect you from intruders who may try to access your computer from the Internet. This is possible because a home router assigns private IP addresses to the computers on its network and these IP addresses are hidden from the Internet.

When you get a broadband Internet connection, your ISP assigns your connection an IP address. An IP address (or Internet protocol address) is a number that's assigned to a computer on a network to identify it. It takes the form of four sets of digits separated by dots. For example, 192.168.1.104 is one such IP address. Each of the four numbers is a value between 0 and 255. The ISP uses your computer's IP address to identify your connection.

To protect your home network from Internet intruders, who can sometimes find that IP address and get to your computer, you can use a home router. Your home router assigns private IP addresses to each of the computers on your home network, using a process called network address translation (NAT). With NAT, the router can identify each computer and recognize when a message is supposed to go from one to another—it knows, from the IP addresses, which is which. So, the computers on your network can visit different parts of the Internet simultaneously. The router keeps track of which computer wants to go where because of the private IP addresses. Hubs and switches don't have this NAT feature, which makes private IP addresses invisible to people on the Internet.

A home router has even more special features—in fact, it's a switch with special features. A ***home router*** is a device that connects computers into a network, and also connects dissimilar networks together (like a home network and the Internet), separating the network traffic and keeping local traffic inside its own network (see Figure 7.5). Like a switch, a router can also handle multiple communications channels.

FIGURE 7.5

A home router is a switch with special features.

Of special interest to home network owners is the home router's ability to connect networks together while keeping local traffic confined. This means that a home router provides a measure of protection for your network, that is, a home router can act as a firewall. It stops messages between people on your home network from getting out, and furthermore stops intruders from getting into your home network from the Internet. See the I-Can box for an explanation of how a home router works as a firewall.

Note that in this section we've been discussing home routers. A router built for large networks is a bit different. It still connects networks together, but isn't a device into which you would plug computers.

WIRED COMMUNICATIONS MEDIA

What Kind of Cables Do I Need?

The most common type of cable used in home networks is Cat 5 cable, which is similar to twisted-pair phone cable. ***Cat 5,*** or ***Category 5, cable*** is a more robust version of ordinary phone cable. Each end of the Cat 5 cable has an RJ-45 connector. One plugs into the Ethernet card on your computer and the other end into your home router. You'll need Cat 5 cable, with a connector on each end, for each computer on the network.

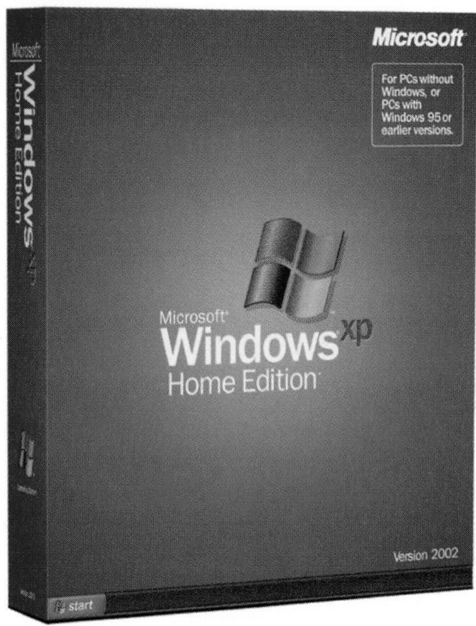

FIGURE 7.6

The Windows operating system that comes on a computer when you buy it is equipped to handle the movement of information in and out of your computer.

NETWORK OPERATING SYSTEM SOFTWARE

Do I Need Any Operating System Software besides Windows?

For a small home network, Windows will do fine (see Figure 7.6). Use Windows 98 SE or a later version. Windows must be installed on all the computers in the network, but that's not usually a problem, since most computers come with Windows already installed.

WIRELESS NETWORK ACCESS

How Do I Get Wireless Access to My Network for My Notebook?

Wireless communication between devices means that information travels as waves through the air from one to the other. As you've already learned in Chapter 6, there are different types of wireless communication between devices. You've already seen Bluetooth and IrDA, also known as infrared. IrDA uses red light below what your eye can see, and Bluetooth uses radio waves. Bluetooth is not the only type of radio wave information transmission system. WiFi is another example. The main difference between these two, from a consumer point of view, is their reach—Bluetooth is good for about 30 feet, while WiFi extends about 300 feet.

You might use Bluetooth in your car. For example, you might wirelessly connect your cell phone, PDA, and notebook computer. But inside your house, where distances between devices are greater, you'd probably need WiFi.

WiFi is a standard for transmitting information in the form of radio waves over distances of up to 300 feet, often used for wireless access to networks. You'll see WiFi-capable devices like PDAs and notebook computers advertised by companies that sell computers and computer components.

did you know?

The only countries in which the number of females who use the Internet outnumber the males are the United States and Canada. American and Canadian men, however, on average, spend more time online than women.[6]

Wireless Access to a Wired Network

To get wireless access to your wired home network, you'll need a device called a wireless network access point. A ***wireless network access point*** or ***wireless access point*** (sometimes referred to as a ***WAP***) is a device that allows computers to access a network using radio waves. A wireless access point has a transmitter and a receiver for bi-directional flow of informa-

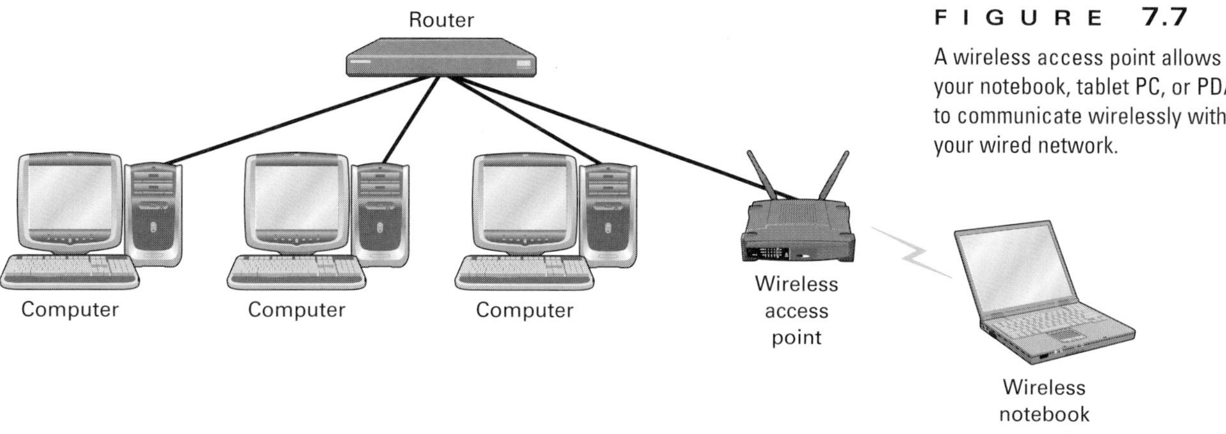

FIGURE 7.7

A wireless access point allows your notebook, tablet PC, or PDA to communicate wirelessly with your wired network.

tion. It also has an antenna that radiates outgoing radio waves through the air and captures incoming waves.

You can attach your wireless access point in the same way you attach your computers. That is, you use a cable with RJ-45 connectors on each end, connecting one end into the router, and the other into the wireless access point (see Figure 7.7). For your notebook to access the network, you would need a wireless PC Card (also called a WiFi card). A WiFi card incorporates a transmitter, a receiver, and an antenna, just as the wireless access point does. This way, the wireless access point and the PC Card can swap information back and forth. Tablet PCs, notebook computers, and newer PDAs usually have WiFi built in for easy transfer of information.

Completely Wireless Network

Many home network wireless access points are routers too, so you can set up your wireless network the same way you did the wired one—with the exception of the cables. But, you don't even need a wireless router to connect a small number of computers together. First, you need to put a wireless network card into each desktop computer. You can get wireless network cards for PCI slots in desktop computers or a wireless network adapter that plugs into a USB port on the outside of your computer. Second, make sure that all wireless devices are within, at most, 300 feet of each other. The distance varies according to the number and types of obstacles in the way. For example, a house has walls and furniture that shorten the distance you can have between wireless devices. To learn more about wireless networks and communications, complete the "Wireless Communications" tutorial on your SimNet Concepts Support CD and visit the Web site for this text at www.mhhe.com/i-series.

REASONS TO HAVE A HOME NETWORK
What Are the Advantages of Having a Home Network?

We've already mentioned that a home network allows you to share an Internet connection as well as hardware and files. With the increasing popularity of mobile devices, swapping information between computer devices without removable storage media (like floppy disks, Zip disks, CDs, or DVDs) is becoming ever more important.

Sharing an Internet Connection

You can share one broadband Internet connection among several computers by connecting your DSL, cable, or satellite modem to your home router (see again Figure 7.4 on page 197). Instead of connecting one more computer, you're connecting a network—the Internet. A word of caution: Before you hook up a network to a single Internet connection, make sure that it's not a violation of the contract you signed with your ISP.

Sharing Hardware and Folders

To share a printer on your home network, connect it to one computer with a printer cable and let the other computers access the computer with the printer by turning on the printer sharing option.

To share files, you need to use the file sharing option in Windows. ***File sharing*** means that you can share the files on your computer with others who are part of your network. You actually share whole folders or drives, rather than individual files. For information on how to turn on file sharing and printer sharing, see the Consumer Q&A at the end of this chapter.

Transferring Information Between Devices

Transferring information from one computing device to another now has a new dimension. Mobile computing devices like PDAs and tablet PCs have very few, if any, of the removable storage media that desktop and notebook computers do. This means that you need a network more than ever to be able to transfer information between them. Also, since our newest information devices are mobile, it would be nice to be able to wirelessly sync the devices from anywhere in your home without having to hook up cables first. To "sync" devices such as a PDA and a notebook computer means to copy file additions or changes made on one device to the other so that the files are the same (or synchronized). To learn more about home networks, visit the Web site for this text at www.mhhe.com/i-series.

SECTION 7.2

making the grade

1. A(n) ____________ network has a small number of computers that can share hardware or files.
2. An Ethernet card is the most common type of ____________.
3. A(n) ____________ is the connector on the end of a network cable that you plug into a network card.
4. You can connect a wireless access point to your wired computer by plugging it into your ____________.
5. A wireless PC Card has a transmitter, a receiver, and a(n) ____________ just like a wireless access point does.

7.3 LARGE NETWORKS

In this section, we'll shift focus from the small networks that you create and control yourself to large ones that affect you in some way. Some merely store information about you; others serve your needs, like helping you work on a course assignment; and still others improve your life—cellular telephone networks, for instance.

ORGANIZATIONAL NETWORKS

How Are Organizational Networks Different from Home Networks?

In a peer-to-peer home network all computers are equal. Each one has its own files and devices that it can let other computers share. In a business environment, you'll probably use a client/server network instead of a peer-to-peer network, unless you run a small business with very few computers.

A ***client/server network*** is a network in which one or more computers are servers and provide services to the other computers, which are called clients. The server or servers have hardware, software, and/or information that the client computers can access (see Figure 7.8). Servers are usually powerful computers with large storage systems. Depending on the network, the server could be a high-end PC, a minicomputer, or even a mainframe. Large companies often have several servers, each of which may perform a different task or serve different parts of the company. It's usually cheaper and more efficient to have software on a server where everyone can access it because

- A network license allowing people on the network to use a software package is usually cheaper than buying separate copies of software for each computer.
- It's easier to update one server copy of software than to update hundreds or even thousands of separate copies.
- Control and security of software and information is easier if they're on the server. For example, when you log into a network, the server can check that your access is authorized.

Client/Server Networks

There are more physical implementations of client/server networks than models of cars on the road. Conceptually, however, all large networks work on the same principle as little ones. You still need network cards, communications media, and network operating systems on all the computers in the network. And you need at least one connecting device—a hub or switch—to tie the computers together.

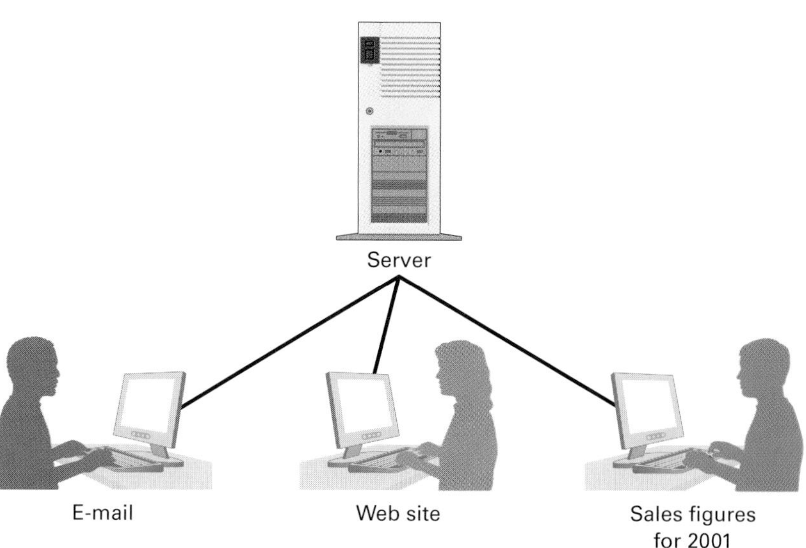

FIGURE 7.8

A server provides services to the other computers on the network, which are called clients.

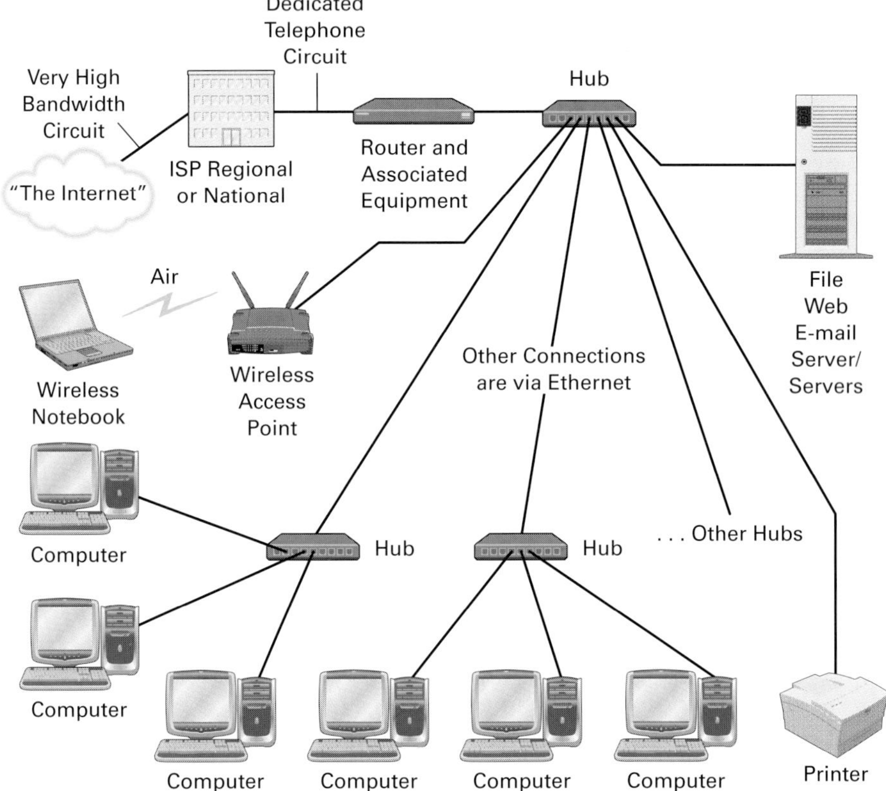

FIGURE 7.9

A large network has more hubs, switches, and routers than a small home network, and is much more complex to implement.

This is not to say that large networks are simple to build and maintain—they most definitely are not. The number of considerations goes up exponentially with the size of the network. For a client/server network, you need a special operating system for the servers. You may have to install special network processors. You also have to consider which communications media and protocols to use. As you learned in Chapter 3, a communications protocol is a set of rules that every computer follows to transfer information. TCP/IP (Transport Control Protocol/Internet Protocol), for example, is the protocol that computers connected to the Internet have to use to be able to talk to the other computers. It's quite a simple concept—if the computers don't all speak the same language they can't communicate.

Figure 7.9 shows a typical network for a business. A large network might span many states or even be scattered all over the world. To learn more about client/server networks, complete "The Client/Server Relationship" tutorial on your SimNet Concepts Support CD.

did you know?

Of the 8,413,854 domains on the Internet, 53 percent or 4,453,807 are commercial (.com) sites.[7]

How Organizations Use Networks

Regardless of how a business network is physically constructed, the objective is to allow people to have access to information and devices and to communicate—the same reasons you had for creating your home network. Businesses use different methods of achieving these objectives, since they have so many more computers that serve a large number of people with diverse needs.

One way that businesses use networks is to provide a locally accessible information resource for members of the organization, called an intranet. An ***intranet*** is an internal organizational Internet that is guarded

i-series insights — *Ethics, Security & Privacy*

Big Brother in England: A Network of Cameras

In England, almost every town, from the teeming city of London to the smallest hamlet, has surveillance cameras on the corners of buildings and built into street lamps. Victoria Station, one of the most famous spots in London, has about a dozen cameras in its vicinity. *The Economist,* a British publication, says that 1.5 million cameras monitor Britons, and on average, a citizen is recorded by these cameras 300 times a day.

The surveillance has three uses: (1) It continuously monitors street activity, (2) it stores images of events for possible future use, and (3) it identifies wanted persons.

The cameras in the surveillance network deliver images to a monitoring center where officials keep an eye on what's happening on the streets. The monitoring centers are also connected to a server with a huge database of photos of people wanted by the police. The images captured by cameras are fed to software that compares each one with the pictures in the database and signals when a match is found. The images are then stored in case they're needed in the future.

The implications of this collection of facial images are far-reaching. Scotland Yard shares its information with other crime-fighting organizations. For example, British police, and those in many other countries, work with Interpol, the international crime-fighting organization.

against outside access by special security hardware and/or software called a firewall. Consider again your home network where you have a broadband modem connected to your home router. In effect, you have a private network in your home, connected to another network (the Internet). Your home network is protected by your home router, which can, and most often does, act as a firewall. So, in effect, you have an intranet at home that only people in your house can access.

But internal access to a network is usually not sufficient for an organization. Consider your educational institution. Certainly, some information and access must stay within the institution, but it's also necessary for certain people, not employed by the school, to be able to access the system. This sort of network access is called an extranet. An ***extranet*** is an extension of an intranet that allows other organizations and people access to information and application software on an internal intranet. Again, consider your home network as an example. You can most likely access your institution's registration and enrollment system from your home through the Internet. In that case, you're accessing your school's extranet, not as an employee, but as someone else who needs access.

Another way you may access your institution's network is through the use of a course delivery system like Blackboard, WebCT, eCollege, or Jones International. Course delivery systems allow students and instructors to communicate and work together, by providing, at a minimum, a place where students can retrieve course materials. They also allow synchronous (same time) and asynchronous (different time) interaction. That is, you communicate back and forth like you would in any chat room, or you can leave messages and materials where others can access them.

To learn more about how intranets and extranets work, complete the "Intranets and Extranets" tutorial on your SimNet Concepts Support CD. To learn more about administering a network and working with network software, complete the "Network Software and Network Administration" tutorial on your SimNet Concepts Support CD.

FIGURE 7.10

A collaboration system allows people to work together even if they're in different parts of the world.

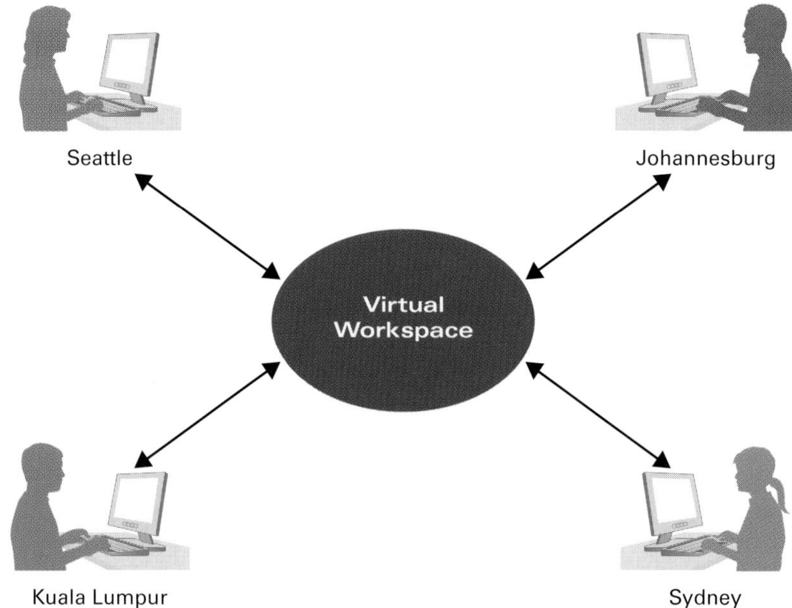

A system designed to allow people to work together in this way is called a collaboration system. A ***collaboration system*** is software that allows people to work together. Any system that incorporates e-mail, chat rooms, instant messaging, e-mail, and/or any other form of communication and exchange is a collaboration system. It's often a feature of an extranet.

One of the major application areas of collaboration systems is in B2B e-commerce. As you saw in Chapter 2, e-commerce is simply traditional business in a new form. It's conducted in cyberspace, but is still based on relationships—which means people working together. Web-based collaboration tools use the power of the Internet to enable people to work together effectively and efficiently (see Figure 7.10).

Groove and NextPage are both examples of a special kind of collaboration system software called a peer-to-peer collaboration system. A ***peer-to-peer collaboration system*** is software that enables people to communicate and share documents between peers without going through a central server. It's based on the Napster principle, which was the first system that allowed people to exchange files (music) with each other straight from the participants' computers. The music was not stored on Napster's server. Peer-to-peer collaboration systems are used extensively in B2B e-commerce, where companies need to access each other's files to work together effectively. See Chapter 14 for an expanded discussion on this topic. To learn more about network technologies, visit the Web site for this text at www.mhhe.com/i-series.

There's a huge market for people who are skilled in networking, from network managers to technicians. If you're interested in becoming a technician, you can get certification training for the Microsoft and Novell networks (to name just two). If you want to design networks or be a network administrator, you'll need a degree in information systems or computer science.

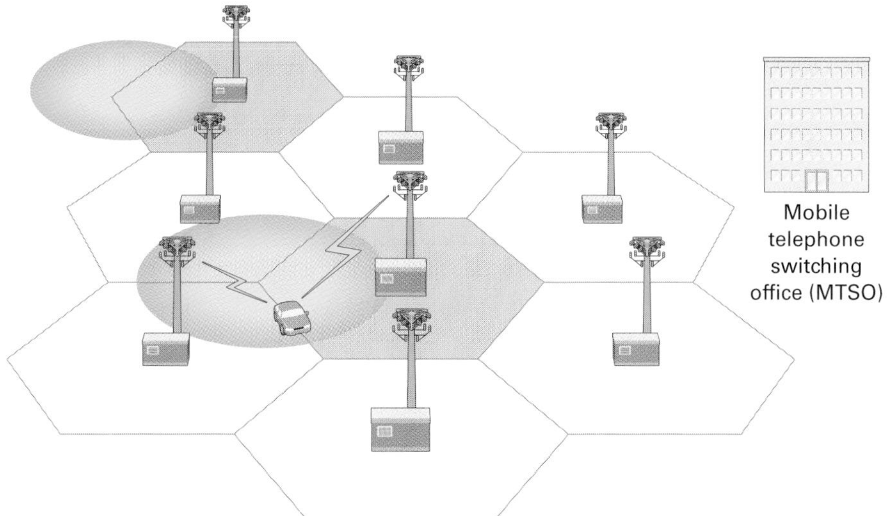

FIGURE 7.11

A cell phone network divides up its coverage area into cells, which are laced into a grid. Each cell has its own base station with an antenna and other equipment that make cell phone calls possible. Nonadjacent cells can use the same frequency.

CELLULAR TELEPHONES—WORLDWIDE WIRELESS NETWORKS

How Do Cell Phones Work?

Some businesses build one or more networks for their own employees, others allow access to select groups, and still others build networks and sell access to them to consumers. Two of the wireless networks most used by consumers are cellular telephone networks and global positioning systems.

Cell phones are actually wireless two-way radios. Two-way radios differ from the radio in your car in that you can't talk back to your car radio—it's a one-way transmission. Cell phones send and receive information in the form of radio waves, using a range of frequencies. Just as your favorite radio station has a frequency and no other radio in the vicinity can use that frequency, a cell phone gives you your own frequency when you want to make a call. There wouldn't be enough frequencies for all the people who want to use cell phones except for the clever reuse of frequencies.

The way it works is that an area of coverage is divided into hexagonal "cells" (hence the term cell phone), each of which cover an area equivalent to about 10 square miles (see Figure 7.11). Nonadjacent cells can use the same frequency at the same time. With this system, millions of people can talk on cell phones at the same time.

Each cell has a base station. When you turn on your cell phone it (1) listens for the ***system identification code (SID)***—a unique number that the Federal Communications Commission (FCC) assigned your carrier; and (2) sends its own identification number to the base station, which picks it up with its antenna, which is usually located on a tower. When you make a call, the number you key in goes to the base station, too.

If your cell phone doesn't hear any SID at all, it means that it can't communicate with any base station. That's why you get that no-service message. You can't make or take a call unless your cell phone is in contact with a base station.

When your cell phone locates an SID, it may be from your carrier's base station or from that of another carrier. If the cell phone SID and the base station SID match, then the base station belongs to your carrier. In this case, the base station sends your cell's identification to its ***mobile telephone switching office (MTSO),*** which stores it in its database so that it can find you when calls come in for you.

practically speaking

Selecting a Cell Phone

In selecting a cell phone and carrier you need to ask yourself two very important questions: (1) Where will I use my phone? and (2) How will I use it? This leads to considerations like whether you want an analog or digital phone; regular cellular or PCS; extent of your coverage area; and additional services.

Analog vs. digital: In the beginning, cell phones worked on an analog system. Now, they're mostly digital because that allows calls to be compressed more easily when they're moving between phones, increasing the number of simultaneous calls possible. Some parts of the country still operate on the analog system only. If you buy an analog cell phone, you can be reasonably sure that it will work in all the areas covered by your carrier. However, if you choose an analog phone, you'll be sacrificing lots of nice features and transmission quality. Alternatively, you can get a dual-mode phone that will use digital where available, and analog otherwise.

Regular cellular vs. PCS: PCS or personal communications service is a completely digital system that emphasizes personal use of the cell phone for services such as paging, caller-ID, sending e-mail and photos, and Web access.

Extent of coverage area: Within the United States, there are three types of cellular phone networks, and you can't use a phone for one type on another type. You can also get world phones if you travel overseas (see the Consumer Q&A at the end of this chapter for more on the three types of cell phone networks).

Features: The features available for cell phones are many and varied. Each carrier has its own list. When you're buying a cell phone, try out all the features before you buy.

If the SID that your cell phone locates does not match the cell phone's SID, the cell phone knows it's roaming. In that case the base station again sends your cell phone's identification to its MTSO, which then contacts your carrier's MTSO with information on your whereabouts.

As you move, the base station tracks your cell phone and hands over control to another base station when you move into another cell area.

GLOBAL POSITIONING SYSTEMS (GPS)

How Does GPS Work and What Can It Do for Me?

A ***global positioning system (GPS)*** is a navigational system that uses satellites to tell you where you are, how fast you're going, and what direction you're headed in. GPS is funded by and controlled by the U.S. Department of Defense (DOD), although thousands, if not millions, of civilians use GPS worldwide. GPS is another example of a wireless network from which you, as a consumer, can benefit relatively inexpensively. And, why not? After all, taxpayers have already paid for the system.

How GPS Works

GPS consists of three major parts: satellites, receivers, and ground control stations. The satellite part has 24 satellites, each completing its own orbit every 12 hours at about 12,000 miles above the earth (see Figure 7.12). The receivers are the GPS devices that we use to find out where we are. The ground control part consists of five ground stations, located in different parts of the world, that monitor the system.

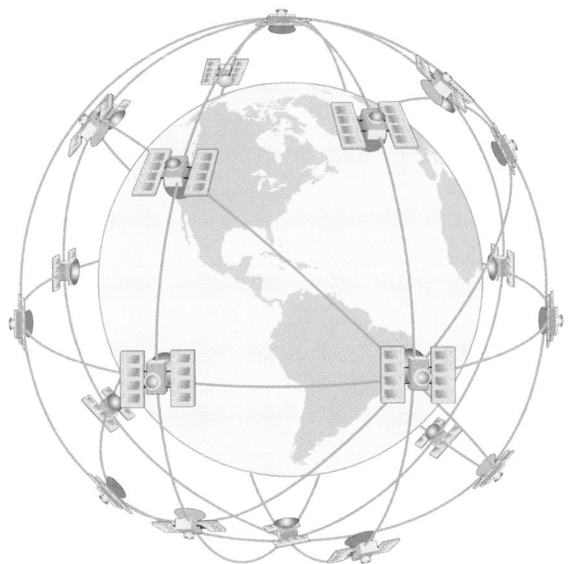

FIGURE 7.12

12,000 miles above the earth, 24 Department of Defense global positioning satellites orbit the earth.

GPS works like this. Say you were somewhere and didn't know where. Then someone told you that you were 720 miles from Casper, Wyoming; that you were also 701 miles from Detroit, Michigan; and 816 miles from Brownsville, Texas. When you draw three circles, with radii corresponding to the distances, on a map, the three will intersect in only one place—your location. This is a method of pinpointing a location called triangulation—you're in the center of a triangle (see Figure 7.13).

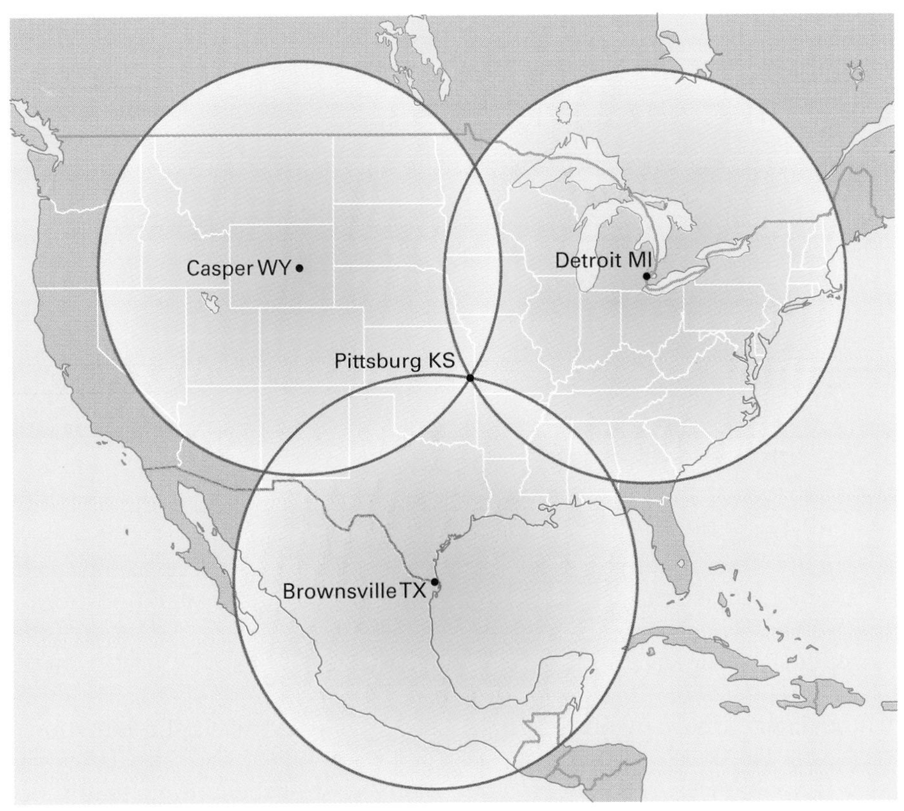

FIGURE 7.13

Given three circles each with a known radius that intersect, you can pinpoint a location.

The method that the GPS uses is a little more complex, since in space we're dealing with spheres, which are three-dimensional. But the general principle is the same. Using the known positions of at least three or four satellites, your GPS receiver can pinpoint your location on earth with considerable accuracy.

Uses of GPS

Police, fire, and emergency medical teams have GPS receivers in their vehicles pinpointing their exact location, which is then transmitted back so the unit closest to the emergency can be sent to help. Newer autos have map displays as an option. The map displays rely on GPS receivers and a map database. People use GPS receivers to keep track of the best fishing spot in the lake, or to find the exact spot where something fell overboard. If you lose something out the window of your car, you can note the exact spot so that you can find it when you go back.

People are even using GPS receivers to keep track of where their children are. A system called *Whereify* is a pager/cell phone/GPS that can relay information to parents on the whereabouts of their children. You can use a GPS to tell the tow truck exactly where to come to get you out of the ditch, and you can even use it to improve your golf game by measuring the precise distance between the ball and the pin, thus enabling you to choose the right club for the shot.

The three largest GPS receiver device companies are Magellan, Garmin, and Trimble. You can also buy a GPS card for your PDA that includes map information.

SECTION 7.3

making the grade

1. A network in which one or more computers provide services to the other computers is called a(n) ___________ network.
2. A(n) ___________ is an internal organizational Internet that is guarded against outside access by a firewall.
3. A system that allows people to work together and incorporates e-mail, chat rooms, and so on is called a(n) ___________.
4. A(n) ___________ is a navigational system that uses satellites to tell you where you are and how fast you're going.
5. A cellular telephone is actually a two-way ___________.

7.4 COMMUNICATIONS MEDIA

The objective of a business network is to move information from one place to another, and to facilitate the sharing of both information and hardware. For consumers, a network is nice to have; for businesses, it's a matter of survival. Businesses must be able to reliably move information across town or between continents.

Whatever the case, information must travel over some path from its source to its destination. ***Communications media*** are the paths, or physical channels, in a network over which information travels. In your home network, you have a choice of Cat 5 cable or WiFi (wireless). Businesses have more choices. Actually, so do you, but most of them are prohibitively

Wired	Wireless
• Cat 5 twisted-pair cable (variation on phone cable)	• Infrared, Bluetooth, and WiFi for short distances
• Optical fiber cable (uses light pulses to transfer information)	• Microwave for medium distances • Satellite for long distances

FIGURE 7.14
Communications media can be wired or wireless.

expensive for regular consumers. Businesses, however, need, and can pay for, the speed, capacity, and reach that other communications media afford.

All communications between computers are either wired or wireless (see Figure 7.14). ***Wired communications media*** transmit information over a closed, connected path. ***Wireless communications media*** transmit information through the air.

BANDWIDTH
What Does Bandwidth Mean?

Before discussing the various types of communications media, we must first address bandwidth. The ***bandwidth,*** or capacity, of the communications medium refers to the amount of information that a communications medium can transfer in a given amount of time. You measure the capacity of a communications medium in bits per second (bps), thousands of bits per second (Kbps), or millions of bits per second (Mbps). To learn more about bandwidth, complete the "Bandwidth and Data Transmission" tutorial on your SimNet Concepts Support CD.

The top speed at which a telephone modem can move information is about 56 Kbps, that is, 56,000 bits per second. For a DSL modem, speeds vary from 144 Kbps (144,000 bits per second) to 1.54 Mbps (1,540,000 bits per second), and can even go as high as 6.0 Mbps. Bandwidth is comparable to the size of a drinking straw—the fatter the straw, the more liquid you can drink in a given period of time.

WIRED COMMUNICATIONS MEDIA
What Kinds of Wired Communications Media Are There?

Wired communications media are those that connect devices with cables of some kind. Twisted-pair and optical fiber are the types of cabling you'd normally find in business computer networks. Optical fiber is not generally used in home networks since it's expensive to install and maintain.

Twisted-Pair

Twisted-pair cable comes in several varieties. The Cat 5 that you read about in connection with home networks earlier in this chapter is one type. Most of the world's phone system is twisted-pair and since it's already in place, it's an obvious choice for networks.

The simplest type of twisted-pair phone cabling (Cat 1) provides a slow, fairly reliable path for information at up to 64 kilobits per second (Kbps), while a better type (Cat 3) provides up to 10 megabits per second (Mbps).

Cat 5, or Category 5, cable provides a much higher bandwidth than ordinary phone cable, so it's the most widely used cabling for data transfer in today's business networks (see Figure 7.15). Cat 5 is relatively inexpensive and is fairly easy to install and maintain.

FIGURE 7.15
Cat 5 twisted-pair cable (like phone wire, except more robust) is used for connecting computers in home and business networks.

However, twisted-pair of any kind is relatively easy to tap into and so it's not very secure. It's even possible to access the information by simply detecting the signals that "leak" out.

A second disadvantage of twisted-pair cabling is the distinct possibility of distortion in the information during transfer. Distance, noise on the line, and interference tend to cause information to be lost or damaged. For example, a crackle that changes a credit card number from 5244 081**1** 2643 741 to 5244 081**0** 2643 741 is more than a nuisance; in business it means retransmitting the information or else applying a charge to the wrong person's credit card.

Optical Fiber

If you've ever made a phone call to Western Europe from the United States, your message probably went under the Atlantic ocean in the form of light through optical fiber cable. ***Optical fiber cable*** is the fastest and most efficient medium for wired communication, using a very thin glass or plastic fiber through which pulses of light travel. Information transmission through optical fiber works rather like flashing code with a light through a hollow tube.

Optical fiber cable's advantages are size (one fiber has the diameter of a human hair); capacity (exceeding 1,400 Mbps); much greater security; and no leakage of information. Attempts at tapping are pretty easy to detect since installing a tap noticeably disrupts service on the line. However, optical fiber is very expensive and difficult to install and maintain.

WIRELESS COMMUNICATIONS MEDIA

Are There Wireless Media in Addition to Those for Home Networks?

Home networks use types of wireless communications that are effective for relatively short distances. These are infrared, Bluetooth, and WiFi, and we discussed these concepts earlier in this chapter and in Chapter 6. Large, organizational networks need to be able to send information wirelessly for much greater distances than do home networks. For example, an organization might need a way of transmitting information across rugged terrain, to the other side of the world, or when one or more parties may be in motion. Wireless communications radiate information into the air to be picked up by an antenna. Security is a big problem since the information is available to anyone in the radiation's path. However, wireless encryption methods are good, and getting better.

Medium Distances

Microwave communications media are line-of-sight information transmission media. That is, the microwave signal cannot follow the curved surface of the earth. So, to send the information on earth over a distance of more than about 20 miles you'd have to use repeaters (see Figure 7.16). A ***repeater*** is a device that receives a radio signal, strengthens it, and sends it on. (You've probably seen microwave towers—they're the tall towers with several little dishes on them that are sometimes part of industrial complexes.) Microwave signals have difficulty getting through walls or trees or other solid objects, so there must be a clear path from sender to receiver.

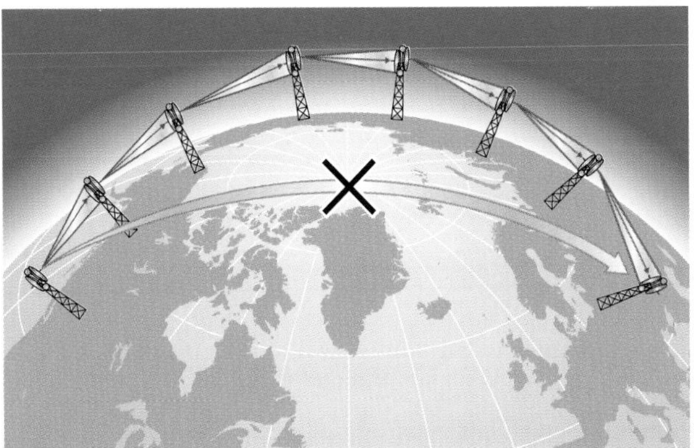

FIGURE 7.16

Microwave transmission is a line-of-sight type of wireless communications medium.

Long Distances

If you've ever made a phone call from the United States to anywhere in Asia, your message was most likely relayed by communications satellites. There's a delay between the moment that you're finished talking and when the other person responds. That's because your message has to go up 22,500 miles into the air, bounce off the satellite, and come back down to earth to your conversation partner. Satellite links are very expensive, and are generally not affordable for most consumers.

Communications satellites are actually microwave repeaters in space. They solve the problem of line-of-sight since the transmission shoots up into the sky in a straight line and then shoots back down to earth again (see Figure 7.17). Since satellites are so high, an array of them can cover essentially the whole earth (as the two dozen GPS satellites do).

You may have satellite radio service in your car. If so, you know that you're never completely out of range of your favorite satellite radio station (as long as you stay within the contiguous United States), although you may experience momentary breaks in transmission.

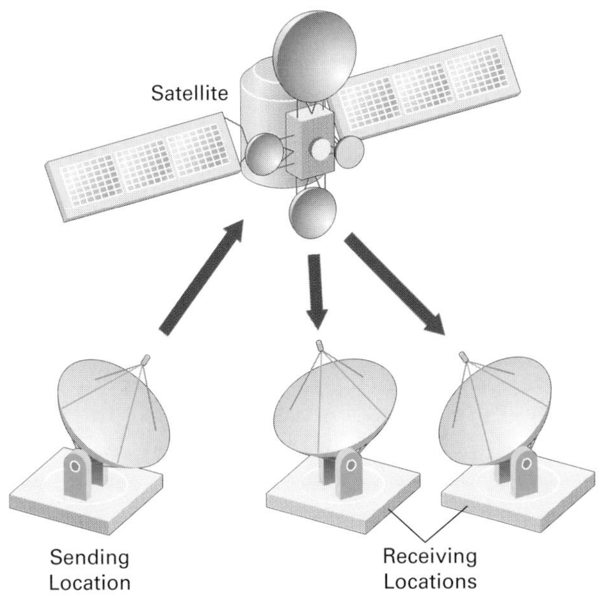

FIGURE 7.17

A satellite allows you to send information wirelessly over long distances.

Satellite communications are cost effective for moving large amounts of information, especially given a large number of receiving sites. You'd also use satellite communications to connect land-based networks in far-flung locations or to connect moving vehicles to each other or to the organizational network.

SECTION 7.4

making the grade

1. The paths in a network over which information travels are called ___________.
2. ___________ refers to the rate at which a communications medium transfers information.
3. Cable that transfers information in the form of light pulses through a hollow tube is called ___________.
4. Communications media that transmit information over a closed, connected path are called ___________.
5. ___________ communications media transmit information through the air.

7.5 CONSUMER Q&A

1. Does It Matter What Type of Cable Modem I Get if I Want to Share a Broadband Internet Connection?

Cable, DSL, and satellite modems often come with both Ethernet and USB connectors. If you're planning on sharing a broadband Internet connection, you need to use an Ethernet connector to plug in to your home router, since that's the device that enables sharing.

2. How Do I Turn On File and Device Sharing?

When you turn on file and/or printer sharing, other computers on your network can access your computer. It's not difficult to turn on sharing, although different versions of Windows do it slightly differently.

First, go to the **Control Panel** and choose Network & Dialup. Then choose **Local Area Connection,** and click on **Properties,** and put the checkmark in the little box beside **File and Printer Sharing for Microsoft Networks.** The system will then want to reboot.

Then you need to specify the drive or folder you want to share. Point to the appropriate drive or folder, then click the right mouse button and choose the **Sharing and Security** option. From there, you can specify whether the others on your network may access each drive, folder, or file. When you turn on the file sharing option on your computer for a folder, that folder appears in the Windows Explorer lists of the other computers.

When you have highlighted folders and printer to be shared, they appear in Windows Explorer with an open hand at the bottom of the icon associated with the folder or device.

If you want to restrict access to your folders, you'll need to password protect your folders. You may choose a blank password, in which case the person requesting the file won't be prompted for a password.

You go through a similar process to share a device. Say you want to share a printer. You go to the **Control Panel** in the **Start** menu, choose printers, highlight the one you want to share, and click the right mouse button as before.

3. Which Cell Carriers Use Which Type of Cell Networks?

Within the United States, there are three types of cellular telephone networks, and you can't use a phone designed for one type on another type. The three types are:

- GSM, used by most of the world, is also what Cingular, Nextel, and T-Mobile use in this country. Note that even though GSM is the standard used by the rest of the world, the frequencies it uses are different. Europe, Asia, and Australia use the 900 MHz and 1,800 MHz bands, and North and South America use the 1900 MHz band. World phones are tri-band, meaning that they function in all three frequency bands.
- CDMA (code division multiple access) is used by Sprint PCS and Verizon Wireless.
- TDMA (time division multiple access) is used by AT&T and Cingular.

Note that while Cingular uses two types of networks (TDMA and GSM), you still can't use their TDMA phone on their GSM network, or vice versa.

7.6 SUMMARY AND KEY TERMS

A ***computer network (network)*** is a collection of computers that supports the sharing of information, software, and hardware devices. The four basic components of networks are ***network interface cards (NICs)*** in each computer, one or more connecting devices to tie the computers together, wires or waves to provide paths for the information to travel, and ***network operating system software (NOS)*** to direct the movement of information in and out of the computers.

You can set up a ***peer-to-peer network*** at home so that you can share information and devices like printers between several computers. For a home network, you would use ***Ethernet cards*** as network interface cards, a ***home router*** as a connecting device, ***Cat 5 cable*** as a pathway for information moving between devices, and the Windows operating system as the network operating system.

If you want wireless access to your home network, you would probably use the ***WiFi*** wireless standard, so that the wireless access point on your network and the PC Card in your notebook computer would both be WiFi compatible. With a home network you access the drives, folders, or printers on one computer from another. You can also share a broadband Internet connection among several computers.

Organizational networks operate on the same principles as home networks, but they are much more complex. A business network is usually a ***client/server network,*** in which one or more computers are servers and provide services to the other computers which are called clients. Organizations use networks three ways:

- Businesses use networks internally to enable employees to be productive—as in providing access to databases and other business records. These networks are called ***intranets.***

- Businesses use networks to manage dealings with customers, suppliers, and others, allowing more efficient use of time and resources. This type of network is often called an ***extranet.***
- Businesses also use networks to provide a service to customers, as cellular telephone carriers do.

When people work together electronically, they are using a ***collaboration system.*** A collaboration system is a system that incorporates e-mail, chat rooms, instant messaging, e-mail, and/or any other form of communication and exchange.

Two types of wireless networks that consumers use a lot are cell phone networks and global positioning systems. Cellular telephones are two-way radios that send and receive information wirelessly. The area serviced by a cell phone carrier is divided into hexagonal cells, each of which has an antenna and other equipment that serve any customers in that cell. A ***global positioning system (GPS)*** is a navigation system that uses satellites to tell you where you are, how fast you're going, and what direction you're headed in. GPS has three major components: satellites, receivers, and ground control stations. The GPS device that you carry around is the receiver component.

Communications media are the paths, or physical channels, in a network over which information travels. The two major categories are ***wired communications media*** and ***wireless communications media.*** Wired communications media include twisted-pair cable and ***optical fiber cable.*** Wireless communications media include Infrared, Bluetooth, and ***WiFi*** for short distances; ***microwave communications media*** for medium distances; and ***communications satellites*** for long distances.

To learn even more about the information in this chapter including network technologies, wireless devices, and home networks, visit the Web site for this text at www.mhhe.com/i-series.

KEY TERMS

bandwidth (p. 211)
Cat 5 (Category 5) cable (p. 199)
client/server network (p. 203)
collaboration system (p. 206)
communications media (p. 210)
communications satellite (p. 213)
computer network (network) (p. 194)
Ethernet card (p. 198)
extranet (p. 205)
file sharing (p. 202)
global positioning system (GPS) (p. 208)
home router (p. 199)
intranet (p. 204)
local area network (LAN) (p. 196)
microwave communications media (p. 212)
mobile telephone switching office (MTSO) (p. 207)
network hub (hub) (p. 198)
network interface card (NIC or network card) (p. 195)
network operating system (network OS or NOS) (p. 195)
optical fiber cable (p. 212)
peer-to-peer collaboration system (p. 206)
peer-to-peer network (p. 197)
repeater (p. 212)
RJ-45 connector (Ethernet connector) (p. 198)
switch (p. 198)
system identification code (SID) (p. 207)
WiFi (p. 200)
wired communications media (p. 211)
wireless communications media (p. 211)
wireless network access point (wireless access point or WAP) (p. 200)

review of terminology

Multiple Choice

1. A device that connects computers into a network, and can also segment a network is called
   a. a switch.
   b. a home router.
   c. a hub.
   d. a GPS.
   e. none of the above.

2. The type of cable that is a robust version of phone cable and is used for networks is
   a. Cat 5 cable.
   b. optical fiber cable.
   c. file sharing cable.
   d. communications cable.
   e. none of the above.

3. The wireless standard used for networks over distances up to 300 feet is called
   a. Bluetooth.
   b. WiFi.
   c. IrDA.
   d. RF.
   e. none of the above.

4. A(n) __________ is the device that allows computers to wirelessly access a wired network.
   a. satellite communications media
   b. microwave communications media
   c. wireless network access point
   d. radio wave
   e. infrared sequence

5. An Ethernet PC Card is
   a. a video card.
   b. a sound card.
   c. a wireless network access card.
   d. the type of network card you'd have in a desktop computer.
   e. the type of network card you'd have in a notebook computer.

6. An extranet is
   a. the service that your ISP provides for mobile computing.
   b. a network that is internal to a company's employees.
   c. a network that allows access to a company's network by customers and suppliers.
   d. the parts of the Internet that people don't visit a lot.
   e. none of the above.

7. A carrier's cellular telephone coverage area is divided into
   a. counties.
   b. states.
   c. hexagonal cells.
   d. square cells.
   e. rectangular cells.

8. Satellite communications media are used
   a. as part of a home network.
   b. as part of a business network.
   c. as part of a government network.
   d. as b and c.
   e. as a, b, and c.

9. A system that incorporates e-mail, chat rooms, and instant messaging is a(n)
   a. collaboration system.
   b. extranet.
   c. intranet.
   d. computer network.
   e. none of the above.

10. A client/server network
    a. is used by businesses.
    b. has one or more computers that are servers.
    c. has lots of client computers.
    d. helps avoid duplication of information on multiple computers.
    e. all of the above.

True/False

11. ____ A GPS is a navigational system that tells you where you are and how fast you're going.

12. ____ The Windows operating system can perform the network function of moving information in and out of computers in a peer-to-peer network.

13. ____ A cellular telephone does not need to be in contact with a base station to make and receive calls.

14. ____ A peer-to-peer network is the type of network that businesses usually use.

15. ____ The bandwidth of a communications medium measures its capacity to move information in a given period of time.

Take this quiz online at www.mhhe.com/i-series and get instant feedback.

QUESTIONS AND EXERCISES

1. The Eurostar Train System and Computer Networks

There are various brick-and-mortar networks that people use every day. There's the U.S. postal system, the federal government system, thousands of school systems, and so on. The common characteristic that all these networks, and computer networks, too, have in common is that they are connected and share information and other effects.

Look at the picture below of part of the European rail system. The routes shown are served by the Eurostar train which travels underwater from the mainland of Europe to England through the Channel Tunnel (Chunnel). Match the components of the Eurostar system in the table below to network components.

Transportation Term	Network Term
Rails	
People in the train cars	
The railroad station in Lille	
The cities of London and Paris	
Railway stations in London and Brussels	
A Hovercraft (a vehicle that propels itself forward by floating on a cushion of air over land and water) that leaves from the coast of France and stops in Ashford, England	

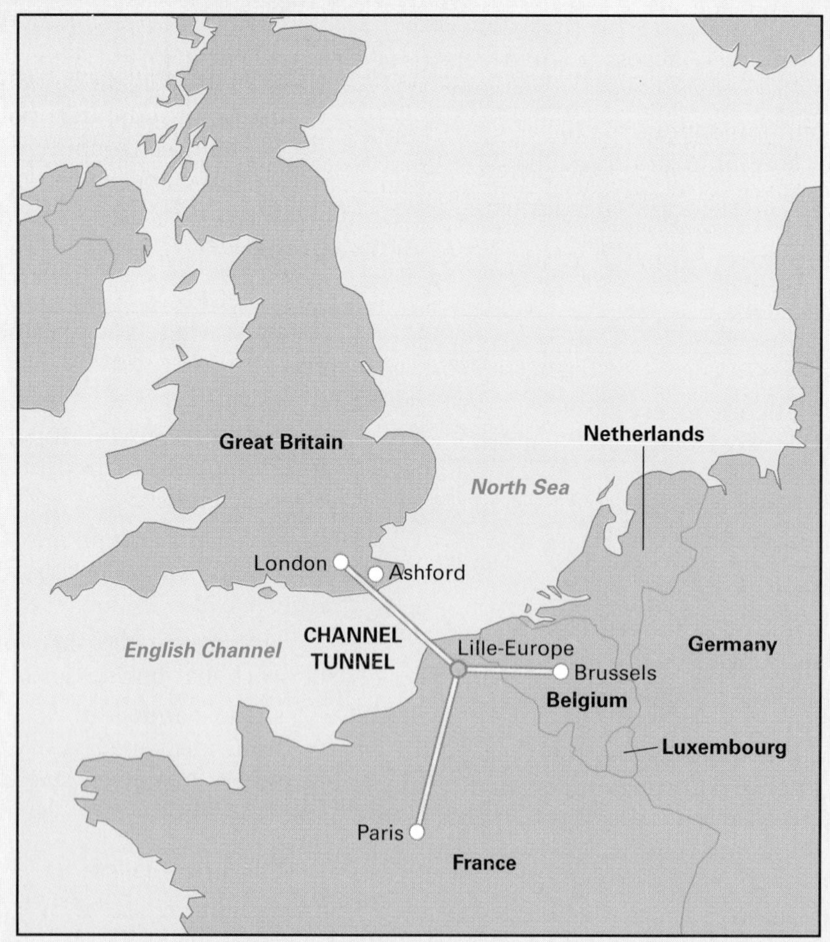

2. Moving Information from Here to There

In Chapter 6, you read about the journey of information from a storage device like the Archos to your speakers. The information was stored as 1s and 0s, and as it moved between computer components, it changed its form, until it eventually became music you could hear.

Now consider the movement of a music file around networks and perform the following tasks.

a. List the steps you would have to take to make a music file on one computer available to the other computers on that network (*Hint:* you have to "share" it, and there may be more than 3 steps).

Step 1: ______________________________

Step 2: ______________________________

Step 3: ______________________________

b. Trace the journey of a music file from a storage device on your computer to the speakers on another computer on your home network. (*Note:* There may be more than 4 stops in the journey.)

The music file moves:

from	to
1.	
2.	
3.	
4.	

c. Trace the journey of an e-mail you send, with a music file attached, from your computer to the recipient's computer in another state. (*Note:* There may be more than 4 stops along the way.)

The e-mail moves:

from	to
1.	
2.	
3.	
4.	

e-commerce

1. Finding the Right Cell Phone

As you know from reading this chapter, you have a lot of choices when it comes to cell phones. Look at a national cell phone carrier site like one of the following:

- Verizon—www.verizon.com
- Sprint—www.sprint.com

Then, find a local cell phone carrier's Web site and compare the two based on the following criteria:

a. Do caller ID, call waiting, caller ID blocking, and call forwarding cost extra? If so, how much?
b. Can you get text messaging?
c. Does the company offer alerts (such as from ESPN) when something of interest to you happens?
d. Are you able to send photos with your phone?

2. Buying Groceries Online

In many areas of the country, you can have groceries delivered within 90 minutes when you order online, depending on where you live.

For this exercise, we'd like you to connect to two of the following Web-based grocery sites:

- Groceronline—www.groceronline.com
- Groceries Express—www.grocexp.com
- Netgrocer—www.netgrocer.com

As you're at each of these sites, do some grocery shopping and answer the following questions:

a. Can you shop for groceries by category such as "fresh fruits and vegetables"?
b. Can you easily add and remove items from your electronic grocery shopping cart?
c. What is the delivery schedule for your groceries? Same day? Two days? Longer?
d. What sort of "extra" delivery charge is there for your Web groceries?

3. Buying and Renting Videos

Videos are another hot electronic commerce aspect of the Web. When you buy or rent videos on the Web, you'll be able to choose from VHS or DVD. Connect to a couple of the sites listed below and see what you can find.

- Blockbuster—www.blockbuster.com
- Columbia House—www.columbiahouse.com
- Video.com—www.video.com

As you visit each site, perform the following tasks and answer the following questions:

a. Search for a video by name. Do you have to know the exact name?
b. Search for videos by category. What categories are available?
c. Search for videos by actor. Do you have to know the name of the actor, or can you choose from a list?

ethics, security & privacy

1. Should Big Brother Be Allowed to Watch Us?

In this chapter, in the I-Series Insights box, you read about camera surveillance in England, the country that is widely believed to have the largest camera-surveillance network in the world. Opinions in England differ as to whether such surveillance is a good or bad thing. Opponents feel that the system is an invasion of privacy and violates the rights of law-abiding citizens. Those in favor point to a huge reduction in crime (95 percent in car theft alone) as proof that street cameras make England a safer place to be since they enable the police to stop crimes in progress. Also, a videotape of the actual commission of a crime provides ironclad evidence for prosecutors, increasing their conviction rate and ability to get criminals off the street.

More and more cameras are going up in the United States. We're already used to security cameras in Wal-Mart stores (they're in the dark globes that hang from the ceiling). Las Vegas is famous for having cameras in casinos that watch employees and customers. Many buildings that are accessible by the public have cameras in hallways, elevators, and even in offices.

However tolerant we are of cameras in stores and casinos, surveillance by agents of law enforcement is usually more difficult for people in this country to accept. At the 2001 Super Bowl, police, with the agreement of the NFL, focused video cameras on the faces of tens of thousands of spectators as they entered the stadium. The images were sent to computers, which, using facial recognition software, compared the images to a database of pictures of suspected criminals and terrorists.

These actions of the Tampa Police Department caused an outcry from privacy advocates. A police spokesperson defended them, saying it's legal and permissible to take pictures of people in public places, since you have no expectation of privacy in a public place. The American Civil Liberties Union (ACLU) protested the surveillance of people by a government agency without court authorization.

What do you think about surveillance in public places?

a. Should stores and casinos and other businesses be allowed to keep tabs on customers with cameras? Why or why not?

b. Should law enforcement be allowed to monitor citizens without having to show cause and without a court order? Why or why not?

c. The surveillance of the citizenry by British law enforcement was grudgingly accepted in the beginning as a means of preventing terrorism. It has not yet been shown that any terrorist act was averted or that any terrorists were caught by the presence of cameras. Based on these results, would you accept widespread monitoring of citizens as a protection against terrorism in this country? Why or why not?

d. Facial recognition systems have been dropped by several government agencies after it was determined that they don't work very well. Do you think that because facial recognition is imperfect, we don't really need to worry about our privacy being invaded by such systems? Why or why not?

on the web

1. Find Out What It Would Cost to Build Your Own Home Network

Build your own home network on paper. Assume you have four desktop computers and a notebook computer and you want to link them together. Go to the Web and find information on

- Home routers
- Ethernet cards
- Cat 5 cable with RJ-45 connectors
- Wireless access points

Find at least two sources for each of these components and calculate the most and the least expensive system. If you have a broadband Internet connection, find out whether your ISP has any objection to connecting a home network to their system.

2. Investigate Satellite Radio

At the time this book was being written, there were two satellite radio providers: Sirius and XM. Do a little Web surfing and find out if there are any others now. Find out

- What you have to buy to install each type (usually an antenna and a receiver).
- How much the system would cost initially.
- How much the monthly subscription is.
- What kind of features the receiver has (for example, does it tell you the name of the artist and the song?).
- Whether you can get a portable model (a "boom box").

3. Find Out about Firewalls

Go to the Web and find out about software and hardware that protect your computer and home network, respectively.

a. If you have only one computer connected to the Internet, then a software firewall like Zone Alarm will most likely be enough protection from intruders. Find three different firewall software packages on the Web. A good place to start looking would be the sites that sell anti-virus software. Compare the firewall software on price and features. Some sites to try are as follows:
   - Symantec—www.symantec.com
   - TREND Micro—www.trendmicro.com
   - Virus List (a virus encyclopedia)—www.viruslist.com

b. If you have a home network, then you'd be well advised to check into a hardware firewall. One place to look is at the LinkSys site (www.linksys.com) or any site that sells computer hardware.

4. Find Out What Network Terms Mean

Search the Web and find out what the terms below mean. They're all common terms pertaining to networks.

a. bandwidth shaper
b. ping
c. DNS server
d. gateway
e. packet
f. packet sniffer
g. encryption
h. e-mail alias
i. multiplexor
j. file transfer protocol (FTP)
k. full duplex
l. handshake
m. leased line
n. ISDN

group activities

1. Find Out What Makes Servers Special

Compare a high-end desktop computer designed to be a network server and a typical computer designed for a single individual. What's the difference in the CPU chips? What's the difference in price? How many CPUs are there in the server? Is there a difference in the memory (the amount and type) in the two machines? How about the hard disk drives? Is there any sort of automatic backup on the server? Would you like such an automatic backup system on your computer? Why or why not?

2. Research Your Institution's Network

In organizational networks, the backbone is often optical fiber cable. The backbone is the main highway along which information moves from one place to another. It works like the motor highway system, where the interstate system joins the major cities, and other roads branch off, joining smaller cities and towns.

What sort of backbone to install on a network is one of the many decisions that network administrators have to make when planning or upgrading a network. Find out what decisions the network administrators at your institution, or another large organization, have made. Ask the technical people

- How many servers there are on the network.
- How many clients there are on the network.
- How many hubs, switches, and/or routers there are.
- What type of backbone the network has.
- Whether wireless access is possible, and if so, how many wireless access points there are and how their locations were determined.

3. Investigate Which GPS Would Suit Your Needs

The big sellers of GPS receivers are Garmin, Magellan, and Trimble. They all sell small, hand-held devices that help you not get lost by telling you where you are, or help you mark a spot, or help you get to where you're going. If you don't want a separate device, you can get an adapter card for your PDA.

Your task is twofold. First, find out what features you can buy in a GPS. Find GPS receivers from the three big manufacturers, or others. List five features they have in common and three more that are unique to one manufacturer.

Second, find three PDAs that have GPS built-in or for which GPS adapters are available. List five features that these PDA GPSs have.

4. Try Using a Collaboration System

Work on a project with your group without ever having a face-to-face meeting. Write an article on Spam, computer viruses, or some other abuse in cyberspace.

You can use any electronic tools available such as phones, e-mail, instant messaging, your institution's course delivery system (like Blackboard), or any other tool at your disposal. Keep a log of when and where each communication took place, its duration, and who was involved.

Your report will then consist of the text of the report and a listing of contact dates and times between team members.

crossword puzzle

Across

7. Scripting language based on Visual Basic
9. The scrambling of information
10. Enables Web clients to interact with all Web servers
12. Combination of XML and HTML
13. "Friends & Family" marketing is an example
14. Puts the "s" on https://
17. HTML tag for bold, italics, and the like
20. Ad that appears under your browser screen
21. Ensures that transactions are secure and legitimate
22. Combination of HTML, VBScript, and specific commands
23. Saying no to alternative uses of your personal information
26. Technology-enabled commerce
29. Mobile technology-enabled commerce
31. Server for WAP-enabled devices
33. Tag for creating hyperlinks

Down

1. Common ad on many Web pages
2. Filtering in which you rate products
3. What allows you to format HTML elements separately from content
4. Program for transferring information
5. Type of editor in which you see the result
6. Filtering in which you are placed in an affinity group
8. Rate at which Web site visitors order a product or service
10. Programming languages that use the power of a user's Web browser
11. Count of visitor information
15. Client-side Web programming language
16. File that contains your Web page
18. Stores information about your e-commerce purchases
19. Language used to create Web pages
20. Server-side scripting language for creating dynamic sites
24. HTML tag for making information—such as titles—stand out
25. Markup language for wireless devices
27. The ease of use of a Web site
28. Markup language that uses customized tags
30. Opposite of #23 across
31. Communications protocols for wireless devices
32. Ad that appears on your screen outside your current browser

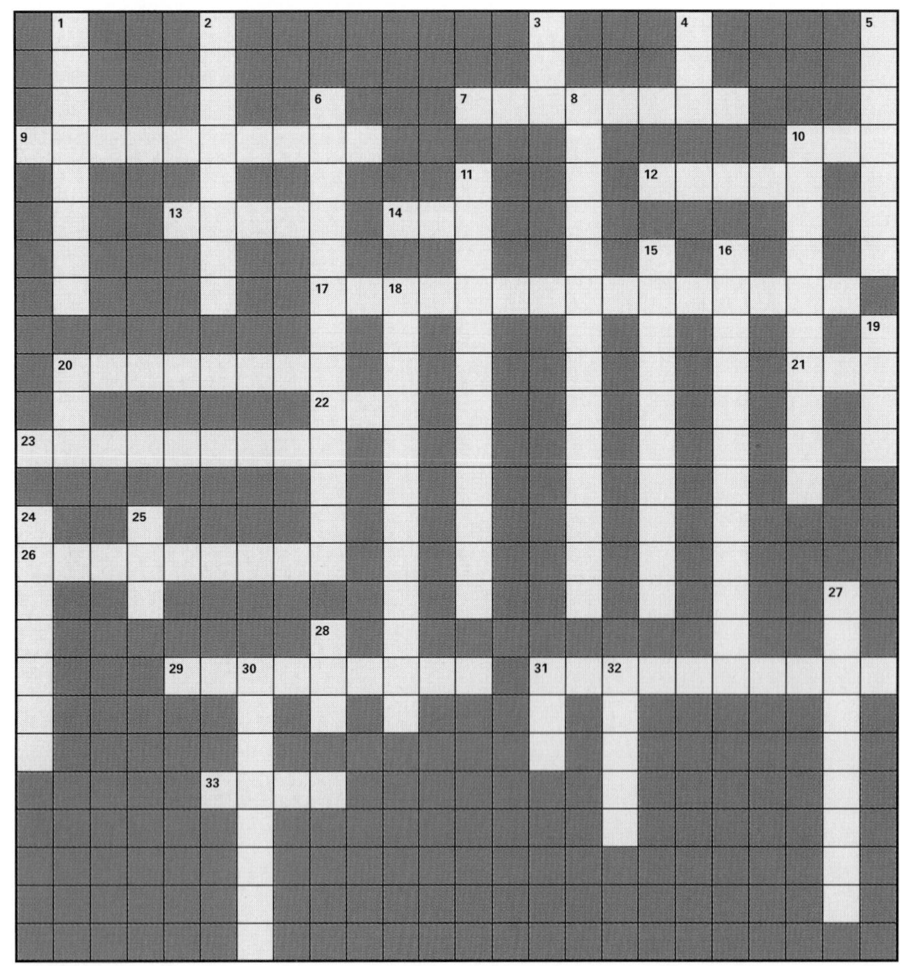

CHAPTER eight

8

E-Commerce and Web Site Development

How Do You Harness the Power of the Web?

SIMNET CONCEPTS SUPPORT

did you know?

Selling products and services on the Web is big business. Companies want to make it easy for you to place orders on their Web sites. People who can develop Web sites that generate sales are in high demand.

in *response to concern that using wireless devices while driving is dangerous, IBM and automakers are developing systems that won't let you send e-mail or make phone calls when they detect you're driving on an icy road.*[1]

a *resource for those new at Web design is the HTML Writers Guild (www.hwg.org), a leading training organization with 150,000 members in more than 160 countries.*

the *first online holiday shopping spree—Christmas 1998—helped Amazon.com reap __??__ in annual sales. Amazon.com led all e-retailers in 2002 with __??__ in sales.*[2]

To find out just how much money Amazon.com makes in e-commerce sales, visit www.mhhe.com/i-series.

Student Learning Outcomes

After reading this chapter, you should be able to:

1. List and describe the ways in which B2C e-commerce businesses personalize your shopping experience on the Web.
2. Define how B2C e-commerce businesses create Web sites that are "sticky."
3. Describe the various marketing and advertising strategies B2C e-commerce businesses use to reach you.
4. Discuss your payment options for making e-commerce purchases and the methods e-commerce businesses use to ensure the security of those transactions.
5. Describe how to publish and maintain a Web site.
6. Discuss how Web developers use XHTML, XML, CSS, and other Web technologies to make e-commerce and m-commerce Web sites.
7. Compare and contrast client-side Web programming languages with server-side Web programming languages.

In Chapter 2, we briefly touched on electronic commerce when we introduced you to the Web and the Internet. In this chapter, we will further explore the world of e-commerce by addressing two major topics: (1) business to consumer e-commerce activities and (2) Web site authoring and management. Let's remind you of the following definitions:

- ***Electronic commerce (e-commerce)***—really just commerce, but it's commerce that technology facilitates and enhances.
- ***Business to consumer electronic commerce (B2C e-commerce)***—occurs when a business sells products and services through e-commerce to customers who are primarily individuals.
- ***Business to business electronic commerce (B2B e-commerce)***—occurs when a business sells products and services through e-commerce to customers who are primarily other businesses.

In this chapter, we'll focus first on B2C e-commerce and what it takes to be successful in that arena. We'll then follow with a discussion of what you need to know to create and manage your own Web site. To learn more about B2B e-commerce, complete the "B2B and E-Commerce" tutorial on your SimNet Concepts Support CD.

did you know?

It's *possible for consumers to "try on" digitized clothes online. Lands' End added a virtual model feature to its Web site in 2000 and boosted new sales 26 percent.*[3]

8.1 KEYS TO SUCCESS IN B2C ELECTRONIC COMMERCE

As a typical e-commerce consumer, you'll participate in B2C e-commerce, in which businesses sell products and services to you. To be successful in the e-commerce world, those businesses must still follow sound business principles. That is, successful B2C e-commerce businesses must personalize your shopping experience, create Web sites that you want to visit frequently (called "sticky" Web sites), and effectively market and advertise their sites.

PERSONALIZING THE SHOPPING EXPERIENCE

How Do B2C Businesses Create Personalization for Me through a Computer?

Have you ever been to a store that tracks what you buy and then recommends items that you might like? This is called *personalization* and it's cer-

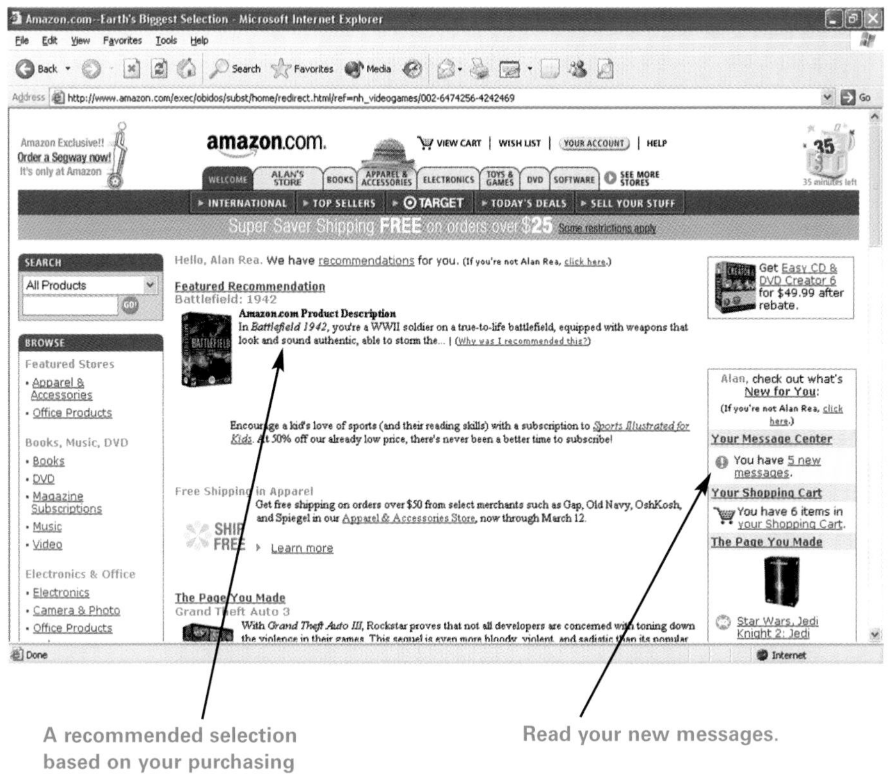

FIGURE 8.1

Your customized Web page at Amazon.com will look different from this one. It will contain product offerings specific to your own purchasing and searching histories.

tainly possible on the Web. ***Web personalization*** is the process of customizing a Web page or series of Web pages according to a customer's preferences. For example, you can create your own account at Amazon.com (see Figure 8.1). Through it, Amazon.com tracks your purchasing preferences, searching preferences, shipping information, and more. In doing so, Amazon.com provides a customized Web page with products you might like based on what you've already purchased (and/or searched for).

Some of this information about you is kept in a *cookie*. Recall from Chapter 4 that a cookie is a file of information that a Web site stores on your hard disk. For Amazon.com, the cookie stores your log-in ID as well as computer-generated codes that locate information about you in Amazon.com's database.

As you shop at Amazon.com, you buy products by placing them in your shopping cart. A ***shopping cart*** is actually software that stores information about your e-commerce purchases. When you're ready to pay the first time you use Amazon.com, you have to enter such information as your billing and shipping address. That information is then permanently stored in your account. If you shop again at Amazon.com, it may use some of your cookie information to find your billing and shipping address so that you don't have to enter that information again.

CREATING "STICKY" WEB SITES

What Strategies Do B2C Businesses Use to Keep Repeat Customers?

All businesses need repeat customers, and it's no different for B2C e-commerce businesses. In the electronic world, businesses want to create "sticky" Web sites that people want to visit often and never leave once they

FIGURE 8.2

Amazon.com's "sticky" Web site provides you with many easy-to-use features.

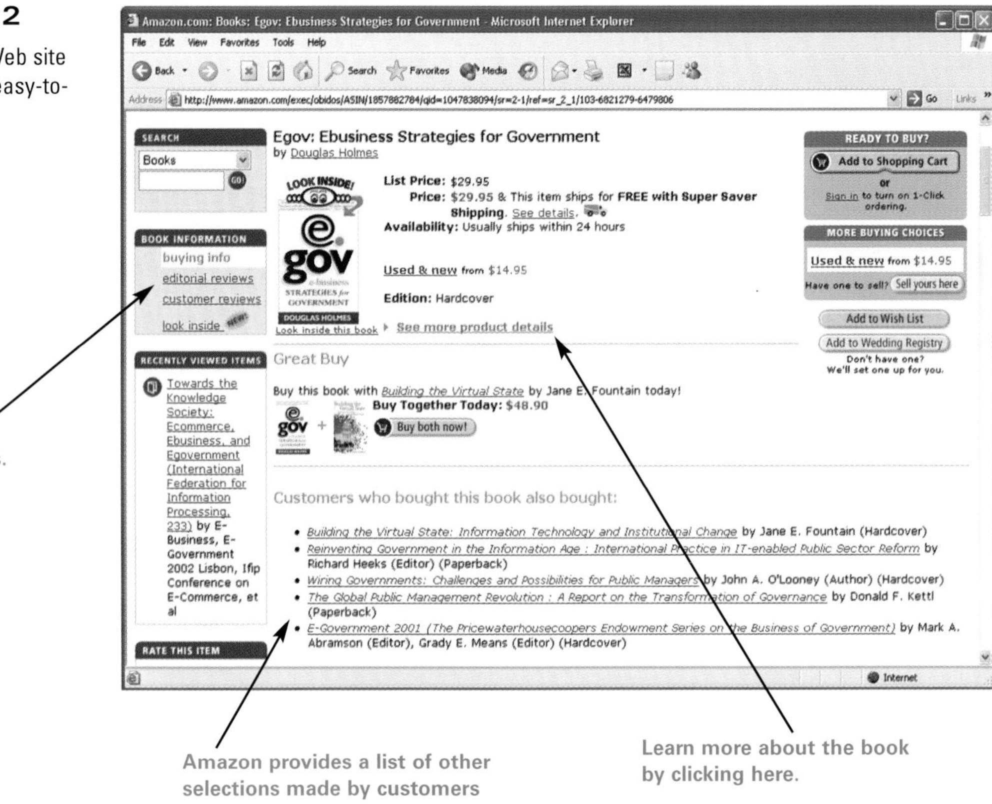

are there. To create "sticky" Web sites, B2C e-commerce businesses strive for a high degree of usability (displaying product and service offerings in an electronic catalog) and m-commerce support.

Usability refers to how easy it is to use a Web page or site. Figure 8.2 shows how Amazon.com has mastered usability. You can choose to buy one of its recommendations or something entirely different. There are ways to manage your account, check how much you've purchased, and even change your recommendations and preferences. So, Amazon.com has achieved a high level of usability—and made it easy for you to shop there.

Not only that, Amazon.com presents its product and service offerings in an ***electronic catalog,*** an electronic product or service presentation in which you enjoy a rich combination of media. For example, if you find a CD you like at Amazon.com, you can listen to clips of the music tracks.

M-commerce, or ***mobile e-commerce,*** allows you to use wireless devices such as smart phones or PDAs to buy and sell products and services through Web e-commerce. M-commerce provides another method for accessing a Web site and ordering its products or services without sitting in front of a desktop or notebook computer. If you could visit a Web site with great usability with your smart phone or PDA and order products you like, would you? Most people would, so many sites are developing content just to support m-commerce.

To learn more about B2C e-commerce and m-commerce, complete the "E-Commerce and Shopping Online" and "Internet Appliances" tutorials on your SimNet Concepts Support CD.

did you **know?**

Would *you like to help preserve the world's classic literature in electronic form? Project Gutenberg volunteers have converted thousands of books so that nearly all hardware and software can read them.*

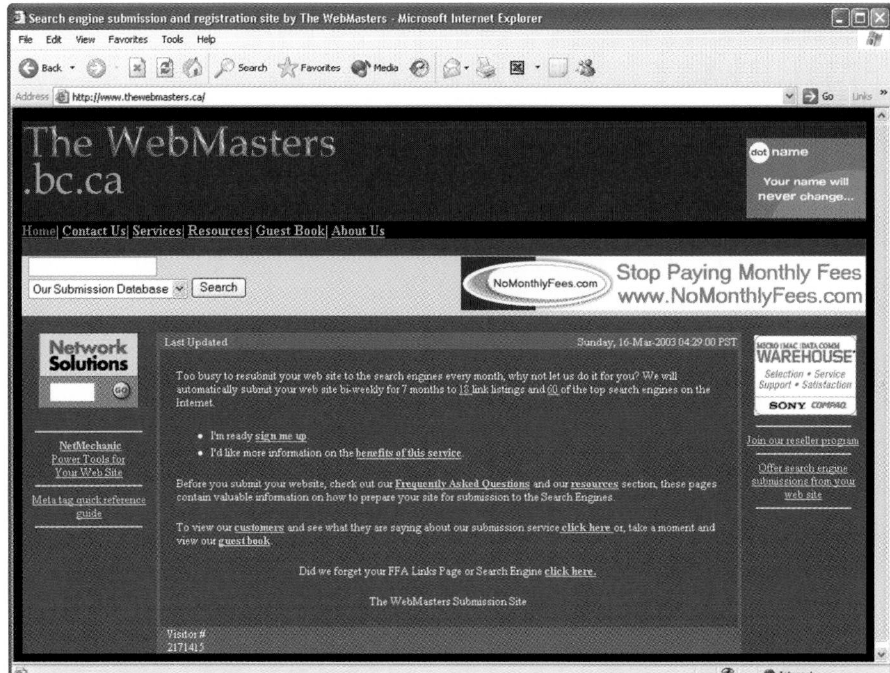

FIGURE 8.3

The WebMasters will register your site free of charge with 60 different search engines.

MARKETING AND ADVERTISING THROUGH OTHER SITES

How Do B2C Businesses Create Partnerships to Increase Their Customer Base?

Of course, it does a Web site no good to be "sticky" if you don't visit it the first time. So, B2C e-commerce businesses undertake numerous marketing and advertising strategies just to get you to their sites.

Registering a Site with Search Engines

Most important, these businesses register their sites with search engines (and you can register yours too). In Chapter 2 we discussed search engines, special tools on the Web that give you the ability to find Web sites by key word or words or by asking questions. The cost for registering your site with a search engine can range from free to several thousand dollars per year. For example, Yahoo! Express is a service that gets your site listed on Yahoo! and guarantees Web traffic within 7 days. You can also pay additional fees to have your site appear at the top of a search or category list.

If you're just starting your e-commerce business, you can register your site for free on many sites with services provided by the likes of The WebMasters (www.thewebmasters.ca, see Figure 8.3). Completely free of charge, The WebMasters will register your site with 60 different search engines. Of course, it won't guarantee you any traffic as Yahoo! Express does.

Banner Ads and Click-Throughs

Another mechanism for advertising a Web site is a banner ad. A ***banner ad*** is a graphical advertisement (often including movement and animation) that will take you to another site if you click on it. Some banner ads may also appear in the form of a pop-up ad or a pop-under ad. A ***pop-up ad*** is a small Web page containing an advertisement that appears on your

FIGURE 8.4

Many B2C e-commerce businesses place banner ads on other sites to attract customers.

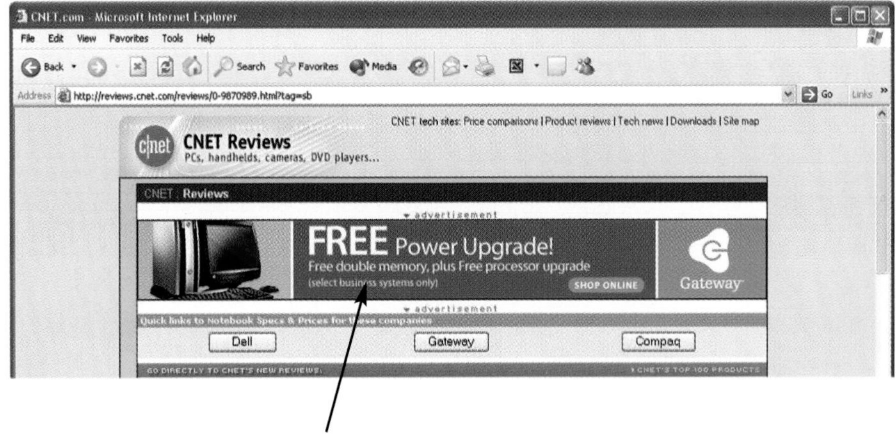

This banner ad is targeted to individuals who read CNET and also make computer purchases.

computer screen outside the current Web site loaded into your browser. A ***pop-under ad*** is a form of a pop-up ad that you do not see until you close your current browser window. Both pop-up and pop-under ads are designed to draw attention to their content by appearing where you don't expect them.

Most ads (especially banner ads) target a specific audience. In Figure 8.4, for example, the banner ad is for Gateway memory and a processor upgrade. This ad appears on CNET (www.cnet.com), a site people interested in technology frequently visit.

To monitor the effectiveness of banner and pop-up ads, e-commerce sites track click-throughs. A ***click-through*** is information that is captured when you click on an ad to go from one Web site to another. For payment purposes, the business that placed the ad must pay the hosting site for every click-through. So, you can actually sell ad space on your e-commerce site and make money by recording the click-throughs and charging the target e-commerce site appropriately. In Figure 8.4, CNET would charge Gateway every time someone starts at CNET and then clicks on the banner ad to go to Gateway.

Affiliate Programs

Many businesses also choose to advertise their sites through other sites by way of an affiliate program. An ***affiliate program*** (or an ***associate program***) allows an e-commerce business to sell goods and services via another Web site. Let's say you create a B2C e-commerce Web site about online gaming. On your site you recommend books, software, and gaming items (controllers and the like) through an affiliate program such as Affiliate.net from Barnes & Noble (www.bn.com). For every person who "clicks through" from your site to Barnes & Noble and purchases something, you get a commission. So, you can actually make money just by creating a "sticky" Web site that people visit and then click on links to other affiliate sites.

did you know?

Teenagers *and young adults likely will be first to demand the convenience of mobile commerce. Since they're comfortable with mobile instant messaging, experts predict they won't hesitate to order a Big Mac from a PDA.*[4]

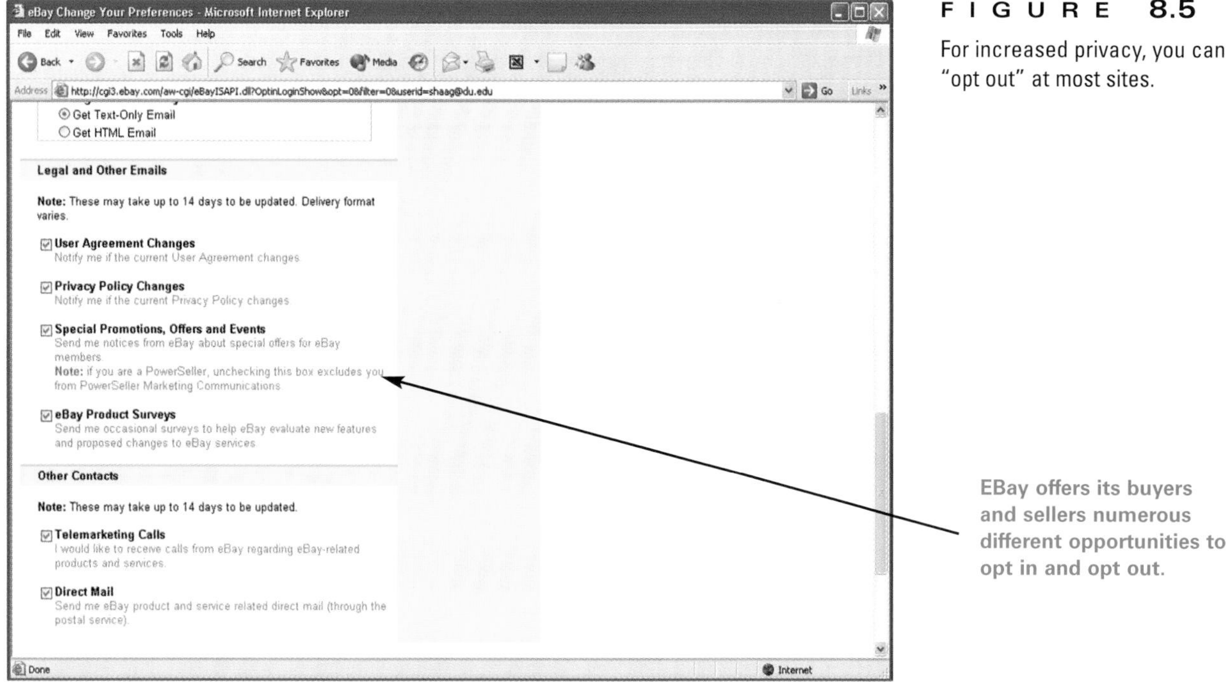

FIGURE 8.5

For increased privacy, you can "opt out" at most sites.

MARKETING TO AND THROUGH CUSTOMERS

What Marketing Can I Expect to See while at a B2C Site?

As people visit a B2C e-commerce Web site (and hopefully buy products and services), those businesses want to utilize their customers and their information to facilitate other marketing activities. Key topics here include opting in and opting out, viral marketing, personalization filtering, and pop-up ads. As we just discussed pop-ads are designed to catch your attention because they appear in places where you don't expect them. So, B2C e-commerce sites do use pop-up ads to draw your attention to "great" (supposedly) deals.

Opting In and Opting Out

Click-throughs usually record basic information about you, such as what site you came from and the date and time. But when you purchase a product, an e-commerce Web site will want even more information—your name, e-mail address, phone number, age, gender, likes and dislikes, and payment information as well.

But did you know that most businesses allow you some control over the information they collect about you? They give you the choice of "opting in" or "opting out" (see Figure 8.5). ***Opting in*** is when you give permission for alternative uses of your personal information. ***Opting out*** is when you say no to alternative uses of your personal information.

Would you rather have businesses ask you first before using your information (i.e., give you the ability to opt out) or simply assume you are willing to allow them to use it?

FIGURE 8.6

Many sites offer free promotional items and the chance of winning prizes in exchange for your personal information, which they use in viral marketing.

did you know?

A key moment in e-commerce history was the introduction of the downloadable Netscape browser in 1994, two years after the creation of its forerunner Mosaic. Consumers finally had point-and-click access to the Web.[5]

Viral Marketing

Some e-commerce businesses let you play games and have the chance of winning money or prizes in exchange for your personal information. An example is www.grab.com (see Figure 8.6).

These sites then use your name and e-mail address for their promotional purposes and sell it to other businesses as well. This is the concept of viral marketing. ***Viral marketing*** is a set of techniques that e-commerce businesses use to gather personal information about you, use that information in their own promotional campaigns, and sell that information to other e-commerce businesses. If you participate in viral marketing as a consumer, your e-mail will soon be full of advertisements and offers from hundreds—if not thousands—of e-commerce businesses. Some you may be interested in; some you may not.

A variation of viral marketing is one in which you provide a business with contact information of other people. Many telephone service providers have such programs that offer you a discounted rate if you provide information on other people (to which the providers will then market their services).

Personalization Filtering

No matter how a B2C e-commerce business gathers information about you, it will attempt to use that information to provide you with a personalized offering of products and services. Businesses achieve this through *personalization filtering,* which includes:

- ***Collaborative filtering***—a method of placing you into an affinity group of people with the same characteristics. Then, likes and dislikes are associated with all members of that group. Amazon.com is very good at collaborative filtering.
- ***Psychographic filtering***—which anticipates your preferences based on the answers you give to a questionnaire. This method is more personal than collaborative filtering.

practically speaking

Are You Addicted to the Internet?

Do you glance at the clock and realize that you've spent more time than you wanted to surfing the Web? Do you find yourself checking e-mail throughout the day and being disappointed when you don't have any? Do you find yourself looking forward to more time on the Internet? If you answered yes to any one of these questions, you may be addicted to the Internet. You just can't seem to get enough of it, and, when you try to quit, you can't.

Dr. Kimberly Young is one of the first "cyber-psychologists." She is a professor at the University of Pennsylvania and author of articles and books on cyber-addictions. On her Web site (www.netaddiction.com), Dr. Young notes that cyber-addiction takes many forms—cyber-relationships, online gambling, and excessive chat room use. Over 60 percent of the respondents to a survey of Dr. Young's who were deemed addicted to the Internet spent their time in interactive activities such as chat rooms and other virtual environments.

New forms of Internet addiction appear each day. They include day trading on the stock market, Internet gaming use, and excessive Web surfing for information. Dr. Young suggests answering certain questions to determine if you're addicted:

- How often do your grades or schoolwork suffer because of the amount of time you spend online?
- How often do you check your e-mail before something else that you need to do?
- How often do you find yourself anticipating when you will go online again?
- How often do you lose sleep because of late-night log-ins?

Internet addiction is serious. Although it's very different from being addicted to a substance (a chemical or physical dependence), psychological addiction can be very powerful and very difficult to break. With the increase in the number of ways the Internet can be accessed such as through cell phones and PDAs, anyone can get an "Internet fix" anytime and anywhere.

If you're wondering if you have an Internet addiction, go to the NetAddiction Web site and take its survey.

- ***Adaptive filtering***—which asks you to rate products or situations and also monitors your actions over time to find out what you like and dislike.
- ***Profile filtering***—which requires that you choose terms or key words, providing a personal picture of you and your preferences.

All the above issues we've just discussed are central to the success of a B2C e-commerce business, which must personalize your shopping experience, create sticky Web sites, and effectively reach you through various marketing and advertising strategies. The first goal is to get you to the site. The second goal is to increase the business's conversion rate. A ***conversion rate*** is the percentage of potential customers who visit a site and then become actual customers by making a purchase. If the conversion rate for your B2C e-commerce business is high, you're more likely to be successful. If not . . .

SECTION 8.1

making the grade

1. A(n) ___________ is an electronic product or service presentation in which you enjoy a rich combination of media.
2. A(n) ___________ is a small Web page containing an advertisement that appears on your computer screen outside the current Web site loaded into your browser.
3. ___________ is when you give permission for alternative uses of your personal information.
4. A(n) ___________ is the percentage of potential customers who visit a site and then become actual customers by making a purchase.

8.2 PAYMENT METHODS AND SECURE TRANSACTIONS

The e-commerce world is just like the brick-and-mortar world. You have to pay for what you want, and you need to know that your transactions are secure.

PAYMENT OPTIONS

As a Consumer, How Do I Pay for Purchases on the Internet?

As you might guess, you can't use folding cash to pay for products or services at a B2C e-commerce site. You have mainly the options of using your credit card or using a financial cybermediary. In the future, you'll be able to use digital cash, which we'll discuss in Chapter 11.

FIGURE 8.7

PayPal is the leading financial cybermediary in the e-commerce world.

i•series insights *Ethics, Security & Privacy*

Security, Privacy, and Trust in E-Commerce

If you read *The Wall Street Journal* or follow the stock market, you know that e-commerce will continue to grow. But e-commerce does face some challenges. Most important, many people still don't trust participating in e-commerce on the Web. And that hesitancy is warranted. Before you join the e-commerce bandwagon, keep the following in mind.

Security

From the very beginning, you'll want to check regularly that each of your e-commerce transactions is secure. In general, look for https:// or the lock icon on your screen. Check your credit card statements carefully.

Privacy

As Web sites collect more information about you, you're relinquishing privacy in return for convenience. Monitor how they can use your personal information and decide whether to submit this information in return for information and services. Check the privacy policies at the e-commerce Web sites you shop. Do they sell your buying habits to other companies? What happens to this information if the company merges with another?

Trust

Whether the e-commerce Web site adheres to industry's privacy codes may determine if you can trust it. Look for a TRUSTe logo, which means that the Web site follows certain standards. TRUSTe is a nonprofit organization that sets privacy standards and monitors its member Web sites for violations of privacy standards. You can learn more about TRUSTe at www.truste.org.

Financial cybermediaries are Web-based companies that make it easy for one person to pay another person or Web-based business over the Internet. One of the best known (and a true e-commerce success story) is PayPal (www.paypal.com, see Figure 8.7 on the previous page). PayPal is widely used by people participating in auctions on eBay. (And now, eBay owns PayPal.) When you create a PayPal account, you enter basic personal information including your credit card information and/or your checking account information.

When you make a purchase on the Web, you can use your PayPal account and request that money be sent to the PayPal account of the other person or business (provided that the recipient also has a PayPal account). Likewise, if you sell something on the Web, the purchaser can pay you by requesting that money be deducted from his/her account and placed in your account. At any time, given that you accumulate money in your PayPal account, you can request that a check be cut and sent to you or that money from your PayPal account be transferred into your checking account.

SECURE TRANSACTIONS
How Do I Know My Payments Are Safe and Secure?

Many people have chosen not to make purchases on the Web because they fear that both their personal information and credit card information are vulnerable to interception and eventual use for the wrong reasons (such as identify theft, which we'll discuss in the next chapter). To ensure that personal and transaction information is secure, most B2C e-commerce businesses employ Secure Sockets Layers and Secure Electronic Transactions.

FIGURE 8.8

To ensure secure transactions, many e-commerce businesses use a Secure Sockets Layer (SSL) to transmit personal and financial information.

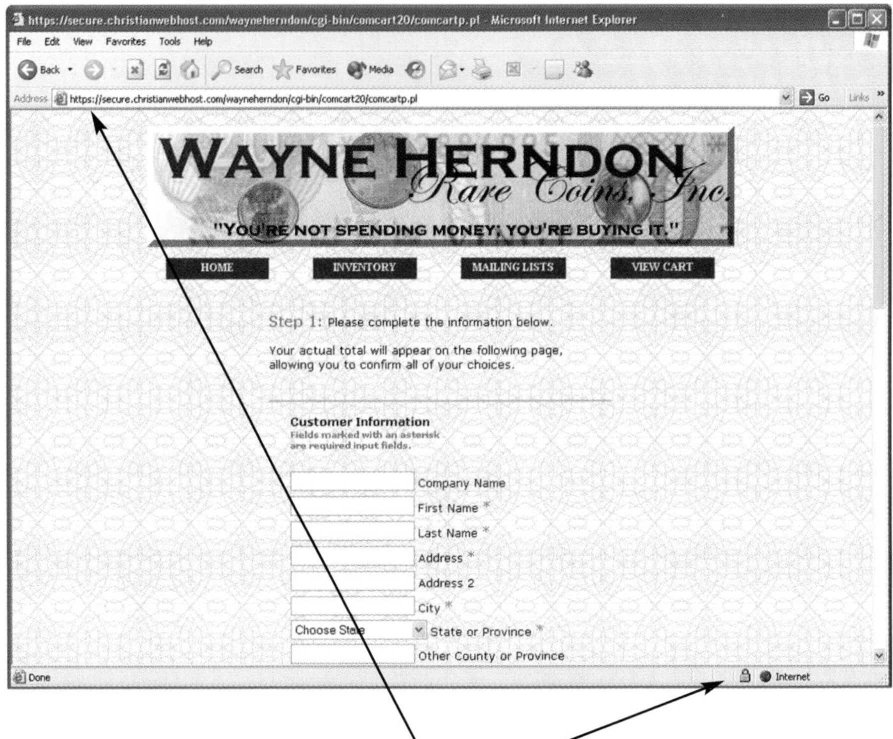

You can determine if a site uses a Secure Sockets Layer (SSL) by finding the "s" in http:// or the lock icon in the lower right corner of your browser.

A ***Secure Sockets Layer (SSL)*** (1) creates a secure and private connection between a Web client and Web server, (2) encrypts the information, and (3) then sends the information over the Internet. ***Encryption*** scrambles information so that it cannot be read without the right decryption key. *Decryption keys* are simply the instructions concerning how to unscramble the information. SSLs do provide good security for transferring information and are used widely by e-commerce sites. You can tell your information is being transferred via SSL if you see that the Web site address for the server starts with https:// (notice the inclusion of the "s") as opposed to just http:// (see Figure 8.8). You may also see a lock icon appearing in the bottom portion of your Web browser window if your information is being transferred via SSL.

A ***Secure Electronic Transaction (SET)*** is a transmission security method that ensures transactions are legitimate as well as secure. Much like an SSL, an SET does encrypt information before sending it over the Internet. And, taking it one step further, an SET enables a merchant to verify a customer's identity by securely transmitting credit card information to the business that issued the credit card for verification. SETs are endorsed by major e-commerce players including MasterCard, American Express, Visa, Netscape, and Microsoft.

The authors of this textbook are frequent purchasers of products and services on the Web, and we believe that most transactions are safe, especially those involving your personal and credit card information. Notice that we said "most." Certainly, no transmission of information—in either the physical world or the e-commerce world—is absolutely safe and secure, and in both worlds you should take care. In the chapter to follow, we'll discuss at great length the issues surrounding security and privacy. Nonetheless, we would encourage you to set your fears aside and participate in e-commerce activities (if you like shopping on the Web).

making the grade

SECTION 8.2

1. ___________ are Web-based companies that make it easy for one person to pay another person or Web-based business over the Internet.
2. A(n) ___________ creates a secure and private connection between a Web client and Web server.
3. ___________ scrambles information so that it cannot be read without the right decryption key.
4. A(n) ___________ enables a merchant to verify a customer's identity by securely transmitting credit card information to the business that issued the credit card for verification.

8.3 WEB AUTHORING AND WEB SITE MANAGEMENT

We toured the Web in Chapter 2, and in this chapter you have explored many aspects of e-commerce. Web developers created most of the e-commerce sites we have looked at. ***Web developers*** are technical professionals who create Web sites. Web developers work with graphics, multimedia, text, and programming languages. Some specialize in certain technical areas while others like to do it all. Recently, we found more than 2,000 jobs for Web developers on Monster.com, so there are numerous job opportunities if you choose this career.

But to create a good Web site you don't have to be a Web developer. All you need is a fundamental knowledge of HTML. ***HTML (Hypertext Markup Language)*** is the basic language you use to create Web pages. Remember, a Web page is a specific portion of a Web site that deals with a certain topic. In this section we'll introduce you to the basics of HTML and other Web tools that will help you develop a Web page, such as an e-resume so you can market your skills and knowledge to potential employers. In Appendix B and on the Web site that supports this text (www.mhhe.com/i-series) you can learn more about HTML and building Web pages. You can also learn more about HTML by completing the "HTML—The Language of the Internet" tutorial on your SimNet Concepts Support CD.

HTML

How Do I Create a Web Page?

HTML lets you decide what information will appear on your Web page and how it will look. To format your page, you place commands in angle brackets < > to tell the Web browser what, where, and how you want the information to appear. We call these commands HTML tags. ***HTML tags***

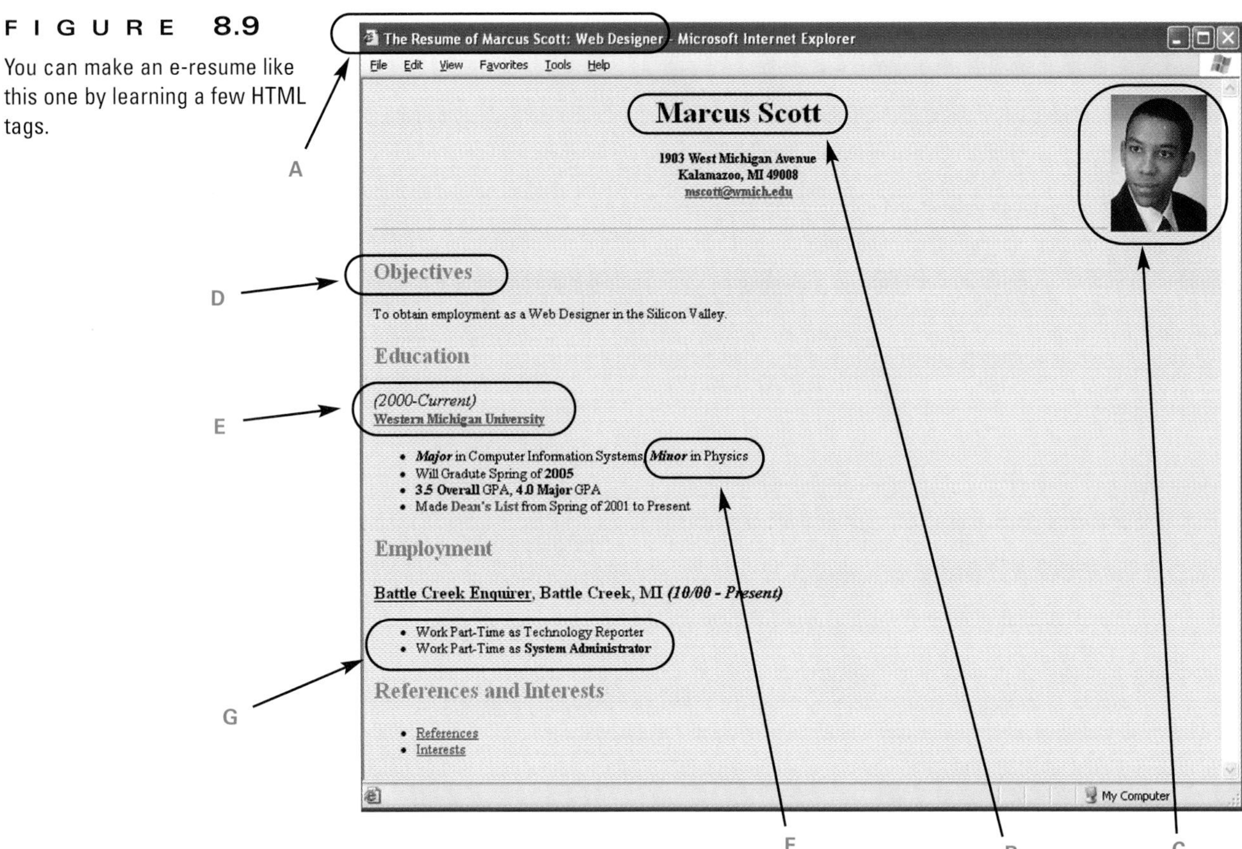

FIGURE 8.9

You can make an e-resume like this one by learning a few HTML tags.

specify the layout and presentation of information on a Web page. Figure 8.9 shows a Web page with an e-resume and Figure 8.10 on the opposite page shows the HTML document that created it.

An ***HTML document*** is a file that contains HTML tags and the information you want to appear on your Web page. Thus, a Web page is simply an HTML document visually displayed in a Web browser. As we explore how Marcus created his e-resume in Figure 8.9, you can compare the HTML tags (in Figure 8.10) by matching the letters in each figure.

While creating your HTML document, you'll use several formatting tags including basic formatting tags, heading tags, and font tags. ***Basic formatting tags*** are HTML tags that tell a Web browser how to display text. You can use tags such as bold (**<b>** and **</b>**) or strong (**<strong>** and **</strong>**) and italics (**<i>** and **</i>**) or emphasis (**<em>** and **</em>**). ***Heading tags*** are HTML tags that make certain information, such as titles, stand out on your Web page. Heading tags range from **<h1>** and **</h1>** to **<h6>** and **</h6>,** with **<h1>** being the largest.

When you create any Web page, you usually want to present text in the most concise manner. ***List tags*** are HTML tags that allow you to present information in the form of a list, either numbered (using **<ol>** and **</ol>**) or unnumbered (using **<ul>** and **</ul>**). Notice that Marcus included in his e-resume links (some in the form of lists) to his other Web pages as well as related Web sites using link tags. ***Link tags*** are HTML tags you use to create links from your Web page to other sites, pages, downloadable files such as audio and video, and e-mail.

In order for employers to find your e-resume, you'll want to make sure search engines can find your Web page. You need to help search engines

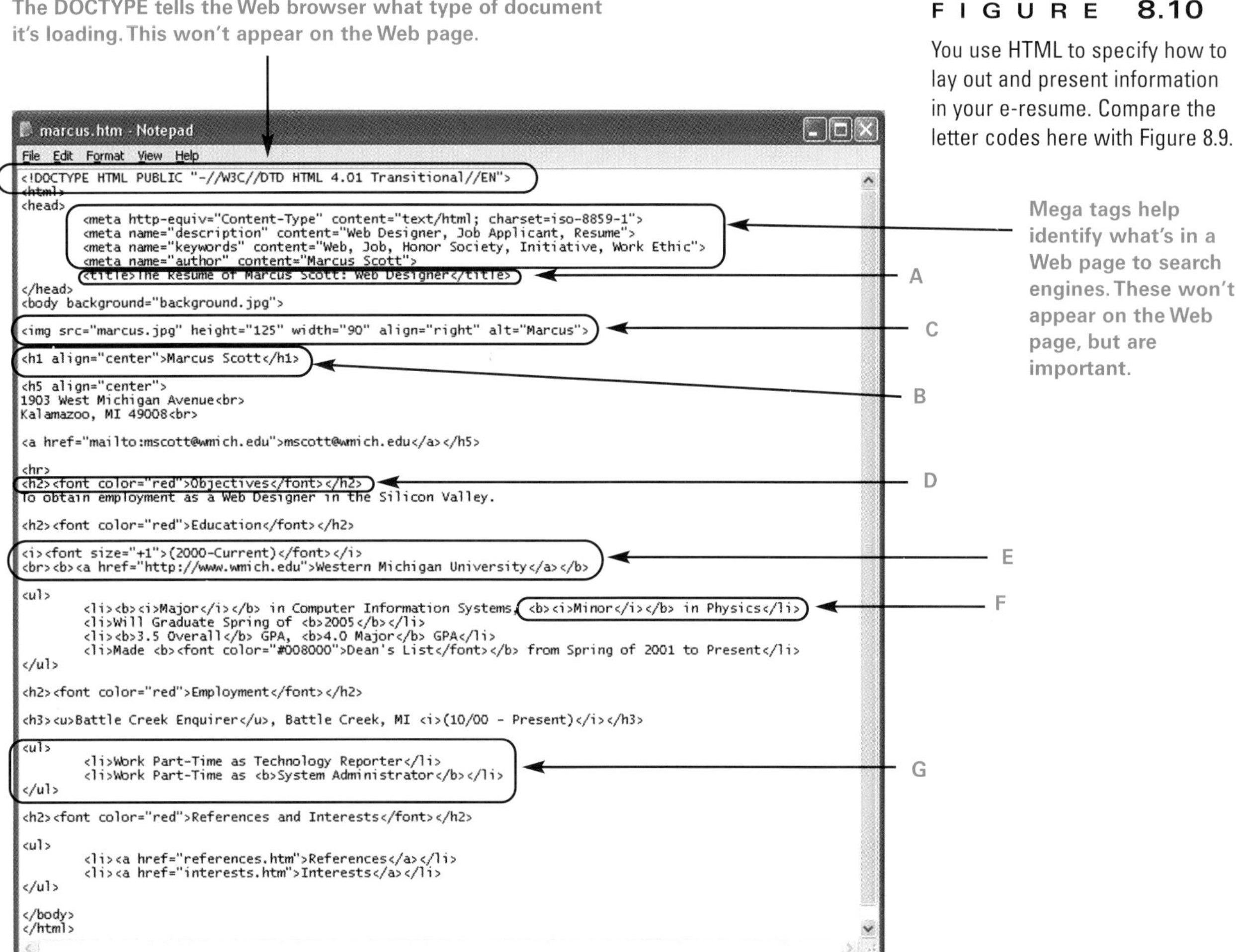
The DOCTYPE tells the Web browser what type of document it's loading. This won't appear on the Web page.
marcus.htm - Notepad
File Edit Format View Help
Mega tags help identify what's in a Web page to search engines. These won't appear on the Web page, but are important.
A
B
C
D
E
F
G

```
<!DOCTYPE HTML PUBLIC "-//W3C//DTD HTML 4.01 Transitional//EN">
<html>
<head>
	<meta http-equiv="Content-Type" content="text/html; charset=iso-8859-1">
	<meta name="description" content="Web Designer, Job Applicant, Resume">
	<meta name="keywords" content="Web, Job, Honor Society, Initiative, Work Ethic">
	<meta name="author" content="Marcus Scott">
	<title>The Resume of Marcus Scott: Web Designer</title>
</head>
<body background="background.jpg">
<img src="marcus.jpg" height="125" width="90" align="right" alt="Marcus">
<h1 align="center">Marcus Scott</h1>
<h5 align="center">
1903 West Michigan Avenue<br>
Kalamazoo, MI 49008<br>

<a href="mailto:mscott@wmich.edu">mscott@wmich.edu</a></h5>

<hr>
<h2><font color="red">Objectives</font></h2>
To obtain employment as a Web Designer in the Silicon Valley.

<h2><font color="red">Education</font></h2>

<i><font size="+1">(2000-Current)</font></i>
<br><b><a href="http://www.wmich.edu">Western Michigan University</a></b>

<ul>
	<li><b><i>Major</i></b> in Computer Information Systems, <b><i>Minor</i></b> in Physics</li>
	<li>Will Graduate Spring of <b>2005</b></li>
	<li><b>3.5 Overall</b> GPA, <b>4.0 Major</b> GPA</li>
	<li>Made <b><font color="#008000">Dean's List</font></b> from Spring of 2001 to Present</li>
</ul>

<h2><font color="red">Employment</font></h2>

<h3><u>Battle Creek Enquirer</u>, Battle Creek, MI <i>(10/00 - Present)</i></h3>

<ul>
	<li>Work Part-Time as Technology Reporter</li>
	<li>Work Part-Time as <b>System Administrator</b></li>
</ul>

<h2><font color="red">References and Interests</font></h2>

<ul>
	<li><a href="references.htm">References</a></li>
	<li><a href="interests.htm">Interests</a></li>
</ul>

</body>
</html>
```

FIGURE 8.10

You use HTML to specify how to lay out and present information in your e-resume. Compare the letter codes here with Figure 8.9.

analyze and categorize your e-resume by using meta tags. ***Meta tags*** provide information for search engines about your Web page.

WEB AUTHORING SOFTWARE

What Should I Use to Write HTML?

Some professional Web developers use Notepad or another text editor, such as vi or emacs, to make sure their HTML documents appear exactly how they want them to look. However, most Web developers instead use specially designed tools, called Web authoring software, to create their HTML documents because they don't want to type out each HTML tag. We discussed Web authoring software in Chapter 3.

WYSIWYG HTML Editors

Some Web developers also like to see what the Web page will look like without loading it into a Web browser. They use WYSIWYG HTML editors. ***WYSIWYG HTML editors,*** or "What You See Is What You Get" HTML editors, display how your Web page will look in a Web browser as you write the HTML document. These editors allow you to change the displayed version, which automatically results in changes to the actual HTML document. To learn more about HTML editors, complete the "HTML Editors" tutorial on your SimNet Concepts Support CD.

Web Site Management Software

Other Web authoring software packages help you not only to develop Web pages but also to maintain your Web pages and Web site. ***Web site management software*** allows you to create, update, and manage all of your Web pages quickly and efficiently. Macromedia Dreamweaver and Microsoft FrontPage are popular Web site management software packages.

Most professional Web developers use Web site management software to develop their Web sites. If this type of job interests you, you should consider learning how to use Web site management software. Visit the Web site for this text (*Life-Long Learning Module A,* "Enhanced Web Development") at www.mhhe.com/i-series for more information.

PUBLISHING AND MAINTAINING YOUR WEB SITE
How Do I Get My Site on the Web?

Once you've built your Web site, you'll want to share it with others. Your e-resume does you no good if a potential employer can't view it. You have some decisions to make about publishing your Web site.

Web Space

You'll need Web space on a Web server to upload your Web site to show others. We discussed Web space and servers in Chapter 2. You'll need an FTP program as well. An ***FTP program*** moves files between computers. In this case, you're moving files from your computer to Web space so people can view them on a Web server. To learn more about Web hosting services, complete the "Web Hosting" tutorial on your SimNet Concepts Support CD.

Maintaining a Web Site

The Web changes fast. Keep your Web site "up to speed" with fresh content. People quickly notice an outdated Web site. Some Web developers embed the modification date on the Web page so people know the information is current. Don't keep dead links, either. Links to other sites fail as the Web changes. If your friend removes her Web site, your link to it dies. Check your links regularly to make sure they work.

SECTION 8.3

making the grade

1. ___________ is the basic language you use to create Web pages.
2. You use ___________ to tell a Web browser how to display text.
3. ___________ provide information for search engines about your Web page.
4. ___________ HTML editors display how your Web page will look as you write the HTML document.
5. A(n) ___________ moves files between computers.

i•can

Build an E-Resume in 10 Minutes

You've seen how Marcus created his e-resume using HTML tags. Now it's time to start your own. Even if you've never done any HTML scripting before, you'll have the start of an e-resume by the time we're done.

Open Notepad or another simple text editor. We don't need the powerful features of a word processing program to write HTML. In some cases, a word processor will attempt to create a Web page for you. This can cause problems when you're writing HTML.

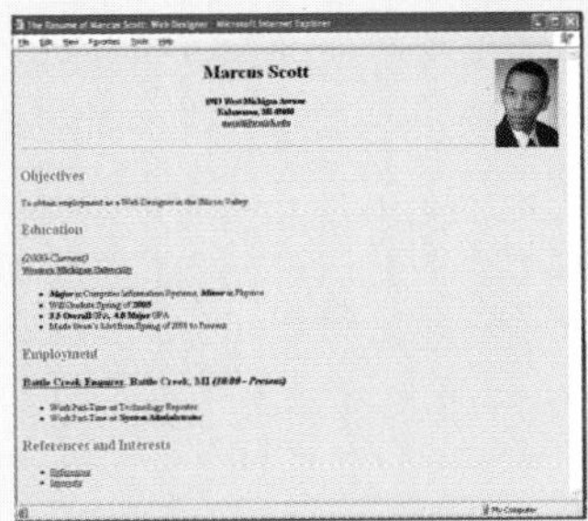

Now go back and look again at Figures 8.9 (on page 238) and 8.10 (on page 239) to refresh your memory. You can retype the code in Figure 8.10 if you'd like, but we've placed a copy online at www.mhhe.com/i-series for you to use. Go ahead and get the HTML document from our Web site.

As you work through the HTML document, notice the help we've provided for you as HTML comments. Anything between a **<!--** and a **-->** won't show up on the Web page. When you're done making changes, save your HTML document as **resume.htm.** To do this in Notepad, click on **File,** then **Save As.** Name the file **resume.htm** and then make sure to select **All Files** for the type. You're now ready to publish your e-resume.

If you'd like to continue creating Web pages, you might want to get a free HTML editor instead of Notepad. You can find many free HTML editors. We did a search on Google for "free +html +editor" and received more than 4,800 hits.

8.4 ADVANCED WEB TECHNOLOGIES

The HTML documents and tags we've discussed work well for basic Web sites and pages. However, for e-commerce and m-commerce, Web developers use many other Web technologies and programming languages. In this section you'll learn about Web technologies that make the Web interactive and useful in a variety of applications. To learn more about programming languages, complete the "Programming Languages" tutorial on your SimNet Concepts Support CD.

CSS (CASCADING STYLE SHEETS)

How Do Web Developers Separate Content from Style?

You'll notice that Marcus used various colors and fonts in his e-resume, such as in the main headings. Instead of using the **<font color="red">** and **</font>** tag, he could have used CSS or Cascading Style Sheets to change the text color. ***CSS (Cascading Style Sheets)*** allow you to format an HTML document's elements separately from its content.

You can use three types of cascading style sheets:

1. ***Inline CSS:*** Inline CSS changes the appearance of a single HTML tag in *one* HTML document. In Figure 8.11 we've changed the color of some text to red using Inline CSS.
2. ***Embedded CSS:*** Embedded CSS changes the appearance of a *single type* of HTML tag in one HTML document. For example, all the **<h2>** tags in Figure 8.11 will be green.
3. ***External CSS:*** External CSS uses a stylesheet file to change a *single type* of HTML tag in an *entire* Web site. In Figure 8.11, our **style.css** file formats all lists and hyperlinks in our Web site.

FIGURE 8.11

Here you can use external, embedded, and inline styles to make each Web page different while still maintaining an overall Web site theme.

A link to the external stylesheet.

An embedded style changes all <h2> tags in this HTML file to green.

An inline style changes this text color to red.

marcus-css.htm - Notepad

File Edit Format View Help

```
<!DOCTYPE HTML PUBLIC "-//W3C//DTD HTML 4.01 Transitional//EN">
<html>

<head>
        <meta http-equiv="Content-Type" content="text/html; charset=iso-8859-1">
        <meta name="description" content="Web Designer, Job Applicant, Resume">
        <meta name="keywords" content="Web, Job, Honor Society, Initiative, Work Ethic">
        <meta name="author" content="Marcus Scott">

<link rel="stylesheet" href="style.css" type="text/css">

<style type="text/css">
        h2 {color: #006600;}
</style>

<title>The Resume of Marcus Scott: Web Designer</title>

</head>

<body background="background.jpg">

<img src="marcus.jpg" height="125" width="90" align="right" alt="Marcus">

<h1 align="center">Marcus Scott</h1>

<h5 align="center">
1903 West Michigan Avenue<br>
Kalamazoo, MI 49008<br>

<a href="mailto:mscott@wmich.edu">mscott@wmich.edu</a>
</h5>

<hr>
<h2>Objectives</h2>
<p style="color: #ff0000">To obtain employment as a Web Designer in the Silicon Valley.</p>

<h2>Education</h2>

<i><font size="+1">(2000-Current)</font></i>
<br><strong><a href="http://www.wmich.edu">Western Michigan University</a></strong>

<ul>
        <li><strong><i>Major</i></strong> in Computer Information Systems, <strong><i>Minor</i></strong> in
        <li>Will Graduate Spring of <strong>2005</strong></li>
        <li style="color: #ff0000"><strong>3.5 Overall</strong> GPA, <strong>4.0 Major</strong> GPA</li>
        <li>Made <strong>Dean's List</strong> from Spring of 2001 to Present</li>
</ul>

<h2>Employment</h2>

<h3><u>Battle Creek Enquirer</u>, Battle Creek, MI <i>(10/00 - Present)</i></h3>

<ul>
        <li>Work Part-Time as Technology Reporter</li>
        <li>Work Part-Time as <strong>System Administrator</strong></li>
```

This formats the font type and color and the background color on our Web site.

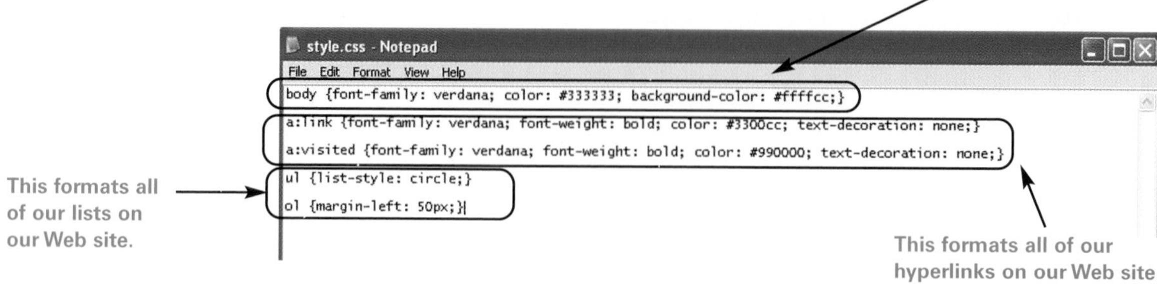

style.css - Notepad

File Edit Format View Help

```
body {font-family: verdana; color: #333333; background-color: #ffffcc;}
a:link {font-family: verdana; font-weight: bold; color: #3300cc; text-decoration: none;}
a:visited {font-family: verdana; font-weight: bold; color: #990000; text-decoration: none;}
ul {list-style: circle;}
ol {margin-left: 50px;}
```

This formats all of our lists on our Web site.
This formats all of our hyperlinks on our Web site.

You should use cascading style sheets in your HTML documents as well. Then many different Web browsers on many different devices (including Internet appliances) can view your Web pages. We discuss designing HTML documents using CSS in greater detail in *Life-Long Learning Module A,* "Enhanced Web Development."

XML (EXTENSIBLE MARKUP LANGUAGE)

How Do E-Commerce Web Sites Organize Their Information?

Earlier in this chapter you saw how Amazon.com enhanced your e-commerce experience with Web personalization. E-commerce sites use Web databases to store information about you and their products. You'll learn more about databases in Chapter 10.

Organizing Content

Many e-commerce Web sites use XML to convert information from Web databases to Web page content. ***XML (Extensible Markup Language)*** is a markup language that uses customized tags to describe how to organize and exchange information between applications. XML organizes the content, XHTML (more on this later), and CSS, respectively, describe the content and what it should look like on the Web page. For one Web page, you'd have an XML file **(.xml),** an XHTML file **(.htm),** and a CSS file **(.css).**

Most Web developers agree that the combination of XML, XHTML, and CSS plays an important role in the future of the Web.

XML Syntax

Unlike HTML, XML has no standard tags. Instead, developers build on a basic XML syntax. ***XML syntax*** is a set of rules and standards used to organize information for XML use. Figure 8.12 is an XML document that a bookstore might use to organize its inventory.

The first line in Figure 8.12 is the XML declaration. The ***XML declaration*** tells Web browsers what XML version you're using. Also, notice in Figure 8.12 that you must open and close every XML tag in a certain order.

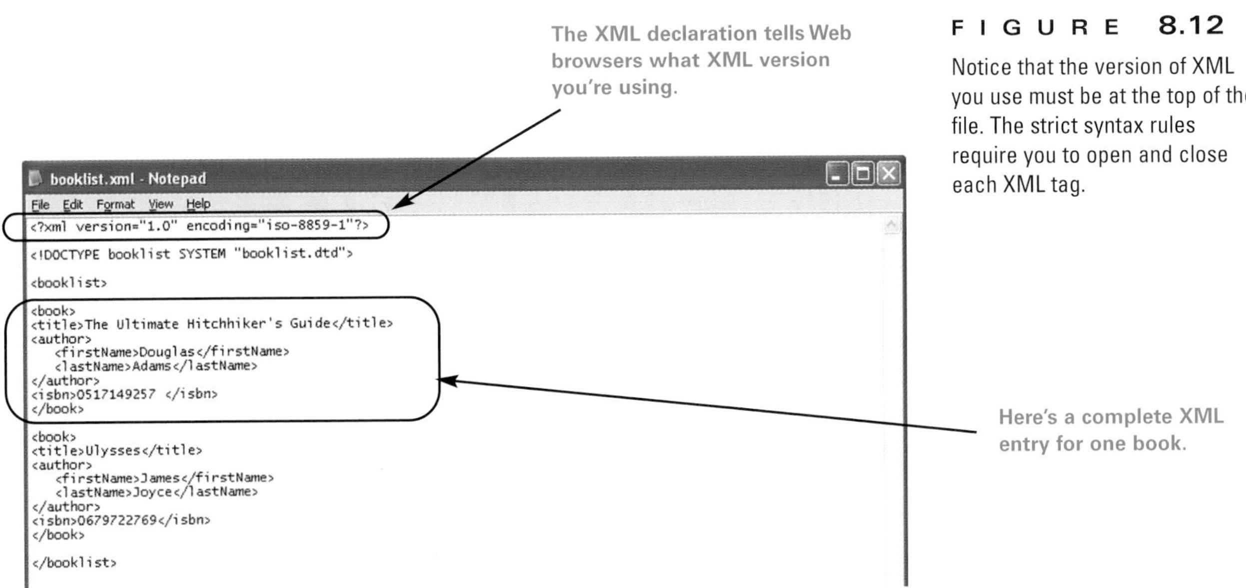
The XML declaration tells Web browsers what XML version you're using.
booklist.xml - Notepad
File Edit Format View Help
Here's a complete XML entry for one book.

```
<?xml version="1.0" encoding="iso-8859-1"?>
<!DOCTYPE booklist SYSTEM "booklist.dtd">
<booklist>
<book>
<title>The Ultimate Hitchhiker's Guide</title>
<author>
   <firstName>Douglas</firstName>
   <lastName>Adams</lastName>
</author>
<isbn>0517149257 </isbn>
</book>
<book>
<title>Ulysses</title>
<author>
   <firstName>James</firstName>
   <lastName>Joyce</lastName>
</author>
<isbn>0679722769</isbn>
</book>
</booklist>
```

FIGURE 8.12

Notice that the version of XML you use must be at the top of the file. The strict syntax rules require you to open and close each XML tag.

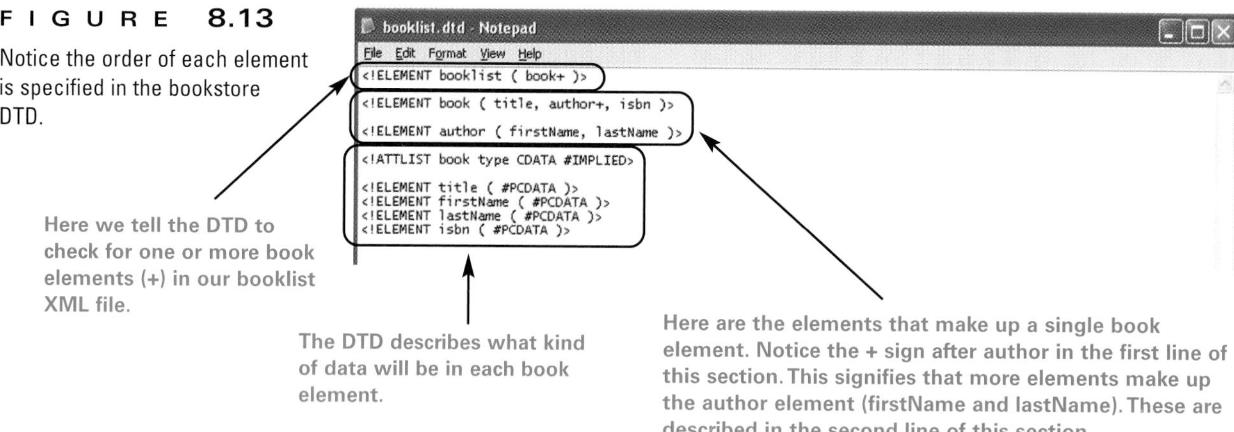
booklist.dtd - Notepad
File Edit Format View Help
<!ELEMENT booklist (book+)>
<!ELEMENT book (title, author+, isbn)>
<!ELEMENT author (firstName, lastName)>
<!ATTLIST book type CDATA #IMPLIED>
<!ELEMENT title (#PCDATA)>
<!ELEMENT firstName (#PCDATA)>
<!ELEMENT lastName (#PCDATA)>
<!ELEMENT isbn (#PCDATA)>
Here we tell the DTD to check for one or more book elements (+) in our booklist XML file.
The DTD describes what kind of data will be in each book element.
Here are the elements that make up a single book element. Notice the + sign after author in the first line of this section. This signifies that more elements make up the author element (firstName and lastName). These are described in the second line of this section.

FIGURE 8.13

Notice the order of each element is specified in the bookstore DTD.

Programmers call these tags elements. An ***XML element*** is one set of XML tags. You must close the XML tag **<book>** with a **</book>** when you're finished with the book element. The same is true with the **<author>, <title>,** and **<isbn>** elements. You must follow XML syntax and open and close the XML tags in the correct order. XML tags are also case-sensitive. An XML document that meets all syntax requirements is called a ***well-formed XML document.***

Valid XML Documents

Even though our bookstore example is a well-formed XML document, it's still not ready for e-commerce. In order for bookstores to share XML documents, they need to adhere to a set of rules defined by all bookstores. An ***XML DTD,*** or ***XML Document Type Definition,*** contains a list of all valid XML elements and their required order. For example, in Figure 8.12 on the previous page, the author element can never appear outside the book element. Figure 8.13 is a DTD for our bookstore XML document. When an XML document adheres to a specific DTD, it's a ***valid XML document.*** You can find out more about XML in *Life-Long Learning Module A,* "Enhanced Web Development," at www.mhhe.com/i-series.

XHTML (EXTENSIBLE HYPERTEXT MARKUP LANGUAGE)

What's the Next Step in Web Site Development?

In Chapter 1 you learned about the options you have to access information over the Web. Perhaps you use a desktop or notebook computer or a cell phone, PDA, or a tablet PC. Whatever device you use, you must be able to read the information you access.

Why XHTML?

Unfortunately, today's HTML won't work on Web browsers on all devices. Cell phones or PDAs can have problems. For example, the text might be too large for your PDA to view more than a few words at a time.

XHTML makes it possible for all devices to view all Web sites. ***XHTML (Extensible HTML)*** combines the strict syntax of XML to organize content with the presentation power of HTML to display information on almost any Internet device. If you write all your HTML documents as XHTML documents, your Web site will work with today's and tomorrow's Web browsers on today's and tomorrow's Internet-accessing devices.

XHTML versus HTML

You'll find five major differences between XHTML and HTML. Notice XHTML's similarity to XML requirements:

1. All XHTML tags need to be lowercase.
2. All XHTML tags have to be correctly closed.
3. All XHTML elements must be properly nested.
4. All XHTML documents must be well-formed.
5. All XHTML documents must be valid.

Figure 8.14 illustrates some of the major differences between HTML and XHTML.

FIGURE 8.14

Even though the resulting Web page looks the same, notice the major differences between the HTML and XHTML code.

	HTML	XHTML
All XHTML tags need to be lowercase.	<BODY> <H2>Hello World</H2> </BODY>	<body> <h2>Hello World</h2> </body>
All XHTML tags have to be correctly closed.	<p>Welcome to my Website. <hr> <p>Please come again. <img src="smile.gif" alt="smile">	<p>Welcome to my Website.</p> <hr /> <p>Please come again.</p> <img src="smile.gif" alt="smile" />
All XHTML elements must be properly nested.	<b><i>Really, I mean it.</b></i>	<b><i>Really, I mean it.</i></b>
All XHTML documents must be well-formed.	<html> <head> <title>My Web Page </title> </head> <body>	<html> <head> <title>My Web Page</title> </head> <body> </body> </html>
All XHTML documents must be valid.	NA	XHTML must be either strict, transitional, or frameset. More on this in *Life-Long Learning Module A,* "Enhanced Web Development." XHTML validity can be checked by submitting the XHTML file to validator.w3.org.

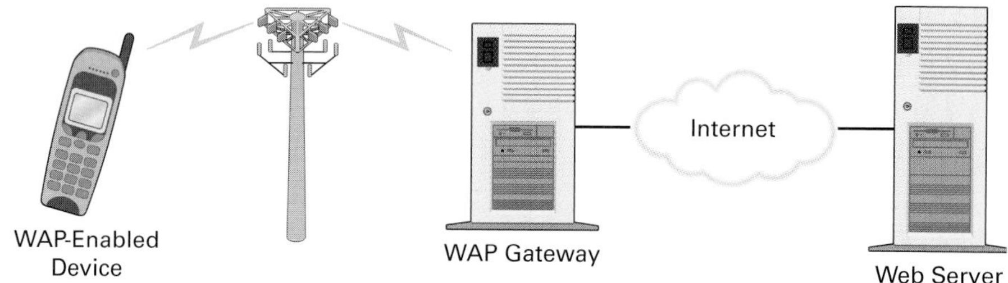

FIGURE 8.15

When you request a Web page on your cell phone, the request goes to a WAP gateway. The WAP gateway searches the Web server for the Web page and then translates the HTML into WML so you can view it.

THE WIRELESS WEB
How Does My Hand-held Device Surf the Web?

In Chapter 1, we discussed computing without wires. And in Chapter 2 and earlier in this chapter you learned about *m-commerce,* which allows you to use wireless devices such as smart phones or PDAs to buy and sell products and services on the Web. Many PDAs and smart phones, as well as cellular phones and other wireless devices, interpret Web information using WAP, or wireless application protocol. To learn more about the wireless Web, complete the "Wireless Communications" tutorial on your SimNet Concepts Support CD.

WAP (Wireless Application Protocol)

WAP (Wireless Application Protocol) is a collection of communications protocols that allows wireless devices to access the Web. Remember, a communications protocol is a set of rules that every computer follows to transfer information.

For WAP to work, you need three items: (1) a WAP-enabled device such as a PDA, (2) a WAP gateway, and (3) a Web server. A ***WAP-enabled device*** is any technology that uses WAP. A ***WAP gateway*** is a server that translates Web pages into a language that WAP-enabled devices can read.

Figure 8.15 shows what happens when you use a WAP-enabled device to access a Web page. The WAP gateway receives the request from the cell phone, searches the Web server for the information, and then translates the information from HTML to WML before sending it back to the cell phone. ***WML,*** or ***Wireless Markup Language,*** is a markup language based on XML that organizes content so WAP devices can read it.

Developing wireless applications for Internet devices is a new career field with vast employment potential. You'll first need to learn a variety of technologies, such as XML, XHTML, CSS, WML, and the Java programming language. We've provided links to resources that will help you in the *Life-Long Learning Module A,* "Enhanced Web Development."

CLIENT-SIDE WEB PROGRAMMING LANGUAGES
How Do I Use a Web Browser's Power?

Your Web browser is a powerful software application. You can use it to pull information off Web servers. In Chapter 2 we talked about how Web clients and Web servers work together.

Web developers know that powerful Web browser applications can do more than just display information using XHTML and XML. But Web developers also want to increase interactivity without placing the entire burden on a Web server's resources. With client-side Web programming languages, Web developers are able to increase interactivity without using Web server resources. ***Client-side Web programming languages*** employ the computing power of users' Web browsers to add functionality to Web

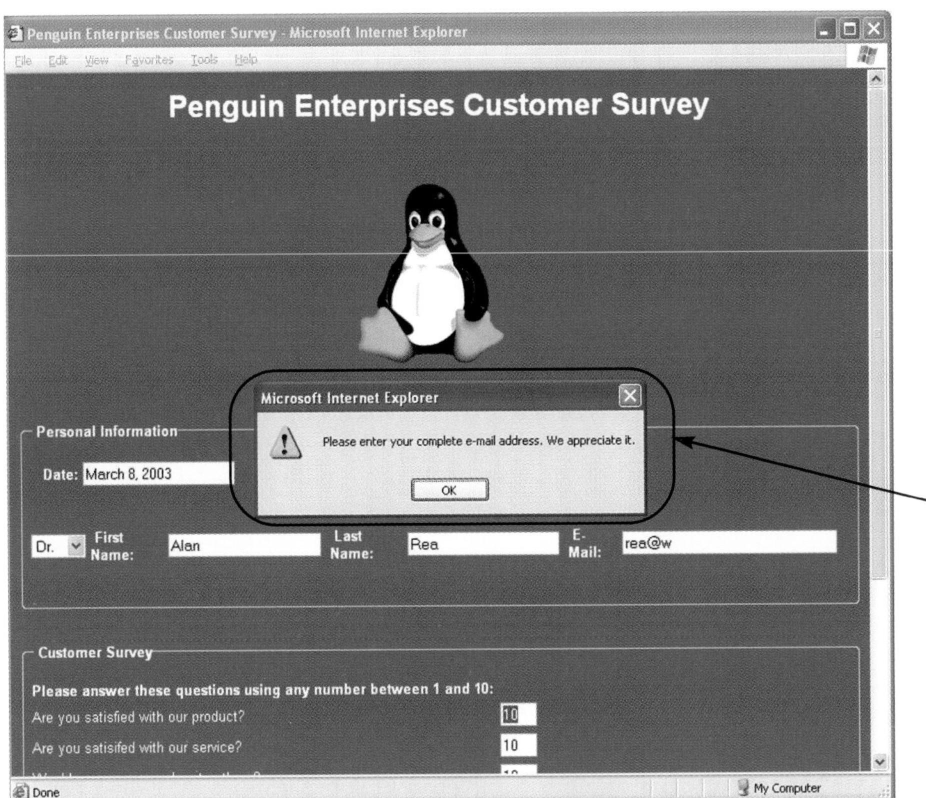

FIGURE 8.16

This Web form uses JavaScript to make sure you enter your e-mail address. If you don't, and try to submit the form, you'll see a message like the one here.

Notice the JavaScript alert box asking us to enter a complete e-mail address.

pages. The most common client-side Web programming language is JavaScript. We'll learn more about programming languages in Chapter 13.

JavaScript

Have you ever been to a Web page with images or text that change when you place your cursor over them? This site is probably using JavaScript. ***JavaScript*** is a scripting language developed by Netscape that you can use to add interactivity and features to a Web page. Web developers create e-commerce shopping carts with JavaScript.

Almost all Web browsers support JavaScript. Web developers write JavaScript in the Web page with HTML. You've probably interacted with JavaScript but may not have been aware of it. For example, on most e-commerce Web sites you have to fill out a Web form to order a product or request information. Web developers use JavaScript to make sure you correctly fill out the form. Figure 8.16 is a sample form that probably looks like a Web form you've seen or filled out before.

SERVER-SIDE WEB PROGRAMMING LANGUAGES

How Do I Supplement the Web with Web Servers?

As powerful as Web browsers are, not all programming is on the client-side. Web developers do need Web servers to run certain applications. ***Server-side Web programming languages*** use Web server resources to retrieve information, process information, and customize Web pages for users. Web developers use the Common Gateway Interface, Active Server Pages, and Hypertext Preprocessor scripts to execute many server-side programs.

CGI (Common Gateway Interface) is a specification that enables all Web clients to interact with all Web servers. Web developers use the CGI specification to transfer and process information between a Web page and the Web server. CGI programs can process information that Web forms collect. CGIs can also access databases and track the number of visitors to a Web page.

ASP, or ***Active Server Pages,*** use a combination of HTML, VBScript, and specific commands to build interactive Web pages. VBScript is similar to JavaScript. ***VBScript*** is a client-side scripting language based on Visual Basic. With ASP, Web developers can customize Web pages by developing interactive elements on the client side (with VBScript). But Web developers can also use ASP to retrieve elements from the server to process forms, interact with databases, and create Web applications such as e-commerce storefronts.

PHP (Hypertext Preprocessor) is a server-side scripting language Web developers use to create dynamic Web pages. It's similar to ASP in what it can do. Instead of the **.asp** extension on files, however, you'll see a **.php** extension.

Certification

We've covered many skills that Web developers need to develop Web sites for e-commerce and m-commerce. Whether it's XHTML, WML, JavaScript, or PHP, Web developers must continually learn new techniques to keep their Web sites competitive. If you want to be a Web developer, you should consider becoming certified. To learn more about careers in IT, complete the "Careers" tutorial on your SimNet Concepts Support CD. Most certifications require you to pass an exam. Some require you to take classes as well. Here are a few:

- Computer Technology Industry Certification: www.comptia.org
- HTML Writers Guild: www.hwg.org
- Linux Certification: www.redhat.com/mktg/rhct-rhce
- Microsoft Certification: www.microsoft.com/traincert
- National Computer Science Academy: www.ncsacademy.com
- World Association of Webmasters: www.joinwow.org/getcertified

SECTION 8.4

making the grade

1. ___________ allow you to format an HTML document's elements separately from its content.
2. ___________ is a markup language that uses customized tags to describe how information should be organized and exchanged between applications.
3. ___________ combines the strict syntax of XML to organize content with the presentation power of HTML.
4. A server that translates Web pages into a language that WAP-enabled devices can read is a(n) ___________.
5. A(n) ___________ is a specification that enables all Web clients to interact with all Web servers.

8.5 SUMMARY AND KEY TERMS

Electronic commerce (e-commerce) is really just commerce, but it's commerce that technology facilitates and enhances. In ***business to consumer electronic commerce (B2C e-commerce),*** there are many keys to success. One is ***usability***—the ease of using a business's Web page or Web site. Businesses need customers to visit and stick with their Web sites, and so they feature:

- ***Web personalization***—customizing a Web page or series of Web pages according to a customer's preferences.
- ***Shopping cart***—helpful software that stores information about your e-commerce purchases.
- ***Electronic catalog***—an electronic product or service presentation in which you enjoy a rich combination of media.
- ***M-commerce***—use of wireless devices such as smart phones or PDAs to buy and sell products and services on the Web.

E-commerce businesses employ a number of marketing and advertising devices and strategies, including:

- Registering a site with search engines so you can easily find it.
- ***Banner ads***—graphical advertisements that will take you to another site if you click on them. ***Pop-up ads*** and ***pop-under ads*** are types of banner ads.
- ***Click-throughs***—information that can be used to monitor the effectiveness of banner ads.
- ***Affiliate programs (associate programs)***—that allow an e-commerce business to sell goods and services via another Web site.
- ***Opting in*** and ***opting out***—offering consumers the opportunity to give or deny permission to use their personal information.
- ***Viral marketing***—techniques that e-commerce businesses use to gather personal information about you, then use that information in their own promotional campaigns, and sell it to other e-commerce businesses.
- Personalization filtering—methods for analyzing information about you including ***collaborative, psychographic, adaptive,*** and ***profile filtering.***

Along the way, you'll eventually have to pay for the products and services you buy. One alternative is to use a ***financial cybermediary***—a Web-based company that makes it easy for one person to pay another person or Web-based business over the Internet—such as PayPal. Whatever you do, e-commerce businesses will attempt to ensure the security of your personal and financial information using ***Secure Sockets Layers (SSLs), encryption,*** and ***Secure Electronic Transactions (SETs).***

Creating e-commerce Web sites is big business and ***Web developers*** are professionals who do it for a living. At the most basic level, you can create your own Web page using ***HTML (Hypertext Markup Language).***

There are also numerous advanced Web technologies you can use. These include:

- ***CSS (Cascading Style Sheets)***—to format an HTML document's elements separately from its content.

- ***XML (Extensible Markup Language)***—a markup language that uses customized tags to describe how to organize and exchange information between applications.
- ***XHTML (Extensible HTML)***—combines the strict syntax of XML to organize content with the presentation power of HTML.
- ***WAP (Wireless Application Protocol)***—a collection of communications protocols that allows wireless devices to access the Web.
- ***Client-side Web programming languages*** such as ***JavaScript*** and ***VBScript***—employ the computing power of users' Web browsers to add functionality to Web pages.
- ***Server-side Web programming languages*** such as ***CGI (Common Gateway Interface), ASP (Active Server Pages),*** and ***PHP (Hypertext Preprocessor)***—use Web server resources to retrieve information, process information, and customize Web pages for users.

To learn more about e-commerce and the Web technologies that enable e-commerce activities, visit the Web site for this text at www.mhhe.com/i-series.

KEY TERMS

review of terminology

Multiple Choice

1. __________ asks you to rate products or situations and also monitors your actions over time to find out what you like and dislike.
   a. Adaptive filtering
   b. Profile filtering
   c. Collaborative filtering
   d. Psychographic filtering
   e. Web personalization
2. An e-commerce business that sells goods and services via another Web site is participating in
   a. viral marketing.
   b. an affiliate program.
   c. Web personalization.
   d. collaborative filtering.
   e. m-commerce.
3. Active server pages build interactive Web page by using
   a. HTML.
   b. VBScript.
   c. specific commands.
   d. all of the above.
   e. none of the above.
4. The specification that enables all Web clients to interact with all Web servers is called
   a. ASP.
   b. PHP.
   c. CGI.
   d. CSS.
   e. WML.
5. Information that is captured when you click on an ad to go from one Web site to another is called
   a. a conversion rate.
   b. usability.
   c. viral marketing.
   d. a click-through.
   e. opting in.
6. __________ employ the computing power of users' Web browsers to add functionality to Web pages.
   a. Server-side Web programming languages
   b. Client-side Web programming languages
   c. ASPs
   d. PHPs
   e. None of the above
7. __________ CSS changes the appearance of a single type of HTML tag in one HTML document.
   a. Inline
   b. External
   c. Internal
   d. Embedded
   e. Active
8. An example of a client-side Web programming language is
   a. CGI.
   b. ASP.
   c. PHP.
   d. JavaScript.
   e. collaborative filtering.
9. __________ is a client-side scripting language based on Visual Basic.
   a. VBCS
   b. VB language
   c. VB Uniform Language
   d. Visual Basic Client
   e. VBScript
10. Technical professionals who create Web sites are called Web
    a. developers.
    b. techies.
    c. engineering specialists.
    d. technicians.
    e. specialists.

True/False

11. ____ Tags such as those indicating bold, strong, and emphasis are included in the category of basic formatting tags.
12. ____ Businesses that sell to customers who are primarily individuals are participating in C2B e-commerce.
13. ____ An HTML document is a displayed version of a Web page within a Web browser.
14. ____ You can use link tags to create links from your Web page to other sites, pages, downloadable files such as audio and video, and e-mail.
15. ____ M-commerce allows you to participate in e-commerce in metropolitan areas (hence the "m" in m-commerce).

Take this quiz online at www.mhhe.com/i-series and get instant feedback.

1. Defining a B2C E-Commerce Business

In the late 1990s, everyone rushed to join the B2C e-commerce world by setting up shop on the Web. Unfortunately, few of those businesses built solid plans on which to operate. This is your opportunity to prove you're better.

You are to create a business plan for a new B2C e-commerce business. Focus your business on one major set of products (e.g., sporting goods) you would like to offer. As you define your new e-commerce business, perform the following:

a. Search the Web, create a list of competitor Web sites, and perform an analysis of those Web sites from the point of view of Web personalization.
b. Search the Web and create a list of affiliate or associate programs you can join.
c. On paper, define the structure of your electronic catalog and include descriptions of the types of media you will employ.
d. Create a list of Web sites on which you believe you would benefit by placing banner ads.
e. Define a viral marketing technique that will enable you to gather information about your customers and visitors. Describe how you would use that information to increase the quality of your marketing efforts.
f. Determine a list of suppliers from whom you can order your products. Search the Web for these suppliers and determine which, if any, have a B2B Web site through which you can order your products.
g. Determine the cost of registering your site with three search engines that are <u>not</u> free.
h. On paper, design the home or main page for your Web site. Be sure to include your logo, product categories, any services you will provide (such as customer service), images that will attract the attention of your audience, and so on.

You also need to create a path-to-profitability (P2P). That is, you must forecast your expenses, create a series of sales projections, and determine a break-even point (basically, the point at which you're not losing money but you're not making any money either).

To help you with this, we've created a P2P spreadsheet and placed it on the Web site that supports this text at www.mhhe.com/i-series (select **Chapter 8** and then **P2P**). When you find the link for the file **P2P.xls,** click once on it to download and save it to your computer. Then, start Excel. The spreadsheet is self-explanatory and you should be able to complete it in about 30 minutes. What is your break-even point? Is it realistic or reasonable for you to assume that your business will be successful? Why or why not?

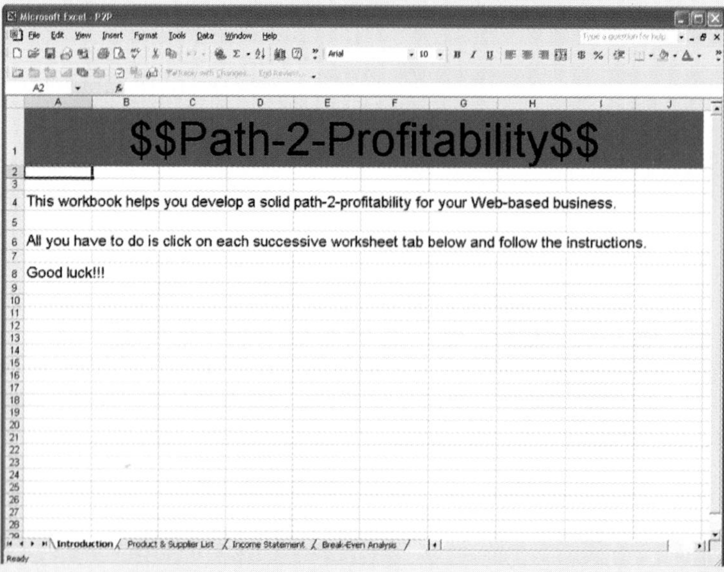

2. Creating a Web Page with Style

We've noted in this chapter that Web developers use XHTML and CSS to create Web sites viewable by many Internet devices. You can create a Web site using XHTML and CSS as well.

Go to our Web site at www.mhhe.com/i-series (select **Chapter 8** and then **Project Data Files**). Download **Website.zip** and then extract it. You should find the following files in the **Web** folder:

- **page1.htm**
- **page2.htm**
- **pages.css**

Open each file in Notepad and read the help we've placed in the comments. You're now ready to change the Web pages using CSS. As you go through each step, note whether you use an inline, embedded, or external style.

a. Change the style for all pages so that:
   - Page backgrounds are gray with dark green 12 point Arial text.
   - All level 1 headings are red.
   - All level 2 headings are blue.

b. Change the first **h1** tag in **page1.htm** to purple.

c. Change the background color of **page1.htm** to white.

d. Change the color of all **h2** tags in **page2.htm** to green.

Remember to save your new files as **All Files** as you did in this chapter's I-Can feature box.

3. Organizing Information with XML

In this chapter, you looked at how a bookstore used XML to organize its inventory. But to experience the power of XML, you need to see it in action. Go to the Web site at www.mhhe.com/i-series (select **Chapter 8** and then **Project Data Files**). Download **games.xml** and save the file to your computer.

If you were to open the **games.xml** file in Internet Explorer, you'd expect to see something like Figure 8.12 on page 243. However, it won't be the same because the **games.xml** file is not well-formed. It's up to you to make the changes in the **games.xml** file so that it will work. Make sure to look at the **games.xml** file comments for hints.

When you've found all of the errors, save the **games.xml** file and then open it in Internet Explorer. You should see a Web page like the one below.

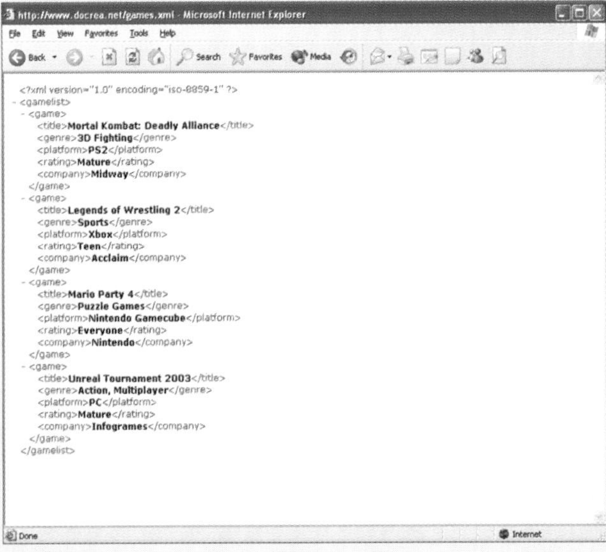

e-commerce

1. Getting Your Site on a Search Engine

One of the real keys to success for an e-commerce business is to effectively advertise by registering through various search engines. Connect to at least two of the following Web sites that provide registration to search engines:

- AutoSubmit.com—www.autosubmit.com
- Submit pro—http://businessweb.com.au/add-it/pro
- Microsoft bCentral Submit It!—http://addurl.com/
- Ark Webs—www.arkwebs.com/aw/submit.htm
- 360 Traffic—www.360traffic.com

After you read through a couple of those sites, answer the following questions:

a. Is there a level of search engine registration that is free?

b. Are there one or more levels of search engine registration that require you to pay a fee?

c. How many search engines will the site provide registration to?

d. What are the major search engines that the site will provide registration to?

2. Using Personal Portals

Many Web sites allow you to personalize their sites by creating an account and selecting the items you want to appear on your Web page. You can select weather, news, sports, or other information. Some of the more popular Web sites are:

- MSNBC—www.msnbc.com
- ESPN.com—www.espn.com
- The Weather Channel—www.weather.com

Look at the above Web sites and then answer the following questions:

a. What personalization do these sites permit?

b. Are there limits to what you can do? For example, can you arrange the page content to suit yourself?

3. Buying Clothes/Return Policies

Buying clothes on the Internet is similar to buying them by mail order in that you can't try them on first. To overcome this problem, most e-tailers, like mail-order merchants, let you send garments or shoes back if, for any reason, you don't want to keep them.

Look at four clothing and/or shoe e-tailers and answer the questions that follow. You can use your own preferred Web sites or these:

- Eddie Bauer—www.eddiebauer.com
- Old Navy—www.oldnavy.com
- Nordstrom—www.nordstrom.com
- Nike—www.nike.com
- Customatix—www.customatix.com

a. Does the site have a measurement guide explaining the measurements that correspond to sizes?

b. Does the site tell you whether you can get your money back or store credit only?

c. Can you design your own shoes at the shoe sites? (Hint: Try the Customatix.com Web site.) Can you return the shoes if you find you don't like them?

d. Do the shoe sites have detailed foot-measuring methods?

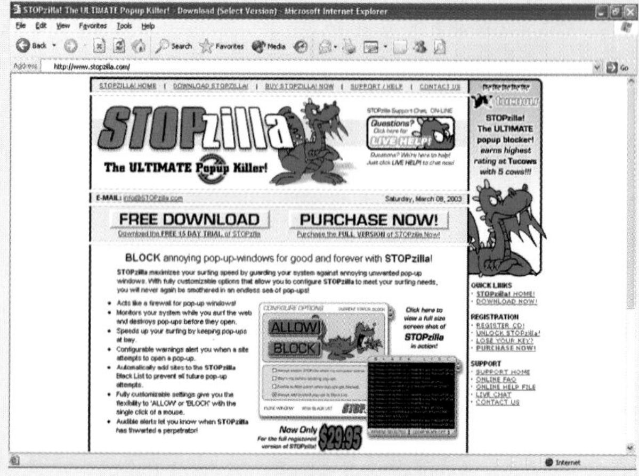

ethics, security & privacy

1. To Pop-Up or Not: Effective or Annoying?

Pop-up and pop-under ads are fairly new to the Web, but their use is growing each day. Many Web users don't enjoy ads popping up on their screen or hiding behind a Web page. Many times these ads use so much bandwidth they slow down Web surfing. Excessive ads also can crash browsers and computers if they take up too much system resources. Companies such as Earthlink offer services and software to stop pop-up and pop-under ads on your computer.

If pop-up and pop-under ads are so annoying, why do Web sites use them? The answer is simple—they work. More people shop at e-tailers who advertise this way. Web surfers notice pop-up and pop-under ads more often than the typical banner ad. Thus, they more frequently click through and purchase something.

Search the Web for sites that discuss the pop-up and pop-under issue. You might be surprised at all the information you find. After you've done some research, answer the following questions:

a. What is your opinion of pop-up and pop-under ads? Do you find them effective? Do you find them annoying?
b. Many Web sites argue that without advertising such as with pop-up and pop-under ads, they would need to charge for access. Would you rather pay a fee than experience pop-up and pop-under ads?
c. If you're against pop-up and pop-under ads, discuss some alternatives. If you're in favor of pop-up and pop-under ads, discuss better ways to implement them.

2. Are Cookies Bad for You?

The *New Yorker* cartoon illustrates how most people view surfing the Web. Most think they can move from site to site without leaving information about themselves.

This is not true. Many sites write "cookies" or small text files to the "cookie folder" on your computer. Cookies for a specific Web site might include when you visited a site, what Web pages you looked at, and any information you gave the Web site, such as your name and e-mail address. Each time you return to that Web site, it can access the cookie it wrote to your hard drive. Some companies set the cookies to "expire" after some time, but others leave them on your computer for as long as possible. Most companies use cookies responsibly in order to personalize your Web experience at their sites. As you consider the use of cookies on the Web, answer the following questions:

a. Did you know companies were storing information about you and your activity at their sites? What do you think about this?
b. Most Web sites use cookies to personalize a visit for you. The result may be you don't have to log in, or your local weather and favorite sports team automatically appear. Which do you prefer: having a personalized visit or having privacy?
c. If you answered that you prefer privacy in the preceding question, would you consider turning off cookies? Some Web sites won't work at all. Is this sacrifice worthwhile?
d. Do Web sites have a right to use cookies? Why or why not?
e. Some companies have found ways to track Web surfing from site to site instead of just at their own. Now, you leave a "cookie trail" at all the sites you visit. If you listen to a certain kind of music at one site, there is a possibility that when you visit a Web CD store, that type of music CD will appear on your Web page. Is this something you want to happen? What are the possible effects of this?

"On the Internet, nobody knows you're a dog."

on the web

1. Evaluating an E-Commerce Experience

In this chapter we considered what makes an effective e-commerce experience. We discussed how Amazon.com uses techniques such as Web personalization, an electronic catalog, and good usability to create a sticky Web site that you'll want to visit repeatedly. Amazon.com also uses personalization filtering to help create a unique shopping experience for you. And Amazon.com takes security measures, such as SSL, to keep personal and credit card information from prying eyes.

Of course, Amazon.com is only one of many e-commerce Web sites that you can shop. Find a Web site that interests you and analyze how effective it is at e-commerce. Although you might find other criteria by which to analyze the site, you should include the following in your investigation: personalization, usability, stickiness, and security.

2. Analyzing Advertising

Banner ads, pop-up and pop-under ads, and affiliate programs are all techniques e-commerce sites use to generate business via a click-through. You've seen all three types of ads in your Web travels. Now it's time to analyze how effective these ads are.

Pick three Web sites that contain these types of ads. Make sure to find at least one type of each ad. Then answer the following questions for each Web site:

a. Are the ads targeted to a specific audience or interest? Our example in Figure 8.4 (on page 230) shows the Gateway ad on CNet. This audience is interested in technology.

b. Do the ads work as you expected? When you click on one are you taken to a Web site that allows you to purchase the advertised product or service?

c. Would you have clicked on the ad if this assignment didn't require it? In other words, do you pay attention to these ads or do you ignore them? Make sure to explain your answer.

3. Exploring Web Development Resources

Web developers use XHTML, XML, CSS, JavaScript, and WML (along with other technologies) to create successful e-commerce and m-commerce Web sites. As an aspiring Web developer you'll discover that some of the best resources for these technologies are on the Web.

Choose three Web technologies from this chapter that interest you. Then find three Web resource sites for each technology. List each Web resource along with a three- to four-sentence description of what it offers. Share your findings with the class.

4. Watching the Wireless Web

Surfing the Web and buying items with hand-held devices (m-commerce) is growing in popularity. It's already successful in Japan and many European countries. People in the United States are beginning to use the wireless Web as well.

Search the Web for current wireless Web news. Since it's a quickly changing technology, you'll find that information varies daily. List the top three Web sites for wireless Web information you've found. Include a brief paragraph about each Web site. Share these Web sites with the class. You might even combine your findings to create your own wireless Web resource page.

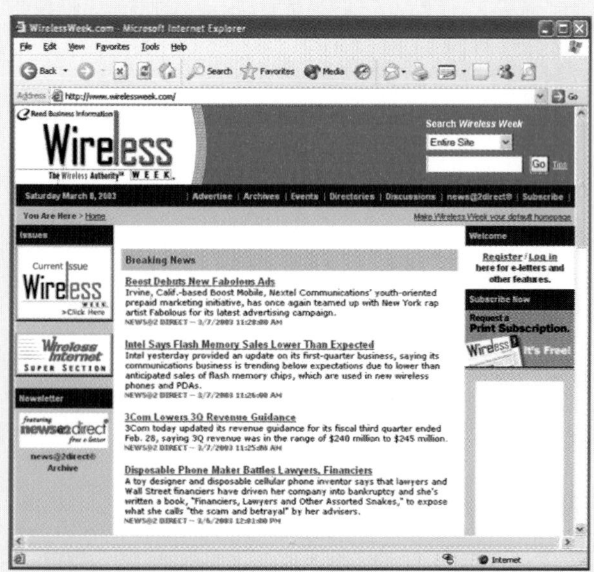

group activities

1. Exploring Job Opportunities

People skilled in advanced Web technologies such as XML, WML, and XHTML are among the most highly sought after in the IT field. After searching Monster.com, we completed the second column in the table below concerning the number of jobs available requiring various advanced Web technology skills.

Your task is twofold. First, search Monster.com for job openings requiring advanced Web technology skills and complete the third column. Second, search another Web-based job database for similar job openings and complete the fourth column. Is the number of job openings for each advanced Web technology skill increasing, decreasing, or staying consistent? Why do you believe these trends exist?

Web Technology	Monster.com as of June 2003	Monster.com as of ____________	____________ as of ____________
CSS	315		
XML	2328		
XHTML	47		
WAP/WML	46		
JavaScript	1184		
CGI	338		
ASP	3873		
PHP	240		

2. Surveying Web Site Development Habits

Conduct a survey of computer users in regard to their development of a personal Web site. As a group, prepare a list of questions to use. Below, we've provided several that you should definitely include.

a. Do you have a personal Web site?
b. What service (e.g., school, Yahoo!, etc.) do you use as a Web host?
c. What general categories of information and content are on your Web site?
d. How often do you update your Web site?
e. How many images do you have on your Web site?
f. How did you create your Web site—by writing HTML, using Web authoring software, or some other means?
g. Does your site include the use of any advanced Web technologies such as XML or CSS? If so, which are they?

3. Surveying E-Commerce Habits

Conduct a survey of computer users and their e-commerce habits. As a group, prepare a list of questions to use, such as:

a. How often do you buy things on the Web? If you don't, why not?
b. Which e-commerce Web sites do you use?
c. What is your favorite e-commerce Web site and why?

You can go to your school's computer labs, visit the dorms, or ask people questions as you walk around campus. Prepare your findings using presentation software for the class. Were your findings a surprise? Are more or fewer people using e-commerce than you thought? If you have the chance, ask a friend at another school to do the same survey. Do your results differ?

crossword puzzle

Across

2. The kind of hacker who is hired to hack
4. ______-of-service
6. Malicious software
11. A virus that isn't
12. ______ Use Doctrine
15. A hacker who seeks to cause harm to a lot of people
17. A virus that attaches to Word or Excel
18. Software designed to cause annoyance or damage
20. It monitors Internet traffic
21. The set of principles and standards we use in deciding what to do in situations that affect other people
23. National Crime Information Center
24. Key ______ software
25. A small file that a Web site puts on your hard disk
26. Illegally copied software
27. These hackers don't usually do damage; they are just seeking a ______

Down

1. These good-guy hackers wear this type of hat
3. The right to be left alone if you want to be
5. ______ Web browsing service
7. Making an e-mail look as though it came from someone other than the sender
8. A hacker who wants to send a political message
9. Someone who breaks into other people's computers
10. A virus that spreads itself
12. Keeps intruders out
13. This theft steals your financial good name
14. You should report Internet fraud to this government agency
15. Protects the expression of an idea
16. A cyber vandal wears this color hat
19. Junk e-mail
20. ______ bunny
22. Web sites use Web ______ to monitor surfers
25. Hackers for hire

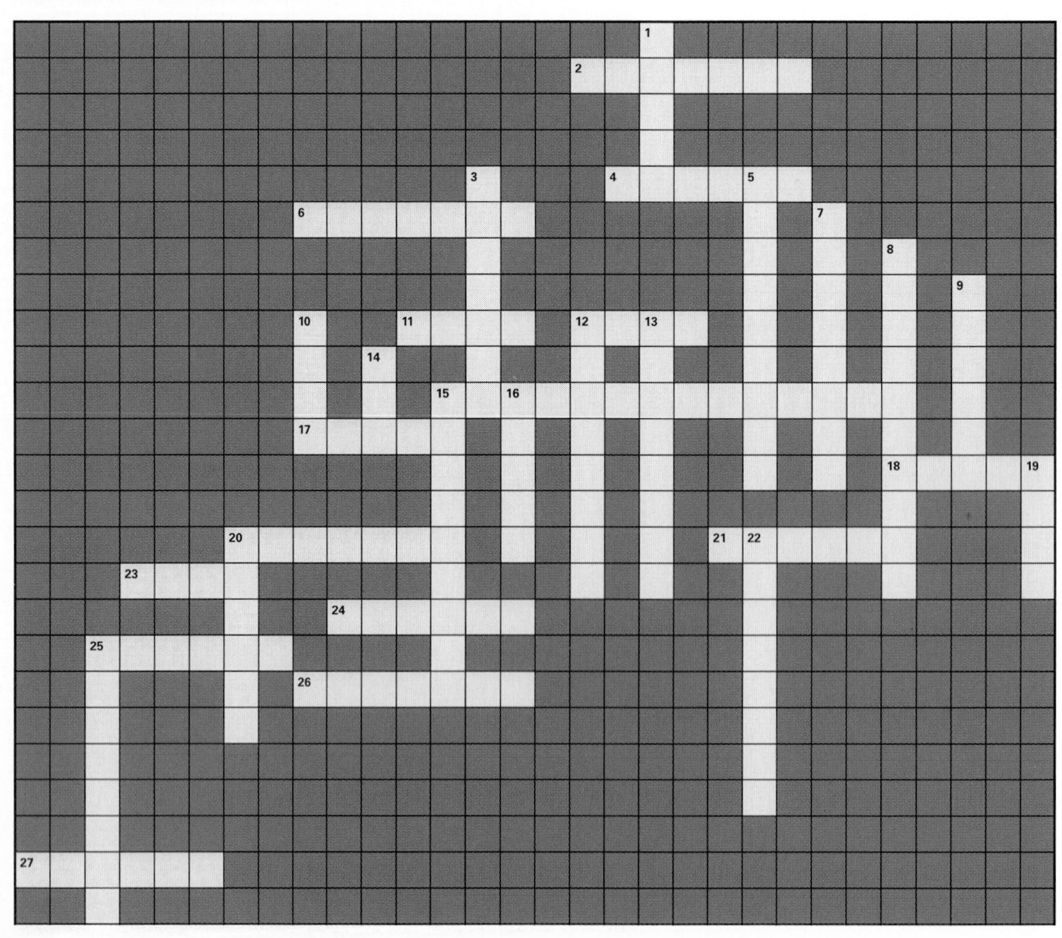

CHAPTER nine

9

Ethics, Security, and Privacy

What's Right, What's Wrong, and How Do I Protect Myself?

SIMNET CONCEPTS SUPPORT

- Privacy Issues (p. 272)
- Security Issues (p. 281)

did you know?

Computers are a force for great good but can also be used for unethical and even criminal acts. The increasing power and speed of computers enhance our productivity and freedom but also make us more vulnerable.

the *American Management Association says that 78 percent of U.S. companies electronically monitor their employees. Sixty-three percent watch their Internet use, 47 percent store and review e-mail, 15 percent watch workers with video, and 12 percent record and review phone messages.*[1]

between *700,000 and 1.1 million people became victims of identity theft in 2001.*[2]

the *Slammer (also called the Sapphire) worm spread with lightning speed in January 2003. The number of computers infected doubled every 8.5 seconds in the first minute of the attack. More than 75,000 computers were contaminated within __??__ minutes of the worm's January 25 release.*[3]

To find out how many minutes it took the Slammer worm to infect 75,000 computers, visit our Web site at www.mhhe.com/i-series.

Student Learning Outcomes

After reading this chapter, you should be able to:

1. Define ethics and describe what it means to use computers in an ethical fashion.
2. Define copyright, Fair Use Doctrine, and pirated software.
3. Identify and describe five types of threats in cyberspace.
4. Describe the seven types of hackers and what motivates each group.
5. Define privacy and identify ways in which it can be compromised.
6. Describe what you can do to protect yourself in cyberspace.

The "gift of fire" is how Sara Baase describes computers in her book on computers and ethics. Like fire, computers are a tremendous force for good. Computers free you from all sorts of paperwork drudgery. They enable you to do so many things faster and better. They give you convenience and accessibility. Computers even save lives: Without computers, many of the diagnostic and corrective medical procedures in use today wouldn't be possible. However, as with fire, there's a downside. Computers can be used as weapons to cause harm, to steal, to hurt people.

9.1 ETHICS

Computers are tools that you use to communicate and interact with other people. What you do when you interact with other people affects them in ways big and small. Our societal rules regarding how we interact with one another fall into two categories:

- *Ethics* covers those actions that have serious consequences in the lives of others. These are the sorts of actions that you label "right" or "wrong."
- *Manners* color our day-to-day behavior toward others in situations whose effects are not likely to be far-reaching. These are behaviors you might label either "polite" or "rude."

Ethics and manners are the rules and guidelines that are developed or that evolve over time in a society with the intention or effect of enhancing our human coexistence.

ETHICS IN THE USE OF COMPUTERS

How Do I Use My Computer Ethically?

Your behavior while using a computer is an extension of your sense of ethics in other parts of your life. As an ethical person, you try to live by certain principles, but from time to time you'll face ethical dilemmas. These are situations in which determining what the "right thing" is becomes a difficult matter. Ethical dilemmas usually arise in situations in which you have to reconcile conflicting demands, responsibilities, and goals.

Consider this dilemma: A young woman is engaged to a young man who has developed a medical condition that causes him constant pain. Medicine is available to treat this illness and relieve the pain, but it's very expensive and the young man doesn't have insurance to cover it. The young woman hasn't much money either. If the man had the medicine he could lead an almost normal life, but without it he's seriously disabled. The young woman has the skills necessary to break into the local pharmacy's computer and get the medicine. She knows how to alter the records to show that the medicine is paid for and get it sent to her fiancé.

did you know?

The *last man to be conscripted into the U.S. armed forces was called up on Valentine's Day, 1972.*[4]

But she knows that hacking (breaking into someone else's computer) and theft are unethical—not to mention illegal. On the other hand, someone she cares deeply for is suffering and she has the ability to fix it quickly and easily. What does she do? That will depend on her ethics.

Ethics is the set of principles and standards we use in deciding what to do in situations that affect other people. Sometimes these principles are so strongly and widely held that they have become laws. Murder is an example. In cyberspace, the same ethical rules that apply in the brick-and-mortar world also apply.

In general we can say that it's unethical to

- Use your computer to harm others. It may or may not be illegal, but it's certainly unethical.
- Use your computer to steal.
- Abuse your power. As is true in the brick-and-mortar world, in cyberspace certain people know and can do more than others. However, the ability to do something doesn't give you the right to do it.
- Use or access someone else's computer resources without permission.
- Copy copyrighted software either for your own use or to give to others. It's also illegal. This is the law that's probably broken the most often in the world of computing.

Copyright

A ***copyright*** is a type of legal protection accorded to intellectual property (see Figure 9.1). A copyright protects an expression of an idea. People who write music usually copyright their compositions. A copyright means that although other people may of course use the same musical notes or even phrases in their creations, no one else can sell music that is too similar to the copyrighted tune or song. Again, if you invent a cool video game and you copyright it, you can't prevent others from developing their own video games, but they can't sell a game that looks too much like yours.

Furthermore, you can't just borrow or tape copyrighted material for your own use. It's illegal to copy a copyrighted video game or other software, a picture, text, video, or anything else, without permission, whether it's on the Internet or not. This would be making someone else's expression of an idea your own without asking permission or paying to do so.

FIGURE 9.1

You may not copy copyrighted material without permission.

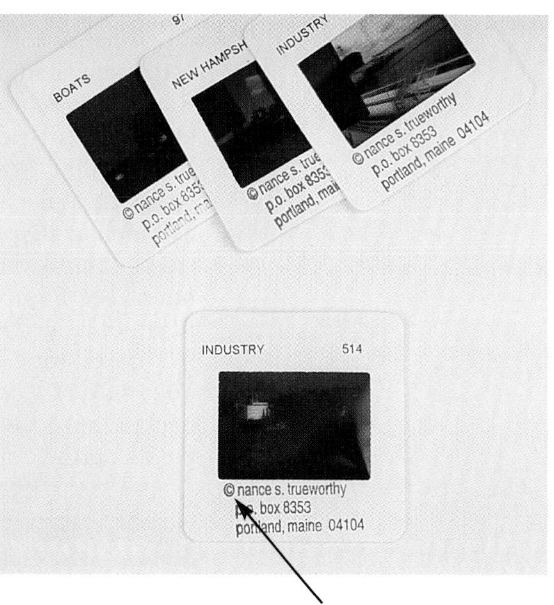

If you see this symbol, it's protected by a copyright.

Fair Use Doctrine

Having a copyright doesn't mean that you have absolute rights to your intellectual product under every circumstance. There are certain exceptions. For example, a TV program could show your video game without your permission. This would be an example of the use of copyrighted material for the creation of new material—the TV program—and, under the Fair Use Doctrine, it's perfectly legal.

FIGURE 9.2

The creator of the software determines what others may do with it.

Type	Your Rights
Copyright	Buy a license to use it
Shareware	Try before you buy
Freeware	Use, copy, share
Public domain	Use, copy, share, sell

The ***Fair Use Doctrine*** defines the situations in which copyrighted material may be used. These include copyrighted works used in the creation of a new work and, within certain limits, for teaching purposes. Generally, the determining factor in copyright disputes is whether the copyright holder has been or is likely to be denied income based on the infringement. Courts will also consider other factors such as how much of the work was used and for what purpose. For instance, a teacher may copy only a specified amount, or number of words, of a story or book to hand out to students without getting permission from the author.

When you buy copyrighted software, what you're paying for is the right for you, the buyer, to use it. Generally, by breaking the shrink-wrap on the package you're agreeing to the copyright statement. Actual copyright terms vary among software publishers. Some software companies state emphatically that you may not install the software on more than one computer—even if the additional computers are yours and no one else ever uses them. Other companies allow you to put a copy of the same software on multiple machines—as long as only one person is using the given software package at any one time.

To copy software and give it to a friend in violation of the copyright statement would be copyright infringement and the copy is pirated software. ***Pirated software*** is copyrighted software that is copied and distributed without permission of the owner. Furthermore, copyright law demands that you protect copyrighted material, so knowingly letting someone make a copy of your computer game would violate copyright law as much as if you had done the copying yourself. Not all software is copyrighted, however. Software can also be shareware, freeware, or public domain (see Figure 9.2). Refer back to Chapter 3 for details. For more on downloadable freeware and shareware, visit www.mhhe.com/i-series.

There's one universal exception to all software copyright statements. You may always make one copy of copyrighted software to keep for backup purposes. After that, the number of legal copies you may make depends on the copyright agreement that comes with the software package.

SECTION 9.1

making the grade

1. The set of principles and standards we use in determining what to do in situations that affect other people is called ___________.
2. The ___________ says that copyrighted material may be used in certain specified situations.
3. When you buy copyrighted software, you're buying only the ___________ to use it.
4. ___________ is copyrighted software that is copied and distributed without the permission of the owner.

i-series insights *Ethics, Security & Privacy*

The E-Mail You Send Can Get You Fired

When you use e-mail, remember that it's not private. There are no laws protecting e-mail like those that protect snail mail. If you are using the company computer system at your job to send e-mail, be aware that your employer has the right to monitor your messages. Courts have consistently ruled in favor of employers in cases involving employer monitoring of employee e-mail.

Many people have lost their jobs because they thought their e-mail at work was private. Here are some recent examples.

- The *New York Times* fired more than 20 people for sending or forwarding e-mail that the paper considered offensive.
- The First Union Bank fired 7 employees for the same reason.
- The Dow Chemical Company investigated complaints about inappropriate e-mail and, as a result of the inquiry, hundreds of employees stood accused of sending and receiving such e-mail. When it was all over, 50 employees had been fired, some of whom had worked for Dow for more than 10 years.
- The Nissan Motor Corporation fired two people who received and saved sexually suggestive messages.

Apart from getting you fired, what you write in an e-mail can also be used against you in a court of law. For example, in 1991, a police officer involved in the Rodney King beating sent an e-mail message to a friend stating that he hadn't beaten anyone that badly in a long time. He mistakenly thought his e-mail was private. Of course, he was mistaken about a lot of things.

When deciding what to put into an e-mail message, a good policy to follow is "if in doubt, leave it out." If you don't, it could cost you your job.

9.2 THREATS IN CYBERSPACE

Computers are weapons and targets of computer crime. They're weapons in that computers are used to steal money, customer lists, personal identities, credit card numbers, and so on. They're used to spread slander, harass people, and snoop into private files. None of these are new crimes of course; they've just taken on a new, electronic form.

Computers are also the targets of computer crime. Some people, popularly called hackers, make determined efforts to get access to other people's computers. Their reasons vary. Some hackers merely want to prove they can break in, others want to cause annoyance or damage, and still others want to steal information.

First we'll take a look at the ways in which people use computers to commit crimes, and then we'll examine some of the exploits of hackers.

COMPUTERS AS WEAPONS
How Can People Steal Online?

Theft by computer takes many forms. It could be credit card fraud, identity theft, or some sort of scam.

Credit Card Fraud

Stealing your credit card number, rather than the card itself, is much safer for thieves. If you notice your credit card is missing, you'd inform the credit card company and have the card canceled. But if someone steals just the number, you have no way of knowing that your card has been compromised—until you get the bill. Thieves can get your credit card number in one of several ways (listed on the next page).

FIGURE 9.3

Sites that encrypt information will let you know that their sites are secure.

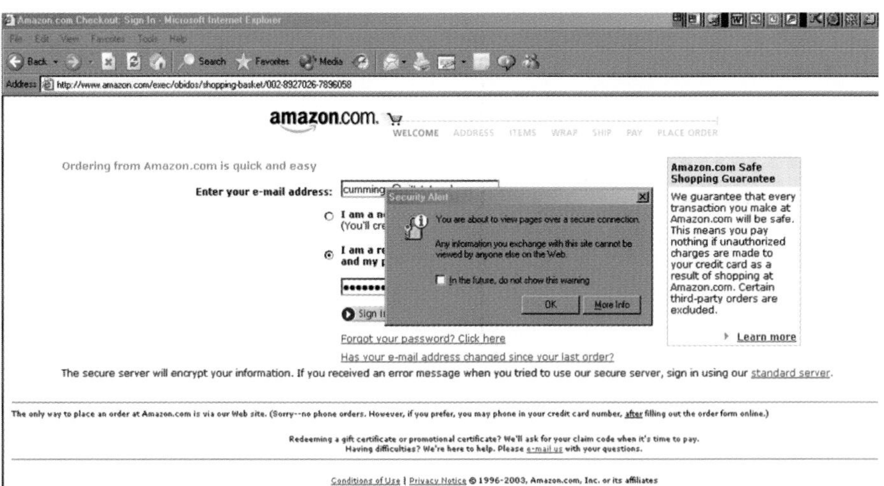

- First, thieves can use skimmers, which are small devices that scan the number off credit cards. The drawback is that the thieves have to get your name and address elsewhere.
- Second, they can buy magnetic strip readers, which read the name, number, expiration date, and a unique code off the card as well as the number.
- Third, they can sometimes break into databases of credit card bureaus, banks, or other institutions that keep credit card records.

When you shop on the Internet, be sure you're on a secure site before you volunteer your credit card number. It's possible for thieves to get credit card numbers that are traveling from one computer to another unless the information is encrypted (converted into a secret code). To decrypt, or read the code, the receiving Web site must have the decryption key. You'll usually see a warning box that pops up before you enter a secure site (see Figure 9.3). You'll know the site is secure if you see an "s" on the end of the http (https://) (see Figure 9.4 on the opposite page). Your Web browser will also usually show a small lock in the bottom right-hand corner.

A person armed with your social security number, driver's license, and a fake credit card can get credit or debit cards in your name. Experts estimate that this happens to thousands of people in the United States every day. Theft costs all of us a lot of money, since to cover the cost of purchases made on stolen or faked credit cards, credit card companies raise interest rates and charges.

did you know? *A network with a fast connection could generate up to 30,000 copies of the Slammer worm per second, which accounts for its lightning-fast proliferation.*[5]

Identity Theft

Imagine that you've been working and earning money for 20 years. You've always paid your bills on time and have a very good credit rating. Now imagine a thief trolling for a good mark. This person is looking for someone like you—a person with good credit.

So, having found you, the thief steals your financial identity and becomes you—on paper. This is when your problems start and you probably won't even know it. The thief runs up a huge credit card debt, takes out loans, writes bad checks, travels to exotic destinations, all the while pretending to be you, financially speaking.

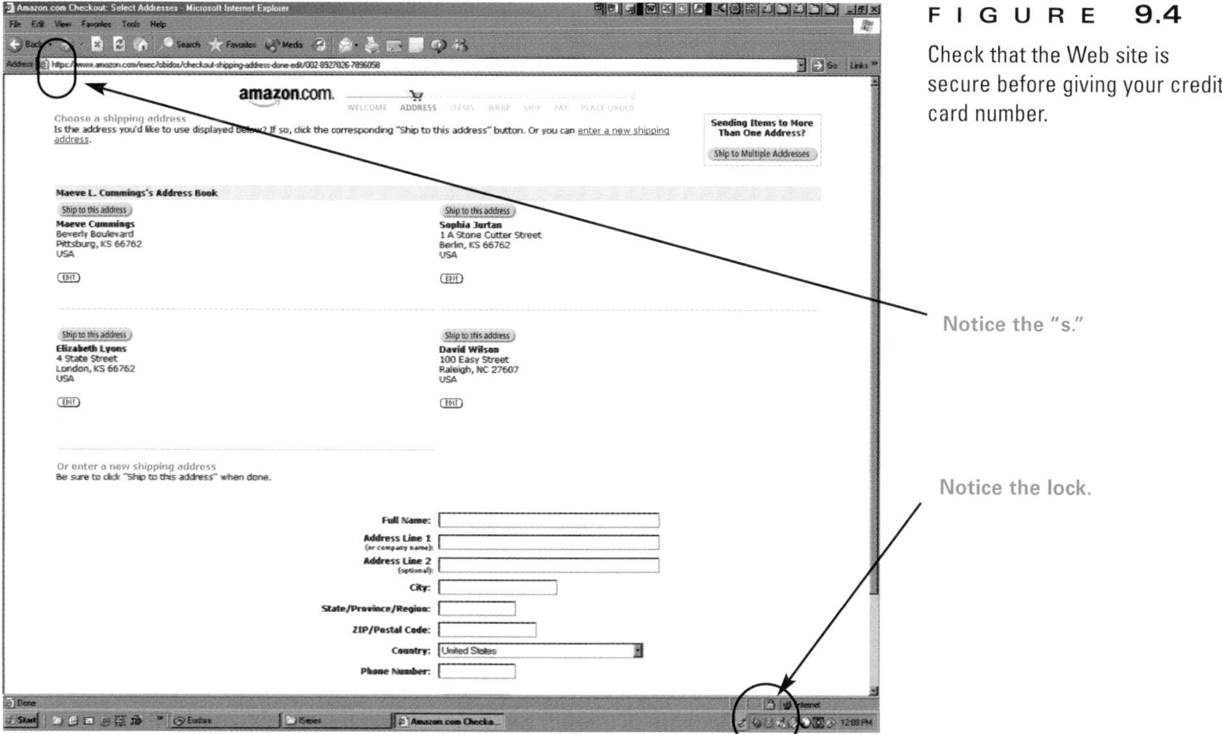

FIGURE 9.4

Check that the Web site is secure before giving your credit card number.

Then one day you find your financial reputation is ruined. You can't cash a check, your credit cards are refused, and you can't get a bank loan. This is when you discover that you've become the victim of identity theft. ***Identity theft*** is the impersonation by a thief of someone with good credit. The thief essentially uses the victim's credit to steal products and services. If you're the victim, you won't usually have to pay the debts, but your financial good name no longer exists. Often times, your only choice is to shut yourself down financially. That means you have to start building a good financial reputation again. And it's not that simple. It's hard to get a second social security number and driver's license since these numbers are designed to stay with you for life.

Since social security numbers are the key to finding almost all other information about you, experts suggest that you be very careful with your social security number and not use it as your driver's license number or have it printed on your checks.

Up to 1.1 million people were victims of identity theft in 2001, according to the Federal Trade Commission (FTC). The agency also estimates that identity theft costs the business community $17,000 per victim. Furthermore, it will probably cost you, as an identity theft victim, about $1,000 in out-of-pocket expenses. And that's not all. You will probably spend months or even years trying to straighten out the mess caused by someone stealing your financial identity.

Dot-Cons

Many criminals who used to operate in the brick-and-mortar world have moved their operations to cyberspace, and new crooks have joined them. There, they can work in a more protected, more comfortable environment.

FIGURE 9.5

The Federal Trade Commission (FTC) is on the trail of Internet criminals and publishes a list of the Top 10 Online Frauds (www.ftc.gov).

Dot-Con Scams

- **Travel/vacation fraud:** You're offered a luxury trip with all sorts of "extras" at very low prices. Then you find that what you get is much lower quality than was promised. Or, you're hit with hidden charges after you've paid.

  FTC says: Make sure you have all promises in writing, including the cancellation policy, before you sign up.
- **Bogus business opportunities:** You see an offer to stay at home, be your own boss, and earn big bucks. But then you find that the scheme is a bust and you're probably worse off than before.

  FTC says: Check with others who have started businesses with the company. Get all promises in writing and get an attorney or accountant to check the contract.
- **Online auction fraud:** In this case you get something less valuable than what you paid for, or you might even get nothing at all.

  FTC says: Always use a credit card or an escrow service.
- **Internet service provider scams:** You get a check for a small amount ($3 or $4) in the mail and cash it. Then you find you're trapped into long-term contracts with ISPs that exact huge penalties if you cancel.

  FTC says: Read ALL the information about the check before you cash it and watch for unexpected charges.
- **Credit card fraud:** You get an offer which says you can view adult-oriented Web sites for free if you provide a credit card number—just to prove you're over 18. Then your credit card bill has charges for goods and services you never purchased.

  FTC says: Always examine your credit card statement carefully for unauthorized charges. You'll only have to pay up to $50 of the charges if your card was misused.
- **Web site design/promotions—Web cramming:** You start getting billed for Web pages that you didn't even know that you had, or are offered a "free" Web page and then incur phone charges without realizing it.

  FTC says: Review your telephone bills and challenge any charges you don't recognize.
- **Multilevel marketing/pyramid scams:** You're promised that you can make money through products and services you sell as well as those sold by people that you recruit into the program.

  FTC says: Avoid plans that require you to recruit distributors, buy expensive inventory or commit to a minimum sales volume.
- **Business opportunities and work-at-home scams:** You get notices of deceptive earnings claims by e-mail, on Web sites, and in print ads promoting business opportunities.

  FTC says: Talk to other people who started the business through the same company, get all the promises in writing, and study the proposed contract carefully before signing. Get an attorney or accountant to take a look at it, too.
- **Health care frauds:** You get claims about medications and treatments, which are not sold through traditional suppliers, but are "proven" to cure serious and even fatal health problems.

  FTC says: Consult a health care professional before buying any "cure-all" that claims to treat a wide range of ailments or offers quick cures and easy solutions to serious illnesses.

did you know? Ninety *percent of women who walk into a department store immediately turn to the right.*[6]

The scams they perpetrate include get-rich-quick schemes, travel and vacation fraud, phone fraud, health care fraud, and many others (see Figure 9.5 on the opposite page). Here are some specific examples:

- Buy and sell votes: During the 2000 presidential election, a Chicago-based Web site was offering a "presidential vote auction." In other words, you could sell your vote, which incidentally, is illegal. Payment was offered ($12.38 for an Illinois vote and $19.61 for a California vote) in exchange for a promise to vote a certain way. It's not clear how the buyers of the votes were going to verify that the vote sellers kept their end of the bargain.
- The CD-Universe blackmail case: Criminals broke into CD-Universe's customer database and stole thousands of credit card numbers. They then threatened the company that they would publish the credit card list on the Internet unless CD-Universe paid them ransom money. The company refused and the criminals duly published the credit card numbers.
- McDonald's payroll system: This case involved a 15-year-old who broke into McDonald's payroll records and gave raises to his friends.
- Stock price manipulation: A junior college student put false rumors on the Internet about Emulex Corporation, a California-based technology company. The stock price plummeted and he bought up lots of stock. When the panic subsided and the price went back up, he sold the stock and made a tidy profit.

COMPUTERS AS TARGETS
How Do People Attack Computers?

There's lots of malware floating around in cyberspace. ***Malware*** is malicious software that is designed by people to attack some part of a computer system. Two of the most notorious types of malware are viruses and denial-of-service attacks.

Viruses

The term "computer virus" is a generic term for lots of different types of destructive software that spreads from file to file. A ***computer virus (virus)*** is software designed intentionally to cause annoyance or damage. There are two types of viruses, benign and malignant. The first type of virus displays a message or slows down your computer but doesn't destroy any information.

Malignant viruses, however, do damage to your computer system. Some will scramble or delete your files. Others shut your computer down, make your Word software act strangely, or damage the compact flash memory in your digital camera so that it won't store pictures anymore.

One common type of computer virus is the macro virus. ***Macro viruses*** are viruses that spread by binding themselves to software such as Word or Excel. If your computer is infected, and you send an infected file to someone else as an e-mail attachment, the recipient's computer will get the virus as soon as the attachment is opened. The virus will then make copies of itself and spread from file to file, destroying or changing the files in the process. You can also get infected if you download an infected file from the Internet or open a file on an infected disk.

FIGURE 9.6

The Love Bug worm gets busy once it's released in your computer.

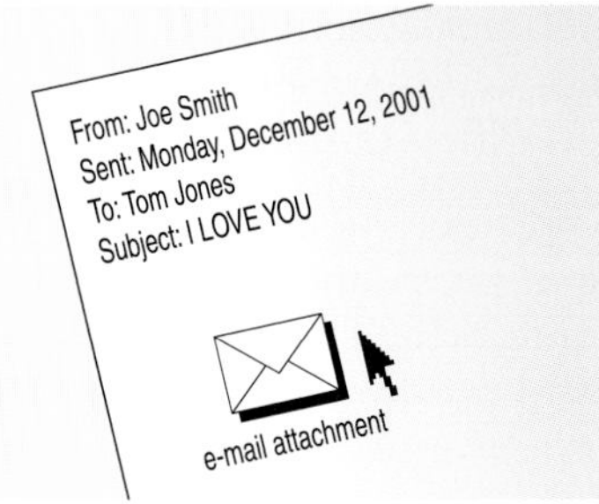

1 The virus arrives in an e-mail.

2 When you open the attachment, you turn the virus loose in your computer.

3 It goes to your address book to mail itself to all your friends.

4 The virus starts destroying files.

5 The virus looks for passwords that it can send back to its creator.

A ***worm*** is a computer virus that spreads itself, not only from file to file, but from computer to computer via e-mail and other Internet traffic. A worm finds your e-mail address book and sends itself to the e-mail addresses in your list. One of the more famous worm viruses was called the "Love Bug." It arrived in your e-mail as an attachment. The subject of the e-mail was "I LOVE YOU"—a message that's hard to resist. Take a look at Figure 9.6 to see what it did.

A virus can't do anything unless the virus instructions are executed. That usually means that you have to open the attachment to become infected because that's where the harmful code is. So be very careful about opening up an attachment if you're not sure what it is and where it came from. Also, be aware that some e-mail programs have the ability to execute macros (small blocks of code) and these may be executed when you open the e-mail itself, releasing the virus. Consult your e-mail program vendor for more information.

There are even virus hoaxes. A ***virus hoax*** is e-mail distributed with the intention of frightening people about a nonexistent virus. People who get such an alert will usually tell others, who pass the information on. The effect of the hoax is to cause people anxiety and lost productivity. The cost to companies can be very severe since business must be suspended while computer professionals spend time and effort looking for a non-existent

did you know?

More *than 2,500 left-handed people are killed every year on account of using right-handed products.*[7]

virus in hundreds, perhaps thousands, of computers on one or more networks.

Viruses are scary, but a virus can't hurt your hardware, your monitor or processor, except in rare, isolated cases. Viruses can't hurt any files they weren't designed to attack either. For example, a virus designed for Microsoft's Outlook generally doesn't infect Qualcomm's Eudora or any other e-mail application. Viruses can't infect files on write-protected disks.

Denial-of-Service Attacks

Many e-businesses have been hit with denial-of-service attacks. ***Denial-of-service (DoS) attacks*** cause thousands of access attempts to a Web site over a very short period of time, overloading the target site and shutting it down. The attacks may come from one or many thousands of computers. In either case the objective is to flood the targeted computer, usually belonging to an e-business, with so many access attempts as to prevent legitimate customers from getting into the site to do business. One such DoS is the "Ping of Death" (see Figure 9.7 for details on how it works). E*Trade, Amazon.com, and Yahoo!, among others, have been victims of the "Ping of Death."

For some companies, such as online stockbrokers, denial-of-service attacks can be disastrous. The timing of stock trading is often crucial, and it matters very much whether the sell or buy order goes in this hour or the next. And since stockbrokers need a high level of trust from customers to do business, the effect of having been seen to be so vulnerable is very bad for business.

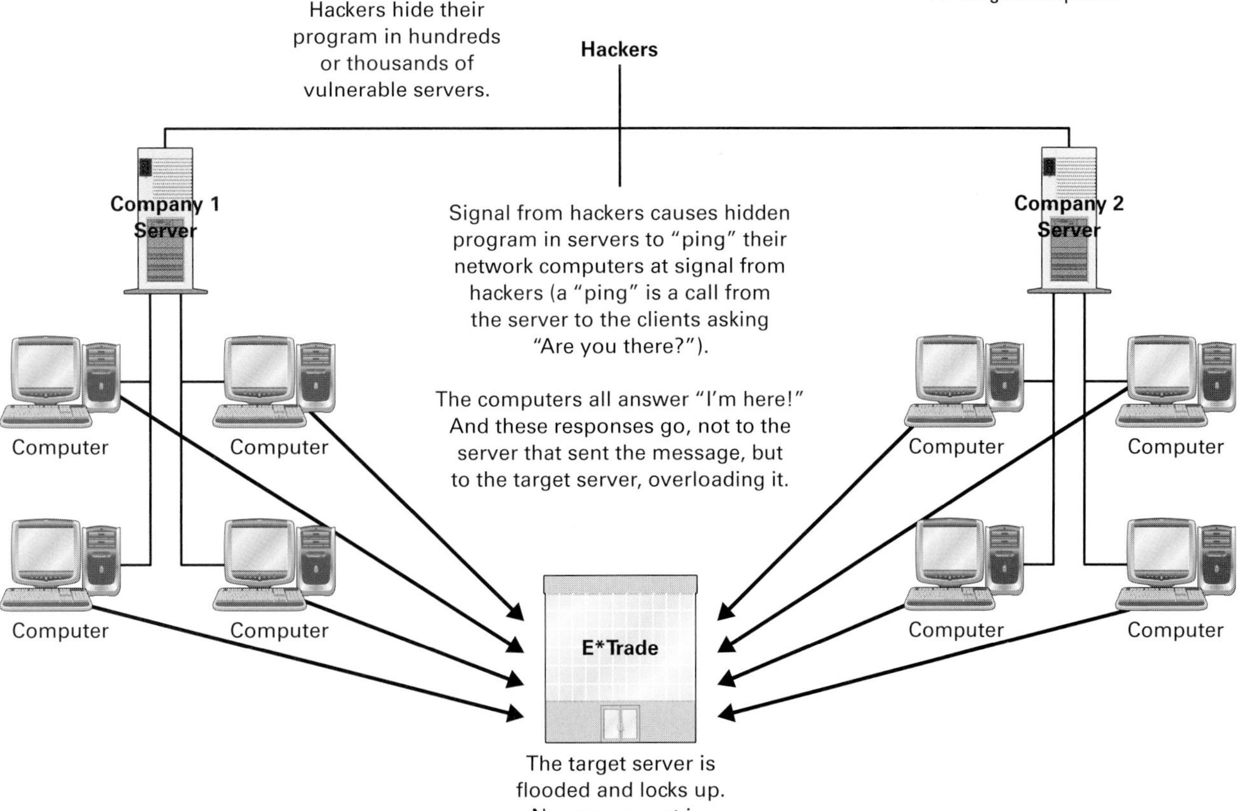
Hackers hide their program in hundreds or thousands of vulnerable servers.
Hackers
Company 1 Server
Company 2 Server
Signal from hackers causes hidden program in servers to "ping" their network computers at signal from hackers (a "ping" is a call from the server to the clients asking "Are you there?").
The computers all answer "I'm here!" And these responses go, not to the server that sent the message, but to the target server, overloading it.
Computer
Computer
Computer
Computer
Computer
Computer
Computer
Computer
E*Trade
The target server is flooded and locks up. No one can get in.

FIGURE 9.7

The objective of a denial-of-service attack is to shut down the target computer.

Combination Worm/DoS

A form of worm first discovered in July 2001 combined the worm's ability to propagate and denial-of-service attack's ability to bring down a Web site. The first worm of this kind was called "Code Red." It attacked only servers (the computer on a network that provides services to the other network computers) running specific system software. Code Red again used e-mail address books to send itself to lots of computers, but it was very efficient, with the ability to infect as many as 500,000 other servers per day. When it infected a server it had two tasks to perform. First, it defaced the server for 10 hours before going dormant. Second, it initiated 99 separate threads (or tasks), which all scanned (sought out) other servers to infect for 19 days. On day 20 all infected computers launched denial-of-service attacks against a White House Web server. The White House found out about the impending attack, and foiled it by changing its IP address.

This type of worm has the potential to do an extraordinary amount of damage. Code Red affected the performance of network equipment and caused slowdowns for cable Internet providers. Code Red cost an estimated $2.4 billion in prevention, detection, and cleanup, even though it didn't destroy files or otherwise do much damage. What has computer security experts worried is that the potential for this particular type of malware is very great and future versions may carry a much nastier payload.

The Code Red worm doubled the number of computers it infected every 37 minutes. Eighteen months later in January 2003, a much faster Code Red–type worm, called the SQL Slammer or Sapphire worm, spread much faster. It doubled the number of computers it infected every 8.5 seconds in its first minute, spreading worldwide in about 10 minutes. It caused disruption to financial, transportation, and governmental institutions. It almost cut off Web access in South Korea completely and shut down a number of Bank of America ATMs. Again, the payload was not destructive—apart from bringing down a lot of computers—but the potential for harm of such an attack is enormous.

THE PERPETRATORS
Who Spreads Viruses and Denial-of-Service Attacks?

People who break into computer systems are often called hackers. ***Hackers*** are very knowledgeable computer users who use their knowledge to invade other people's computers. There are many types of hackers, classified according to motivation.

Thrill-Seeker Hackers

Thrill-seeker hackers are hackers without evil intentions, who may even follow a "hackers' code," so that they often report the security leaks to their victims. These people are cyberspace joy riders. Even though they break into computers illegally, their intent and thrill lies in the achievement itself, and their reward is usually the admiration of their fellow hackers.

Black-Hat Hackers

Black-hat hackers are hackers with malicious intent—they're cyber vandals. They exploit or destroy the information they find, steal passwords, or otherwise cause harm. These are the hackers who deliberately cause trouble for people they don't even know by creating viruses and bringing down computer systems.

An example is a 16-year-old black-hat hacker who was sentenced to detention for 6 months after he hacked into military and NASA networks. He

did you know? The *most expensive commercial ever made was the 1984 Apple Macintosh commercial. Costing about $1 million, it ran only once—during the 1984 Super Bowl.*

caused the systems to shut down for three weeks. He intercepted more than 3,000 e-mails and stole the names and passwords of 19 defense agency employees. He also downloaded temperature and humidity control software worth $1.7 billion that helps control the environment in the international space station's living quarters.

Crackers

Crackers are hackers who hack for profit. They're often hired to break into a system to get information for blackmail, bribery, or revenge. Crackers are the people who engage in corporate espionage.

Hacktivists

Hacktivists use the Internet to send a political message of some kind. The message might be a call to end world hunger, an alteration of a political party's Web site exhorting you to vote for the opposition, or a slogan for or against a particular religious or national group.

Hacktivism is becoming a common response to disagreements between nations. When a U.S. military plane made an emergency landing in China and a dispute arose about the return of the crew and plane, U.S. hackers started to attack Chinese Web sites, and Chinese hackers returned the favor, targeting government-related sites. During the 2003 war with Iraq, hacktivists on each side of the conflict attacked Web sites on the other side.

Cyberterrorists

A ***cyberterrorist*** is a hacker who seeks to cause harm to a lot of people or to destroy critical systems or information. Possible targets of violent attacks would be air traffic control systems and nuclear power plants and anything else that could harm the infrastructure of a country. At a less lethal level, a cyberterrorist act would include shutting down e-mail or some part of the Internet or destroying government records, perhaps on social security benefits or criminals.

Script Bunnies

Script bunnies or ***script kiddie***s are people who would like to be hackers but don't have much technical expertise. They download click-and-point software that automatically does the hacking for them. An example is the young man who started the Kournikova virus in Holland. That virus was very similar to the Love Bug worm in that when your system was infected, the worm sent itself to all the people in your Outlook address book. Tens of millions of people received e-mail with the infected attachment, and a large number of those opened the attachment hoping to see a picture of Anna Kournikova, the attractive Russian tennis player.

White-Hat or Ethical Hackers

The thrill-seeker hackers used to be called white-hat hackers. But lately the term "white-hat" is increasingly being used to describe hackers who legitimately, with the knowledge of the owners of the IT system, try to break in to find where the vulnerable areas are located and to fix them. These ***white-hat*** or ***ethical hackers*** are computer security professionals who are hired by the company to find and fix the parts of a network that might be vulnerable to hackers. For more on hackers, visit www.mhhe.com/i-series.

SECTION 9.2

making the grade

1. ___________ theft is the impersonation by a thief of someone with good credit.
2. A(n) ___________ is a very knowledgeable computer user who uses his or her knowledge to invade other people's computers.
3. A computer ___________ is software designed intentionally to cause annoyance or damage.
4. When thousands of computers overload a target site by trying to access it at the same time, the target site may be a victim of a(n) ___________ attack.

9.3 PRIVACY MATTERS

There's lots of personal information about you, and everyone else, on the Internet—so much, in fact, that you would hardly believe it—and so much that many people are becoming increasingly concerned about what they see as an assault on their privacy. ***Privacy*** is the right to be left alone when you want to be, to have control over your own personal information, and not to be observed without your consent. It's the right to be free of unwanted intrusion into *your* private life.

Most of us value our privacy, but we know that there are intrusions that are just a part of life. For example, businesses such as the electric company can send a bill to your home whether you want one that day or not, so they don't have to leave you alone completely.

If the neighbors see you going to school at certain times each day and notice how you're dressed, you'd probably just consider that to be part of living in a community. You probably wouldn't win a lawsuit to prevent people from looking out their own windows at you. But if they were looking in your windows, you might have a case. To learn more about your privacy, complete the "Privacy Issues" tutorial on your SimNet Concepts Support CD.

INVASION OF PRIVACY BY OTHER PEOPLE

Can Others Observe What I Do on My Computer?

Just as people physically spy on others, invade their privacy by going through their mail, look in their cabinets, follow them, and so on, for malicious or curious reasons, they can also spy on your computer activities and invade your privacy electronically. Motives for electronic spying might range from idle curiosity to an attempt to get your password or to access something else important they have no right to. Obviously, if you suspect some such attempt to violate your privacy, you're well within your rights, and would be well advised, to see what's going on. Another unfortunately common situation in which you might want to check up on computer activity would be if you suspected that your minor child was in electronic contact with someone or something undesirable, or if you thought that someone was using your computer without permission.

did you know?

February *1865 and February 1999 were the only months in recorded history not to have a full moon.*

Snooping by Others

Many Web sites offer programs, collectively referred to as "snoopware," to help people monitor what's happening on their computers.

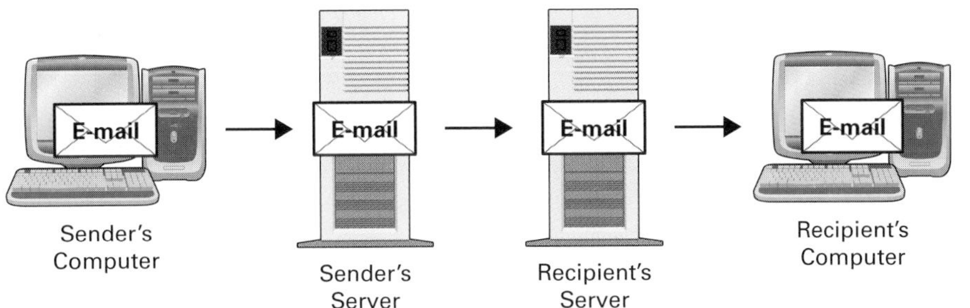

FIGURE 9.8

The e-mail you send is stored on many computers.

For general snooping you can get key logger software and install it on the computer you want to monitor. ***Key logger,*** or ***key trapper, software*** records keystrokes and mouse clicks. It records e-mail, instant messages, chat room exchanges, Web sites you visit, applications you run, and passwords you type in on that computer. Spector Pro is an example of this type of monitoring software and from the same software company you can also get eBlaster, which will actually e-mail you activity reports—every 30 minutes, if you like. Be careful if you go snooping that you're not breaking the law. Of course, the ethics of it you'll have to decide for yourself. Family members (other than the parents of minor children) and friends don't have unlimited rights to monitor each other.

Also available for monitoring computer use are screen capture programs that periodically record what's on the screen. (They get the information straight from the video card.) These don't trap every single screen, just whatever is on the screen when the capturing program activates, but they still give whoever is doing the monitoring a pretty good idea of what the computer user is up to.

E-Mail Is Not a Private Matter

As you're probably well aware, e-mail is completely insecure. It might as well be written on a postcard for all the privacy it has. Beyond that each e-mail you send is copied and stored, at least temporarily, on four or more different computers (see Figure 9.8). When you write an e-mail, it's stored first in the computer you're using. Second, it's stored by your e-mail server—the computer through which it gets onto the Internet. Third, it's stored on the recipient's computer, and fourth, it's probably archived on the recipient's e-mail server.

INFORMATION ON YOUR BUYING HABITS AND PREFERENCES

How Do Companies Get Information about Me?

Sometimes you exchange some of your privacy for something you want. You have to give your name, address, and social security number to get a driver's license. So you're giving up some personal information, hence some privacy, in exchange for the privilege of being able to drive. In order for businesses to offer products and services that you want, to sell them to you, and to send them to you, they need to have information about you.

Should you be able to look at the information that companies have about you? Should you be able to change things that are wrong? Should you be able to delete information you don't want them to have? Europeans think so. The European Union has implemented the Directive on Protection of Personal Data. The rights accorded citizens of member countries include the right to know the marketer's source of information, the right to check personal information, the right to correct it, and the right to specify that information can't be used for direct marketing.

Before computer use was so widespread, massive amounts of paper records were collected and kept. But the paper system naturally limited the amount of information collected and its accessibility. Cross-tabulation isn't easy with paper files. The people who collected information about your health stored it in one place; those who recorded your grocery shopping habits kept the information somewhere else. With computers, multiple types of information can be cross-referenced quickly and easily, creating a picture of you that is quite detailed and, in the opinion of many, too intrusive. Many companies are worried about protecting the privacy of their customers. So much so, in fact, that 150 of Fortune 500 companies now employ Chief Privacy Officers (CPO), whose responsibility it is to guard the privacy of personal information that the company stores.

Companies get information about your preferences and identity three ways: (1) from information you explicitly provide, (2) from information organizations collect through contact with you, and (3) from information about you that organizations get from other organizations (see Figure 9.9).

FIGURE 9.9

There are three ways businesses can get information about you.

• Information you volunteer such as when you register for sweepstakes at a store or at a Web site.
• Information that organizations collect based on your contact with them. Credit card companies have information on what you buy, and Web sites can see what pages you look at and for how long.
• Information that organizations can buy from one another.

Information You Volunteer

Some ways in which you provide personal information to organizations are

- *Contests and promotions:* If you've ever signed up for a contest at your local supermarket, you've offered personal information to the store in exchange for a chance to win.
- *Warranty cards and rebate offers:* When you send in a warranty card or respond to a rebate offer, you give the manufacturer information about your buying habits along with your name and address.
- *Registration at Web sites:* If you've ever registered at a Web site to receive products or services or to enter a contest, you've given the Web site personal information.

There's personal information on most adults in hundreds of databases. Using the Internet to access databases that sell personal information, you can find out virtually anything about anyone. You can find out what people earn, where they live, how much they paid for their home, where they lived before, and so on. There are few laws restricting this information; see Figure 9.10 on the opposite page for examples of existing laws on privacy.

Information Collected by Contact

When you use credit cards or checks, you're giving the store information about yourself, which can be linked to your receipt showing your buying habits and preferences. Not surprisingly, the companies with the largest databases of personal information are those that have direct contact with

U.S. Laws on Information

- The **Privacy Act** restricts what information the federal government can collect; allows people to access and correct information on themselves; requires procedures to protect the security of personal information; and forbids the disclosure of name-linked information without permission.
- The **Freedom of Information Act** says that citizens have the right to access the information that federal agencies have collected on them.
- The **Computer Matching and Privacy Protection Act** says that government agencies can't compare certain records trying to find a match. However, most records are not covered by this act.
- The **Bork Bill** (officially known as the **Video Privacy Protection Act**) prohibits the use of video rental information on customers for any purpose other than that of marketing goods and services directly to the customer.
- The **Communications Assistance for Law Enforcement Act** requires that telecommunications equipment be designed so that authorized government agents are able to intercept all wired and wireless communications being sent or received by any subscriber. The Act also requires that subscriber call-identifying information be transmitted to a government agency when and if required.
- The **Health Insurance Portability and Accountability Act (HIPAA)** to keep patient information confidential. Final rules governing HIPAA were announced in February 2003 and gave large health care organizations until April 2005 to comply, while smaller ones get an extra year.
- The **Financial Service Modernization Act** requires that financial institutions protect personal customer information and that they have customer permission before sharing such information with other businesses.

FIGURE 9.10

The United States doesn't have a consistent set of laws protecting citizens from misuse of information. Current laws apply only to certain groups or industry segments.

consumers—retailers, financial services companies, and telecommunications companies. The Federal Trade Commission says that 92.8 percent of Web sites gather at least one type of identifying information, at least your name or e-mail address. More than half collect at least one type of demographic information, perhaps your gender or age. Those with the largest databases include the Chase and First Union banks and retailers such as Wal-Mart, the Limited, and Sears. In fact, Wal-Mart has the largest data warehouse outside the government with about 101 terabytes of information. It uses the information to keep hundreds of stores stocked with products in the colors, sizes, and prices attractive to consumers living in the vicinity of each store.

Retailers and banks collect and keep information to make decisions about how to run their businesses. Web sites do the same thing, except they collect information on you by observing you at their sites. They see which Web pages you go to, how long you stay there, what you buy, and so forth, and make judgments about your needs and interests from that information. They sometimes even store information about you on your own hard disk drive in the form of "cookies."

A ***cookie*** is a small text file containing specific information about you that a Web site stores on your computer's hard drive. This information is always helpful to the site that placed it there. Sometimes it's helpful to you too. For example, if you want to repeatedly visit a site that requires an ID and password, a cookie can keep that information and provide it to the Web site so that you don't have to type it in every time. When you visit that Web site, your Web browser looks for the cookie information for that Web site. If it finds it, your Web browser sends the information on to the Web

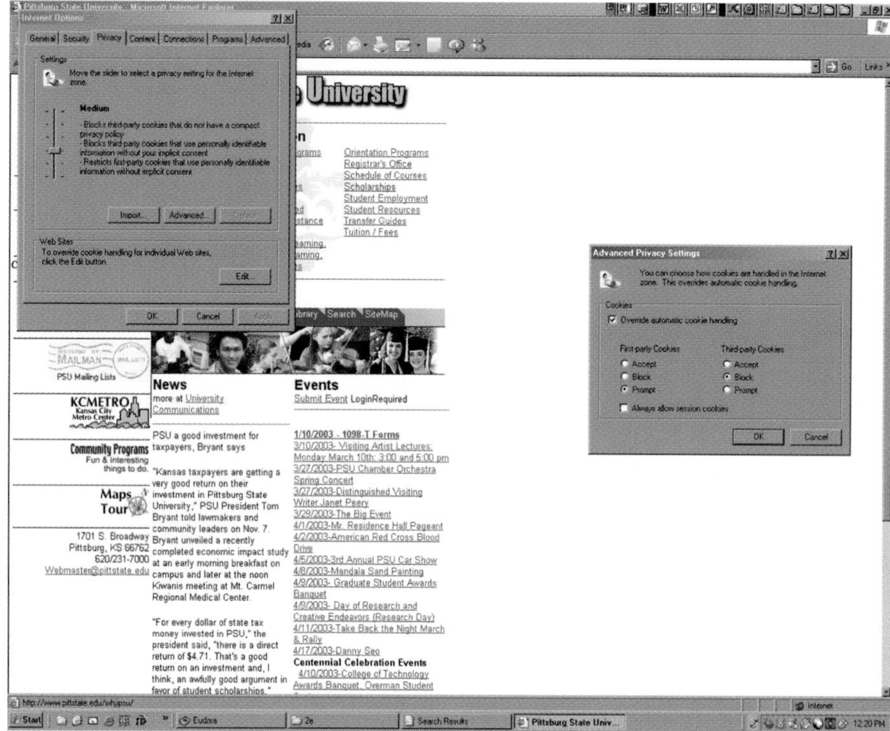

FIGURE 9.11

You can set your Web browser to accept cookies, to refuse cookies, or to warn you when a Web site attempts to set a cookie.

site. If you put products into a wish list or an electronic shopping cart, that information stays in a cookie so that the next time you visit the site, that site can access the information. When you buy a product or take it out of the shopping cart, the cookie on your hard disk is altered accordingly.

You can turn cookies on and off, and best of all, you can get your Web browser to tell you when a site wants to send you a cookie (see Figure 9.11).

Information Sold from One Company to Another

Many companies with huge databases of information sell that information to others. Credit card companies sell information on consumers although many claim that they don't sell personal information with names attached. There are companies that specialize in the collection and sale of information. Retail companies like big spenders. Market researchers know that there are certain online consumers who spend $8,000 or more every year, for instance, and commercial online companies will pay to find out who these people are.

Among the Web companies that collect information, the most famous are DoubleClick and Engage. They follow you around the Web and then sell the information on your activities to other Web sites that want to sell you products and services. Some companies also collect information from chat rooms and discussion groups. So, a prospective employer wanting to know more about you can, for a fee, get access to what you have said in these cyber environments.

Web sites can tell who you are by looking at cookie information, but that's not the only way they keep track of you. They can also use sniffers. A ***sniffer*** is software that sits on the Internet analyzing traffic. The software tries to find out who you are. It tries several approaches until it finds one that works.

Would you be interested in increasing Energy Levels by 84%?
Would you like to increase your Muscle Strength by 88%?
While at the same time reducing Body Fat by 72%?

Of course you would! We offer Wonder Drink, the Most Potent Formula available to help you achieve all of this and more!

In thousands of clinical studies, our Wonder Drink has been shown to accomplish the following:

- Reduce body fat and build lean muscle without exercise!
- Remove wrinkles and cellulite!
- Lower blood pressure and improve cholesterol profile!
- Improve sleep, vision, and memory!
- Restore hair color and growth!
- Strengthen the immune system!
- Increase energy and cardiac output!
- All this in only 6 months of usage!!!

Testimonial:
"As a straight-ahead bicycle racer, I used to have to wait a minute and a half after sprinting for my heart rate to come down to where I could sprint again. After a month on Wonder Drink, I can now sprint again after only 45 seconds! Wonder Drink cut my waiting time in half!" —Ed Caz, CA

FIGURE 9.12

Spam is electronic junk mail.

Armed with information on who you are, the software can engage in *Web tracking.* It can track what pages you visit, how long you stay there, what files you download, and what documents you open. This information is then stored in a database, where it can be analyzed along with information from other Web visitors.

Companies use this information in many ways. They make business decisions with it, they define target markets, they send you advertising, and so on. Companies can send you either customized or mass advertising. If companies know who you are and think you're likely to shop with them, they display ads on a site that you're likely to visit. If they increase their click-through count (the number of people who click on the ad) by only one-half of one percent, they're happy and consider their advertising dollars well spent.

Mass advertising is the posting of ads where lots of people are likely to see them, such as TV advertising. On the Web, mass advertising reaches you when you visit a Web site or comes to you by junk e-mail, which is called "spam" (see an example in Figure 9.12).

Spam is electronic junk mail or unsolicited mail, usually from commercial businesses attempting to sell you products and services. The Dotcons, or scams, are heavy users of spam, which often sends out to 10,000 or more people at the same time. It's cheap and easy since lists of e-mail addresses are readily available and so is bulk e-mail software. A *Newsweek* article says that one successful bulk e-mail company that sends out spam for other companies e-mails about 3 million messages every day. Spam constitutes almost half of all e-mail traffic.

Spammers often "spoof" their addresses to make it hard for you to find them. ***Spoofing*** is forging the return address on an e-mail so that the e-mail message appears to come from someone other than the sender. Spammers can also relay their spam through several different servers, making it difficult to trace. Most ISPs in the United States have bans on spamming, so spammers send e-mail through "blind" relays. These are computers in countries on the other side of the world that redirect e-mail, making it very hard to trace.

i•can

Protect Information on Old Hard Drives

Dataquest, a hard disk drive manufacturer, estimates that for every 10 new hard drives sold, 7 old ones are discarded. Many of these disks are recycled and sold for a few dollars in thrift shops, on eBay, and at auctions. And many of those disks have valuable information on them.

Here are just two examples. The Pennsylvania Department of Labor and Industry sold used computers that still had thousands of files with information about state employees. A woman in Nevada bought a used computer only to find that it had prescription records on 2,000 pharmacy customers, which included names, social security numbers, and lists of all the medications they had purchased at that pharmacy.

Remember that the delete action does not get rid of a file. It just alters the name of the file to mark the space that the file occupied as available for reuse. To get rid of a file completely, you could destroy the disk drive, perhaps melt it down for maximum effect. However, this wastes a resource that someone else could use. So, before you pass on your old hard disk, you could use a special overwriting program (there are many free ones on the Internet) that changes every single bit on the disk obliterating the previous contents. Government agencies run their overwriting programs several times (up to seven) on each storage medium to make sure that no information is left behind.

GOVERNMENT RECORDS

What Information Does the Government Keep on Individuals?

The various branches of government need information to administer entitlement programs, social security, welfare, student loans, law enforcement, and so on. Government agencies have about 2,000 databases containing personal information on individuals. It's fairly safe to assume that any time you have contact with any branch of government, someone will subsequently store information about you. For example, if you get a government-backed student loan, you must provide personal information such as your name, address, income, parents' income, and so on. That information is then stored with other pertinent facts, such as the school you're attending, the bank dispersing the loan, and later your repayment records. Following are some other examples of government agencies that collect a lot of information.

The ***NCIC (National Crime Information Center)*** is a huge database with information on the criminal records of more than 20 million people. You've often heard about someone being arrested for a grievous crime after a routine traffic stop for some minor infraction like a broken taillight. The Oklahoma City bombers were caught this way. Usually the arrest comes about after the officer stops the car and runs a check on the license plate and driver's license through the NCIC, finding an outstanding warrant.

The IRS (Internal Revenue Service) has income information on all taxpayers. The IRS also has access to other databases. For example, the IRS keeps track of vehicle registration information so that they can check up on people buying expensive cars and boats to make sure they're reporting a corresponding income level.

The Census Bureau collects information every 10 years on all the U.S. inhabitants the agency can find. Everyone is requested to fill out a census form, and some people get a very long and detailed form requiring them to disclose a lot of personal information. The information that the Census Bureau collects is available to other government agencies and even to commercial enterprises.

making the grade

1. __________ is the right to be left alone when you want to be.
2. A(n) __________ is software that analyzes Web traffic.
3. __________ is electronic junk mail.
4. __________ is forging the return address on e-mail.

9.4 HOW TO PROTECT YOURSELF

Cyberspace is a great place to visit. You can work, shop, and play there. But you have to be just as careful as you are in the brick-and-mortar world.

SECURITY BEFORE YOU ENTER CYBERSPACE

How Do I Protect My Computer and Files?

Here are three rules you should remember: (1) If it can be stolen, lock it up. (2) If it can be damaged, back it up. (3) If it can come in and do damage, block it.

Now that many people use notebooks, the number of computers that are stolen is skyrocketing. You can buy security cable with padlocks for your notebook to make it harder to steal when it's not by your side. The cable and padlocks are like those you see in department stores for expensive products that the store wants you to be able to look at but not take without paying for.

The best protection for files is backups. Losing hardware, a Zip disk, or hard drive, is seldom your biggest problem. The real value is most likely in the files. Replacing those may well be much more expensive in time and effort than replacing the hardware.

Make sure you have anti-virus software to detect and remove or quarantine viruses. There are many types of anti-virus software available for sale on the Internet and in computer stores.

Snooping by Others

If you're on the receiving end of snoopware and want to disable activity-monitoring programs like Spector Pro, you can get a free program from www.idcide.com called the *Privacy Companion* or one called *Who's Watching Me* from www.trapware.com.

E-Mail Is Never Private

Since e-mail is so insecure, some people like to encrypt their e-mail, and there are many products on the market that will do the job. ZixMail is an example. Others are CertifiedMail, PrivacyX, and SafeMessage. Disappearing Email gives you a slightly different type of e-mail protection. This software is free and sends a self-destructing message with the e-mail so that the e-mail deletes itself after the period of time you specify. Before the recipient opens the e-mail the Disappearing Email software checks with the Disappearing server that the e-mail hasn't passed its expiration date. However, you can defeat this feature by copying the text out of the e-mail and pasting it somewhere else.

SECURITY IN CYBERSPACE TRANSACTIONS

How Do I Protect Myself in Cyberspace?

If you buy goods and services on the Web, you need to do what you do in the brick-and-mortar world—use common sense.

Credit Card and Identity Theft

- Give your credit card number only to reputable companies that you trust.
- Use only secure sites, i.e., those with https://.
- Never give out your social security number unless the law demands it. Your social security number is the key to most information about you.
- Use passwords of at least 10 characters and numbers.
- Use different passwords for different systems/sites.

Dot-Cons

- Be very skeptical about claims of extraordinary performance or earnings potential.
- Always read the fine print.
- Always look at the site's privacy policy.
- Be wary of a company that doesn't clearly state its name, address, and phone number.
- Immediately report any fraudulent, deceptive, or unfair practices to the Federal Trade Commission (see Figure 9.13 on the opposite page).

Protecting Personal Information

Don't give out personal information without thinking about it first. Think about whether you want the recipient to have this information, keeping in mind that you lose control of the information once you hand it over. Look for the privacy policy of the site you're dealing with. But be aware that the bankruptcy courts have held that customer records are assets that may be sold to pay off debts.

Anti-Tracking Software

You can avoid being tracked while you're surfing by using ***anonymous Web browsing (AWB).*** Surfsecret and Anonymizer are examples. They hide your identity from Web sites that you visit. It's a kind of reverse spoofing, where you hide your address from the Web, rather than Web sites hiding their e-mail addresses from you.

Avoiding Spam

Spam can be very irritating. The more times you give your e-mail address to e-commerce businesses and post it to online message boards, the more spam you can expect to get. A general rule is not to believe anything that spammers say—including how to get off their list. By replying, even to the "unsubscribe" option, you're really just confirming that your e-mail address is active.

did you know?

Of Americans who get music off the Internet, 92 percent use free services, 1 percent use pay services, and 7 percent use both.[8]

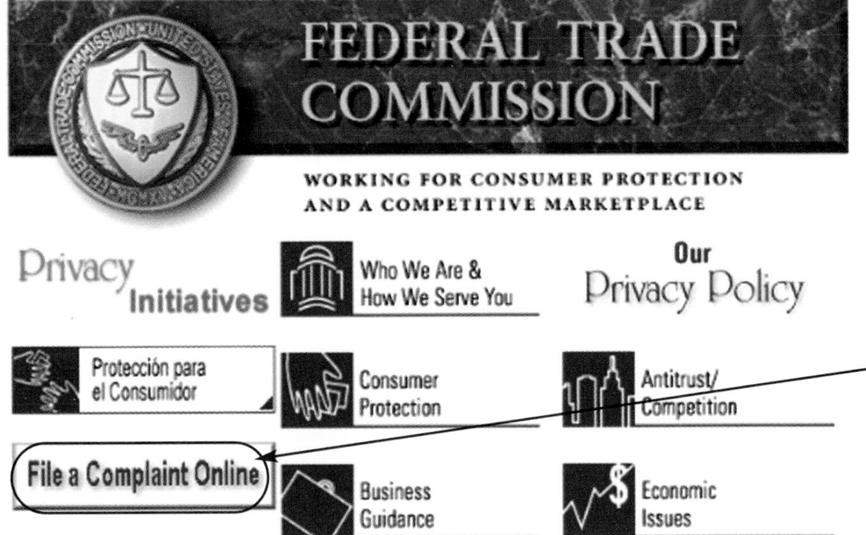

FIGURE 9.13

You should report any fraudulent, deceptive, or unfair business practices to the FTC.

Protecting a Computer or Network from Intruders

A ***firewall*** is hardware and/or software that protects a computer or network from intruders. The firewall examines each message as it seeks entrance to a network, like border guards checking passports. Unless the message has the "right" markings, the firewall prevents it from entering the network.

If you have just one computer, firewall software is probably enough to protect your system and information from intrusion when you're connected to the Internet. The firewall software permits nothing to enter or leave that shouldn't. For example, McAfee has firewall software called Personal Firewall (available at www.mcafee.com). Another product is Zone Labs' ZoneAlarm (available at www.zonelabs.com) and you can download the basic edition free.

If you have more than one computer with a cable modem or a DSL connection, you would be well advised to invest in a hardware firewall. With a home router, such as Linksys (www.linksys.com), you can link all your computers to the router and to each other. Then the router will check all incoming traffic and deny access to any that looks suspicious. To learn more about security, complete the "Security Issues" tutorial on your SimNet Concepts Support CD.

making the grade

SECTION 9.4

1. A(n) __________ is hardware and/or software that protects a computer or network from intruders.
2. __________ software prevents your being tracked while you're surfing.
3. The __________ tracks consumer fraud of all kinds.
4. Your __________ is the key to most information about you.

9.5 SUMMARY AND KEY TERMS

Ethics is the set of principles and standards we use in deciding what to do in situations that affect other people. Our ethics in how we use computers is an extension of our ethics in the other parts of our lives.

A ***copyright*** protects the expression of an idea. The ***Fair Use Doctrine,*** however, says that you may use copyrighted material in certain situations. ***Pirated software*** is copyrighted software that is copied and distributed without the permission of the owner.

When computers are misused, they may be the weapons or targets of the misdeed. As weapons, computers can be used in credit card theft, in ***identity theft,*** or to run scams promising you great deals or wealth. As targets, computers are attacked by other computers with ***malware,*** which includes ***viruses (macro viruses, worms,*** or even ***virus hoaxes), denial-of-service (DoS) attacks,*** and combination worm/DoS attacks.

The people who specialize in attacking computers are called ***hackers.*** Hackers have many reasons for their actions. They can be ***thrill-seeker hackers*** (joyriders in cyberspace), ***black-hat hackers*** (cyber vandals), ***crackers*** (hackers for hire), ***hacktivists*** (politically motivated), ***cyberterrorists*** (terrorists in cyberspace), ***script bunnies*** or ***script kiddies*** (who download destructive code from the Web), or ***white-hat*** or ***ethical hackers*** (computer security professionals hired to protect a network).

Privacy is the right to be left alone when you want to be, to have control over your own personal information, and not to be observed without your consent. Your privacy can be assailed from various sources. First, other people can spy on you using key logger or key trapper software. Second, businesses collect information on you. Third, government agencies collect information on citizens for various reasons.

Tools that businesses use on the Internet include ***sniffers,*** software that sits on the Internet analyzing traffic; ***cookies,*** which are small text files of information placed on your hard disk by a Web site that you visit; and ***spam,*** which is electronic junk mail.

To protect yourself in cyberspace, you can get software to detect snooping by ***key logger software.*** You should be very careful of personal information, especially your social security number. Be wary about entering into a deal that looks too good. Avail yourself of AWB or anti-tracking services when you're on the Web, and put a ***firewall*** on your system or network.

Visit the Web site for this text at www.mhhe.com/i-series to learn more about freeware, shareware, and hackers.

KEY TERMS

anonymous Web browsing (AWB) (p. 280)
black-hat hacker (p. 270)
computer virus (virus) (p. 267)
cookie (p. 275)
copyright (p. 261)
cracker (p. 271)
cyberterrorists (p. 271)
denial-of-service (DoS) attack (p. 269)
ethics (p. 261)
Fair Use Doctrine (p. 262)
firewall (p. 281)
hacker (p. 270)
hacktivist (p. 271)
identity theft (p. 265)
key logger (key trapper) software (p. 273)
macro virus (p. 267)
malware (p. 267)
NCIC (National Crime Information Center) (p. 278)
pirated software (p. 262)
privacy (p. 272)
script bunny (script kiddie) (p. 271)
sniffer (p. 276)
spam (p. 277)
spoofing (p. 277)
thrill-seeker hacker (p. 270)
virus hoax (p. 268)
white-hat or ethical hacker (p. 271)
worm (p. 268)

review of terminology

Multiple Choice

1. What can you NOT do with freeware software?
   a. copy the software
   b. change the software
   c. sell the software
   d. give away the software
   e. You can do all of the above.

2. The information that a Web site places on your hard disk is called a
   a. spam.
   b. sniffer.
   c. cracker.
   d. cookie.
   e. firewall.

3. Spoofing is
   a. spreading jokes on the Internet.
   b. sending unsolicited e-mail.
   c. forging the return address on e-mail.
   d. collecting personal information.
   e. none of the above.

4. A company can get information
   a. directly from you.
   b. from contact with you as a customer.
   c. from a third party who collected the information.
   d. from all of the above.
   e. from none of the above.

5. Threats in cyberspace include
   a. credit card theft.
   b. identity theft.
   c. get rich quick scams.
   d. viruses.
   e. all of the above.

6. A virus hoax is
   a. a worm that pretends to do damage.
   b. e-mail distributed with the intention of frightening people about a nonexistent virus.
   c. software that cannot be damaged by a virus.
   d. the spreading of a virus.
   e. none of the above.

7. A typical virus will generally damage
   a. your printer.
   b. all the software on your computer.
   c. your processor.
   d. files on write-protected disks.
   e. none of the above.

8. White-hat hackers are
   a. thrill-seeker hackers.
   b. the same as cyberterrorists.
   c. people without much technical expertise.
   d. hired to test a system for vulnerabilities.
   e. none of the above.

9. The NCIC is
   a. the database that Wal-Mart uses for customer information.
   b. the IRS income tax database.
   c. a law governing health care information.
   d. a database used by law enforcement agencies.
   e. a type of firewall.

10. An anonymous Web browsing service
    a. protects the identity of the Web site you are visiting.
    b. protects the identity of your computer from the Web site you are visiting.
    c. keeps your personal information (such as age and gender) from being relayed to the Web site you are visiting.
    d. guarantees that you will not get any spam.
    e. does none of the above.

True/False

11. ____ Your e-mail is completely private.

12. ____ Federal law says that no one can use your personal information without your permission.

13. ____ Anti-virus software prevents people from developing viruses.

14. ____ A copyright protects the expression of an idea.

15. ____ A firewall protects the privacy of your personal information completely.

Take this quiz online at www.mhhe.com/i-series and get instant feedback.

QUESTIONS AND EXERCISES

1. Sensible Internet Use and Good Manners

In the table below is a list of actions that you can take while using the Internet. For each, state whether this is something you should or should not do, and state why. Also state whether taking or not taking the action is a matter of ethics (E), common sense (S), or good manners (M).

Action	Yes	No	E/ S/ or M	Justification
Should you				
• treat people in cyberspace with the same courtesy and respect that you would in the brick-and-mortar world?				
• knowingly pass on a virus as long as it doesn't do any real damage?				
• use the MM-DD-YY date format in your correspondence with people all over the world?				
• edit out irrelevant parts of messages that you're quoting to others?				
• expect people to answer your e-mail immediately?				
• use lots and lots of acronyms like FYI (for your information), IMHO (in my humble/honest opinion), and BTW (by the way)?				
• be careful of what you say about others, realizing how easy it is to forward e-mail?				
• give your ID or password to anyone who asks for it?				
• assume that your e-mail is private?				
• be careful about addressing e-mail, since it can seem that you're sending e-mail to only one person, when in fact you're sending it to a group?				
• use offensive language and call people names?				
• take e-mail messages off the server and store them on your own system?				
• send copies of everything you receive to everyone you know?				
• access the e-mail of others without permission?				
• send huge attachments to your e-mail friends?				
• forward personal e-mail to others without the author's permission?				
• put a subject heading in your e-mail so that the recipient has a good idea of what the message is about?				
• send off-color jokes and pictures in e-mail?				
• hack into CNN's computer network?				

2. Napster, Kazaa, and Other Music Sites

(1) Napster, the site that launched a firestorm in the music industry and revolutionized collaboration, was started by 19-year-old Northeast University student Shawn Fanning, who set up a Web site with software that allowed people to link their computers together and share their music in MP3 format. The site kept a list of the people who shared their music through Napster, and also provided search capabilities so that you could easily find someone online who had the music you wanted.
(2) The Recording Industry Association of America (RIAA) representing 18 recording companies including the "Big Five"—Sony, Warner, Universal, BMG, and EMI—filed suit to stop Shawn and Napster. The basis for the legal action was that Napster provided a service that enabled and facilitated piracy of music on an enormous scale. You have to show injury in such a case, and RIAA claimed that Napster's piracy facilitation was cutting into its $14-billion-a-year sales.
(3) Napster referred to the Audio Home Recording Act of 1992, which allows people to copy music for personal use. Napster said it wasn't guilty of copyright infringement since no music was stored on its site, so it didn't give any music to anyone.
(4) Napster was removed from the Web under an appeals court order in July 2002. However, other music swapping sites, like Kazaa, Grokster, and Morpheus, sprang up to take its place. The music industry has initiated litigation to stop those sites too, but their task will be much harder this time. The newer sites are more sophisticated, offering other files, including software, movies (some that are playing in theaters), and videogames as well as music. The sites don't keep track of who's downloading what, and they claim that they can't be held responsible for what people do on their site, if they don't know about it.
(5) Also these newer sites have no central servers to track and control the transfer of files between people, as Napster did. Niklas Zennstrom, one of the creators of Kazaa, says that the only way that Kazaa can be shut down is if everyone who uses it removes the music-sharing software from their computers, which is, to say the least, unlikely.

Look at the table below. Now reconsider the account of Napster and Kazaa you have just read. In the table below, identify as many of the key terms or key concepts as you can that appeared in the Napster-Kazaa story. Specify the paragraph number where the concept appears. For those that do not appear, on a separate sheet add sentences to the story to include them and in the table show the paragraph number.

Term or Concept	Is Concept Already There?	Paragraph Number Where It Appears in the Current Story or Your New Edition
Sniffer		
Spoofing		
Virus		
Fair Use Doctrine		
ID Theft		
Copyright		
Privacy		
Ethical computer use		
Cookie		
Web tracking		
Spam		
Firewall		
Worm		
Denial of service		
Pirated software		

e-commerce

1. Browsing the Web Anonymously

You know that organizations can collect information on you as you surf the Web. They can put a cookie onto your computer, note your IP address (i.e., the unique address that your ISP assigns your computer), and note your e-mail address in messages you send. However, you can hide your Web surfing tracks by using anonymous Web browsing software. Below are some anonymous Web browsing sites. Look at these or other sites and answer the questions that follow the list of sites.

- Anonymizer—www.anonymizer.com
- iClean—www.internet-privacy-software.org/iclean.asp
- Idsecure—www.idzap.com
- SafeWeb—www.safeweb.com

a. Do you have to pay for the service? If so, how much?

b. Does the software offered automatically delete or block cookies?

c. Does it block and/or remove ads?

2. Renting a Hotel Room

You can find lots of hotel information on general travel sites such as www.expedia.com or www.travelocity.com. Here are some hotel-chain Web sites. Visit a few of them and answer the questions that follow.

- Marriott International—www.marriott.com
- Motel 6—www.motel6.com
- Super 8—www.super8.com
- Hilton Group—www.hilton.com

a. Which chains have hotels in other countries? On what continents do they offer hotel rooms?

b. Which hotel chains have properties in your hometown or in the town where you're going to college?

c. Can you get airline miles for staying at any of these chains?

d. Which Web sites give you a picture of the rooms?

3. Making Airline Reservations

Almost all airlines sell tickets on their Web sites. But you can also go to general travel sites and compare flight times and prices there. For some of the best deals, you should check out the sites that compare prices for you, such as www.farechase.com or www.airlineguides.com.

Look at the following airline Web sites and answer the questions that follow.

- American Airlines—www.aa.com
- Delta Airlines—www.delta.com
- Southwest Airlines—www.southwest.com
- United Airlines—www.ual.com

a. Pick a destination at least 1,000 miles from where you are now and compare prices, number of stops, and how long it takes you to get to the destination airport.

b. Did any of the sites give you a list of cities they serve? How were you able to choose from the list of cities?

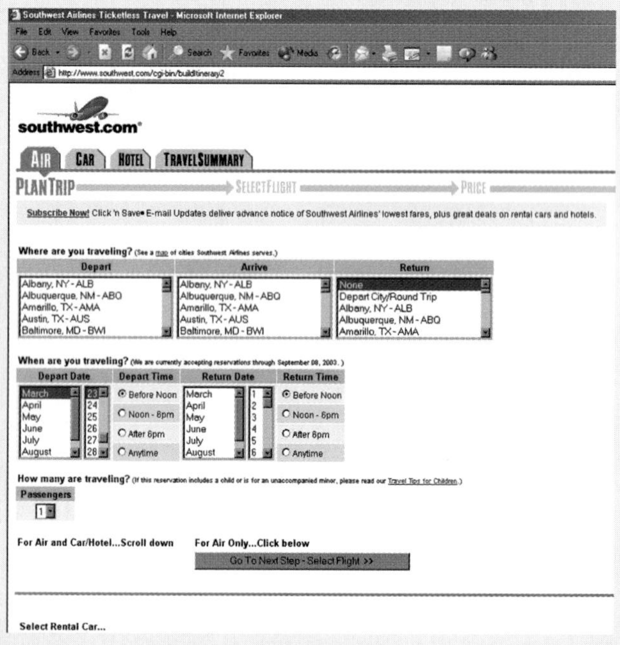

ethics, security & privacy

1. Expedia.com Helps to Find the Killer

In St. Louis, Missouri, a mass murderer was on the loose and had already killed 10 women. The police were not even close to finding the killer. The only clue they had was a set of tire tracks.

The murderer, meanwhile, was getting bolder and more confident, so much so that he actually wrote to a newspaper reporter about his killing spree. He went so far as to enclose a map of where the bodies of seven other murder victims were buried. The newspaper reporter at first thought he had a prankster on his hands, but notified the police anyway, and turned the letter and map over to them. The police discovered bodies of the young women in the exact location that the map indicated. But how would they find the killer?

They couldn't tell much about the sender from the letter, but the map was distinctive. It was recognized by one of the officers as being the type of map available on the travel site Expedia.com, which is owned by Microsoft. The police contacted Microsoft and requested a list of IP addresses of computers that had accessed the site within a few days of when the letter was mailed.

Microsoft was able to give the police the names and billing addresses of those who could be suspects. (The company keeps the names, credit card numbers, and billing addresses of those who book travel through Expedia.com.) The police narrowed down the list and got a warrant to search the house of the most likely suspect.

When they arrived at his house with a search warrant, they found a car with tires that matched the prints taken from one of the crime scenes. In the basement of the suspect's house, they found duct tape and other effects used in the crimes. The man was arrested. He hung himself in his cell just before his trial was to begin.

Consider the following questions:

a. Do you think that it was ethical for Microsoft to hand over names and addresses of customers? Whichever way you answer, do you think you'd feel differently if the police came to your door and asked if they could search your home so that they could rule you out? Why did you answer as you did?

b. Would it have been all right to search the suspect's house if the police had not had a court order? Why or why not?

c. How would you feel about law enforcement agencies being able to monitor e-mail and other Internet traffic, simply as a precaution, to try to spot wrongdoing?

d. The European Union is considering a law to give border police access to e-mail and Internet use by citizens. The law would mean that police could access any and all e-mail and Internet usage information from ISPs simply by requesting it. No court would be needed. Would you support the creation of such a law in this country? Why or why not? What if this law were proposed to protect you from terrorism?

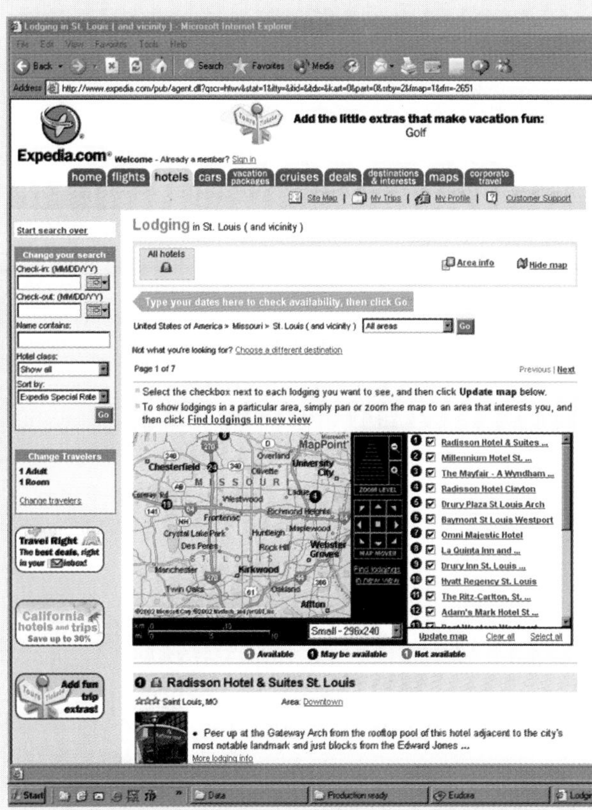

on the web

1. Want to Know Your IP Address?

Every computer that is connected to the Internet has an IP address. An Internet Protocol (IP) address is a unique number that has four groups of up to three digits between 0 and 255 (for example, 192.168.1.104). Some computers always have the same IP address. This is called a static IP address. Sometimes, depending on the network or ISP, a computer gets a dynamic IP address. That means that the IP address changes constantly. (The network administrator or the ISP has a list of who had what IP address when, so you can still be tracked.) Several sites on the Web will tell you your IP address and sometimes even more information, like your name and the institution you're accessing the Web from. Check out these. What were you able to find out?

- What Is My IP—
  www.whatismyip.com/indexbody.cfm
- Internet Help—
  www.internet-help.net/ip-address.htm

2. Codes of Ethics

Various professional organizations have codes of ethics. The accounting profession, for example, has a thick book with small print called Generally Accepted Accounting Principles. This book includes rules for how accountants should deal with difficult situations that might arise during performance of their professional duties. The Association for Computing Machinery (ACM), which is an organization for computing professionals, has a similar, although much simpler, set of codes. Go to the ACM site at www.acm.org and summarize the guidelines cited there for members of ACM and computing professionals.

3. Parental Control Software Packages

To protect your family, you can get software that prevents children from connecting to undesirable sites. The software launches when a person starts the Web browser. This software looks at every Web address that you try to connect to in two ways. First, it compares the address to its database list of thousands of objectionable sites. If the address is on that list the software blocks the retrieval of the site. Second, if it doesn't find the address in the list, it checks the content of the site, looking for specific words that might indicate an objectionable site.

Search the Web and find at least two different parental control software packages. What features do they include? Are they free to download?

4. What Polymorphic Viruses Are Floating around Cyberspace?

In the wake of the Love Bug worm, a new and potentially deadly worm called NewLove popped up. This worm had two new features. First, it buried its destructive logic somewhere that makes it much harder to find. NewLove disabled Windows and made other files unusable. Second, it changed its code every time it succeeded in infecting a computer, adding some code randomly and growing with each infection. It didn't spread very far, but caused a stir within the IT community because of the ability to change its code. It was a new kind of virus called a *polymorphic virus*. A polymorphic virus changes itself to evade detection. Essentially it encrypts itself to evade detection by anti-virus software, but changes the way it does it each time.

Visit the Web and look up five currently active polymorphic viruses. For each one find out

a. the name of the virus.
b. what it does.
c. the name of anti-virus software that finds it.
d. the symptoms of infection.

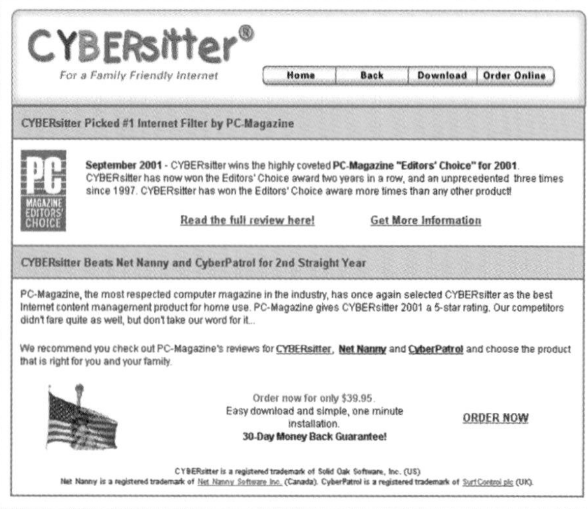

group activities

1. How Does HIPAA Protect Your Personal Health Information?

The final requirements of the Health Insurance Portability and Accountability Act of 1996 were announced in February 2003, although compliance is not required until 2005 or 2006, depending on the size of your health care institution. Find out what these requirements are and how they protect you. Write a one-page report on what you find.

2. Helping a Friend

Suppose you fully intend to spend the evening working on an Excel assignment that's due the next day when a friend calls who is stranded miles from home and desperately needs your help. It takes most of the evening to pick up your friend, bring him home, and return to your studying. You're so tired when you get home, all you can do is just fall into bed and sleep.

The next day your friend, who completed his assignment earlier, suggests you just make a copy of his, put your own name on it, and hand it in as your own work. Should you do it? Isn't it only fair that since you helped your friend, your friend should do something about making sure you don't lose points because of your generosity? What if your friend promises not to hand in his own work so that you can't be accused of copying? Your friend wrote the assignment he has given you so there's no question of copyright infringement. What will you do? Explain.

3. Providing Personal Information

Each member of your group should think of three times he or she provided personal information in exchange for something. Make a table of what information each person gave and what they received for providing the information. Were all the exchanges perfectly legitimate? Were any of them more problematic for any reason?

4. Ethics and Laws

Sometimes what's legal might still be unethical. Think of five laws, past or present, at home or abroad, that you would consider unethical to obey and state why. Then think of five behaviors that are legal, past or present, at home or abroad, that you would nevertheless consider unethical to engage in and state why.

5. Debating Privacy

The European Parliament has decreed that citizens of all its member countries have the following rights:

- The right to know where a marketer obtained personal information.
- The right to look at any personal information that any company has.
- The right to correct any inaccurate information.
- The right to prevent personal information from being used for direct marketing.
- The right to never have sensitive information such as race, religion, and sexual orientation divulged without express permission.

Half of your group should take the privacy advocate's side and give reasons why these rights should be written into U.S. law. The other half should take the opposing viewpoint and give reasons why this might not be a good thing for this country.

6. Digital Signatures and Certificates

Digital signatures are a way of protecting electronic messages, like e-mails, on their journey through cyberspace. It's an anti-tampering device. The basis of a digital signature is that a set of characters in the message is used in arithmetic operations to generate a unique "key" for that message. When the message arrives, the recipient performs the same operations in the exact order and the result should be the original message. If it's not, then the message has been tampered with.

Digital signatures are often used in conjunction with digital certificates. What are digital certificates? Do some research and write a one-page report on digital certificates and how they're used.

crossword puzzle

Across

2. Information about a field
3. Graphical tool for answering questions
5. Logical collection of files
6. Primary key of more than one field
9. Customizable Web site
11. AI data-mining tool
12. Most important key in a database file
14. Software for working with a database
17. Group of related fields
18. For data entry into a database
22. Manipulating information to support decision making
23. Unrefined information
24. Narrative form of #3 across
26. Knowledge in the business world
27. Graphical tool for designing a database
28. Primary key of one file in another file

Down

1. Database for storing Web addresses as objects
4. Opposite of #22 across
5. Collection of information from multiple databases
7. Structure and properties of a database table
8. Databases that support e-commerce
10. Newest database model
13. Meaningful data
15. These make up a record
16. Collection of files
19. Enables applications to talk to each other
20. Manipulating information in a data warehouse
21. Seller of information
25. Subset of a data warehouse

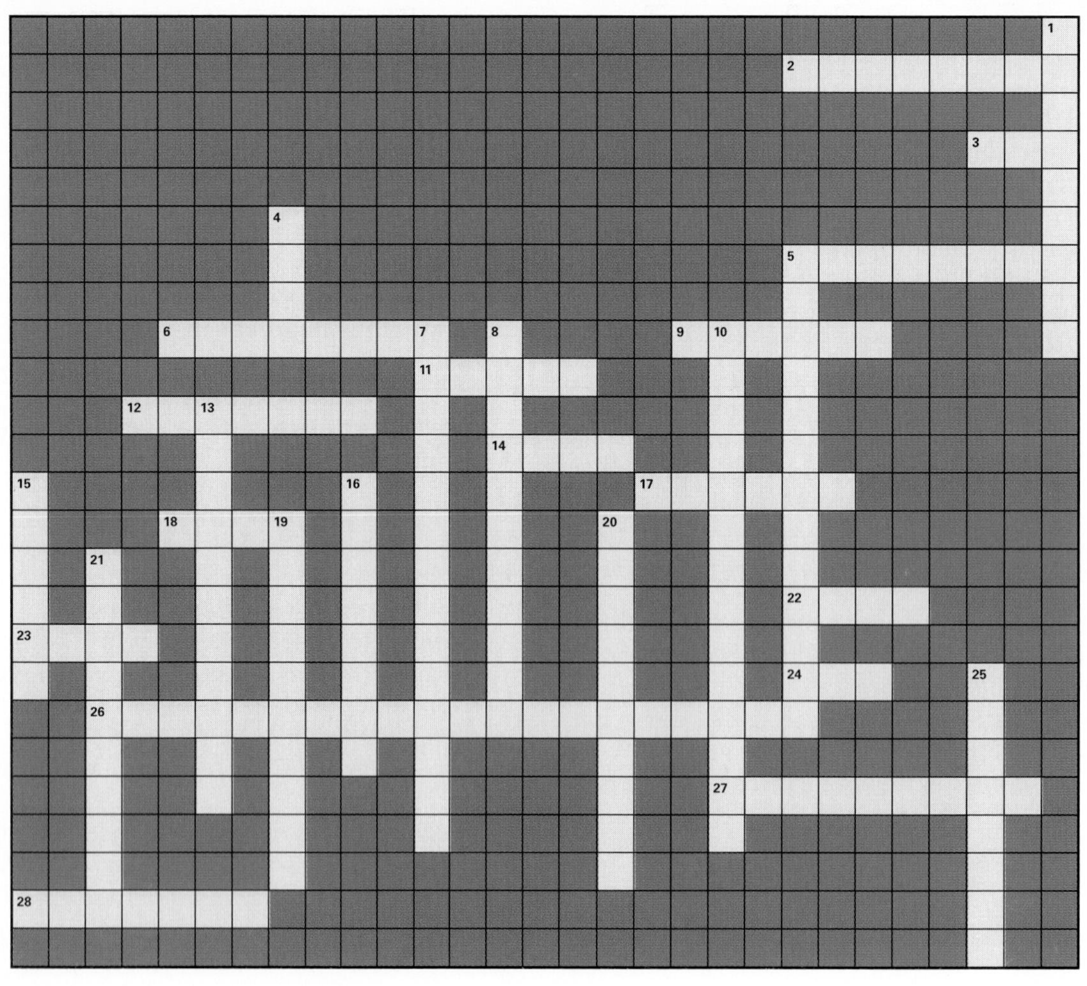

CHAPTER ten 10

Databases and Data Warehouses

How Do You Organize Large Amounts of Information?

SIMNET CONCEPTS SUPPORT

- Database Applications (p. 293)
- Managing Data (p. 293)
- Database Management Systems (pp. 293, 299)
- Designing Relational Databases (p. 295)
- Types of Database Organizations (p. 297)
- Privacy Issues (p. 309)
- Security Issues (p. 309)
- Data Mining (p. 310)

did you know?

No doubt about it—we are in the *information age.* Technologies such as databases, DBMSs, data warehouses, and data-mining tools that help people organize, manage, and sift through huge volumes of information are vitally important. Almost any category of information you can think of is probably stored somewhere in a database or data warehouse. Many of these are freely available on the Web.

adherents.com *(www.adherents.com) provides congregation statistics for over 4,200 religions, churches, denominations, religious bodies, faith groups, tribes, cultures, movements, ultimate concerns, etc.*

u *UFO Database (www.larryhatch.net) provides a database of UFO information including cataloging and mapping features as well as the ability to perform statistical analyses.*

roller *Coaster DataBase (www.rcdb.com) provides a searchable database of information on over ___??___ roller coasters throughout the world.*

To find out how many roller coasters and their information are stored in Roller Coaster DataBase, visit the Web site for this text at www.mhhe.com/i-series.

Student Learning Outcomes

After reading this chapter, you should be able to:

1. Describe the difference between data and information and the logical structure people use to organize data and information.
2. Define key relational database concepts including field properties, primary keys, compound primary keys, foreign keys, and integrity constraints.
3. Describe the role of an entity-relationship diagram in defining the structure of a database and the relationships among the tables.
4. List the major components of a database management system and describe their roles.
5. Discuss how Web databases support various e-commerce functions.
6. Describe how data warehouses and data-mining tools help create business intelligence.

Businesses and individuals alike need technology tools to help them effectively organize their information so they can access and use it for a variety of purposes. In this chapter, we'll explore databases and data warehouses as technology tools for organizing information. And we'll also explore database management systems and data-mining tools as technology tools for accessing and using information in databases and data warehouses.

10.1 DATA, INFORMATION, AND THEIR STRUCTURES

You arrive at the airport excited about taking a vacation. You need to remind yourself when your plane is leaving and find out which gate. After checking in at the ticket counter you look at your boarding pass and head to your gate.

DATA VERSUS INFORMATION

Is Data Different from Information?

Your boarding pass has provided you with essential information, such as the gate number and departure time (and without it you wouldn't be able to get on the plane, either).

This information comes from data the airline keeps about flights, departures, gate assignments, and so on. Take a look at Figure 10.1. There you can see the difference between data and information. ***Data*** are distinct items providing descriptions of people, places, and/or things that may not have much meaning to you, depending on their context. For example, in Figure 10.1, you can see the items NW843, 1140, and 23, but you

FIGURE 10.1

The difference between data and information is extraordinary. Which would you rather look at to find your flight?

Data

NW843, MSP, ANC, 1140, 1444, 6.4, 757, 23

Information

Flight Information							
Flight	**Origin**	**Destination**	**Departure**	**Arrival**	**Flight Time**	**Airplane**	**Gate**
NW 843	Minneapolis (MSP)	Anchorage (ANC)	11:40 AM	2:44 PM	6 hr. 4 min	Boeing 757	23

don't know what they mean. Once someone organizes these data in the appropriate context, it becomes clear that your flight (NW 843) leaves at 11:40 A.M. from gate 23. The data have been transformed into information. ***Information*** is organized data whose meaning is clear and useful to you in a given context. Both presentations in Figure 10.1 contain the same items, but one is more useful than the other, because one is meaningfully organized for you. Which would you rather use when trying to find your flight?

LOGICAL STRUCTURES

How Do People and Organizations Organize Their Data?

Because of the vast amount of data and information that people and organizations work with on a daily basis, data and information must be organized in a logical fashion, as follows (see Figure 10.2):

- ***Field***—the smallest piece of data, which may be information in a given context. In Figure 10.1, your flight number (NW 843) is a field.
- ***Record***—a group of logically related fields. In Figure 10.1, all the fields that make up the information concerning your flight information constitute your flight record.
- ***Data file*** (which we generally refer to as a *file*)—a group of logically related records. From an organizational point of view (Northwest Airlines in this case), the **Flight Information** file would have records concerning all its flights, including departure and arrival information.
- ***Database***—a logical collection of files. Again, if you consider Northwest Airlines, its database would consist of a file with flight information, a file with crew information, a file with customer information, and so on.
- ***Data warehouse***—a collection of information from internal and/or external sources (mostly databases) organized specifically for generating business intelligence to support decision making.

FIGURE 10.2

The logical hierarchy for storing data and information includes fields, records, files, databases, and data warehouses.

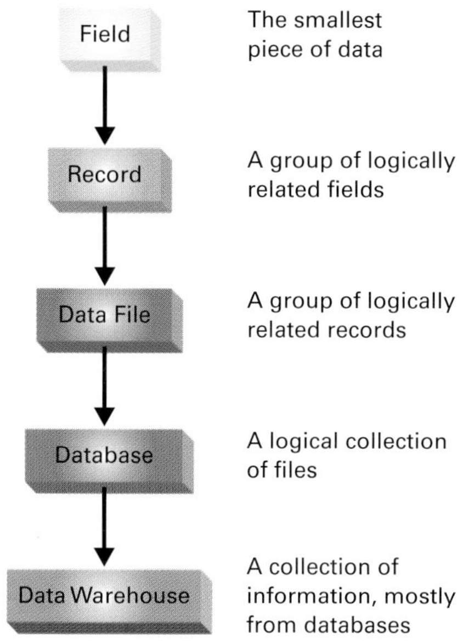

Field — The smallest piece of data

Record — A group of logically related fields

Data File — A group of logically related records

Database — A logical collection of files

Data Warehouse — A collection of information, mostly from databases

In the first part of this chapter, we'll deal specifically with databases. In the final part, we'll talk in more detail about data warehouses. To learn more about databases, complete the "Database Applications," "Managing Data," and "Database Management Systems" tutorials on your SimNet Concepts Support CD.

making the grade

SECTION 10.1

1. Information is organized ___________ whose meaning is clear and useful to you in a given context.
2. The smallest piece of data is a(n) ___________.
3. A record is a group of logically related ___________.
4. A(n) ___________ is group of logically related records.
5. A(n) ___________ is a logical collection of files.

10.2 RELATIONAL DATABASES

At the database level, the most popular method for organizing and storing information is the ***relational database model*** which stores information in files or tables that have rows and columns. Let's consider a database example for Retread Auto, a small business that sells used cars and also provides service work only for the cars it sells. In Figure 10.3, we've provided a sample of Retread Auto's database. This is a database we created in Microsoft Access, the most popular personal technology tool for creating and working with databases. Microsoft Access refers to *files* as *tables,* so we'll use the term *table* as well.

RELATIONAL DATABASE CONCEPTS

What Do I Need to Know about Relational Databases?

In Figure 10.3, you can see that Retread Auto's database consists of three tables—**Car, Customer,** and **Service.** Within the **Car** table, you'll find six records which appear in separate and distinct rows. Each record contains seven fields—**VIN Number, Car Type, Year, Color, Mileage, Price,** and **Customer ID.**

Field Properties

For each field in a table of a database you must specify a field property. A ***field property*** is the type of information in a field (for example, numeric, date, and currency). So, the field property for **VIN Number** is text because it contains both alphabetic and numeric information. Likewise, the field property for **Price** is currency because it contains financial information.

FIGURE 10.3

Retread Auto used three tables to create its database.

Car : Table

VIN Number	Car Type	Year	Color	Mileage	Price	Customer ID
HQ1294N8493	Honda Civic	1998	Green	45021	$14,025.00	1122
JD5768D6473	Geo Metro	1994	Red	67009	$6,348.00	9999
MJ4563H9485	Jeep Cherokee	1995	Blue	101034	$8,032.00	4388
PD4356G4357	BMW 325i	1999	Silver	24000	$23,995.00	2333
PJ4987D2591	Buick Skylark	1982	Black	97500	$4,500.00	9999
ZZ9384N3746	Chevy Camaro	1997	Black	88000	$12,999.00	6717
		0		0	$0.00	0

Tavis Marten owns the Jeep Cherokee.

Customer : Table

Customer ID	First Name	Last Name	Address	City	State	Zip	Phone
1122	Manny	Smith	3453	Ada Avanue	MI	49053	(616)555-2255
2333	Roberta	Lott	47 Michigan Avenue	Climax	MI	49034	(616)555-4821
4388	Tavis	Marten	122 Annondale Dr.	Kalamazoo	MI	49008	(616)555-4587
6717	Susie	Jones	8675 State Street	Portage	MI	49024	(616)555-7435
9999	Blank	Customer				0	
0						0	

Service : Table

VIN Number	Date In	Date Completed	Service Performed	Total Bill	Customer Paid
HQ1294N8493	11/4/2003	11/4/2003	Oil Change	$23.95	☑
HQ1294N8493	12/1/2003	12/2/2003	Front End Alignment	$47.95	☑
ZZ9384N3746	1/17/2004	1/21/2004	Engine Overhaul	$795.00	☐
				$0.00	■

Primary Keys

For each table in a database you must specify a primary key. A ***primary key*** is a field in a database table that uniquely identifies a record in that table. Take a look at the **Customer** table. Its primary key is **Customer ID.** So, each **Customer ID** in the **Customer** table must be unique.

Can you guess what the primary key is for the **Service** table? It is a combination of **VIN Number** and **Date In.** Why? Because it's possible that Retread could service the same car on different days. So, you can't just use **VIN Number.** This is an example of a compound primary key. A ***compound primary key*** occurs in a database table when two or more fields together uniquely identify each record.

Foreign Keys

To create the best possible database, all tables within it must be logically associated through the use of foreign keys. A ***foreign key*** is a primary key field of one database table that also appears in another database table. Notice that **Customer ID** is the primary key field for the **Customer** table. Notice also that **Customer ID** appears in the **Car** table. In this instance, the **Customer ID** in the **Car** table tells us which customer purchased a particular car and is an example of a foreign key.

Following the logic of foreign keys, Retread must establish a relationship between the **Service** table and one of the other tables. Can you find the foreign key that creates that relationship? It is **VIN Number. VIN Number** is the primary key of the **Car** table and also appears in the **Service** table.

Integrity Constraints

An ***integrity constraint*** is a rule that helps ensure the quality of information in a database. For example, when first creating its database, Retread Auto could specify that the **Mileage** field in the **Car** table cannot be zero or negative. Therefore, no one could ever add a car to the database and enter its mileage as zero or a negative number.

Another form of an integrity constraint is a foreign key. By specifying that **Customer ID** is the primary key in the **Customer** table and also a foreign key in the **Car** table, no one can enter a **Customer ID** in the **Car** table that does not also exist in the **Customer** table. That's a powerful way of ensuring the quality of information in Retread's database.

RELATIONSHIPS IN RELATIONAL DATABASES
What Kinds of Relationships Can I Create in a Database?

One of the key differences between a database and a spreadsheet application is your ability to create relationships. As you've just read, you create relationships by defining foreign keys. These foreign keys can then help you implement integrity constraints, thus ensuring the quality of the information in your database.

Our focus here is to briefly introduce you to the considerations necessary for effectively designing a database. To learn more, complete the "Designing Relational Databases" on your SimNet Concepts Support CD.

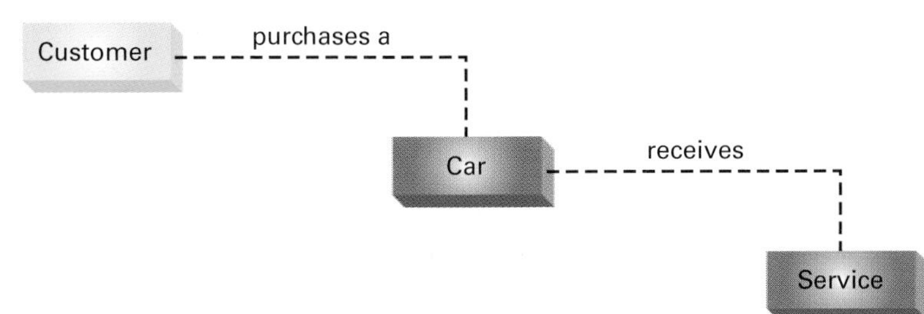

FIGURE 10.4
Retread Auto's E-R diagram shows the relationships among the tables in its database.

Entity-Relationship Diagrams

As you go about defining the structure of a database and the relationships among the tables, you create an entity-relationship diagram. An ***entity-relationship (E-R) diagram*** is a graphical representation of the tables in a database and the relationships among the tables. In Figure 10.4, you can see the E-R diagram for Retread Auto's database.

Notice first that each table is represented by a rectangle. Then, between the tables for which a logical relationship exists you add a dotted line and some sort of verb. So, **Customer** "purchases a" **Car,** and a **Car** "receives" **Service.** If you think about it, these statements make perfect business sense.

At this point, the E-R diagram alerts the people at Retread Auto that there must be foreign keys in the database. Because a relationship exists between the **Car** and **Customer** tables, the primary key in the **Car** table (**VIN Number**) must appear as a foreign key in the **Customer** table or the primary key in the **Customer** table (**Customer ID**) must appear as a foreign key in the **Car** table. Likewise, because a relationship exists between the **Car** and **Service** tables, one of those tables must have a foreign key in it that appears as a primary key in the other table.

Types of Database Relationships

There are three types of relationships in a database: one-to-one, one-to-many, and many-to-many. With E-R diagramming, you represent a "one" with a straight line (|) and a "many" with a crow's foot (<).

A ***one-to-one relationship*** means that *one* record in a database table can only be related to at most *one* record in another database table. For example, if you created a database to track what cars were assigned to various reserved parking spaces on your campus, there would be a one-to-one relationship between a car and a reserved parking space. That is to say, a car can only be assigned one reserved parking space, and a reserved parking space can have only one car assigned to it.

A ***one-to-many relationship*** means that *one* record in a database table can be related to *many* records in another database table. Notice that there is a crow's foot on the top side of the **Car** table and a straight line on the right side of the **Customer** table in Figure 10.5 on the opposite page. This is an example of a one-to-many relationship. You would interpret it as:

- A **Customer** can purchase many **Cars.**
- A **Car** can be purchased by only one **Customer.**

did you know?

The *U.S. Patent and Trademark Office database includes all patents dating from 1790, a total of more than 6.5 million.*

practically speaking

There Is More than One Database Model

The relational database model is the most popular database model in use today. Other database models that you may hear about from time to time include hierarchical, network, and object-oriented.

The ***hierarchical database model*** creates a hierarchy of relationships among records in a database such that a "child" record can have only one "parent" record, but a "parent" record can have many "child" records. A good example might be your school. You probably have several different high-level academic units at your school such as Business and Economics, Engineering, and Liberal Arts. Each of those would have departments within it. Each department can be within only one high-level academic unit. So, the high-level academic unit is the "parent" and the departments are the "children."

The ***network database model*** is similar in structure to the hierarchical database model except that each child can have more than one parent. For example, your school may have some instructors who teach classes for several different departments. If so, one of those instructors might belong to several different departments and thus has many "parents."

The ***object-oriented database model*** uses objects to represent people, places, and things. Objects contain both information and the procedures necessary to manipulate the information. Your stereo system is an object-oriented system. Your CD player contains both the music on the CD and the procedures for obtaining the music from the CD.

Of the three models, the newest is the object-oriented database model, and it represents a substantial career opportunity for you. Businesses need skilled IT specialists who can define and work with objects, object-oriented databases, and object-oriented database management systems. Many of today's newer programming languages such as Java are entirely based on object-oriented concepts. If you're interested, see what your school offers in the way of object-oriented classes (and definitely read Chapter 13). To learn more about the different types of databases, complete the "Types of Database Organizations" on your SimNet Concepts Support CD.

C careers

These statements make logical sense. It is entirely possible that a given customer may purchase many cars from Retread Auto. A car, however, can be purchased by only one customer. (Here, we are making the assumption that a car cannot have two owners at the same time.)

Finally, a ***many-to-many relationship*** means that *many* records in a database table can be related to *many* records in another database table. From a technical point of view, you cannot have many-to-many relationships in the same database, so you won't find any in Retread Auto's database.

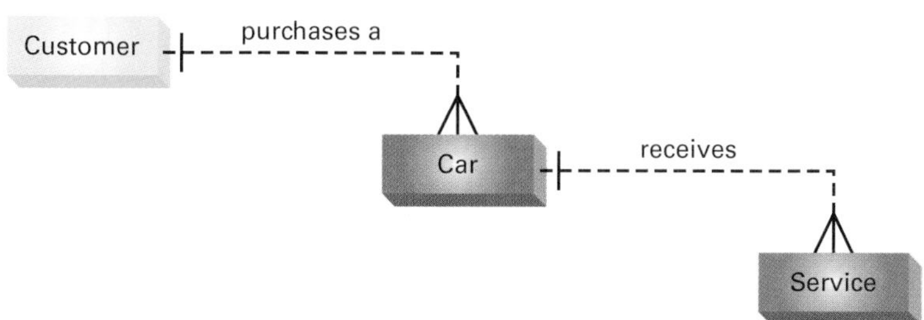

FIGURE 10.5

This new E-R diagram for Retread Auto's database defines the type of relationships that exist between the tables.

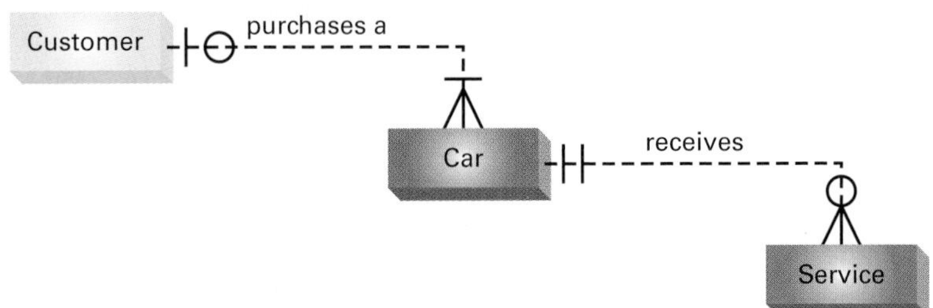

FIGURE 10.6

In this final E-R diagram, you can see the minimum values for each of the relationships in Retread Auto's database.

Minimum Values in a Database

Our E-R diagram in Figure 10.5 on the previous page shows only the tables and the types of relationships that exist between them. If you look now at Figure 10.6, we've added minimum values to the relationships. *Minimum values* for relationships in a database can be zero (represented with a small circle) or one (represented with a straight line). We also place these marks just inside the notations for defining "one" and "many" relationships.

Let's consider again the relationship between **Car** and **Customer.** Because we placed a straight line next to the crow's foot on the top side of the **Car** table, it means: A **Customer** can purchase many **Cars** and a **Customer** must purchase at least (or at a minimum) one **Car.** That is to say, Retread Auto has no customers in its database who have not purchased at least one car. Again, that makes sense from a business point of view because Retread Auto services only cars it sells.

Read in reverse, the relationship between **Car** and **Customer** is: A **Car** can only be purchased by one **Customer** and a **Car** may have yet to be purchased by a **Customer.** Again, this makes sense. It is possible for Retread Auto to have a car on its lot that has not been sold.

The ability to design the correct structure of a database (including defining tables, their relationships, their types of relationships, and the minimum values of relationships) is a highly sought-after skill in the IT field. If you're interested in designing and working with databases, check your school's catalog for courses related to databases and database management systems.

SECTION 10.2

making the grade

1. The ___________ stores information in files or tables that have rows and columns.
2. A(n) ___________ is the type of information in a field.
3. A(n) ___________ occurs in a database table when two or more fields uniquely identify each record.
4. A(n) ___________ diagram is a graphical representation of the tables in a database and the relationships among the tables.
5. A(n) ___________ relationship means that one record in a database table can be related to many records in another database table.

10.3 DATABASE MANAGEMENT SYSTEMS

To create, manage, and use the tables in Retread Auto's database, we need a database management system. A ***database management system (DBMS)*** is application software that allows you to arrange, modify, and extract information from a database. All DBMSs include a data definition subsystem, data manipulation subsystem, application generation subsystem, and data administration subsystem. You can learn more about DBMSs by completing the "Database Management Systems" tutorial on your SimNet Concepts Support CD.

DATA DEFINITION SUBSYSTEM

How Do I Define the Structure of a Database and Its Tables?

The ***data definition subsystem*** of a DBMS helps you define the tables in a database and the relationships among them. Some people refer to the data definition subsystem as the *Data Definition Language* or *DDL.* When you define a database table, you first create its data dictionary. A ***data dictionary*** defines the structure and properties of a database table.

In Figure 10.7 we've provided a screen that shows the data definition subsystem for the **Car** table in the Retread Auto database. Notice that we identified **VIN Number** as the primary key by placing the Key icon beside it. In the bottom part of the screen, you can see the field properties for the **Mileage** field in the **Car** table. Because it is a numeric field, we set the number of decimals to zero and provided the validation rule of "**>0.**" This is an integrity constraint and ensures that no car is entered into the **Car** table with a mileage that is zero or negative.

For each table in a database, you must first create the data dictionary just as we have done for the **Car** table.

Defining Relationships among the Tables

After you define the data dictionary or structure for each individual table in a database, you then need to define the relationships that exist among those tables. At this point, you are defining the presence of foreign keys, or the primary keys of one table that will appear in another table.

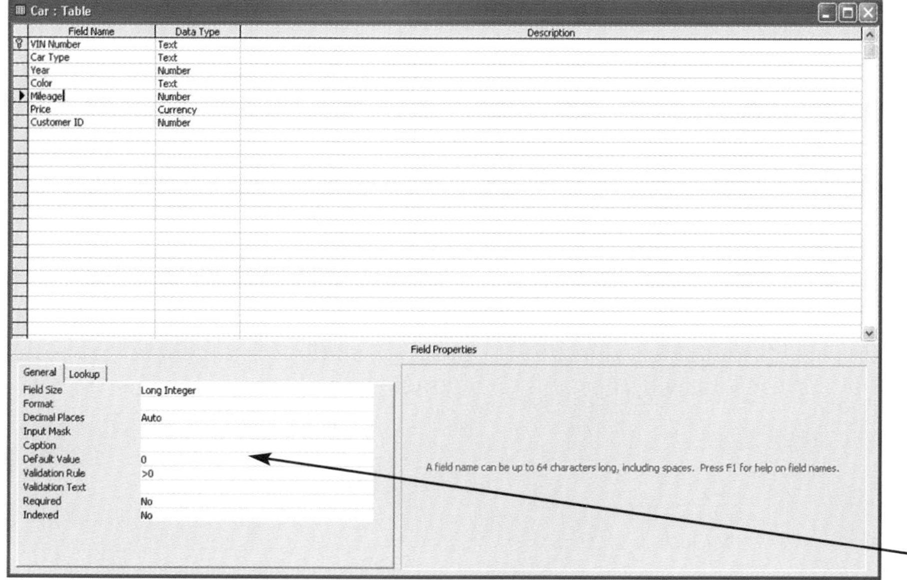

FIGURE 10.7

For each table in a database, you must first define its data dictionary. This is the data dictionary for Retread Auto's **Car** table.

This is the data dictionary for the **Mileage** field. Notice that it cannot be zero or less than zero.

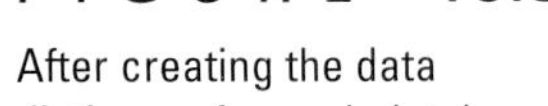

FIGURE 10.8

After creating the data dictionary for each database table, you must define the relationships that exist among the tables.

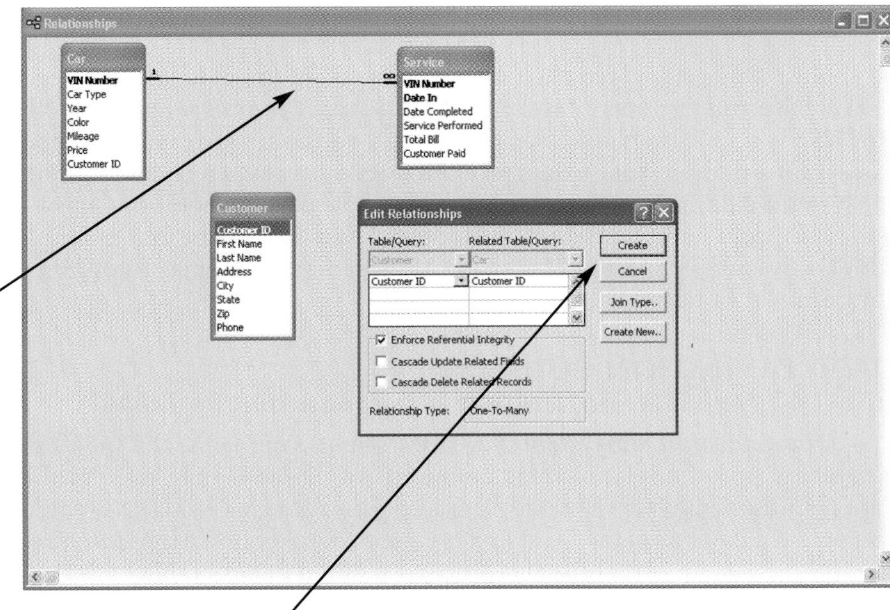

This shows the relationship between **Car** and **Service.**

Once we click on the **Create** button, Access will create the relationship between **Car** and **Customer.**

In Figure 10.8, we've provided a screen capture of how you achieve this in Microsoft Access. Access represents the "one" side of relationship with a "1" and the "many" side of the relationship with an infinity symbol (looks like an 8 on its side). All you have to do is click on and drag the primary key from the table which will have the "one" side of the relationship and drop it onto its counterpart in the table which will have the "many" side of the relationship. We have done that in Figure 10.8 by dragging the primary key of **Customer ID** from the **Customer** table and dropping it on **Customer ID** in the **Car** table.

Microsoft then presents a **Relationships Dialog** box. In it, we will click on the **Enforce Referential Integrity** box and then the **Create** button. In doing so, Access will require that any **Customer ID** entered into the **Car** table also be present in the **Customer** table. This again is a method of enforcing integrity constraints which will help ensure the quality of the information in a database.

After creating that relationship, you would follow a similar process to create the relationship between the **Car** and **Service** tables. Figure 10.8 shows the result of doing this.

did you know?

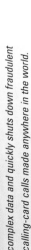

An object-oriented database (called Sheriff) analyzes complex data and quickly shuts down fraudulent calling-card calls made anywhere in the world.

DATA MANIPULATION SUBSYSTEM

How Do I Use a DBMS to Enter and Query Database Information?

The ***data manipulation subsystem*** of a DBMS helps you enter information into a database, query it to find information, and generate reports. Database users will most often interact with these tools when using a DBMS.

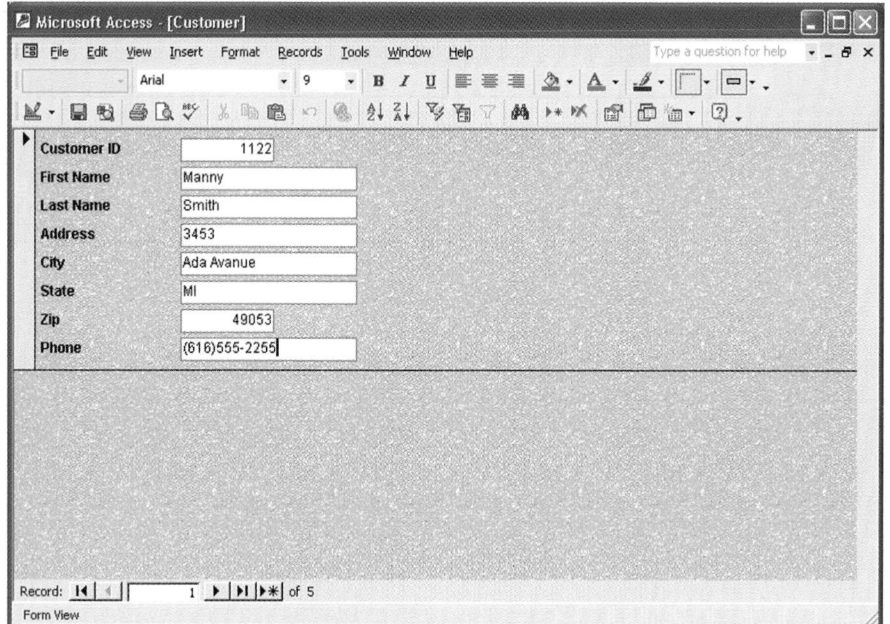

FIGURE 10.9

This database form allows people at Retread Auto to add, change, and delete information in the **Customer** table.

Database Forms

You can enter information into a database table much as you would using a spreadsheet, seeing rows for each of the records and column headings that include the field names. However, a better way is to use a database form. A ***database form*** is a graphical interface that makes it easy to add, change, and delete information.

In Figure 10.9, we have provided a database form that you can easily develop for entering information into Retread Auto's **Customer** table. The database form allows you see one record at a time. You can click in any field and change its contents. Using the buttons across the bottom of the database form, you can:

- Go to the first record
- Go back one record
- Go forward one record
- Go to the last record
- Add a new record

As you define a database form, you can determine a number of its characteristics including the background color and texture. If you want to get really "user friendly," you could even add Retread Auto's logo to the database form. This sort of customization further encourages users to take full advantage of the DBMS.

Querying Information in a Database

Sometime you will need to find information in a database. For example, the employees of Retread Auto might want to find out who purchased a 1995 Blue Jeep Cherokee or obtain a list of services on a given date. Of course, with a database that contains only a few records in each table neither of these is a difficult task. But if you have a database with thousands of records, you might want to take advantage of a query-by-example tool.

FIGURE 10.10

This QBE will answer the question: Who bought what car?

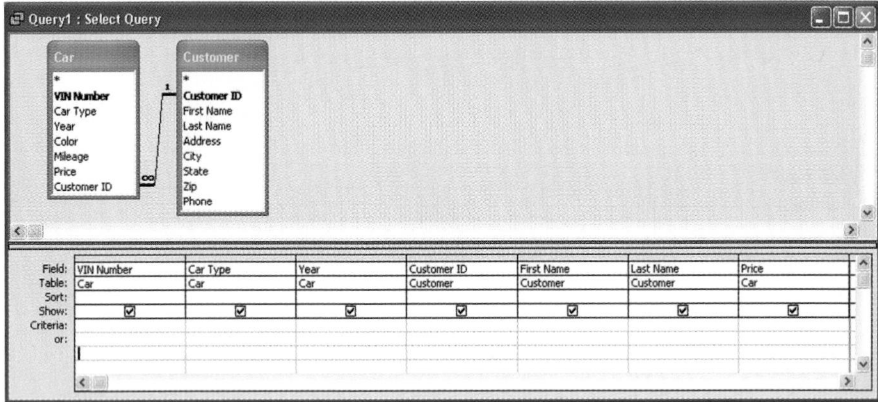

A ***query-by-example (QBE) tool*** allows you to graphically represent what information you'd like to see from a database. Consider the question: Who bought what car? In Figure 10.10 we used a QBE tool to answer that question. In this example, the QBE tool pulls information from the **Customer** and **Car** tables of the Retread Auto database. Using the one-to-many relationship between the tables, the DBMS is able to link all sold cars by a customer's ID number. Each time you run, or execute, the query, the DBMS will generate the information you want.

Another method of querying a database is to use SQL. ***Structured Query Language (SQL)*** is a standardized query language for most DBMSs. The SQL statement that would provide the same information as the QBE in Figure 10.10 would be:

```
SELECT  Car. [VIN Number], Car. [Car Type], Car.
        Year, Customer. [Customer ID], Customer.
        [First Name], Customer. [Last Name], Car.
        Price
FROM    Customer INNER JOIN Car
ON      Customer. [Customer ID] = Car. [Customer
        ID];
```

Most often, typical database users will opt for a QBE tool instead of SQL because SQL is harder to learn.

Generating a Report

You use a ***report generator*** to create a report in a database environment. Typical report generators will allow you to specify what information you want in a report, the order in which it will appear (perhaps alphabetically or sorted by date), and various reporting options such as a title and subtotals. You can even use the results of a query to generate a report.

In Figure 10.11 on the opposite page we've provided a sample report that the employees at Retread Auto can generate. Once employees define a particular report that they find useful, they can save the format of the report under a special name (such as "Weekly Sales by Car Type"). At the end of each week, employees simply select that report and the report generator will include any information on sales that occurred for the week.

OTHER DBMS SUBSYSTEMS
What Else Can a DBMS Help Me Do?

The two remaining subsystems of a DBMS include the application generation subsystem and the data administration subsystem. In organizations of any size (especially those concerned with the security of database in-

did you know?

The *U.S. Census Bureau presents a dynamic POPClock on the Web that shows real time changes (by the second) for the populations of the United States and the world. It is viewable only in Netscape Communicator.*

acquires the target business's information. If a business ever "folds up" and ceases to exist, that business's information can be sold to pay off its creditors. Many organizations, such as the Electronic Frontier Foundation (www.eff.org), can help you with privacy concerns and questions. To learn more about privacy and security, complete the "Privacy Issues" and "Security Issues" tutorials on your SimNet Concepts Support CD.

making the grade

SECTION 10.4

1. A(n) __________ supports the access to, modification of, and presentation of information through a Web browser.
2. A(n) __________ database stores each Web address as an object linked to its respective Web page.
3. __________ is a software application that works between two or more different software applications and allows them to talk to each other.
4. A(n) __________ is a Web page for which you define the content you want to see.

10.5 DATA WAREHOUSES AND BUSINESS INTELLIGENCE

Such great tools for organizing and storing large volumes of information, databases and DBMSs support both OLTP and OLAP. ***Online transaction processing (OLTP)*** is the processing of information to support some sort of transaction such as the purchase of a product. ***Online analytical processing (OLAP)*** is the manipulation of information to generate business intelligence and support decision-making tasks. ***Business intelligence*** is knowledge about your customers, competitors, and internal operations that can help you make more informed and effective decisions.

With a DBMS you can work with only one database at a time, however. So, if you need business intelligence derived from information in multiple databases, you need a data warehouse and data-mining tools.

DATA WAREHOUSE FEATURES

How Does a Data Warehouse Differ from a Database?

A ***data warehouse*** is a collection of information from internal and/or external sources (mostly databases) organized specifically for generating business intelligence to support decision making. For example, a bank might be trying to segment its customer base in an effort to aim specific products and services at those customers most likely to buy them. The bank would have historic and current information on its customers in its own databases. It might buy information about outstanding debt and credit ratings from a credit bureau and information about competitors' products and services from a public database. Then the bank would bring all this information together into a data warehouse so that personnel could analyze the information to decide whom to target, how to price products and services, and how to market them.

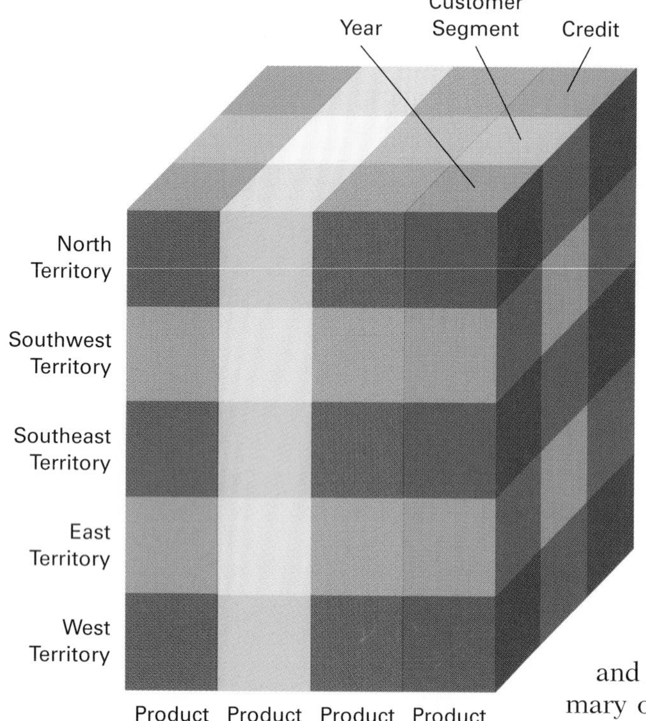

FIGURE 10.16

A data warehouse is multidimensional with layers of rows and columns.

Another company might want to bring together only internal database information. That company might want to combine sales and customer demographic information to derive various forms of business intelligence (see Figure 10.16).

A data warehouse is different from a database in that it is *multidimensional* with layers of columns and rows. This allows you to look at relationships within the information that are not easy to see in a two-dimensional structure. Consider the small yellow subcube in the top row, first layer, and second column of Figure 10.16. That subcube would contain sales by year (the layer) for the North territory (the row) for Product Line #2 (the column). As you view the data warehouse from different perspectives (called *turning the cube)*, you can view the information from its various perspectives.

Data warehouses, then, directly support OLAP and not OLTP. That is, each subcube contains a summary of information gathered from other sources. The data warehouse does not contain information in great detail but rather presents summaries that help you quickly see relationships and trends. Because the information is summarized, you cannot perform OLTP with a data warehouse.

DATA-MINING TOOLS
What Tools Do I Use to Manipulate a Data Warehouse?

Data mining is the process of extracting information from a data warehouse for decision-making purposes. It's the process of searching and exploring information electronically to discover new information and relationships. In a data warehouse environment we call the tools you use to perform data mining ***data-mining tools.*** They include query-and-reporting tools, multidimensional analysis tools, statistical tools, and data-mining agents (see Figure 10.17). To learn more, complete the "Data Mining" tutorial on your SimNet Concepts Support CD.

Query-and-Reporting Tools

Query-and-reporting tools for a data warehouse are similar to QBE tools, SQL, and report generators in the typical database environment. Most data warehousing environments support simple and easy-to-use data manipulation tools such as QBE, SQL, and report generators. Most often, data warehouse users use these tools to generate simple queries and reports.

FIGURE 10.17

Data-mining tools help you perform data mining in a data warehouse.

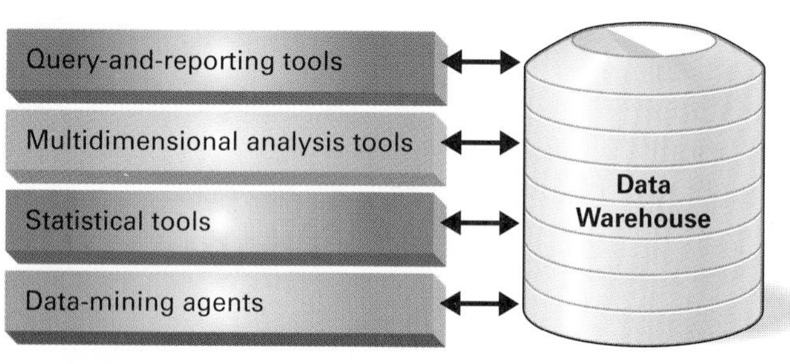

Multidimensional Analysis Tools

Multidimensional analysis (MDA) tools are slice-and-dice techniques that allow you to view multidimensional information from different perspectives. As you slice and dice your way through data warehouse information,

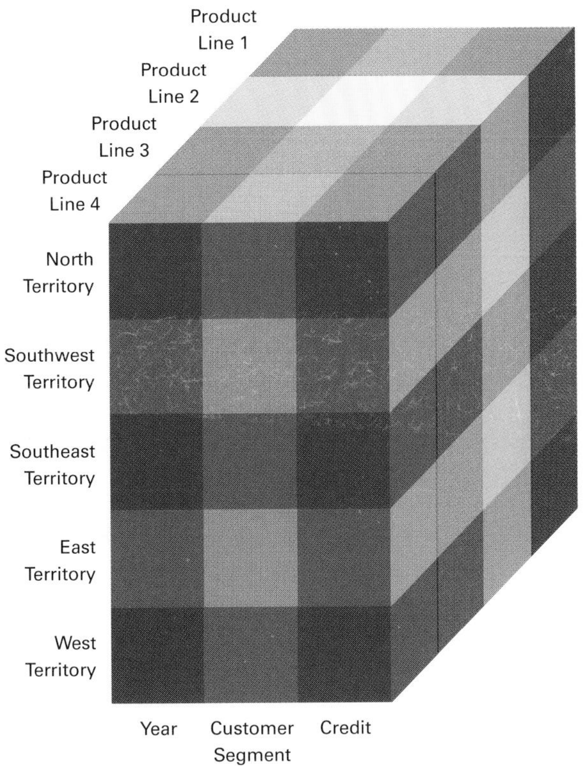

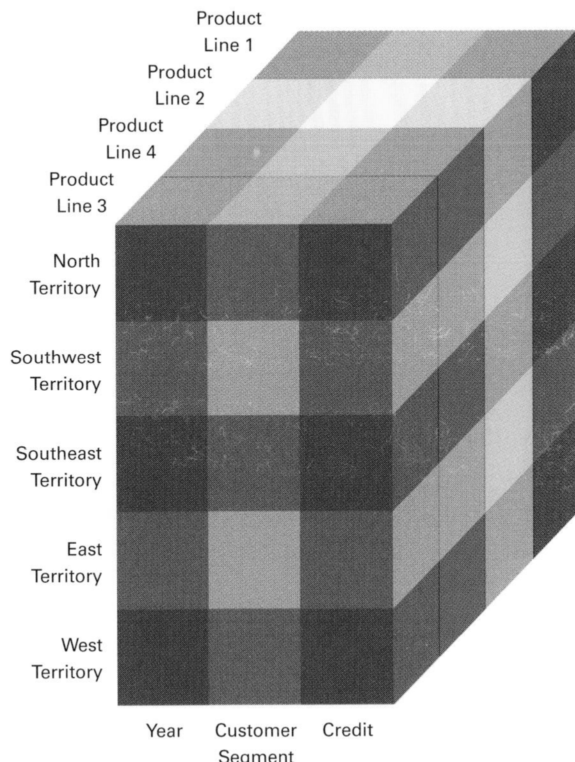

FIGURE 10.18

Multidimensional analysis (MDA) tools help you view information in a data warehouse from different perspectives.

you are in fact turning the cube. If you refer back to Figure 10.16, you could rotate the cube by 90 degrees to the left (clockwise on the horizontal axis).

The result is shown in Figure 10.18. As you can see the y-axis now contains information by year, customer segment, and credit. The x-axis still contains information by territory. And the z-axis (or depth axis) now contains information by product line. The ability to rotate the cube provides you with more perspectives on the information.

Likewise, you could use MDA tools to move layers to the front. For example, in the left data warehouse in Figure 10.18 the front layer is for Product Line #4. If you requested to see similar information for Product Line #3, your MDA tools would bring that layer to the front, moving the layer for Product Line #4 to the second layer (the right data warehouse in Figure 10.18).

Statistical Tools

Statistical tools help you apply various mathematical models to the information stored in a data warehouse to discover new information. For example, in the data warehouse in Figure 10.16 you could perform a time series analysis of sales by year across a given product line to see if a trend existed.

Data-Mining Agents

Data-mining agents help you discover new information, trends, and relationships within a data warehouse without necessarily applying a specific mathematical model. Data-mining agents are a subset of artificial intelligence. We'll talk more about data-mining agents and artificial intelligence in Chapter 15.

FIGURE 10.19

From a central data warehouse, an organization can create numerous data marts, each with a special focus.

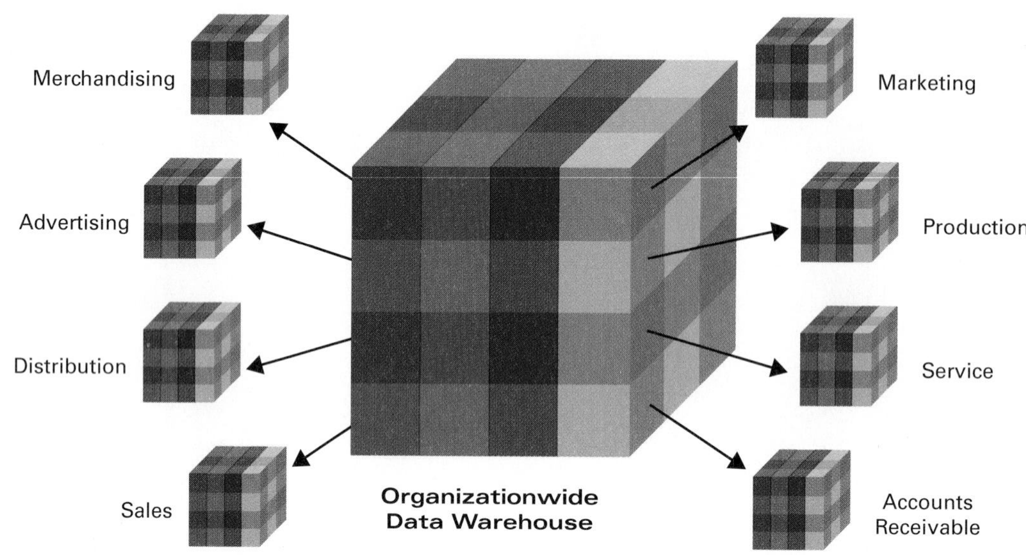

DATA MARTS

How Is a Data Mart Different from a Data Warehouse?

A ***data mart*** is a miniature data warehouse with a special focus. Most data warehouses are perceived as organizationwide, containing summaries of all the information that an organization tracks and uses. Not everyone in an organization needs a complete data warehouse, however. Production may need a data mart that doesn't contain information concerning advertising and marketing strategies. Conversely, the advertising department may need that information but not information concerning work-in-progress and shipping schedules (which production would need).

So, many organizations build numerous data marts that contain only the information that specific people, units, or departments may need (see Figure 10.19). As with a complete data warehouse, a person using a data mart still has the ability to use the entire data-mining tool set—multidimensional analysis tools, query-and-reporting tools, statistical tools, and data-mining agents.

SECTION 10.5

making the grade

1. ___________ is the processing of information to support some sort of transaction such as the purchase of a product.
2. A(n) ___________ is a collection of information from internal and/or external sources (mostly databases) organized specifically for generating business intelligence to support decision making.
3. ___________ is the process of extracting information from a data warehouse for decision-making purposes.
4. ___________ for a data warehouse are similar to QBE tools, SQL, and report generators in the typical database environment.
5. A(n) ___________ is a miniature data warehouse with a special focus.

10.6 SUMMARY AND KEY TERMS

It is the information age and all businesses (and people) are storing vast amounts of data and information. ***Data*** are distinct items providing descriptions of people, places, and/or things that may not have much meaning to you, depending on their context. ***Information*** is organized data whose meaning is clear and useful to you in a given context. The organization for data and information follows a typical hierarchy:

- ***Field***—smallest piece of data.
- ***Record***—group of logically related fields.
- ***Data file***—group of logically related records.
- ***Databas***e—a logical collection of files.
- ***Data warehouse***—a collection of information from internal and external sources (mostly databases).

The most popular method of storing information is to use the ***relational database model,*** which stores information in files or tables that have rows and columns. Important concepts within the relational database model include:

- ***Field property***—the type of information in a field (e.g., currency or date).
- ***Primary key***—a field in a database table that uniquely identifies a record in that table.
- ***Foreign key***—a primary key field of one database table that also appears in another database table.
- ***Integrity constraint***—a rule that helps ensure the quality of information in a database.

When you define the structure of a database, you create an ***entity-relationship diagram,*** a graphical representation of the tables in a database and the relationships among the tables. Types of database relationships include ***one-to-one, one-to-many,*** and ***many-to-many.***

A ***database management system (DBMS)*** is the application software that allows you to arrange, modify, and extract information from a database. A DBMS includes the following four subsystems:

1. ***Data definition subsystem***—helps you define the tables in a database and the relationships among them. You use this subsystem to create the ***data dictionary.***
2. ***Data manipulation subsystem***—helps you enter information into a database, query it to find information, and generate reports. Facilities within this subsystem include ***database forms, query-by-example (QBE) tools, SQL,*** and ***report generators.***
3. ***Application generation subsystem***—contains tools for generating transaction-intensive software.
4. ***Data administration subsystem***—contains tools for managing the overall database environment.

Databases play a very important role in electronic commerce as well as internal operations. Key e-commerce database topics include:

- ***Web database***—supports the access to, modification of, and presentation of information through a Web browser.
- ***Middleware***—software application that works between two or more different applications and allows them to talk to each other.

- ***Hypertext database***—stores each Web address as an object linked to its respective Web page.
- ***Personal portal***—Web page for which you define the content you want to see.

Data warehouses, the next step up from databases, are collections of information from internal and/or external sources (mostly databases) organized specifically for generating ***business intelligence*** to support decision making. Most data warehouses are perceived as organizationwide. If a particular department needs a smaller data warehouse, you would create a ***data mart,*** a miniature data warehouse with a special focus.

Data mining is the process of extracting information from a data warehouse for decision-making purposes. You perform data mining with four different ***data-mining tools:***

- ***Query-and-reporting tools***—similar to QBE tools, SQL, and report generators in the typical database environment.
- ***Multidimensional analysis (MDA) tools***—slice-and-dice techniques that allow you to view multidimensional information.
- ***Statistical tools***—help you apply various mathematical models to discover new information.
- ***Data-mining agents***—help you discover new information, trends, and relationships in a data warehouse without necessarily applying a specific mathematical model.

To learn more about databases, database management systems, data warehouses, data-mining tools, and your privacy visit the Web site for this text at www.mhhe.com/i-series.

KEY TERMS

application generation subsystem (p. 303)
business intelligence (p. 309)
compound primary key (p. 295)
data (p. 292)
data administration subsystem (p. 304)
data broker (p. 308)
data definition subsystem (p. 299)
data dictionary (p. 299)
data file (p. 293)
data manipulation subsystem (p. 300)
data mart (p. 312)
data mining (p. 310)
data-mining agent (p. 311)
data-mining tool (p. 310)
data warehouse (p. 293)
database (p. 293)
database administrator (DBA) (p. 303)
database form (p. 301)
database management system (DBMS) (p. 299)
entity-relationship (E-R) diagram (p. 296)
field (p. 293)
field property (p. 294)
foreign key (p. 295)
hierarchical database model (p. 297)
hypertext database (p. 306)
information (p. 293)
integrity constraint (p. 295)
many-to-many relationship (p. 297)
middleware (p. 305)
multidimensional analysis (MDA) tool (p. 310)
network database model (p. 297)
object-oriented database model (p. 297)
one-to-many relationship (p. 296)
one-to-one relationship (p. 296)
online analytical processing (OLAP) (p. 309)
online transaction processing (OLTP) (p. 309)
personal portal (p. 306)
primary key (p. 295)
query-and-reporting tool (p. 310)
query-by-example (QBE) tool (p. 302)
record (p. 293)
relational database model (p. 294)
report generator (p. 302)
statistical tool (p. 311)
Structured Query Language (SQL) (p. 302)
Web database (p. 305)

review of terminology

Multiple Choice

1. A group of logically related fields is called a
   a. record.
   b. data file.
   c. database.
   d. data warehouse.
   e. data mart.

2. A(n) ___________ is a field in a database table that uniquely identifies a record in that table.
   a. foreign key
   b. field property
   c. primary key
   d. secondary key
   e. unique key

3. Not allowing an hourly wage to be zero or negative is an example of a(n)
   a. foreign key.
   b. primary key.
   c. compound primary key.
   d. integrity constraint.
   e. file.

4. When one record in a database table can only be related to at most one record in another database table, the relationship is called a
   a. one-to-many relationship.
   b. one-to-one relationship.
   c. many-to-one relationship.
   d. many-to-many relationship.
   e. compound relationship.

5. To create a data dictionary, you use the
   a. application generation subsystem.
   b. data administration subsystem.
   c. data manipulation subsystem.
   d. data definition subsystem.
   e. data dictionary subsystem.

6. The data manipulation subsystem of a DBMS consists of
   a. database forms.
   b. QBE tools.
   c. SQL.
   d. report generators.
   e. all of the above.

7. To create a report in a database environment you use
   a. a QBE tool.
   b. SQL.
   c. a database form.
   d. a report generator.
   e. the data administration subsystem.

8. The manipulation of information to generate business intelligence and support decision-making tasks is called
   a. OLAP.
   b. OLTP.
   c. OLQP.
   d. OLBI.
   e. none of the above.

9. Business intelligence is knowledge about
   a. your customers.
   b. your competitors.
   c. your own internal operations.
   d. all of the above.
   e. only a and b above.

10. Data-mining tools that are slice-and-dice techniques allowing you to view multidimensional information from different perspectives are called
    a. data-mining agents.
    b. statistical tools.
    c. MDA tools.
    d. query-and-reporting tools.
    e. none of the above.

True/False

11. ____ A primary key is a foreign key field of one database table that also appears in another database table.

12. ____ DBMS software is application software that allows you to arrange, modify, and extract information from a data warehouse.

13. ____ A query-by-example (QBE) tool is a graphical version of SQL.

14. ____ Data brokers are companies that search many databases and return information to you.

15. ____ Statistical tools apply subjective reasoning to the information stored in a data warehouse to discover new information.

Take this quiz online at www.mhhe.com/i-series and get instant feedback.

QUESTIONS AND EXERCISES

1. Designing a Database

Building a solid entity-relationship diagram is a key to your success in implementing a database that you can then use to store, organize, and massage information. In short, you must correctly define primary keys, foreign keys, and relationships among the various database tables.

The dean of the business school at a private college in the Northeast has asked you to help in creating an entity-relationship diagram and defining primary keys, foreign keys, and relationships for a database that will track departments, instructors in each department, and what courses each instructor is qualified to teach. There will be three tables in this database application (given below). For each, include what you believe would be the primary key (there are no compound primary keys).

Table	Description	Primary Key
Department	An academic unit that teaches classes. A department example is Finance.	
Instructor	The people within each department responsible for delivering classes, advising students, and so on.	
Course	A topic of study delivered as a class in which students enroll.	

a. In the E-R diagram below you are to enter the table names in the rectangles. Then, draw a dotted line between the tables for which a relationship exists. Finally, you are to describe each relationship with some sort of verb just as we did in Figure 10.4 on page 296.

b. Once you've identified the relationships, your task is now to add the appropriate notations for describing the types of relationships (one-to-one, one-to-many, and many-to-many). As we did in Figure 10.5 on page 297, use a straight line (|) to represent a "one" and a crow's foot (<) to represent a "many."

c. Now you need to identify the minimum values for each of the relationships. As we did in Figure 10.6 on page 298, use a small circle to represent a "zero" minimum value and a straight line (|) to represent a "one" minimum value.

d. Because there are relationships in your E-R diagram, you must identify the necessary foreign keys. For each relationship you created (by drawing a dotted line to connect two tables), describe which primary key of a given table would be present in the other table as a foreign key and provide justification for your reasoning.

e. Finally, write a narrative description of
   - The relationships you identified in a above.
   - The types of relationships you identified in b above.
   - The minimum values you identified in c above.

2. Defining the Timeliness of Data Warehouse Information

When you create a data warehouse, you need to consider how often you must update the information within it. The information in most data warehouses is static, meaning that you must request when and how often a software utility should filter through the various databases and update the information in a data warehouse.

Some data warehouses may need to have their information updated only monthly (or perhaps even yearly). Others may need to be updated on a minute-by-minute basis. Below, we've provided several scenarios in which a data warehouse might be used. Your task is to determine for each scenario how often the data warehouse information must be updated. Limit your selections to: minute-by-minute, daily, weekly, and monthly. The descriptions of the scenarios are short, leaving you to consider many other facets. So, for each one provide some justification concerning your decision.

Scenario	Update How Often?	Why?
A data warehouse that helps determine how to allocate the printing of reports across several printers on a network based on demand.		
A data warehouse that helps your school determine how to adjust class sizes to meet enrollment requests by students.		
A data warehouse that sends real-time weather alerts to private citizens notifying them of significant changes in weather conditions.		
A data warehouse that helps betting organizations in Las Vegas predict the scores of professional football games.		
A data warehouse that helps a business adjust the timing of its radio advertisements in light of demographic changes.		
A data warehouse that helps product planners monitor the success of a new product line in the clothing retail industry.		
A data warehouse that helps a kitchen manager adjust production levels of food in a school cafeteria.		
A data warehouse that helps a bank adjust rate offerings on its CDs (certificates of deposit).		
A data warehouse that helps an auto parts store determine the forecasted demand for various types of tires.		
A data warehouse that helps a video store manager determine how many copies of a new video to buy.		
A data warehouse that helps the IRS determine how many audit workers to have on staff as "tax season" approaches.		

e-commerce

1. Obtaining a Free Credit Report

Different databases contain a variety of different information. One type of database on the Web that might interest you is a database that contains your credit report. Up until a couple of years ago, you had to pay a Web site to provide you with a credit report. Not anymore—now you can obtain a free credit report from numerous sites. Below we've listed several such sites.

- Freecreditreport.com—www.freecreditreport.com
- CreditExpert—www.creditexpert.com
- FreeCreditProfile—www.freecreditprofile.com
- Free Credit Report—www.reports-credit-free.com

Visit a couple of the sites and answer the following questions for each.

a. Can you really get a credit report for free?
b. Are there any strings attached?
c. What sort of information do you have to provide (such as your social security number)?
d. How do you receive your credit report? Online? Via e-mail? Other?

How easy do you think it is for someone to impersonate you at one of these sites and obtain your credit report fraudulently? Is there anything you can do to ensure that this doesn't happen?

2. Getting Tutored on the Web

It only makes sense—you can find just about any information you want on the Web, especially for helping you with class work—so, why not be able to get online tutoring assistance? You can. Many Web sites provide online assistance, while others will help you find tutors in your area. Below are four tutor-oriented sites.

- Elance Online—www.elance.com/c/cats/main/categories.pl?mid=PO3I&rid=POD5
- Computer Science Tutoring by E-mail—www.cstutoring.com
- TutorNation.com—www.tutornation.com
- Tutor.com—www.tutor.com

As you visit each site, answer the following questions:

a. Does the site provide online tutoring?
b. Will the site help you find a tutor in your area?
c. What are the costs of tutoring or matching services?
d. How do you pay for services?
e. For what topics can you find tutoring assistance?
f. What sort of credentials does the site offer?

Let's think about this for a moment. Tutoring is a very individualized activity that usually requires a lot of one-on-one interaction. Do you think you can receive the same level of quality over the Web? Why or why not?

3. Using Interlibrary Loan

You've spent hours doing research for your paper. After searching databases, you have a list of books and articles that will help. You trudge off to the library and begin your search.

But you can find only some of the books and magazines that you need. Instead of giving up, try interlibrary loan. Interlibrary loan is a service that lets member universities share books and articles with each other. Here are a few:

- Library of Congress—www.loc.gov/rr/loan
- OhioLink (all Ohio universities)—olc1.ohiolink.edu
- Penn State University—www.libraries.psu.edu/iasweb/ill/illmain.htm
- Western Michigan University—www.wmich.edu/library/interlib-loan.html

After looking at these Web sites, go to your school's library Web site and look for information on interlibrary loans. Answer the following questions:

a. What are your library's policies on requesting books? Do they differ from those of the Web sites listed above?
b. What are your library's policies on requesting articles? Do they differ from those of the Web sites listed above?
c. How long will it take you to get a book? An article?

ethics, security & privacy

1. How Secure Is Your Personal Information?

Databases are an important part of e-commerce. Without them, businesses wouldn't be able to have interactive Web catalogs or process your credit card payment. Businesses couldn't keep their inventories stocked or tell you about items that might interest you.

Yet all this convenience comes with a price. It's the risk of people breaking into e-commerce Web sites. Crackers attack regularly. Most attempts fail, but some don't. Consider these questions that relate to database security:

a. Would you work with or provide information to a business that a cracker had broken into? What if the business demonstrated it had improved its security after the break-in?
b. Who should be responsible for protecting data? Many businesses assume the software they use can withstand an attack. They blame the software developers when a cracker finds a vulnerability.
c. Software developers blame businesses that don't monitor their daily "bug reports" on software systems. Bug reports discuss vulnerabilities and offer solutions. Should businesses be responsible for keeping their software current? Or should software developers notify businesses? Who should keep the system updated?

Many Web sites and organizations also inform people about software vulnerabilities and the latest cracks into e-commerce systems. Should you be responsible for monitoring the latest problems with database security?

2. CRUD—Defining Who Can Do What with Database Information

In the technology world, we use the acronym *CRUD* to specify who can access and use various pieces of information in a database. CRUD stands for **Create, Read, Update,** and **Delete.**

Consider the issue of your information at your school. Who should be able to change (update) your major? Who should be able to view (read) your address? Who should be able to drop (delete) you from a class in which you're currently enrolled? These are important questions to ask and important questions to answer.

In the left column of the table below are specific pieces of information about you. In the columns to the right are different groups of people at your school (including you). Your task is to complete the interior part of the table by placing a C, R, U, and/or D in the appropriate cells. Some cells may have multiple letters. After you complete this task discuss with your classmates whether and how your answers differ.

	You	Other Students	Your Instructor	Your Advisor	Registrar's Office	Financial Aid
Name						
Phone number						
E-mail address						
Declared major						
GPA						
Family income						
Parking violations						
Books you've checked out from the library						
Classes you're taking						
Grades in completed classes						

on the web

1. Using Webopedia to Learn More about Technology

Webopedia (www.webopedia.com) is a Web-based database about technology. It includes a powerful search feature that allows you to learn more about technology by exploring various topics and reading definitions. Connect to Webopedia, perform searches on the following terms, and read their definitions and descriptions:

- Database
- DBMS
- SQL
- QBE
- Hypertext database

How different are Webopedia's definitions and descriptions from the ones we provided in this text? Did any of Webopedia's definitions help you better learn about a particular term? If so, which term and why? How would you rate your overall experience in using Webopedia? Do you think it's a good resource from which to learn about technology terms? Why or why not?

2. Researching Data Warehouses and Data-Mining Tools

Data warehouses and data-mining tools are among the newer technologies that businesses have recently embraced. As businesses strive to provide more customized and tailored products and services, it's vitally important to create good business intelligence on which to base decisions. There are a number of data warehousing and data-mining tools available to businesses. Below, we've listed a few.

- BusinessObjects—www.businessobjects.com
- SAS—www.sas.com
- Cognos—www.cognos.com
- Informatica—www.informatica.com
- Brio—www.brio.com

Using the Web, you are to do some research on each of these products and prepare a short report for the class concerning the major focus of each tool. For example, SAS provides great statistical tools for use in a data warehouse environment.

3. Finding a DBMS for Your PDA

Today, you can also get a DBMS for your PDA. These are obviously much different from personal and organizational DBMSs that provide great functionality and capability. PDA DBMSs include:

- abcDB Database (www.pocketsoft.com)
- Data On The Run (www.biohazardsoftware.com)
- FileMaker Mobile (www.filemaker.com)
- HanDBase Professional (www.handbase.com)
- MobileDB (www.mobiledb.com)
- SmartList To Go (www.thinkdb.com)

Do some Web research on these PDA DBMS tools. Which seems to be the leader? Do any of these allow you to "sync" information with a personal DBMS such as Microsoft Access? Do any of them list a maximum number of records you can store in a database?

4. Researching Database Security

Protecting data is an ongoing challenge for many DBAs. Most businesses use specific software and techniques to protect valuable information from competitors, hackers, and others who could benefit from the stolen information. Search the Web for three sites that discuss the importance of database security. Share the Web sites with the class. Also, list five steps you can take to check for database security on the Web. Finally, search a popular job database Web site such as Monster.com for DBA openings. Read through a few of the job descriptions. How many did you find that emphasize database security as a necessary qualification?

5. Finding a Free DBMS

Many people use Microsoft Access because it's included in their Microsoft Office software. But what if you don't have Access? Are there other DBMSs you can use? Are they free (or available at a low cost)? Search the Web and find at least three free DBMSs. Explain to the class what types of DBMSs you found. Would you use any of them? Why or why not?

group activities

1. Evaluating Popular Personal DBMSs

We believe the ability to use a personal DBMS is becoming more essential everyday in finding a good job. All businesses want you to possess expertise in word processing, spreadsheet, and presentation software. Many more are now beginning to place a high priority on your ability to use a personal DBMS. Below are seven well-known personal DBMSs.

- Alpha Five
- askSam Professional
- FileMaker Pro
- Microsoft Access
- MyDatabase
- Paradox
- QuickBase

Your group's task is twofold. First, research these DBMSs and create a comparative report of their features. As you do, include the following as minimum considerations and issues:

- The latest version number
- Security features
- Support for SQL
- Export information to HTML format
- Support for mail merge
- Support for creating relationships among tables
- Report wizard support
- Form wizard support

Second, perform seven different searches on Monster.com for job openings that include these personal DBMSs in their descriptions. Build a table that compares how many companies are seeking individuals who know these tools. Along with your table include a recommendation concerning which personal DBMS tool you think students should learn.

2. Digging for Databases

Compile a list of databases that people use on your campus. Ask your friends if they use any databases. Go to computer labs and see what databases are on computers. Ask professors if they use any databases in their research. Search the library's Web site for reference databases or ask a reference librarian what databases are available. For each database note its name, purpose, and location. What did you find about the number of databases on campus? Present your findings to the class.

3. Defining the Structure of a Data Warehouse

Data warehouses can contain many different dimensions of information. In the data warehouse in Figure 10.16 on page 310 there are five dimensions of information—territory, product line, year, customer segment, and credit. On the Web site that supports this text (www.mhhe.com/i-series, select **Chapter 10** and then **Project Data Files**), we've provided a spreadsheet of housing information. The name of that file is **Housing.xls.** You'll need to download that file and use it for this exercise.

The file contains a variety of information on new houses being built in the Detroit area. You are to perform the following:

a. Define which dimensions of information would be important to a real estate agent trying to determine which type of houses to sell.
b. Define which dimensions of information would be important to a new housing developer trying to determine which type of houses to build.
c. Define which dimensions of information would be important to a bank trying to determine how to create loan packages for people buying those homes.

You are not limited to just the dimensions of information presented in the spreadsheet. If you feel you need additional information to complete the tasks above, specify what those dimensions would be and from where you would have to obtain that information.

crossword puzzle

Across

1. Chip in your body
4. First step in ASR
6. Type of technology that uses living tissue
7. ______ home appliance
10. Computer that may be a piece of clothing
11. Automatic speech ______
13. Your breath, for example
14. Third step in #11 across
15. 3-D simulation
16. Technology at the atomic level
20. #1 across that assumes physiological functions
21. VR device for your feet

Down

2. Second step in #11 across
3. System of low-orbiting satellites
5. CPUs that work in more than binary
8. Also called digital cash
9. VR device that covers your field of vision
12. Storage device that uses 3-D technology
17. Service provider of application software
18. 3-D room
19. VR device for your hand

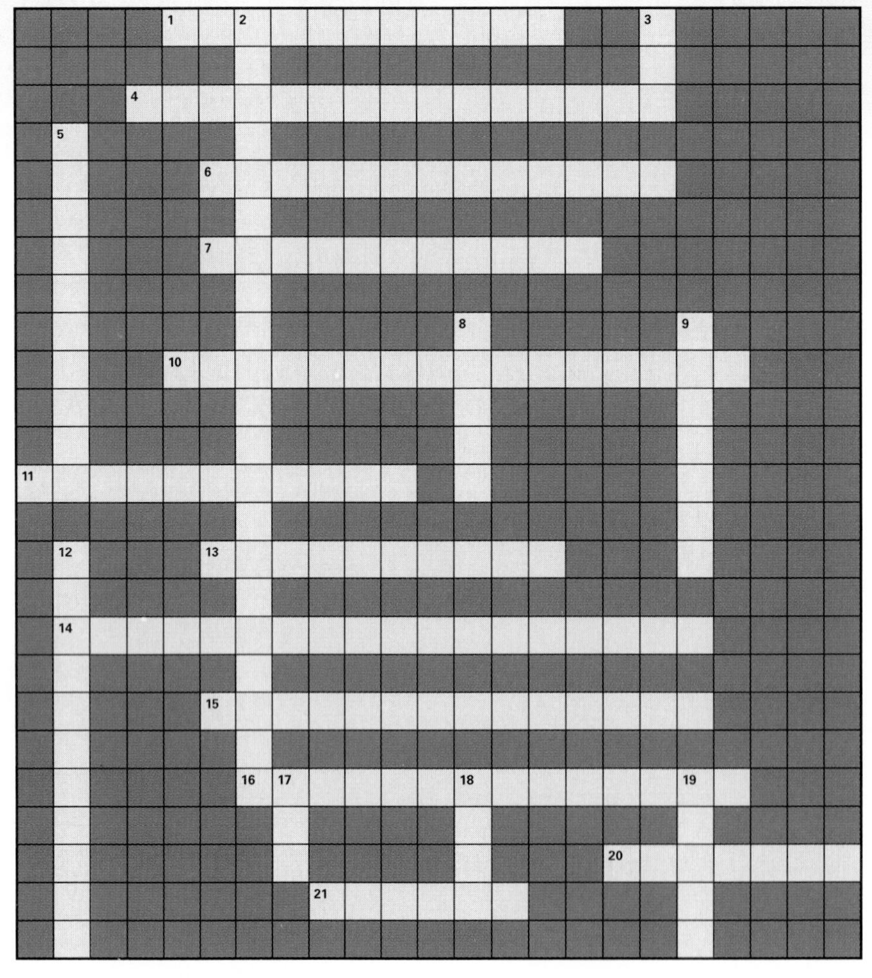

CHAPTER eleven 11

Emerging Technologies

Can You See Them Coming?

SIMNET CONCEPTS SUPPORT

- Virtual Reality and Artificial Intelligence (p. 328)

did you know?

Technology is changing at a phenomenal pace on a daily basis and so is how we incorporate it into our lives. Not long ago, only one in every three homes in the United States had a computer. Today, one in every three homes in the United States boasts at least two computers, many with networks. But not only is the extent to which we use technology increasing—so is the number of new emerging technologies on the horizon.

the *U.S. Government spends more than $600 million annually on nanotechnology research.*[1]

inphase, *a Colorado-based company, is working on a holographic storage device (much smaller than a DVD) that will hold up to 20 movies.*[2]

the *Labor Coach is special contraction software that you can install on a PDA that monitors the contractions of an expectant mother.*[3]

because *of the widespread use of electronic forms of payment (e.g., online bill paying), retail payments by "writing a check" dropped from 85 percent in 1979 to __??__ percent in 2000.*[4]

To find out what percentage of retail payments were still in "written" form in 2000, visit www.mhhe.com/i-series.

Student Learning Outcomes

After reading this chapter, you should be able to:

1. Describe how automatic speech recognition, virtual reality, biometrics, and thought-control user interfaces will change how you interact with technology.
2. Define multi-state CPUs and holographic storage devices and identify the changes they will bring about in technology.
3. Describe how e-cash will work on the Internet and discuss the challenges to making e-cash a common reality.
4. Describe emerging technologies and uses of technology on the Internet including renting software from ASPs, personalization through push technologies, and the Internet-enabled home.
5. Discuss the potential benefits and drawbacks of cutting-edge technologies such as CAVEs, membrane-based technologies, nanotechnologies, biochips, and implant chips.

As we all know, technology is changing every day. New versions of software become available, prices drop for hardware, and that same hardware becomes smaller, faster, and better. But such changes in existing technology are just the tip of the iceberg. In this chapter we survey some new and emerging technologies (several truly are cutting-edge) and look at how those technological innovations will change your life (see Figure 11.1).

On the horizon, there are emerging technologies (and innovative uses of technology) that will dramatically change how you interact with your computer and forever change how you live your life. For the most part, these new technologies and the changes they will bring are inescapable.

For even more information on new technologies that are emerging every day, visit *Life-Long Learning Module D,* "New Technologies Impacting Your Life," and *Life-Long Learning Module E,* "Computers in Your Life Tomorrow."

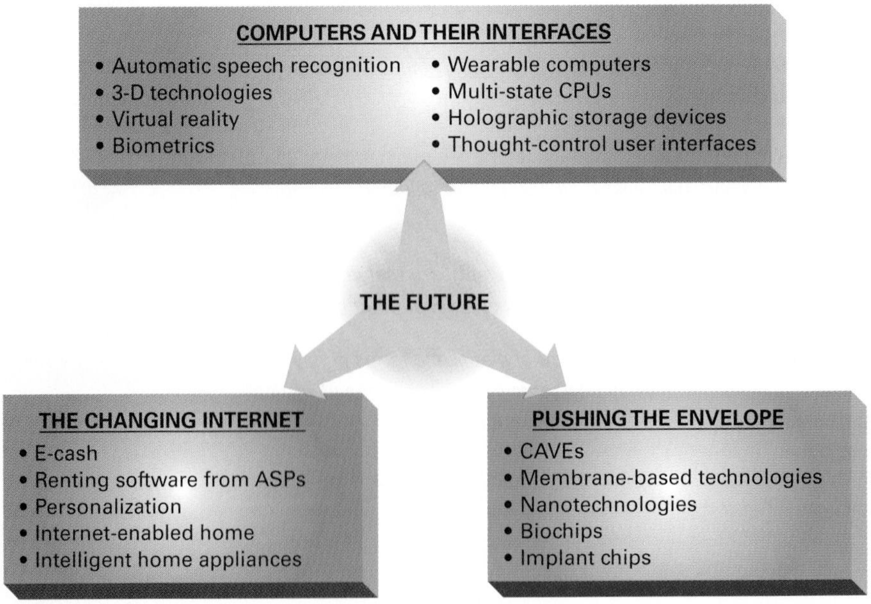

FIGURE 11.1

Emerging technologies such as biometrics and implant chips will dramatically change your life.

COMPUTERS AND THEIR INTERFACES
- Automatic speech recognition
- 3-D technologies
- Virtual reality
- Biometrics
- Wearable computers
- Multi-state CPUs
- Holographic storage devices
- Thought-control user interfaces

THE FUTURE

THE CHANGING INTERNET
- E-cash
- Renting software from ASPs
- Personalization
- Internet-enabled home
- Intelligent home appliances

PUSHING THE ENVELOPE
- CAVEs
- Membrane-based technologies
- Nanotechnologies
- Biochips
- Implant chips

11.1 COMPUTERS AND THEIR INTERFACES

Some of the most visible emerging technologies are those that (1) fundamentally change the technology itself or (2) change the way you interface or interact with your computer. Right now, you carry around relatively small and lightweight notebook computers, tablet PCs, and PDAs. And you use seemingly productive input and output devices such as mice, styluses, keyboards, and the like. In the future, expect all that to change with the emergence or increased quality of automatic speech recognition, 3-D technologies, biometrics, wearable computers, multi-state CPUs, holographic storage devices, and thought-control user interfaces.

AUTOMATIC SPEECH RECOGNITION
When Will I Talk to My Computer?

In the movies at least, for many years now, people have been carrying on conversations with their computers. To a certain extent, you can expect that to become an everyday reality in your lifetime. (But no, your computer won't try to take over.) Automatic speech recognition is the emerging technology that will help you talk to your computer.

An ***automatic speech recognition (ASR)*** system captures your speech and can distinguish your words and word groupings to form sentences. ASR systems include many IT components such as a microphone (an input device), a sound card (another piece of hardware), software to distinguish your words, and databases that contain words and language rules. An ASR system uses these components to process your speech in three steps (see Figure 11.2).

- **Step 1 Feature Analysis—*Feature analysis*** in ASR captures your words as you speak, converting the digital signals of your speech into phonemes. A *phoneme* is the smallest unit of speech, essentially a syllable. In Figure 11.2, you can see that the ASR system captured the word "Do" and converted it into the phoneme "dü." The phonemes are then passed to step 2.

FIGURE 11.2

Automatic speech recognition (ASR) is a three-step process.

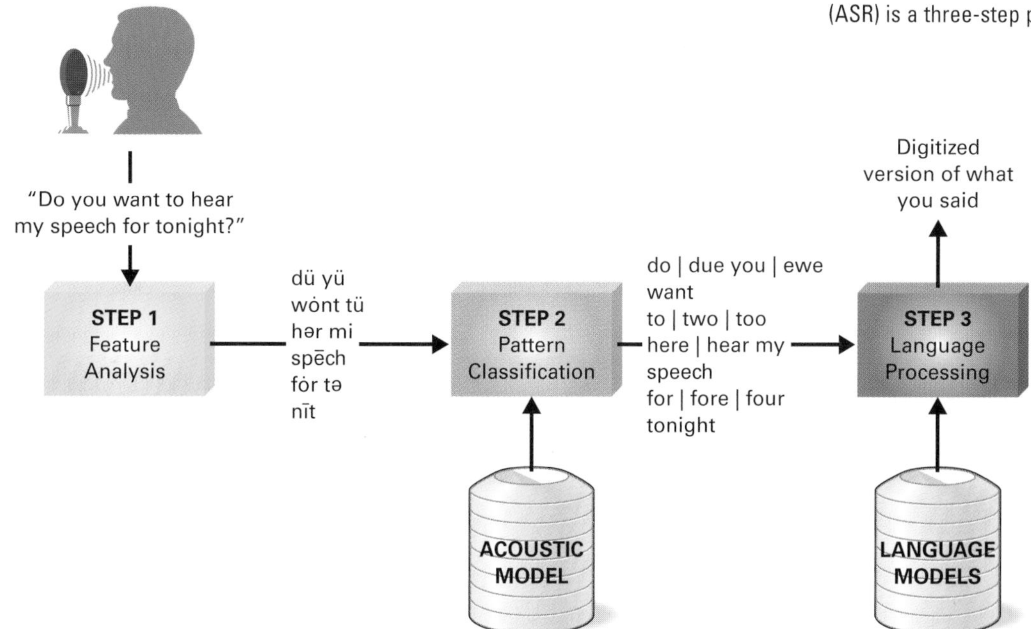

- **Step 2 Pattern Classification—*Pattern classification*** in ASR attempts to recognize your spoken phonemes by locating a matching phoneme (or phoneme sequence) among words stored in an acoustic model database. An acoustic model database is your ASR system's vocabulary. For the phoneme "dü," pattern classification may find multiple words such as "do" and "due." Whatever the case, it sends all possible matching phonemes to step 3.
- **Step 3 Language Processing—*Language processing*** in ASR attempts to make sense of what you're saying by comparing the possible word phonemes to rules in a language model database. Your language model database includes grammar rules, task-specific words, and sentences you might frequently use. As an example, in Figure 11.2 you're asking a question. So, your language model database would determine that your first spoken word is "do" and not "due."

Language processing is the key step. When you listen to someone, you can easily determine which words they're using within the context of your conversation. That's difficult for a computer. Consider the sentence, "Fruit flies like a banana." What does that mean? Well, in the gardening Olympics (if there is such a thing), that statement implies that if you were to toss a piece of fruit in the air, it would "fly" in the same way a banana would. More realistically, though, it means that a winged insect called a fruit fly is particularly fond of the taste of a banana.

Automatic Speech Recognition Today and Tomorrow

ASR is already all around you. Most telephone service providers use ASR when you call information to obtain a phone number. Most cell phones today include some sort of ASR so you can speak a person's name instead of entering a phone number. Many of today's new intelligent home appliances (which we'll discuss later) have some ASR. So, all you have to say is "cold water, delicate rinse, no fabric softener," and your washing machine sets itself appropriately.

The latest release of Microsoft Office (Office 2003) has greatly integrated ASR into almost all of its applications. You can install and train the Office 2003 ASR system in about 15 minutes. You can also buy many commercially available and good ASR systems for around $100 (see Figure 11.3). ASR systems are just one of the many emerging technologies that will change how we interact with technology. Just think of the possibilities of how you can interact with a computer if you don't have to use a clunky mouse and keyboard. You can read more about ASR systems on the Web site that supports this text at www.mhhe.com/i-series.

FIGURE 11.3

There are numerous good commercially available ASR systems.

ASR System	Publisher	Web Site
ViaVoice	IBM	www-3.ibm.com/software/speech/
Dragon NaturallySpeaking	ScanSoft	www.scansoft.com/naturallyspeaking/
SpeechMagic	Philips	www.speech.philips.com/

3-D TECHNOLOGIES
Will My Computer Show Me Things in "Real Life"?

Throughout this text—especially in Chapters 3 and 8—we've discussed three-dimensional technologies and VRML (Virtual Reality Modeling Language). These technologies help give you the illusion that you're participating in a true three-dimensional world through your computer.

Formally defined, ***three-dimensional (3-D) technologies*** present information to you in such a way that you have the illusion that the object you're viewing is actually in the room with you. You can see the depth of the image, turn it to reflect different angles and perspectives, and in some way understand the density of the object. We introduced you to the concepts of 3-D technologies and what it takes to create 3-D graphics in Chapter 3. For a list of Web sites with 3-D presentations of information, visit the Web site for this text at www.mhhe.com/i-series. And don't forget that you may have to download and install a plug-in or player to view the 3-D presentations on many of those sites.

What's the emerging technology that takes advantage of 3-D technologies? It's virtual reality (and a few others we'll talk about later).

Virtual Reality

Virtual reality (VR) is a three-dimensional computer simulation in which you actively and physically participate using special input and output devices such as gloves, headsets, and walkers. We refer to these types of devices as *immersion 3-D technologies* (see Figure 11.4).

A ***glove*** is an input device that captures the movements of your hand and fingers. A ***headset*** (also called a ***head-mounted display*** or ***HMD***) is a combined input and output device that (1) captures the movement of your head from side to side and up and down and (2) includes a special screen that covers your entire field of vision. A ***walker*** captures the movement of your feet and body as you walk or turn in different directions. Some walkers can adjust their tension making it harder for you to walk depending on the situation. So, if you were in a VR game and walking through a swamp, the resistance of the walker would increase.

FIGURE 11.4

Virtual reality makes use of special input and output devices such as gloves, headsets, and walkers.

Virtual reality applications are very popular in games such as flying an airplane, skiing snowy slopes, and even playing golf. The business world uses virtual reality for a variety of purposes. Volvo, for example, lets you virtually experience a car wreck to learn how air bags work. Many airlines use virtual reality to train pilots how to react to mechanical failures and adverse weather conditions.

There are some drawbacks to virtual reality. After participating in virtual reality, many people experience simulator sickness, eye strain, and a form of déjà vu. In the latter, some people experience *VR flashbacks* several hours later which often cause a temporary disassociation with "real" reality. In spite of those shortcomings, we believe virtual reality is an emerging technology destined to take its place in your future.

practically speaking

The Best Applications of Virtual Reality

Imagine a world in which the color blue feels like sandpaper, a world in which the only furniture you can sit on must be green, or a world in which a pin dropping on the floor sounds like the cracking of thunder. That's the real world for a person with autism. Autism is a disease that interferes with the development of the part of the brain that processes sensory perceptions. Some autistic people do indeed feel things (sandpaper grinding across the skin) when they see colors.

For autistic people, the world is a mishmash of objects that make no sense to them when they have to deal with them all at once. For example, if you place two differently colored chairs in front of an autistic person and tell him or her that they are both chairs, that person may become confused and disoriented.

A simple world is the best world for individuals suffering from autism. But our world is not simple. Many researchers are using virtual reality to teach autistic people to deal with everyday life.

In a virtual reality simulation, researchers can eliminate all forms of background noise, colors, and objects, except those that they want the autistic person to focus on. As the autistic person becomes comfortable with a simple virtual reality simulation, new objects or colors can be introduced without the usual adverse side effects. This allows the autistic person to gradually move from dealing with a simple environment to an environment that includes many objects and colors.

Virtual reality is indeed an emerging and cutting-edge technology, and will dramatically change the way we live our lives and interact with technology. When most people think of virtual reality, they think of games and fun, such as experiencing a roller-coaster ride while sitting in a recliner chair. And there'll be much money made with those types of virtual reality applications.

But the best uses of virtual reality won't necessarily be for fun or make anyone rich. Instead, they'll help people cope with everyday life. That's true for all the new technologies—it's a multibillion-dollar industry, but perhaps we would all do better to let the money take care of itself, and think more about how technology can aid people in everyday life.

There are career opportunities for you within the realm of 3-D technologies. We have noticed a consistent and marked increase in the number of job openings for people skilled in the development of virtual reality and VRML applications. If you like building virtual worlds, consider learning virtual reality and VRML. To learn more about virtual reality, complete the "Virtual Reality and Artificial Intelligence" tutorial on your SimNet Concepts Support CD.

BIOMETRICS
Will We Ever Get Rid of Passwords?

Today, the standard security mechanism is a password. You have to remember it, and you need to change it frequently. But that will soon change with the emerging technology of biometrics. ***Biometrics*** is the use of physical characteristics—such as your fingerprint, the blood vessels in the retina of your eye, or perhaps the sound of your voice—to provide identification. Already, biometrics is widely used in high-security environments such as military installations.

The concept is quite simple. You can copy someone's password, but you can't copy a fingerprint or iris scan. Many banks are currently converting ATMs to the use of biometrics, specifically, an iris scan. When you open an account and request ATM use, the bank doesn't issue you an ATM card. Instead, your iris is scanned and a copy of it captured. To use an ATM, you allow the machine to scan your iris and it matches you to your account. You can then perform whatever transaction you wish.

There are also biometric devices that you can attach to your computer—you have to provide your fingerprint for scanning and verification before your computer will turn on (see Figure 11.5).

Biometrics is moving way beyond use just for identification. Consider these real-world applications in place today (see Figure 11.6):

FIGURE 11.5

Some keyboards come equipped with biometric scanning devices for fingerprint identification. Other fingerprint ID devices can be plugged directly into your computer.

- **Internet-enabled toilets—**these toilets use your physiological output to capture readings (e.g., white-cell count, red-cell count, sodium level, and sugar level) and send that information via the Internet to your doctor's computer. Your doctor's computer can then analyze that information to determine if you're getting sick.
- **Custom shoes—**several shoe stores, especially those that offer fine Italian leather shoes, no longer carry any inventory. When you select a shoe style you like, you place your bare feet into a box that scans the shape of your feet. That information is then used to make a custom pair of shoes for you. It works extremely well if your feet are slightly different from each other in size or shape (as is the case with most people).
- **Custom wedding gowns—**following the custom-fit shoe idea, many bridal boutiques now do the same thing for wedding dresses. Once the bride chooses the style she likes, she steps into a small room that scans her entire body. That information is used to create a wedding dress that fits perfectly.
- **Custom bathrobes—**some high-end spa resorts now actually have patrons walk through a body-scanning device upon check-in. The scanning device measures the patron's body characteristics and

FIGURE 11.6

Shoes, wedding dresses, and bathrobes are just a few of the many clothing products that can be custom-made with the help of biometrics.

then sends that information to a sewing and fabricating facility that automatically creates a custom-fit bathrobe.

Biometrics promises to forever change how we live our lives. Consider the use of Internet-enabled toilets. From a good perspective, your doctor can diagnose early symptoms of an illness. From another perspective, your employer or school could use Internet-enabled toilets to check for drug and alcohol use. Is this an invasion of your privacy? What if you use an Internet-enabled toilet in your home to ensure that the caretaker of your children isn't using drugs or alcohol? Is that an invasion of your caretaker's privacy? Do you have the right to check your children's caretaker for drug and alcohol use?

WEARABLE COMPUTERS
How Portable Will Technology Become?

Although some technology today is considered very small and portable, it will become even more so in the future, to the extent that you may someday "wear" your computer. A ***wearable computer*** is a fully equipped computer that you wear as a piece of clothing or attached to a piece of clothing similar to the way you would carry around your cell phone on your belt.

In reality, wearable computers are not some far-fetched cutting-edge technology that will take years to arrive. Today, Charmed Technologies and Xybernaut® (just to name a few) are already manufacturing and selling wearable computers (see Figure 11.7). The leader in this area is Xybernaut (www.xybernaut.com) with its line of poma® wearable computers. The poma includes an optical mouse, one-inch square screen that covers one of your eyes, 128MHz processor, 32MB of RAM, Compact Flash slot, USB port, and support for the addition of micro drives and wireless modem cards.

FIGURE 11.7

As technology becomes increasingly smaller, expect to wear your computer.

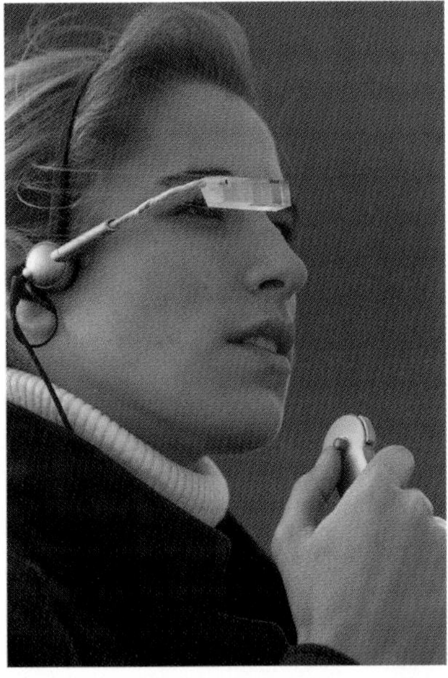

Some wearable computers don't even look like computers.

Charmed Technology wants you to wear your CPU on your belt.

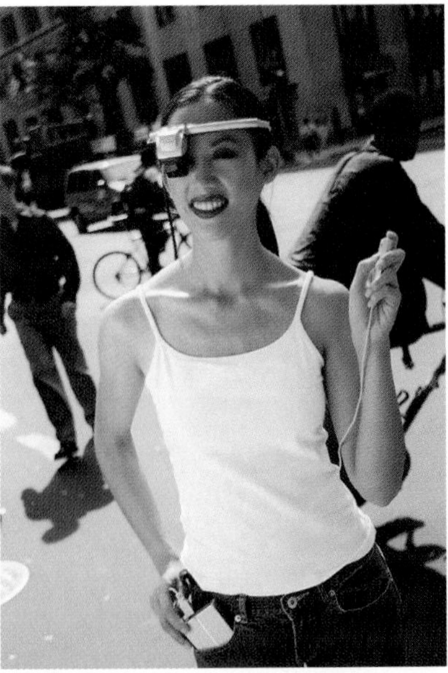

Xybernaut's wearable poma clips onto your belt and includes a small screen that covers one of your eyes.

With the increased use of wearable computers, society must address a number of issues. For example, you're probably familiar with pending legislation that would make it against the law to use a cell phone while driving a car. If passed, will that legislation need to be eventually modified to include wearable computers? After all, poma's wearable computer does include a screen that covers one of your eyes.

What happens when technology advances to the point that regular reading glasses can accept and display wireless communications from a wearable computer? Could regular reading glasses become a display device such that someone could cheat on an exam by having someone else send e-mail messages through a wearable computer to the reading glasses? These are the types of issues you'll deal with in your lifetime.

CPUs AND STORAGE DEVICES

What Hardware-Specific Changes Can I Expect to See?

Daily, scientists and researchers are working on ways to make hardware devices such as CPUs and storage devices faster, smaller, and more efficient. In this area, you can expect to someday see multi-state CPUs and holographic storage devices.

Multi-State CPUs

Right now, CPUs are binary-state, capable of working only with information represented by a 1 or a 0. That greatly slows processing. What we really need to increase speed are CPUs that are multi-state. ***Multi-state CPUs*** work with information represented in more than just two states, probably ten states with each state representing a digit between 0 and 9. When multi-state CPUs do become a reality, your computer will no longer have to go through many of the processes associated with translating characters into binary and then reversing the translation process later. This will make them much faster. Of course, the true goal is to create multi-state CPUs that can also handle letters and special characters without converting them to their binary equivalents.

Holographic Storage Devices

Right now, storage devices store information on two-dimensional surfaces, but research in the holographic realm will change that, and ***holographic storage devices*** will store information on a storage medium that is composed of 3-D crystal-like objects with many sides or faces (see Figure 11.8). On each face, information can be stored. This is similar in concept to small cards that you may have seen which change the picture or image as you view the cards from different angles. Technically, a different

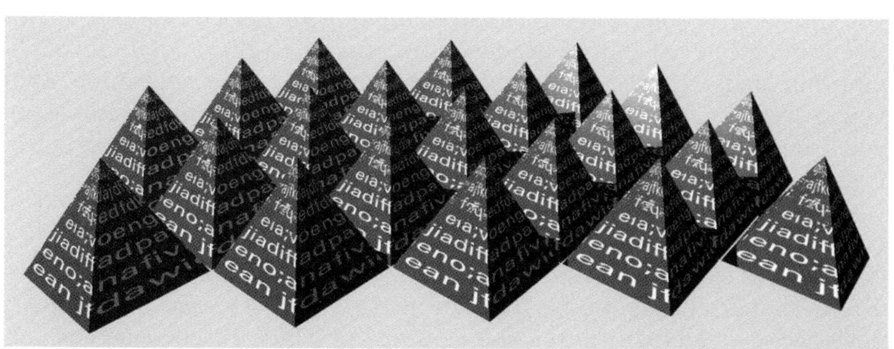

FIGURE 11.8

Holographic storage devices will store information using 3-D crystal-like objects as the storage media.

i•can

Distinguish between Technology Advances and Their Impacts

You might be asking which emerging technology you should primarily be focusing on. The answer is none of them. Rather, we believe you should focus on the real and potential impacts of all types of emerging technologies.

For example, just think how many sight- and movement-challenged people will be able to effectively use technology because of speech recognition and speech synthesization. (Speech synthesization produces voice output from text.) Think how much richer and more meaningful your education will be in subjects such as Greek and Roman cultures, forestry management, and various foreign languages if you can virtually experience places and events through virtual reality.

And think about biometrics and thought-control user interfaces. How will your life change when those two emerging technologies become a reality? What happens when thought-controlled user interfaces become wireless and you don't even have to wear a sensing device on one of your fingers? Will you someday be able to turn on your TV and change the channels just by *thinking* commands? Will that mean control of the TV is no longer determined by who has possession of the remote control?

We do believe you should keep an eye open toward what new technologies are emerging. You should then focus on how those technologies can and will impact your life.

picture or image has been stored on different faces of crystal-like objects. As you turn the card, you see the different faces of the crystal-like objects, and thus a different image or picture.

If and when holographic storage devices do become a reality, you may be able to store an entire set of encyclopedias on a single crystal that may have as many as several hundred faces. Think how small technology will become then.

THOUGHT-CONTROL USER INTERFACES

What's beyond Voice-Control User Interfaces?

Right now, you use a graphical user interface (GUI) to interact with your computer. In the very near future, that will change to a voice-control user interface through automatic speech recognition. You'll simply say which programs you want to start (Internet Explorer for example) and speak information and commands. While surfing the Web, you'll say a Web site address followed by the command **Go.** But what if you didn't even have to speak commands and information? What if your computer could capture what you're thinking?

One really cutting-edge technology that aims to bring that to reality is *The Mind Drive,* made by Discovogue (www.other90.com). When using *The Mind Drive,* you slip a small sensing device onto one of your fingers. As you think commands and information, the sensing device captures 70 different bio-electrical signals produced by your mind that radiate throughout your body. Those are processed and interpreted to determine what you're thinking. If you're using word processing software for example, all you'll have to do is "think" the contents of your term paper and it will begin appearing on your screen.

Discovogue is already using *The Mind Drive* to control movement in video games—all you have to do is think commands such as "left," "right," "faster," and so on. *The Mind Drive* is also used in music composition software—change the tempo by thinking it. In Figure 11.9 on the opposite page, we've listed many of the applications for which Discovogue has perfected *The Mind Drive.*

did you know? For *about $50, your veterinarian will place an implant chip in your pet.*

Application	Description
MindSkier	3-D downhill slalom skiing
MindBowling	3-D bowling
PinballMind	3-D pinball
MindGames	Brain teasers
Fib	The equivalent of a lie-detector test
MindMusic	Create and modify original music compositions

FIGURE 11.9

The Mind Drive is already available for many types of software.

You'll probably see the wide-scale production and use of thought-control user interfaces in your lifetime.

So, what's your take on all these emerging technologies that will fundamentally change technology itself and how you interact with your computer? Are you fast at typing or would you rather use speech recognition? Can you ever foresee a time when your computer will capture your thoughts? Is technology becoming so important that you need to wear it all the time like a regular piece of clothing? Do you want an Internet-enabled toilet monitoring your physical well-being?

making the grade

SECTION 11.1

1. During ___________, ASR attempts to recognize your spoken phonemes by locating a matching phoneme (or phoneme sequence) among words stored in an acoustic model database.
2. Special input and output devices for virtual reality include gloves, headsets, and ___________.
3. An Internet-enabled toilet is an example of one device that makes use of ___________.
4. Multi-state CPUs work with information represented in more than just ___________ states.
5. *The Mind Drive* is an example of one device that makes use of a(n) ___________ user interface.

11.2 THE CHANGING INTERNET

Without a doubt the most explosive and visible aspect of technology is the Internet. Over the next several years, you will witness an unbelievable number of changes with respect to the Internet. You'll also see the emergence of many new Internet-based trends and Internet-enabled technologies. Among those will be e-cash, renting software from ASPs, true personalization, and the Internet-enabled home.

E-CASH

Will We Ever Do Away with Folding Cash and Coins?

Using cash or checks to pay for products in an electronic commerce world is a bit of an oxymoron, like jumbo shrimp, freezer burn, even odds, and ill health. There ought to be a better way. You can use a credit card to buy

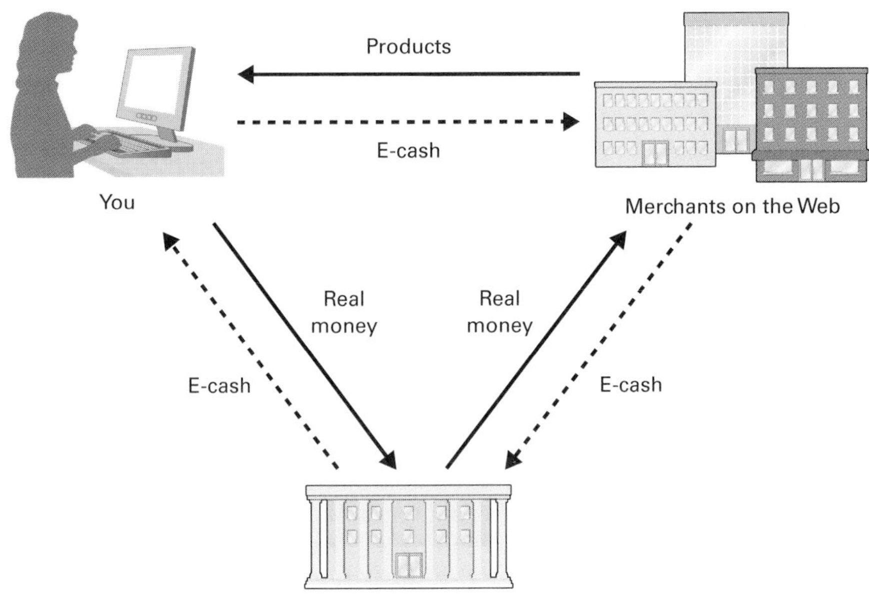

FIGURE 11.10

E-cash facilitates transactions on the Web by using files that represent money.

products on the Web, but you still receive a paper credit card balance statement, and you must write a check to pay your balance.

The alternative is e-cash. ***E-cash (electronic cash*** or ***digital cash)*** is exactly what its name implies—an electronic representation of cash, which is nothing more than a file that says you have a certain amount of money in electronic form with which you can buy products on the Web by sending the e-cash file to a merchant.

To use e-cash on the Web, the first thing you have to do is obtain e-cash from an electronic bank (see Figure 11.10). You can buy e-cash in a variety of ways—send real cash through the mail, provide your debit or credit card number as if you were making a regular purchase, or actually open an account with the electronic bank and request that an amount of e-cash be deducted from your account and sent to you.

Once you have your e-cash, all you have to do is find a product to purchase on the Web and send the appropriate number of e-cash files to the merchant. For example, a $40 purchase would require that you send two $20 e-cash files. In turn, the merchant can use the e-cash to purchase products and services from other merchants or return it to the electronic bank for real money.

did you know? From *2001 to 2002, adult-oriented spam more than doubled to 8 percent of all e-mail messages.*[5]

What's Holding Up E-Cash?

E-cash and its use look simple enough. And someday it will be commonplace. But we first have many hurdles to overcome.

- **Anyone Can Be an Electronic Bank**—The FDIC and FSLIC have yet to establish strict guidelines by which an organization can become an electronic bank and offer e-cash. Be careful here—buy e-cash only from an established and well-known electronic bank.

- **There Are No E-Cash Standards—**Many electronic banks on the Web are offering their own versions of e-cash. So, e-cash from one electronic bank will look different from another electronic bank's e-cash. This makes merchants hesitant—dealing with different forms of e-cash is almost like accepting different forms of international currency.
- **Merchants Must Have Accounts with Electronic Banks—**To accept e-cash, a merchant must have an account with an electronic bank. This is necessary if the merchant wants to convert the e-cash to real money.
- **E-Cash Makes Money Laundering Easy—**E-cash files include no information about you. So, the owner of e-cash can use it for any purpose and it can't be traced. This will make money laundering very simple on the Web.
- **E-Cash Is Easy to Lose, Impossible to Replace—**E-cash is a file on your hard disk. If your hard disk crashes and you lose your information (some of that information is actually e-cash), you've lost your money. Don't expect an electronic bank to replace it.

The single biggest drawback to the use of e-cash is simply the acceptance by the consumer market at large that e-cash is safe to use. There is justification for that hesitation. Consider this: Someone can fairly easily intercept your e-mail as it moves over the Internet. Isn't it entirely possible then that someone could intercept (and essentially duplicate and steal) your e-cash as it moves over the Internet? The answer is yes, although there are many ways in which your e-cash is securely hidden (through encryption and the like). As we discussed in Chapter 8, techniques such as Secure Sockets Layers (SSLs) and Secure Electronic Transactions (SETs) are essential not only for credit card–based e-commerce transactions but also for e-cash–based transactions as well.

In spite of these hurdles, we firmly believe that e-cash will become the standard form of currency on the Web within the next 10 years or so. What do you think?

RENTING SOFTWARE FROM APPLICATION SERVICE PROVIDERS

Will I Always Have to Buy Software?

As more technology choices become available to you (smart phones, PDAs, tablet PCs, and the like), you'll probably opt to use many different devices to satisfy your computing needs. As technology becomes increasingly smaller, you may not have the capacity necessary on every device to store all your software needs. And even if "small" technologies can store all your software needs, do you really want to purchase that software for each of your different technology devices?

These sorts of issues have given rise to the notion of renting application software instead of buying it. Many businesses now do rent some software instead of buying it and installing it on every single technology device within the organization. Those businesses use an application service provider.

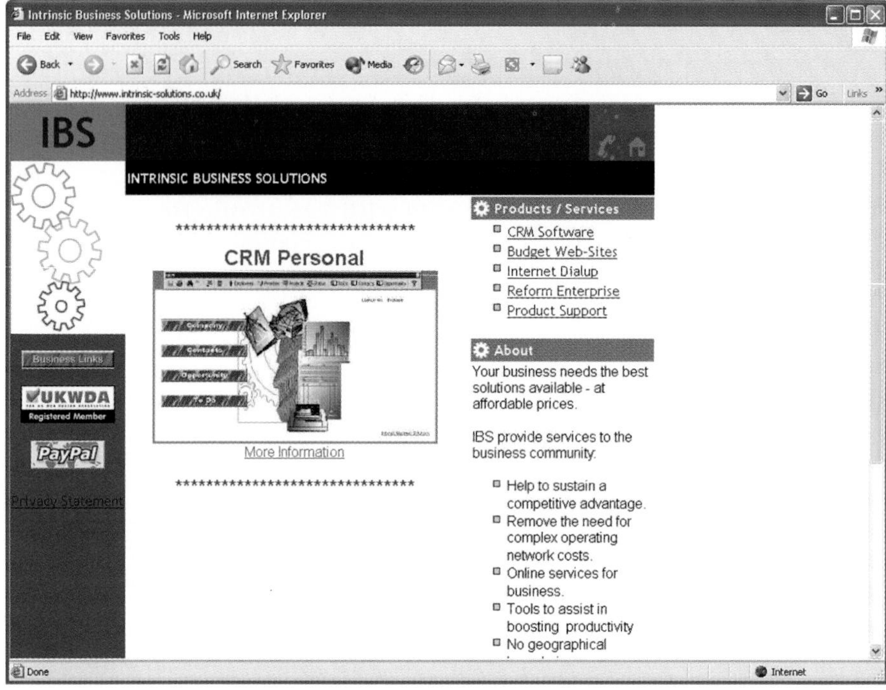

FIGURE 11.11

Application service providers (ASPs) such as Intrinsic Business Solutions offer Web-based software solutions in many areas including customer relationship management.

An ***application service provider (ASP)*** is a company that provides software, storage, and other services for other businesses and individuals to use. For example, Intrinsic Business Solutions (located in the UK) is an ASP that offers Web-based customer relationship management (CRM) solutions for small and medium-sized companies (see Figure 11.11). As a small business, you may not be able to afford a powerful CRM system made by companies such as Firstlogic or Blue Martini. You then have only two choices—write your own CRM software (which is extremely time-consuming and expensive) or rent CRM software from an ASP. If you choose the latter and, for example, select Intrinsic Business Solutions as your ASP, you will receive a secure Internet connection to the ASP's servers, which contain the CRM software and storage facilities for storing your customer files of information.

Then, from anywhere, you and your sales force can access the Internet; you can use the ASP's CRM software and work with your customer files of information.

Let's focus, for a moment, on your personal use of an ASP (see Figure 11.12 on the opposite page). In the future, APSs will provide personal productivity software for you to use (for a fee, perhaps $.25 per session) and storage so you can store your files on their Web servers as opposed to your personal technologies.

For example, you may be in an airport and need to build a spreadsheet with your PDA. Your PDA, however, may not have a complete version of Excel. So, you would use your PDA to connect to the Internet and a personal ASP. With your PDA, you would then use the personal APS's Excel software to create your spreadsheet. You could then save your spreadsheet to the ASP's server. When you finally get back to your office, you would use your computer, connect to the same ASP, and retrieve your spreadsheet and save it to your computer.

There are obviously many issues you'll have to consider when deter-

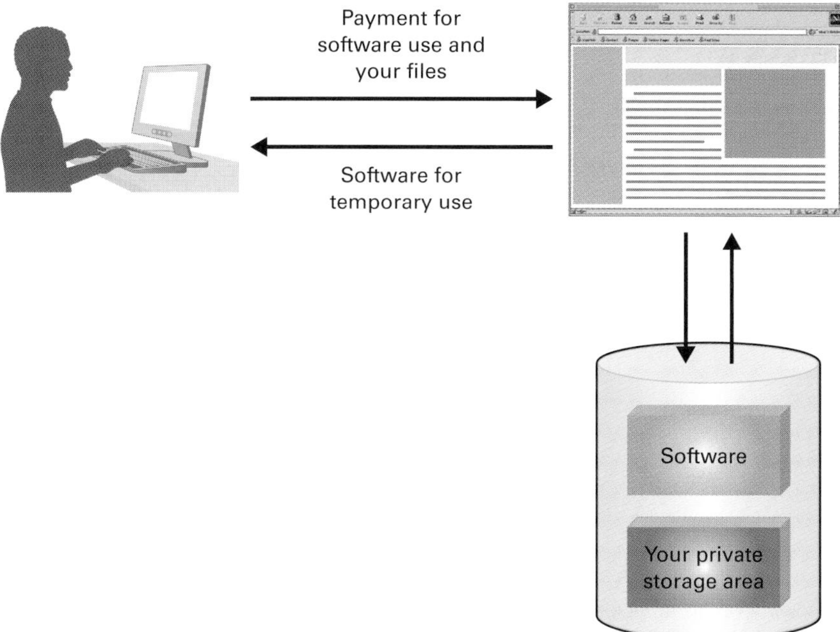

FIGURE 11.12

For a very small fee (perhaps $.25 per session), you'll be able to use a variety of technology tools while renting personal productivity software from an application service provider (ASP) and using that ASP's servers to store your files.

mining whether or not to use a personal ASP. For example, will you really need to buy a desktop, notebook, or tablet PC computer with a large amount of disk storage? If you use a personal ASP, you'll essentially be storing much of your software and information on the ASP's servers.

You'll also need to consider privacy and reliability. If all your information is on a Web-based server, it will be easier for someone to gain access to it (for the wrong reasons) than if you stored all your information on your home computer. When considering reliability, you need to think about what happens if the personal ASP's Web site goes down. How will you perform your work?

In spite of many potential drawbacks, we believe the advantages are far greater. We certainly expect personal ASPs to become a part of your everyday life in the future.

PERSONALIZATION

When Will Spam Become Truly Personalized?

Consider the following scenario. You're driving home from work on Tuesday and get a call on your cell phone. It's a computer-generated voice telling you that you're within a couple of miles of your favorite video rental store. That store has noticed that you usually rent drama movies on Tuesday and a new drama movie has just arrived. All you have to do is press 1 on your cell phone to reserve a copy and press 2 to get driving directions to the video rental store.

FIGURE 11.13

The global positioning system (GPS) is a collection of low-orbiting satellites that can "triangulate" your position, speed, and direction of movement.

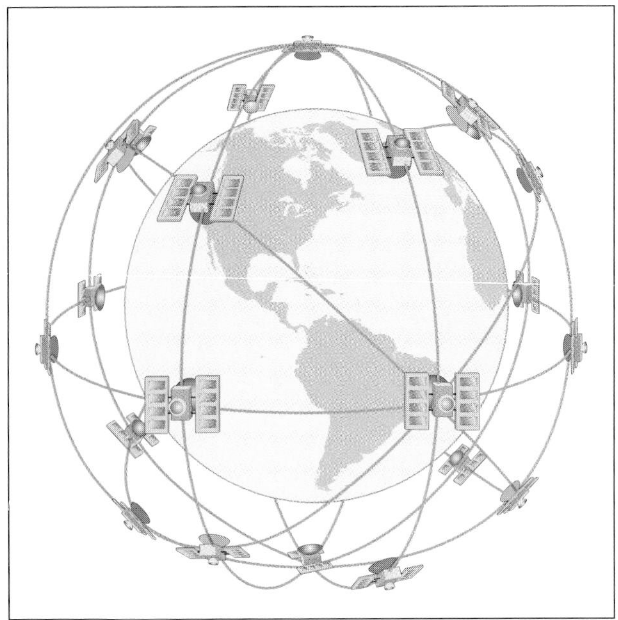

We believe this "scenario" will soon become a reality because of numerous technologies. First, your cell phone will be GPS-enabled. The ***global positioning system (GPS)*** is a navigational system that uses satellites to tell you where you are, how fast you're going, and what direction you're headed in (see Figure 11.13). Using GPS, the local video rental store can determine where you are and which direction you're traveling. (If you're going to work, the store's computer won't call you because most people don't rent movies on the way to work.)

When the video rental store does notice you in its general vicinity, it will trigger a series of software applications that review your video rental history. Your video rental history will be stored in a *data warehouse* (we discussed these in Chapter 10) that might include multiple dimensions such as day of the week, time of the day, and movie category (see Figure 11.14 on the opposite page). If the store's computer notes that you rent movies from a certain category on the day and during the time that you're driving, it will then search its database to determine if any new movies have arrived that you might like to see.

It will also check your video rental history to determine if you've already rented the new movie. Finally, the store's computer will check to see if it has previously called you to inform you of the new movie. If you've already rented the movie or been called and informed of the new movie, the store's computer will not call you.

That's a very realistic example of how personalized businesses can become in offering you products and services. You'll never get a phone call for a new movie in a category you don't usually rent from. You'll never receive a phone call at 3 P.M. on a Saturday if you don't usually rent movies around that time on that day. And you'll never receive the same message twice. Think of how different this is from spam.

Do you like this idea? Do you want to receive a cell phone call while driving home informing you of a new movie? If you don't, then you'll simply "opt out" of this service. If this does appeal to you, you'll obviously have to "opt in" to this type of use of your personal information.

did you know?

Many *teachers use Plagiarized.com (www.plagiarized.com) to help them evaluate the work of students in search of text copied directly from Web documents.*

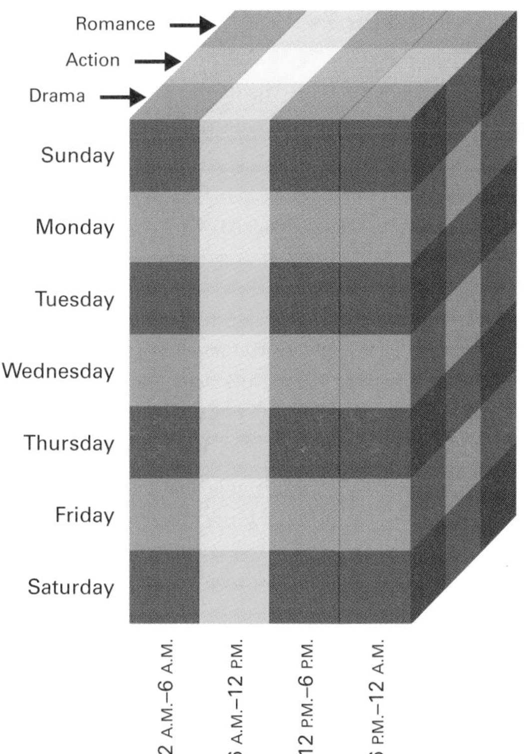

FIGURE 11.14

Using a data warehouse, businesses will be able to better track what you want and when you want it.

Earlier in this chapter we discussed how biometrics will enable businesses to personalize products for you such as bathrobes and shoes. But some products don't need mass customization. Instead, businesses offering commoditylike products such as videos and books just need to know what you want and when you want it. They will know this information about you because of technology.

This particular use of technology is an example of a "push" environment. Right now, you mainly work in a "pull" environment in which you visit Web sites and request information and products. In a push environment, businesses will know you so well that they'll be able to push products and information to you tailored to your likes and dislikes. Here are a few questions for you to ponder.

- How important will "opting in" and "opting out" become in the future?
- Could your school provide this type of service to tell you which classes you need to take?
- Could your school provide this type of service to tell you when a seat is open in a previously closed class that you need to take?
- If your cell phone is GPS-enabled, can any organization track your movements?
- Is a push environment always better than a pull environment or will we need a combination of the two?

YOUR INTERNET-ENABLED HOME
How Will My Home Take Advantage of the Internet?

Right now, your home has all the familiar input and output devices, most of which have "wired" connections and are not connected to each other in the form of a productive network—light switches, stereo controls, kitchen units, washer and dryer timers, sprinkler system controls, and so on. When your home does become completely technology based, it will be (1) wirelessly networked, (2) a part of the Internet, (3) speech enabled, and (4) characterized by intelligent home appliances (see Figure 11.15).

Your home of the future will have a wireless network comprising all your electronic devices, everything from your refrigerator to your tablet PC and PDA. From any of your traditional computer devices anywhere in your home you'll be able to turn on the TV, adjust the volume of your stereo, stop your water sprinklers, turn on the oven, and perhaps even add 10 minutes to the fluff cycle of your clothes dryer. We believe that Bluetooth—which currently works well for wireless connections up to 30 feet—may become the standard for connecting all your electronic devices. Of course, most homes are larger than that, so Bluetooth will have to work for increased distances (which we believe will happen).

Your home will have one central point that connects your wireless network to the Internet. This will enable many future innovations. For example, from any Internet connection anywhere in the world you'll be able to control all your home electronics. You'll probably even be able to connect to a Web site and view Web cam images of your home. You'll receive all your information—newspapers, magazines, e-mail, etc.—through that one single connection to the Internet.

Your wireless network will be speech enabled. When you walk into a room, you'll say "lights" and the room will come alight. Some new homes now have sensors that turn the lights on and off automatically as you enter or leave a room. This is another application of biometrics, and you'll need to decide if you want biometric-controlled or speech-enabled functionality for your lights.

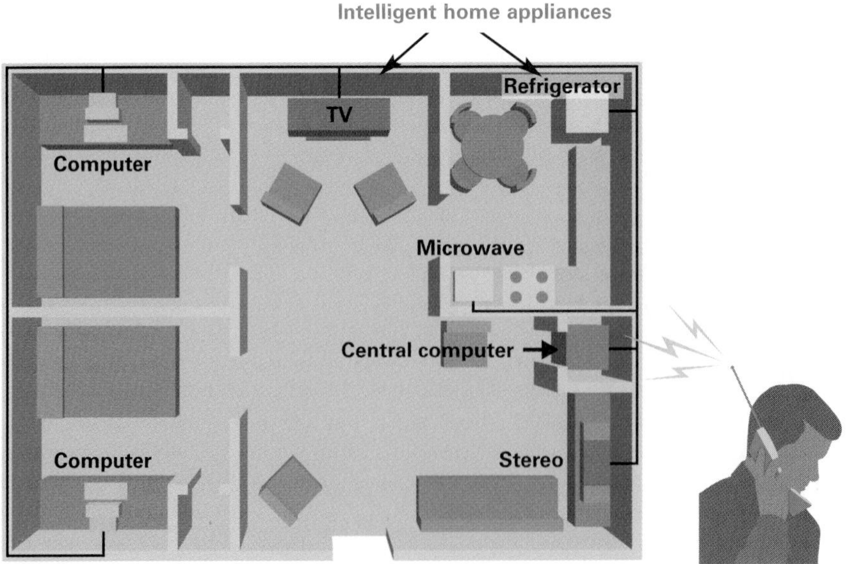

FIGURE 11.15

Homes of the future will be wireless, a part of the Internet, speech enabled, and characterized by intelligent home appliances.

Finally, your future home will have intelligent home appliances. An ***intelligent home appliance*** contains embedded computer technology that controls numerous functions and is capable of making some decisions. Smart vacuum cleaners will automatically adjust their settings based on the naps or densities of your carpet, varying densities and weights of dirt, and collection bag fullness. Clothes washers will automatically balance loads and determine dirt content to add detergent. Your refrigerator will smell the milk going bad and send a message to your PDA or cell phone to buy more milk.

When considering the home of the future, you need to let your imagination run wild. The possibilities and innovations are astounding.

making the grade

SECTION 11.2

1. ___________ is an electronic representation of cash.
2. A(n) ___________ is a company that provides software, storage, and other services for other businesses and individuals to use.
3. The ___________ is a navigational system that uses satellites to tell you where you are, how fast you're going, and what direction you're headed in.
4. A(n) ___________ contains embedded computer technology that controls numerous functions and is capable of making some decisions.

11.3 PUSHING THE ENVELOPE

In a chapter like this, you should really start to think "beyond your ears" (that's our version of thinking outside the box). So, let's step out and look at some really cutting-edge technologies.

CAVES

What's beyond Virtual Reality?

Earlier in this chapter, we introduced you to holographic storage devices that will use crystal-like objects to store information on multiple surfaces. Another type of holographic device is a CAVE. A ***CAVE (cave automatic virtual environment)*** is a special 3-D virtual reality room that can display images of other people and objects located in other places and CAVEs all over the world.

There are two main types of CAVEs. The first displays images on all four walls to give you the illusion that you're in a particular environment. For example, you could give a speech in this type of CAVE and have people who are watching your presentation in various locations displayed on the walls. That would give you the illusion of being in a large auditorium. That type of CAVE has been around for a very long time and is not really an emerging technology.

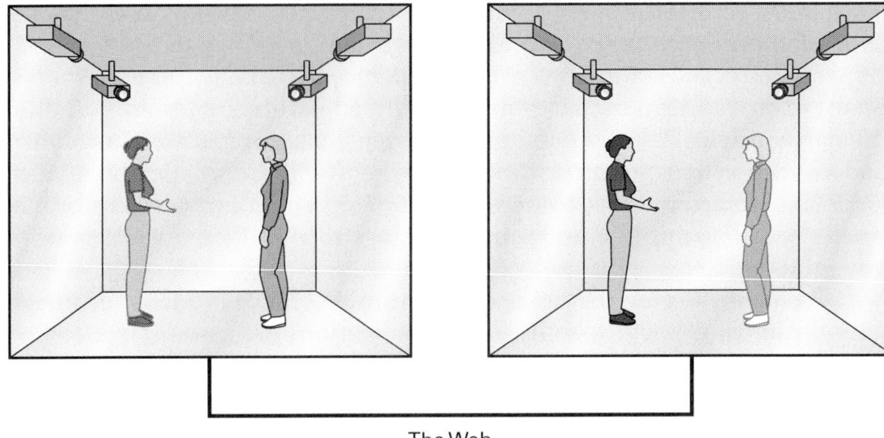

FIGURE 11.16
CAVEs will give you the illusion that you're with someone miles away.

With the other type of CAVE (which truly is a cutting-edge technology), you enter one CAVE while someone else enters another. Numerous digital camera/projection units capture you both, send the images to the opposite CAVEs, and re-create your 3-D likenesses (see Figure 11.16). Then, you and the other person see and carry on a normal conversation with each other. In essence, each of you feel as if you and the other person are in the same room.

Unlike basic virtual reality, you won't need to wear any special gear such as gloves, headsets, or walkers. You'll simply enter a CAVE and be placed in literally any virtual environment along with one or more other persons. Consider these questions.

- How can businesses use CAVEs to increase the quality of customer service?
- How will CAVEs increase the quality of online learning and/or distance education?
- Will the use of CAVEs positively or negatively impact the travel industry?
- How do you think the entertainment industry will incorporate the use of CAVEs into movies and video games?

MEMBRANE-BASED AND NANOTECHNOLOGIES
Is It Possible to Store Information in Living Tissue?

Right now, technology is manufactured using various metals and metal alloys. In the future, you can expect to see the emergence of membrane-based technologies. ***Membrane-based technologies*** store and manipulate information within living tissue cells. That may sound really wild, but the concept is quite simple. The idea is to control tissue cells and their electronic states such that we can alter whether an individual cell represents a 0 or a 1 (the basics of binary information). In doing so, living tissues can become storage devices that increase in size as we need more space and decrease in size as we need less storage space.

In the medical field, it is already possible to control the electronic state of a single cell. The process is very expensive and lacks the true organization capabilities necessary to store and retrieve information from millions of cells. This is the point at which nanotechnology becomes important.

did you know? New *grocery shopping carts have remote radio-controlled devices on them that lock the wheels (to prevent theft) when the cart leaves a 300-ft. radius of the store.*

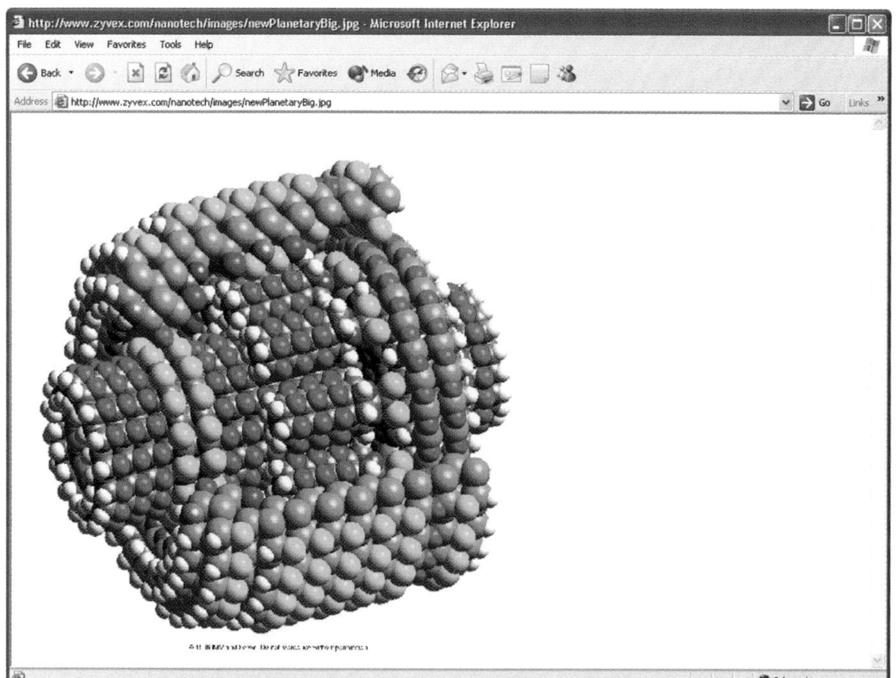

FIGURE 11.17

Nanotechnologies and membrane-based technologies seek to create elaborate structures of molecules, atoms, and living tissue cells that can self-assemble, store information, and perform processes.

Nanotechnology is the study of controlling individual atoms and molecules to (1) create computer chips that are hundreds of times smaller than current chips and (2) encourage those atoms and molecules to "self-assemble" into new forms. Currently, the best chip manufacturers can do is to make circuit elements with a width of 130 nanometers. A nanometer is one hundred-thousandth the width of a human hair. Nanotechnology aims to create circuit elements that are only one nanometer in width, essentially 130 times smaller than current technologies.

The "self-assembly" characteristic focuses on giving atoms and molecules the information and ability to organize themselves according to what we want them to do or represent. This brings us back to membrane-based technologies because science has proved that cells do contain some basic level of intelligence.

Membrane-based technologies and nanotechnologies are a very mind-boggling cutting-edge area of research. But you don't really need to understand their technical workings or the theories behind them to begin to ask some thought-provoking questions.

- Can we increase brain capacity by inventing ways for people to store information in their skin and other tissues?
- If technology controls what atoms, molecules, and tissue cells store as information, might it be possible for someone to literally hook you up to a computer and read your information?
- If we can control information within tissue cells, might you never again need a storage device because you can use your tissue to store information?
- Will we stop "manufacturing" computer devices and start "giving birth" to them?

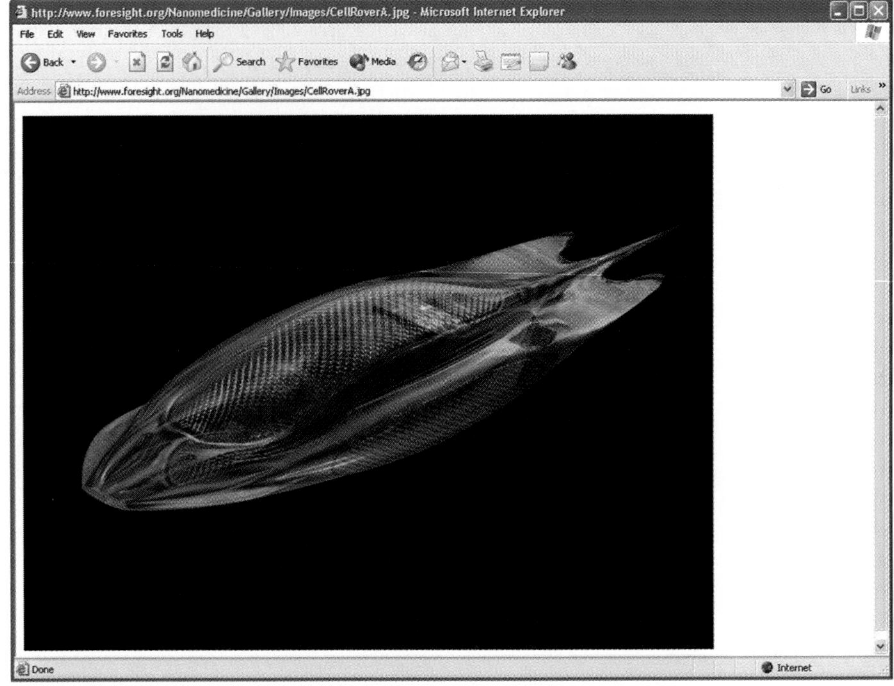

FIGURE 11.18

Biochips such as the cell rover will be able to move through the human body performing such tasks as destroying bacteria and dispensing medication.

BIOCHIPS

How Will Emerging Technologies Impact the Medical Field?

While we're on the subject of the integration of technology and the human body, let's talk about biochips. A ***biochip*** is a technology chip that can perform a variety of physiological functions when inserted into the human body. For example, there are implant chips that block pain for people who suffer severe spinal injuries. Doctors are exploring the use of biochips to help paralyzed people walk. And there are even biochips that can help people see.

Many of these biochip devices in the future will not be stationary within the human body. Instead, they will move through the blood vessel structure—for example, seeking out bacteria to destroy. They may even move to the appropriate part of the body to dispense medication at the right time (see Figure 11.18).

Biomedical engineering is the name often given to this field of technology (specifically, biochips) that supports the functioning of the human body. We believe there are significant career opportunities in biomedical engineering. If you like technology and also other science subjects such as biology and chemistry, we would encourage you to consider a biomedical engineering career.

IMPLANT CHIPS

Can Biochips Be Used to Track My Movements?

Biochips are designed to take over and perform physiological functions such as blocking pain. Implant chips are entirely different. An ***implant chip*** is a technology-based microchip—containing at a minimum personal information but also perhaps GPS-tracking capabilities—implanted into the human body. So, implant chips serve two purposes. First, they may

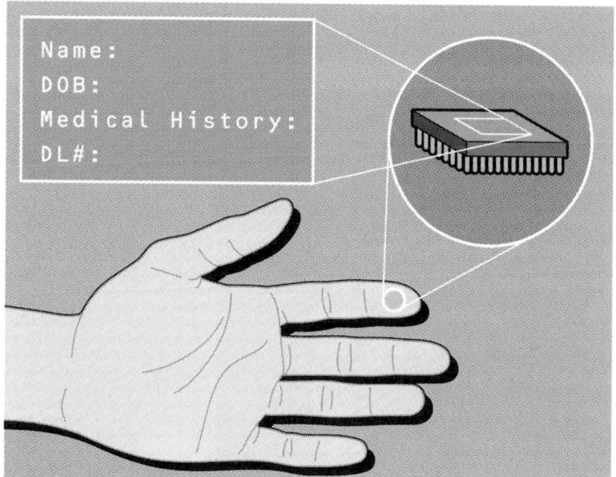

FIGURE 11.19

Implant chips in your body may contain all your vital information.

contain vitally important information about you (see Figure 11.19). If you get ill while on vacation, a doctor can scan your chip and view your complete medical history, including any allergic reactions you may have to certain types of drugs. That's the smaller and more acceptable use of implant chips.

On a grander and more thought-provoking scale, many people propose that these chips be GPS-enabled and used to track the movement of people by satellite. This has raised much concern in the area of privacy. Most people don't want the government or any organization to have the ability to monitor their movements. But there are arguments for it. For example, we could easily locate missing or kidnapped children. If someone were to break into your house, the police could tell you who it was.

From a somewhat morbid point of view, it is entirely possible that someone could surgically remove your implant chip. In doing so, that person might be able to take on your identity. After all, the scanning of implant chips may become the primary mechanism for verifying your identity while at an ATM, registering for school, and a variety of other functions.

You will definitely have to wrestle with the issue of implant chips in your lifetime. Already, a family of four in Florida has adopted the use of implant chips that are GPS-enabled. The parents felt the benefits of being able to track their children far outweighed the potential disadvantages. To read more about implant chips and consider some interesting questions, read the I-Series Insights box on the next page.

That ends our brief tour of the future. We don't have a crystal ball, of course, and neither does anyone else. Some of the emerging technologies we've discussed are surely destined to take their place in your future—speech recognition or digital cash. Others face the uncertainty common to all technological innovations. We encourage you always to look toward the future, not only for the interest of reading about emerging technologies, but in light of your possible career choices or changes, to understand the potential impacts (both good and bad) on your life of new technology, and to stay alert for how it may help you be more productive and effective.

i•series insights — *Ethics, Security & Privacy*

Do You Really Want a Chip in Your Body?

Implant chips are the central issue of much debate, mainly in the area of privacy. On an implant chip, you can store a wealth of information about yourself, including your medical history and other forms of personal information. Then, if you ever need that information, it can easily be scanned.

Most people are in favor of that use of the technology. But many want it to stop there, while others see more applications. For example, that same implant chip could be used (in conjunction with satellites) to track the movements of people. So, we could easily find lost skiers and hikers, tell who burglarized a home, and find a lost or kidnapped child. Those sound like good uses of technology.

If we can track anyone anywhere, however, what's to stop certain people or organizations from tracking others for the wrong reasons? Couldn't the government easily follow you wherever you go? Couldn't your school easily track you to see where you are when you're supposed to be in class? Couldn't the ATF (Bureau of Alcohol, Tobacco, and Firearms) use those implant chips to determine who should be able to drink alcohol or own a gun?

What do you think? Is this a technology that we should repress or ignore because it can potentially be used in a bad way? Or should we move forward with its use while enacting legislation to control its use?

SECTION 11.3

making the grade

1. A(n) ____________ is a special 3-D virtual reality room that can display images of people and objects located in other places.
2. Membrane-based technologies store and manipulate information within ____________.
3. ____________ is the study of controlling individual atoms and molecules to (1) create computer chips that are hundreds of times smaller than current chips and (2) encourage those atoms and molecules to "self-assemble" into new forms.
4. A(n) ____________ is a technology chip that can perform a variety of physiological functions when inserted into the human body.

11.4 SUMMARY AND KEY TERMS

Emerging technologies and new uses of existing technologies surface every day. How those emerging technologies and uses of technology impact our lives is even more important than the technological changes themselves.

Emerging technologies that (1) fundamentally change the technology itself or (2) change the way you interface or interact with your computer are listed on the next page.

- ***Automatic speech recognition (ASR)***—a system that captures your speech and can distinguish your words and word groupings to form sentences.
- ***Three-dimensional (3-D) technologies***—present information to you in such a way that you have the illusion that the object you're viewing is actually in the room with you.
- ***Virtual reality (VR)***—a three-dimensional computer simulation in which you actively and physically participate using special input and output devices such as gloves, headsets, and walkers.
- ***Biometrics***—the use of physical characteristics—such as your fingerprint, the blood vessels in the retina of your eye, or perhaps the sound of your voice—to provide identification.
- ***Wearable computers***—fully equipped computers that you wear as a piece of clothing or attached to a piece of clothing similar to the way you would carry your cell phone on your belt.
- ***Multi-state CPUs***—work with information represented in more than just two states, probably 10 states with each state representing a digit between 0 and 9.
- ***Holographic storage devices***—store information on a storage medium that is composed of 3-D crystal-like objects with many sides or faces.
- Thought-control user interfaces—devices capable of capturing and interpreting your thoughts.

The Internet, its technologies, and uses of the Internet are changing just as rapidly. These include:

- ***E-cash (electronic cash*** or ***digital cash)***—an electronic representation of cash.
- Renting personal productivity software from an ***application service provider (ASP).***
- Personalization—the ability of organizations to push personalized products, services, and information to you through such technologies as the ***global positioning system (GPS)*** and data warehouses.
- Your Internet-enabled home—wirelessly networked, speech enabled, and characterized by ***intelligent home appliances.***

Finally, there are numerous cutting-edge technologies that will dramatically change your life if they become a reality.

- ***CAVEs (cave automatic virtual environments)***—special 3-D rooms that can display images of people and objects located anywhere in the world such that you and they feel you're in the same room together.
- ***Membrane-based technologies***—store and manipulate information within living tissue cells.
- ***Nanotechnologies***—control individual atoms and molecules to (1) create computer chips that are hundreds of times smaller than current chips and (2) encourage those atoms and molecules to "self-assemble" into new forms.
- ***Biochips***—technology chips that can perform a variety of physiological functions when inserted into the human body.

- ***Implant chips***—technology-based microchips implanted into the human body.

To learn more about automatic speech recognition systems and 3-D Web sites, visit the Web site for this text at www.mhhe.com/i-series.

KEY TERMS

application service provider (ASP) (p. 336)

automatic speech recognition (p. 325)

biochip (p. 344)

biometrics (p. 328)

CAVE (cave automatic virtual environment) (p. 341)

e-cash (electronic cash, digital cash) (p. 334)

feature analysis (p. 325)

global positioning system (GPS) (p. 338)

glove (p. 327)

headset (head-mounted display, HMD) (p. 327)

holographic storage device (p. 331)

implant chip (p. 344)

intelligent home appliance (p. 341)

language processing (p. 326)

membrane-based technology (p. 342)

multi-state CPU (p. 331)

nanotechnology (p. 343)

pattern classification (p. 326)

three-dimensional (3-D) technologies (p. 327)

virtual reality (VR) (p. 327)

walker (p. 327)

wearable computer (p. 330)

review of terminology

Multiple Choice

1. Automatic speech recognition consists of
   a. feature analysis.
   b. pattern classification.
   c. language processing.
   d. all of the above steps.
   e. none of the above steps.
2. During features analysis, your ASR system converts the digital signals of your speech into
   a. words.
   b. sentences.
   c. phrases.
   d. phonemes.
   e. paragraphs.
3. The special device in virtual reality that captures the movements of your hand and fingers is called a(n)
   a. headset.
   b. HMD.
   c. glove.
   d. walker.
   e. mitt.
4. Storage devices composed to 3-D crystal-like objects with many sides or faces are called
   a. 3-D storage devices.
   b. holographic storage devices.
   c. crystal storage devices.
   d. imaging storage devices.
   e. nanotechnologies.
5. Biometrics include
   a. fingerprint identification devices.
   b. Internet-enabled toilets.
   c. devices for creating custom-fitting shoes.
   d. devices for creating custom-fitting wedding dresses.
   e. all of the above.
6. CPUs that work with information represented in more than just two states are called
   a. digital CPUs.
   b. multi-faceted CPUs.
   c. holographic CPUs.
   d. multi-state CPUs.
   e. multi-digital CPUs.
7. *The Mind Drive* is an example of a product that uses a
   a. voice-control user interface.
   b. GUI.
   c. thought-control user interface.
   d. mind-control user interface.
   e. heat-map-control user interface.
8. The single biggest drawback to the use of e-cash is that
   a. the consumer does not yet believe that e-cash is safe to use.
   b. anyone can become an e-bank.
   c. e-cash is easy to lose.
   d. e-cash is impossible to replace.
   e. e-cash makes money laundering easy.
9. Your Internet-enabled home of the future will probably be
   a. wirelessly networked.
   b. a part of the Internet.
   c. speech-enabled.
   d. characterized by intelligent home appliances.
   e. all of the above.
10. Technology chips that can perform a variety of physiological functions when inserted into the human body are called
    a. biochips.
    b. implant chips.
    c. physiological chips.
    d. biological implant chips.
    e. none of the above.

True/False

11. ____ During language processing, your ASR system compares possible word phonemes to rules in an acoustic model database.
12. ____ HMDs are special input devices in virtual reality that capture only the movement of your head from side to side and up and down.
13. ____ Xybernaut makes a wearable computer called a poma.
14. ____ Virtual reality (VR) is a two-dimensional technology.
15. ____ Implant chips contain information about you but cannot be used to track your movements.

Take this quiz online at www.mhhe.com/i-series and get instant feedback.

review of concepts

QUESTIONS AND EXERCISES

1. Creating a Timeline for Emerging Technologies and Their Uses

Below is a list of 20 emerging technologies and emerging uses of technologies we discussed in this chapter. In what order do you think they will become a common reality? In the middle column provide a number between 1 and 20. The number 1 will represent the technology or use of technology you believe will become a common reality first, and the number 20 will represent the one you believe will become a common reality last. Essentially, you're building a timeline for the emerging technologies and emerging uses of technology.

In the right-hand column you are to provide a year by which you believe these technologies and uses of technologies will become a common reality. This column of information will be in the same order as the middle column of information.

Emerging Technology/Use	Timeline Number	No Later Than
Automatic speech recognition		
Virtual reality		
Biometrics (identification)		
Biometrics (for creating customized products)		
Wearable computer		
Multi-state CPU		
Holographic storage device		
Thought-control user interface		
E-cash		
Rentable personal productivity software		
Personalization through push		
Wirelessly networked home		
Speech-enabled home		
Intelligent home appliance		
CAVE		
Membrane-based technology		
Nanotechnology		
Biochip		
Implant chip (information only)		
Implant chip (for tracking)		

2. Matching Occupations with Emerging Technologies

Below, we've provided a table with three columns. The first column contains a list of occupations such as air traffic controller and school teacher. In the middle column you are to list the emerging technologies we discussed in this chapter that each occupation could benefit from the use of. In the right-hand column you are to provide a description of how each occupation would use the emerging technologies you listed in the middle column.

Occupation	Emerging Technologies	Description of Use
Air traffic controller		
School teacher		
Emergency medical technician		
Police officer		
Soldier		
Doctor		
Lawyer		
Accountant		
Airplane pilot		

e-commerce

1. Understanding New Government Initiatives to Use the Web

The U.S. Government (thanks in part to the President's Management Agenda or PMA) is undertaking numerous new initiatives to take advantage of the Web in the delivery of products, services, and information to citizens, businesses, and internal governmental agencies.

Connect to FirstGov at www.firstgov.gov. While you're there, look around and answer the following questions:

a. What services are available online for citizens?
b. What services are available online for businesses?
c. What services are available online to internal governmental agencies?
d. What sort of information is provided if you need to contact someone in the federal government?
e. Does the site provide links to state and local governmental agencies? If so, how are those links organized?
f. Are some services categorized by age of citizens (e.g., Web pages just for kids or senior citizens)?
g. After reviewing the site, are you more or less inclined to interact with the federal government via the Web? Justify your answer.

2. Making Long-Distance Phone Calls

Someday you may never pay for another long-distance phone call. By paying only your ISP monthly fee, you'll be able to use the Web to make "free" long-distance phones calls. Sound too good to be true? Well, it's already happening and many people are doing it. Below, we've provided four Web sites that support using the Web for making long-distance phone calls.

- Eurocall—www.eurocall.com
- DialPad—www.dialpad.com
- InetPhone—www.inetphone.com
- Net2Phone—www.net2phone.com

Connect to any one of the sites and answer the following questions:

a. Are calls really free or do you have to pay some sort of fee? If you have to pay a fee, what is it?
b. What sort of special computer equipment do you need to make a Web-based phone call?
c. Can you make local calls as well as long-distance calls?
d. Can you use a cell phone to make phone calls on the Web?
e. Does the person you're calling also have to be connected to the Web when you call him or her?

3. Taking College Courses on the Web

You've probably had an instructor who places materials on the Web for you to use. You may have taken exams over the Web or joined in Web discussion groups. But did you know that many schools offer entire classes over the Web? Some schools even offer online degrees. You could go to college without ever leaving home. We've listed some of these Web sites:

- The Open University—www.open.edu
- The University of Phoenix—www.phoenix.edu
- Capella University—www.capella.edu

As you look at these schools, consider these questions:

a. What types of courses or degrees do they offer?
b. Can you get the degree you're pursuing at an online school?
c. Would you rather get your degree at an online school than at the school you attend now? Why or why not?
d. Can you think of people who might benefit from taking courses online? Who might they be? What are the benefits?
e. What would be the differences between taking a course online and taking one in a classroom?
f. What would be the differences between getting an entire degree online and getting one where you are now?

ethics, security & privacy

1. Tracking Customer Movement with Body Heat Maps

Several retail stores are currently exploring the possibility of using body heat maps to track customer movement. Body heat maps are an extension of biometrics. As it turns out, each person's body has a unique signature in the form of a heat map. When you enter a store, the store will capture your body heat map and then track you throughout the store. When you buy products, those products will be associated with—for instance—how long you reviewed them on the display, whether or not you compared them with competing or complementary products, and whether or not a sales associate helped you review the products.

Because this is a realistic possibility, answer the questions below and be prepared to justify your answers in a class debate.

a. Should organizations have the right to capture your unique body heat map as you enter and use their facilities?
b. Should organizations first obtain your permission before using your body heat map to track you?
c. Would you enter a store if you knew that your body heat map was being used to monitor and track your activities?
d. Should your school be able to capture your body heat map as you enter a classroom to take an exam and then use that heat map to verify your identity?

2. DNA Testing

In the movie *Gattica,* biometrics was carried to its extreme logical conclusion. In that movie, all people were identified through a quick check of their DNA. A girl on a date even had her boyfriend's DNA checked for any flaws or deficiencies. People were given jobs according to their DNA testing. Those people with DNAs that showed physical or mental deficiencies of any kind were given simple tasks such as collecting trash. Those with good DNAs were given the opportunity to work in an office, make a lot of money, and live a nice life.

Consider, answer, and debate the following questions:

a. Should we use DNA testing as the ultimate form of biometrics? It will certainly make it almost impossible for anyone to imitate you.
b. Should we use DNA testing to determine which types of jobs people should have?
c. Should we use DNA testing to determine which schools people are allowed to go to?
d. Should the poultry industry be allowed to use DNA testing on chickens and other forms of fowl to determine which birds will yield you the greatest nutritional value?
e. In general, isn't DNA testing another form of discrimination, no matter how it's used?

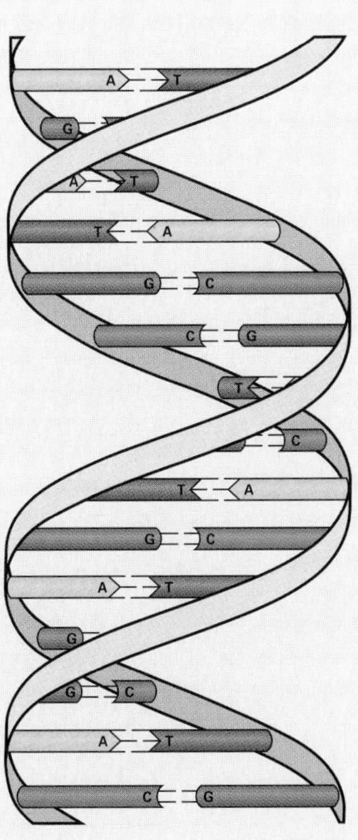

on the web

1. Finding Virtual Reality Applications

Virtual reality is certainly finding its way onto the Internet. You can download virtual reality applications, buy special virtual reality input and output devices, and even interact with virtual reality applications while on the Web. For this project, you are to perform two tasks. First, search the Web for virtual reality applications that you can interact with while on the Web. Make a list of at least five different applications you find including their Web sites. Only two of those virtual reality applications can be in the area of gaming such as downhill skiing and marksmanship. Second, you are to create a list of five different virtual reality applications that you were not able to find on the Internet but believe would have some value to a business (i.e., not personal virtual reality applications). For each of the five, define how the virtual reality application would work and what benefits a business would derive.

2. Determining the Capabilities of Xybernaut's Newest Poma Wearable Computer

Xybernaut, right now, seems to be the leader in the development of wearable computers with its line of poma computers. Visit Xybernaut's Web site at www.xybernaut.com and research the capabilities of its newest poma computer. At a minimum, answer the following questions:

a. What is the speed of its CPU?
b. How much RAM can it have?
c. How many ports does it have and what kinds are they?
d. What operating system does it use?
e. What pointing and other input devices can you use?
f. What is its screen resolution?
g. What application software can you use?

3. E-Publishing on the Web

E-publishing is an emerging technology that we didn't discuss specifically in this chapter. E-publishing is simply the development, authoring, distribution, and use of traditional print products in electronic form. For example, you can now buy some textbooks in electronic form and download them to your computer. Do some research on the Web concerning e-publishing. What organizations seem to be leading the way? What Web sites offer e-books? Can you find fiction, nonfiction, textbooks, and magazines? What measures are e-publishers implementing to ensure that you pay for your e-book and then don't make a copy of it for someone else? What's a rocket book? What's a soft book?

4. Using Electronic Coupons

When you receive your local Sunday newspaper, it probably comes with a host of coupons you can clip and take to the store. When we finally arrive at completely electronic newspapers, those coupons will also have to be electronic. Right now, you can find electronic coupons on the Web. Connect to Coupons.com at www.coupons.com. What sorts of coupons did you find? How are they organized? How do you download the coupons and print them? Now, connect to your favorite search engine and types in "coupons." What other sites did you find that offer electronic coupons?

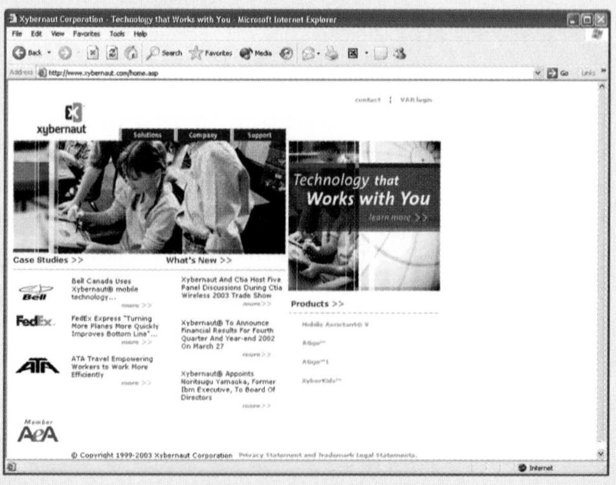

group activities

1. Researching Voice-Controlled Cell Phones

Voice-controlled user interfaces are becoming more and more common each day on a variety of technologies. One such technology is cell phones. Do some research and find at least three cell phones that support a voice-controlled user interface. Create a short report that includes the following information for each cell phone:

a. Manufacturer name
b. Brand name and model
c. Price for the cell phone
d. Pricing levels for the cell phone service
e. Number of telephone numbers you can store and access using a voice-controlled user interface

Do you have a voice-controlled user interface? Have you ever owned a cell phone that did not support a voice-controlled user interface? How much easier is it to say a person's name instead of typing in a phone number or scrolling through a phone list?

2. Blocking Spam

Spam is a real problem for most people. It's basically junk e-mail offering you everything from get-rich-quick schemes to herbal supplements that will revitalize your body. There are, however, software products that can help you block unwanted spam. You are to research the spam-blocking tools we've provided below and prepare a short report for your class detailing their capabilities and their differences. You are also to recommend to your class which spam-blocking software product you believe everyone should use.

- Junk Spy (www.junkspy.com)
- MailWasher (www.mailwasher.net)
- Matador (www.mailfrontier.com)
- Norton Internet Security (www.symantec.com)
- SpamAssassin (www.deersoft.com)
- SpamButcher (www.spambutcher.com)
- SpamCatcher (www.mailshell.com)
- SpamKiller (www.spamkiller.com)

3. Creating Three-Dimensional Graphs

Creating two-dimensional and pseudo three-dimensional graphs in spreadsheet software such as Excel or Lotus 1-2-3 is easy. Using your spreadsheet software, type in the following information:

Territory	Sales in $ millions
East	10
West	12
North	31
South	17
International	4

Create the following graphs: (1) a two-dimensional bar graph of sales, (2) a two-dimensional bar graph of sales with the bars running horizontally, (3) a three-dimensional bar graph, (4) a two-dimensional pie chart, and (5) an exploded three-dimensional pie chart. You should be able to create just the first graph and then simply change the graph or chart type to view the other four. Do the three-dimensional graphs do a better job of conveying information or are they simply more appealing to the eye?

4. Researching Intelligent Home Appliances

Take a short trip to a local appliance store. What sort of intelligent home appliances are for sale? For each appliance you find, write down its characteristics, how the embedded computer technology can make decisions, and whether or not the appliance is voice-controlled. For each that you find, also find a corresponding appliance that is not "intelligent." What's the price difference? Does the increased functionality of the intelligent home appliance make you want to spend more money?

crossword puzzle

Across

3. Quick and risky conversion method
4. Feasibility assessment—can you meet deadlines?
7. Opposite of #22 down
9. Development performed by users
11. ______ testing—does the system work correctly?
12. Method of converting one portion of a system at a time
13. Method of converting only select users
14. SDLC phase in which you assess initial feasibility
15. Delegating work to someone else
17. Software for a specific industry
18. Process of building a model
21. SDLC phase in which software is written
24. SDLC phase that focuses on logical system requirements

Down

1. Software for a variety of industries
2. Graphical depiction of steps in software
5. Structured systems development approach
6. Most important document in outsourcing
8. SDLC phase in which you bring the new system to life
10. SDLC phase in which you focus on physical system requirements
16. Feasibility assessment—do you have the expertise?
18. A model
19. Safe conversion method in which you run two systems
20. Feasibility assessment—do you have the money?
22. Programmer who writes OS software
23. Chief information officer

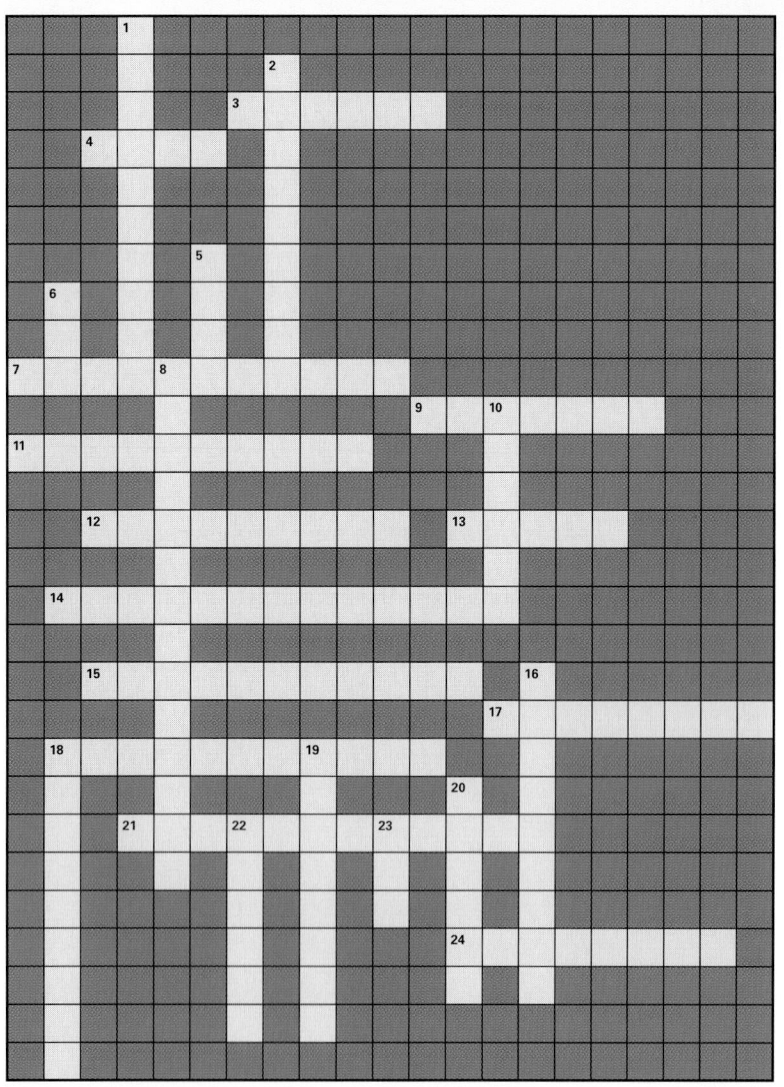

CHAPTER twelve 12

Systems Development

Why Is Packaged Software Sometimes Not Enough?

SIMNET CONCEPTS SUPPORT

- Systems Development Overview (p. 362)
- Project Management Applications (p. 363)

did you know?

One of the greatest organizational challenges today is to effectively design, develop, and implement a new computer system. Building a computer system is almost as much an art as it is a science.

microsoft's *"old" Windows 95 operating system is 11,236,344 lines of code.*

microsoft *spent 9,234,455 hours developing Windows 95 (49 minutes per line of code).*

microsoft *spent 2,333,345 hours testing Windows 95 (12.5 minutes per line of code).*

microsoft *programmers consumed __??__ pizzas while writing Windows 95—that's one slice of pizza for every __??__ lines of code.*

To find our just how many pizzas Microsoft programmers consumed and how many lines of code they had to produce between each piece of pizza, visit www.mhhe.com/i-series.

Student Learning Outcomes

After reading this chapter, you should be able to:

1. Discuss why organizations develop computer systems.
2. List the six phases within the systems development life cycle (SDLC) and describe the major purposes of each.
3. Define the people who are included on most project development teams.
4. Describe the reasons why modeling systems from both a logical and physical perspective is important.
5. Define end user development and how it differs from the traditional systems development life cycle (SDLC), and the advantages and disadvantages of end user development.
6. Describe why organizations choose to outsource systems development and the major steps in outsourcing.

Software doesn't just magically appear. First someone has to determine a need for it. Then someone has to specify in excruciating detail how the software must work, what information it should capture and display, and the steps within each process. Next, someone must write the actual software code. Then, it has to be tested, tested, and retested. And that covers only the software aspect—there's just as much to do for hardware.

Many organizations today have spent billions of dollars developing computer systems, from seemingly simple payroll systems to elaborate customer-integrated systems that run on the Web. These are not trivial efforts.

In this chapter, we'll focus on how organizations go about developing new computer systems. Although you may not want to develop computer systems for a living, this is still an important topic for you. Why? Mainly because you'll be using the systems. If they meet your needs, you'll be more productive. If they don't meet your needs, you'll experience many hours of frustration.

12.1 WHY ORGANIZATIONS DEVELOP SYSTEMS

Before we explore *how* organizations build computer systems, let's first answer the following question: "*Why* do organizations need computer systems?" That's a really great question; after all, if you don't know why you're developing something, you may question the need for it. Organizations today develop new computer systems for three primary reasons:

1. To become more efficient.
2. To level the competitive playing field.
3. To achieve an advantage through innovation.

did you know? The *U.S. federal government IT budget in 2003 was slightly over $60 billion.*

DEVELOPING SYSTEMS TO BECOME MORE EFFICIENT

Do Organizations Develop Systems Just for Efficiency?

Many organizations today develop systems designed specifically to be more efficient in their internal processes. For example, Avon developed a document-imaging system to gather and process input from orders. In previous years, order entry clerks had to type in handwritten information from orders. With the new document-imaging system, Avon reported that accuracy improved by 76 percent, productivity improved by 75 percent, order-processing times decreased by 76 percent, and order-entry costs decreased by 65 percent.

Systems developed for the sake of internal efficiency, as in the case of Avon, are not designed to yield a market advantage but rather to add to the survivability and the bottom line of an organization by making the organization more productive.

DEVELOPING SYSTEMS TO LEVEL THE COMPETITIVE PLAYING FIELD

Do Organizations Develop Systems Just to Stay Up with the Competition?

In many instances, organizations develop new systems to stay competitive in the marketplace. This is typically a "reactionary" measure after an organization sees that a competitor has developed a new system and decides it should develop its own. For example, several years ago shipping organizations such as UPS and the U.S. Postal Service noticed that FedEx had developed a system that enabled customers to electronically request a parcel pickup and to track the parcel through the shipment process by simply accessing the Web and entering a parcel tracking number (see Figure 12.1).

Just to stay competitive and not lose customers to FedEx, UPS and the Postal Service and others were forced to develop similar systems. This may not seem like the ideal circumstances under which to develop a new system (and it isn't), but sometimes organizations find themselves having to react to what the competition is doing.

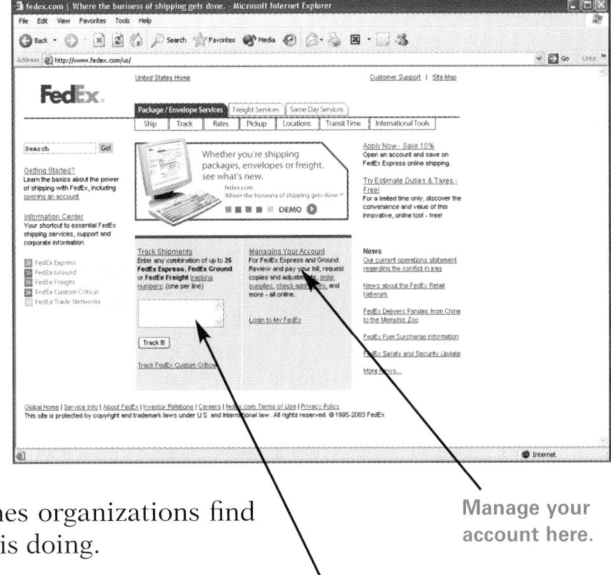
Manage your account here.
Track packages here.

FIGURE 12.1

FedEx's customer-oriented parcel tracking software helped it achieve a competitive advantage in the marketplace.

DEVELOPING SYSTEMS TO ACHIEVE AN ADVANTAGE THROUGH INNOVATION

Can Organizations Achieve an Advantage by Developing a New System?

The best reason for an organization to develop a new system is for the purpose of gaining an advantage in the marketplace through innovation. Our previous example of FedEx is a good one. FedEx developed its new customer-oriented parcel tracking software (which is an example of a customer-integrated system) to achieve an advantage over its competitors. Until UPS and the others were able to develop similar systems, FedEx attracted many new customers (away from its competition).

By their very nature such new systems also increase the efficiency of an organization. Because of its customer-oriented "do it yourself" software, FedEx was able to reduce the number of people handling incoming phone calls for parcel pickup and tracking.

Another excellent example of achieving an advantage through the development of a new computer system is self-scanning systems at grocery stores. Again, these new systems allow customers to process their own grocery purchases, scanning items and paying. People needing only a few grocery items specifically visit stores with self-scanning facilities because they believe they can get through the checkout line more quickly.

SECTION 12.1

making the grade

1. Many organizations today develop some systems just to be more ___________ in their internal processes.
2. When organizations develop new systems just to stay competitive, it is typically a(n) ___________ measure.
3. The best reason for an organization to develop a new system is for the purpose of gaining a(n) ___________ in the marketplace through innovation.

12.2 THE TRADITIONAL SYSTEMS DEVELOPMENT LIFE CYCLE

The most common way in which organizations develop systems today is through the traditional systems development life cycle. The ***traditional systems development life cycle (SDLC)*** is a structured step-by-step approach to developing systems that creates a separation of duties among technology specialists and users. In the SDLC, users (such as yourself) are the business process experts and quality control analysts, whereas the technology specialists are responsible for the actual design, construction, and support of the system.

It's like having a home custom built. You are the expert in what you want and it's up to you to ensure that the house is built to meet your needs and specifications. The builder, including all the various crews, is then responsible for the actual design and construction of your home along the lines you have laid out.

Using the SDLC, your organization follows six phases (see Figure 12.2):

1. Investigation
2. Analysis
3. Design
4. Construction
5. Implementation
6. Support

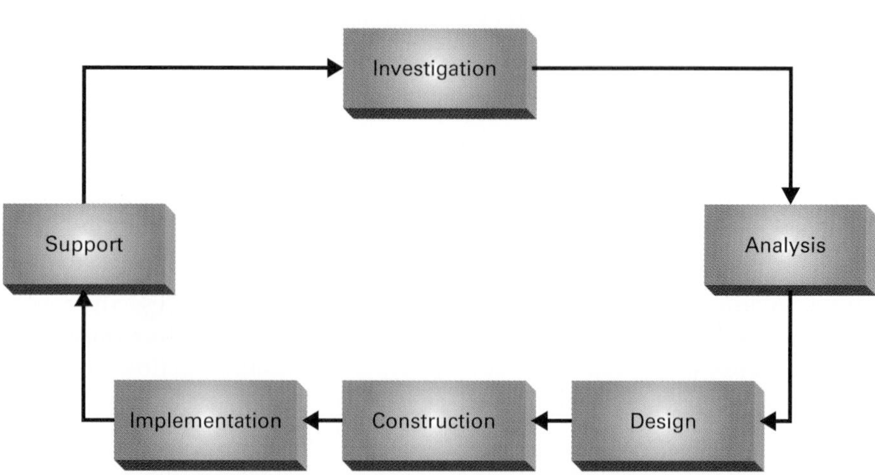

FIGURE 12.2

The traditional systems development life cycle (SDLC) has six phases.

To illustrate some key concepts and techniques in the SDLC, let's follow the Richmond Blood Center as it went about developing a new system for tracking donors, inventory, and requests from local hospitals. The Richmond Blood Center is a nonprofit organization that maintains an inventory of blood by accepting donations and fills requests for blood from local hospitals. Please review Figure 12.3.

FIGURE 12.3

The Richmond Blood Center needs a new system for tracking donors, inventory, and requests from local hospitals.

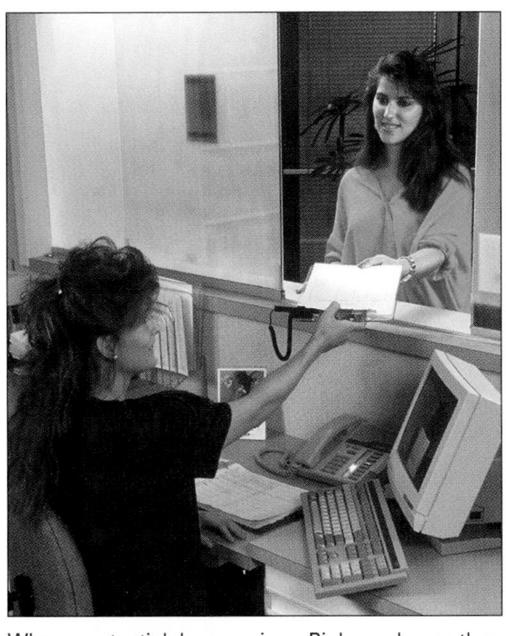

When a potential donor arrives, Richmond goes through a series of checks. For a new donor, Richmond gathers a variety of information, including name, address, age, and medical history. If the new donor is not acceptable, Richmond provides a written reason why and the donor is excused. For a repeat donor, Richmond verifies that enough time has elapsed since that donor last gave blood. If enough time has not elapsed, Richmond provides a written statement to that effect and the donor is excused.

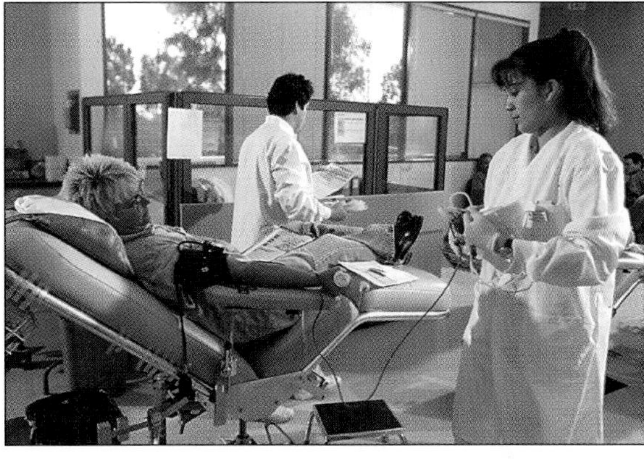

Donors who are acceptable are then taken to a waiting room, and, from there, on to a donating room. Once the donor has given blood, Richmond logs the pint of blood into its inventory and updates information for the donor.

Periodically, Richmond receives requests for blood from local hospitals. If Richmond has sufficient blood in inventory, it fills the requests and updates its blood inventory information. If there is insufficient inventory, Richmond backlogs the requests. On a daily basis, Richmond evaluates the backlogged requests to see which—if any—it can fill.

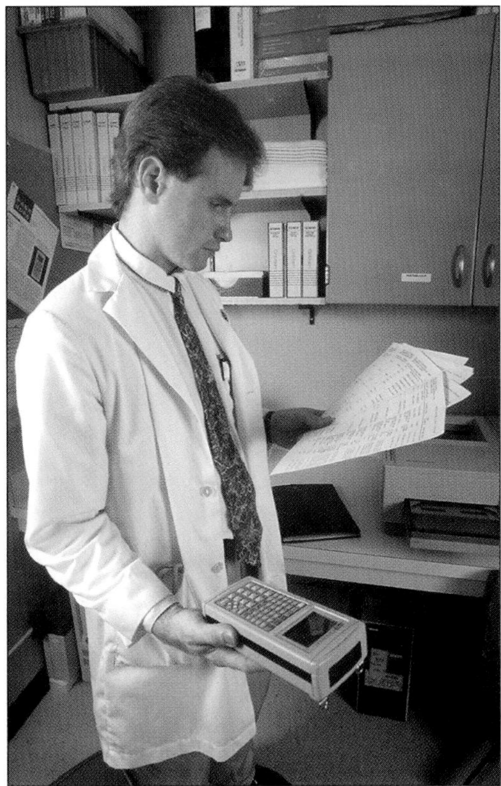

On a daily basis, Richmond checks its inventory status by blood type. If inventory levels for any blood type fall below 10 pints, Richmond generates appeal letters to previous donors with the given blood type.

SYSTEMS INVESTIGATION

How Does the Systems Development Process Begin in an Organization?

Here, we'll introduce you to the broad steps and considerations within each phase of the SDLC. To learn more about the SDLC, complete the "Systems Development Overview" tutorial on your SimNet Concepts Support CD.

In the first phase of the SDLC—***systems investigation***—you seek to lay the foundation for the systems development process by performing four tasks (see Figure 12.4). All four tasks are equally important, but at the outset defining the problem or opportunity is most crucial.

A ***problem/opportunity statement*** is a concise document that describes the exact nature of the problem or opportunity and provides broad statements concerning how the proposed system will benefit the organization. What is key here is that you define the problem or opportunity and not symptoms. Many systems development efforts fail today because people don't truly understand the nature of the problem or opportunity. So, they end up developing a system that treats only symptoms.

Second, you must create an *initial feasibility assessment* from several points of view, taking into account the time, technical, and fiscal aspects.

- A ***time feasibility assessment*** determines if your organization can develop the proposed system while meeting certain deadlines.
- A ***technical feasibility assessment*** determines if your organization has access to or can acquire the necessary hardware and software for the proposed system.
- A ***fiscal feasibility assessment*** determines if your organization has sufficient resources to develop the proposed system and if the total cost of those resources falls within an allocated budget.

If the proposed system is infeasible for any of the above reasons, you may choose to abandon its development or seek other development means such as end user development and outsourcing (which we'll discuss in later sections).

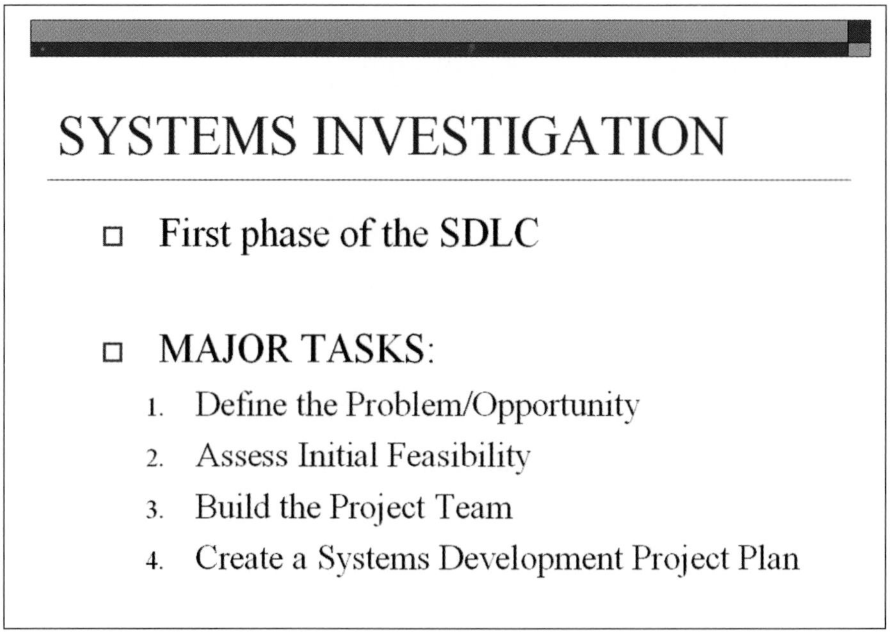

FIGURE 12.4

Systems investigation is the phase that starts the systems development life cycle (SDLC).

SYSTEMS INVESTIGATION
First phase of the SDLC
MAJOR TASKS:
1. Define the Problem/Opportunity
2. Assess Initial Feasibility
3. Build the Project Team
4. Create a Systems Development Project Plan

Once you've determined that a proposed system is feasible, it's time to build a project team. Most project teams include the following people:

- *A champion*—a ***system champion*** is a management person within your organization who (1) believes in the worth of the system and (2) has the "organizational muscle" to pull together the necessary resources. This may often be the chief information officer. A ***chief information officer (CIO)*** is the person within your organization who oversees the use of information as a resource.
- *Several users*—users are simply those people who will eventually be responsible for interacting with the system on a daily basis.
- *One or more systems analysts*—a ***systems analyst*** is a technology specialist who understands both technology and business processes. This person is responsible for gathering requirements from users and ensuring that other specialists understand those requirements.
- *One or more programmers*—a ***programmer*** is a technology specialist whose expertise lies in taking user requirements and writing software to match those requirements. Your team may include both ***application programmers*** (programmers who write application software) and ***system programmers*** (programmers who write operating system and utility software).
- *One or more hardware specialists*—a hardware specialist has expertise in different types and platforms of hardware, perhaps networking units or server computers.
- *Project manager*—the ***project manager*** is the person who oversees the project from beginning through implementation and support.

All these people are vitally important to the systems development process, with perhaps the most important being the systems analyst. A systems analyst must be able to speak two languages—business and technical. That person is responsible for creating the communications bridge between users (business process experts) and technology experts.

As the fourth and final task, you must create a *systems development project plan*. A ***systems development project plan*** is a document that includes a list of the project team, the problem/opportunity statement, the project budget, the feasibility assessments, and project timetable (see Figure 12.5). In each subsequent phase of the SDLC, you'll revisit this project plan and perhaps update it in light of new considerations. Most project teams use project management software such as Microsoft Project to help them effectively manage the project plan and organize all of the documents associated with the development of a specific project. To learn more about project management software, complete the "Project Management Applications" tutorial on your SimNet Concepts Support CD.

At the Richmond Blood Center, a nonprofit organization, gaining a competitive advantage in the marketplace was not a concern. It had a manual and paper-based process for tracking donors, handling blood requests from hospitals, managing inventory, and generating appeal letters that worked well enough. The real goal of the new system was simply to streamline processes to work more efficiently and thus productively.

FIGURE 12.5

The systems development project plan is the document you create in systems investigation.

1. **Problem/Opportunity Statement**
2. **Feasibility Statement**
   - Time
   - Technical
   - Fiscal
3. **Project Team**
   - Champion
   - Users
   - Systems Analysts
   - Programmers (Application and System)
   - Hardware Specialists
   - Project Manager
4. **Project Budget**
5. **Project Timetable**
   - Milestones

SYSTEMS ANALYSIS
How Does an Organization Study the Current System?

The ***systems analysis phase*** of the systems development life cycle (SDLC) involves modeling how the current system works from a logical (not physical) point of view, identifying its weaknesses and the opportunities to improve, creating a logical model of the new system, and reviewing the project plan (see Figure 12.6).

There are two keys here. First, you can't simply ignore the current system. It undoubtedly has some value. And when you model it, you can gain insight into its weaknesses and opportunities for improvement.

Second, the real goal of systems analysis is to develop an understanding of the current and proposed system from a logical, not physical, point of view. That is, at this point you shouldn't concern yourself with technical issues such as hardware and software. You should focus first on business processes and business information without regard to the hardware and software that does or will support them. In doing so, you allow your business needs to drive your technology decisions, not the other way around.

During this phase, you can employ a variety of modeling techniques—one of the more popular ones is data flow diagramming. ***Data flow diagramming (DFD)*** is a modeling technique for illustrating how information moves through various processes and how people outside the system provide and receive information. In Figure 12.7 on the opposite page you can see a data flow diagram (DFD) for the Richmond Blood Center. Notice that it really has no starting or ending point and that it makes no reference to technology. So, DFDs are great tools for modeling a system from a logical perspective without regard to any of its physical or technical characteristics. In a DFD, processes are represented as circles and information repositories are represented as rectangles. Players that are external to the system are also represented as rectangles.

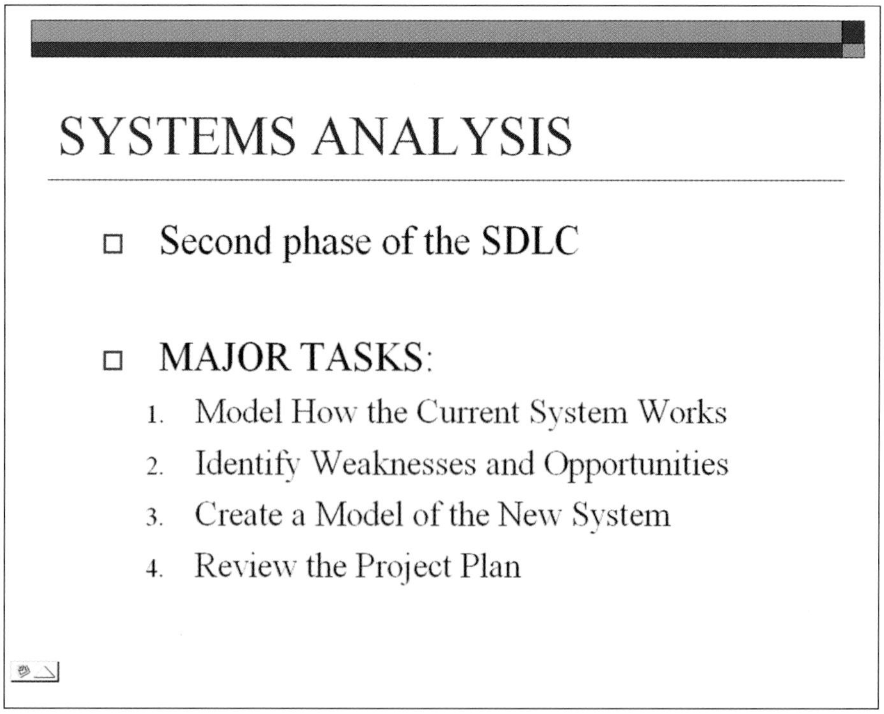

FIGURE 12.6

During systems analysis, you logically model the current and proposed systems.

SYSTEMS ANALYSIS

- Second phase of the SDLC
- MAJOR TASKS:
  1. Model How the Current System Works
  2. Identify Weaknesses and Opportunities
  3. Create a Model of the New System
  4. Review the Project Plan

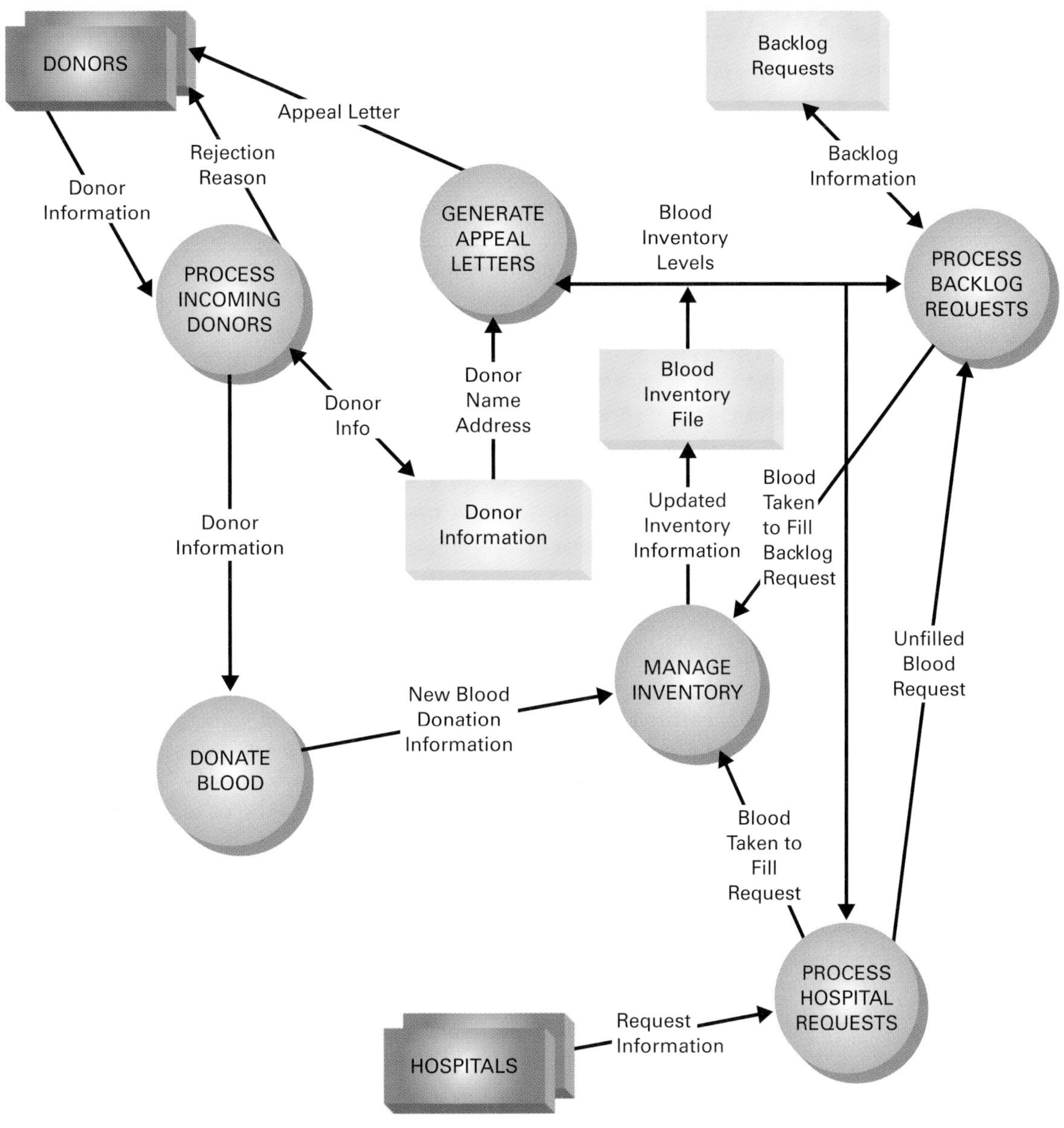

FIGURE 12.7

The Richmond Blood Center data flow diagram (DFD) shows major processes and the flows of information among them.

It was during this process that the receptionist for the Richmond Blood Center noted that repeat donors often became a bit miffed after driving to the blood center to give blood only to find that not enough time had elapsed since their last donation. So, the receptionist suggested that creating a Web site might be a good idea. Then, donors could type in a special password and determine if it was time to give blood again.

SYSTEMS DESIGN

How Does an Organization Create a "Blueprint" for the New System?

The ***systems design phase*** of the systems development life cycle (SDLC) involves generating several alternative technical solutions for the new logical model, selecting the best technical alternative, developing detailed software specifications, and—once again—reviewing the project plan (see Figure 12.8). Most of the work during this phase is performed by the technology specialists. Your role becomes one of reviewing the technical alternatives, the chosen technical alternative, and the software specifications to ensure that they meet your logical business needs.

As the technology specialists generate the software specifications, they will often create sample input screens, sample report formats, and program flowcharts. It is your responsibility to review all of these. A ***program flowchart*** is a graphical depiction of the detailed steps that software will perform. In Figure 12.9 on the opposite page you can see a partial program flowchart for the Richmond Blood Center for the software that accepts a hospital request for blood, determines if it can be filled and backlogs the request if it cannot be filled, or fills the order and updates the inventory to reflect that inventory has been reduced.

There are numerous other ways besides program flowcharting to create software specifications. We'll be covering some of these in the next chapter on programming and programming languages.

In generating and evaluating technical designs, your project team will probably look at such options as creating an *intranet,* a completely private system that runs on a network or perhaps a system that runs on a Web site for everyone on the Web to see and use. Whatever the case, there are more alternatives than you can imagine. It's up to your technology specialists to identify a group of the best, and then it's up to the entire project team (including users) to choose absolutely the best one given the constraints of your project plan.

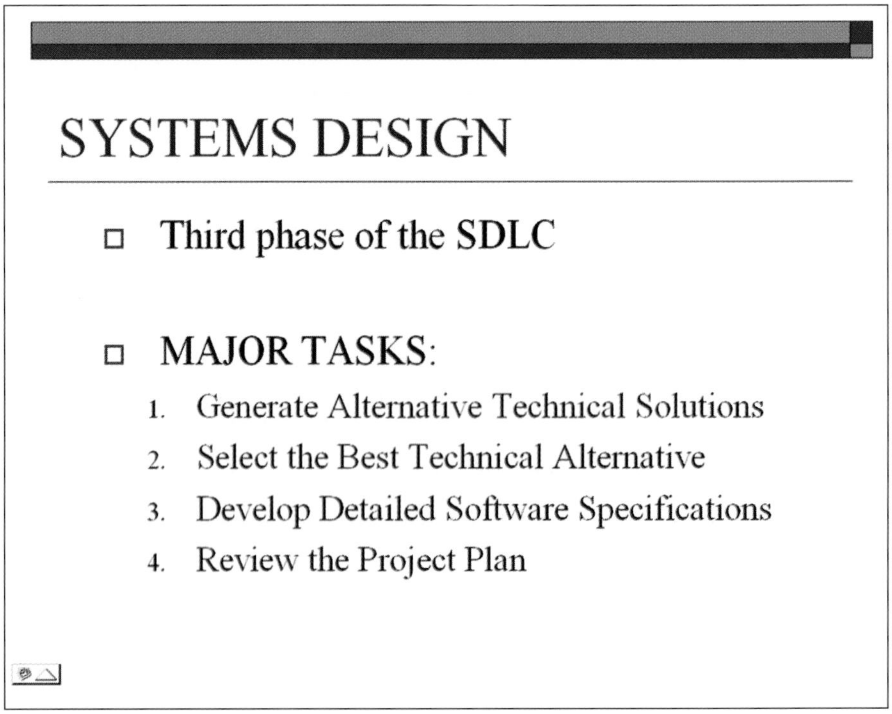

FIGURE 12.8

During systems design, you build the technical blueprint for the new system.

SYSTEMS DESIGN

- Third phase of the SDLC
- MAJOR TASKS:
  1. Generate Alternative Technical Solutions
  2. Select the Best Technical Alternative
  3. Develop Detailed Software Specifications
  4. Review the Project Plan

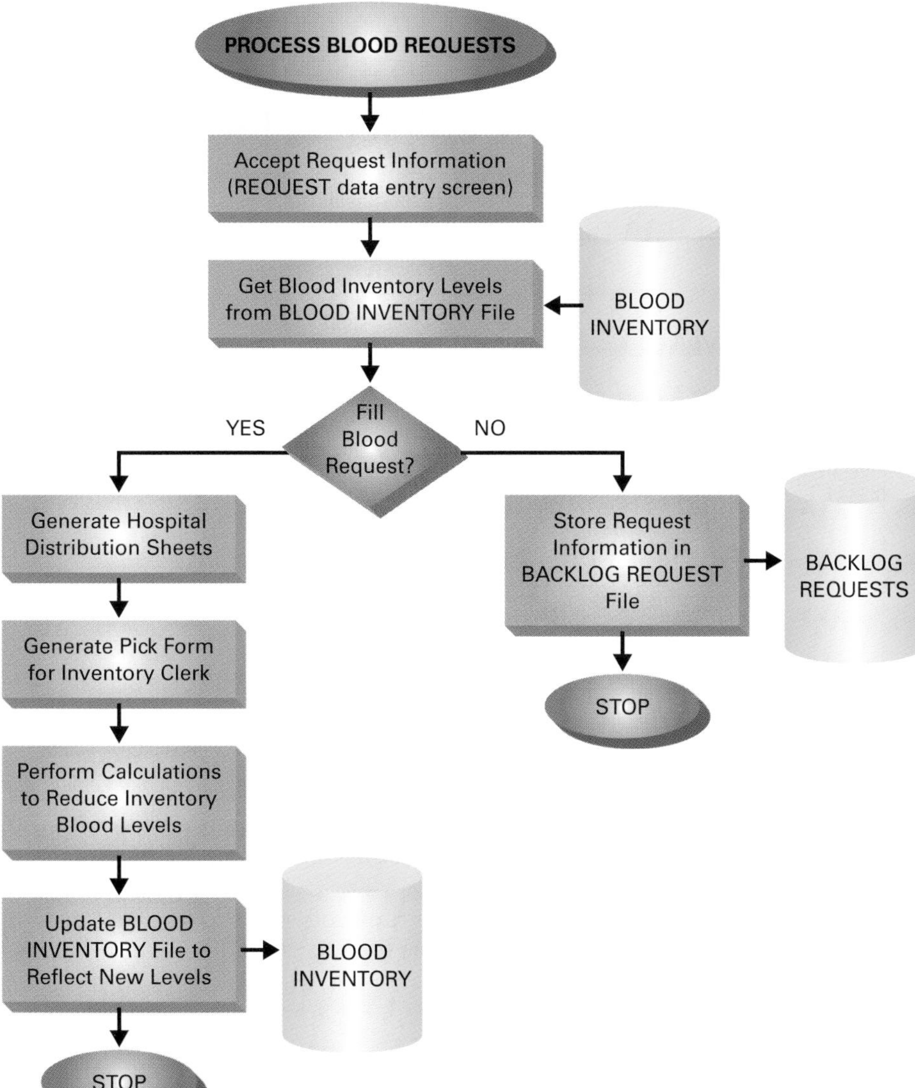

FIGURE 12.9

This flowchart shows the process the Richmond Blood Center follows for blood requests from hospitals.

If you're interested in a career as an IT specialist, generating flowcharts and technical designs for a proposed system, you have numerous opportunities available to you. Organizations of all sizes need skilled IT architects who can design technical solutions. But keep in mind that the best IT technical architects also understand every facet of business operations including accounting, finance, production, and others.

SYSTEMS CONSTRUCTION
How Do Technology Specialists Build the New System?

The goal of the ***systems construction phase*** of the systems development life cycle (SDLC) is to actually create the new system. This will involve a number of tasks including acquiring and installing any new hardware, writing software, testing the software, and reviewing the project plan (see

FIGURE 12.10

During systems construction, you actually build the new system.

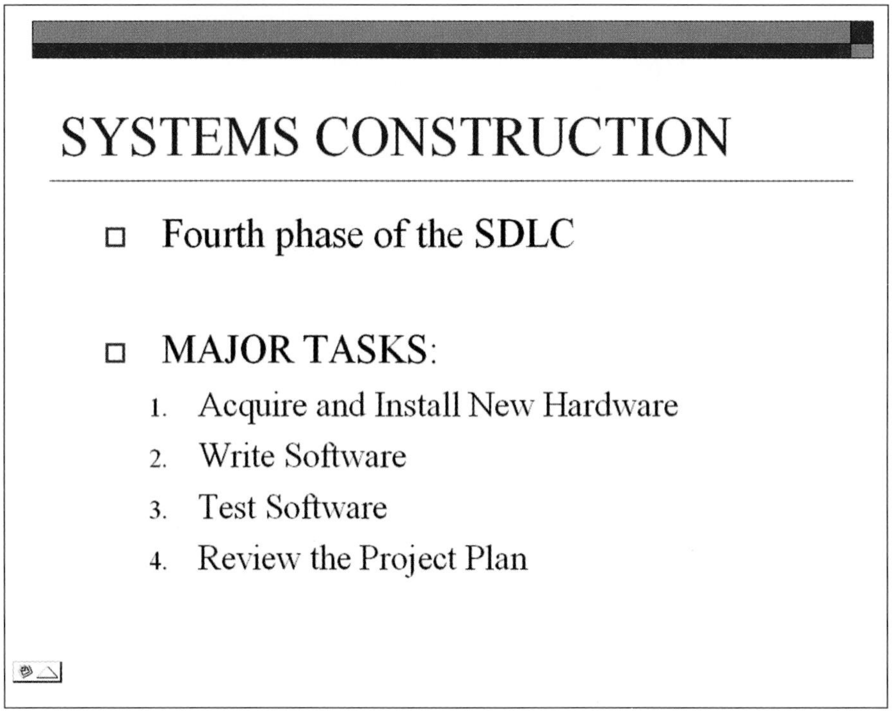

SYSTEMS CONSTRUCTION

- Fourth phase of the SDLC
- MAJOR TASKS:
  1. Acquire and Install New Hardware
  2. Write Software
  3. Test Software
  4. Review the Project Plan

did you know? On its busiest day in December, MasterCard International processes over 16 million transactions.[1]

Figure 12.10). This is the phase in the SDLC that requires the most time. According to most experts, 80 to 90 percent of all efforts are devoted to this phase. Why? Because writing and testing software is a labor-intensive task.

Writing software requires that programmers use the software specifications and a programming language or tool to actually create the working software. That is no small task. Consider this—the typical large organization payroll software includes somewhere between 500,000 and 1 million lines of software code. And all that code must work perfectly.

That's also why testing is so important during this phase. As a user, you'll be called on to test the software. At this point, you'll need to make sure that the software doesn't allow you to enter bad information (such as a series of numbers for a name or the letter "Q" for a blood type). You'll also want to test the software for range validity—for example, the system for the Richmond Blood Center should not allow the entry of new donors who are under the age of 18. Basically, you have to look at every field and determine what it cannot accept and then try it.

As you do this, hardware specialists will be acquiring, installing, and testing any new hardware. Eventually, you'll have to test the software again (in the next phase) on the new hardware under operational conditions.

SYSTEMS IMPLEMENTATION

What Steps Must an Organization Take to Start Using the New System?

The ***systems implementation phase*** of the systems development life cycle (SDLC) involves training users, converting existing information to the new system, converting users, acceptance testing, and reviewing the project plan (see Figure 12.11 on the opposite page). At this point, your project team brings the new system to life in your organization. The project team

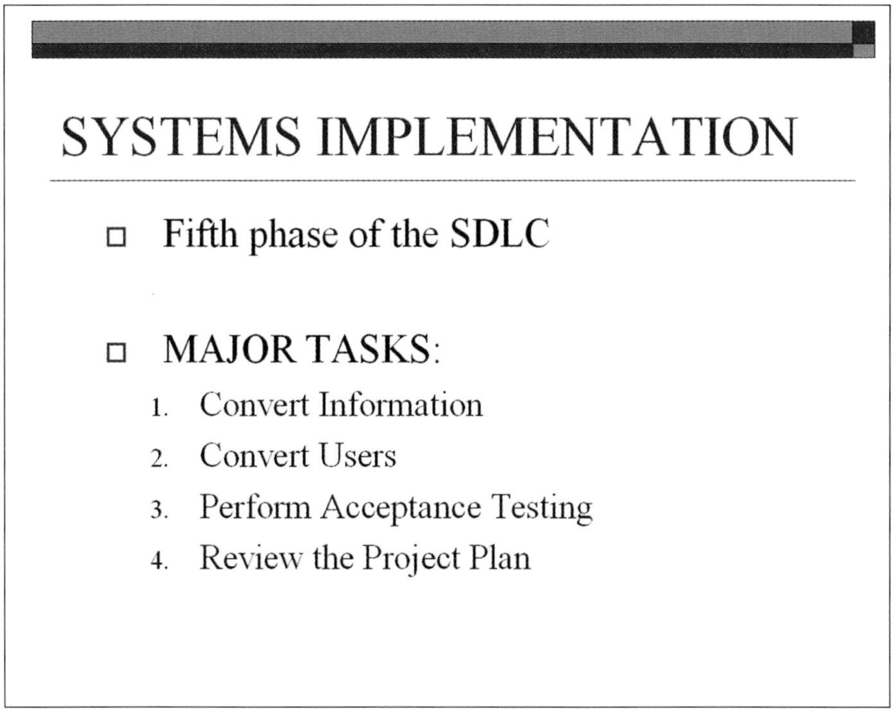

SYSTEMS IMPLEMENTATION

- Fifth phase of the SDLC
- MAJOR TASKS:
  1. Convert Information
  2. Convert Users
  3. Perform Acceptance Testing
  4. Review the Project Plan

FIGURE 12.11

During systems implementation, you test the new system and bring it to life in your organization.

installs the new software on the new hardware, trains all users how to use the software, and goes through a process of acceptance testing.

Acceptance testing is a formal, documented process in which users use the new system, verify that it works correctly under operational conditions, and note any errors that need to be fixed.

A key in this phase is moving from the old way of doing things to the new system. We call this *conversion*. There are four popular conversion methods:

1. ***Parallel conversion***—you run both the old and new systems until you're sure the new system works correctly.
2. ***Plunge conversion***—you unplug the old system and use the new system exclusively.
3. ***Pilot conversion***—you target a select group of users to convert to the new system before converting everyone.
4. ***Piecemeal conversion***—you target only a portion of the new system for conversion, ensure that it works correctly, and then convert the remaining system.

Each method has its advantages and disadvantages. For example, parallel conversion is the safest but also the most expensive procedure. Plunge conversion (sometimes called "cold turkey" conversion) is the cheapest but also the most dangerous if the new system fails. Many organizations combine two or several methods. For example, an international organization may convert its home office in Tokyo using a parallel conversion method before converting the rest of its offices (pilot approach).

The Richmond Blood Center, because its old system was paper-based, decided to use a parallel conversion method. So, employees at each process gathered and recorded information using both the old paper system and the new computerized system until it was verified that the new system worked correctly.

SYSTEMS SUPPORT

What Happens When the New System Needs Modification?

No system is ever complete. The way your organization works and the processes it performs are constantly evolving and changing. So, your computer systems must change as well. It may be that your systems are fairly robust and adaptable to change. But it is entirely possible that a given system may need a complete overhaul at some time.

During systems support, your tasks are four-fold (see Figure 12.12). First, your organization must provide a formal mechanism for the periodic review of the system. Your organization will be interested in answering such questions as "Does this system still support the overall business goals?" and "Do modifications need to be made to this system in light of changes to business processes?" These are very important questions, and your organization should provide answers to them on a frequent basis.

Second, users of the system may notice changes that need to be made. Some of these are quite simple, such as adding a new report. Others may be more complex, such as adding new business rules to meet federal reporting requirements for tax purposes. Whatever the case, your organization must provide a formal mechanism through which users can request changes. You can certainly achieve this by creating a change request form or by holding meetings in which users provide feedback concerning the system and its operation.

Third, as changes are proposed your organization must evaluate them and determine which (if any) to undertake. As we've stated, even seemingly minor modifications require time and money. Your organization must constantly balance proposed changes against limited resources.

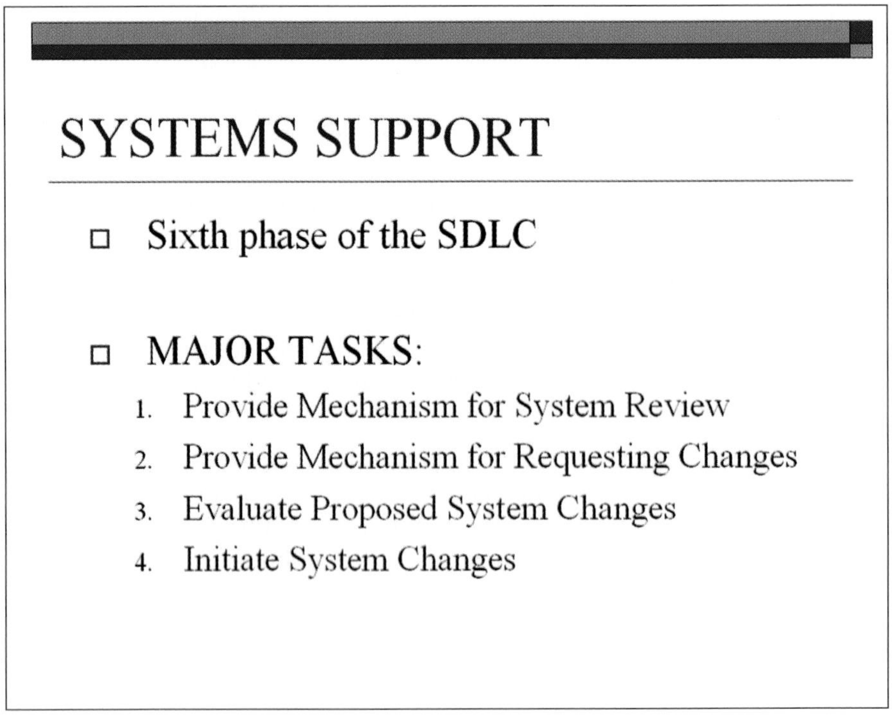

FIGURE 12.12

Systems support includes a variety of ongoing tasks.

SYSTEMS SUPPORT

- Sixth phase of the SDLC
- MAJOR TASKS:
  1. Provide Mechanism for System Review
  2. Provide Mechanism for Requesting Changes
  3. Evaluate Proposed System Changes
  4. Initiate System Changes

i•can

Understand My Roles in Each Step of the SDLC

Most people in any organization are not IT specialists—perhaps they are like you, seeking to have systems developed that will make you more productive so you can do a more efficient and effective job. This surely doesn't mean that you should take a backseat role in the SDLC. On the contrary, you should actively strive for the best outcome by participating in the various phases of the SDLC as a

- Business process expert.
- Quality control analyst.
- Manager of other people.

In the early phases of the SDLC you'll be acting as a business process expert, providing vitally important information concerning how the current system works or doesn't work and what features you would like to see in the new system. Without this sort of input from you and everybody else, the project team will never be able to build a system that meets your needs.

In later phases of the SDLC, as technology specialists take over much of the development responsibilities, your role will shift to one of a quality control analyst, in which you review and verify the work of the IT specialists. Again, without your input here, the IT specialists will not be able to design, develop, and implement a system that meets your intended needs.

Finally, in all phases you'll have to take into consideration the productivity of those people you are managing. As a manager of a department or unit, one of your primary responsibilities is to ensure that the employees you're overseeing have the right IT systems to make them more productive.

Finally, your organization must initiate system change. This is usually achieved in one of two ways. First, if the change is minor, such as adding a report, the new requirements would go immediately to the construction phase for the writing and testing of the necessary software. On the other hand, major changes may require you to start the SDLC all over again with the investigation phase. This often occurs when the technology on which the original system was built becomes obsolete and hard to maintain (see Figure 12.13). If this is the case, starting over may very well be the best way to implement change.

For a period of time after implementation, support costs may be relatively high for further user training and eliminating "bugs."

Nearing the end of the useful life of a system, support costs will begin to skyrocket. It's definitely time to consider a complete overhaul.

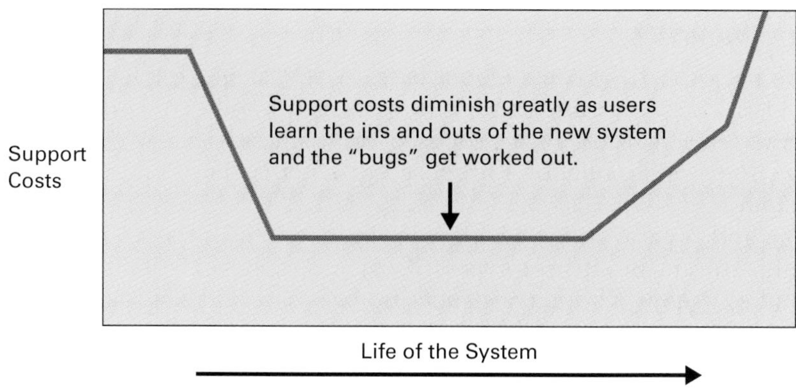
Support costs diminish greatly as users learn the ins and outs of the new system and the "bugs" get worked out.
Support Costs
Life of the System

FIGURE 12.13

Support costs for a system vary over time.

SECTION 12.2

making the grade

1. A(n) ___________ feasibility assessment determines if your organization can develop the proposed system while meeting certain deadlines.
2. A(n) ___________ is a technology specialist who understands both technology and business processes.
3. ___________ is a modeling technique for illustrating how information moves through various processes and how people outside the system provide and receive information.
4. Using the ___________ conversion method you literally unplug the old system and use the new system exclusively.

12.3 END USER DEVELOPMENT AND PROTOTYPING

The systems development life cycle (SDLC) is the most popular way organizations develop computer systems. Two other popular alternatives are outsourcing (which we'll discuss in the next section) and end user development. ***End user development*** is the development and support of computer systems by users (such as yourself) with little or no help from technology specialists.

End user development is growing in popularity. Today, it's estimated that most organizations have so many new proposed systems that it would take them an average of five years to complete them all. So, many organizations are empowering employees to develop many smaller systems themselves. This is the concept of end user development.

You must be prepared for this. Although you won't be developing large-scale systems that support hundreds of users, you'll probably be developing smaller systems such as a customer information tracking system for the marketing department or perhaps a maintenance scheduling system for equipment on the production floor. These are definitely important systems.

did you know? Almost 70 percent of all business *software running today was developed in the language COBOL.*

PROTOTYPING

Will I Follow the SDLC while Performing End User Development?

When you perform the process of end user development, you'll almost always build prototypes. ***Prototyping*** is the process of building a model that demonstrates the features of a proposed product, service, or system. A ***prototype,*** then, is a model of a proposed product (which can be a computer system).

People and organizations perform prototyping all the time. Automobile manufacturers build prototypes of cars to demonstrate safety features. Building contractors construct models of bridges to test their strength in adverse weather conditions. Your instructor may give you sample test questions for an upcoming exam. Those sample questions are a model or prototype of what you can expect.

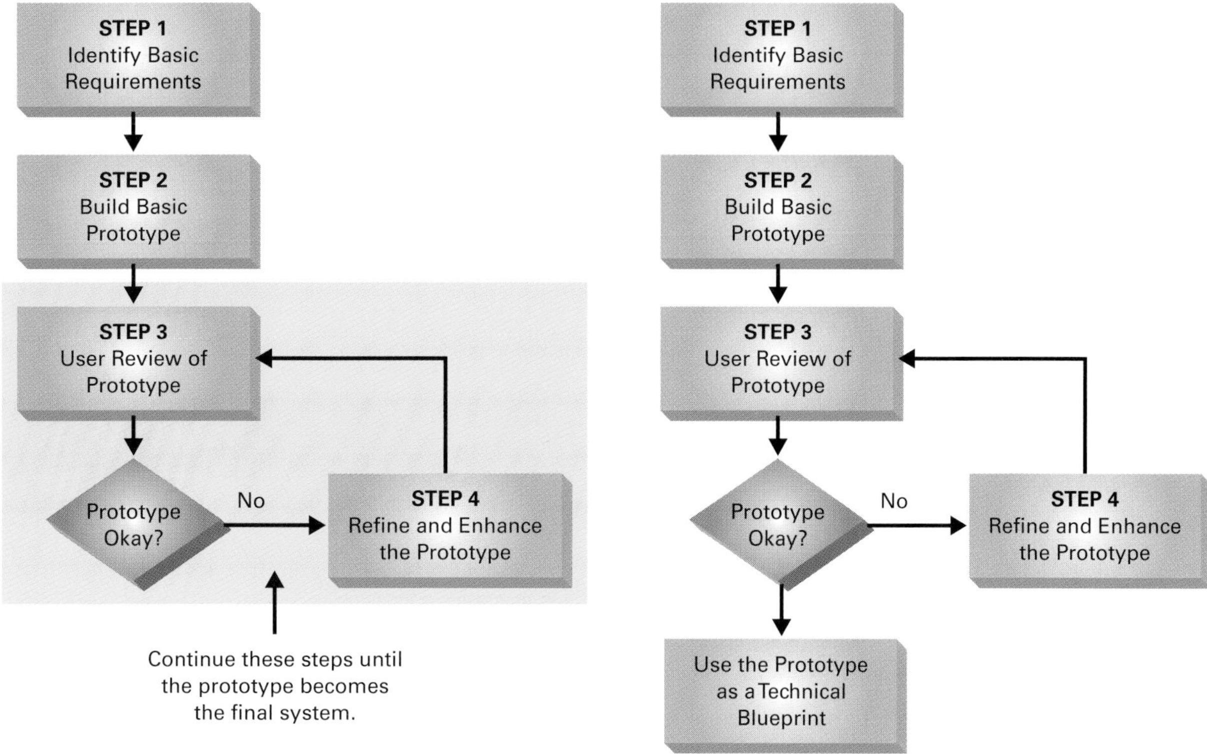

FIGURE 12.14

In prototyping, you start with basic requirements and continually add new features and processes.

In systems development, prototyping is an iterative process (see Figure 12.14) in which you

1. Identify the basic requirements of the system.
2. Build a prototype from basic requirements.
3. Have other users review the prototype and suggest changes.
4. Refine and enhance the prototype until it's complete.

The iterative process occurs between steps 3 and 4. So, as your fellow users review your prototype and suggest changes, you refine and enhance your prototype and then have the users once again review the updated prototype. This iterative process continues until the prototype is complete and can become the final system (see the left side of Figure 12.14).

Prototyping is also widely used in the SDLC. However, as the right side of Figure 12.14 shows, the final prototype in the SDLC acts only as the technical blueprint from which the eventual system is developed. So, during the SDLC, prototyping is used for the analysis and design phases. For end user development, you'll most often use prototyping for analysis, design, and construction.

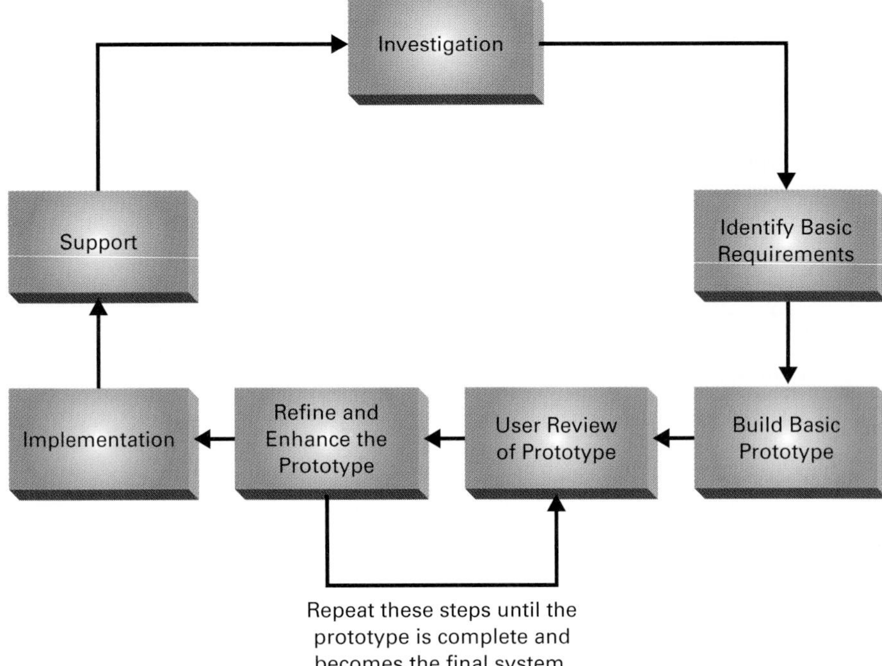

FIGURE 12.15
End user development looks similar to the traditional systems development life cycle (SDLC).

THE END USER DEVELOPMENT PROCESS
What Steps Will I Follow while Performing End User Development?

In Figure 12.15, you can see the phases of end user development including the prototyping process. It's actually quite similar to the SDLC, except that analysis, design, and construction are replaced by the four steps of prototyping.

During end user development—as its name implies—the burden of all development tasks falls on your shoulders. These tasks include identifying potential hardware and choosing the best, writing any necessary software, training other users, converting existing information to the new system, testing the new system, and completely documenting how the new system works, just to name a few.

These are not insignificant tasks, and you shouldn't take them lightly. End user development is an empowering process. But it comes with increased responsibility.

END USER DEVELOPMENT ADVANTAGES AND DISADVANTEGES
Is There a Good Side and a Bad Side to End User Development?

As always, there are two sides to the coin. End user development has both advantages and disadvantages. The advantages of end user development include

- *Encouraging active user participation*—when users develop their own system, they participate more in its development.
- *Improving requirements determination*—users essentially tell themselves of the systems requirements in end user development.
- *Strengthening user sense of ownership*—no matter what you do, if you do it yourself, you take pride in your work.

did you know? The *average American depends on more than 264 computers per day.*

- *Increasing the speed of systems development*—smaller systems do not lend themselves well to the SDLC and can benefit from end user development with prototyping.

If you're not knowledgeable and careful, however, end user development can lead to problems:

- *Undeveloped systems*—end users may lack the necessary expertise in IT development to complete a system.
- *"Privatized" systems*—end users often develop systems that do not take into account what the entire organization needs.
- *Subpar systems*—end users often choose technologies they are comfortable with as opposed to more optimal technologies.
- *Short-lived systems*—end users may not fully document a system, making it difficult to make changes in the future.

making the grade SECTION 12.3

1. ___________ is the development and support of computer systems by users with little or no help from technology specialists.
2. A(n) ___________ is a model of a proposed system.
3. In prototyping, you must first identify the ___________.
4. In prototyping, the iterative process occurs between steps ___________ and ___________.

12.4 OUTSOURCING

A final alternative to developing a computer system is outsourcing. ***Outsourcing*** is the delegation of work to a group outside your organization for (1) a specified length of time, (2) a specified cost, and (3) a specified level of service.

Outsourcing is big business, and not just limited to the technology area. According to a Yankee Group survey of 500 companies, 90 percent stated that they had outsourced at least one major business function and 45 percent stated that they had outsourced some major portion of their technology environment. In just the IT area, a survey estimated that outsourcing exceeded $120 billion in the year 2000.

As you can see in Figure 12.16, there are various ways an organization can outsource some of its IT operations:

1. Purchasing ***horizontal market software,*** or general business software that has application in many industries. Horizontal market software includes accounts receivable, payroll, inventory management, logistics, and customer relationship management.

FIGURE 12.16
Outsourcing systems development can take on many forms.

2. Purchasing ***vertical market software,*** or software that is unique to a particular industry. In the medical field, for example, an organization can purchase radiology software, nursing scheduling software, and patient admission software. These types of applications are definitely unique to the medical field (you wouldn't buy nursing scheduling software to help you schedule production equipment on a manufacturing floor).
3. Hiring an outsourcing vendor to develop software from scratch—when no prewritten software is available, an organization may choose to hire an organization to create the system from scratch.

THE OUTSOURCING PROCESS

How Is the Process of Outsourcing Different from and Similar to the SDLC?

In most instances, outsourcing is similar to the systems development life cycle (SDLC), except that your organization turns over much of the design, construction, implementation, and support steps to another organization. However, your organization is still responsible for investigation, analysis, and a few new steps centered on a *request for proposal* (see Figure 12.17).

Systems Investigation

No matter who will develop the proposed system, you must always perform systems investigation. Recall from our discussion of the SDLC that systems investigation includes performing an initial feasibility assessment. It is while assessing the initial feasibility of a proposal that you might target a system for outsourcing.

For example, you could determine that your IT specialists haven't enough time or resources to build a system. You could also determine that your organization doesn't possess the expertise to develop a given system. You may also find that it's simply cheaper to buy prewritten horizontal or vertical market software than it is to develop it from scratch. These are all good reasons why your organization would target the development of a proposed system for outsourcing.

FIGURE 12.17

Like end user development, outsourcing looks similar to the traditional systems development life cycle (SDLC).

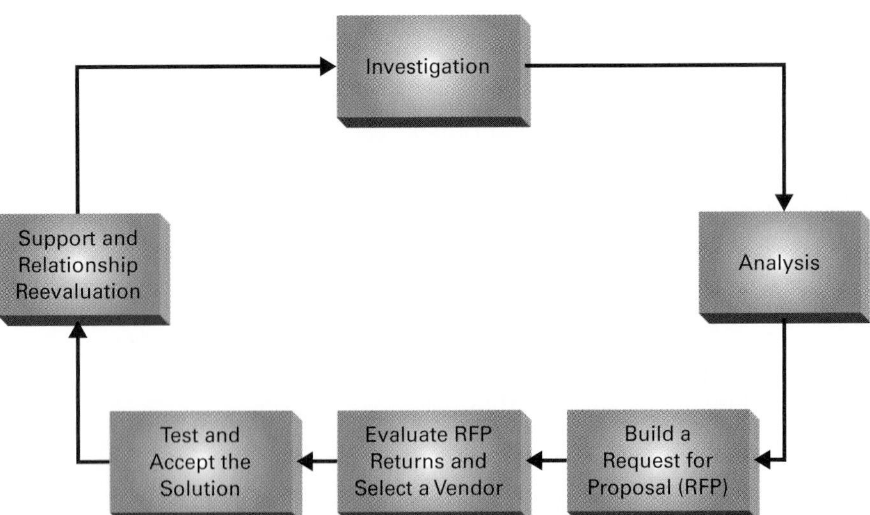

Systems Analysis

As with systems investigation, you must still perform the systems analysis phase for any proposed system. The documentation you create during systems analysis will become the foundation for the most important outsourcing document—a request for proposal.

Build a Request for Proposal (RFP)

To tell an outsourcing vendor what you want, you must create a request for proposal. A ***request for proposal (RFP)*** is a formal document that outlines your logical requirements for the proposed system and invites outsourcing vendors to bid on its development.

An RFP is not a small document—some will exceed several hundred pages and require months for your organization to create. Here, take all the time you need. The more complete and thorough your RFP, the more likely an outsourcing vendor will be able to define and develop a system that meets all your needs. Figure 12.18 shows the general outline of content for an RFP.

FIGURE 12.18

A request for proposal (RFP) is the most important document in outsourcing.

1. **Organizational Overview**
2. **Problem Statement**
3. **Description of Current System**
   - Business Processes
   - Hardware
   - Software (Application and System)
   - Information
   - System Interfaces
4. **Request for New System Characteristics**
   - Hardware
   - Software
   - Business Processes
   - Information
   - System Interfaces
5. **Request for Implementation Plan**
   - Training
   - Conversion
6. **Request for Support Plan**
   - Hardware
   - Software
   - Training
7. **Request for Development Time Frame**
8. **Request for Statement of Outsourcing Costs**
9. **How RFP Returns Will Be Scored**
10. **Deadline for RFP Returns**
11. **Primary Contact Person**

Evaluate Request for Proposal Returns and Select a Vendor

Once you receive RFP returns from several potential outsourcing vendors, you must evaluate those and decide on which outsourcing vendor to use. Again, this is not a simple process. One outsourcing vendor may be the cheapest but may not offer a system with everything you want. Another outsourcing vendor may offer exactly the system you want but cannot develop it within your desired time frame.

Once you've chosen an outsourcing vendor, a lengthy and legal process follows during which you must create a legally binding document that both organizations sign stating exactly what work is to be carried out, how and when payments will be made, the project time frame, and how your organization can get out of the contract if the outsourcing vendor is not living up to its end. With that legal document in place, the outsourcing vendor will set out to create the system you want.

Test and Accept the Solution

Once the outsourcing vendor has completed the system, it will turn it over to you for testing and acceptance. It is during this time that you'll completely test the software, train users, convert old information to the new system, and convert users to the new system (through one or some combination of the parallel, plunge, pilot, and piecemeal conversion methods).

Your most important task here is to completely test the software. If something doesn't work right, do not accept the system. Instead, have the outsourcing vendor fix the problem(s) immediately.

i•series insights *Ethics, Security & Privacy*

Outsourcing Gone Bad

Outsourcing can be a very effective systems development technique. It enables your organization to focus on its unique core competencies and hire another organization to perform processes, take over business activities, and also develop systems that are important but not in a strategic sense. For example, your school may outsource its food operations and perhaps security. Why? Because your school is not in the business of providing food—it's in the business of providing you with an education. So, your school can focus on that primary task and let someone else make your lunch.

But there are significant downsides to outsourcing for systems development related to the competence of the outside source. For example, Duke Power Co. hired an outsourcing vendor to develop a customer relationship management system. The outsourcing vendor did deliver the system but it didn't work correctly. The vendor then wanted another two years to make modifications. Duke Power had no choice but to abandon the project, and it lost $12 million in the process.

This problem of course occurs in all business environments. A couple of years ago GE was all set to introduce a new washing machine, but it couldn't because GE had outsourced some of the parts development and the vendor was late in delivering the parts. So, GE had to delay its product introduction and lost money on marketing and advertising.

It may not always be true that if you want something done right you should do it yourself. But just because you hire someone else to do your work doesn't necessarily mean that it will get done right or on time.

Systems Support and Relationship Reevaluation

As you move forward in using the new system, you'll want to provide for the many support tasks we discussed with the SDLC, including performing a periodic review of the system, providing a formal mechanism through which users can request changes, and evaluating their worth.

Most important, you'll want to constantly reevaluate your relationship with the outsourcing vendor. Many such organizations include support and maintenance activities as part of the overall cost of the system. Is the outsourcing vendor providing support when it stated it would? Is the outsourcing vendor willing to help you evaluate the worth of proposed changes as it stated it would?

If you're considering a career in the IT field, you may very well go to work for an outsourcing vendor, creating systems for other organizations. If so, you need to learn in great detail how the SDLC works, how it is affected by outsourcing, and how to create an RFP response.

SECTION 12.4

making the grade

1. ___________ is the delegation of work to a group outside your organization.
2. ___________ market software is general business software that has application in many industries.
3. ___________ market software is software that is unique to a particular industry.
4. The most important document in the outsourcing process is a(n) ___________.

12.5 SUMMARY AND KEY TERMS

Organizations need computer systems today for three reasons: (1) to remain efficient, (2) to level the competitive playing field, and (3) to achieve an advantage through innovation. Your participation in the systems development process is important because you are (or will be): (1) a business process expert, (2) a quality control analyst, and (3) a manager of other people.

The most common way in which organizations develop systems is through the ***traditional systems development life cycle (SDLC)***—a structured step-by-step approach to developing systems that creates a separation of duties among technology specialists and users. The SDLC includes six phases:

1. ***Systems investigation***—laying the foundation for the systems development process. In it you create a problem/opportunity statement; perform time, technical, and fiscal feasibility assessments; gather a project team; and create a systems development project plan.
2. ***Systems analysis***—modeling how the current system works, identifying weaknesses and opportunities, creating a model of the new system, and reviewing the project plan.
3. ***Systems design***—generating several alternative technical solutions, selecting the best alternative, developing detailed software specifications, and reviewing the project plan.
4. ***Systems construction***—creating the new system, including acquiring and installing any new hardware, writing software, testing software, and reviewing the project plan.
5. ***Systems implementation***—training users, converting existing information to the new system, converting users, acceptance testing, and reviewing the project plan.
6. ***Systems support***—maintaining and supporting the system over time.

Because most organizations don't have the IT resources to develop all proposed systems, they are turning to end user development. ***End user development*** is the development and support of computer systems by users (such as yourself) with little or no help from technology specialists. As you perform this process, you'll most often be ***prototyping,*** building a model that demonstrates the features of a proposed system. As you continually refine the prototype, you eventually create a complete and working system.

Still other organizations are turning to outsourcing. ***Outsourcing*** is the delegation of work to a group outside your organization for (1) a specified length of time, (2) a specified cost, and (3) a specified level of service. The most important document in outsourcing is a request for proposal. A ***request for proposal (RFP)*** is a formal document that outlines your logical requirements for the proposed system and invites outsourcing vendors to bid on its development.

KEY TERMS

acceptance testing (p. 369)
application programmer (p. 363)
chief information officer (CIO) (p. 363)
data flow diagramming (DFD) (p. 364)
end user development (p. 372)
fiscal feasibility assessment (p. 362)
horizontal market software (p. 375)
outsourcing (p. 375)
parallel conversion (p. 369)
piecemeal conversion (p. 369)
pilot conversion (p. 369)
plunge conversion (p. 369)
problem/opportunity statement (p. 362)
program flowchart (p. 366)
programmer (p. 363)
project manager (p. 363)
prototype (p. 372)
prototyping (p. 372)
request for proposal (RFP) (p. 377)
system champion (p. 363)
system programmer (p. 363)
systems analysis phase (p. 364)
systems analyst (p. 363)
systems construction phase (p. 367)
systems design phase (p. 366)
systems development project plan (p. 363)
systems implementation phase (p. 368)
systems investigation (p. 362)
technical feasibility assessment (p. 362)
time feasibility assessment (p. 362)
traditional systems development life cycle (SDLC) (p. 360)
vertical market software (p. 376)

review of terminology

Multiple Choice

1. A(n) ___________ feasibility assessment determines if your organization has access to or can acquire the necessary hardware and software for the proposed system.
   a. time
   b. technical
   c. fiscal
   d. outsourcing
   e. organizational

2. During systems investigation, you
   a. define the problem/opportunity.
   b. assess initial feasibility.
   c. build a project team.
   d. create a systems development project plan.
   e. perform all of the above steps.

3. The person within your organization who oversees the use of information as a resource is called the
   a. CEO.
   b. CFO.
   c. CIO.
   d. CCO.
   e. CPO.

4. A programmer who writes operating system software is called a(n)
   a. application programmer.
   b. computer system programmer.
   c. operating system programmer.
   d. system programmer.
   e. OS programmer.

5. The phase of the SDLC in which you model systems from a logical point of view is the
   a. systems investigation phase.
   b. systems analysis phase.
   c. systems design phase.
   d. systems construction phase.
   e. systems implementation phase.

6. The phase of the SDLC in which you generate and evaluate several different technical alternatives is the
   a. systems investigation phase.
   b. systems analysis phase.
   c. systems design phase.
   d. systems construction phase.
   e. systems implementation phase.

7. During systems construction, you
   a. model the new system from a logical point of view.
   b. model the new system from a technical point of view.
   c. perform acceptance testing.
   d. write and test software.
   e. establish a project team.

8. Acceptance testing occurs in which phase of the SDLC?
   a. systems investigation phase
   b. systems analysis phase
   c. systems design phase
   d. systems construction phase
   e. systems implementation phase

9. The conversion method in which you target a select group of users to convert to the new system is called
   a. parallel conversion.
   b. plunge conversion.
   c. pilot conversion.
   d. piecemeal conversion.
   e. micro conversion.

10. The conversion method in which you target only a portion of the new system for conversion is called
   a. parallel conversion.
   b. plunge conversion.
   c. pilot conversion.
   d. piecemeal conversion.
   e. micro conversion.

True/False

11. ____ Fiscal feasibility assessment determines if your organization has the facilities to house the hardware for a proposed system.
12. ____ A programmer who writes application software is called an application programmer.
13. ____ A program flowchart is a graphical depiction of the detailed steps that software will perform.
14. ____ Using the parallel method of conversion, you run both the old and new system until you're sure the new system works correctly.
15. ____ Using the traditional SDLC, you outsource the design and implementation phases.

Take this quiz online at www.mhhe.com/i-series and get instant feedback.

review of concepts

QUESTIONS AND EXERCISES

1. Understanding Your Roles in Each Step of the SDLC

As a non-IT specialist, your roles during each phase of the SDLC differ. Primarily, you will be some combination of (1) a business process expert in that you provide information concerning how the current system works and how you want the new system to work, (2) a quality control analyst in that you review and verify that the project team is developing the new system with the features you want, and (3) a manager of other people in that you must take into account the needed productivity of people you manage. In each row (SDLC phase) in the table below, you are to allocate a total of 100 points according to the extent to which you think you would participate in that SDLC phase as a business process expert, quality control analyst, and manager of other people. That is, the sum of the values you provide in every row must sum to 100 at the end.

SDLC Phase	Business Process Expert	Quality Control Analyst	Manager of Other People	Total
Systems Investigation				= 100
Systems Analysis				= 100
Systems Design				= 100
Systems Construction				= 100
Systems Implementation				= 100
Systems Maintenance				= 100

2. Understanding the Relationships among the SDLC and a Request for Proposal

In Figure 12.18 on page 377, we provided an outline of a request for proposal (RFP). You'll notice that in many ways it looks very similar to the SDLC. In the table below, identify which phases of the SDLC most closely correspond to each element of an RFP.

Elements of a Request for Proposal (RFP)	Phase(s) of the SDLC
1. Organizational overview	
2. Problem statement	
3. Description of the current system	
4. Request for new system characteristics	
5. Request for implementation plan	
6. Request for support plan	
7. Request for development time frame	
8. Request for statement of outsourcing costs	
9. How RFP returns will be scored	
10. Deadline for RFP returns	
11. Primary contact person	

3. Identifying Steps within Phases of the SDLC

For each of the following steps in the left column identify in which phase of the SDLC they occur (given in the right column). Some of these are a bit "tricky" as we haven't specifically addressed them in the chapter. You'll have to think on your own and be prepared to justify your answers.

Step	SDLC Phase
A. _____ Build the project team	1. Systems Investigation
B. _____ Create a model of the new system	2. Systems Analysis
C. _____ Write software	3. Systems Design
D. _____ Initiate system changes	4. Systems Construction
E. _____ Identify weaknesses and opportunities	5. Systems Implementation
F. _____ Create a systems development project plan	6. Systems Support
G. _____ Select the best technical alternative	
H. _____ Provide a mechanism for requesting changes	
I. _____ Model how the current system works	
J. _____ Assess initial feasibility	
K. _____ Develop detailed software specifications	
L. _____ Train users	
M. _____ Perform acceptance testing	
N. _____ Acquire and install new hardware	
O. _____ Convert users	
P. _____ Generate several alternative technical solutions	
Q. _____ Define the problem/opportunity	
R. _____ Provide a mechanism for system review	
S. _____ Convert information	
T. _____ Evaluate proposed system changes	
U. _____ Choose a conversion method	
V. _____ Decide to outsource the systems development process	
W. _____ Build sample screens and reports	
X. _____ Document the workings of the new system	
Y. _____ Decide to completely abandon the new system	

e-commerce

1. Researching Horizontal Market Software

Horizontal market software is big business. Many large-scale organizational horizontal market software packages in such areas as customer relationship management, inventory management, and accounting can sell for $1 million or more. Below, we've listed several well-known vendors of horizontal market software.

- PeopleSoft—www.peoplesoft.com
- SAP—www.sap.com
- JD Edwards—www.jdedwards.com
- Baan—www.baan.com
- Oracle—www.oracle.com

Choose a particular vendor from the above list and do some fact finding on the Web. As you do, answer the following questions.

a. For what sort of applications does the vendor provide horizontal market software (e.g., accounting, oil and gas, inventory, etc.)?

b. Does the vendor provide case studies that detail the success of various organizations while using its software?

c. Can you find a price listing for the vendor's horizontal market software?

d. Does the vendor provide support for its software such as implementation, maintenance, and training?

2. Buying Sports Gear

Sports is big business on the Web. You can check scores, visit your favorite team, and even place legal bets on games around the world. You can also find sites dedicated to selling you sports gear—equipment you need for playing sports, sports memorabilia, and sports apparel such as sweatshirts and T-shirts. Below, we've listed three such sites.

- Gear.com—www.gear.com
- Foot Locker—www.footlocker.com
- Sports Fan—www.sportsfan.com

Visit two of these sites and answer the following questions.

a. Can you find sports equipment? If so, for what sports?

b. Can you find sports memorabilia?

c. Can you find sports apparel?

d. Is the sports apparel "official" merchandise of a certain league?

e. Can you search for products by team name? By player name? By sport?

f. Do any of these sites give you the ability to read about players or perhaps talk with them in a chat room? How about live video?

g. Can you watch games at any of these sites or perhaps highlights of games?

3. Buying Event Tickets

You may want to go to a concert, a football game, a rodeo, an opera, a dog show, wrestling, show jumping, or some other event. If so, you can probably find tickets for these events on the Web, and buying tickets on the Web is often easier than over the phone. You pick your event, enter the number of seats you want, and specify your desired price level. The site will tell you if seats are available and offer you a map of the stadium or arena and allow you to select your seats. Here are some sites to look at (pick one and answer the questions that follow).

- Tickets.com—www.tickets.com
- Ticket Master—www.ticketmaster.com
- Sports-Hospitality.com—www.sports-hospitality.com
- Culturefinder.com—www.culturefinder.com

a. Does the site provide tickets for more than 10 different types of events?

b. Does the site offer tickets primarily for one category of events, sports, concerts, etc.?

c. Does the site offer events in a particular city?

d. Does the site have a privacy statement?

ethics, security & privacy

1. When Should You Consider Ethics, Security, and Privacy while Developing a System?

As you learned in this chapter, there are six phases in the traditional systems development life cycle (SDLC). During each phase, you must consider various aspects of ethics, security, and privacy. Consider that your school is going to build a system that allows you to specify which classes you would like to take in a given term. Your school will then use that information to build a schedule of classes that will meet all students' needs. Sounds pretty good—you'll never have another class time conflict and you'll be able to get the classes you need each term.

In the table below, we've listed the six phases of the traditional SDLC. It is your task in the right column to record several ethics, security, and privacy issues for each phase that your school should consider as it sets out to develop the new system.

SDLC Phase	Ethics, Security, and Privacy Issues
Investigation	
Analysis	
Design	
Construction	
Implementation	
Support	

2. What to Do When Software Produces the Wrong Result

People create software. And people make mistakes. So, it's entirely possible that some software will not work correctly. What should you do when that happens? How responsible is an organization for its software that doesn't work right? What you do about it or what the organization does may be a question not of law but of ethics. It may be difficult to determine the correct course of action. Consider the scenarios below. For each, determine what action you would take (if any) and determine what action the organization should take (if any).

a. Your state's lottery software accidentally generates thousands of winning numbers. You have one of those numbers.

b. Your state's lottery software accidentally generates thousands of winning numbers. You have a ticket but not a winning number.

c. Your organization's payroll software overpays you by $10.

d. Your organization's payroll software overpays you by $100.

e. Your organization's payroll software overpays you by $1000.

f. A grocery store scanning system doesn't charge you enough for a certain product. You notice the error when you get home.

g. A grocery store scanning system charges you too much for a certain product. You notice the error when you get home.

on the web

1. Researching IT Outsourcing Vendors

As you learned in this chapter, IT outsourcing is very prevalent in the business world. No matter what industry you choose as a career, your organization will most probably outsource some of its IT functions—everything ranging from call centers to complete systems development and support. Using your favorite search engine, type in the terms "IT" and "outsourcing." As you peruse through some of the many Web sites of IT outsourcing vendors, make a short report for your class that includes the following information:

- A list of IT outsourcing vendors and the industries in which they specialize.
- The types of services those outsourcing vendors sell.
- A list of IT outsourcing vendors who focus solely on Web development.

Now, search the Web again for outsourcing vendors, this time focusing on only those vendors that market their services to educational institutions such as your school. What vendors did you find? What sorts of applications do they provide outsourcing for (e.g., enrollment and registration)?

2. Understanding Degrees of Freedom

Within the context of developing IT systems for the Web, "degrees of freedom" measures how many clicks it would take someone to eventually find the information he/she wanted. So, you must carefully design the overall structure of a Web site in order to minimize degrees of freedom. Connect to your school's Web site and count the degrees of freedom (i.e., number of clicks) it takes you to perform the following:

a. View your transcript
b. View your schedule of classes
c. View the master schedule of classes for the next term
d. Change your personal information such as your address
e. View degree requirements.

How well is your school doing with respect to minimizing degrees of freedom?

3. Finding Free Flowcharting and Data Flow Diagramming Tools

There is indeed a lot of free software on the Web, including everything from checkbook software to card games. You can also find a variety of freeware for drawing diagrams such as flowcharts and data flow diagrams (DFDs). Search the Web for one or two examples of this type of software and download one to your computer. Now, try to re-create the drawings in Figures 12.7 and 12.9 on pages 365 and 367. How successful were you? Did you find the drawing tool easy or difficult to use?

4. Building Synergistic Teams

Most systems development efforts are successful because they were carried out by people who worked effectively as a team. You've probably experienced this in school. Some of your projects may have been great because you could work easily with your other team members. And you may have been on a team that never seemed to get anywhere for a variety of reasons. So, to effectively develop systems or work on any kind of team, you need to choose team members carefully. Do some research on the Web for team-building information. As you find sites that discuss the characteristics of a good team, create a list of helpful suggestions for creating the best team.

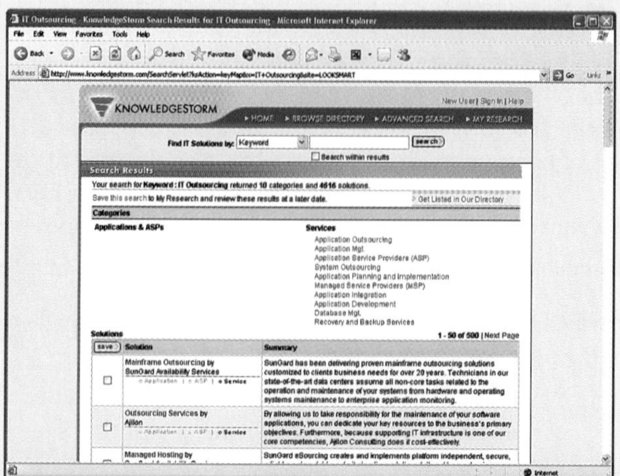

group activities

1. Creating a Program Flowchart

Consider the process that your state requires you to go through to obtain a driver's license—from beginning to end including taking a driver's education course, passing a written exam, and so on. Using Figure 12.9 on page 367 as a guide, create a flowchart that details the steps you must follow to obtain a driver's license. Using the same flowchart in Figure 12.9 as a guide, now create a flowchart that details the steps your state requires you to go through to periodically update your driver's license. Based on your two flowcharts, can you find any sequences of steps that could be facilitated by IT? Could your state make the processes easier for citizens by performing some of the steps over the Web? If so, what steps would those be and how would your flowchart or flowcharts change?

2. Identifying Outsourcing at Your School

Outsourcing isn't limited to just the realm of IT. Businesses today outsource almost everything. Your first task is to review all your school's operations and determine which are outsourced. Think broadly here—your school may be outsourcing its food operations, security, bookstore operations, and many other activities. Once you create the list of outsourced activities at your school, perform a little research for each and answer the following questions:

a. To whom is the activity outsourced?
b. What is the duration of the outsourcing contract?
c. What sort of metrics does your school use to ensure that the outsourcing vendor is performing its job correctly?
d. Does the outsourced activity directly impact you as a student? If so, how?

3. Everyday Prototyping

Throughout your life, you've performed the process of prototyping many times. For example, you may have created a resume, had several people evaluate it, and then refined it for another round of reviews. Think of at least three more instances in which you've performed prototyping. For each example, answer the following questions:

a. What basic requirements did you start with?
b. Who reviewed the prototype?
c. Approximately how many times did you refine and enhance the prototype?
d. What was the role of technology as you performed prototyping? If you didn't use any technology, could you have benefited from its use? Why or why not?

4. Creating a Data Flow Diagram for a Vending Machine

In Figure 12.7 on page 365, we provided a data flow diagram (DFD) for the Richmond Blood Center. Now it's your turn to attempt to draw a DFD. For your exercise, consider a vending machine that sells candy bars. The external players will include the person who fills the machine and empties the money and consumers such as your group. What are the processes you identified (there should be approximately five to seven)? What information repositories did you identify? Compare your DFD with that of another group. How similar and different are the two DFDs?

Now, create another DFD for the same vending machine. This time, consider a vending machine that doesn't accept money, but rather one you call with your cell phone. These types of vending machines are common in many parts of Europe. When you want to buy something in these vending machines, you essentially make a phone call to a computer system that triggers the machine so that you can make a selection. That same computer system then charges your cell phone bill for your purchase.

crossword puzzle

Across

4. Sun's 3GL programming language
5. Another name for a loop
8. Numerical value that tracks loops
10. Contains all object properties and methods
11. Represents input, processing, and output
15. Integrated Development Environment
16. An exact copy of an object class
18. Specific steps to solve a problem
21. Instructions and explanations for software
22. Visual Basic for Applications
23. Simultaneously translates source into object code
26. Mistakes in a software code's grammar
27. Graphical depiction of software steps
29. Converts assembly into machine language
30. Translating your algorithm

Down

1. Small fix to a software problem
2. Information that comes from an external source
3. Executes a task within a software application
5. Passing properties and methods from a class to an object
6. Concurrent Versions System
7. This is the "P" in IPO
9. A common name for software errors
10. Computer Aided Software Engineering tool
12. Uses English to outline the necessary steps to solve a problem
13. Execute lines of code in the order they appear
14. Finding errors in software code
17. Tests a true or false condition
19. Object-Oriented Programming
20. A word or symbol programmers use to store values
24. Allows you to manipulate object properties
25. Words that a language keeps for its own use
28. Rapid application development

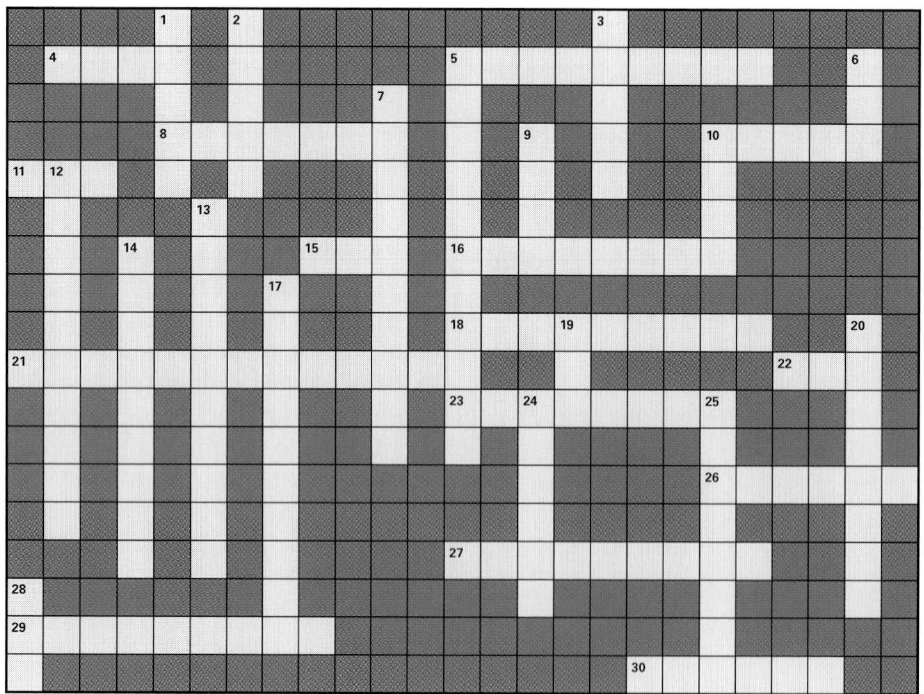

thirteen

CHAPTER

13

Computer Programming

How Can You Create Your Own Software?

SIMNET CONCEPTS SUPPORT

- Programming Languages (p. 405)
- Object-Oriented and Visual Programming (p. 411)

did you know?

For as long as computers have been around, programmers have challenged themselves to make software that effectively tells computers what to do. In this chapter you'll learn about the processes programmers use to write software and you'll try your hand at programming.

how *would you like to tackle a semester's worth of programming in one afternoon? That's the challenge at the world finals of the Association for Computing Machinery's International Collegiate Programming Contest, sponsored by IBM, which gives teams five hours to solve eight problems.*[1]

Star Trek *fans also love to code. They're working on creating a programming language for Klingon computer systems. It's called* var'aq.[2]

programmed *to be the world champion at chess, the computer Deep Junior can process __??__ chess moves per __??__. It was enough to end the six-game chess match with number one human chess player, Garry Kasparov, in a draw.*[3]

To find out just how fast Deep Junior can process chess moves, visit www.mhhe.com/i-series.

Student Learning Outcomes

After reading this chapter, you should be able to:

1. Understand how programmers investigate, analyze, and design software solutions to solve problems.
2. Identify the basic coding control structures used in programming.
3. Identify various common coding errors.
4. Understand how programmers test, implement, and maintain software.
5. Discuss programming language generations and characteristics.
6. Understand object-oriented programming concepts.
7. Discuss programming frameworks, such as Sun Microsystems's Java Platform Technologies and Microsoft's .NET

In Chapter 12, we presented a broad overview of the systems development process. One of the most time-consuming aspects of the process is writing the software, which occurs in the construction phase.

In this chapter, we'll explore how programmers solve business challenges so users can be more productive. We'll also look at basic programming techniques and how programmers create, test, and implement software.

You'll also learn about programming languages' history and characteristics and we'll show you the newest programming languages and frameworks designed to meet your software needs.

13.1 A PROGRAMMER'S VIEW OF INVESTIGATION, ANALYSIS, AND DESIGN

Let's assume you're an applications programmer for Penguin Enterprises. You've just joined the project team responsible for creating a new payroll system. In this section, we'll look at the preliminary phases of the systems development process—investigation, analysis, and design—from your point of view.

SYSTEMS INVESTIGATION

How Can a Programmer Help Lay the Foundation for a New Systems Development Effort?

Recall from Chapter 12 that there are four key tasks performed in systems investigation: defining the problem/opportunity, assessing initial feasibility, building the project team, and creating a systems development project plan. As a programmer, your primary focus should be on defining the problem/opportunity for the project team. To write the software correctly, you'll need to understand the exact nature of the problem or opportunity (see Figure 13.1 on the opposite page).

Once users (in this case, people in the Payroll department) have answered all the questions to your satisfaction, you can present your portion of the problem/opportunity statement to the project team. Notice that the problem/opportunity statement has no programming terms. Rather, you focus on how the software will incorporate the business logic necessary for the application. ***Business logic*** is a set of rules used to govern a business process. In this case the process is how to correctly calculate employee pay. Your program will need to incorporate the business logic to work effectively.

did you know?

The operating system Linux—typically found only in powerful networked computers—is coming to electronics. That should make everything from cell phones to TVs cheaper, since Linux companies don't collect royalties.[4]

Client's Request

Please create software to calculate employees' payroll.

Questions to Ask

Your Question	Client's Response
How often are employees paid?	Weekly.
Are they paid by the hour or salaried?	Both, but this program will only be for the hourly employees.
How much can an employee make per hour?	No more than $75 an hour and no less than $10.
Do the employees earn overtime?	Yes. Any hours over 40 are paid as time and a half.
How much overtime can an employee have?	An employee can work no more than 80 hours total in one week.
Will this program need to print out the paychecks?	No. Just send the information to Payroll. It will run the checks the same time it does the salaried paychecks.
What about employee benefits?	No. Payroll already has software for this as well.

Problem/Opportunity Statement

Create a program that gets an employee's name, pay rate, and number of hours worked in one week.

Assume that employees are hourly workers.

If an employee works over 40 hours in a week, calculate for overtime pay. No employee can work over 80 hours in one week. No employee can earn less than $10 an hour or more than $75 an hour.

Send the weekly payroll totals to the Payroll department so it can calculate benefits and print the paychecks. Make sure that this software's output is portable to the Payroll software.

FIGURE 13.1

As a programmer, you'll frequently create problem/opportunity statements. Make sure to note the steps in the process. If you are careful to completely define the problem/opportunity statement, there's less chance of an error later in the systems development process.

SYSTEMS ANALYSIS

How Does a Programmer Model the Logical, Not Physical, System?

During systems analysis, your focus as a programmer is on the information and information-processing requirements of the new system. You want to develop these specifications logically, without worrying about the physical details (covered in the technical solution) such as amount of storage space, type of network software, the speed of the CPU, or the amount of available computer memory.

So, in analysis you need to define: (1) what information will go into the software, (2) how the software will process the information, and (3) what information the software will generate. In the previous chapter, you saw how to do this with a data flow diagram. However, programmers use other techniques as well called pseudocode and program flowcharts.

Pseudocode

You don't concern yourself with the physical details of a system during systems analysis. You also don't worry yet about how your software will interact with the computer's operating system.

At this stage, you focus on what the program should do. For this you can write pseudocode. ***Pseudocode*** uses English statements to create an outline of the necessary steps for a piece of software to operate. Programmers call these steps an algorithm. An ***algorithm*** is a set of specific steps that solves a problem or carries out a task. An algorithm is like a cooking recipe. It lists the necessary steps to create a main dish or dessert. In our case, the sweet reward is a working piece of software.

When you read about SQL statements in Chapter 10, you learned to use a form of structured English to ask the DBMS to perform tasks. You used specific words such as **SELECT, FROM,** and **SORT.** Pseudocode is like structured English, but it's not as strict. As a programmer, you can choose whatever words and notations work best for you as long as they're not ambiguous.

Look at the pseudocode for the payroll software in Figure 13.2. Notice that even though there's no set of rules for writing pseudocode, the pseudocode in Figure 13.2 does follow guidelines that programmers agree are important, for example, using simple English, putting only one command on a line, and bolding important words.

FIGURE 13.2

Pseudocode is one method programmers use to express an algorithm.

```
START PROGRAM

GET INPUT FROM EMPLOYEE (NAME, HOURS WORKED, PAY RATE)

CHECK IF INPUT MEETS EMPLOYER'S CONDITIONS

  If Hours Worked > 80 hours Then
    Inform the user to see manager or re-enter hours

  If Pay Rate < $10 OR Pay Rate > $75 Then
    Inform the user to see manager or re-enter pay rate

CALCULATE EMPLOYEE'S PAY

  If Hours Worked <= 40 Then
    Weekly Pay = Hours Worked * Pay Rate
  Else
    Overtime = Hours Worked – 40
    Overtime Pay = Overtime * Pay Rate * 1.5
    Weekly Pay = (Pay Rate * 40) + Overtime Pay

DISPLAY RESULTS ON SCREEN

ASK EMPLOYEE IF INFORMATION IS CORRECT
  If information is correct Then
    Submit Information to Payroll
  Else
    Have Employee Repeat Process

STOP PROGRAM
```

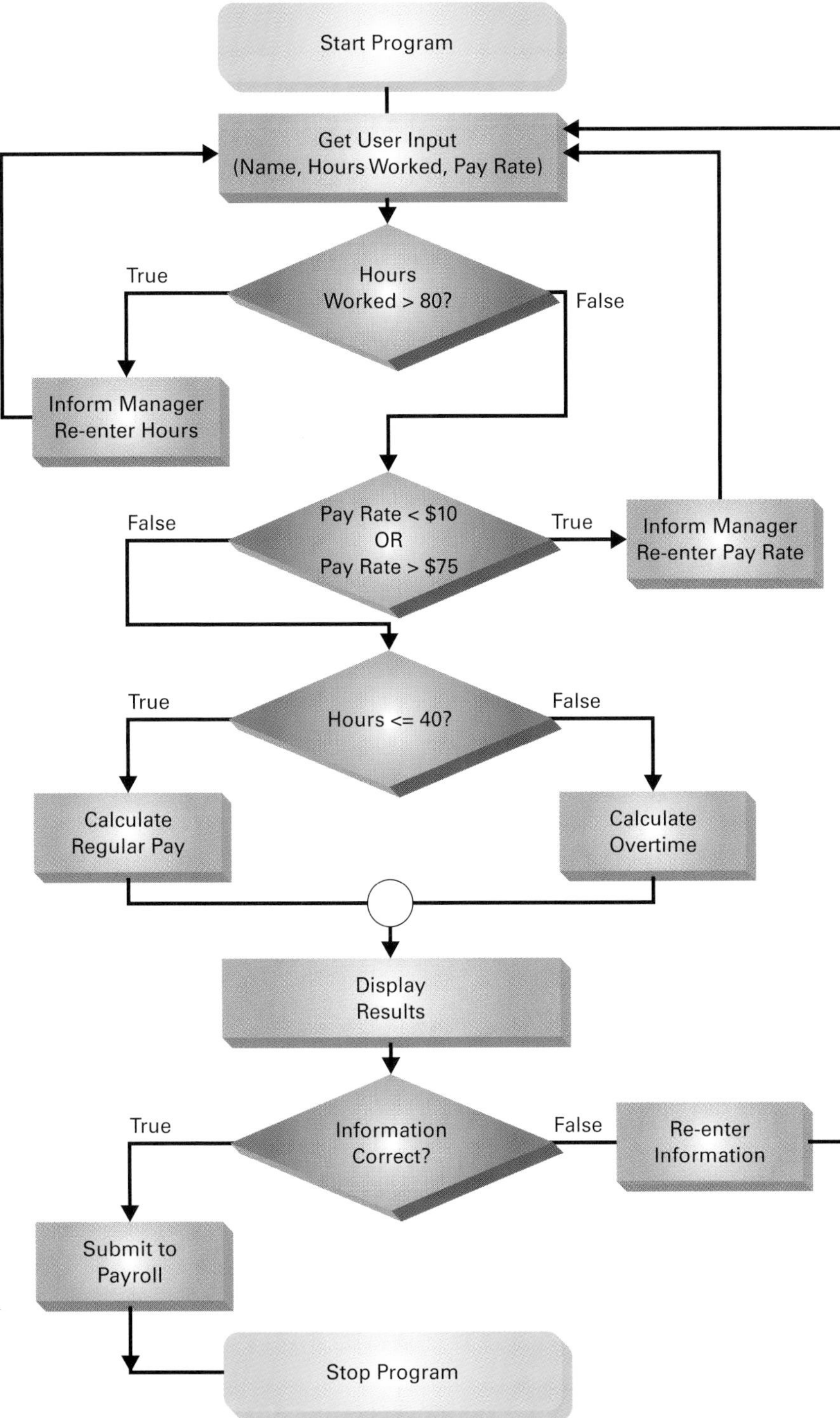

FIGURE 13.3

Program flowcharts graphically express algorithms.

Program Flowcharts

Programmers also use program flowcharts to plot the software's algorithm. As we discussed in Chapter 12, a ***program flowchart*** is a graphical depiction of the detailed steps that software will perform. Unlike pseudocode, which has less structure, in flowcharts programmers must use symbols. Figure 13.3 shows the payroll software flowchart. Compare the flowchart in Figure 13.3 with the pseudocode in Figure 13.2. You'll see identical logic in each.

Testing the Algorithm

After you've completed your algorithm, check its logic. In the payroll software, calculating overtime for anyone working more than 20 hours instead of more than 40 hours would be a logic error. A ***logic error*** is a mistake in the way an algorithm solves a problem.

Logic errors can be hard to find once you begin writing your program, so it's best to catch them in the algorithm. Programmers check their algorithms by inputting test data and checking the logic by hand or with a calculator. Come up with some test data (employee name, hours worked, and pay rate) and run it through our pseudocode (Figure 13.2 on page 392) or program flowchart (Figure 13.3 on page 393). Did everything work as expected? If it didn't, programmers stop the process and return to the algorithm to find out what went wrong. Maybe there's a mistake in the arithmetic or some steps in the process are out of place (or missing). If it does work, you're ready to move to the next step in the process—designing the software.

SYSTEMS DESIGN
How Does a Programmer Create a Technical Design for New Software?

As you move into design, it's time to convert your logical description of the proposed software into technical software specifications. Now you must concern yourself with the physical characteristics of the system, such as the filenames, variable types and names, and the programming language you'll use to write the software.

During design, programmers will also build a software prototype to demonstrate software features. We discuss prototyping later in this section. If you'd like to learn more about prototyping, visit the Web site for this text at www.mhhe.com/i-series.

Basic Software Needs

You learned that in the analysis phase you must know what information will go into the software, how it will process that information, and what will result. In other words, you're looking at input, processing, and output. You're familiar with devices that provide input (keyboards and mice) and output (monitors and printers) on your computer. Your computer system itself (specifically, your CPU and RAM) does all of the processing. Therefore, all software must work with these three concepts to be successful.

- ***Input*** is information that comes from an external source and enters the software. Input can come from your typing on your keyboard, from records in a database, or from clicking on a button or icon with your mouse.
- ***Processing*** manages information according to the software's logic. In other words, processing is what the software does to the input it receives. This can be anything from adding a few numbers together to mapping the earth's climate. In the payroll software, processing involves calculating an employee's pay.
- ***Output*** is the information software produces after it has processed input. Output can appear on a computer screen, in a printout, or in records in a database.

did you know? Here's *when writing code is like brain surgery: A computer-controlled robot developed in Singapore can drill a hole through the skull more precisely and quickly than surgeons can to remove brain tumors.*[5]

Input	Processing	Output

Hours_Worked
Pay_Rate
	If Hours_Worked <= 40
	Weekly_Pay = Hours_Worked * Pay_Rate
	Else
	Overtime = Hours_Worked – 40
	Overtime_Pay = Overtime * Pay_Rate * 1.5
	Weekly_Pay = (Pay_Rate * 40) + Overtime_Pay
	End If
		Weekly_Pay
		Overtime
		Overtime_Pay

FIGURE 13.4

An IPO table assists programmers as they design software.

Input-Process-Output Tables

As you work with input, processing, and output in the design phase, you can include them in input-process-output (IPO) tables. An ***IPO (input-process-output) table*** shows what information a piece of software takes in, how it processes the information, and what information it produces. We've created such a table in Figure 13.4.

Prototyping

Before starting the next phase of writing the software, programmers present prototypes to the potential users. In Chapter 12, you learned that prototyping is the process of building a model that demonstrates the features of the proposed product, service, or system. Programmers show users what the software will do first to avoid having to make major changes later.

Programmers use a variety of methods to illustrate how users will interact and use the program. Story boards show users what the program interface will look like. Programmers also can show a series of tasks a user might follow to accomplish a goal.

Programmers might also use software mock-ups created with software development environments. Ultimately, programmers want to get as much user input as possible at this stage so they can improve software features and functions, as well as avoid writing unnecessary software code.

making the grade

SECTION 13.1

1. ____________ is a set of rules used to govern a business process.
2. You use ____________ to create an outline of the necessary steps for a piece of software to operate.
3. A(n) ____________ is a set of specific steps used to solve a problem or carry out a task.
4. A(n) ____________ is a mistake in the way an algorithm solves a problem.
5. ____________ is the information software produces after it has processed input.

13.2 WRITING COMPUTER SOFTWARE

After you test your algorithm, determine basic software needs, and design an approved prototype, it's time to write the software. This is the construction phase, the fourth phase of the systems development life cycle (SDLC). In this section, we'll show you some of the basic programming techniques and structures you'll need to create software.

CODING

How Do I Explain My Algorithm to the Computer?

Once you've written your algorithm using pseudocode or a program flowchart, it's time to explain your algorithm in terms a computer can understand. To accomplish this, you'll write software using a programming language. A ***programming language*** contains specific rules and words that express the logical steps of an algorithm. We'll identify the many languages later in the chapter.

Most programmers call writing the software program "coding." ***Coding*** is when you translate your algorithm into a programming language. Figure 13.5 shows the Penguin Enterprises payroll software and part of the software code. We wrote this software in Visual Basic (VB) because it's a popular programming language and works with the Microsoft Windows. Other programming languages, such as Java, might work as well. The complete software program is available at the text Web site at www.mhhe.com/i-series.

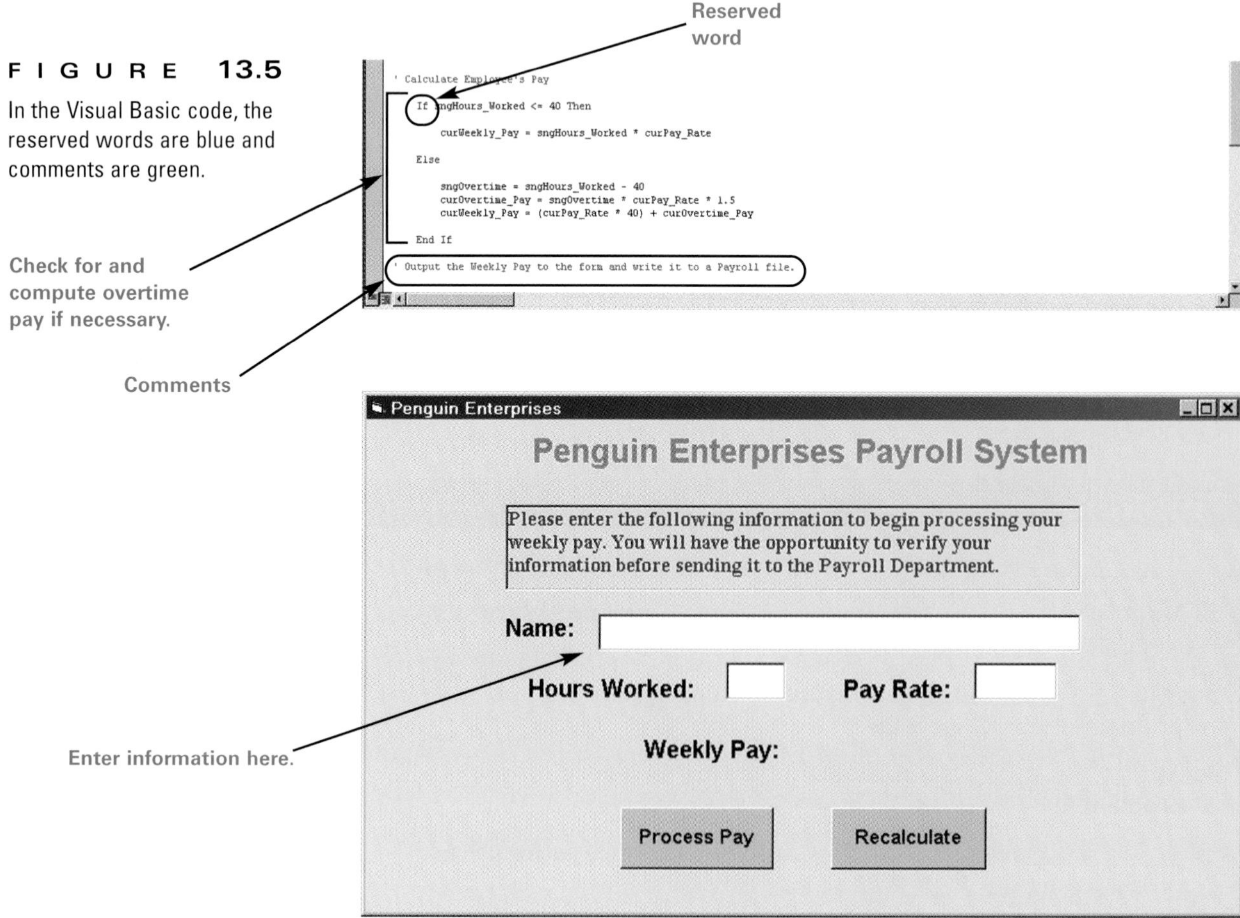

FIGURE 13.5

In the Visual Basic code, the reserved words are blue and comments are green.

Notice that some words appear blue. These are reserved words. ***Reserved words*** are commands that a programming language has set aside for its own use. In Figure 13.5 on the previous page, you'll notice **If** is colored blue. **If** is a reserved word VB uses to create a logical test. For example, the code determines whether an employee should receive overtime pay by using **If.** Notice also that many lines start with a single apostrophe (') and are a different color (green). Programmers call these lines comments. ***Comments*** are explanations that tell other programmers what's happening in software code. The computer ignores comments when it runs the code.

Finally, note how the programmer has indented and arranged the code. You know exactly which lines go with the **If** and which go with **Else.** Programmers write code like this so other programmers can easily read the code. Just like comments, the computer ignores spaces and indentations when it runs the code.

CONTROL STRUCTURES
How Do I Tell the Computer How to Read My Algorithm?

Unless told otherwise, most computers will read code like you're reading this textbook. Programmers refer to this as sequential execution. ***Sequential execution*** is when a computer performs each line of software code in the order it appears.

However, computers didn't always read code this way. It wasn't until programming languages adopted control structures that you could assume a certain sequence of execution. ***Control structures*** specify the order in which a computer will execute each line of software code. Let's look at the three basic control structures you can use.

Sequence Control Structure

The sequence control structure is the most basic. The ***sequence control structure*** makes sure that a computer executes software code from top to bottom, left to right. It enforces sequential execution and is present in most programming languages. Figure 13.6 is an example of how the sequential control structure works. The oval marks the start of the program (and another marks the end). Each rectangle represents an instruction or action in the software code. Notice that once the program starts it must follow each instruction until the program stops.

But what happens if the logic in your algorithm requires the program to execute the code in a different order or skip sections if a certain condition exists? For this you'll need other control structures: selection or repetition. We'll discuss these two control structures below. You can see all three types of control structures in action at the text Web site at www.mhhe.com/i-series.

FIGURE 13.6

The sequence control structure is the most basic programming control structure.

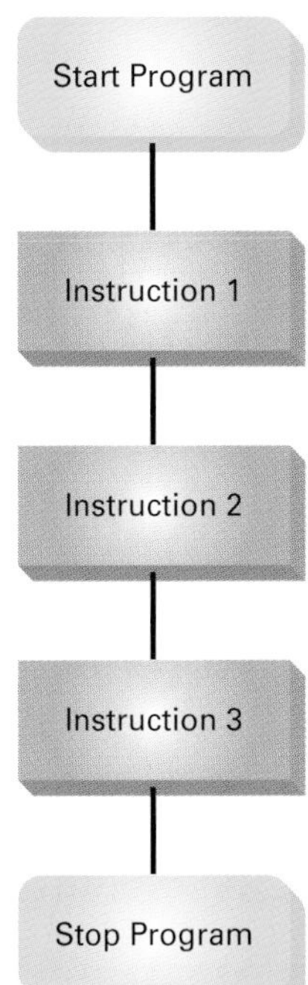

Selection Control Structure

Every day you make decisions. Should you sleep in or should you go to class? Should you study or go out with your friends? Should you eat that last piece of pizza? You make your decision based on the answer to a condition: Are you sleepy? Do you have a test? Are you hungry? A ***condition*** is an exisiting situation. Your decision is similar to how software uses a selection control structure. A ***selection control structure*** tests a condition to decide how a computer will execute software code.

FIGURE 13.7

The selection control structure makes a decision based on a condition. In this code, it's the numbers of hours worked.

```
If  Hours_Worked <= 40 Then
  Weekly_Pay = Hours_Worked * Pay_Rate
Else
  Overtime = Hours_Worked - 40
  Overtime_Pay = Overtime * Pay_Rate * 1.5
  Weekly_Pay = (Pay_Rate * 40) + Overtime_Pay
End If
```

In this code, you only pay an employee overtime if Hours_Worked is NOT less than or equal to 40. In other words, they worked more than 40 hours.

In our payroll software, we asked how much each person worked. If it's more than 40 hours, we calculate overtime; if it's less than or equal to 40, we don't. Based on that condition the software decides what code to execute. Figure 13.7 shows how the code handles this condition.

Look at the **If, Then, Else,** and **End If** reserved words in Figure 13.7. These reserved words are part of the if-then-else statement. The ***if-then-else statement*** tests a condition in software code that results in a true or a false. If an employee has worked 40 hours or less, the statement under the **If** is executed and the statements under the **Else** are bypassed. If an employee has worked more than 40 hours, the statement under the **If** is bypassed and the statements under the **Else** are executed.

Figure 13.8 is a flowchart of the if-then-else statement. After we start the program, notice that a diamond represents the tested condition. If someone has worked more than 40 hours (overtime) we go to the left. If they have worked 40 hours or fewer, we go to the right. After we perform the correct calculation, the flowchart joins the process path (the circle) and ends the software code. Of course, many times the answer is not always a yes or a no, a true or a false. For that, we need to use a case control statement.

FIGURE 13.8

The if-then-else statement tests a true or false condition and executes code depending on the result.

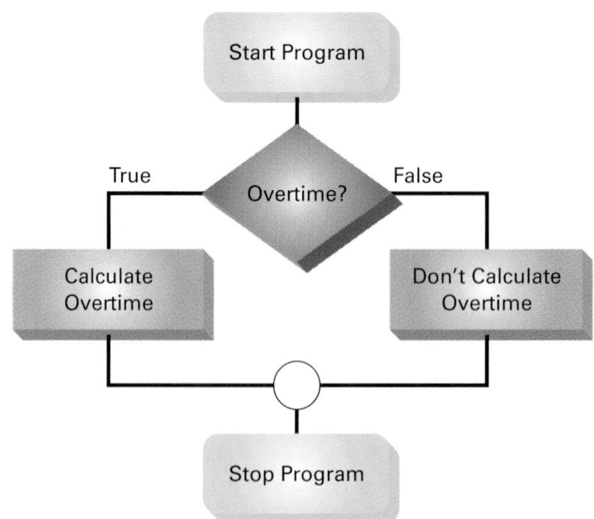

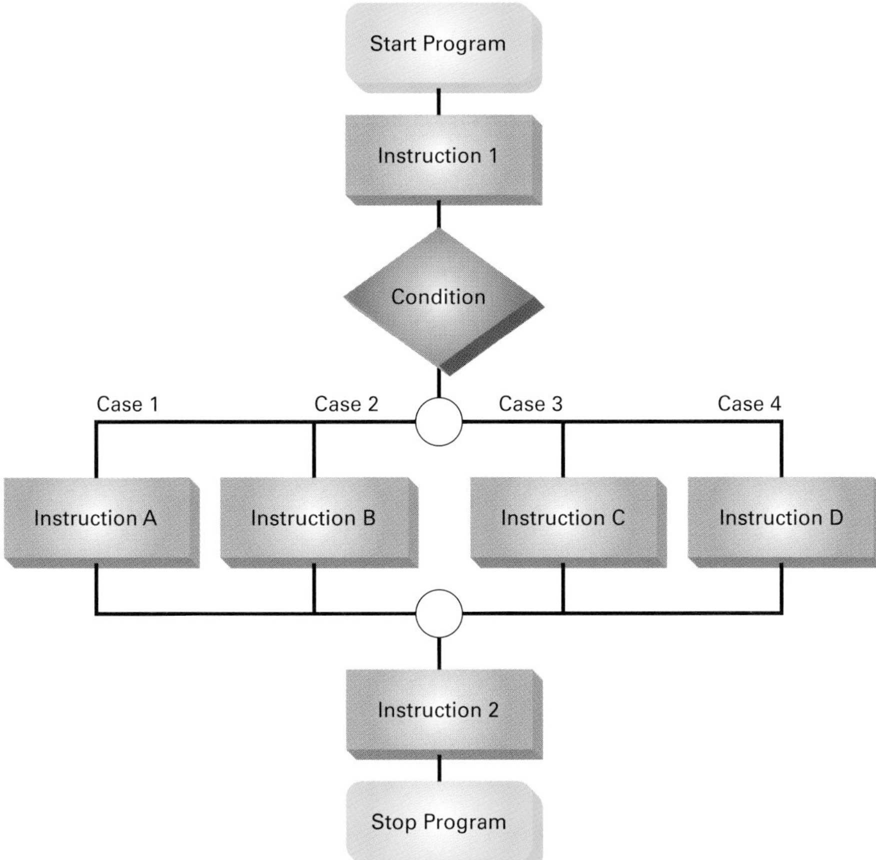

FIGURE 13.9

The case control statement (or switch statement) tests a condition that has more than a true or false answer.

The ***case control statement*** (or ***switch statement***) tests a condition that can result in more than a true or false answer. For example, you might need to determine shipping costs based on an item's weight. Figure 13.9 shows the case control statement in action.

Repetition Control Structure

Have you ever read the instructions on a shampoo bottle? You'd most likely see (1) Lather, (2) Rinse, (3) Repeat if necessary. You're to use the shampoo until you meet a condition (let's assume it's clean hair).

Similarly, in coding, the ***repetition control structure*** instructs a piece of software to repeat a series of instructions until it fulfills a condition or while a condition exists. Programmers also call the repetition control structure an ***iteration control*** or simply a ***loop.*** There are three variations of repetition control structures: (1) the do-while statement, (2) the do-until statement, and (3) the for-next statement.

The ***do-while statement*** repeats a portion of software code as long as a certain condition exists. If the condition is true, the software program executes the lines of code. It then tests the condition again. If it's still true, the software program executes the code again.

In contrast, the ***do-until statement*** repeats a portion of a software code as long as a certain condition doesn't exist (it's false).

The ***for-next statement*** repeats a portion of software code a precise number of times. The for-next statement uses a counter to check the condition. A ***counter*** is a numerical value that tracks the number of iterations in a software code.

FIGURE 13.10

Programmers use loops when they need to repeat a process a certain number of times or as long as a condition does or doesn't exist.

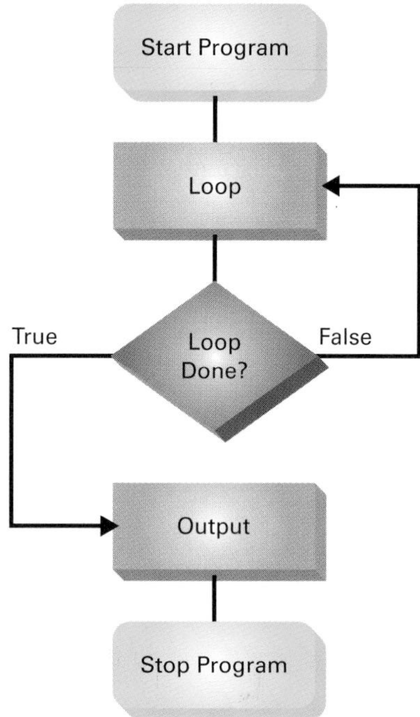

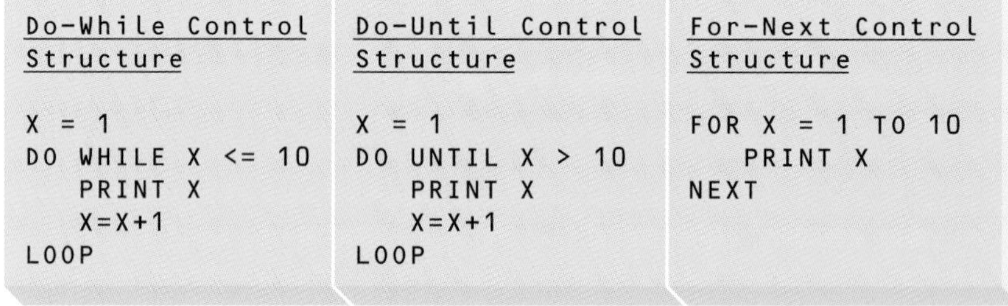
All three loops will print the numbers 1-10

Do-While Control Structure	Do-Until Control Structure	For-Next Control Structure
X = 1 DO WHILE X <= 10 PRINT X X=X+1 LOOP	X = 1 DO UNTIL X > 10 PRINT X X=X+1 LOOP	FOR X = 1 TO 10 PRINT X NEXT

Figure 13.10 above illustrates the differences and similarities of do-while, do-until, and for-next statements. They all achieve the same result—printing the numbers 1 through 10 on the screen.

SECTION 13.2

making the grade

1. A(n) ___________ contains specific rules and words that express the logical steps of an algorithm.
2. ___________ are commands that a programming language has set aside for its own use.
3. You use ___________ to tell other programmers what's happening in software code.
4. When a computer executes software code from top to bottom, left to right, it's following the ___________.
5. A(n) ___________ tests a condition in software code that results in a true or a false.

i-series insights *Ethics, Security & Privacy*

Programming Backdoors

You know how difficult it can be to write just a few lines of code that result in a working, bug-free software program. Imagine that you're working on a project team whose job is to create software containing millions of lines of code. How can you make sure that if something bad happens when you run the program, you'll be able to stop it and fix it? You might consider creating a backdoor. A ***backdoor*** is an undocumented method a programmer uses to gain access to a program or a computer.

The concept is simple. Programmers create a command that allows them to enter a program or a computer and fix any errors or check up on the program. There's a downside to this—people other than the programmers can find the backdoor and use it for purposes other than maintenance or troubleshooting. Hackers routinely find backdoors in software and exploit their discovery. Maybe they just explore the program, but maybe they decide to take information.

Backdoors can cause other problems. Many viruses use backdoors to access e-mail or credit card information or steal information from corporate databases. What programmers designed to help can become hurtful instead.

But backdoors are definitely helpful. When programs cease to work and there's a possibility of a system crash, programmers can use a backdoor to enter the program and save important information. Perhaps a hacker seizes control of a company's Web server. A backdoor could help the company take its server back.

We list Web sites and references on programming backdoors at www.mhhe.com/i-series. You must decide whether you think programming backdoors is beneficial or too risky.

13.3 TESTING, IMPLEMENTING, AND MAINTAINING SOFTWARE

In the remaining systems development life cycle, you'll need people to help you test your software (phase 4—construction), implement it in your organization (phase 5—implementation), and provide you feedback so you can maintain the software over time (phase 6—support).

TESTING SOFTWARE
How Do I Make Sure a Piece of Software Works?

You tested your algorithm before you began coding, but now you'll want to test—or debug—your written code. ***Debugging*** is the process of finding errors in software code. ***Bugs*** are a common name for software errors. When you debug your code, you look for syntax, run-time, and logic errors.

Syntax Errors

Syntax errors are mistakes in a software code's grammar. Just as misspelling a word is a mistake when writing, misspelling a command word or forgetting to close a module will cause a syntax error. If you're supposed to use a semicolon (;) and you use a colon (:) instead, you've made a syntax error.

Run-Time Errors

Run-time errors are mistakes that occur when you run the software code. Software not displaying a window correctly is a run-time error. Another common error is not matching variables in a calculation. A ***variable*** is a word or symbol programmers use to store values in a software program. When you try to add a variable that contains a number and one that contains a letter, you get a run-time error.

FIGURE 13.11

A major task for programmers is debugging the code. In many development environments syntax errors appear in red.

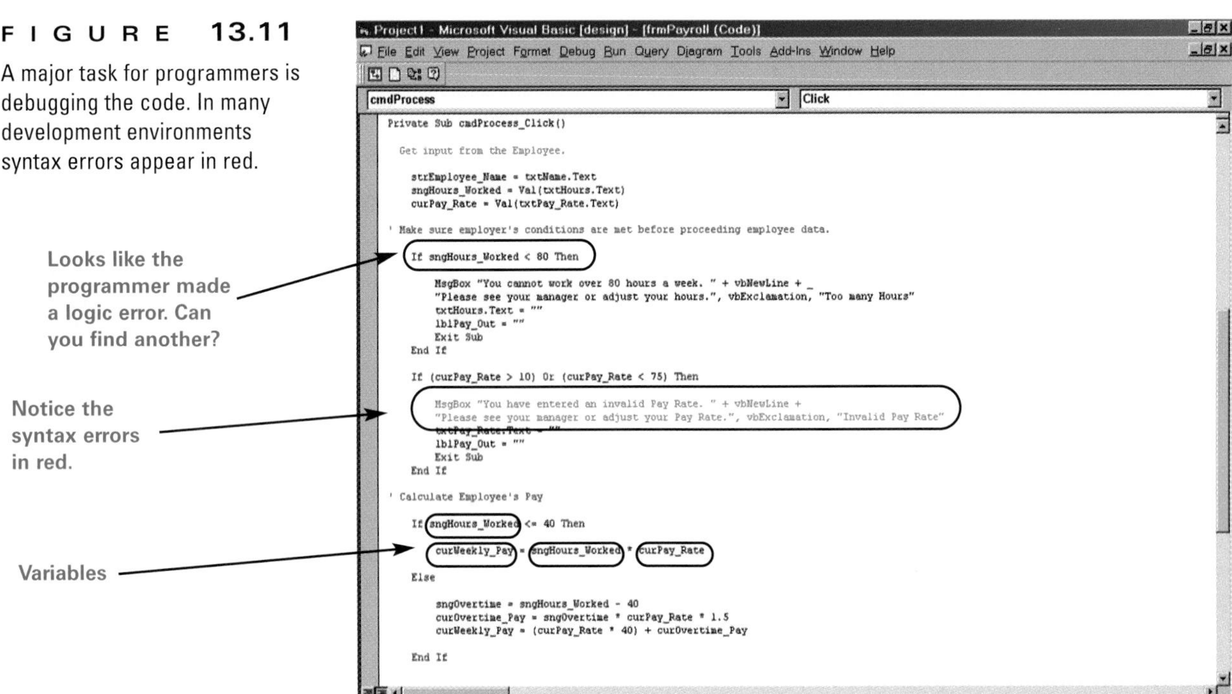

Logic Errors

You checked for *logic errors* when you designed your algorithm. Remember that a logic error is a mistake made in the way an algorithm solves a problem. You should test for logic errors as part of the debugging process. Figure 13.11 has some common programming errors. Notice the logic error marked in the program. What happens when this software checks how many hours the employee worked?

End User Testing

After programmers have fixed the errors, users will test the software to make sure it meets their needs. As we discussed in Chapter 12, users must test it and "sign off" that the software works correctly. This is called *acceptance testing.*

SOFTWARE DEVELOPMENT ENVIRONMENT

How Do I Find Errors and Manage My Code?

You could write code in a simple text editor such as Notepad. However, most programmers use a software development environment. A ***software development environment*** is an application that provides programming tools to debug and manage software programs. You'll also hear programmers refer to a software development environment as an ***integrated development environment (IDE).***

Debugging Help

In Figure 13.11, some code is in red. You know that this identifies syntax errors in the code. If you were to execute this code, you'd also get run-time errors. The software development environment helps you identify where these errors are in the software code. And although they're not easy to see,

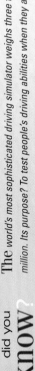

did you know? The world's most sophisticated driving simulator weighs three tons and costs $81 million. Its purpose? To test people's driving abilities when they are drunk. Researchers at the University of Iowa hope the findings will lead to fewer crashes and deaths.[6]

logic errors exist. Unlike a syntax or a run-time error, the software development environment won't alert you to a logic error. We've placed the code for Figure 13.11 at www.mhhe.com/i-series so you can find all the errors.

Managing Development

Many software development environments also help you manage your software development. Some have powerful programming features, such as graphical interfaces and tools to help link the software to other software. For example, you could make sure that your payroll software works with the Payroll department's software.

Because of its power, programmers use the software development environment to create working prototypes for end user testing and feedback. These prototypes aren't completely functional like the the final software application, but they provide enough information for users to make decisions.

As discussed in Chapter 12, end users can "try out" a prototype to see if the software meets their needs. If it doesn't, the programmer makes changes and sends out another prototype. Programmers refer to this as rapid application development. ***Rapid application development (RAD)*** uses prototypes to test software components until they meet specifications.

In certain organizations, programmers use sophisticated CASE tools (see Figure 13.12). ***CASE,*** or ***computer aided software engineering, tools*** are software applications that help prepare reports, draw program flowcharts, and generate software code for prototypes. Programmers use CASE tools to incorporate the entire software development process into one development environment. CASE tools are not available for every programming language.

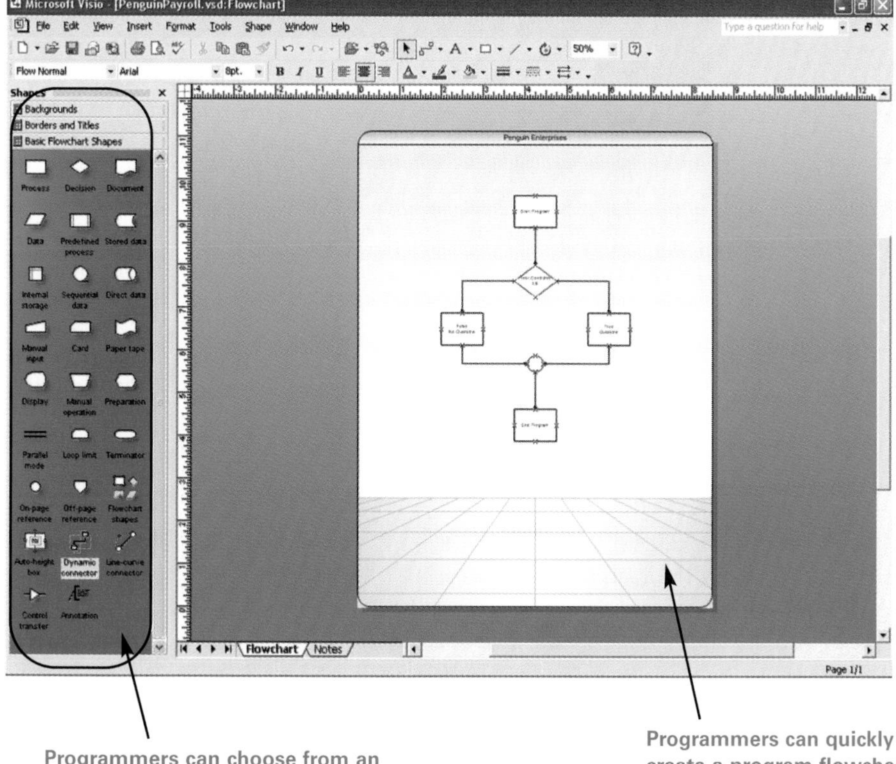

FIGURE 13.12
Microsoft Visio is one of the CASE tools available to programmers.

As programmers code software, they make many changes to meet users' needs and fix errors. Many times programmers want to examine an earlier version of their code when new errors occur or a user requests new features. To manage the changes between code versions, some programmers use a CVS. A ***CVS (Concurrent Versions System)*** is an open source software tool that tracks all changes to a project's code. CVS is especially useful for a programming team working on software code because it records each team member's major code changes.

IMPLEMENTING SOFTWARE
How Can I Make Sure There's a Smooth Transition?

Once programmers write and test the software code to everyone's satisfaction, they release it to technical support personnel who then install the software application on users' computers. However, the programmer's job still isn't complete. A programmer must write documentation. ***Documentation*** is a collection of instructions and explanations relevant to a piece of software. Programmers must produce or help produce various forms of documentation during software implementation. These are comments, program manuals, and user manuals.

As we discussed earlier, *comments* are explanations within code that tell other programmers what's happening. Comments can be a single line or a large portion of text explaining what's happening in a section of code. Programmers write comments as they code the software and must now check their comments for accuracy.

Programmers also must create documentation for other programmers. The ***program manual*** is a technical manual for programmers. It can be print or electronic. The program manual contains the problem/opportunity statement, algorithms, flowcharts, and copies of older versions of the code.

Usually a programmer doesn't write the user manual. Instead companies employ technical writers. ***Technical writers*** explain concepts and procedures to nontechnical software users. The technical writer works with programmers to produce the user manual. The ***user manual*** tells users how to use a software program. User manuals can be a book, but more frequently they come on a CD or are on the company's Web site.

MAINTAINING SOFTWARE
How Do I Keep Software Fresh?

In Chapter 12 you learned about systems support and maintenance. As a programmer, you help support and maintain a system by making sure the software functions correctly and meets business needs. To do this, you'll need to code and implement software patches and updates.

In the support phase, employees use the software. They might find a problem with how the software interacts with a system or another piece of software. Maybe the payroll software doesn't connect to and send information to the payroll system in the correct format. If it's a minor fix, programmers will patch the software. A ***software patch*** is a small fix to a problem using a piece of software code.

When patches are no longer enough, programmers must upgrade software. A ***software upgrade*** is a substantial revision of existing software to improve its usefulness. Often software companies release upgrades because they've made major improvements since the last version. For example, Microsoft Office 2003 is an upgrade to Microsoft Office XP.

did you know?

Sitting *too long at your computer can be deadly, doctors say. A New Zealand man who spent 12 to 18 hours a day at his computer died after a blood clot formed in his leg veins and then traveled to his lungs. Researchers suggest the condition be called "e-thrombosis."*[7]

making the grade

1. __________ is the process of finding errors in software code.
2. __________ are mistakes in a software code's grammar.
3. __________ is an open source software tool that tracks all changes to a project's software code.
4. The __________ is a technical manual for programmers.
5. A(n) __________ is a small fix to a problem using a piece of software code.

13.4 PROGRAMMING LANGUAGES

Earlier when we needed to write the Penguin Enterprises payroll software, we had to pick a programming language. We chose Visual Basic based on our system requirements and how the software had to function. In this section, we'll explore programming language generations and look at programming language characteristics. Understanding these concepts will help you choose the right programming language for your next coding project. To learn more about programming languages visit the Web site for this text at www.mhhe.com/i-series and complete the "Programming Languages" tutorial on your SimNet Concepts Support CD.

PROGRAMMING LANGUAGE GENERATIONS

How Have Languages Evolved?

In international business, people use English more often because it's more widely understood. Programmers have hundreds of programming languages to choose from, but they use some languages more often because of their flexibility and portability. ***Portability*** means a programming language has the ability to work on a variety of computer hardware and operating systems.

Because of the diversity of computer systems available today, programmers must think about portability when deciding which programming language will work best in a given situation. To help you make this decision, you'll need to know something about how programming languages have evolved.

Machine Language

Just as you can't understand a language you've never learned, a computer can't understand any language but its own. A ***machine-dependent language*** is a programming language that works only on a specific computer system and its components. Languages that work only on a certain computer system are low-level languages. A ***low-level language*** requires programmers to code at a basic level that a computer can understand.

The most basic programming language is machine language. ***Machine language*** is a machine-dependent, low-level language that uses binary code to interact with a specific computer system. If you thought about writing the payroll software in machine language (which you wouldn't), you'd write it in binary code because binary code is the only language computers can understand.

FIGURE 13.13

This assembly language program prints "Hello World" on the screen. It works only on a specific computer system.

```
.text
.align 4
.global start
start:
mov 0, %o0
set string, %o1
mov 14, %o2
mov 4, %g1
ta 0
mov 0, %o0
mov 1, %g1
ta 0
.align 4
string:
.ascii "Hello, World!\n"
```

You learned about binary code in Chapter 6. Remember, binary code is a series of 1s and 0s grouped together to represent what we want the computer to do. Programmers don't use binary to code software, but they must translate all software code into machine code so computers can use it.

Assembly Language

Since no human can effectively code in binary, programmers developed another low-level programming language: assembly language. ***Assembly language*** is a machine-dependent, low-level language that uses words instead of binary numbers to program a specific computer system. Programmers can use words such as **start** or abbreviations such as **mov** (move) to tell the computer what to do. Figure 13.13 is assembly language that tells a computer to print "Hello World" on your screen.

For the computer to read assembly language you must run the code through an assembler. An ***assembler*** is a utility program that converts assembly language into machine language that the computer can then use to run software.

Third Generation Languages

Can you imagine the task of writing assembly language for every type of computer today? Neither can programmers. Instead they use programming languages that many different computers can understand. These are machine-independent languages. A ***machine-independent language*** is a programming language that works on different computer systems regardless of their components.

With machine-independent languages, you can use words closer to human language to code software. Programmers use reserved words, such as **ADD, DIVIDE,** and **PRINT,** and mathematical symbols such as (+) and (–) for addition and subtraction. A ***high-level language*** allows programmers to use words and symbols closer to human language to code software.

Machine independence and high level in these languages distinguish them from machine and assembly languages. The move to these languages (in the 1950s) marks another generation: third generation languages. A ***third generation language (3GL)*** is a machine-independent, high-level procedural language that uses human words and symbols to program diverse computer systems. All 3GLs are also procedural languages. A ***procedural language*** requires that a programmer write code to tell software what to accomplish and how to accomplish it.

Fourth Generation Languages

With a 3GL you can use words resembling human language. However, you still specifically instruct the software *what* to do and *how* to do it because 3GLs are procedural languages. Fourth generation languages, on the other hand, are nonprocedural languages. A ***nonprocedural language*** requires that a programmer write code to tell the software only what it should accomplish. So a ***fourth generation language (4GL)*** is a machine-independent, high-level nonprocedural language that uses human words and symbols to program diverse computer systems. Experts are using Natural language to instruct a computer and make programming easier. ***Natural languages*** are human languages that can program a computer.

PROGRAMMING LANGUAGE CHARACTERISTICS
What Distinguishes Languages from Each Other?

You can see how programmers can distinguish languages depending on the generation the languages come from. Programmers can determine if they should use a machine-dependent or a high-level language for a task. But how can you determine which language you'd need to write a software application program for a Windows operating system? You'd probably pick a 3GL, since machine language or assembly language wouldn't be as portable for the many computers that use various Windows operating systems. But how would you know which 3GL to use? Should you use Visual Basic, Java, or C++? To make this decision you'll need to know a bit more about programming language characteristics.

Compiled

You know that computers can understand only machine language (binary). So when you code in a high-level language such as C++ you must get your code into a form the computer can understand. With assembly language you can use an assembler. With a high-level language you use a compiler. A ***compiler*** simultaneously translates high-level programming languages into machine language. In other words, your 3GL or 4GL is completely translated into machine language all at once before it's run by a computer.

When you write your code in a programming language, you're writing the source code. Your ***source code*** contains all the commands and comments a programmer used to code the software. You can read the source code if you open it in a development environment. The ***object code*** is the machine language the computer uses to run your program. To get from the source code to the object code, you must compile your source code into the object code. Only computers can read the object code. Most software development environments come with a compiler.

Interpreted

With other programming languages, such as JavaScript (discussed in Chapter 8), the computer uses an interpreter to convert the source code into object code. An ***interpreter*** translates one line of source code into object code at a time. In other words, the computer translates a line of source code into object code, then executes it, and then goes to the next line of code and repeats the process. Running interpreted software on a computer does take longer than running compiled software. With the speed of today's systems, however, the loss isn't noticeable.

Scripted

Because today's computer systems can run interpreted languages efficiently, you'll see many programs written with scripting languages. A ***scripting language*** is an interpreted programming language that works within another application to perform tasks. Programmers call these tasks macros. A ***macro*** is a scripting language program that executes a task or set of tasks within a software application.

In Chapter 12, you learned that end user development is one way some businesses choose to develop software applications. Since many businesses use the Microsoft Office suite of applications, Visual Basic for Applications is often the choice for end user development. ***Visual Basic for***

FIGURE 13.14

With some minor changes to convert from VB to VBA, you can now use the Penguin Enterprises payroll program in Microsoft Excel.

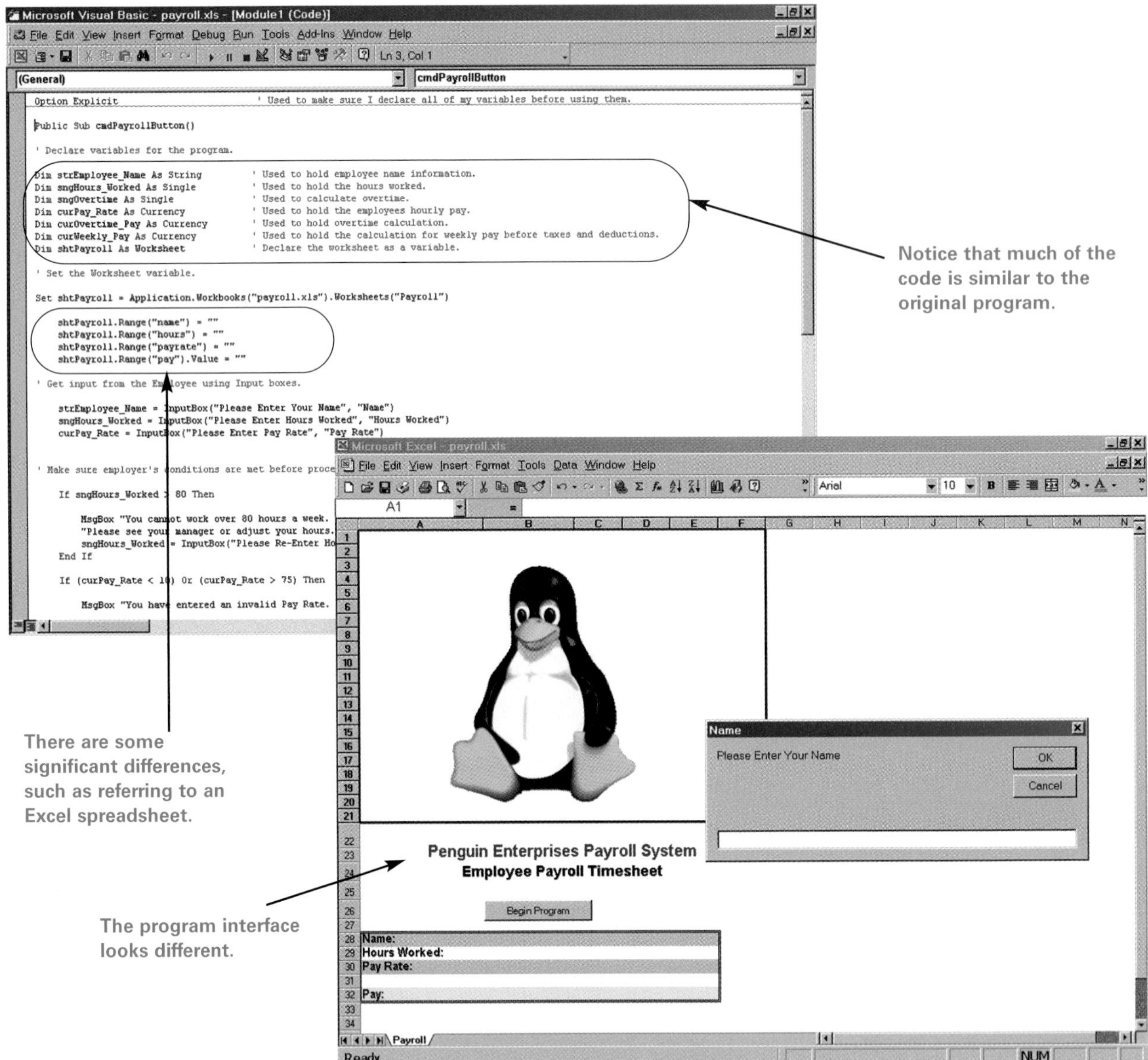

Applications (VBA) is an interpreted scripting language that works within Microsoft Office applications. For example, you can use VBA in Microsoft Excel to create a payroll spreadsheet macro (Figure 13.14) much like the payroll software created in Visual Basic.

Event-Driven

An ***event-driven language*** responds to actions users perform on the program. It's an event when you click on a button, use a pull-down menu, or scroll down a window. In an event-driven language, each of these events triggers an action. GUI programmers primarily use event-driven programming languages.

making the grade

1. __________ is when a programming language can work on a variety of computer hardware and operating systems.
2. __________ language is a machine-dependent, low-level language that uses words instead of binary numbers to program a specific computer system.
3. A(n) __________ simultaneously translates high-level programming languages into machine language.
4. A(n) __________ is a scripting language program that executes a task or set of tasks within a software application.
5. A(n) __________ language responds to actions users perform on the program.

13.5 PROGRAMMING FRAMEWORKS

You've learned a lot about the basics of programming in this chapter. You investigated a business problem, analyzed it, and designed a solution for it. You learned how to write basic software code and how to test, implement, and maintain your software. Finally, you have the skills to determine the best programming language for the task at hand.

In this final section you'll learn about how programmers use programming frameworks. A ***programming framework*** is a collection of software tools you use to create a complete business solution. The two most important programming frameworks are Sun's Java Platform Technologies and Microsoft's .NET. Since both of these are based on object-oriented programming, we'll start this section with a brief discussion of object-oriented concepts.

OBJECT-ORIENTED PROGRAMMING
How Can I Reuse Parts of Programs?

When you interact with the world, it's at an object level. When you drive a car, you know how to use the accelerator pedal to make it go, the brakes to make it stop, and the steering wheel to turn. You don't need to know that when you push the accelerator, a gas mixture goes through the fuel injector, which speeds up the revolutions per minute in the engine, which makes the drive shaft spin more quickly, and so on. All you need to know how to do is interact with objects: accelerator, brakes, or steering wheel. Someone (engineers, in this case) has "coded" everything else.

Object-oriented programming (OOP) allows you to interact with objects when you code software. In procedural languages like COBOL, you'd have to write the entire program code for the car to accelerate. In OOP all you need to know is that when you give the car more gas, the car will go faster. Plus, in OOP you know that you can use the accelerator with any car you drive. Being able to use the same technique with any "car object" you encounter hints at the power of object-oriented programming.

Objects

Objects are an important component of object-oriented programming. A ***programming object*** is an item that contains properties and methods to

practically speaking

Language Translators

You now see the many decisions you must make when translating an algorithm into error-free software. Whether it's choosing the correct programming language or debugging and testing the code, there's no room for error. Can you imagine the challenge to code software that can translate one human language to another? Consider the following mistakes people made *without* the help of software:

- When KFC wanted to translate its slogan "finger-lickin' good" into Chinese, it came out as "eat your fingers off."
- Scandinavian vacuum manufacturer Electrolux launched an ad campaign in the United States with the slogan "nothing sucks like an Electrolux."
- When General Motors tried to sell the Chevy Nova in South America, people didn't buy it. "No va" means "it won't go" in Spanish. GM changed the name to Caribe for its Spanish markets.

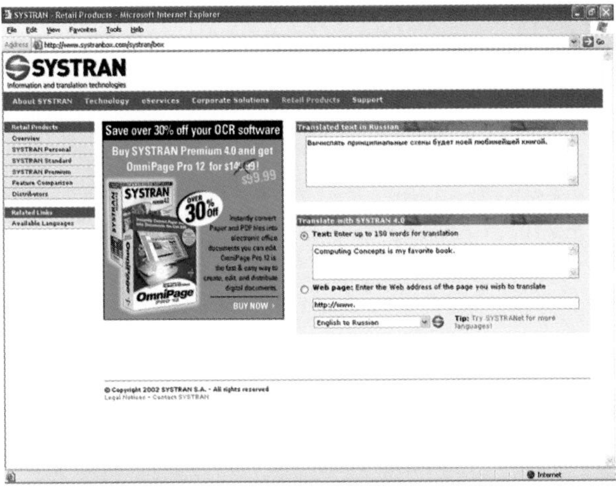

These examples show that translating one language into another is tricky—even for people with huge resources.

Language translator software can help. This software will translate Web pages, e-mail letters, reports, manuals, and books into another language. You also can get multilingual word processors, encyclopedias, dictionaries, and writing tools. And some Web sites will translate text for a fee.

For translation of short blocks of text, try SysTran's Web site (www.systransoft.com/), which can translate your text into various languages. If your text requires foreign characters, make sure you install them on your computer before you start. Both Netscape and Internet Explorer can show Web sites in languages other than English. You just have to add the language to your browser.

Be careful about using language translation software if you don't know the target language well. If you're in doubt, be sure to check your work with someone who's fluent in the translated language.

---

manipulate that information. For example, a car object would have the properties of model type, engine, color, tires, steering, year made, condition, fuel level, etc. An ***object property*** is an identifying characteristic of an object. An ***object method*** allows you to manipulate the properties. For example, a **fill up** method allows you to make sure the car has enough fuel.

Classes and Instances

But the power of OOP doesn't stop with a single object. Programmers create a generic car object that contains all possible properties and methods about cars. In OOP, this makes it an object class. An ***object class*** is an object that contains all of the properties and methods a programming object can possess. Now whenever you want to create another car object, you simply need to create an instance of the car class. An ***object instance*** is an exact copy of an object class.

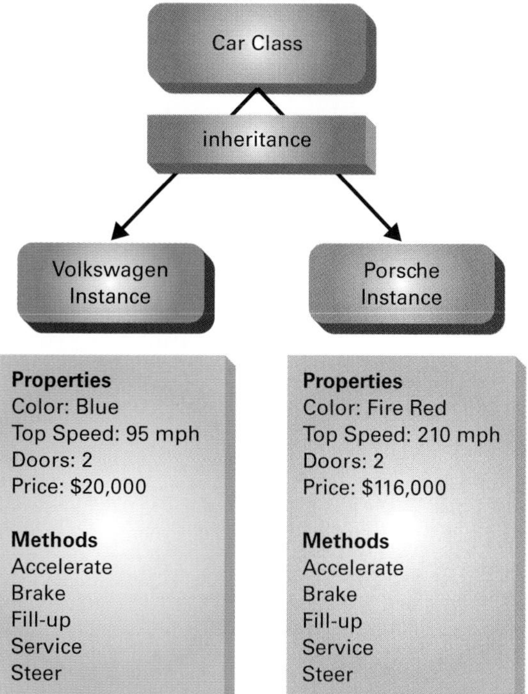

FIGURE 13.15

In this example two car instances inherit all of the properties and methods of the car class.

In OOP, programmers call this process of class copying *inheritance*. ***Inheritance*** is the passing on of properties and methods from a class to an object. Programmers use inheritance to quickly and efficiently create similar objects with the same types of properties and methods. Figure 13.15 shows how you'd view cars in OOP. To learn more about OOP, complete the "Object-Oriented and Visual Programming" tutorial on your SimNet Concepts Support CD.

JAVA PLATFORM TECHNOLOGIES
How Can I Deploy Comprehensive Software Solutions?

Java is an object-oriented 3GL programming language developed by Sun Microsystems. Sun developed Java to work on all computer operating systems that can use the Java Virtual Machine. Today, you can use Java on many computers and Internet appliances, as well as on the Web as Java applets.

Sun has created a variety of programming frameworks (called platform technologies) based on Java. These programming frameworks help programmers create software solutions for business applications, enterprise software, and mobile devices.

Programmers most frequently use the Java 2 Platform Standard Edition (J2SE) programming framework when they need a Java platform technology. This framework includes many of the standard Java tools, such as compilers to create applications and Java applets.

Large-scale businesses use the Java 2 Platform Enterprise Edition (J2EE) programming framework to create enterprise software solutions. Programmers use the J2EE to create applications and systems for companies to use over their intranets and extranets. We'll discuss how important large-scale systems are to businesses in Chapter 14.

Programmers use the Java 2 Platform Micro Edition (J2ME) programming framework to create software for technologies such as smart cards, pagers, phones, PDAs, and Internet appliances. The J2ME promises to add many features to hand-held devices in the future.

MICROSOFT .NET

How Can Microsoft Help Me Create Comprehensive Solutions?

Many programmers use Microsoft's software development environment to write their code. We used the Visual Basic development environment to code our Penguin Enterprises payroll application. Microsoft .NET is the next generation of development environments. With .NET, Microsoft has created a programming framework that will allow businesses to create applications and systems that work almost anywhere. To accomplish this, Microsoft uses a combination of development tools, servers, XML Web services, and smart client software.

The Visual Studio .NET is the major tool for programmers in Microsoft's new framework. ***Visual Studio .NET*** is a software development environment that allows programmers to write code in Visual Basic, C++, or C# for the .NET framework. All applications that programmers write in the Visual Studio .NET environment will work in the .NET framework no matter which language they choose to write their software code.

We've discussed the various types of servers throughout the text. You're familiar with Web and FTP servers, but Microsoft .NET relies on a vast array of specialized servers to deliver applications and information. We've included more information about these specialized servers at the text Web site at www.mhhe.com/i-series.

At the heart of Microsoft .NET are the XML Web services. In Chapter 8, you learned how XML helps organize content and exchange information between applications. XML Web services enable the Microsoft .NET framework to share information not only between .NET applications but also with other software applications.

Microsoft .NET allows all applications developed in the programming framework to share information. .NET enables you to access the same information on your computer, digital phone, Tablet PC, or PDA. Moreover, .NET provides similar applications for each device so you don't need to learn a new software program for each device. As smart client use increases, .NET will allow you to share information among all .NET-enabled devices (see Figure 13.16).

FIGURE 13.16

Microsoft .NET enables all devices to share applications and information among each other.

SECTION 13.5

making the grade

1. A(n) __________ is a collection of software tools used to create a complete business solution.
2. A(n) __________ is an item that contains properties and methods to manipulate that information.
3. A(n) __________ is an exact copy of an object class.
4. __________ is a software development environment that allows programmers to write code in Visual Basic, C++, or C# for the .NET framework.

13.6 SUMMARY AND KEY TERMS

As a programmer, you have many responsibilities and tools to work with as you develop software during the systems development life cycle. During the investigation phase, you'll develop a problem/opportunity statement that incorporates ***business logic***—the steps used to govern a business process.

In analysis, you often use ***pseudocode*** (English statements to create an outline of an algorithm for a piece of software) or ***program flowcharts*** (graphical depictions of the algorithm). An ***algorithm*** is a set of specific steps to solve a problem or carry out a task.

During design, you can use ***IPO (input-process-output) tables*** to show what information is ***input,*** how to ***process*** that information, and what information is then ***output*** (displayed or printed). You also must test your algorithms to make sure there are no ***logic errors***—mistakes in the way the algorithm solves the problem. During the design phase, you also create basic prototypes to demonstrate to users what the software might do.

In the construction phase you begin coding. ***Coding*** occurs when you translate your algorithm into a ***programming language*** (specific rules and words that express an algorithm). All programming languages have ***control structures,*** including:

- ***Sequence control***—executes instructions from top to bottom and left to right.
- ***Selection control***—makes a logical decision based on an existing condition (these include if-then-else and case statements).
- ***Repetition control***—instructs the software program to repeat a series of instructions until you fulfill a condition or while a condition exists (these include do-while, do-until, and for-next statements).

When testing software, you find software errors or ***bugs.*** Software errors include ***syntax errors*** (mistakes in the programming language's grammar), ***run-time errors*** (mistakes that occur when you run the software code), and ***logic errors.***

Many programmers today write software in a ***software development environment***—an environment that provides programming tools to debug and manage software programs. You'll also hear programmers call this an ***integrated development environment.*** Another software development tool is a CASE tool. ***Computer aided software engineering (CASE) tools*** help prepare reports, draw flowcharts, and generate software code from prototypes. Many programmers keep track of all their software code changes with an open source tool called a ***CVS (Concurrent Versions System).***

Implementing software involves preparing ***documentation***—a collection of instructions and explanations. Programmers also help ***technical writers*** prepare ***user manuals*** to tell users how to use the software program.

Maintaining software often involves creating ***software patches*** (a small fix to a problem) and ***software upgrades*** (a substantial revision of existing software).

Depending on your system and software needs, you can choose from ***machine, assembly, third generation (3GL),*** and ***fourth generation (4GL) languages.*** If it's a 3GL, you'll need to ***compile*** or ***interpret*** the ***source code*** to create ***object code.*** More than likely you'll use an ***event-driven language*** that responds to users' actions, such as clicking a button.

Many programmers are beginning to use ***programming frameworks***—a collection of software tools to create complete business solutions. Sun's Java Platform Technologies and Microsoft's .NET are the two most popular programming frameworks. Both of these frameworks use object-oriented programming (OOP).

Programmers use ***object-oriented programming*** to interact with objects as they code the software. They can manipulate ***object properties,*** or characteristics, as well as ***object methods*** which allow you to manipulate properties. Programmers also create an ***object instance,*** or an exact copy of an object class. An ***object class*** is an object that contains all of the properties and methods a programming object can possess.

To learn more about programming and programming languages, visit the Web site for this text at www.mhhe.com/i-series. We also provide additional resources for this chapter on topics including:

- Programming languages
- Sample software code

KEY TERMS

algorithm (p. 392)
assembler (p. 406)
assembly language (p. 406)
backdoor (p. 401)
bug (p. 401)
business logic (p. 390)
case control statement (or switch statement) (p. 399)
CASE, or computer aided software engineering, tools (p. 403)
coding (p. 396)
comment (p. 397)
compiler (p. 407)
condition (p. 397)
control structure (p. 397)
counter (p. 399)
CVS (Concurrent Versions System) (p. 404)
debugging (p. 401)
documentation (p. 404)
do-until statement (p. 399)
do-while statement (p. 399)
event-driven language (p. 408)
for-next statement (p. 399)
fourth generation language (4GL) (p. 406)
high-level language (p. 406)
if-then-else statement (p. 398)
inheritance (p. 411)
input (p. 394)
integrated development environment (IDE) (p. 402)
interpreter (p. 407)
IPO (input-process-output) table (p. 395)
iteration control (p. 399)
Java (p. 411)
logic error (p. 394)
loop (p. 399)
low-level language (p. 405)
machine language (p. 405)
machine-dependent language (p. 405)
machine-independent language (p. 406)
macro (p. 407)
natural language (p. 406)
nonprocedural language (p. 406)
object class (p. 410)
object code (p. 407)
object instance (p. 410)
object method (p. 410)
object property (p. 410)
object-oriented programming (OOP) (p. 409)
output (p. 394)
portability (p. 405)
procedural language (p. 406)
processing (p. 394)
program flowchart (p. 393)
program manual (p. 404)
programming framework (p. 409)
programming language (p. 396)
programming object (p. 409)
pseudocode (p. 392)
rapid application development (RAD) (p. 403)
repetition control structure (p. 399)
reserved word (p. 397)
run-time error (p. 401)
scripting language (p. 407)
selection control structure (p. 397)
sequence control structure (p. 397)
sequential execution (p. 397)
software development environment (p. 402)
software patch (p. 404)
software upgrade (p. 404)
source code (p. 407)
syntax error (p. 401)
technical writer (p. 404)
third generation language (3GL) (p. 406)
user manual (p. 404)
variable (p. 401)
Visual Basic for Applications (VBA) (p. 408)
Visual Studio .NET (p. 412)

review of terminology

Multiple Choice

1. A graphical depiction of an algorithm is called
   a. pseudocode.
   b. a logical structure.
   c. a program flowchart.
   d. a GUI layout.
   e. a programming framework.

2. A(n) __________ shows what information a piece of software takes in, how it processes information, and what information it produces.
   a. program flowchart
   b. algorithm
   c. control structure
   d. software development environment
   e. IPO table

3. __________ is when you translate your algorithm into a programming language.
   a. Pseudocode
   b. Coding
   c. Compiling
   d. Interpreting
   e. Debugging

4. __________ specify the order in which a computer will execute each line of software code.
   a. Conditions
   b. Switch statements
   c. IPO tables
   d. Control structures
   e. Reserved words

5. __________ are mistakes that occur when you run the software code.
   a. Run-time errors
   b. Logic errors
   c. Syntax errors
   d. Bugs
   e. Iterations

6. __________ uses prototypes to test software components until they meet specifications.
   a. Prototypical infusion
   b. A CASE tool
   c. Software development environment
   d. Rapid application development (RAD)
   e. CVS

7. A(n) __________ is a substantial revision of existing software to improve its usefulness.
   a. software patch
   b. software upgrade
   c. CVS
   d. debugging version
   e. implementation

8. __________ require a programmer to write code to tell the software what it should accomplish but not how it should accomplish it.
   a. 3GLs
   b. Procedural languages
   c. Machine languages
   d. Assembly languages
   e. Nonprocedural languages

9. A(n) __________ translates one line of source code into object code at a time.
   a. interpreter
   b. compiler
   c. assembler
   d. scripter
   e. 3GL

10. A(n) __________ is an object that contains all of the properties and methods a programming object can possess.
    a. object property
    b. object method
    c. programming framework
    d. OOP
    e. object class

True/False

11. ____ Sequential execution is when a computer performs each line of code according to a set condition.

12. ____ A counter is a numerical value that tracks the number of iterations in a software code.

13. ____ Logic errors are mistakes in a software code's grammar.

14. ____ A 3GL is a machine-independent, high-level procedural language.

15. ____ An object property allows you to manipulate an object.

Take this quiz online at www.mhhe.com/i-series and get instant feedback.

QUESTIONS AND EXERCISES

1. Developing Pseudocode to Solve a Business Process

As a programmer on a systems development team, you need to develop a logical design for the program you'll create. In this chapter, we showed you how programmers take a problem/opportunity statement and translate it into an algorithm using pseudocode or a program flowchart.

Here's your chance to practice your logic skills. You need to develop an algorithm for the CyberTik ticket ordering program. This program will charge users a certain price depending on what type of event they want to attend and how many tickets they buy. We've created the problem/opportunity statement below. You create the pseudocode.

CyberTik Problem/Opportunity Statement

- Create a program that requests a user's name, date, and type of event and the number of tickets the user wants to order.
- If a user wants a ticket to a sporting event, then the cost is $25 per ticket. If a user wants a ticket to a concert, then the event is $30 per ticket. All other tickets cost $20.
- If a user orders more than five tickets, the user gets a 5% discount.
- After the user selects the type and number of tickets, calculate the total cost.
- Display the tickets ordered and the user's information on the screen.
- Ask the user if the information is correct.
- If the information is correct, process the order. If it's not correct, start over.

Remember, you should follow some basic guidelines when writing your pseudocode. To refresh your memory, look on page 392. You should also think about what type of control structures you'll need to create your program logic.

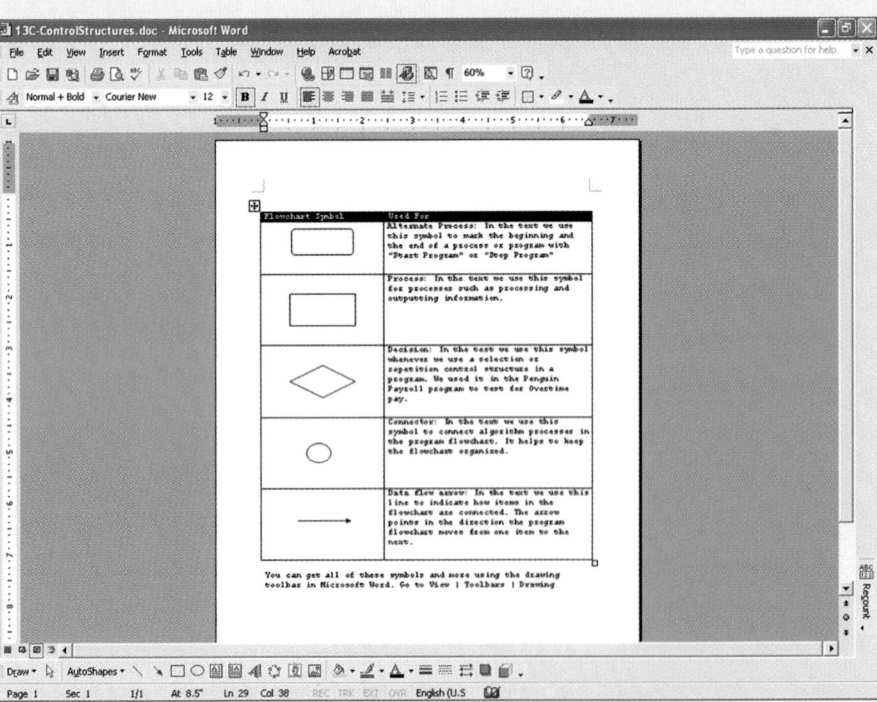

2. Creating the Correct Control Structure

In this chapter we looked at how control structures specify the order in which a computer will execute each line of code in a software program. Creating correct control structures can be challenging. Perhaps you need to test a condition to see how a computer should execute code (selection) or maybe you need to run a series of instructions a certain number of times (repetition).

Of course, the best way to learn about control structure is to practice. Go to the Web site at www.mhhe.com/i-series. (Select **Chapter 13**, **Project Data Files**, and then **ControlStructures.doc**.) Once you download this file, open it up in Word. You'll find symbols for the program flowcharts in this file along with explanations of how to use each one.

Using the symbols, create three program flowcharts that reflect the control structures written in each pseudocode to the right.

a. START PROGRAM
GET USER INPUT (NAME, ADDRESS)
DISPLAY RESULTS ON SCREEN
STOP PROGRAM

b. START PROGRAM
GET USER INPUT (HUNGRY?)
If HUNGRY =YES **Then**
Eat
Else
Don't eat
DISPLAY RESULTS ON SCREEN
STOP PROGRAM

c. START PROGRAM
COUNT TO 10
For Count = 1 to 10
Next
DISPLAY RESULTS ON SCREEN
STOP PROGRAM

3. Debugging a Software Program

As a programmer, you'll need to make sure your software works as it should. Debugging software is a major part of programming. You'll need to know how to identify and fix syntax, run-time, and logic errors.

The best way to learn about debugging software code is to practice. Go to the Web site at www.mhhe.com/i-series. (Select **Chapter 13**, **Project Data Files**, and then **DebugPayroll.xls**.) Once you download this file, open it up in Excel. If you see a warning about a macro, go ahead and allow it to work since we are a trusted source. Otherwise, you won't be able to complete the assignment.

The Excel spreadsheet contains the Penguin Payroll VBA macro discussed on pages 408–409. To see the macro code, press **Alt+F11** on your keyboard. You'll see there are many syntax errors (marked in red) in this code. You'll need to fix these as well as the run-time and logic errors. *Make sure to read the programmer's comments for help.*

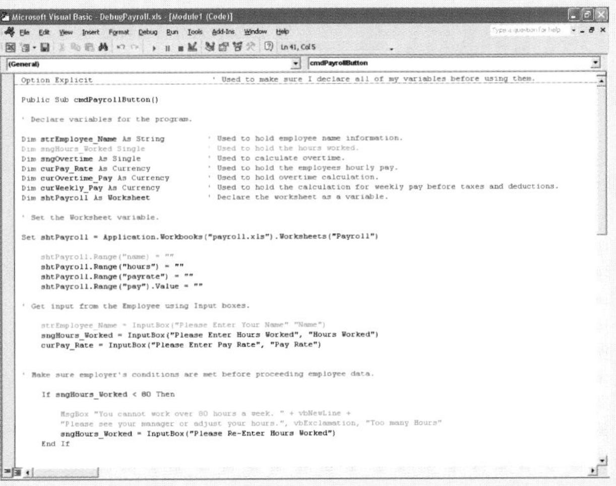

e-commerce

1. Exploring Technical Certifications

If you spend time learning a technical skill, such as a programming language or a network operating system, you'll want to let potential employers know you meet certain standards. Many technology companies have developed exams to test your skill level. If you pass an exam (or series of exams), you become a certified professional.

Job applicants who are certified in certain technologies have an edge on those who aren't. Certification is a way to demonstrate you have the necessary technical skills to succeed. We've listed a few Web sites to help you learn more about certification:

- Cisco—www.cisco.com/warp/public/10/wwtraining
- Java—suned.sun.com/US/certification
- Microsoft—www.microsoft.com/traincert
- Novell—www.novell.com/training/certinfo
- RedHat—www.redhat.com/training/rhce/courses

After looking through these sites, answer the following questions:

a. What types of certifications did you find?
b. How many exams do you need to pass for each certification? How much did they cost?
c. Can you take classes to learn about the technology before taking the exam?
d. Go to www.monster.com and www.dice.com. Search for jobs that require your chosen certification. What types of jobs did you find?

2. Buying a Car

Buying a car has typically been an "experiential" shopping excursion. That is, most people really need to drive different cars, get a feel for how they handle, and just smell the interior.

More people are using the Web to research cars, finance options, and car dealers before making that trip to the lot. When you step into the dealer's showroom, you can know exactly what the dealer paid for the car you want and how the dealership and the car rate in overall customer satisfaction. Below, we've listed four Web sites where you can find this information:

- AutoWeb—www.autoweb.lycos.com
- autobytel—www.autobytel.com
- CarsDirect—www.carsdirect.com
- Yahoo! Autos—autos.yahoo.com

Determine a car you'd like to own, visit each site, and answer the following questions.

a. How do you search for a car?
b. Does the site inform you of the closest dealer who has the car you want?
c. Can you simply buy your car on the Web and have it delivered to your driveway?
d. What about financing options?
e. Does the site provide unbiased rankings of automobiles? What about dealership rankings?
f. Would you ever consider buying a car on the Web without first test-driving one at a local dealership? Why or why not?

3. Renting a Car

Instead of buying a car, maybe you just need one for the weekend or for a vacation. Choose the type of car you'd like to rent using the following sites:

- Alamo—www.alamo.com
- Avis—www.avis.com
- Enterprise Rent-A-Car—www.enterprise.com
- Hertz Car Rental—www.hertz.com

Using what you found out about your car at the sites above, answer the following questions:

a. Can you rent a car in every state in the United States? Are some states more expensive than others?
b. Can you rent a car overseas?
c. Do they give you maps and/or weather information?
d. Do they have frequent user programs? Is it easy to enroll in one?

ethics, security & privacy

1. How Secure Is Your Software?

You've seen how many lines of software code it takes to make a basic application work effectively. The Penguin Enterprises payroll program is small compared to many software applications, yet it's possible to make many errors in its few lines of code.

Most software programs contain millions of lines of code. Programmers work to make sure that their code is as bug-free as possible. However, it's impossible to catch 100 percent of the bugs. Instead, many software companies release programs to you when only a majority of the bugs have been found. Then, the companies release software patches as they find additional bugs. Many of the bugs found won't do much except to cause your software not to work properly.

However, some bugs allow hackers to access information, crash your computer, or acquire information from you. If you haven't kept your software up to date with patches, when you connect to the Internet or share files, you might be allowing your software to do things it shouldn't.

Visit the following Web sites to learn more about bugs:

- MSDN Bug Center—msdn.microsoft.com/bugs/default.asp
- Redhat Bugzilla—bugzilla.redhat.com
- SANS Security Alert—www.sans.org/newsletters/sac

Answer the following questions:

a. Were you aware that there were so many bugs in the software you might be using? Does this make you think differently about how you use your software?
b. Did you see any bugs that pertain to your computer software?
c. Why do you think that companies release software with bugs in it? Would you wait for new software until after programmers had found all the bugs? How long would you wait?
d. Most software vendors release patches on their Web site to fix bugs. Find some newer bugs on one of the lists above and then see if the software vendor has issued a bug-fix patch.

2. To Install or Not to Install: That's the Question

You read about ethical, security, and privacy violations almost every day. Hackers, software pirates, and identity fraud all make headlines. Yet we don't always think about the decisions programmers, systems analysts, and software engineers quietly make on a daily basis.

Suppose you landed a job as programmer at a good company. On your first day your manager hands you an application package. She asks you to customize the application with macros and then install the customized application on all the computers in the business. When you ask about the software licensing agreement, your manager tells you not to worry about it. You're not quite sure what your manager means by this. What do you do? You want the job, but you're not sure if this request is ethical (or legal). How can you get some guidance?

Fortunately, there are ethical standards for IT professionals to follow. These come from the Association for Computing Machinery (ACM), the Institute of Electrical and Electronics Engineers (IEEE), and the British Computer Society (BCS):

- ACM Code of Ethics and Professional Conduct—www.acm.org/constitution/code.html
- IEEE Code of Ethics—www.ieee.org/about/whatis/code.html
- BCS Codes of Practice—www.bcs.org/codes

Choose one of the societies listed above and then use its guidelines to answer the following questions:

a. What should you do according to the standards you chose?
b. What is your response to your manager?
c. How could you use the standards to support your response to your manager?
d. Can you think of other ethical IT dilemmas you may encounter as an IT professional or even as a computer user?

on the web

1. Exploring Programming Frameworks

In this chapter you learned how software tools in programming frameworks can help programmers develop complete business solutions. Two of the most-used programming frameworks are Microsoft's .NET and Sun's Java Platform Technologies. Visit the Web sites below:

- Java—java.sun.com/products
- .NET—www.microsoft.com/net/basics

Use the following questions to prepare a PowerPoint presentation:

a. What programming languages does the Java framework use? What about .NET?
b. If you wanted to develop a software program for a Palm OS PDA, which programming framework would you use? Why?
c. If you wanted to develop a software program for a Tablet PC, which programming framework would you use? Why?
d. What do you see as some of the major differences between the two programming frameworks? Make sure to explain your answer.

2. Finding a Programming Job Online

Programmers are in high demand. Search job Web sites for programming jobs. Start with these Web sites:

- ComputerJobs.com—www.computerjobs.com
- Dice.com—www.dice.com
- Monster.com—www.monster.com

Consider the following questions:

a. What types of jobs do you find?
b. Are they what you expected?
c. What types of skills, education, and experience are employers looking for?
d. What types of certifications are employers asking for?
e. Are employers seeking knowledge about certain languages more than others?

Create a PowerPoint presentation that lists the five most interesting jobs you found. You should also discuss the answers to the above questions in your presentation.

3. Exploring Programming Resources

Most programmers specialize in only a few of the hundreds of available programming languages. You'll find there are many good programming resources, such as tutorials, sample code, and programming tips on the Web.

Choose two programming languages—C++, COBOL, Java, and Visual Basic are just a few—and find at least three Web resource sites for each. List each Web resource site's location along with a three- to four-sentence description of what it offers. Share your findings with the class.

4. Finding Code on the Web

Many programmers will share code (or portions of it) on the Web. Other programmers take this code, modify it, and then use it. The Web site www.vbcode.com is one example of this type of programming resource for Visual Basic.

Find five Web sites that share or discuss programming languages. Consider the following questions:

a. Were you able to download the complete code for a program? If so, why do you think programmers made it available? If not, why do you think they haven't shared it?
b. Did programmers share code from certain programming languages more often than others? Which ones? Why do you think this is the case?
c. Can you think of reasons why you shouldn't share code with other programmers? And when you shouldn't use code from other programmers?

group activities

1. Investigating and Designing Solutions

Businesses routinely ask programmers to investigate a business problem and design a solution to the problem. In this chapter you learned how to investigate a problem by asking questions to create a problem/opportunity statement. Using the problem/opportunity statement, you then proceeded to write pseudocode to create the logical model for a software program.

As a group, find a problem that needs solving using software. Perhaps you need to find a better way to organize your music files or you need to track membership and dues in a student club. Whatever the problem, ask questions to create a problem/opportunity statement.

Using the statement, prepare pseudocode or a flowchart to solve the problem. Finally, decide what programming language you'll use to code your algorithm. Make sure to explain why you chose the language that you did.

Prepare a PowerPoint presentation discussing the entire process. Include the logical model in your presentation.

2. Exploring Programming Majors

You've learned about the various careers and certifications you can pursue as a programmer. What types of majors might you declare in school to help you become a programmer? Is Computer Science the only choice? What about Information Systems or Computer Engineering? You can choose from many majors that will help you become a programmer.

In addition to your own school, investigate at least five more schools to find out what types of programming-related majors they offer. Prepare a chart of schools and majors. Also, list some of the classes that the schools include as part of their major. Answer the following questions:

a. What's the most common programming-related major you found?
b. What types of classes seem to be common for all the programming-related majors?
c. What type of specialties does each major allow you to choose from?

3. Interviewing a Programmer

Find a programmer on your campus or at a local business. Prepare a set of questions about her or his job responsibilities, methods of coding software, and certifications. You might want to ask if the programmer's software development life cycle is the same or different from the one in the text. Or maybe identify what types of programming languages the programmer prefers and why. Make sure to work as a group to prepare a list of questions before conducting the interview.

Interview the individual. Present your findings to the class. Make sure to compare your findings with other groups. Do the different programmers' roles vary? Did they all mention specific programming languages? What about how the programmers conduct software development? Was it the same as in the text?

4. Deciding on Proprietary versus Open Source Software

In this chapter we discussed programming languages and how programmers can use a language to create software. Currently, there's much discussion among programmers about proprietary versus open source software. You'll see this debate primarily between Microsoft and Linux advocates.

Compare and contrast the philosophy behind proprietary software such as Windows with open source software such as Linux. Which would you use for your operating system? What about application software or utilities?

As a group, compare a proprietary and open source operating system, word processing application, spreadsheet, and DBMS. Which type would the group use? (You can choose proprietary for some and open source for others.) Make sure to explain your answers.

crossword puzzle

Across

1. Highest level of management
5. Report that summarizes information
8. Software that supports groups
10. System that processes transactions
13. Software that helps with the execution of meetings
14. Flow of information that includes directions and strategies
15. Report that shows "out of the norm" information
16. TPS that customers use
17. Group ______ database
19. Information that describes the surroundings of an organization
20. Information that is quantifiably known
23. System that helps analyze problems and take advantage of opportunities
24. Software in which you can capture notes on a presentation
27. System that alerts people to potential problems and opportunities
28. Internal Internet

Down

2. Report that compares sets of information
3. Collective personality of a nation or group of people
4. Level of information
5. Information that anyone can access as they need to
6. Opposite of #20 across
7. Person who works outside the office
9. Flow of information that moves among departments and teams
10. Organization that operates throughout the world
11. Lowest level of management
12. Computing environment that places technology in the hands of those who need it
18. Report given by week, for example
21. Flow of information that describes the internal aspects of the organization
22. Middle management
25. Information describing how the organization is doing based on its transactions
26. #28 across open to certain business partners

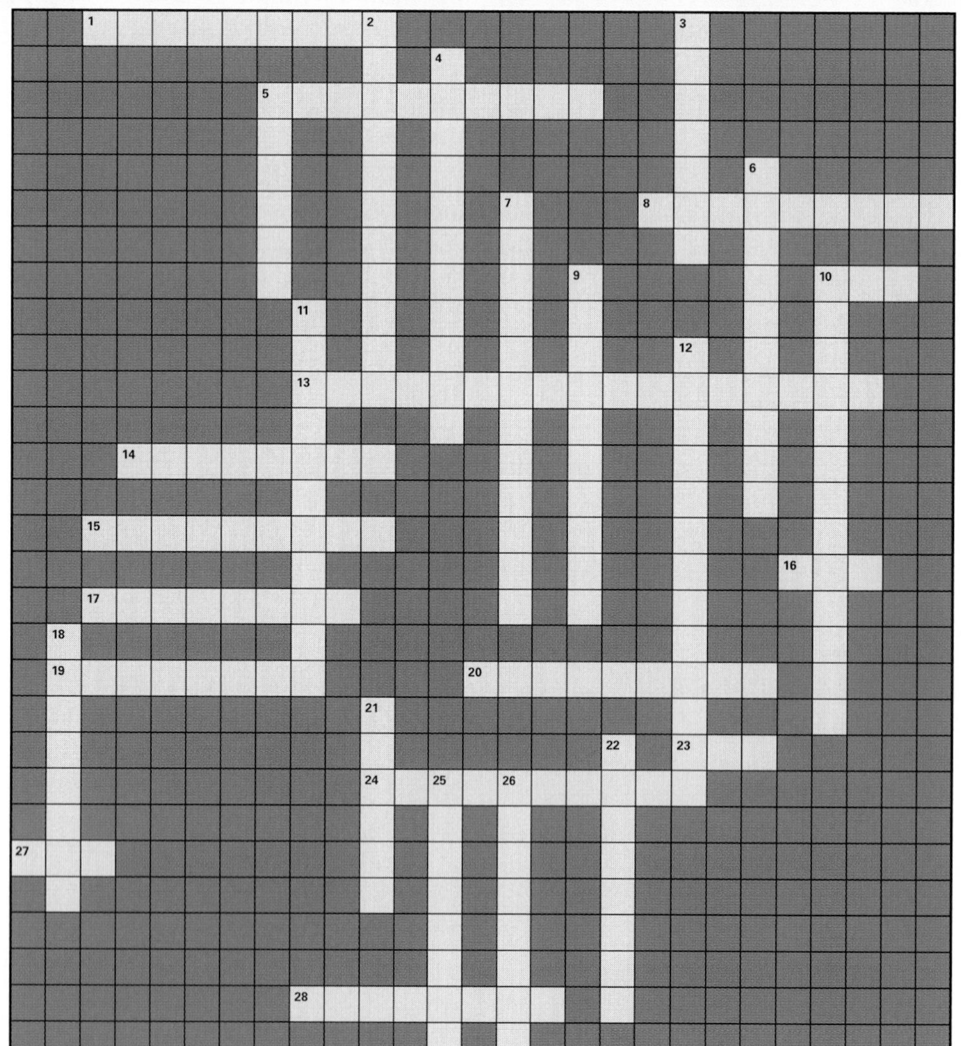

fourteen

CHAPTER

14

Organizational Information Systems

Why Are Computers the Heavy Artillery in Business?

SIMNET CONCEPTS SUPPORT

- CAD Applications (p. 437)
- Financial Management Applications (p. 437)
- Intranets and Extranets (p. 438)

did you know?

Almost all businesses today require the use of computers and information technology. Many businesses use the technology simply to be more efficient and effective, an obvious advantage. Others go further and use the technology to find innovative ways to beat the competition.

dell *Computer provides immediate access to information through IT. Because of that, it carries only three to four days of inventory, compared to the industry standard of about 45 days.*[1]

charles *Schwab has placed technology in the hands of its customers and allows them to manage their own money and make their own stock trades. Schwab's 3 million customers manage more than $250 billion in assets and trade more than $11 billion in securities each week.*[2]

metLife *also provides information and services to its customers. According to George Foulke, vice president of IT for MetLife, it costs just __??__ to serve a customer via the Internet, while it costs several __??__ when customers speak with a person on the phone.*[3]

To learn about the difference in cost between serving a customer via the Internet versus by phone, visit the Web site for this text at www.mhhe.com/i-series.

Student Learning Outcomes

After reading this chapter, you should be able to:

1. Describe the typical structure of an organization and the nature of information technology and information within it.
2. Define the types of IT systems that help an organization track information.
3. Discuss how management information systems and executive information systems support the needs of managers.
4. Describe how various technologies support organizational logistics.
5. Define how technology can help an organization spread out nationally and around the globe.

Computers today are the heavy artillery in business. In the information age, knowledge is power. Remember the old saying, "What you don't know can't hurt you." Well, in business today the new saying is, "What you don't know can and will put you out of business."

Computers and technology are the tools businesses use to gather, store, manage, and manipulate vitally important information. This information includes (1) transactions with customers and other businesses, (2) knowledge about the competition and other external forces, and (3) knowledge about how the business works internally. Successful businesses today keep a wealth of information about all three, and they provide employees with the technology and technology know-how to access and use that information.

As you prepare to move into the business world, you need to understand how and why businesses gather, store, manage, and manipulate information with technology. In previous chapters, we've discussed some of these issues, especially in regard to databases in Chapter 10. Now, we want to take a very specific look at the structure of a business and what com-

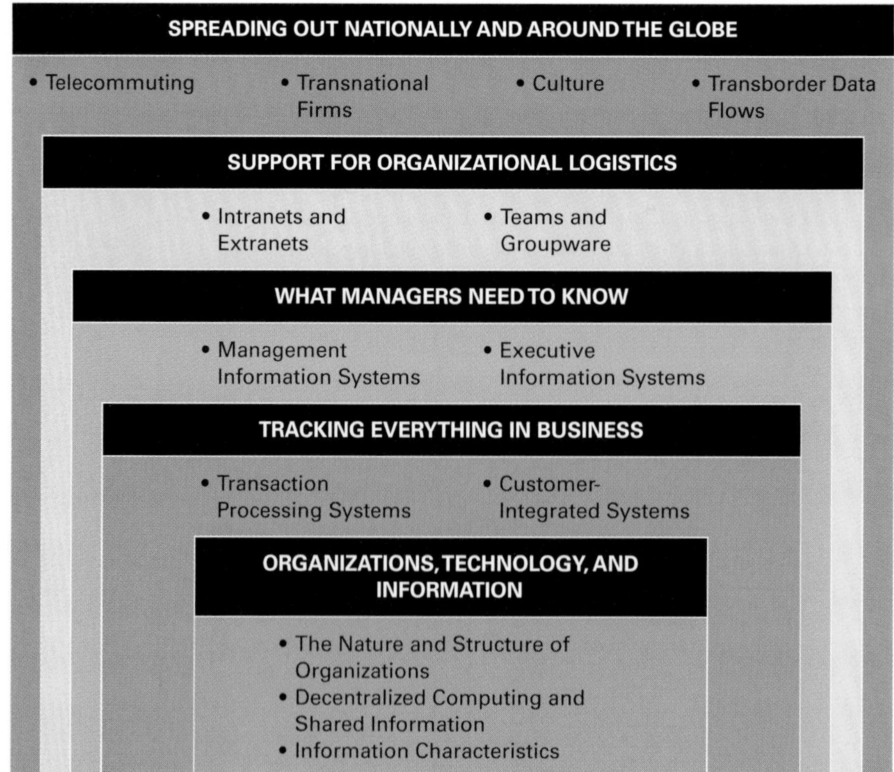

FIGURE 14.1

Your focus in this chapter starts with a look internally at organizations and then expands to businesses spreading out nationally and around the globe.

puter systems businesses use in the information age. Figure 14.1 on the opposite page provides an overview of this chapter.

14.1 ORGANIZATIONS, TECHNOLOGY, AND INFORMATION

The use of technology to manage information in an organization doesn't just happen. It must be carefully thought out and planned. Organizations can't simply decide they need technology because everyone else seems to have it, just as you shouldn't buy a home computer because everyone else seems to have one. Organizations must first understand their nature and structure, the information requirements of their employees, and then how technology can support what they do.

THE NATURE AND STRUCTURE OF ORGANIZATIONS

How Are Organizations "Organized" Today?

A traditional organization is usually viewed as a four-level pyramid (see Figure 14.2). At the top is ***strategic management,*** which provides an organization with overall direction and guidance. Strategic management is responsible for developing the long-range plans of the organization. Typical strategic-level managers include the CEO (Chief Executive Officer), CIO (Chief Information Officer), CFO (Chief Financial Officer), CPO (Chief Privacy Officer), and COO (Chief Operating Officer). It may also include people who have the title "vice president."

The second level of an organization is often called ***tactical management,*** which develops the goals and strategies outlined by strategic management. So, tactical management may set goals for sales over the next several years. The third level is ***operational management,*** which manages and directs the day-to-day operations and implementation of the goals and strategies. So, operational management might determine the sales goals for each region (East, West, North, and South) that would meet the overall sales goals set by tactical management.

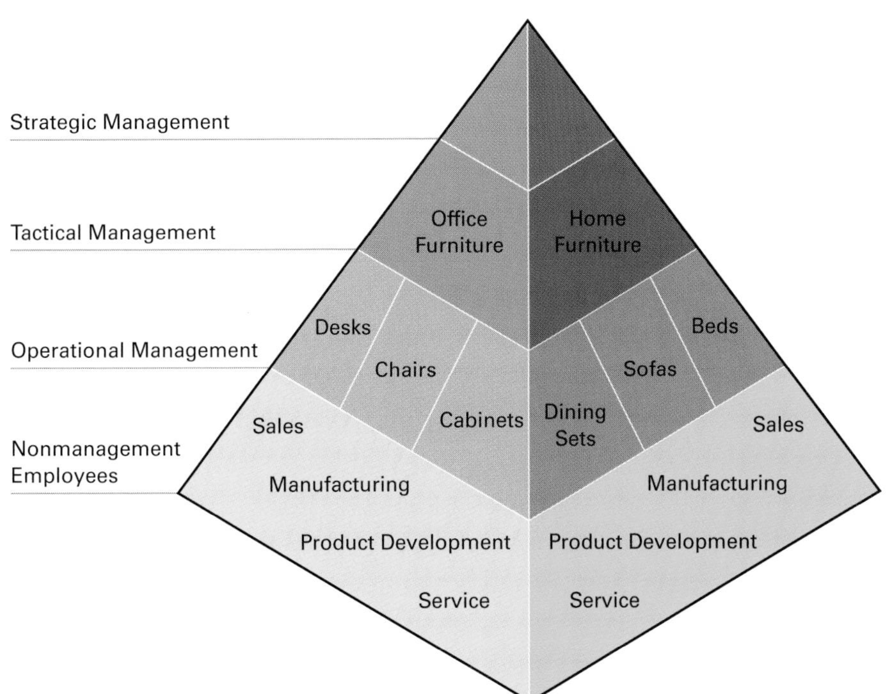

FIGURE 14.2

Typical organizational structures are in the form of a pyramid with several levels.

At the fourth level of an organization are nonmanagement employees, those people who perform all the productive daily activities such as order processing, manufacturing line work, customer service, and so on. You should notice in Figure 14.2 (on the previous page) that organizations also exhibit depth. In our example, the organization is structured according to product lines.

DECENTRALIZED COMPUTING AND SHARED INFORMATION

How Do Organizations Get Technology and Information into the Hands of Their Employees?

In today's business world, technology is in the hands of all employees, so information must be in their hands as well. All employees—regardless of their level—can help an organization be successful, but they can do it only if they can use technology to access the right information. Organizations achieve this goal through the practices of decentralized computing and shared information.

Decentralized Computing

Decentralized computing is the placement of technology into the hands of those people in an organization who need it in order to do their jobs effectively and efficiently. This is really all about empowering employees through the use of technology. If you need access to information, then your organization should provide you with the technology to access it. Organizations need to train employees to use the technology in the most efficient and optimal way, too.

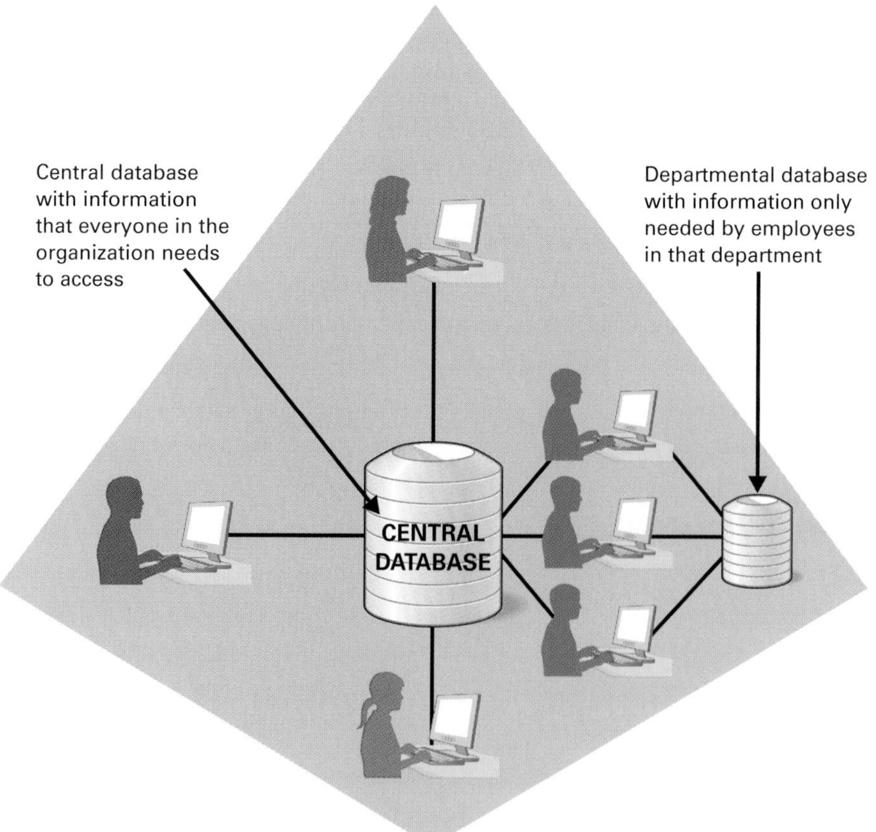

FIGURE 14.3

Decentralized computing and shared information give all employees the ability to access whatever information they need whenever they need it.

Shared Information

Shared information is the concept that employees should have access to whatever information they need when they need it (see Figure 14.3 on the opposite page). For example, sales people need to access inventory information to determine if products are on hand, and they need to access manufacturing information to determine when products will be available.

In a shared information and decentralized computing environment, you'll typically find a large central database that contains all the information anyone may need to access. You'll also find smaller departmental databases that contain information that only employees in a particular department need to access. For example, Bass Brewery—one of England's largest beer manufacturers—uses decentralized computing, shared information, and a state-of-the-art computer system to produce more than 50 types of beer in more than 150 different packages. With the touch of a computer screen, production managers control both the brew house and packaging hall, selecting the volume run, type of beer, and type of packaging. The appropriate recipes alter the contents fed into the vats. Information concerning bottling sizes and labels is sent to the packaging hall. Cleaning fluid is automatically released to the vats in the brew house. The entire process depends on decentralized computing, shared information, and the touch of a finger.

INFORMATION CHARACTERISTICS
Do People in Organizations Have Different Information Needs?

People within an organization have different information needs according to their responsibilities. Thus, information within an organization takes on different attributes and flows in different directions.

Differing Information Needs

Depending on your responsibilities within your organization, you need information of varying specificity, or "granularity." ***Information granularity*** refers to the degree of detail information contains. For example, nonmanagement employees and operational managers need information with a fine level of granularity, perhaps sales on a daily basis. Tactical managers make use of information with a coarser granularity, perhaps sales by product line on a monthly or quarterly basis. Strategic managers work with information that exhibits a very coarse level of granularity, perhaps total sales by year.

So, if you think of an organization from top to bottom, people at the highest or strategic levels need more general information with the coarsest granularity, while nonmanagement or line people who work with daily processes need the finest level of granularity (see Figure 14.4). Strategic managers don't need to know the details of every sale; they need to know total sales by some time period in order to set overall goals and directions. Operational managers and nonmanagement employees need to know the details of every sale because they are charged with the day-to-day business activities.

FIGURE 14.4

Information granularity varies according to the organizational level.

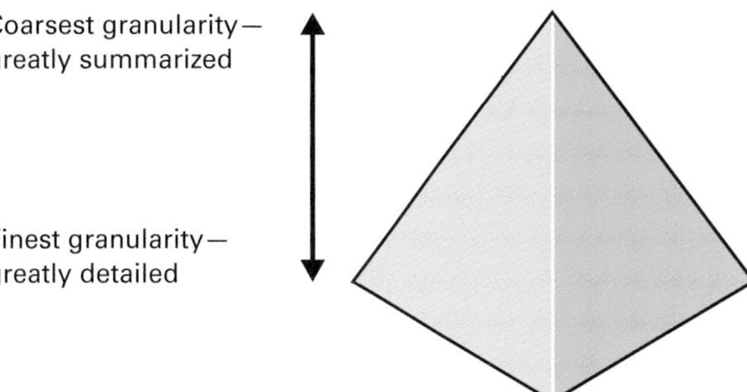

i•series insights *Ethics, Security & Privacy*

Who's Looking at Your Medical Records?

According to one poll, 85 percent of surveyed doctors said that protecting the confidentiality of patient medical records was very essential and high on their priority list. That sounds good, doesn't it? Think again. If there are 35 students in your class, then 85 percent means that 5 of you have doctors who don't care about protecting the confidentiality of your medical records.

Long before the use of computers in the medical field became widespread, record confidentiality was suspect. For example, your doctor's handwritten notes about you could be subpoenaed by a court without your permission or knowledge. This happened to a woman in California whose medical records were subpoenaed after a car accident. Her records revealed that she had given up a child for adoption 30 years earlier, information that should not have been relevant.

Telemedicine—which can electronically transfer your records to any doctor in the country at any time—is a great concept. For example, if you live in Montana and become ill while on vacation in Florida, your medical records can easily be transferred. But beware—perhaps your most sensitive information is now traveling throughout a vast network of computers and computer users.

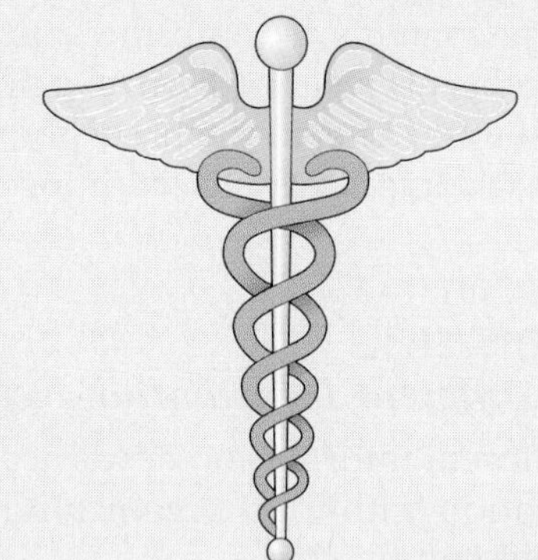

If you're concerned about the confidentiality of your medical records, take action. These suggestions provide a starting point.

1. Never disclose anything to your doctor that is not health-related. It may be recorded in your file, which can be transferred to another organization such as an insurance carrier.
2. Ask your doctor if any of your records can be accessed by individuals or organizations outside his or her office. If they can, ask for what purpose.
3. Always ask to review your medical records for accuracy and content.
4. Ask your doctor to notify you in writing if your records are ever subpoenaed.

did you **know?**

In one year, 440 IRS employees were investigated for browsing through the tax records of neighbors, acquaintances, or celebrities.

Information Attributes

People in different jobs in an organization need information that covers different areas or that describes different aspects of the business. We say that information can be internal, external, objective, or subjective.

Internal information describes specific operational aspects of an organization. ***External information,*** on the other hand, describes the environment surrounding an organization. ***Objective information*** quantifiably describes something that is known, while ***subjective information*** attempts to describe something that is currently unknown.

Let's consider these information attributes within the context of the levels of an organization. Strategic managers need internal and objective information that describes how the organization is performing its activities, albeit objective information with a coarse level of granularity. Strategic managers also need external and subjective information, however. For example, the CFO needs to know how interest rates will probably move in the coming months, which would be external and subjective information.

As you move down through the levels of an organization, people typically need more internal and objective information and less subjective and external information. For example, operational managers and nonmanagement employees may need to know exact sales figures on a daily basis (internal and objective), not projected sales (which would be subjective information), which would serve a strategic planning function.

The Flows of Information

Information in organizations flows continuously in various directions—up, down, and horizontally (see Figure 14.5). The ***upward flow of information*** describes the current state of the organization based on its daily transactions (such as sales). So, people at the lower level of the organization capture that information and store it in the central database. Then, people in the upper levels can access and use that information.

The ***downward flow of information*** consists of the strategies, goals, and directives that originate at one level and are passed to lower levels. So, an overall sales goal might originate at the strategic management level. That goal would flow down to tactical management, which would develop more specific sales goals and pass them to operational management. That level would then develop daily or weekly sales goals and pass them to nonmanagement employees (the lowest level).

The ***horizontal flow of information*** refers to information that passes among various departments. If you consider our organizational structure in Figure 14.2 on page 425, there would be a constant horizontal flow of information between the product development departments in the office furniture and home furniture product lines. Why? Because there is probably some overlap of business intelligence here. Perhaps the office furniture department has determined a way to make a better office chair that can be used by the home furniture product development team to make a better sofa.

FIGURE 14.5

Information within an organization flows up, down, and horizontally.

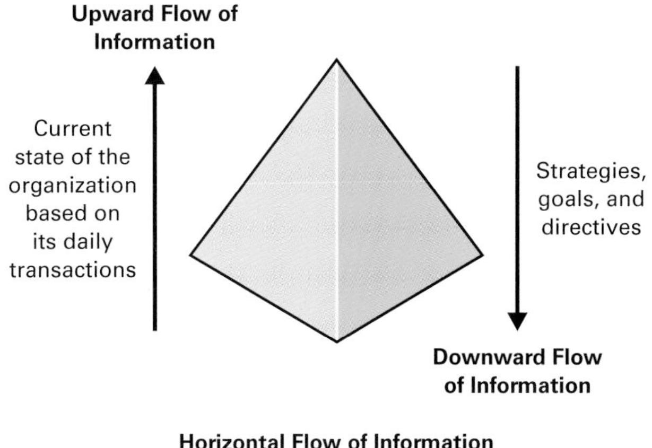

making the grade

SECTION 14.1

1. ___________ management develops the goals and strategies outlined by strategic management.
2. ___________ is the placement of technology in the hands of those people in an organization who need it in order to do their jobs effectively and efficiently.
3. Information ___________ refers to the level of detail the information contains.
4. ___________ information describes the environment surrounding an organization.
5. The ___________ flow of information consists of the strategies, goals, and directives that originate at one level and are passed to lower levels.

14.2 TRACKING EVERYTHING IN BUSINESS

At the very heart of a business are systems that process daily transactions, such as sales to customers, inventory updating, and billing. These systems are most often a business's primary interface to its customers. If these systems don't work correctly or are slow to work, your customers won't be your customers anymore. They'll simply go someplace else to buy their products and services. Computer systems for tracking daily transactions include transaction processing systems and customer-integrated systems.

TRANSACTION PROCESSING SYSTEMS
What Computer Systems Process Daily Transactions?

A ***transaction processing system (TPS)*** is exactly what its name implies—a system that processes transactions that occur within an organization. Types of TPS transactions include processing sales orders, paying accounts payable, creating billing for accounts receivable, tracking hours and generating checks for payroll, and ordering more inventory and raw materials.

At a minimum, a TPS includes hardware and software components for four functions:

1. Gathering input information.
2. Processing information.
3. Presenting information.
4. Storing information.

In Figure 14.6, you can see a TPS order-entry system that performs these four functions, including an optical character recognition (OCR) scanner that helps gather input information from handwritten order-entry forms. Again, these types of systems are vitally important to any and all organizations. If they don't work correctly, your business will lose money and customers. Your goal is to ensure that these systems follow exactly the same sound business logic you would implement if you didn't have the technology. It's up to you to design and maintain your transaction systems so they support your business's needs. As we explained in Chapter 12, you are the business process expert who decides what the systems should do for you and checks to see that they are doing it.

In any organization, once information enters a central database through a TPS, that information can then be used throughout the organization. For example, managers at all levels can generate whatever reports they need to make better decisions.

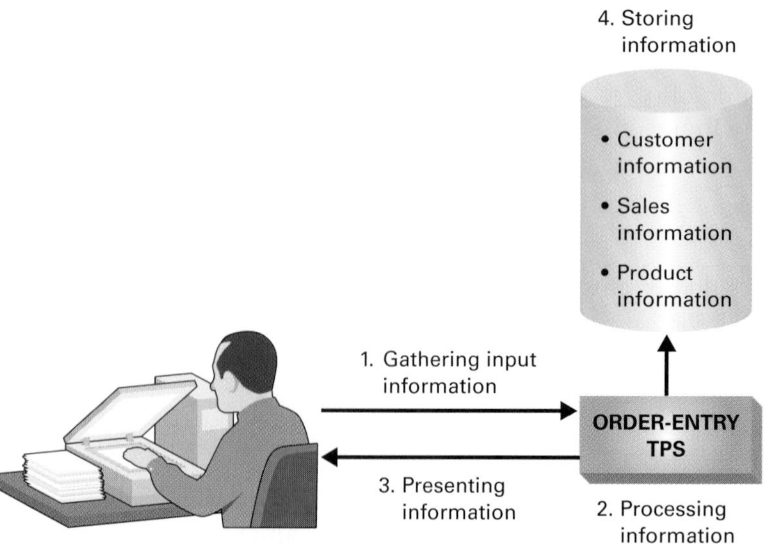

FIGURE 14.6

Transaction processing systems (TPSs) help gather, process, present, and store information.

Transaction processing systems are found in all functions of an organization. And again, these systems must work correctly and efficiently. Not only will your customers leave you if they don't, you could very well go out of business. In the manufacturing industry, losses because of TPS downtime during 1992 were estimated at almost $2.5 billion. In another study, Dr. Stephen Lunce found that most businesses estimated they would lose 50 percent of their revenues if their IT systems failed for only 15 days.

CUSTOMER-INTEGRATED SYSTEMS
Are There Computer Systems That Allow Customers to Process Their Own Transactions?

One of the newest computer systems in the business world today is a customer-integrated system. A ***customer-integrated system (CIS)*** is an extension of a transaction processing system that places technology in the hands of an organization's customers and allows them to process their own transactions. ATMs are perhaps the most common example of a CIS. ATMs provide you with the ability to do your own banking anywhere at any time. What's really interesting is that ATMs actually do nothing "new," but they give you greater flexibility in accessing and using your money.

For a bank, an ATM represents greater customer satisfaction and cost savings. If you're using an ATM instead of a teller inside a bank, then the bank may not need as many tellers. You essentially become your own teller when you use an ATM. It's a win-win situation for everyone.

CISs further decentralize computing power in an organization by placing that power in the hands of customers (see Figure 14.7). For that

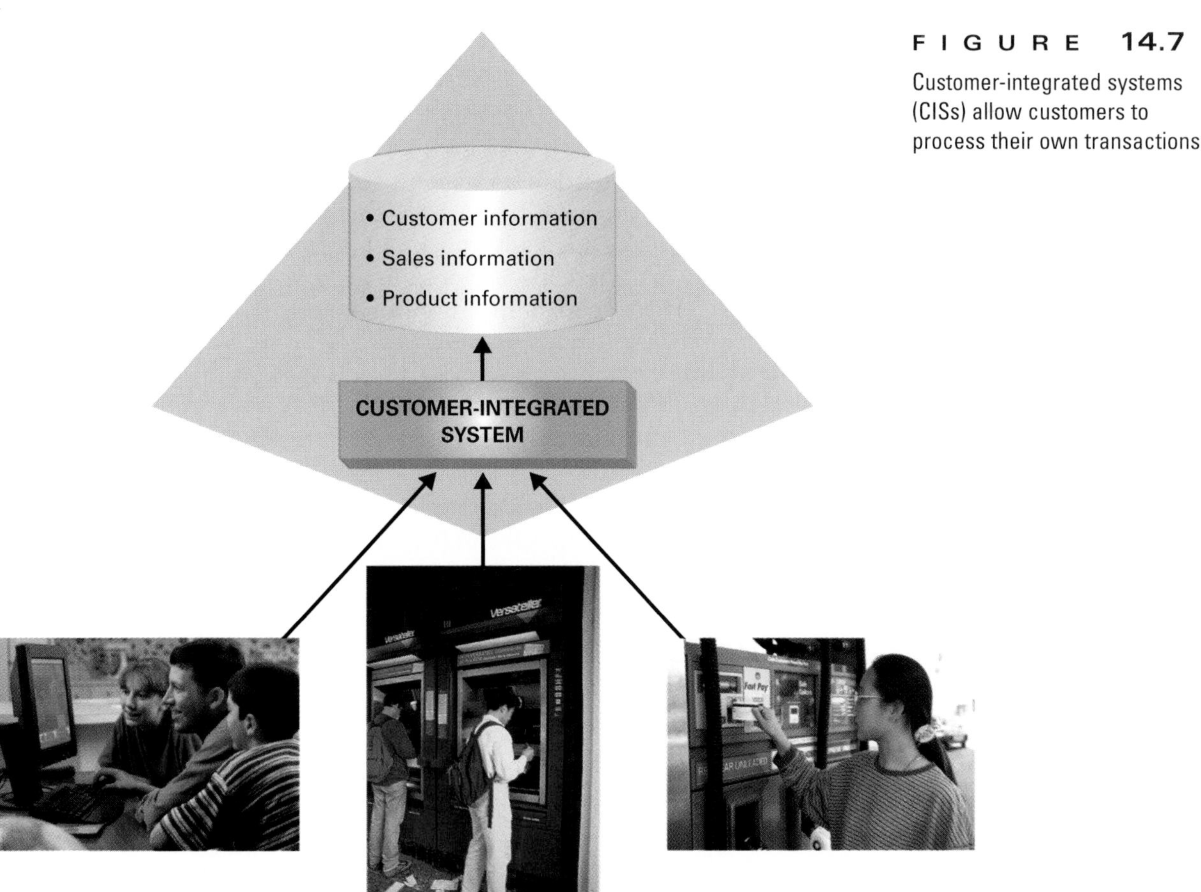

FIGURE 14.7

Customer-integrated systems (CISs) allow customers to process their own transactions.

reason, CISs are also responsible for *communicating* information. Consider ATMs again. You can use an ATM literally anywhere in the world. So, ATMs must include the ability to communicate information from one location to another.

You can find other great examples of customer-integrated systems all over the Web. Throughout this text, you've been experiencing CISs by completing the e-commerce projects at the end of each chapter.

Transaction processing and customer-integrated systems capture vitally important information that helps an organization ensure quality and undertake various reengineering efforts. To learn more about quality and reengineering efforts such as total quality management and business process reengineering, visit the Web site for this text at www.mhhe.com/i-series.

SECTION 14.2

making the grade

1. A(n) ___________ is an extension of a TPS that places technology in the hands of an organization's customers.
2. A(n) ___________ is exactly what its name implies—a system that processes transactions that occur within an organization.
3. CISs further ___________ computing power in an organization by placing that power in the hands of customers.
4. The Web is a common place to find all kinds of ___________.

14.3 WHAT MANAGERS NEED TO KNOW

Before, during, and after daily activities occur within an organization, managers have many responsibilities. Among them is to identify and solve problems, and identify and take advantage of opportunities. But problems and opportunities won't arrive at your desk in an envelope marked "URGENT." Instead, you need to constantly monitor your surroundings. A problem solved before it becomes a problem is the best problem to have. An opportunity that everyone knows about is no longer an opportunity. There are computer systems that can help you with your responsibilities as a manager—these are management information systems and executive information systems.

MANAGEMENT INFORMATION SYSTEMS

What Systems Help Managers Manage?

A ***management information system (MIS)*** is a system that provides periodic and predetermined reports that summarize information. In an organization, this information comes from a database that gathers and stores

did you know?

In *November 2000, pop artist Madonna gave a concert—2,500 people attended the show while 210,000,000 watched it on the Web.*

i•can

Use Technology to Be an Effective Manager

Technology is vitally important in all aspects of a business, perhaps nowhere more so than in the area of supporting managers while they make important decisions.

As a simple example, suppose you're a manager of a local video rental store. Your transaction processing system (TPS) will capture and store information concerning video rentals, inventory orders, late rental returns, and the like. You can then use a management information system (MIS) or executive information system (EIS) to answer the following questions (and many more):

- Which videos haven't rented in the past 60 days? (You might want to place these on the sale rack.)
- Which videos rent the most often and where are they located on the display floor? (You may want to rearrange your store to optimize the renting of certain videos.)
- Which customers consistently return videos late and have to pay a late fee?

Consider the last question—are these "good" or "bad" customers? They're actually the former. When a customer rents a video, the store incurs several costs including employee time to process the rental and whatever costs are associated with charging a credit or debit card. So, when a customer keeps a video an extra day and pays a late fee, there are no direct costs associated with receiving the late fee.

Of course the opportunity cost is that you give up the chance to rent the movie to someone else. As a manager, you'll have to decide which is better. Technology can help you there too.

daily information from transaction processing and customer-integrated systems (see Figure 14.8).

So, MISs are systems that process and create new information (by manipulating existing information) and present information to whoever needs it. MISs are often called *management alerting systems* because they are designed to alert people (usually managers) to the existence or potential existence of problems and opportunities. However, MIS reports can rarely tell you as a manager why a problem has occurred or how to take advantage of an opportunity. That's your job, and that's why an organization is willing to pay you a nice large salary.

FIGURE 14.8

Management information systems (MISs) summarize information contained within a central database.

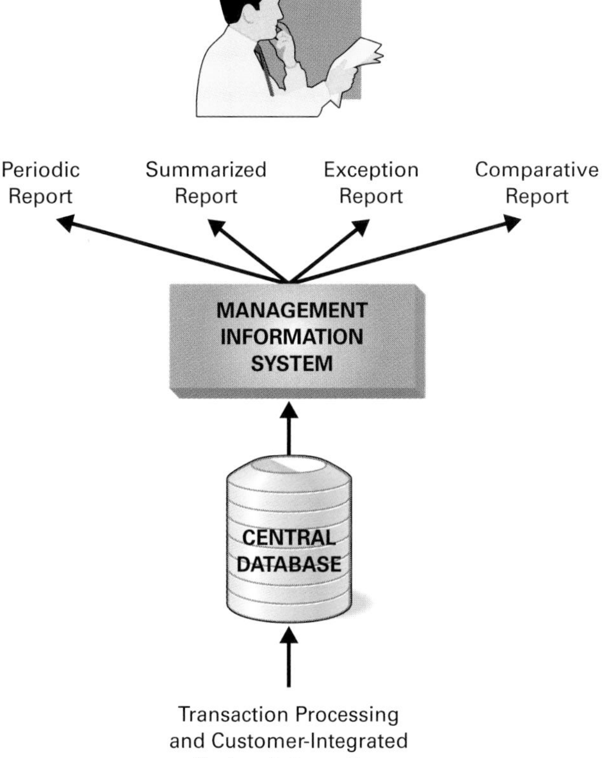

Types of Management Information System Reports

Management information systems provide reports in many different forms—periodic, summarized, exception, and comparative. A ***periodic report*** is a report that is produced at a predetermined time interval—daily, weekly, monthly, yearly, and so on. A ***summarized report*** is simply a report that aggregates information in some way. For example, sales by sales people, returns by product line, and the number of students enrolled in a class are all examples of summarized reports.

An ***exception report*** is a report that shows only a subset of available information based on some selection criteria. For example, a report showing all sales people who did not meet their quotas is an

FIGURE 14.9

An accounting aging schedule is an example of a periodic, summarized, exception, and comparative report.

MAXIMUM OFFICE PRODUCTS
For Period Ending January 31, 2004

CUSTOMER	0–10 Days*	11–30 Days	31–60 Days	61–90 Days	91–120 Days	120+ Days
Shutt's Co.		$ 2,400				
Bellows Meats		700	$300			
Darian Publicity						$2,000
Federal Drivers	$ 1,400					
Jake's Toys	7,000					
Malloy Realty		1,600				
P.J.'s Floral				$600	$200	
Trevor Landscape						
Whitt Federal						
Yellow Truck	9,500					1,500
Zeno Fishery		6,000				
Totals:	$17,900	$10,700	$300	$600	$200	$3,500
Total Sales: $33,200						
% of Total Sales:	53.9%	32.2%	0.9%	1.8%	0.6%	10.5%

*Terms are given 2/10, net 30. $358 total discounted for payments within 10 days.

FIGURE 14.10

Executive information systems (EISs) help managers solve problems and take advantage of opportunities.

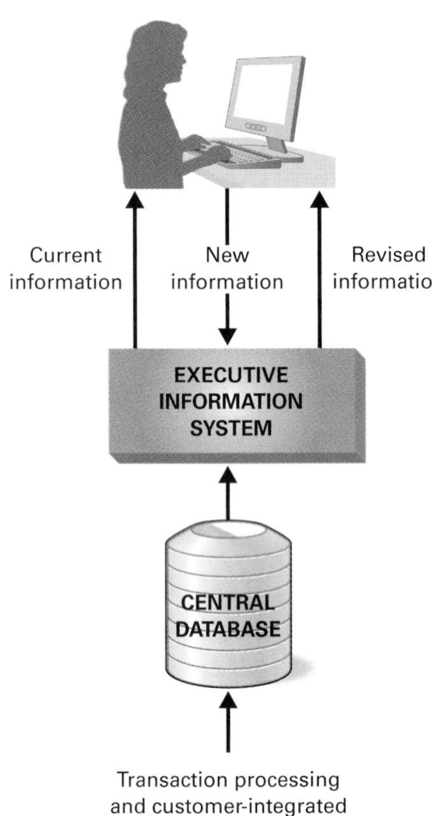

exception report. Finally, a ***comparative report*** is a report that shows two or more sets of similar information in an attempt to illustrate a relationship.

In Figure 14.9, you can see an example of an MIS report that is summarized, periodic, exception, and comparative. In accounting, this type of report is called an "aging schedule." It summarizes sales by customer. It's periodic because it's generated at the end of the month (notice the title). It's an exception report because it groups payments according to when they were made (the selection criterion is time). And it's also a comparative report because it shows percentages of total sales by time period. From this report, do you see any potential or real problems or opportunities?

EXECUTIVE INFORMATION SYSTEMS

What Sort of Computer Systems Help Strategic Managers?

An ***executive information system (EIS)*** is a highly interactive MIS that helps managers solve problems and take advantage of opportunities (see Figure 14.10). Like a management information system, an EIS creates new information (by manipulating existing information) and presents information to the user. Unlike an MIS, however, EISs give you the ability to enter new information and perform scenario analysis such as "what if?" analysis. So, you could view a sales report for last quarter and easily increase sales by 10 percent to understand the net effect on sales for the year.

An EIS allows you to "drill down" through information, as well, to better determine causes of problems and determine how to take advantage of an opportunity. In Figure 14.11 you can see an illustration of drilling down. In the first report, you can see sales by year. By clicking on any year, you can see sales for that year by territory (the second report). Finally, you can click on any territory and see sales by product line within that territory (the third report). So, drilling down is essentially looking first at the forest and choosing which trees to explore.

Calgary Co-op—a small retail chain based in Canada—uses an EIS to effectively compete against the larger chains such as REI, Cub Foods, and Sam's Club. Calgary's EIS constantly displays and updates a large "quick-look monitor board." The board highlights the best and worst product

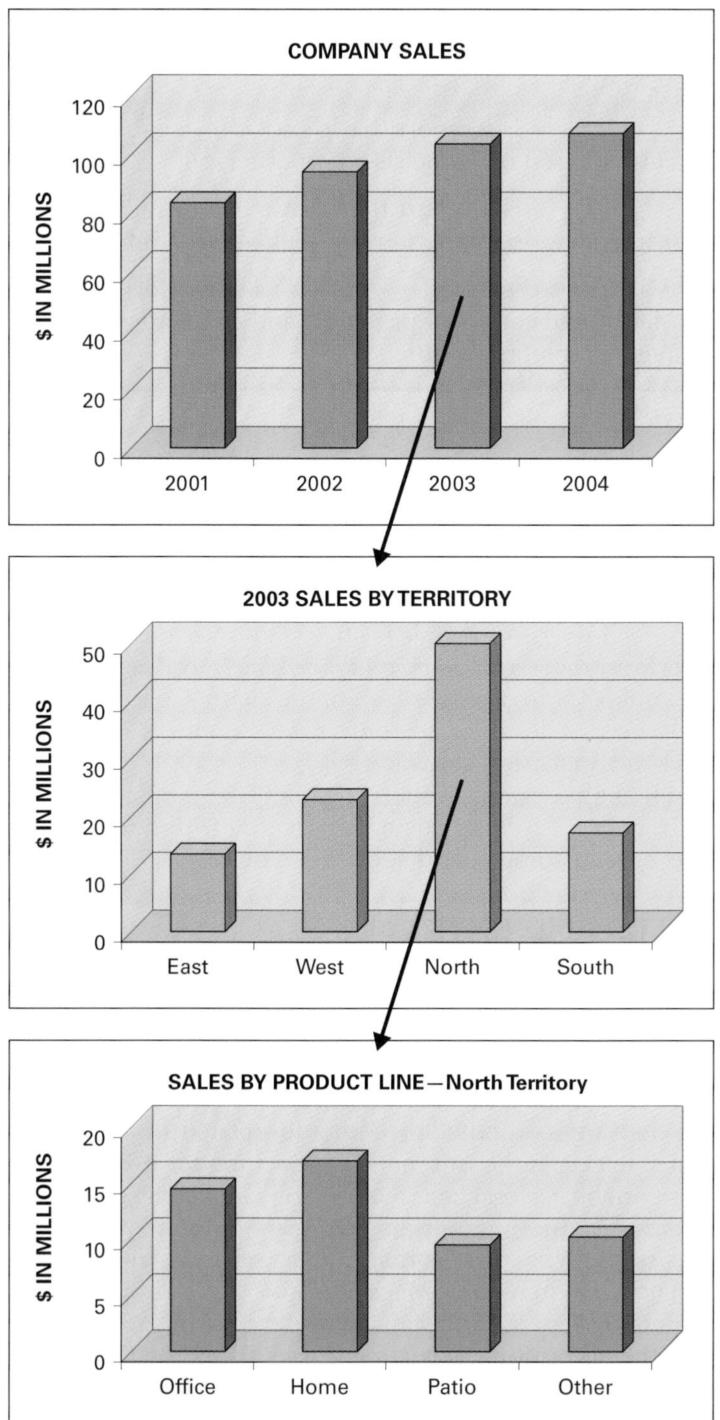

FIGURE 14.11

With an executive information system (EIS), you can "drill down" through information.

performers on a minute-by-minute basis. Calgary's product managers can use their desktop computers to drill down through information to determine why some products are performing poorly and forecast needed inventory levels for products that are moving quickly. With its EIS, Calgary can now analyze sales information in a matter of minutes, a process that once required over two weeks of effort.

SECTION 14.3

making the grade

1. A(n) ___________ is a system that provides periodic and predetermined reports that summarize information.
2. A(n) ___________ is simply a report that aggregates information in some way.
3. A(n) ___________ is a report that shows only a subset of available information based on some selection criteria.
4. A(n) ___________ is a report that shows two or more sets of similar information in an attempt to illustrate a relationship.
5. An EIS allows you to "___________" through information to better determine causes of problems and determine how to take advantage of an opportunity.

14.4 SUPPORT FOR ORGANIZATIONAL LOGISTICS

Businesses today need to move quickly to succeed and survive. Few businesses have the luxury of waiting until decisions can conveniently be made. They need teams of people scattered all over the city, country, and perhaps world to meet and work together. They need to distribute information to employees in a secure fashion no matter where they are. Businesses today need to let their customers and suppliers "inside" the organization to run application software.

This is all about organizational logistics. There are computer systems and technology today to help businesses operate without regard to where their employees, customers, and suppliers may be.

INTRANETS AND EXTRANETS

Can Organizations "Carve Out" Their Own Internet?

From a business point of view, what's the number-one best thing about the Internet? You can undoubtedly answer that question in many ways. From a business point of view, the best thing about the Internet is that it's *platform independent*. That simply means anyone can use any type of operating system and any computer or computer-related device made by any manufacturer to access the Internet. It doesn't matter if you use a Mac, an IBM, a Compaq, or a Nokia cell phone—you can access the Internet.

For businesses, that's important because they employ a variety of different types of hardware and software. For example, the production and design department may use Macs because they provide really great CAD/CAM (computer-aided design/computer-aided manufacturing) software, while the accounting department uses IBMs (or IBM compatibles) because of the wide range of available application software.

did you know? According to the Gartner Group, 30 percent of Americans will be using online banking services by the end of 2007.[4]

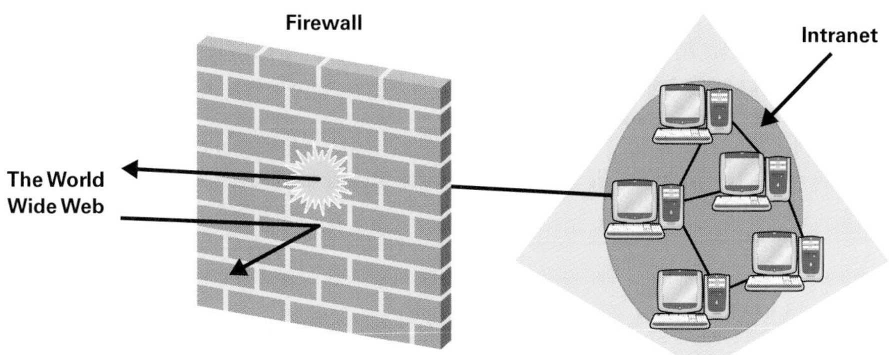

FIGURE 14.12

Intranets use a firewall for protection.

To learn more about CAD/CAM and accounting applications, complete the "CAD Applications" and "Financial Management Applications" tutorials on your SimNet Concepts Support CD.

Many organizations have begun to "internalize" the Internet, essentially creating their own private Internet. To do this, you create an intranet. An ***intranet*** is an internal organizational Internet that is guarded against outside access by special security hardware and/or software called a *firewall* (see Figure 14.12).

With an intranet, you can post sensitive and strategic information for everyone in your organization to see and use, without worrying about that information falling into the hands of your competitors. And intranets look and work exactly like the Internet and Web. You can create elaborate Web pages with links and downloadable files.

U.S. West's intranet—called the *Global Village*—connects over 20,000 employees in 14 different states. The employees can meet in private online chat rooms, exchange documents, and discuss ongoing projects. U.S. West employees can also use the Global Village to request vacation leave, check on their sick day accumulation, and even change their withholding tax. And U.S. West's firewall keeps all the information safe and secure.

Letting Your Suppliers and Customers inside Your Intranet

Carrying the concept of an intranet even further, many organizations are also creating extranets. An ***extranet*** is an extension of an intranet that allows other organizations and people access to information and application software on an internal intranet (see Figure 14.13). For example, you can allow your customers to use your internal order-entry TPS by giving them extranet access to your intranet.

This is a common application for organizations that have other organizations as customers (business to business). In this case, you don't

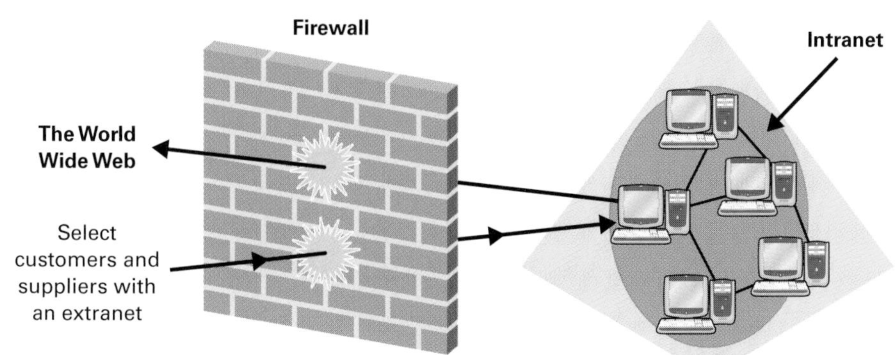

FIGURE 14.13

If you have an extranet, the firewall allows select customers and suppliers to enter your intranet.

want to let just anyone see and use your internal order-entry transaction processing system. So, you provide your organizational customers with extranet access, ensuring that no other organizations or people can use your order-entry TPS.

As the business world moves more toward electronic commerce, intranets and extranets will become commonplace. Over a two-year period, the percentage of businesses reporting they had intranet capabilities grew from 16 percent to 70 percent. To learn more about intranets and extranets, complete the "Intranets and Extranets" tutorial on your SimNet Concepts Support CD.

SUPPORTING TEAMS WITH GROUPWARE

What Computer Systems Help Groups of People Work Together?

A ***workgroup support system (WSS)*** is a system that is designed to improve the performance of teams by supporting the sharing and flow of information. With a WSS, team members can be in the same office or spread out around the globe. This is why we say WSSs support organizational logistics. The foundation of any workgroup support system is ***groupware***—the popular term for the software component that supports team efforts. Popular groupware suites include Lotus Notes/Domino, Microsoft Exchange, Novell Groupwise, and NetSys WebWare. For a review of these suites and a few more, visit the Web site for this text at www.mhhe.com/i-series.

Groupware suites contain software components for supporting the following three functions (see Figure 14.14):

1. Team dynamics
2. Document management
3. Applications development

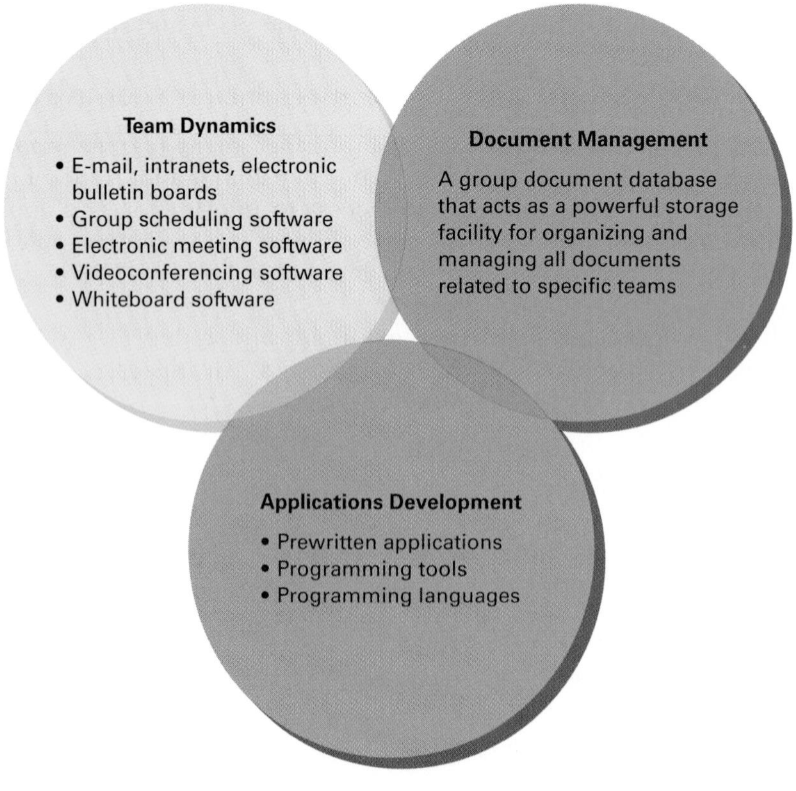

FIGURE 14.14

Groupware supports team dynamics, document management, and applications development.

Team Dynamics
• E-mail, intranets, electronic bulletin boards
• Group scheduling software
• Electronic meeting software
• Videoconferencing software
• Whiteboard software
Document Management
A group document database that acts as a powerful storage facility for organizing and managing all documents related to specific teams
Applications Development
• Prewritten applications
• Programming tools
• Programming languages

Team Dynamics

Team dynamics is the most basic and fundamental support provided by groupware. Team dynamics includes (1) any communications that occur between team members and (2) the facilitation and execution of meetings. For communications, groupware supports such technologies as intranets (which we discussed), e-mail (which you already know about), and electronic bulletin boards.

An ***electronic bulletin board*** is a shared message space where you can post inquiries and schedules for events, and participate in discussion threads and chat rooms. Basically, electronic bulletin boards are bulletin boards with electronic capabilities.

For facilitating and executing meetings, groupware suites include:

- ***Group scheduling software***—provides facilities for maintaining the day-to-day electronic calendars of team members. You can easily use group scheduling software and request a meeting of several team members on a given day. The group scheduling software will look at everyone's calendar, inform you of the best meeting time, send an e-mail to everyone notifying them of the meeting time, and even block that time off on everyone's calendar.
- ***Electronic meeting software***—lets a team have a "virtual" meeting. For example, electronic meeting software helps you develop an agenda and send it to everyone. In turn, other team members read the agenda and provide an electronic response to those items they wish to discuss. This type of meeting can go on for several days and doesn't require that everyone attend an actual meeting in the same place or at the same time.
- ***Videoconferencing software***—allows a team to have a face-to-face meeting when members are geographically dispersed (see Figure 14.15). Videoconferencing software uses video cameras and large-screen monitors to allow everyone to see all the participants. Like electronic meeting software, videoconferencing software doesn't require that everyone attend an actual meeting in the same place.
- ***Whiteboard software***—lets team members meet, view a presentation, and record electronic notes on a large board called a whiteboard. So, you can make a PowerPoint presentation to your team, write on the whiteboard where your presentation appears, and have your writing captured as notes and sent to all team members.

FIGURE 14.15

Videoconferencing software allows people to meet face-to-face while in different locations.

We recommend that you make every effort to take classes while in school that teach you how to use the software tools listed above. Business today is all about teams—you can go a long way in the business world if you know how to use team-oriented technology tools.

Document Management

Perhaps the most critical component of any groupware suite is document management, achieved through a group document database. A ***group document database*** is a powerful storage facility for organizing and managing all documents related to specific teams. An organizationwide group document database may include documents from many different teams, some of which may be shared among many of the teams (see Figure 14.16).

Because of the sharing of information, group document databases support many levels of security to control access to documents. In our example in Figure 14.16, the production team would have access to its documents as well as the shared documents, but not to documents specific to the distribution team.

Your team can store, access, track, and organize a wealth of information in a group document database. You can include word processing documents, spreadsheets, PowerPoint slides, and even audio and video files. Some groupware suites allow you to search all these file types for a specific word. In doing so, it will return to you the location of the word, even to the point that it will tell you where in a video a certain word appears.

FIGURE 14.16

In a group document database, different teams can share information and protect private information.

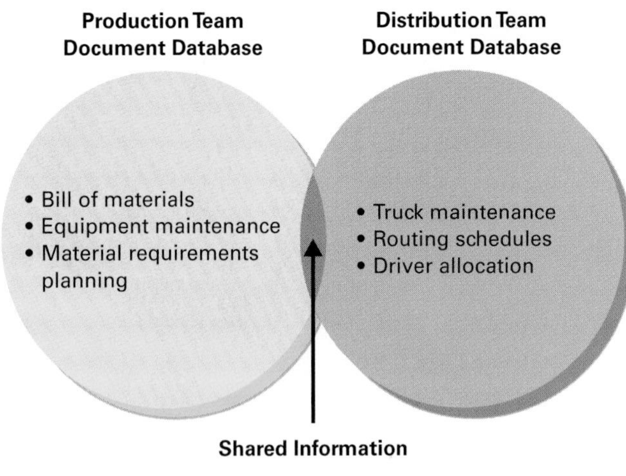

Applications Development

Finally, groupware suites provide you with software development tools so your team can build applications quickly. These tools come in the form of prewritten applications (such as customer relationship management) and actual programming tools and languages. You can use these programming tools and languages to build applications from scratch or modify the existing prewritten applications. We discussed the process of creating software and applications in Chapters 12 and 13.

SECTION 14.4

making the grade

1. A(n) ___________ is an internal organizational Internet that is guarded against outside access by special security hardware and/or software.
2. A(n) ___________ is an extension of an intranet that allows other organizations and people access to information and application software on an intranet.
3. ___________ is the popular term for the software component that supports team efforts.
4. ___________ software provides facilities for maintaining the day-to-day electronic calendars of team members.
5. A(n) ___________ is a powerful storage facility for organizing and managing all documents related to specific teams.

14.5 SPREADING OUT NATIONALLY AND AROUND THE GLOBE

Very few businesses today are "local." No matter what you do, you may have national and international customers, suppliers, employees, and (most important) competition. On a national scale, there are over 290,000,000 people in the United States. But there are over 6,300,000,000 (that's 6+ billion) people worldwide. Why not go after that vast international market? Why not start by capturing more of those 290,000,000 U.S. consumers? And while you're going after that bigger market, consider letting your employees work wherever they need to through telecommuting.

TELECOMMUTING

Do All Employees Have to Work in a Central Office?

Telecommuting is another business innovation supported by technology. ***Telecommuting*** is the use of various technologies (especially telecommunications technologies) to allow employees to work in a place other than a central location. So, ***telecommuters*** are people who work outside the central office some of the time while connected to the central office through technology.

Telecommuting is big business. Over 15 million people in the United States telecommute at least 50 percent of their workweek. And that number is expected to grow by 20 percent per year for the next several years.

For some jobs, telecommuting makes obvious sense. For example, sales people need to be "on the road" and in front of their customers more than they need to be sitting in an office. So, many in today's sales workforce are telecommuters. But there are other jobs that are not so obvious for which telecommuting is a great fit.

For example, JCPenney lets catalog sales people work from home. These people simply wait in their homes for the phone to ring. As a customer, when you call the 800 number to order JCPenney merchandise from its catalog, your phone call is routed to someone's home. That person uses a computer (which is connected to the central database at JCPenney) to take your order. In Figure 14.17 you can see that almost every business segment plans on implementing telecommuting in the near future.

FIGURE 14.17

It seems that all industries plan to implement telecommuting.

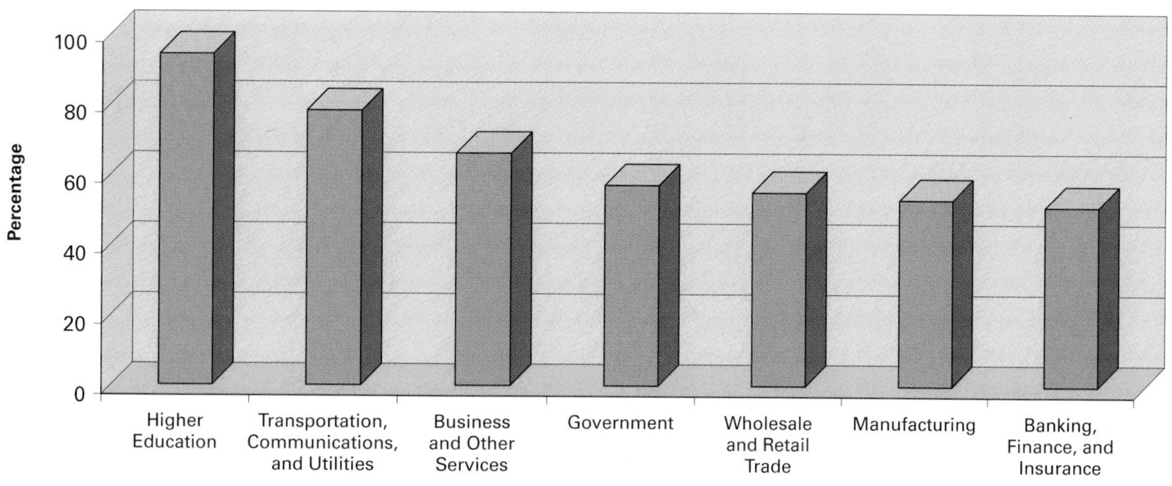

FIGURE 14.18

Before implementing any telecommuting program, always ask yourself why, what, who, how, and where.

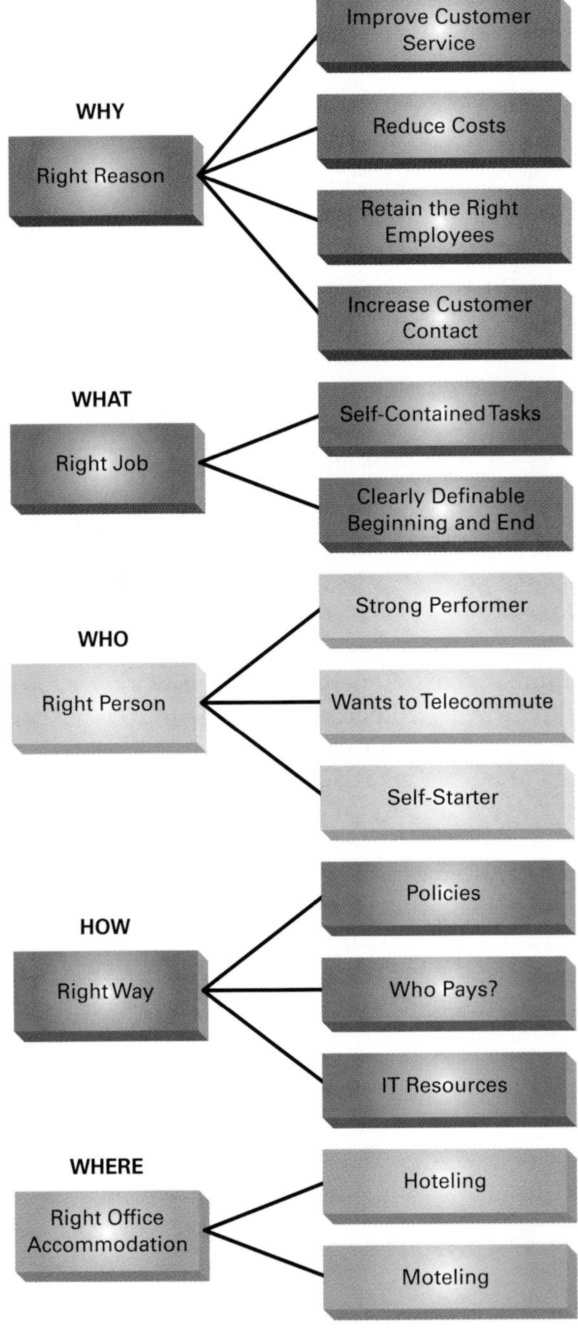

did you know? There are 4 billion people in the world whose per capita income is less than a tenth than that of the United States.[5]

You must implement telecommuting carefully. Not everyone will make a good telecommuter. And some types of jobs don't lend themselves to telecommuting. When considering telecommuting in your organization, ask yourself five questions (see Figure 14.18):

- Why would you want to implement a telecommuting program? Good reasons include improving customer service, reducing costs, retaining employees, and increasing customer contact. A bad reason is because everyone else is doing it.
- What jobs or projects are suited to telecommuting? Good telecommuting jobs and projects include those with self-contained tasks and a clearly definable beginning and end.

- Who is best suited to telecommuting? Characteristics of good telecommuters include strong performers, a desire to telecommute, and self-starters.
- How can you best implement telecommuting? You must consider new policies that you'll need to have in place, who pays for mobile technology and perhaps office furniture in a telecommuter's home, and what new IT resources you'll need to handle the necessary telecommunications.
- Where will you locate telecommuters when they do come into the office? You have a variety of options here including hoteling (equipped offices that telecommuters reserve in advance) and moteling (equipped offices that are allocated on a first-come, first-serve basis).

Answering these five questions will definitely help you develop a successful telecommuting program.

TRANSNATIONAL FIRMS
What Businesses Operate throughout the World?

A ***transnational firm*** produces and sells products and services in countries all over the world, so much so that it's difficult to know which country is the firm's home country. That's certainly true for Honda, an auto manufacturer headquartered in Japan that is now producing more cars outside than inside Japan. In fact, Honda exports more cars from the United States than does General Motors, Ford, or Chrysler. Did you know that?

Operating internationally, a business benefits in many ways. It gains access to a larger market of customers. It can utilize a larger workforce that may be cheaper than in its home country. It can also tap into the intellectual expertise of a workforce in a given country. That's true of many "U.S." software publishers who write and produce much of their software in such countries as India and Pakistan.

To effectively produce and sell products and services all over the world, a transnational firm faces many challenges. These include issues surrounding transborder data flows and cultural differences (see Figure 14.19 on the following page).

Transborder Data Flows

Transnational firms must consider their information and technology assets as they operate around the globe. The popular term for this is *transborder data flows*. But transborder data flows don't just deal with "data" (or information). They also deal with the technology that supports the movement of information.

As organizations begin to move information around the world, they must consider political and legal barriers. For example, in Canada banks cannot transmit financial information out of the country for processing. Instead, it must first be processed in Canada. So, banks with ATMs in Canada must also have processing centers in Canada to process the transactions as they occur. Other countries choose to transmit ATM transaction information to processing centers in the United States. That information is then processed in the United States and transmitted back to the original country.

FIGURE 14.19

Differences in culture are challenging for businesspeople and communicators.

Culture is the collective personality of a nation or society that encompasses language, traditions, currency, religion, history, music, and acceptable behavior. Consider these cultural differences:

Gestures:

A raised or a waggling hand:

- In the United States, it says "goodbye."
- In India and South America it's a beckoning gesture.
- In much of Europe it's a signal for "no."

Handshake:

- United States: Should be firm and strong.
- East Africa: Light palm touch with the fingers hardly bending.
- Morocco: Kiss the back of the hand being shaken.

Insulting Gestures:

- United States: Middle finger thrust upward.
- Britain: First two fingers thrust upward with the palm of the hand facing the body.
- Italy: First and little finger form "horns" to signify the object of the insult being gored by a bull.
- Turkey: Whole arm, with clenched fist, thrust out aggressively.

For more cultural oddities, visit the Web site for this text at www.mhhe.com/i-series.

As organizations move information around the globe, they must also consider the quality and type of technology. Some countries have high-quality technology for moving information, while others do not. And some countries have slow-moving phone lines only for moving information, while others support satellite transmission. Whatever the case, transborder data flows are a challenge for any transnational firm.

SECTION 14.5

making the grade

1. ___________ is the use of various technologies to allow employees to work in a place other than a central location.
2. A(n) ___________ produces and sells products and services in countries all over the world.
3. ___________ is the collective personality of a nation or society.
4. ___________ is the popular term for considering the movement of information around the globe and the technologies that do it.

practically speaking

You Need to Speak Multiple Languages

Business today is increasingly global. As instructors and advisors, we are frequently asked by students how they can best prepare to enter the global marketplace. Of course, we believe that you should learn everything you can about technology as well as business in general (accounting, finance, marketing, logistics, production, and so on).

We also firmly believe you should learn to speak a foreign language (if you don't already know one). Most all businesses today—regardless of their size or industry—seek people with solid business skills who can speak a foreign language. People with a second (or third) language help a business explore new international markets and compete for more consumer dollars around the world. They also help an organization market to different ethnic groups within the United States. You've probably used an ATM that allows you to select from among different languages. Such technologies and the processes they support were developed by people with multiple language skills.

While you're in school, learn a foreign language and learn it well. It can be a significant career opportunity for you.

14.6 SUMMARY AND KEY TERMS

Computers are the heavy artillery in business, supporting everything from tracking internal quality information to transborder data flows.

An organization typically consists of four levels:

- ***Strategic management***—which provides an organization with overall direction and guidance.
- ***Tactical management***—which develops the goals and strategies outlined by strategic management.
- ***Operational management***—which manages and directs the day-to-day operations and implementation of the goals and strategies.
- Nonmanagement employees—who actually perform daily activities.

Today, organizations employ a combination of ***decentralized computing*** and ***shared information*** so that employees can access whatever information they need. That information may be ***internal, external, objective, subjective,*** or some combination of the four. And as information moves throughout the organization, it does so in an upward, downward, and/or horizontal fashion.

Computer systems help organizations track all types of information:

- ***Transaction processing system***—a system that processes transactions that occur within an organization.
- ***Customer-integrated system***—an extension of a transaction processing system that places technology in the hands of an organization's customers.
- ***Management information system***—a system that provides periodic and predetermined reports that summarize information.
- ***Executive information system***—a highly flexible management information system that helps managers solve problems and take advantage of opportunities.

Computer systems and technologies can also support organizational logistics:

- ***Intranet***—an internal organizational Internet that is guarded against outside access by special security hardware and/or software called a firewall.
- ***Extranet***—an extension of an intranet that allows other organizations and people access to information and application software on an internal intranet.
- ***Workgroup support system***—a system that is designed to improve the performance of teams by supporting the sharing and flow of information (includes the software component of ***groupware***).

Finally, computer systems and technologies support organizations as they spread out nationally and around the globe. In either case, technology supports ***telecommuting***—the use of various technologies (especially telecommunications technologies) to allow employees ***(telecommuters)*** to work in a place other than a central location. A ***transnational firm*** produces and sells products and services in countries all over the world. To do this, transnational firms face the challenges of cultural differences and transborder data flows.

On the Web site for this text at www.mhhe.com/i-series, we've provided a great deal of support. There, you can learn more about:

- Total quality management and business process reengineering
- Groupware suites
- Cultural oddities

KEY TERMS

comparative report (p. 434)
culture (p. 444)
customer-integrated system (CIS) (p. 431)
decentralized computing (p. 426)
downward flow of information (p. 429)
electronic bulletin board (p. 439)
electronic meeting software (p. 439)
exception report (p. 433)
executive information system (EIS) (p. 434)
external information (p. 428)
extranet (p. 437)
group document database (p. 440)
group scheduling software (p. 439)
groupware (p. 438)
horizontal flow of information (p. 429)
information granularity (p. 427)
internal information (p. 428)
intranet (p. 437)
management information system (MIS) (p. 432)
objective information (p. 428)
operational management (p. 425)
periodic report (p. 433)
shared information (p. 427)
strategic management (p. 425)
subjective information (p. 428)
summarized report (p. 433)
tactical management (p. 425)
telecommuter (p. 441)
telecommuting (p. 441)
transaction processing system (TPS) (p. 430)
transnational firm (p. 443)
upward flow of information (p. 429)
videoconferencing software (p. 439)
whiteboard software (p. 439)
workgroup support system (WSS) (p. 438)

review of terminology

Multiple Choice

1. The level of management which develops the goals and strategies outlined by strategic management is
   a. operational management.
   b. tactical management.
   c. outlined management.
   d. operations management.
   e. none of the above.
2. Information that describes specific operational aspects of an organization is called
   a. internal information.
   b. external information.
   c. objective information.
   d. subjective information.
   e. granular information.
3. Information that quantifiably describes something that is known is called
   a. internal information.
   b. external information.
   c. objective information.
   d. subjective information.
   e. granular information.
4. Information that attempts to describe something that is currently unknown is called
   a. internal information.
   b. external information.
   c. objective information.
   d. subjective information.
   e. granular information.
5. The __________ flow of information refers to information that passes among various departments.
   a. downward
   b. upward
   c. horizontal
   d. outward
   e. inward
6. The __________ flow of information describes the current state of the organization based on its daily transactions.
   a. downward
   b. upward
   c. horizontal
   d. outward
   e. inward
7. A shared message space where you can post inquiries and schedules for events, and participate in discussion threads and chat rooms is called a(n)
   a. electronic message space.
   b. electronic bulletin board.
   c. ftp site.
   d. whiteboard.
   e. videoconference.
8. __________ software allows a team to have face-to-face meetings when members are geographically dispersed.
   a. Group scheduling
   b. Electronic meeting
   c. Videoconferencing
   d. Whiteboard
   e. Group document
9. __________ software lets team members meet, view a presentation, and record electronic notes on a large board.
   a. Group scheduling
   b. Electronic meeting
   c. Videoconferencing
   d. Whiteboard
   e. Group document
10. A(n) __________ is a system that is designed to improve the performance of teams by supporting the sharing and flow of information.
    a. TPS
    b. CIS
    c. MIS
    d. WSS
    e. EIS

True/False

11. ____ Operational management provides an organization with operational direction over a period of two to five years.
12. ____ Shared information is the concept that employees should have access to whatever information they need when they need it.
13. ____ A periodic report is a report that is produced at only one time interval.
14. ____ Telecommuters are people who work outside the central office some of the time while connected to the central office through technology.
15. ____ Electronic meeting software lets you have face-to-face meetings with members who are geographically dispersed.

Take this quiz online at www.mhhe.com/i-series and get instant feedback.

QUESTIONS AND EXERCISES

1. Identifying Responsibilities of IT Systems

In the table below, we've listed the major types of computer systems we discussed in this chapter in the rows. The columns identify five major information-processing tasks—gathering, presenting, processing to create new information, storing, and communicating. Identify which of the information-processing tasks each system is primarily responsible for by placing a "P" (for primary) in the appropriate cell or cells. If you think a given system includes one or more secondary responsibilities, place an "S" in the appropriate cell or cells. It is quite possible that a given row will have several Ps and several Ss. It's also quite possible that a given column will have several Ps and several Ss.

System	Gathering	Presenting	Processing to Create New	Storing	Communicating
Transaction processing					
Customer-integrated					
Management information					
Executive information					
Workgroup support					

2. Identifying Information Types for a Convenience Store

Types of information include internal, external, objective, and subjective. Often you need them all to make an effective decision. Consider a local convenience store that sells gasoline. What information does it need to set the price per gallon? Complete the table below by listing the specific pieces of information in the appropriate area.

INTERNAL

EXTERNAL

OBJECTIVE

SUBJECTIVE

Next, you are to identify at least five pieces of information that fall into at least two of the types of information. What are they? Don't all pieces of information fall into at least two types of information?

3. Identifying Report Features within a Management Information System

Below is a spreadsheet that contains expense information for Benjamin & Samuel Connolly Enterprises. The report includes expenses by category and by month up through May.

Microsoft Excel - Ben-Sam Connolly Enterprises

BENJAMIN & SAMUEL CONNOLLY ENTERPRISES
EXPENSE REPORTING ENDING MAY 3, 2004

EXPENSE CATEGORY	JAN	FEB	MAR	APR	MAY	YTD TOTAL	04 BUDGET	TOTAL BUDGET REMAINING	BUDGET REAMINING PER MONTH
01 - OFFICE									
Supplies	$ 78.56	$ 124.93	$ 98.46	$ 77.56	$ 103.33	$ 482.84	$ 1,200.00	$ 717.16	$ 102.45
Copier	$ 55.00	$ 55.00	$ 55.00	$ 78.00	$ 55.00	$ 298.00	$ 605.00	$ 307.00	$ 43.86
Meeting Food	$ -	$ 125.00	$ 405.00	$ 75.00	$ -	$ 605.00	$ 500.00	$ (105.00)	$ (15.00)
Subscriptions	$ 55.00	$ -	$ -	$ -	$ 25.00	$ 80.00	$ 100.00	$ 20.00	$ 2.86
01 - OFFICE TOTAL	$ 188.56	$ 304.93	$ 558.46	$ 230.56	$ 183.33	$ 1,465.84	$ 2,405.00	$ 939.16	$ 134.17
02 - TRAVEL									
Airline Tickets	$ 1,275.00	$ -	$ 750.00	$ 200.00	$ -	$ 2,225.00	$ 7,500.00	$ 5,275.00	$ 753.57
Meals	$ 125.00		$ 75.00	$ 125.00	$ -	$ 325.00	$ 1,200.00	$ 875.00	$ 125.00
Entertainment	$ 675.00		$ 500.00	$ -	$ -	$ 1,175.00	$ 1,500.00	$ 325.00	$ 46.43
Rental Car	$ 325.00		$ 200.00	$ 175.00	$ -	$ 700.00	$ 3,500.00	$ 2,800.00	$ 400.00
02 - TRAVEL TOTAL	$ 2,400.00	$ -	$ 1,525.00	$ 500.00	$ -	$ 4,425.00	$ 13,700.00	$ 9,275.00	$ 1,325.00
03 - ADVERTISING									
Newspaper	$ 125.00	$ 125.00	$ 125.00	$ 500.00	$ 125.00	$ 1,000.00	$ 5,000.00	$ 4,000.00	$ 571.43
Web	$ 100.00	$ 450.00	$ 200.00	$ 100.00	$ 350.00	$ 1,200.00	$ 2,500.00	$ 1,300.00	$ 185.71
Radio & TV	$ 5,000.00	$ 5,000.00	$ 5,000.00	$ 5,000.00	$ 5,000.00	$25,000.00	$ 15,000.00	$ (10,000.00)	$ (1,428.57)
03 - ADVERTISING TOTAL	$ 5,225.00	$ 5,575.00	$ 5,325.00	$ 5,600.00	$ 5,475.00	$27,200.00	$ 22,500.00	$ (4,700.00)	$ (671.43)
04 - CONTRACT									
Web Dev. Work	$ 500.00	$ 1,000.00	$ 500.00	$ 500.00	$ 500.00	$ 3,000.00	$ 2,500.00	$ (500.00)	$ (71.43)
04 - CONTRACT TOTAL	$ 500.00	$ 1,000.00	$ 500.00	$ 500.00	$ 500.00	$ 3,000.00	$ 2,500.00	$ (500.00)	$ (71.43)
MONTHLY TOTAL	$ 8,313.56	$ 6,879.93	$ 7,908.46	$ 6,830.56	$ 6,158.33				
2003 MONTHLY TOTALS	$ 7,556.13	$ 7,284.00	$ 7,800.00	$ 7,115.50	$ 6,500.00				

The report above is an example of what you might typically receive from a management information system (MIS) at the end of each month. It's also an example of a summarized, periodic, exception, and comparative report. In the table below, identify the elements of the report that make it summarized, periodic, exception, and comparative.

SUMMARIZED ELEMENTS

PERIODIC ELEMENTS

EXCEPTION ELEMENTS

COMPARATIVE ELEMENTS

e-commerce

1. Doing Business with the Federal Government

Businesses can certainly benefit today by doing business with the federal government. More so than ever before, it's a relatively easy process to establish your business as a government contractor. The best place on the Web to start for this is at FirstGov at www.firstgov.gov. Connect to that site and answer the following questions:

a. How do you register your business as a government contractor?
b. In what ways can you look up government contracts on which you can bid?
c. How can you participate in the government auctioning of old, seized, and other types of merchandise?
d. What sorts of opportunities are available for small businesses?
e. What sorts of opportunities are available for ethnically diverse businesses?

2. Reading Books Online

If you like reading, you'll be pleased to know that you can find a wealth of reading material on the Web. You can download books onto your computer and read them on-screen or print out the pages. On some sites you can read the book right there on the Web site. If you'd like to have a more portable online book, you can buy an e-book, which is a little hand-held screen into which you can download books. You can then take the e-book with you on a plane flight, to bed, up into the hills, or wherever you like to read. You can also download a book to your PDA.

For e-book reading devices check out www.eBook-Gemstar.com. With an e-book reading device you can read in the traditional manner, but you get more than just words on a screen. You can do key word searches, make annotations, and consult a built-in dictionary. eBook-Gemstar even has a built-in modem so that you can download books using a phone line. There's enough memory for about 20 books and you can upgrade to many times more than that. A big advantage of online books is that you can adjust the text size to suit your needs.

Look at these sites, then answer the questions that follow, for each site:

- Glassbook—www.glassbook.com
- CyberRead—www.cyberread.com
- eBooks 'n Bytes—www.ebooksnbytes.com

a. Do these sites let you download to your computer or do you need an e-book device?
b. Can you read the book online at these sites?
c. Do you have to pay for the online book?
d. If you have to pay for the book, can you read a sample and can you get book reviews?

3. Putting Your Book on the Web

You want to write the great American novel. Or maybe you'd like to publish your poems or your mom's recipes. Most publishing houses won't talk to you, but you always have the Web.

To publish a book on the Web, you can convert it to HTML and put it up as Web pages. However, for a fee, there are companies that will publish your book, market it, and make printed copies for people who want it. Take a look at these:

- Iuniverse—www.iuniverse.com
- XLibris—www.xlibris.com
- Trafford Publishing Service—www.trafford.com

Consider the following questions:

a. What are the advantages of using a service like this?
b. Are there disadvantages?
c. Do you think writers should consider these options or use a more traditional route? Why or why not?
d. Would you buy a book from one of these Web sites? Would you order an electronic or print copy? Why?

ethics, security & privacy

1. Do Organizations Really Trust You to Provide Accurate Information?

Many people are somewhat concerned about how businesses use their information. They may fear that they will soon begin to receive a lot of spam or that a business will sell their private and personal information to other businesses. Let's look at it from the other perspective. Do businesses trust you to provide accurate information? Answer the questions below.

a. When interviewing with potential employers, do they take your word that you have a college degree?
b. If you deposit several checks, does the bank trust you to correctly add the amounts?
c. When you register for a class that has a prerequisite, does your school assume that you have actually taken the prerequisite class?
d. When buying a house and negotiating a loan, does the bank assume that the price you're paying for the house is correct and not inflated?
e. When insuring your car, does the insurance company assume that you have a good driving record?
f. When you file your taxes, does the IRS assume that you've correctly reported all your income over the past year?

The answer to each of these questions is probably no. Why? Not because of true "distrust" on the part of organizations, but rather because organizations can't afford to have dirty information—information that's not accurate.

On the other hand, you probably "trust" most organizations more than you think. For example, do you keep all your credit card receipts and compare them to your bill at the end of the month? Do you record all your long-distance phone calls and compare them to your monthly bill? When you receive your tuition bill from your school, do you pull out your calculator and verify that the amounts were added correctly?

Your task is to identify at least three instances (not using the ones we just mentioned) in which you trust organizations to provide accurate information about you or to you.

2. The Ethics of Business Process Reengineering

Many times, a business process reengineering (BPR) effort not only streamlines processes but also puts people out of a job. Indeed, many businesses have undergone BPR efforts and been able to cut hundreds of employees. The question becomes an ethical one. Should employees lose their jobs because a business finds a better way to use fewer employees and more technology? Should businesses be responsible for "retooling" employees and finding them other jobs? For each of the following real-life BPR efforts that have reduced the number of employees, be prepared to justify what you think the organization should do with displaced employees.

a. Wireless meter reading—no longer do meter readers have to walk through a neighborhood. Instead, just a few drive through and capture the readings with wireless technologies.
b. Computer-aided manufacturing—essentially robotics in manufacturing that make many assembly line workers unnecessary.
c. Self-scanning at a grocery store—meaning that fewer checkout clerks are needed.
d. School registration on the Web—which means your school doesn't need as many clerks to register you for classes.
e. Electronic tax filing—meaning the government will need fewer IRS workers.
f. ATMs—so banks don't have to have as many tellers.
g. Automated directory assistance—so phone companies don't have to have as many operators.

on the web

1. Researching Groupware

Technology—mainly workgroup support systems and groupware—can help a team be more effective in what it does—processing transactions, preparing a report, making a decision, and so on. Below is a list of some of the more popular groupware tools today and their respective Web sites.

- Lotus Notes/Domino—http://domino.lotus.com/ldd/products.nsf/products/notesdomino
- Microsoft Exchange—http://www.microsoft.com/exchange/default.asp
- Novell Groupwise—http://www.novell.com/products/groupwise
- Netscape—http://wp.netscape.com/suitespot/v3.5

Visit the sites for a couple of those groupware tools and answer the following questions:

a. Do they support videoconferencing?
b. Do they support a group document database?
c. What sort of security do they provide for allowing team members to access information?
d. Do they work on intranets, extranets, both, or neither?

If you had to buy one, which would it be and why?

2. Researching Your School's Education Delivery Tool

Most schools use some type of education delivery tool such as WebTV, Blackboard, or eCollege. Do some fact finding at your school concerning which education delivery tool it uses and answer the following questions.

a. What is the tool?
b. What is the cost of the site license of the tool?
c. Is the site license cost incremental with respect to the number of classes and/or number of students?
d. Is the tool intranet-based, extranet-based, or both?

What's your view of your school's education delivery tool? Do you like it? Why or why not?

3. Learning about Quality Awards

Organizations wanting to improve their quality and demonstrate it to their customers often follow the guidelines of various quality awards. Two such awards are the Baldrige Award and the Deming Award. Choose one and do a little research on the Web. Your report should include (1) the nature of the award, (2) the criteria for winning the award, (3) the organization which sponsors the award, and (4) past winners of the award. Does winning a quality award really mean that an organization produces quality? Does it mean that an organization will be successful? What Web sites did you find that were the most comprehensive in covering quality awards?

4. Illustrating Executive Information System "Drilling Down"

On the Web site for this text at www.mhhe.com/i-series (click on **Chapter 14** and then **Project Data Files**), you'll find a spreadsheet named **CH14eis.xls**. It includes information concerning a call center. The following specific information is provided:

Column A—the date a call came in

Column B—the employee who answered the call

Column C—the customer who made the call

Column D—the length of the call

Column E—the nature of the call

Your task is to develop a series of three or four graphs that illustrate the concept of drilling down in an EIS. So, your first graph should provide highly summarized information, and your last graph should provide the most detail. You can refer back to Figure 14.11 on page 435 for an example of drilling down with an EIS.

group activities

1. Comparing Self-Scanning Systems at a Grocery Store and ATMs

You can find numerous customer-integrated systems (CISs) on the Web. You can also find them in many other places—self-check-in systems at the airport, pay-at-the-pump fuel stations, ATMs, and self-scanning systems at a grocery store. Consider the latter two. If necessary, visit a local grocery store and try the self-scanning system if you haven't already. Answer the following questions.

a. Which is easier to use and why?
b. Which do you believe provides the greatest savings to the organization? Why? How did you measure the savings?
c. Which do you believe provides the greatest convenience to the customer? Why? How did you measure the "convenience"?
d. Which do you believe will be the first to completely replace its "human equivalent"? What are the human equivalents to ATMs and self-scanning systems at a grocery store?
e. Which do you believe has the greatest likelihood of surviving over the long haul?

To be effective, CISs must be "idiot proof." That is, they have to be so easy to use that no one needs to be trained to effectively use them. Most people agree that ATMs are easier to use than self-scanning systems at the grocery store. Why do people believe this?

2. Building Management Information Systems Reports

On the Web site for this text at www.mhhe.com/i-series (click on **Chapter 14** and then **Project Data Files**), you'll find a spreadsheet file called **CH14mis.xls**. It contains a list of real estate transactions for an area of the country. The following specific information is provided:

Column A—name of county in which the home resides

Column B—name of builder of the home

Column C—year in which the home was built

Column D—asking price for the home

Column E—selling price for the home

Column F—days it took to sell the home

Your task is to download that file (the instructions are on the Web site), use your spreadsheet software, and generate MIS reports. You must generate at least five reports—one summarized, one exception, one comparative, one periodic, and one that's some combination of at least two of the others. Did any of your reports reveal problems or opportunities?

3. Types of Information for Setting Interest Rates

Consider a bank that offers interest rates on CDs. Banks do have some flexibility in setting those interest rates. What sort of information do you think a bank uses to set interest rates? Complete the table below. In the first column, identify specific information that would go into the decision-making process. In the remaining columns, place a check mark identifying what type of information it is.

Information Used	Internal	External	Objective	Subjective

crossword puzzle

Across

4. An expert system is also a(n) ______ -based system
8. An algorithm of evolution
9. A user agent is also called this
11. Logic that's not cut and dried
14. Finding information in a data warehouse
15. A system with rules
16. No formula for this type of decision
17. Shopping bot or ______ agent
18. Has information in layers
21. A bot that finds stuff for you to buy
23. How information is stored in a GIS

Down

1. A network that sees a pattern
2. A representation of reality
3. This agent is not dumb
5. A decision made with a formula
6. Data resides here
7. Monitoring-and-surveillance agent
10. Artificial intelligence
12. The interface you use
13. Intelligence that's not natural
19. The person who runs the expert system
20. Used with a GIS
22. Used to analyze information
24. A machine that imitates humans

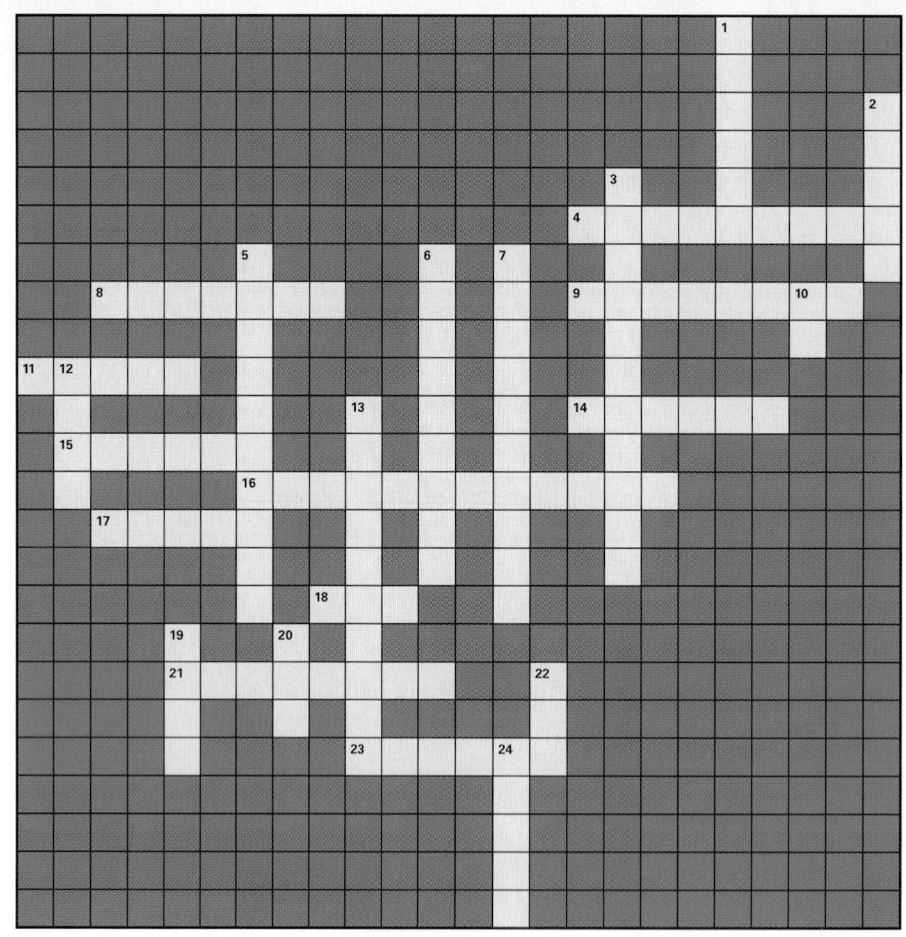

CHAPTER fifteen 15

Computer Brainpower

How Can You Use Your Computer to Help You Think?

SIMNET CONCEPTS SUPPORT

did you know?

All day, every day, businesses make decisions—big ones and small ones. Computer systems can help in the decision-making process by providing fast and accurate analysis capabilities. Here are some examples.

a *national insurance company used a DSS to analyze its risk exposure when insuring drivers with histories of DUIs. The company discovered that married male homeowners in their forties with only one conviction were rarely repeat offenders. The company used that information to increase its market share without increasing its risk exposure.*[1]

the *fabric in the clothes that you buy accounts for about 40 percent of the cost of the garment, so it's important to the manufacturer to waste as little as possible. Genetic algorithms are used to solve the problem of laying out the pieces and cutting the fabric to minimize waste.*[2]

visa, *MasterCard, and many other credit companies use neural networks to spot fraud in customer accounts. MasterCard estimates that neural networks save it __??__ million dollars annually.*[3]

To find out how much MasterCard saves with neural networks, visit our Web site at www.mhhe.com/i-series.

Student Learning Outcomes

After reading this chapter, you should be able to:

1. Define decision support systems, list their components, and identify the types of situations to which they are applicable.
2. Define geographic information systems and state how they differ from other decision support tools.
3. List the different types of artificial intelligence used in business.
4. Describe expert systems and the type of situation to which they are applicable.
5. Define neural network and genetic algorithm, and explain how each works and the type of situation to which each is applicable.
6. Describe the types and uses of intelligent agents.

You make countless ordinary decisions every day. You also make decisions from time to time that are definitely not everyday decisions—where you should send your college application, what job to take, whom to marry. Your decisions affect your future and every action has consequences. For the serious situations, if you don't make the right decision, you have to fix it—find a way out or a way to live with the consequences.

In the business world, it's no different. Managers make decisions every day, some more consequential than others. In fact, decision making is one of the most significant and important activities in business. Organizations devote vast resources of time and money to the process. Businesses make decisions on issues such as whether to expand the workforce, extend business hours, use different raw materials, or start a new product line.

For many years, computers have been crunching numbers faster and more accurately than people can. A computer can unerringly calculate a payroll for 1,000 people in the time it takes a pencil to fall from your desk to the floor. Because of IT, knowledge workers are free of much of the drudgery of manually handling day-to-day transactions. And now IT power is augmenting brainpower and thought processes in ways previously seen only in science fiction. In fact, IT power—in the form of artificial intelligence—is actually *replacing* human brainpower to a limited degree.

Computer-aided decision-making software falls into three major categories.

1. Decision support software that helps you analyze information to aid your decision making. For example,
   - Specific decision support systems such as those for financial planning.
   - Geographic information systems that show information in map form.
2. Artificial intelligence software that can make decisions or perform tasks for you on its own. Examples of this software are
   - Expert systems
   - Neural networks
   - Genetic algorithms
   - Fuzzy logic
3. Intelligent agent software that handles repetitive tasks such as searching and retrieving, and monitoring.

did you know?

The *first CD pressed in the United States was Bruce Springsteen's "Born in the USA" in September 1984.*[4]

15.1 DECISION SUPPORT SOFTWARE

In this section we'll first examine a relatively simple decision situation to see how decision support software can help you. Then we'll discuss decision support systems (DSS) in general. We'll finish with geographic information systems which show information in map form. But first a few words about types of decisions.

Decisions can be structured or unstructured or somewhere in between (see Figure 15.1). A ***structured decision*** is one that you can make by applying a formula. With a structured decision you punch in the right numbers, do the arithmetic correctly, and get the right answer—guaranteed. An ***unstructured decision*** is one for which there is no guaranteed way to get a precise right answer. In fact, there may be many "right" answers. You can only guess since none of us knows for sure what the future holds (psychics notwithstanding). In reality, most decisions have structured and unstructured parts. The following situation is an example.

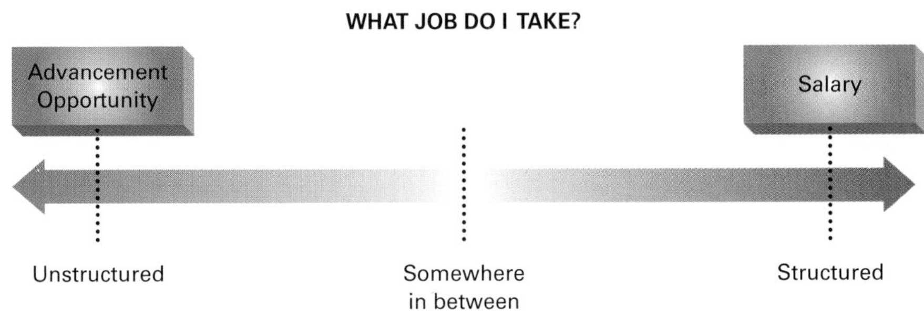

FIGURE 15.1
Decisions range from the totally unstructured to the totally structured. Most decisions fall somewhere in between.

DECISION MAKING WITH PERSONAL PRODUCTIVITY SOFTWARE

How Could I Use a Decision Support System?

Suppose you're trying to decide on financing for a car that costs $10,000. Your choices are

- Three years at 8.25 percent interest.
- Four years at 9.25 percent interest.
- $1,000 down and three years at 8 percent interest.

Which option should you take? This is an example of a decision that has structured and unstructured parts. The structured part is calculating the monthly payments and what the total amount you pay for the car will be when you're finished making the payments.

The unstructured part of this car-buying decision is determining what's best for your financial situation. That's not as easy as applying a formula. This decision requires knowledge about your current financial situation, assumptions about the future, and some good guesses.

An ordinary spreadsheet, such as Microsoft's Excel, is an example of software that you can use to construct your own decision support system and analyze your options. You can look at the numbers, try different possibilities, and compare the results. But first, you need to build an amortization table which shows, in tabular form, the progress of your loan during the loan period.

The amortization table will be the basis of your DSS (see Figure 15.2). To construct it, you need to know what information is important and understand the relationships inherent in that information. For example, you need to relate principal, interest rate, loan term, and payments. Fortunately, Excel has a function (the **PMT** function) to calculate your payment. You need to know that car loan interest rates are usually quoted as yearly rates, but for the Excel **PMT** function you need to divide the annual rate by 12 to achieve a monthly rate, since car payments are usually monthly.

When you've entered the data and formulas, you're ready to analyze the information—that's the decision support part of the exercise. You would enter different values for the variables to see how the payments and total amount you'll pay for the car vary. The amortization table enhanced with the ability to change values and view the results constitutes a decision support system.

When you've tried several different values, you'll have a concrete basis for making your decision. This type of analysis is called a "what-if analysis" and helps you to decide between different options.

FIGURE 15.2

You can use a spreadsheet to analyze your car-buying options.

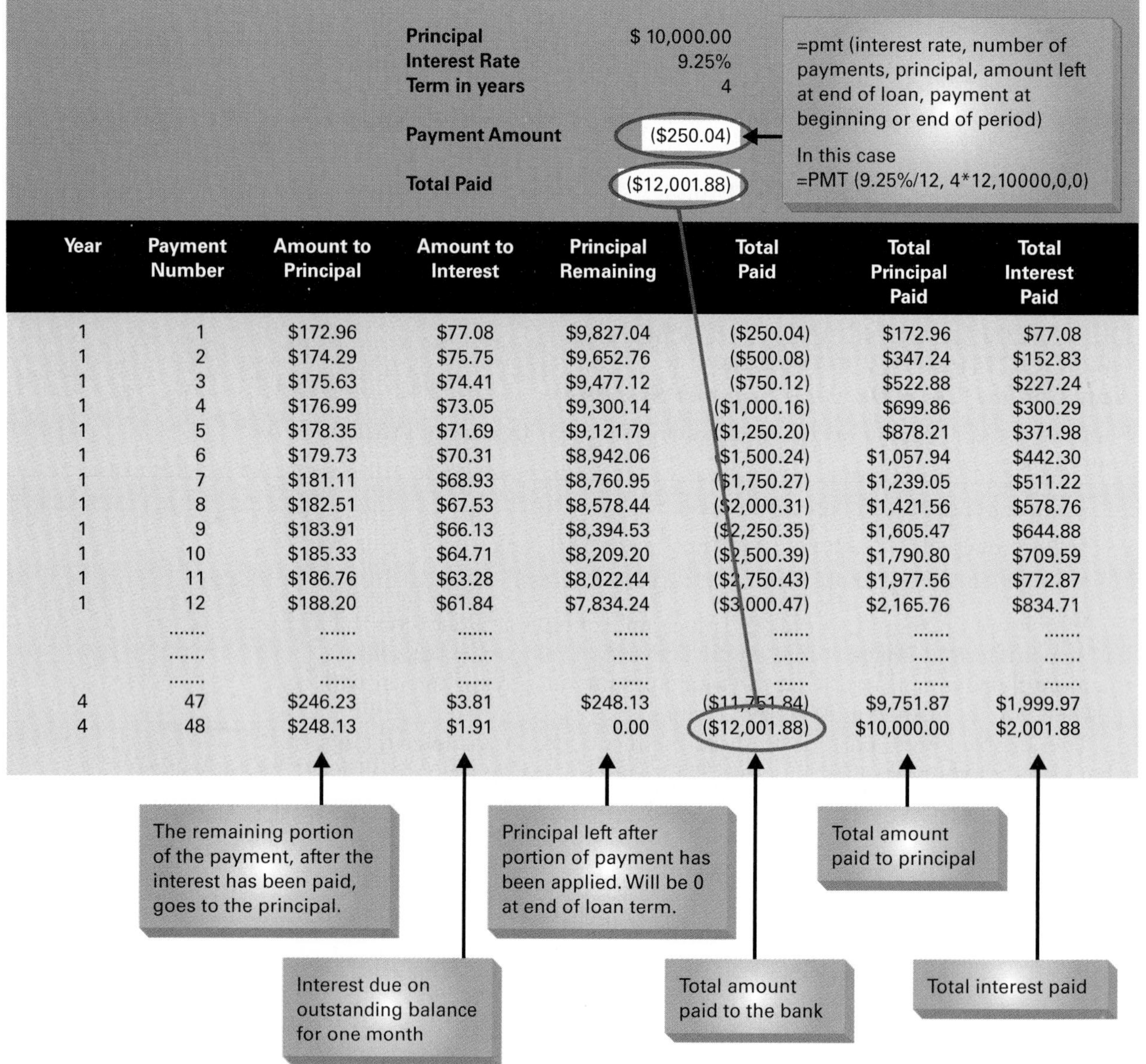

Principal	$ 10,000.00
Interest Rate	9.25%
Term in years	4
Payment Amount	($250.04)
Total Paid	($12,001.88)

Year	Payment Number	Amount to Principal	Amount to Interest	Principal Remaining	Total Paid	Total Principal Paid	Total Interest Paid
1	1	$172.96	$77.08	$9,827.04	($250.04)	$172.96	$77.08
1	2	$174.29	$75.75	$9,652.76	($500.08)	$347.24	$152.83
1	3	$175.63	$74.41	$9,477.12	($750.12)	$522.88	$227.24
1	4	$176.99	$73.05	$9,300.14	($1,000.16)	$699.86	$300.29
1	5	$178.35	$71.69	$9,121.79	($1,250.20)	$878.21	$371.98
1	6	$179.73	$70.31	$8,942.06	($1,500.24)	$1,057.94	$442.30
1	7	$181.11	$68.93	$8,760.95	($1,750.27)	$1,239.05	$511.22
1	8	$182.51	$67.53	$8,578.44	($2,000.31)	$1,421.56	$578.76
1	9	$183.91	$66.13	$8,394.53	($2,250.35)	$1,605.47	$644.88
1	10	$185.33	$64.71	$8,209.20	($2,500.39)	$1,790.80	$709.59
1	11	$186.76	$63.28	$8,022.44	($2,750.43)	$1,977.56	$772.87
1	12	$188.20	$61.84	$7,834.24	($3,000.47)	$2,165.76	$834.71
	....	....	....	....	....	....	....
	....	....	....	....	....	....	....
	....	....	....	....	....	....	....
4	47	$246.23	$3.81	$248.13	($11,751.84)	$9,751.87	$1,999.97
4	48	$248.13	$1.91	0.00	($12,001.88)	$10,000.00	$2,001.88

	Options	Payment	Total Cost of Car
Option 1	$10,000 @ 8.25% for 3 years	$314.52	$11,322.66
Option 2	$10,000 @ 9.25% for 4 years	$250.04	$12,001.88
Option 3	$9,000 @ 8% for 3 years with $1,000 down	$282.03	$10,152.98 (to the bank) + $1,000 (down)

FIGURE 15.3

With option 3 you'll pay the lowest total amount for the car, but the lowest monthly payments come from option 2.

The lowest payments come from the second option of $10,000 at 9.25 percent for four years (see Figure 15.3). And the lowest overall total cost of the car is in the third option ($1,000 down and $9,000 at 8 percent for three years). The shorter the loan term, the less it costs in the long run, other things being equal.

Of course, getting those numbers is only half the battle. You still have to decide what's right for you. You may not have $1,000 right now that you can use as a down payment. You may be living on a restricted budget that makes the lowest possible payments your immediate concern. You'll also need to estimate your financial future. The idea of a DSS is to let you look at alternatives, taking all relevant circumstances into consideration, so that you can make a more informed, and therefore better, decision. To learn more about using your spreadsheet software as a DSS, complete the "Spreadsheet Applications" tutorial on your SimNet Concepts Support CD.

DECISION SUPPORT SYSTEMS

What's a Decision Support System?

In Chapter 10, you learned how data mining can help you make business decisions by giving you the ability to slice and dice your way through massive amounts of information. Actually, a data warehouse with data-mining tools is one type of computer-aided decision support software.

The term *decision support system,* used broadly, means any computer-aided system that helps you make decisions. However, there's also a more restrictive definition. It's rather like the term *medicine.* Medicine can mean the whole health care system or it can mean cough syrup, depending on the context.

In its narrowest sense, a ***decision support system (DSS)*** is software that uses models, information, and an interactive user interface to help you make decisions. A DSS lets you look at information in different ways to help you come to a conclusion about what the best course of action might be for a certain situation. Usually a DSS is software that requires a lot of input from you (see Figure 15.4).

You Contribute . . .	. . . and Gain the Advantages of a DSS
• Experience	• Increased productivity
• Intuition	• Increased understanding
• Judgment	• Increased speed
• Knowledge	• Increased flexibility
	• Reduced problem complexity
	• Reduced cost

FIGURE 15.4

Decision support software helps you make the most of your own decision-making talents.

FIGURE 15.5

A decision support system helps you analyze options and make a decision.

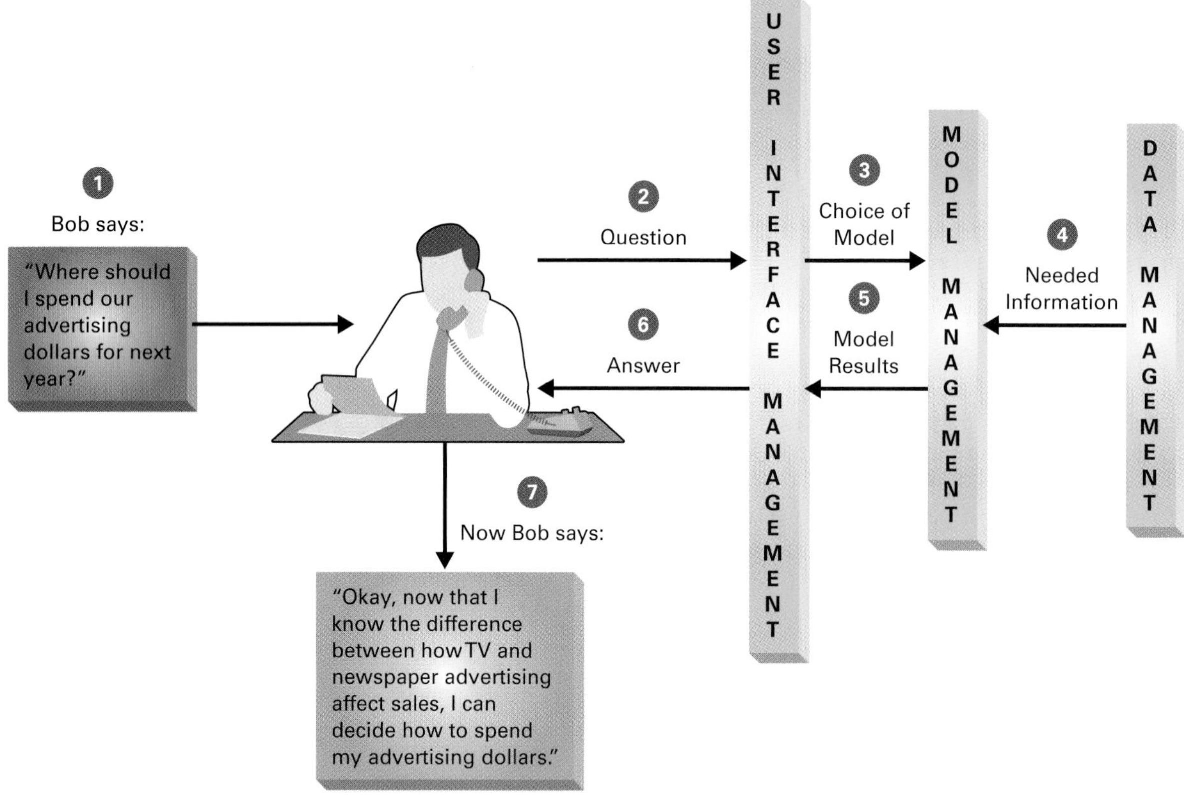

did you know?

Donald *Duck comics were once banned from Finland because he doesn't wear pants.*

Decision Support System Components

Our Excel DSS from the last section has the three features that you expect to find in a DSS. It has a model, data, and a user interface (see Figure 15.5).

1. **Model Management:** The model management component of a DSS handles the models. A *model* is a representation of reality. Model airplanes and cars are small physical versions of the real thing. Mathematical or financial models are representations of the relationship between variables. In our example, the formulas of the amortization table form the model. The model is simply the mathematical representation of how the different values, such as the principal and monthly payments, are linked to each other.
2. **Data Management:** Data or information, in this case, consists of the details of the particular case you're interested in and other pertinent information. The information that we used in the example was the numeric values of the variables, that is, the set of numbers that fit each of the three cases—principal, interest rate, and term of the loan.
3. **User Interface Management:** A ***user interface*** is the manner in which you communicate with the software package. It's what you use to manipulate the information. The Excel screen with its rows and columns, menus and buttons, is the user interface in our example. You can use the user interface to change numbers and see the results

of the changes in the DSS we created. A DSS typically has an interactive user interface so that you can change values easily as we did in the car-buying example.

Business Decision Support Systems

There are many other types of decision support systems besides the one we built for the car-buying "what-if" analysis. A DSS is often very sophisticated software for analyzing information. For example, an insurance company constantly assesses its risk when selling different policies. That's why your age, the type of car, and perhaps your marital status will all be factors the company will use to decide how much you'll have to pay for car insurance. For example, someone probably used a DSS to determine that young single men who drive performance vehicles are the most likely to have accidents and how much it costs to insure those drivers. Examples of other business tasks that lend themselves to the use of a DSS are

- Deciding where to spend advertising dollars.
- Analyzing sales trend information.
- Analyzing drug interactions.
- Developing airline schedules.
- Developing asset portfolios.

A DSS usually gets the information it analyzes from the transaction processing systems (which we discussed in the previous chapter) of the organization. But while a transaction processing system (TPS) provides great detail and a management information system (MIS) summarizes what happened, a DSS tries to use the past to peek into the future and decide how best to proceed.

The types of models that a DSS uses include simulation, optimization, goal-seeking, and statistical techniques, as well as "what-if" models (see Figure 15.6). For example, suppose you just bought a newsstand and are trying to decide which newspapers and magazines to stock and how many of each. If you have too few copies of a popular magazine and run out of it, customers will go elsewhere and you'll lose those sales and possibly future sales too. If you have too many copies of the magazine, however, you'll either have to absorb the loss or, at the very least, pay for shipping the extra copies back to the publisher.

You could use a simulation to help you decide. That would involve estimating demand, which may be constant or changing, and calculating the profit or loss at varying levels of inventory. You could "run the stand" electronically for a number of months and see how it turns out.

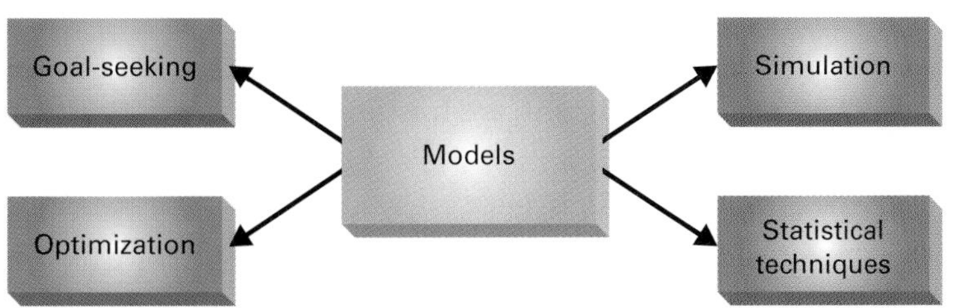

FIGURE 15.6

Types of decision support system models are many and varied.

i•series insights — Ethics, Security & Privacy

Mapping Your Nose

You might be surprised to learn that one of the surgical procedures most prone to malpractice lawsuits is nasal surgery done to alleviate allergy symptoms or to improve breathing. One of the big problems with nasal surgery is simply the location of the nose. It's so close to the eyes and brain that mishaps can turn into tragedies. Occasionally the optic nerve is accidentally cut during nasal surgery, resulting in blindness or near blindness for the patient.

Many nasal surgeries are conducted with an endoscope, a thin, flexible wire with a tiny camera on the tip, which allows the surgeon to "see" inside small tight places such as nasal passages. With the image from the camera displayed on a large monitor, the surgeon can use scalpels, needles, and forceps to perform the necessary procedure.

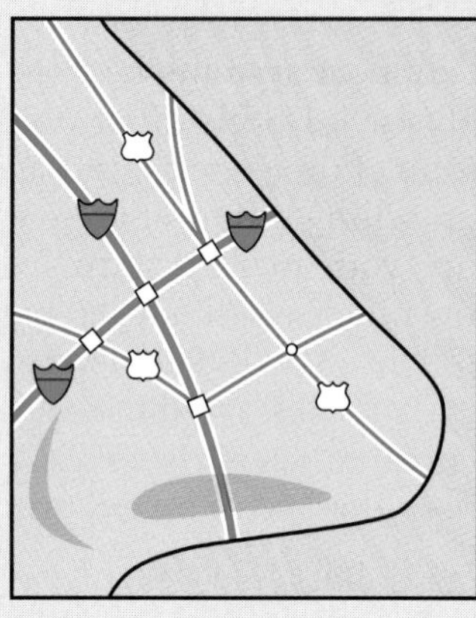

To allow surgeons to train for this tricky procedure, Lockheed Martin has developed a nasal cavity simulation "road map." Many, many razor-thin cross-sectional pictures of actual nasal passages are stored in a database and can be viewed as a three-dimensional picture. To allow surgeons to practice their skills, Lockheed installed this picture of nasal terrain into a mannequin that is used for virtual nasal operations at training hospitals.

The nasal-terrain simulator is an adaptation of a system that Lockheed developed for the Swedish Air Force. That system mapped the terrain of northern Europe. The main alteration that Lockheed made was to shift the emphasis from speed, which the fighter pilots need most, to precision, which the surgeons need most. Whether it's Europe or your nose—good navigation is the key.

Alternatively, you could use an optimization model, which if properly constructed, would give you the optimum number of newspapers and magazines to stock and sell for the greatest profit. Optimization models are used to calculate the most profitable, or least costly, mix of products.

Of course, the accuracy and helpfulness of the results of any model depend on the correctness of the relationships or formulas, how accurate the estimates are, and the validity of any underlying assumptions. For more information on decision support systems, visit our Web site at www.mhhe.com/i-series. You can also learn more by completing the "Financial Management Applications" tutorial on your SimNet Concepts Support CD.

GEOGRAPHIC INFORMATION SYSTEMS (GIS)

What's a Geographic Information System?

Suppose you drive a delivery van. Which of the following would you rather have?

1. A table that shows a list of the pickup and delivery addresses with text information about where each is located.
2. A map that shows the location of all your customers and what you're supposed to pick up or deliver.

Probably you'd rather have the map, as most people would. This kind of flexible map information is called a geographic information system.

did you know? There *are no words in the dictionary that rhyme with orange, purple, or silver.*

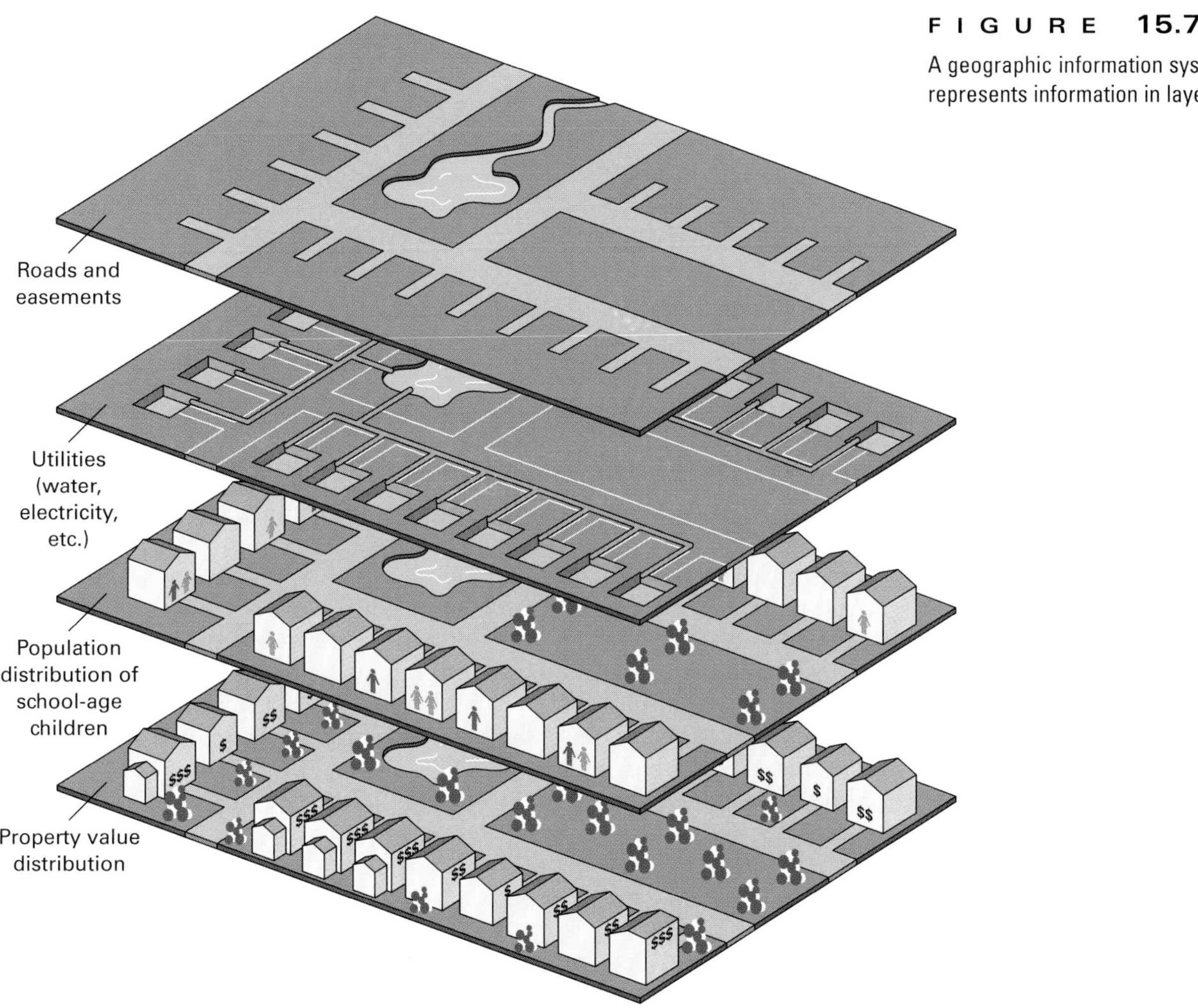

FIGURE 15.7

A geographic information system represents information in layers.

A ***geographic information system (GIS)*** is software that allows you to see information in map form. The value of a GIS is in its visual representation of information. A GIS takes traditional map information and combines it with other information from databases or spreadsheets and represents the information in layers. You can choose the layers you want to see in the picture and thus get a complete image of all the information you need in graphic form (see Figure 15.7). A GIS can take thousands of rows of spreadsheet information and display it in map form, perhaps even with 3-D graphics and animation. You can usually see more information more quickly this way than you could with huge tables.

You can also combine a GIS with a global positioning system. A global positioning system (GPS) is a device that tells you your current latitude, longitude, speed, and direction of movement. Companies that deal in transportation use GISs combined with database and GPS technology. For example, airlines and shipping companies can plot routes with up-to-the-minute information on the location of all their transport vehicles. Hospitals can keep track of where personnel are located by using a GIS and sensors in the ceiling that pick up the transmissions of badges worn by hospital staff. It's almost like *Star Trek* except that the computers don't hold everyday conversations with you.

SECTION 15.1

making the grade

1. Software that has models, information, and a user interface to help you make decisions is called a(n) ___________.
2. A(n) ___________ is a representation of reality.
3. Information is stored in layers in a(n) ___________.
4. A(n) ___________ is a device that tells you where you are.

15.2 ARTIFICIAL INTELLIGENCE

As you saw in the last section, a decision support system augments your own brainpower. It allows you to analyze information as an aid to decision making, but you have to make the final decision.

A different type of computer-aided decision support software is artificial intelligence. ***Artificial intelligence (AI)*** is the science of making machines imitate human thinking and behavior. A robot is an example of an artificial intelligence system. A ***robot*** is an artificial intelligence device with simulated human senses capable of taking action on its own. For example, bomb squads use a bomb-retrieving robot. When they get a report that there's a bomb in a building, they can send in the robot equipped with cameras to "take a look." Some of these robots are also able to disarm or even bring out the bomb by acting on commands sent by remote control. This keeps human beings out of harm's way.

ARTIFICIAL INTELLIGENCE SYSTEMS IN BUSINESS

How Does Business Use Artificial Intelligence?

In business decision making, artificial intelligence is usually in software form. Financial analysts use a variety of artificial intelligence software to manage assets, invest in the stock market, and perform other financial operations. Hospitals use artificial intelligence in many capacities—scheduling staff, assigning beds, and diagnosing and treating illnesses. Many government agencies, including the IRS and the armed forces, use AI. Credit card companies use artificial intelligence to detect credit card fraud, and insurance companies use artificial intelligence techniques and software to ferret out fraudulent claims. Artificial intelligence lends itself to tasks as diverse as airline ticket pricing, food preparation, oil exploration, and child protection.

There is not yet any AI system that can truly replace human thinking, reasoning, and creativity. However, each AI system mimics some specific aspect of human thinking. The major categories of artificial intelligence software that people use in the decision-making process are

- *Expert systems,* which reason through problems and offer advice in the form of a conclusion or recommendation.
- *Neural networks,* which can be "trained" to recognize patterns.
- *Genetic algorithms,* which produce increasingly better solutions to problems in a manner similar to the evolutionary process.
- *Fuzzy logic,* which is a way of reasoning with imprecise or partial information.

did you know? Assuming *that Rudolph was in front, there are 40,320 ways to arrange the other eight reindeer.*

EXPERT SYSTEMS

What's "Expert" about an Expert System?

An ***expert system,*** also called a ***knowledge-based system,*** is an artificial intelligence system that applies reasoning capabilities to reach a conclusion. Expert systems are built for specific application areas, called *domains,* such as diagnosing a disease or determining how to fix a faulty engine. A common type of expert system is a rule-based expert system, which consists of a set of IF . . . THEN questions, called "rules." You answer those questions or rules according to your situation, and the expert system then reaches a conclusion.

Here's an example. Suppose you had an expert system in your car that would tell you what to do when approaching a traffic light. In this case, negotiating traffic lights would be the domain of the expert system. As you approach a green traffic light, you'll most likely proceed on through. If the light is red, you'll stop. If the light is yellow, however, you'll probably try to gauge whether you'll be able to make it through the intersection in time. Your traffic-light expert system would have a set of rules or questions—the kind of questions that you unconsciously ask yourself every time you sit behind the wheel of a vehicle, like "Can I stop without causing havoc or should I continue through the intersection on this yellow light?"

Look at Figure 15.8 for an illustration of the logic of expert system rules. Also in Figure 15.8 is an example of how your computer screen might look during a consultation.

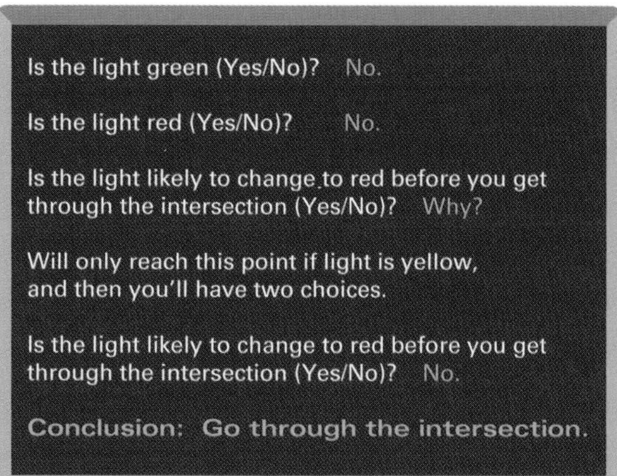

FIGURE 15.8

An expert system asks the user questions and reaches a conclusion based on the answers.

Rule	Question	Yes	No	Explanation
1	Is the light green?	Go through the intersection.	Go to Rule 2.	Should be safe if light is green. If not, need more information.
2	Is the light red?	Go to Rule 4.	Go to Rule 3.	Should stop, may not be able to.
3	Is the light likely to change to red before you get through the intersection?	Go to Rule 4.	Go through the intersection.	Will only reach this point if light is yellow, then you'll have two choices.
4	Can you stop before entering the intersection?	Stop.	Go to Rule 5.	Should stop, but there may be a problem if you can't.
5	Is traffic approaching from either side?	Prepare to crash.	Go through the intersection.	Unless the intersection is clear of traffic, you're likely to crash.

practically speaking

Coplink—A Neural Network Supercop

Federal authorities were looking for a suspect. The only thing they knew about him was that his sister had once reported a domestic dispute with an abusive boyfriend. That's not much to go on—unless you have a way of extracting all cases involving a woman complainant in a domestic violence case who is in the same age group as the suspect and has the same last name. This could involve wading through hundreds, maybe even thousands, of cases—a job that could take months.

But a neural network designed for this task, called Coplink, did the job in less than 30 minutes. The University of Arizona Artificial Intelligence Laboratory has been working on this system since 1997, and as of January 2003 it was being used by six law enforcement agencies. Coplink uses its pattern-identification capabilities to search and match pattern association. The system continuously updates its information, which comes from multiple databases.

The Web site, at www.coplinkconnect.com, is available only to law enforcement agencies and is much more secure than any e-commerce site, according to Hsinchun Chen, the director of the project.

FIGURE 15.9

An expert system is an artificial intelligence system that applies reasoning capabilities to reach a conclusion.

Expert Systems are used in

- *Accounting,* for auditing, tax planning, and so on.
- *Medicine,* to prescribe antibiotics, taking into account the patient's medical history, source of the infection, the price of available drugs, and so on.
- *Process control,* in lithographic printing, for example.
- *Human resource management,* perhaps to determine if the organization is in compliance with federal employment laws.
- *Forestry management,* to plan tree cutting and planting.

You use expert systems mainly to solve one of two kinds of problems: diagnostic and prescriptive (see Figure 15.9). A diagnostic problem asks the question "what's wrong?" For example, if a car's transmission doesn't work, the car mechanic will ask you several questions and based on your answers to those questions he/she will ask some more questions. Eventually the mechanic may be able to tell what the problem is. Prescriptive problems ask the question "what to do?" like our traffic-light expert system did.

NEURAL NETWORKS
Doesn't "Neural" Have Something to Do with My Brain?

A neural network is so called because it simulates the human ability to classify. You learned to differentiate cars from trucks by seeing lots of examples of each type. You learned to look for certain discriminating characteristics, the truck bed or the distinctive cab, and used that information to tell them apart. In other words, you used pattern recognition to tell one type of vehicle from another.

A ***neural network*** is an artificial intelligence system that is capable of learning how to differentiate patterns. You would use a neural network when you have a vast amount of information to analyze and your objective is identification or classification. You train a neural network by feeding it hundreds, or thousands, of examples telling it what category each one belongs to. Then, on its own, the neural network "learns" what characteristics are important in differentiating type A from type B—just as you once did with cars and trucks.

Have you ever received a call from your credit card company asking you if a particular purchase was okay because the purchase was out of the ordinary? If so, the credit card company may well have been responding to its neural network's alert. Credit card companies use neural networks to compare past patterns of credit card usage with incoming purchase transactions. To train the neural network, the company provides it with details of numerous credit card histories and tells it which transactions are fraudulent. Eventually the neural network will learn to identify suspicious transactions on its own.

Another application area of neural networks is in spotting computer viruses. Symantec Corp. has introduced a version of its Norton AntiVirus software, which includes a neural network to help determine if a virus has found its way into your computer. The software, which was developed by IBM, can identify known and even unknown viruses within minutes, allowing the company to provide a fix for the virus faster than the advertised 24 to 48 hours. See Figure 15.10 for more applications of neural networks.

FIGURE 15.10

A neural network is an artificial intelligence system that can learn how to differentiate patterns.

Neural Networks are used

- In airports to find bombs in luggage by detecting their distinctive chemical patterns.
- By medical technicians to check for irregularities in human tissue in an effort to find early warning signs of cancer and other diseases.
- In the business world to assemble stock portfolios, detect fraud, evaluate credit applications, appraise real estate, and even read handwriting.

GENETIC ALGORITHMS

What Does Genetics Have to Do with Computers?

When avid rose growers develop new roses, they usually try to grow a flower with one or more specific characteristics—no thorns, stronger stem, yellow flower, and so on. They combine individual roses that already have the desired characteristics to get a new rose. This is evolution, helped by humans. Believe it or not, businesses use a type of software that is based on the same evolutionary principle, called genetic algorithms. A ***genetic algorithm*** is an artificial intelligence system that mimics the evolutionary, survival-of-the-fittest process to generate increasingly better solutions to a problem.

Many problems exist that have an almost infinite number of possible solutions and it's very hard to find the one that's best. What managers usually do is find a solution that is as good as it can be, given the time constraints of producing it. But with a genetic algorithm, you let the computer use its extraordinary speed to examine many more solutions. The software evaluates these new solutions and, based on the best of those, generates even more solutions, repeating the process until it finds the best one it can.

Let's take an example using business finance. Suppose you were trying to decide what to put into your stock portfolio. You have countless stocks to choose from and a limited amount of money to invest. You might decide that you'd like to start with 20 stocks and you want a portfolio growth rate of at least 7.5 percent.

Probably you'd start by examining historic information on the stocks. You would then combine stocks, 20 at a time, and examine the aggregate return of each group. If you wanted to choose from a pool of 30 stocks, you would have to examine 30,045,015 different combinations. For a 40-stock pool, the number of combinations rises to 137,846,500,000. It would be an impossibly time-consuming, not to mention numbingly tedious, task to look at this many combinations and evaluate your overall return for each one. However, this is just the sort of repetitive number crunching task at which computers excel.

So instead of a pencil, paper, and calculator, you might use a genetic algorithm. You could input the appropriate information on the stocks, such as the number of years the company has been in business, the performance of the stock over the last five years, price to earnings ratios, and other information.

You would also have to tell the genetic algorithm your exact "success" criteria such as stock price growth rate. You could also use a revenue growth rate in the company over the last year of at least 10 percent, a presence in the marketplace going back at least three years, a connection to the computer industry, etc. The genetic algorithm would simply combine and recombine stocks eliminating any combinations that don't fit your criteria and continue the process for several iterations using only the acceptable combinations—in our example those that give an aggregate growth rate of at least 7.5 percent while aiming for as high a stock price growth rate as possible.

A note of caution here: It's important to understand that this method of stock selection is based on past information and assumes that things will not change. That may or may not be a good assumption. See Figure 15.11 for more applications of genetic algorithms.

FIGURE 15.11

A genetic algorithm is an artificial intelligence system that mimics evolution to generate increasingly better solutions to a problem.

Genetic Algorithms are used to

- Minimize the amount of cable that needs to be laid over a wide geographic area.
- Schedule commercials at radio stations.
- Minimize the movement of whiskey casks around a distiller's warehouse.
- Schedule the rotation of trains in France.

FUZZY LOGIC
Is That like Fuzzy Thinking?

Fuzzy logic is a way of dealing with uncertainty and imprecision. If you've ever mistyped a Web address, you've had personal experience of the level of precision that computers require. People, on the other hand, talk in subjective, imprecise ways all the time. You've surely used terms such as "bright lights," "cold winters," "big rooms," "tasty food," and "small cars," and other people pretty much understood what you were talking about. Computer software, however, can't cope with these vague types of terms without fuzzy logic.

Fuzzy logic is a mathematical method of handling imprecise or subjective information. Using fuzzy logic, it's possible for computers to deal with circumstances that are not simple "either/or" situations. Take room temperature for example. Most people would consider a room in which the thermostat is set at 75 degrees Fahrenheit to be warm. If you lower the temperature one degree, the room is still warm. If you keep lowering the temperature until the air in the room is only 40 degrees, most people would say it's cold. At what number of degrees did the temperature go from warm to cold? Was it at 50 degrees, or 60 degrees, or some other number? In truth, there is no hairline warm/cold point. In the real world, the room becomes "less" or "more" warm and gradually becomes "less" or "more" cold. It's this sort of situation that fuzzy logic can handle. If you had a fuzzy logic thermostat, you wouldn't set it to a certain degree setting. You'd set it to "warm" or "cool" and the fuzzy logic would take care of the rest.

did you know? Thirteen *people a year are killed by vending machines falling on them.*[5]

Fuzzy logic is best for situations in which the variables are shifting constantly and a decision must be made quickly. For example, fuzzy logic is built into antilock brakes, giving them control to apply breaking pressure appropriate to the level of skid of the tires. Normally, a computer could handle only input of skid or no-skid, but fuzzy logic adds the ability to differentiate between road surfaces that are a little bit slippery, pretty slippery, and very slippery.

For more information on artificial intelligence, visit our Web site at www.mhhe.com/i-series. If you're interested in the fascinating world of artificial intelligence, you'll find many opportunities from building robots to designing business systems. To learn more about artificial intelligence, complete the "Virtual Reality and Artificial Intelligence" tutorial on your SimNet Concepts Support CD.

making the grade

SECTION 15.2

1. A(n) ___________ is an artificial intelligence system that is capable of learning to differentiate patterns.
2. A(n) ___________ is an artificial intelligence system that mimics the evolutionary process.
3. A mathematical method of handling imprecise or subjective information is called ___________.
4. An artificial intelligence system that applies reasoning capabilities to reach a conclusion is a(n) ___________.

15.3 INTELLIGENT AGENTS, OR BOTS

Do you have a favorite restaurant? Is there someone there who knows you and remembers that you like Italian dressing, but not croutons, on your salad; and ice cream and a slice of cheddar cheese on your apple pie? Does this person familiar with your tastes put a glass of diet cola on your favorite table when you come in the door? If so, he or she has the qualities that artificial intelligence scientists are working on incorporating into intelligent agents. An ***intelligent agent*** (or ***bot***) is software that assists you, or acts on your behalf, in performing repetitive computer-related tasks. Future intelligent agents will most likely be autonomous, acting independently, and will learn and adapt to changing circumstances.

You may not realize it, but you're probably already familiar with a primitive type of intelligent agent—the shifty-eyed paper clip that pops itself up when you're using Word. For example, if your document looks as if it is going to be a business letter—that is, you type in a date, name, and address—the animated paperclip will offer helpful suggestions on how to proceed. Another example of a primitive intelligent agent is the software on Amazon.com's Web site that suggests books to you on the basis of your previous purchases and those of people who bought the books you did.

FIGURE 15.12

There are four types of intelligent agents.

Types of Intelligent Agents
1. Buyer agents or shopping bots
2. User or personal agents
3. Monitoring-and-surveillance agents
4. Data-mining agents

To be truly "intelligent" systems, intelligent agents must be able to learn. For example, if you had an intelligent agent that made travel arrangements for you, it might learn that you like to fly at night. Intelligent agent technology is still in its early stages and there is great disagreement on what actually constitutes an "intelligent agent." Some software that is popularly called "intelligent" doesn't learn, which, according to many, is the foundation of intelligence—natural or artificial.

Intelligent agents usually work in the background, so even while they're working your computer is still available to you for use. For example, your intelligent agent might search the Internet every morning for information about your state senators, your favorite sports team, comic strips you like, and so on, presenting you with a customized newspaper to read with your morning beverage, all while you're reading and answering e-mail.

Currently, you can find hundreds of intelligent agents, or bots, for a wide variety of tasks. There are four basic types of intelligent agents, as shown in Figure 15.12.

- Buyer agents or shopping bots
- User or personal agents
- Monitoring-and-surveillance or predictive agents
- Data-mining agents

BUYER AGENTS

What Do Buyer Agents or Shopping Bots Do?

Buyer agents travel around a network (very likely the Internet) finding information and bringing it back to you. A ***buyer agent*** or ***shopping bot*** is an intelligent agent on a Web site that helps you, the customer, find products and services you want. Shopping bots work very efficiently for commodity products such as CDs, books, electronic components, and other one-size-fits-all products.

MySimon.com is the most successful shopping bot to date with more than a million visitors a month according to Nielsen/NetRatings. MySimon searches for millions of products on thousands of Web sites.

Shopping bots make money by selling advertising space, from special promotions in cooperation with merchants, or from click-through fees, which are payments to the site that provided the link to the merchant site. Some shopping bots give preference to certain sites for a financial consideration. The people who run shopping bot sites have two sometimes conflicting objectives. They want to present as many listings as possible to the consumer in the most useful way, but they also want to make money doing it.

You may have encountered a shopping bot without having specifically requested its services. For example, Amazon.com will offer you a list of books that you might like to buy based on what you're buying now and

did you know? When glass breaks, the cracks move at speeds up to 3,000 miles per hour.[6]

what you have bought in the past. The Amazon site uses an intelligent agent—a shopping bot—to provide this service. Amazon's agent uses a technique called collaborative filtering, which is a way of matching a customer with a group of others who have similar taste, and presenting to you choices that were common in that group.

USER AGENTS

Can I Get an Intelligent Agent that Will Perform Other Tasks?

User agents (sometimes called ***personal agents***) are intelligent agents that take action on your behalf. In this category belong those intelligent agents that already perform, or will shortly perform, the following tasks:

- Check your e-mail, sort it according to priority (your priority), and alert you when good stuff comes through—like college acceptance letters.
- Play computer games as your opponent or patrol game areas for you.
- Assemble customized Web sites with only the information you want appearing on that page (see Figure 15.13). There are several versions of these. A CNN Custom News bot will gather news from CNN on the topics you want to read about—and only those.
- Find information for you on the subject of your choice.
- Fill out forms on the Web automatically for you. They even store your information for future reference.
- Scan Web pages looking for and highlighting the text that constitutes the "important" part of the information there.
- "Discuss" topics with you from your deepest fears to sports.

In the future, user agents for personal use will be available for both your wired and your wireless computer devices. Sprint has recently announced an e-assistant that will carry out verbal requests. We may shortly see personal agents that

- Interact with the personal agents of colleagues to set up a meeting time.
- Incorporate shopping bots and can take your preferences for features on a new car (or anything else) along with a price range and then haggle with car dealers (or their personal agents) to find you the best deal.

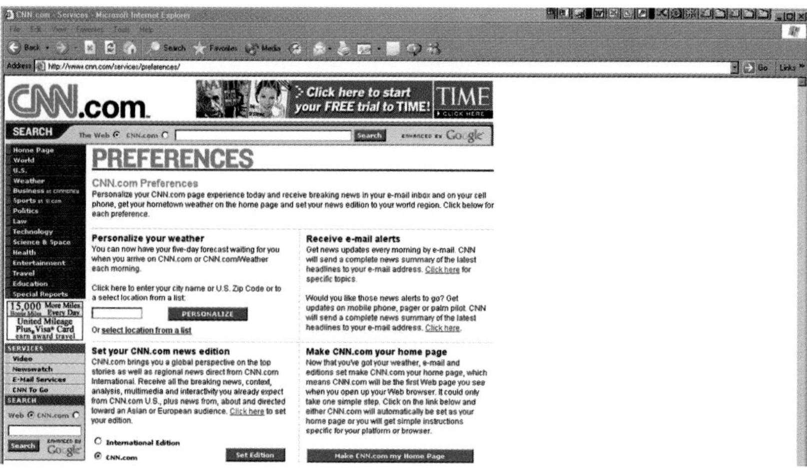

FIGURE 15.13

Some sites will let you personalize how their Web site looks on your computer and what information you see.

MONITORING-AND-SURVEILLANCE AGENTS
What Do These Intelligent Agents Monitor?

Monitoring-and-surveillance agents (also called ***predictive agents***) are intelligent agents that observe and report on equipment. For example, NASA's Jet Propulsion Laboratory has an agent that monitors inventory, planning equipment scheduling, and ordering to keep replacement costs down. Other monitoring agents work on the manufacturing shop floor, finding equipment problems and locating other machinery that will do the same job.

Monitoring-and-surveillance agents are often used to monitor complex computer networks. Allstate Insurance has a network with 2,000 computers. The company uses a network monitoring agent from Computer Associates International called Neugent that watches its huge networks 24 hours a day. Every five seconds, the agent measures 1,200 data points and can predict a system crash 45 minutes before it happens. Neugent combines intelligent agent technology with neural network technology to look for patterns of activity or problems. The neural network part can learn what conditions predict a downturn in network efficiency or a slowing in network traffic. Neugent also watches for attacks from hackers, detecting them early so that they can be stopped.

Another type of monitoring-and-surveillance agent works on computer networks keeping track of the configuration of each computer connected to the network. It tracks and updates the central configuration database when anything on any computer changes, like the number or type of disk drives.

An important task in managing networks lies in prioritizing traffic and shaping bandwidth. That means sending enough network capacity or bandwidth to the most important tasks over those that are secondary. At a university, for example, processing end-of-semester grades might take precedence over Web surfing.

Some further types of monitoring-and-surveillance agents include

- Agents that watch your competition and bring back price changes and special-offer information.
- Agents that monitor Internet sites, discussion groups, mailing lists, and so on, for stock manipulation, insider training, and rumors that might affect stock prices.
- Agents that monitor sites for updated information on the topic of your choice.
- Agents that watch particular products and bring back prices or changes in terms.
- Agents that monitor auction sites for products or prices that you want.

DATA-MINING AGENTS
How Do Intelligent Agents Work in a Data Warehouse?

A ***data-mining agent*** helps you discover new information, trends, and relationships within a data warehouse without necessarily applying a specific mathematical model. You'll recall from Chapter 10 that a *data warehouse* brings together information from lots of different sources. Again, in Chapter 10 you learned that *data mining* is the process of looking through the data warehouse to find information that you can use to take action, like ways to increase sales or keep customers who are considering defecting. Data mining uses many different software tools, including intelligent agents. Data mining is so called because you have to sift through a lot of information for the gold nuggets that will affect the bottom line. This same sort of information-nugget seeking is similar to what the FBI and CIA do when they bring together little bits of information from diverse sources and use the overall pattern to spot trouble brewing or to solve a crime.

The two main objectives of data mining are prediction and discovery. Prediction involves recognizing patterns and recognizing those patterns as they begin to emerge in the information. The process of discovery is to find patterns in information so that characteristics can be categorized into classes. This is just what neural networks do best. So, not surprisingly, neural networks are part of many data-mining tools. And data-mining agents constitute another integral part, since data-mining agents search for information in a data warehouse.

A data-mining agent may detect a major shift in a trend or a key indicator. It can also detect the presence of new information and alert you. Volkswagen uses an intelligent agent system that acts as an early-warning system about market conditions. If conditions become such that the assumptions underlying the company's strategy are no longer true, the intelligent agent alerts managers. For example, the intelligent agent might see a problem in some part of the country that is or will shortly cause payments to slow down. Having that information early lets managers formulate a plan to protect themselves. To learn more about decision support and data mining, complete the "Data Mining" tutorial on your SimNet Concepts Support CD.

making the grade SECTION 15.3

1. The process of extracting new information from a data warehouse is called ___________.
2. Specialized search tools that look at products and prices on many Web sites and bring back information on what they found are called ___________.
3. An intelligent agent that sorts and prioritizes your e-mail is an example of a(n) ___________.
4. Software that assists you, or acts on your behalf, in performing repetitive computer-related tasks is called a(n) ___________.
5. A(n) ___________ agent checks out a network, looking for problems.

15.4 SUMMARY AND KEY TERMS

Information technology can offer help in decision-making in various forms. The major categories of computer-aided decision-making software are (1) decision support software that helps you analyze options; (2) artificial intelligence software that makes the decision for you; (3) and intelligent agents that search and find goods or problems or news articles, or something else of interest to you.

A ***decision support system (DSS)*** is software that uses models, information, and an interactive user interface to help you make decisions. Some business information is easier to comprehend and analyze in map form. A ***geographic information system (GIS)*** is software that allows you to see information in map form.

You don't always need to know enough to do your own analysis. AI systems reach a decision for you. ***Artificial intelligence (AI)*** is the science of making machines imitate human thinking and behavior. There are four major types:

- An ***expert system,*** also known as a ***knowledge-based system,*** is an artificial intelligence system that applies reasoning capabilities to reach a conclusion.
- A ***neural network*** is an artificial intelligence system that is capable of learning to differentiate patterns.
- A ***genetic algorithm*** is an artificial intelligence system that mimics the evolutionary, "survival-of-the-fittest" process to generate increasingly better solutions to a problem.
- ***Fuzzy logic*** is a mathematical method of handling imprecise or subjective information.

For tasks and decision-making that require searching and bringing back information, an ***intelligent agent (bot)*** can help. There are four types:

- A ***buyer agent*** or ***shopping bot*** is an intelligent agent on a Web site that helps you, the customer, find products and services you want.
- ***User agents*** (sometimes called ***personal agents***) are intelligent agents that take action on your behalf.
- ***Monitoring-and-surveillance agents*** (also called ***predictive agents***) are intelligent agents that observe and report on equipment.
- A ***data-mining agent*** operates in a data warehouse discovering information.

Visit the Web site for this text at www.mhhe.com/i-series to learn more about decision support systems and artificial intelligence.

KEY TERMS

artificial intelligence (AI) (p. 464)
buyer agent (shopping bot) (p. 470)
data-mining agent (p. 472)
decision support system (DSS) (p. 459)
expert system (knowledge-based system) (p. 465)
fuzzy logic (p. 468)
genetic algorithm (p. 467)
geographic information system (GIS) (p. 463)
intelligent agent (bot) (p. 469)
monitoring-and-surveillance (predictive) agent (p. 472)
neural network (p. 466)
robot (p. 464)
structured decision (p. 457)
unstructured decision (p. 457)
user agent (personal agent) (p. 471)
user interface (p. 460)

review of terminology

Multiple Choice

1. The objective of data mining is
   a. prediction and discovery.
   b. diagnostic and predictive.
   c. diagnostic and discovery.
   d. prediction and sorting massive amounts of information.
   e. none of the above.

2. Software that lets you see information in map form is a
   a. DSS.
   b. genetic algorithm.
   c. neural network.
   d. geographic information system.
   e. mapping agent.

3. The science of making machines imitate human thinking and behavior is called
   a. artificial intelligence.
   b. genetic algorithms.
   c. neural networks.
   d. geographic information systems.
   e. a bot.

4. A knowledge-based system is also known as a(n)
   a. genetic algorithm.
   b. neural network.
   c. expert system.
   d. geographic information system.
   e. DSS.

5. Software that helps you analyze information so that you can make better decisions is a(n)
   a. monitoring-and-surveillance agent.
   b. DSS.
   c. expert system.
   d. genetic algorithm.
   e. neural network.

6. Intelligent agents can be
   a. shopping bots.
   b. monitoring-and-surveillance agents.
   c. data-mining agents.
   d. all of the above.
   e. none of the above.

7. The extraction of new information from a data warehouse is called
   a. a neural network.
   b. data mining.
   c. visualization.
   d. data marting.
   e. all of the above.

8. Another name for a user agent is a(n)
   a. expert system.
   b. buyer agent.
   c. personal agent.
   d. monitoring-and-surveillance agent.
   e. genetic algorithm.

9. Which of the following is/are example(s) of decision support system models?
   a. "what-if" analysis
   b. goal-seeking
   c. optimization
   d. statistical techniques
   e. all of the above

10. A rule-based expert system
    a. asks a series of questions.
    b. is based on a set of AI rules.
    c. is used in a data warehouse.
    d. is part of a neural network.
    e. is none of the above.

True/False

11. ____ Fuzzy logic is a mathematical method for handling imprecise or subjective information.
12. ____ A shopping bot is a type of data-mining agent.
13. ____ A genetic algorithm is based on the evolutionary process.
14. ____The strength of an expert system is its ability to differentiate patterns.
15. ____ A DSS will make the decision for you.

Take this quiz online at www.mhhe.com/i-series and get instant feedback.

review of concepts

QUESTIONS AND EXERCISES

1. Which Type of Computer-Aided Support Should You Use?

Given the two types of decision support . . .

- Decision support systems for analysis of specific problems
- Geographic information systems that display information in map form

Given the four types of artificial intelligence systems . . .

- Expert systems
- Neural networks
- Genetic algorithms
- Fuzzy logic

Given the four types of intelligent agents . . .

- Buyer agents or shopping bots
- User or personal agents
- Monitoring-and-surveillance agents
- Data-mining agents

Choose the appropriate decision support for the following situations. There may be more than one type of decision support for some of the situations.

Situation	Type(s) of Support	Reason
A. Determine why customer satisfaction levels have dropped.		
B. Fill out tax forms.		
C. Decide where to put a new shopping center.		
D. Determine which of many of thousands of insurance claims are fraudulent.		
E. Find the shortest route to visit the capital cities of all the states in the contiguous United States.		
F. Determine what qualities you need to be accepted as a contestant on a TV game show.		
G. Implement a light-switch system that makes the lighting bright (for studying) and low (for relaxing and chatting).		

2. Be a Human Genetic Algorithm That Puts Nails in Boxes

This project involves packaging nails so that you make the most profit possible (it's a profit-maximizing problem). Say you have 5 types of nails and can make as many as you need of each. These are: 4", 3.5", 3", 2.5", 2", and 1.5". The cost of making each type of nail depends on how big it is. Nail costs and selling prices are listed in the table below along with the weights. The nails will be sold in boxes of up to 30 nails. There must be no more than 10, but no less than 5, of each of three types of nails in each box. The nails in each box should weigh no more than 20 ounces. You're looking for the combination with the highest profit using a trial and error method.

A spreadsheet would be helpful in completing this project. You'll most likely find that you identify some promising paths to follow right away and will concentrate on those to find the best one, which is what a genetic algorithm does.

Nail	Weight	Cost	Selling Price
4"	1 oz	4 cents	8 cents
3.5"	0.85 oz	3.5 cents	6 cents
3"	0.7 oz	3 cents	5 cents
2.5"	0.5 oz	2.5 cents	4 cents
2"	0.25 oz	2 cents	3 cents
1.5"	0.1 oz	1.5 cents	2 cents

3. Extend the Traffic Expert System

One of the big limitations of expert systems is that they can't deal with situations that are not listed in the rules. Demonstrate this by making a list of 10 situations possible at traffic light intersections that the expert system in the text (see p. 465) does not consider. Take two of those and add new rules to accommodate them. As an example, the table below illustrates how the rules would change to accommodate a pedestrian in the intersection.

Rule	Question	Yes	No
1	Pedestrian in front of you?	Go to Rule 5	Go to Rule 2
2	Is the light green?	Drive through	Go to Rule 3
3	Is the light red?	Go to Rule 6	Go to Rule 4
4	Is the light likely to change to red?	Go to Rule 6	Drive through
5	Can you stop in time?	Stop	Swerve to miss pedestrian
6	Can you stop in time?	Stop	Go to Rule 7
7	Is traffic approaching?	Go to Rule 8	Drive through
8	Can you swerve to miss traffic?	Swerve	Prepare to crash

e-commerce

1. Finding the Right Speech Recognition Software

Speech recognition software often incorporates artificial intelligence. It's not unusual to find a speech system that has expert system or neural network features. Following are a few Web sites that offer speech recognition software.

- KnowledgeStorm—www.knowledgestorm.com
- ScanSoft—www.scansoft.com
- Voice Recognition Systems—www.talktoyourcomputer.com

As you consider these and other speech recognition software sites answer the following questions.

a. What are five different application areas for which speech recognition software is available?

b. What special hardware do you need to be able to use speech recognition software?

2. Using Intelligent Agents

Intelligent agents can be Web-based software tools that efficiently find information for you. They can perform repetitive tasks and even do large Web searches while you sleep. The potential of intelligent agents is enormous. Many researchers are developing new types of intelligent agent software to help you work more efficiently on the Web.

But, to be truly "intelligent" systems, intelligent agents must be able to adapt by themselves and be able to act on their own. Furthermore, they must be "sociable" with other intelligent agents. When the time comes that we have such truly intelligent agents, they'll be able to negotiate with each other, so that your shopping bot can make a deal to buy something for you from an intelligent agent at the merchant's site. This sociability feature of intelligent agents is a hot topic in current research. Some artificial intelligence scientists even believe that the only way to create a very sophisticated artificial intelligence system is to have numerous one-purpose agents working together.

There are many sites on the Web devoted to intelligent agents. We've provided two, but you should be able to find many more.

- BotSpot Home Page—www.botspot.com
- UMBC Agent Web—agents.umbc.edu

As you view these sites, answer the following questions:

a. Name five different application areas for which you found intelligent agents?

b. Were any of the intelligent agents available for free? If so, which ones and what do they do?

3. Shopping Bots

All you have to do for extensive comparison-shopping is to send a shopping bot in search of a better deal. Following are some shopping bot sites. Choose three items to search for: one music-related item, one clothing item, and one household item. Search for them with each site. Then answer the questions that follow for each site.

- Bottom Dollar—www.bottomdollar.com
- Yahoo Shopping—shopping.yahoo.com
- Pricing Central—www.pricingcentral.com

a. How many hits did you get at each site for each item?

b. Are tax, postage, and handling charges included in the quoted price?

c. Can you sort in order of price?

d. Does the shopping site specialize in a particular kind of item?

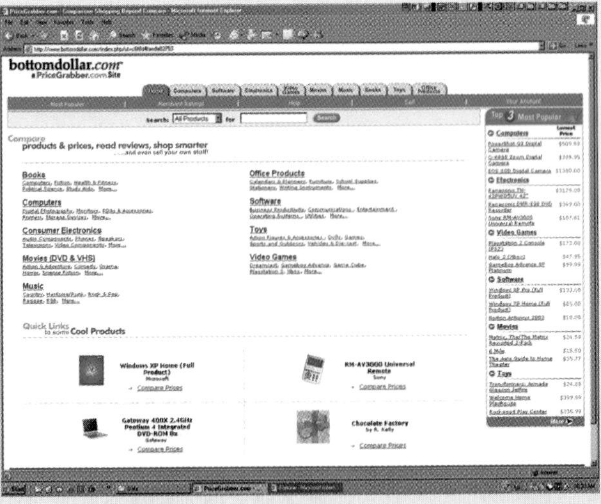

ethics, security & privacy

1. Carnivore and Magic Lantern

DCS-1000 is a sniffer program (see Chapter 9) developed by the FBI to covertly search for e-mails and other computer messages from those suspected of criminal acts. It used to be called Carnivore and can scan millions of e-mails per second. The FBI's computer connects to the suspect's ISP and is controlled and configured remotely by FBI agents. The system can monitor a suspect's e-mail headers and/or content as well as access to FTP and other Internet sites.

DCS-1000 has generated howls of protest from privacy advocates about the danger inherent in invading the privacy of law-abiding citizens. The FBI maintains that to deal with crime in the information age, it has to use the tools of the information age. Privacy advocates want the FBI to publish the DCS-1000 code, but the FBI says that if it were to publish the code, then those who wanted to could defeat it, which in turn would defeat its purpose.

In 2001, the FBI acknowledged an enhancement to DCS-1000 called Magic Lantern, which is key logger software. The FBI installs it by sending the target of an investigation an innocent-looking e-mail that secretly contains the key logger software. Magic Lantern then sends back information to the FBI detailing what the suspect is doing on his or her computer.

Some of the FBI's arguments for keeping DCS-1000 are that it

- Is necessary to fight crime, and its use is very restricted.
- Cannot be installed without the help of the target ISP and remains connected only for the duration of the court order.
- Doesn't look for key words or even search the subject lines of e-mails.
- Is used very sparingly—in the year 2000, it was applied only 16 times. It's used only for serious crimes and only after law enforcement can demonstrate to a judge that it's absolutely necessary.
- Does not look at everyone's e-mail in hopes of finding criminal activity—that would be highly illegal.
- Is necessary to fight foreign terrorists and espionage, dangers that the FBI considers to be the greatest potential cyber-threats to our national security.

Privacy advocates and other groups, while they recognize the FBI's need for surveillance of suspected criminals, don't believe that DCS-1000 has sufficient safeguards in place. Some of their arguments are as follows:

- No one outside the FBI knows exactly how the software works. This means that no one but the FBI can tell if it's actually doing what the court order says it is allowed to do.
- Any searches for specific e-mails mean that the addresses of all e-mail going in and out of an ISP must be scanned. This amounts to government surveillance of e-mail not covered by the court order.
- The chances of examining only a suspect's messages are remote since it's very difficult to capture and reassemble one person's messages when they flow in an information stream shared by many ISP customers.
- A third party could alter, forge, or misroute messages.
- The risk of criminals being able to intercept the system for their own ends is high since the system is operated remotely.

Answer the following questions:

a. Should the FBI be allowed to keep using DCS-1000?

b. Which arguments pro and con do you find convincing? Are there good ones on both sides? Which ones are compelling and which are flawed, and why?

c. Should the Magic Lantern enhancement be removed or does it make good law enforcement sense? Why or why not?

on the web

1. Data-Mining Software

Find three business data-mining tools. Compare them in terms of characteristics and price. Here are a few Web sites you could try:

- IBM's Intelligent Miner—www.4.ibm.com/software/data/iminer
- KD Nuggets—www.kdnuggets.com
- Smart Drill—www.smartdrill.com

2. Types of Decision Support

Go to a Web site such as *InformationWeek*'s at www.informationweek.com or www.techtv.com and look up articles on decision support systems. Classify the articles you find into the categories on the left-hand side of the table below and put the titles of the articles into the right-hand column.

Type of Article	Names
A. Data mining	
B. Financial applications	
C. Manufacturing applications	
D. Global information systems	

3. Bringing Machines to Life

AIBO is a robotic dog and was built by Sony as a toy. But, AIBO is not the only robot around. Honda has a "human companion" robot called ASIMO. On Honda's Web site you can view a Macromedia Flash presentation on ASIMO.

There are various other types of robots too. Hitachi has a vacuum cleaning robot, which is billed as the world's smallest robot. It travels around the room seeking and sucking up dirt from your floors.

Some robots are already available for purchasing and others are still in the prototype stage. You can find lots of information on the Web about robots that are currently available. Check out these or other Web sites for information.

- Honda—asimo.honda.com/inside_asimo.asp?bhcp=1
- 21st Century—www.21stcentury.co.uk/robotics
- Hitachi—www.hitachi.com

At these or other Web sites find five robots (not including AIBO) and answer the following questions.

a. What is the name of the robot?
b. What is the purpose of the robot?
c. Is the robot for sale and if so, how much does it cost?

4. Expert Systems

In the text we discussed rule-based expert systems. These are expert systems that go through lists of questions and use the answers to reach a solution. Not all expert systems are rule-based, however. Case-based reasoning is the basis of another type of expert system, which looks at prior similar situations to find one that matches the problem situation and from that comparison it reaches a conclusion. It works similarly to the way lawyers find previous cases similar enough to a current case to be called a precedent. Find some Web sites that discuss expert systems. Find three expert systems. What are the domains of the expert systems? Does the description say whether these expert systems are rule-based (like the ones discussed in the chapter) or use some other method of handling knowledge, such as case-based reasoning?

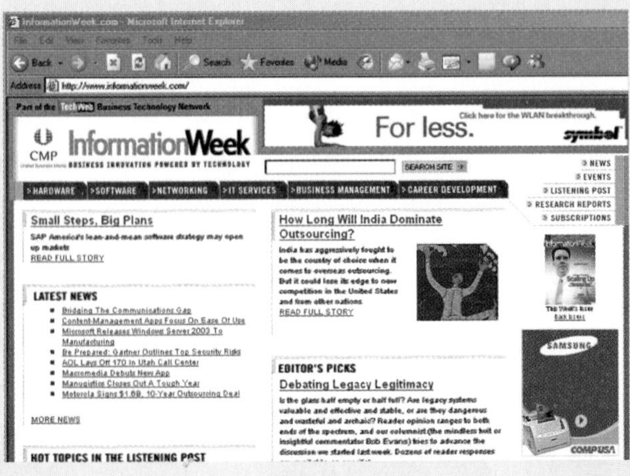

group activities

1. Determining What You Need to Tell a Neural Network

Each of the situations below would be well suited to the classification capabilities of neural networks. Your task is to identify (1) the input to the neural network that would be necessary in each case and also (2) any categories that the neural network would sort the output into.

a. When students apply for admission to a university, they will be admitted, rejected, admitted on probation, or admitted as continuing education students until they have sufficient prerequisites for admission. List 10 characteristics that could be used by the neural network to classify a prospective student and explain why each one is important.

b. An airline wants to decide whether to add flights to its schedule for a particular city. The criteria for the decision will be the comparison of this city to other similar locations. The airline wants to know whether they should have zero, one, or two flights per day to this city.

c. A grocery chain wants to determine which breakfast cereals to carry. List 10 items of input information the neural network would need. Explain why each is important. You should consider the cereal, the location of the store, and the customers.

2. Team Decision Making

Collaborative decision making is becoming an increasingly important part of business decision making. A collaboration system is software that is designed specifically to improve the performance of teams by supporting the sharing and flow of information (you read about such systems in Chapter 7). A collaboration system is not necessarily a computer-aided decision support system, but it is often used as such.

Two of the more popular peer-to-peer collaboration systems are Groove and NextPage. Do some research and write a two-page paper on peer-to-peer collaboration systems for business. Include a description of the evolution of peer-to-peer systems from illegal music sharing to an important business function. Your report should also contain at least two examples of how specific collaboration systems are used and by whom.

3. Deciding on Financing

In Figure 15.2, page 458, is an amortization table that we used to demonstrate the use of a spreadsheet as a decision support system. Recreate that spreadsheet and use it to compare the following house mortgage options.

- **Home Options:** Compare a $75,000 and a $100,000 home.
- **Financing Options:**
  - a. 20 percent down and an interest rate of
    - i. 6.25 percent for 15 years or
    - ii. 6.75 percent for 30 years
  - b. 10 percent down and an interest rate of
    - i. 7.00 percent for 15 years or
    - ii. 7.5 percent for 30 years
  - c. Nothing down and 2 points (i.e., 2 percent of the borrowed amount up front, which is nonrefundable and is added to the borrowed amount) with an interest rate of 9.75 percent for 30 years.

You usually pay closing costs when you buy a house. These charges have some fixed costs and some variable costs. Fixed costs include such things as an appraisal fee for confirming the value of the house, a fee for getting your credit report, hazard insurance, recording fees, a stamp, and various other charges. For the purposes of this assignment, say these fixed costs total $1,986.

Variable costs include items like 6 months of city property taxes (to support schools) of $0.75 per mil ($0.75 for every $1,000 of the price of the house) and perhaps lender's insurance of 0.5 percent of the loan. Use these figures for the variable part of the closing costs for each loan.

Make a table of your results for each of the two home options under the five financing options. For each of the 10 cases, show the closing costs, the monthly payment amount, the amount of interest over the life of the loan, and the total you'll pay for the house under each option.

life-long learning modules

Today's world—both academic and business—is certainly characterized as one of "life-long learning." Simply put, you can't stop learning. Even when you graduate from school and start that perfect job, you need to keep learning to compete effectively.

You must also be a life-long learner in your personal life. You need to stay up-to-date on world events, politics, and other such matters. Our world is changing fast and in so many ways that affect you.

Of course, as you already know from reading this textbook, technology is changing on a daily basis. That means the business world and your personal life are also changing because of new advances in technology. It's up to you to keep pace, in ways that are appropriate for your life and career.

In the following pages, you'll read brief introductions to our *Life-Long Learning Modules,* a comprehensive set of materials you'll find on the Web site that supports this text at www.mhhe.com/i-series. In these *Modules* on the Web, we provide more state-of-the-art information concerning the vast field of information technology.

These *Life-Long Learning Modules* will definitely help keep you current. The information provided in the *Modules* will enhance the material you've been reading. The practical reality of a textbook is that we are constrained in the number of pages we can write. After all, you don't want to buy a text (and carry it around) several thousand pages long. If you've benefited from the discussions in the text, keep on learning at our Web site.

Long after you've finished this class, you'll need to refresh your knowledge and keep on learning. We encourage you to revisit the Web-based *Life-Long Learning Modules.* They're free, full of valuable information, and always up to date.

Please visit us at www.mhhe.com/i-series.

How Do You Make Your Web Site Sizzle?

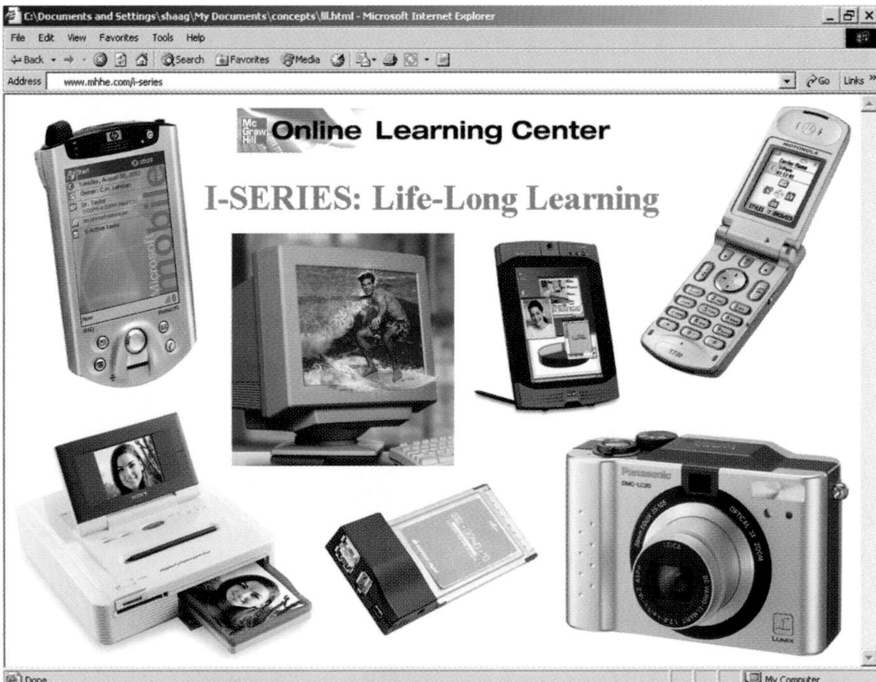

ENHANCED WEB DEVELOPMENT

You know how much the Web is now a part of your life. You can use the Web to find information, buy goods and services, download software, listen to music, watch videos, and play games with friends.

Every day people put more Web sites online. Almost everywhere you look someone has a Web address posted—whether it's on a billboard or a business card. You're probably one of them. After all, we designed some Web pages together in Chapter 8. And you can learn about Web design in Appendix B.

With all the Web sites out there, how can you make yours stand out from the rest? Answers range from the simple to the complex. You can redesign your Web site to make it easier for users to navigate. Or you can add some multimedia to make your Web site more interactive. Perhaps you'd like to learn a new Web programming language to add features to your Web site. Maybe you want to create electronic shopping carts to allow customers to buy things at your own e-commerce business.

In this *Life-Long Learning Module,* we'll show you how you can accomplish all of this and more. And we'll keep you informed of new Web technologies and how to use them on your Web site. Come join us at www.mhhe.com/i-series as we explore making Web sites sizzle.

module a://

Development Tools

Your choice of a Web development tool is an important one if you want to make your site sizzle. And you have many options to choose from. We'll explore many of those in this section including

HTML and WYSIWYG editors (Homesite, BBEdit, Dreamweaver, and FrontPage), image and photo editors (Photoshop, Fireworks, and the GIMP), and Web site management tools such as link checkers and site mapping software. We'll also show you how to get by on $0.00 a day with free and open source software solutions. You can actually plan, develop, and host Web sites using free tools.

Design Guides

Anyone can build a Web site, but doing it effectively is another story. In Web site design you need to define the structure and layout of your Web site before creating it. A well-designed Web site is easy to use, encouraging your readers to visit again and again.

Think of it like creating an advertising flyer. You can easily create a flyer and include all the necessary information. What's key is doing it in such a way that people will not only know exactly what you're selling but also want to buy your products or services.

As you design your site, you should think about important items such as image size and placement, the use of color, and user navigation. We'll discuss these issues and much more at www.mhhe.com/i-series.

Web Scripting and Programming

Web scripting and programming are all about creating interactivity and functionality in your Web site. Interactivity is key to retaining readers. People want to find information on your Web site, but they want to feel that they're in control. Making sure your Web site responds to users' actions will make for a great site.

You should also create a functional Web site. Make it easy for users to find what they need with the smallest amount of effort. You can use a variety of Web scripting and programming languages to make this happen.

Come with us as we show you resources and examples of various languages, such as: XHTML, XML, CSS, WML, JavaScript, VBScript, CGI scripts, ASP, PHP, and Java. We'll also show you scripting and programming tools you can use to write code in these languages.

Multimedia

The technology world is now multimedia. Almost all presentations of information include some combination of text, art, video, sound, and animation. Your Web site can benefit from the use of certain types of multimedia elements. These may include animated GIFs, audio, streaming media, and perhaps even virtual reality. In this section we'll explore these as well as multimedia development tools such as Flash and Shockwave.

Behind the Scenes

As you increase your use of multimedia and other interactive elements, you need to begin to appreciate what goes on behind the scenes. That is, if you understand the technical infrastructure, you can more readily create Web sites that include multimedia and interactivity. Important "behind the scenes" topics include Web servers (and server farms), Web databases, Web security, and Web site architectures. We'll discuss what's behind your Web page at www.mhhe.com/i-series.

Why Do Things Go Wrong?

module b://

CARE AND FEEDING OF YOUR COMPUTER

Your computer is your thinking and working machine, and it needs maintenance and care just like your car. Some of it you do yourself, like filling the gas tank, checking tire pressure, and maybe changing the oil. Some of the upgrading and maintenance tasks that your computer needs you can also take care of yourself. It mostly depends on how technically oriented you are, how much you know about computers, and how much experience you have.

Just as you probably pump your own gas, you'll need to manage your computer storage space yourself, dividing the space into folders and keeping files orderly (as we discussed in Chapter 4). You'll also have to swap out ink or toner cartridges for your printer when the need arises.

Beyond these routine tasks, many people prefer to handle computer maintenance the way most of us take care of car maintenance—get professional help. Perhaps you can change the oil and maybe a tire, but after that you might like a mechanic to take over. Similarly, when you want more memory or a CD-RW drive installed, you might want to bring your computer to a service center or get help from someone who knows more than you do.

At www.mhhe.com/i-series, we'll discuss the care and feeding of your computer and help you decide what you want to do yourself and when you may want professional assistance.

Upgrading Your Hardware and Software

Upgrading your computer can run the gamut from replacing your CPU and motherboard and adding more memory to adding a DVD drive or replacing a mouse with a trackball. If it's a new CPU or more memory you want, you'll have to be sure you have the right kind. You may want a better video card so that gaming or video is faster and of better quality. From time to time, you'll also need to upgrade your software, both application and system. Let us help you decide what you can do yourself and for which tasks you might want professional help.

Troubleshooting

Since a computer is such a sophisticated and complicated machine, there are numerous things that can go wrong with it. Each component has its own special list. For example, if your printer doesn't work, it could be that it's not plugged securely into the wall outlet or into the back of the system unit. It could be that you forgot to install the printer driver or any one of a dozen other things. At www.mhhe.com/i-series, we'll discuss some troubleshooting issues such as common warning beeps, BIOS problems, modem problems, and many more.

Operating System Considerations

Your operating system handles many "behind the scenes" tasks as you use your application software. But just like any other part of your computer, you need to care for and maintain your operating system. For example, you may need to install a new device driver manually when adding new hardware, although if you can plug the device into a USB or Firewire port, you won't usually have to. You may also want to change your screen saver. Your operating system can also help you undelete files, essentially allowing you to retrieve them after performing a delete. Although your operating system isn't a personal productivity tool in the strictest sense, it can in fact help you be more productive as you use your application software. We'll show you many features of your operating system at www.mhhe.com/i-series.

General Maintenance

You can perform many general maintenance tasks yourself. And we would encourage you to do so. If you take your keyboard to a computer repair shop to have it cleaned, you'll probably be charged more than the cost of a new keyboard. On the other hand, you can do it yourself in a matter of minutes with a few simple instructions. In this section we'll explore many general maintenance activities you can perform yourself including cleaning your mouse and monitor, defragmenting your hard disk, and changing printer cartridges. All of these are simple tasks, and we want to help you perform them correctly.

Protection

Finally, you definitely need to protect your computer not only against viruses but also against the harmful effects of weather and even magnets. In this section, we'll discuss the best ways to protect your computer using UPSs, firewalls, and anti-virus software.

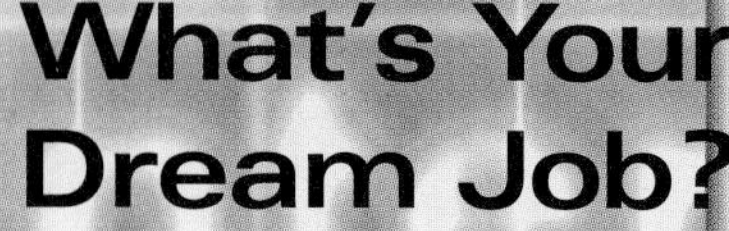

What's Your Dream Job?

module

C://

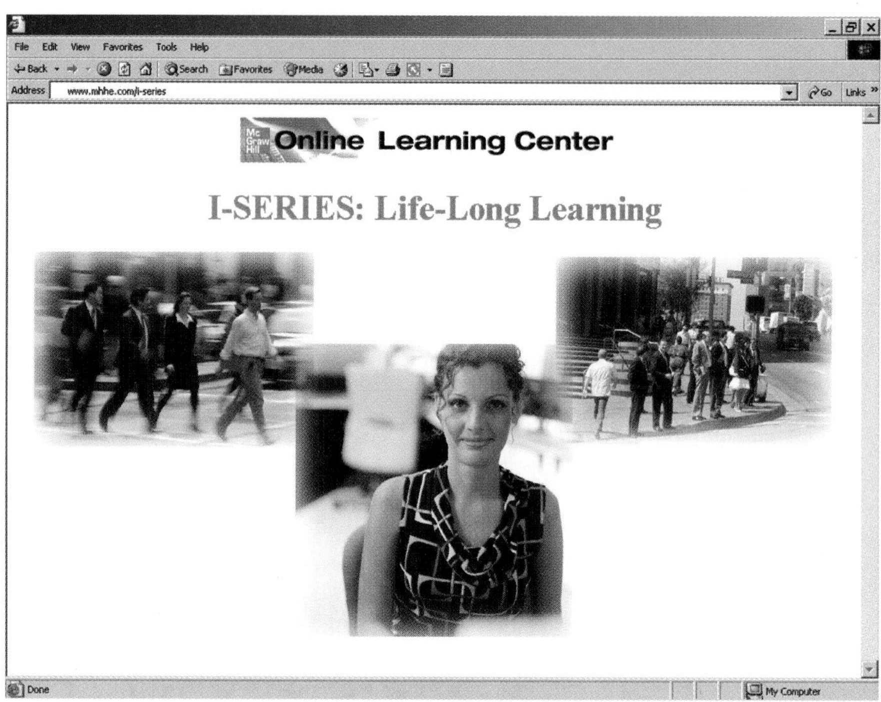

CAREERS IN INFORMATION TECHNOLOGY

The field of information technology can be a great place to work, and the opportunities you have are enormous. Even in today's sluggish economy, IT job opportunities are still growing at a steady pace.

To prepare for a career in information technology you definitely must *prepare.* You need to carefully select your classes and devote your time and energies to making the best grades. You also need to be aware of what jobs are available, what skills and certifications you need, and how you can best position yourself to land your IT dream job.

C careers

We've provided you with a wealth of information in this text. In each and every chapter, you can find one or more "Careers" icons in the side margin that we've placed next to items that address some great careers in technology.

In this *Life-Long Learning Module,* we'll discuss more career opportunities in the field of information technology and what you can do to prepare for them. Today IT specialists are among the highest paid people in any occupation. See how and why at www.mhhe.com/i-series.

Job Titles, Descriptions, and Salaries

The technology field holds a variety of job opportunities for you, but sometimes it's difficult to distinguish among various types of jobs. You might wonder what the difference is between a systems administrator and a systems developer. The field is so new that some job titles seem to overlap or perhaps not make sense.

But the jobs are waiting for you if you know what to look for. Each has its own set of responsibilities and comes with a big paycheck. We'll help you determine what types of jobs are available and which of them interest you.

The Skills You Need

To prepare for an IT job, you need two sets of skills—technology skills and people skills. You can learn the technology skills in classes like the one you're taking. The people skills may be more difficult to acquire.

Technology specialists do need people skills. If you can't communicate with your customers, no one will visit your Web site to buy your products. Or your boss will soon learn that you can't work in a project team. You need a solid people–skill set, and that includes understanding what your colleagues in finance, accounting, marketing, human resource management, production and logistics, and other areas do. We'll explore both technology and people skills at www.mhhe.com/i-series.

Searching for Jobs

The Web is a great place to look for employment. Thousands of Web sites offer searchable databases of job opportunities and internships. Knowing which sites to visit and how to build an electronic and scannable resume are important. In this section, we'll guide you to the better job database sites and offer you points for building an effective scannable and electronic resume.

Learning beyond Your Education

Once you graduate, you can't stop learning. The advancements in technology aren't going to suddenly halt just because you have a diploma in hand. If technology continues to change, then you must be prepared to learn and change with it.

Many IT professionals consistently attend training sessions and conferences. Others seek industry certifications in specific technologies. That's one of the key reasons why we developed these *Life-Long Learning Modules*. At www.mhhe.com/i-series, we'll explore some of the fascinating ways you can stay current with technology.

Thoughts from the Authors

Let it not be said that we (as authors) don't care about you as a student and a person. We do receive royalties for writing this book, but our true love is education. Among the three of us, we have almost 50 years of dedicated teaching experience. Please let us offer you some of our thoughts as you prepare for your future. And if you have some of your own thoughts that you feel would benefit other students, please send us an e-mail at i-series@mcgraw-hill.com. We'd love to hear from you and we'll post your thoughts along with ours.

What's Happening in Your World Today?

NEW TECHNOLOGIES IMPACTING YOUR LIFE

This is a great time to be involved with information technology. You are on the cusp of some fantastic IT breakthroughs that will change the very way we live our lives. IT has improved so many aspects of our lives and its impact is growing every day.

Technology is giving us hope that people without sight will be able to see. Trials are underway which involve connecting a computer directly into the visual cortex of the brain. Researchers are developing exoskeletons that will allow people to walk who are now confined to wheelchairs. Nanotechnologies too small to see will fight diseases and fix broken bones. And new biological fuel cells will soon replace rechargeable batteries. You might never run out of power again.

Less dramatically, wireless Web appliances will let you wander around your house and have Internet access from anywhere—even the shower. A "SmartBox" will sit outside your door ready to receive packages for you from a delivery service like FedEx. It will contact you by e-mail or pager when the package arrives. You'll be able to get a small portable lie detector that uses speech recognition software to sense whether someone is lying to you. If it's hot outside and you want moist towels to cool your brow, we've got computerized dispensers that fit the bill. Most likely, you'll also wear your computer instead of leaving it at home or lugging it in your backpack. You'll use wearable technology to process information on your wristwatch display powered with computer chips in your jacket. This isn't science fiction—all of these products have already been developed.

In this *Life-Long Learning Module,* we'll explore many new technologies in your life today. Join us at www.mhhe.com/i-series.

module d://

Portable and Wearable Computing

Bigger is not always better with technology. As CPUs become more powerful yet smaller, developers are finding ways to help you access the information you need. Want to check e-mail or surf the Web as you lounge by a pool? You don't need a computer anymore. Perhaps you'll use your cell phone or PDA. And soon those may seem cumbersome compared to a portable computer you'll wear on your wrist or access through your eyeglasses. In this section we'll explore what's out there and what's coming.

Internet and Household Appliances

Want to check your e-mail in the kitchen, but you'd rather not set a desktop computer by the sink? You could use a specially designed waterproof device to check e-mail and surf the Web. Such Internet appliances are quickly replacing a second, or sometimes a first, computer in households. And typical household appliances are becoming smarter too. Who ever thought there'd be a day when your refrigerator could remind you by e-mail to buy milk? In this section we'll explore Internet and intelligent home appliances such as smart lock boxes, electronic photo frames and paintings, Web stations, security systems, and much more.

Entertainment Technology

You already know you can use your computer for more than work. You can play video games, leisurely surf the Web for relaxation, listen to music, and watch movies. You can also find other computer-based entertainment technologies such as robotic toys, Playstations, Xboxes, game cubes, and massive multi-user Internet games. We'll discuss these as well as special types of equipment you may need, including game controllers, sound cards, audio systems, and video displays. Come see how you can enjoy entertainment technologies at www.mhhe.com/i-series.

Virtual Reality and Perceptual User Interfaces

Technology is also changing with respect to how we physiologically interface with it. In a few years, you may no longer use a mouse or keyboard to interact with your computer. Instead, you'll use speech recognition, eye-tracking devices, and haptic feedback. Using eye-tracking devices, you'll simply focus on a button and the software will initiate that function. You'll interact with programs simply by talking to them. And, of course, virtual reality will become common (and inexpensive). Come explore these new advancements and many others.

Life-Enhancing and Life-Saving Technologies

Finally, we're beginning to see new life-enhancing and life-saving technologies in many areas of our lives. These new technologies are exploding in the medical field. They include camera pills that you swallow and telemedicine applications such as remote triage virtual reality. Biochips will navigate your body to repair or enhance your muscles, bones, and other tissues. Other new technologies, such as smart highways, will make transportation safer in the automotive industry. Here's your chance to learn more about the latest and greatest life-enhancing and life-saving technologies. You can find them at www.mhhe.com/i-series.

Do You Have a Crystal Ball?

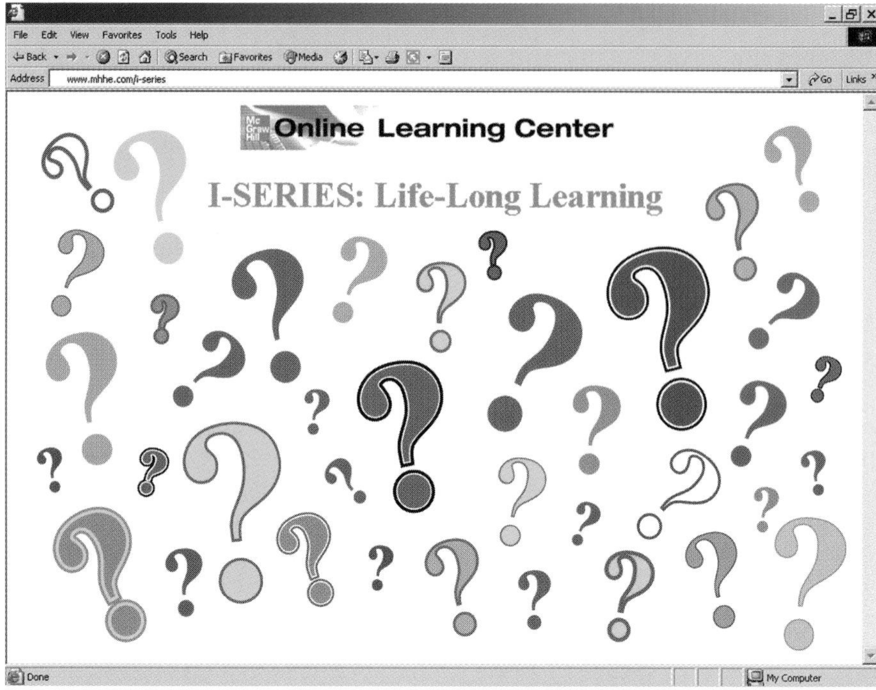

COMPUTERS IN YOUR LIFE TOMORROW

Well, if you do have a crystal ball, we'd certainly like to borrow it sometime. The simple fact of the matter is that no one can predict the future with any real consistency, especially with respect to technology.

However, we can make some statements regarding the future of technology in general. For example, we know that future technologies will begin to incorporate more of your senses (speech for example), just as we discussed in Chapter 11. We also know that complete and high-speed wireless communications are just around the corner. But how those will come about and exactly when is a mystery.

This *Life-Long Learning Module* will take you on a whirlwind tour of what we think the future holds for technology. More important, we want to alert you to how the future of technology will impact your personal life, business life in general, and your own career.

We call these *Life-Long Learning Modules* because we want you to visit them long after you've completed your computer class. The content in this particular module will change frequently and perhaps dramatically. Bookmark it (www.mhhe.com/i-series) and drop back in for a visit from time to time.

module e://

Big Today—How Small Tomorrow?

Technology today is still relatively "big." Although you may think that a PDA that weighs less than a pound is small, tomorrow's PDAs will be about the size of a credit card and weigh about the same amount. Sound too good to be true? Not so—technology tomorrow may become so small that you won't even be aware of its existence. What's even more important is that those "hard to see" computers will process billions and billions of instructions in a single second.

Here Today—Nowhere Tomorrow?

We still live in a world of physical boundaries—homes, states, and even countries. Of course, technologies such as the Web have helped eliminate many of those boundaries. But we have a long way to go. Imagine living in a world where location doesn't matter, a world in which you can run the world's largest organization from your garage or in a wheat field in Kansas. Imagine, too, a world where language limitations are no longer an issue—it's coming sooner than you think. Come with us and explore a "locationless" tomorrow.

Internet Time Today—When Tomorrow?

Just like physical boundaries, we also operate in a world constrained by time. But soon time will also become irrelevant. It's not that we'll operate 24 hours a day—it's that we'll operate without regard for the day of the week, the month of the year, or perhaps even the year. In the virtual world, there are no physical limitations or boundaries—time is one such limitation that will not be present (past or future) in a virtual world. Come with us and explore a "timeless" tomorrow.

See Technology Today—"Transparent Technology" Tomorrow?

By "transparent technology" we mean technology that becomes such an integral and everyday part of our lives that we won't even acknowledge its existence. Think about electricity. Every organization needs it to survive, but how many organizations include electricity in their strategic plan? None, because electricity is transparent in this sense. It's "guaranteed." At www.mhhe.com/i-series, let's explore how technology can become transparent in the business world.

Technology Focus Today—What Tomorrow?

Today, technology is such a hot buzzword that everyone seems to be focusing more on it than on the most important issue—how to use technology for the betterment of people, society, and the business world. Let's take a glimpse into the future and see what it looks like when technology becomes transparent from a societal point of view.

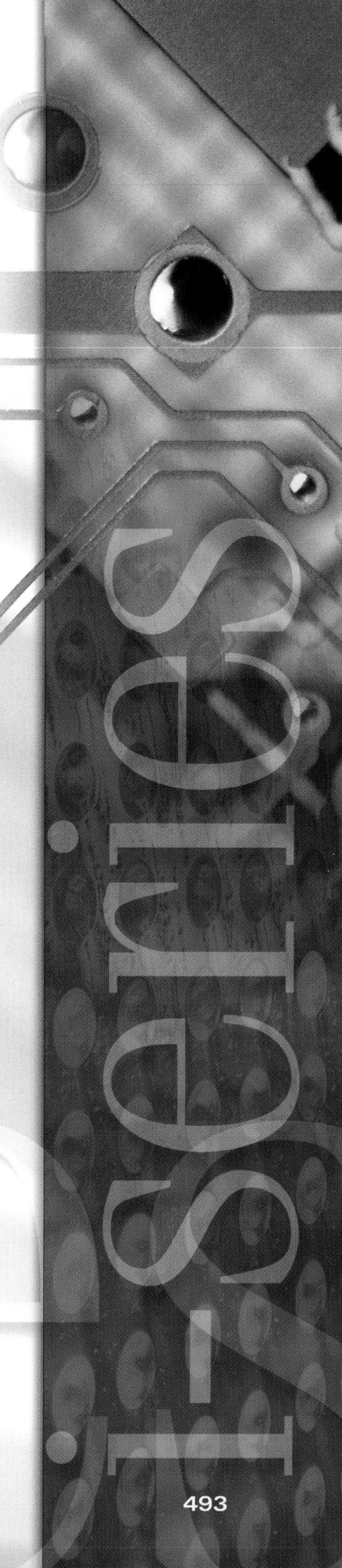

appendix a

The History of Computing

did you know?

Computers—especially personal computers—as you know and use them today have been around only since the mid-1970s. Businesses have used large mainframe computers on a wide-scale basis since the 1950s. But people have had other devices that aid in mathematical processes such as addition and multiplication for almost a thousand years.

moore's *Law states that computing power doubles every 18 months but costs half as much.*

jacquard *Loom in 1801, using an idea based on a weaving loom for creating fabrics, developed one of the first notions of working with information in a binary format.*

ibm *entered the personal computer market in 1981. By the end of 1982, IBM had sold over 835,000 IBM PCs.*

Student Learning Outcomes

After reading this appendix, you should be able to:

1. Describe some of the early "manual automation" computing devices.
2. List the key people and their developments during the first generation of computing technologies.
3. Describe some of the advances that came with the second generation of computing technologies.
4. Define how the integrated circuit enabled both the third and fourth generations of computing technologies.
5. Offer some insights concerning what the fifth generation of computing technologies will hold.
6. Provide a brief historical perspective of the development of personal computers.

A.1 WHEN IT ALL BEGAN

For centuries, people have sought ways to "automate" common mathematical processes such as addition, subtraction, multiplication, and division. Those four core functions support everything we do mathematically.

FIGURE A.1

The abacus is one of the first known devices that people used to help with arithmetic.

As early as 1200 the Chinese were using a device called an ***abacus,*** consisting of rows of beads mounted within a rectangular hand-held device (see Figure A.1). You can definitely argue that the abacus did indeed automate addition, subtraction, multiplication, and division, although it was "manual automation."

In the early 1600s, John Napier (a Scottish mathematician) invented logarithms and a device called Napier's Bones. ***Napier's Bones,*** partially constructed of animal bones, automated multiplication tables by sequencing a series of strips of bones on several different rods (see Figure A.2). In 1621, William Oughtred (an English mathematician) used Napier's logarithms to invent the first slide rule. ***Slide rules*** helped people work with logarithms and perform mathematical operations by "sliding" an interior strip of wood between two stationary strips of wood (Figure A.2).

The abacus, Napier's Bones, and slide rules involved "manual" automation in that the user was responsible for manipulating the instrument's various parts and interpreting the result. ***Mechanical calculators,*** however, the next technological advancement, could autonomously calcu-

FIGURE A.2

Napier's Bones and the slide rule worked on the basis of logarithms to produce mathematical results.

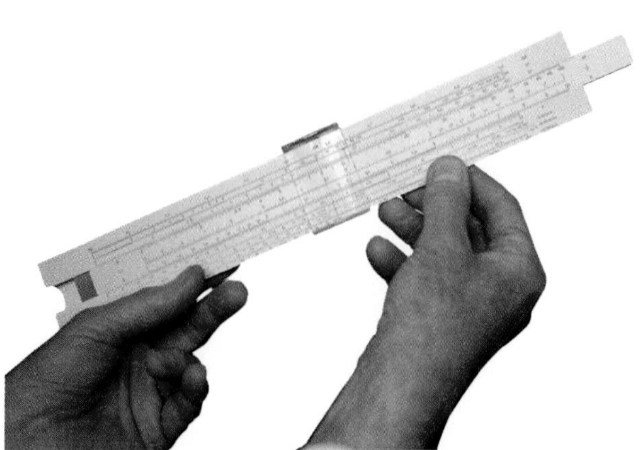

late algorithms once you entered the appropriate information. Notable people and devices in the history of mechanical calculators include:

- **Wilhelm Schickard**—in 1623 developed ***Schickard's Calculator,*** which used a series of interlocking gears each with 10 spokes representing a digit.
- **Blaise Pascal**—in 1642 developed the ***Pascaline,*** which could perform addition, subtraction, multiplication, and division.
- ***deColmar's Arithmometer***—developed in 1820, it was the first mass-produced mechanical calculator.

FIGURE A.3

Charles Babbage's Analytical Engine was the first device to embody such concepts as memory, programming capabilities, and stored data on punched cards.

In 1822 the world caught its first glimpse of a proposed device that worked on a power basis other than pulling gears and levers (as was required by mechanical calculators). The ***Difference Engine,*** developed by **Charles Babbage** in 1822, used steam power to crunch numbers. Babbage, however, never fully completed the Difference Engine before moving on in 1834 to the ***Analytical Engine,*** a general-purpose calculating device that embodied such concepts as memory, programming capabilities, and stored data on punched cards (see Figure A.3). According to many, Babbage's Analytical Engine is the precursor to the modern generations of computing technology.

Using many of Babbage's concepts including punched cards, in the early 1890s **Herman Hollerith** built the ***Hollerith Tabulating Machine,*** which recorded census information for the U.S. government by punching holes into punched cards which could then be read and tabulated by a device consisting of long rods with needles on the end. As a needle passed over a hole in a punched card, it fell through and initiated an action that would capture the information for tabulating. Hollerith's company that produced his tabulating machine became **International Business Machines,** or **IBM,** in 1924.

A.2 FIRST-GENERATION COMPUTING

In the 1930s and 1940s much research was undertaken to develop an electronic computer as opposed to the older mechanical devices that operated on gears and so on. From this research was born the idea of storing information in digital fashion, or as a discrete series of 0s and 1s. The electronic basis for these first-generation computers was the ***vacuum tube*** (see Figure A.4). It is at this point that many computer historians diverge on who was the principal founder of first-generation computers. We'll not debate that topic here but rather alert you to some of the many people instrumental in developing first-generation computers and the characteristics of those computers.

FIGURE A.4

Vacuum tubes were the basis for first-generation computing technologies.

- ***Atanasoff-Berry Computer (ABC)***—an electronic computer developed by **John Atanasoff** and **Clifford Berry** (a graduate student) at Iowa State University during the late 1930s, the ABC was the first electronic computer to work with binary information and is considered by many to be the first real electronic digital computer.
- ***MARK I***—the first electromechanical computer, the MARK I was developed by Harvard University professor **Howard Aiken** in 1944 with the assistance of IBM. It was 51 feet long and 8 feet high.
- ***COLOSSUS***—an electronic device developed in World War II by the Allied forces, COLOSSUS was able to decipher the codes of the German ENIGMA machine. ***ENIGMA*** encoded messages for transmission in such a way that the Allied forces could not, by hand, decipher them. For an interesting presentation of this historical era, you might want to watch the movie *U571*.

FIGURE A.5

The ENIAC weighed 30 tons and was capable of performing 5,000 additions per second.

- ***ENIAC***—the Electronic Numerical Integrator and Calculator (ENIAC) was developed by a team of U.S. scientists in 1943 headed by **John Mauchly** and **J. Prespert Eckert** to calculate trajectory tables for the U.S. Army (see Figure A.5). The ENIAC was over 100 feet long and 10 feet high, weighed 30 tons, and contained over 18,000 vacuum tubes. It could perform an amazing (at the time) 5,000 additions per second.
- ***UNIVAC***—considered the first commercially available electronic computer, the UNIVAC was completed in 1951 by an Eckert and Mauchly joint-venture company. It was later acquired by **Remington Rand.** The UNIVAC was only 15 feet long, 8 feet high, and 9 feet wide. It could perform 2.25 million instruction cycles per second with a RAM capacity of 12,000 characters. Your personal computer today probably has a RAM capacity approaching 1 billion characters of storage.

As you might guess, these first-generation computers suffered because of their size, the amount of heat they generated, and the electricity it took to run them. In some cities, the lights would flicker and dim when one of these early generation computers was turned on.

A.3 SECOND-GENERATION COMPUTING

The second generation of computing began in the late 1940s and lasted through the early 1960s. Second-generation computers worked on the basis of **transistors.** IBM is credited with inventing the first transistor in 1947. Transistors were much smaller than vacuum tubes, produced much less heat, and required much less electricity.

Accompanying the smaller and more powerful second-generation computers came many other inventions. The **high-level programming languages** such as COBOL, which you read about in Chapter 13, were developed during this second generation of computing. A few other notable inventions during the second generation are listed at the top of the next page.

- ***Electronic Recording Machine Accounting (ERMA)***—developed in 1959 by **General Electric,** ERMA was the first technology that could read special characters (see Figure A.6). Banks quickly adopted the use of ERMA to process their growing volume of checks. You could say that ERMA was the foundation (very early) for electronic commerce.
- **American Standard Code for Information Interchange (ASCII)**—ASCII, developed in 1963, was the first important computer industry standard. We still use ASCII today as the standard for representing binary information on personal computers.
- **Compatible computers**—in 1964, IBM introduced a line of "compatible" computers which allowed you to use software and peripheral devices that were not designed for a specific machine. This is what enables you today to take advantage of such concepts as **plug and play** and **hot swap.**

FIGURE A.6

ERMA was the first device to allow organizations such as banks to read special characters.

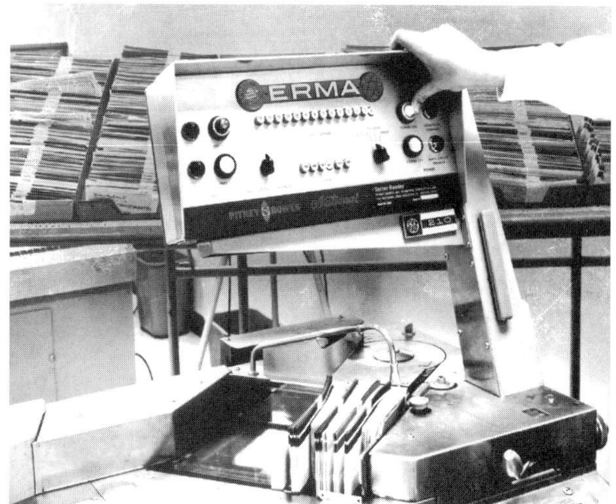

A.4 THIRD-GENERATION COMPUTING

The third generation of computers comprises the early 1960s through the mid-1970s. As with the previous generations of computing technology, the third generation was characterized by another new operating basis—this time, the integrated circuit.

An ***integrated circuit*** incorporates many transistors and electronic circuits on a single wafer or chip. During the third generation, computers became increasingly smaller, faster, and more powerful. In 1965, **Digital Equipment Corporation (DEC)** introduced the first commercially available minicomputer, called the **DEC PDP-8.**

The third generation of computing also ushered in the concept and realization of a network, or collection of connected computers. Standards were quickly developed so networked computers could communicate with each other. As you might guess, it was during this period that the Internet began.

Throughout this third generation of computing, scientists and researchers worked hard to develop integrated circuits with higher capacities. The early integrated circuits could hold 10 to 20 transistors on a chip and were referred to as **small-scale integration (SSI). Medium-scale integration (MSI)** followed not long after and could hold between 20 and 200 transistors on a chip. Finally, **large-scale integration (LSI)** became a reality with up to 5,000 transistors on a chip.

At that point, we stepped into the next generation of computing based on very-large-scale integration.

A.5 FOURTH-GENERATION COMPUTING

The fourth generation of computing began in the mid-1970s and is still with us today (although we are making progress toward the fifth generation). The fourth generation of technology is based on **very-large-scale integration (VLSI)** or what we commonly know as the **microprocessor.**

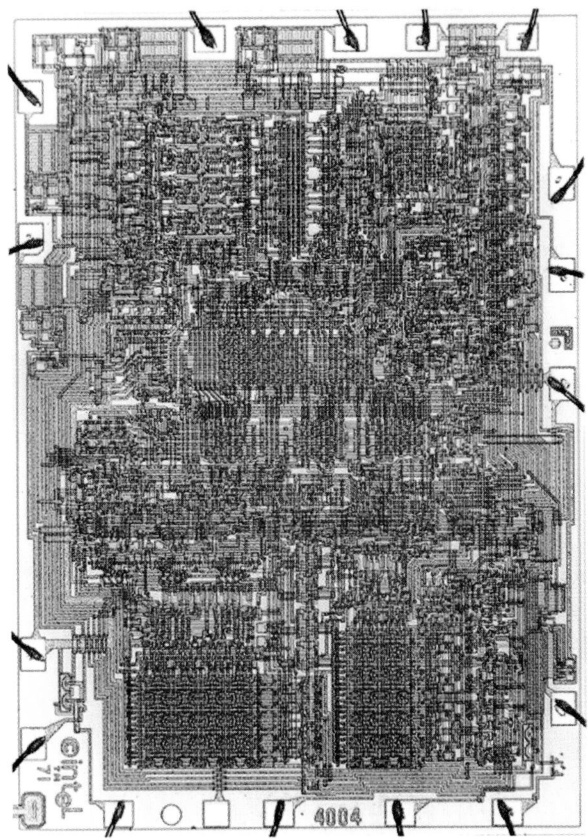

FIGURE A.7

The Intel 4004 was the first general-purpose microprocessor.

Ted Hoff developed the first general-purpose microprocessor, called the **Intel 4004** (see Figure A.7). The Intel 4004 was essentially a complete CPU (with both the control unit and the arithmetic logic unit) and consisted of 2,200 transistors capable of performing 60,000 instructions per second.

The advancements in this generation were simply phenomenal. In 1974, Motorola developed its first microprocessor called the **Motorola 6800.** A few months later, the **MOS 6502** microprocessor chip was developed and became the first used in the Apple II and the Commodore personal computers. So, the microprocessor ushered in the generation of personal computing technologies.

As this generation is dominated by personal computing technologies, we'll talk about those in an upcoming section.

A.6 FIFTH-GENERATION COMPUTING

This is what we are now heading into. It's worth briefly mentioning the next, oncoming generation of computing technologies. No one really knows how or when we'll fully embrace these new techologies. Two of them are especially significant.

The first is ***artificial intelligence (AI),*** the science of making machines imitate human thinking and behavior. We are in the very early stages of AI, making rudimentary advancements in the hope of helping computers think like people. We have a long way to go in the area of artificial intelligence. You can read more about current AI in Chapter 15.

Perhaps one of the greatest changes that we will see in the fifth generation of computing is the development of membrane-based technologies. ***Membrane-based technologies*** store and manipulate information within living tissue cells. The concept is quite simple—all you have to do is control a cell at the molecular level to the extent that it stores a 1 or a 0. The implementation of this, however, is extremely difficult.

If we can achieve the necessary sophistication in membrane-based technologies, you may be able to store information in your skin or other tissue. This, of course, will have far-reaching and unimaginable consequences, both good and bad.

A.7 PERSONAL COMPUTER HISTORY

The original personal computers of the 1970s were not fully assembled, commercially available units, but rather "kits" that computer hobbyists built and put together. The first was the **Mark-8,** developed by **Jonathan Titus** and featured in the July 1974 issue of *Popular Mechanics.*

The first commercially available personal computer (PC) was the **MITS Altair,** which was released in 1975 by **Ed Roberts** and **Micro Instrument and Telemetry Systems (MITS).** The Altair was sold as a kit for $395. It came with 256 bytes of RAM memory (256 bytes, not 256K or 256 thousand bytes). It had no keyboard, no monitor, and no permanent storage device.

In 1977, **Steve Jobs** and **Steve Wozniak,** founders of the **Apple Computer Corporation,** released the **Apple I.** It came with 4K of RAM and sold for about $700. Other companies quickly followed in releasing PCs, including **Atari, Radio Shack,** and **Commodore.** Some PCs came fully assembled, but others came as kits requiring you to assemble them (including screwing in the motherboard, etc.).

In 1981, **IBM** entered the PC market with its **IBM PC 5150,** which quickly became the top-selling PC (see Figure A.8). It used the Intel 8088 microprocessor with a speed of 4.77 MHz. It also came equipped with a single-sided 160KB floppy disk drive. It wasn't until IBM released its **IBM PC XT** a short time later that the first PC came with a hard disk. IBM'S PC XT hard disk had a capacity of 10 megabytes (roughly equivalent to 7 floppy disks of today).

FIGURE A.8

IBM's first personal computer was the IBM PC 5150.

From there, the plot of the story becomes fast, furious, and often confusing. With IBM as the leader, other manufacturers began to develop IBM compatibles or IBM clones. These would eventually spell doom for IBM in the PC market. **Microsoft** (a company you may have heard of) developed the first operating system for the IBM PC. Microsoft went on to gain dominance in the PC operating system and personal productivity software markets.

For a long time, Apple and IBM aggressively fought each other for control of the PC market. IBM eventually won out, although Apple still has a strong presence, and then IBM lost out to the compatibles and clones.

Today, you can buy PDAs that are much faster than the original PCs of the 1970s and 1980s. It wasn't until the mid-1970s that personal computers came with a graphical user interface (GUI) and a mouse. Today, you can set up a home network of computers in about an hour. That wasn't even thought possible without considerable expense and expertise in the early 1990s.

And, of course, you can spend an unbelievable amount of time surfing the Web—for some, too much. Access to the Web is often free, even from home, as long as you have a telephone line.

It's by now almost impossible to conceive of a world without computer technology. We rely on it in so many facets of our personal and business lives. Young children growing up today will never remember a time when this technology wasn't around. In many businesses, our dependence is so great that when computers go down, there's simply nothing to do but sit and wait. It's no wonder there are so many career opportunities in computing, information technology, and related fields awaiting you out there.

To learn more about career opportunities in IT, read *Life-Long Learning Module C* and thumb back through the entire book and find the Careers icons.

appendix b

I-Witness: An Up-Close Look at Building a Web Site

did you know?

Depending on how fast you type, you can create a Web page in about 10 minutes or so. The process is actually quite simple. Once you read this appendix, your Web page can include:

different *sizes of headings to call attention to certain text.*

varying *text sizes and colors.*

a *background of either color or texture (perhaps both).*

links *to other Web pages, downloadable files, and even your e-mail.*

images *such as photos and art.*

lists *that are either numbered or bulleted.*

You can also visit the Web site for this text at www.mhhe.com/i-series to learn more about building a Web page.

SIMNET CONCEPTS SUPPORT

- Web Pages (p. 517)
- HTML—The Language of the Internet (p. 517)

Student Learning Outcomes

After reading this appendix, you should be able to:

1. List and define basic HTML concepts such as an HTML document and structure tags.
2. Use basic formatting tags such as strong, emphasis, and underline.
3. Create headings in a Web page using the heading tag.
4. Adjust text size and color using the font size and color tags.
5. Alter the background of a Web page.
6. Add three different types of links to a Web page.
7. Include and alter the appearance of images in a Web page.
8. Format content within a Web page as a list.

Hypertext markup language (HTML) is the basic language used to create Web pages. In Chapter 8, we briefly introduced you to HTML and Web authoring. HTML allows you to (1) specify the content of your Web page and (2) specify formatting such as bold, underline, and numbered lists. For specifying formatting, you use HTML tags within angle brackets (< and >). So, ***HTML tags*** specify the layout and presentation of information on a Web page.

B.1 HTML BASIC CONCEPTS AND STRUCTURE

To write HTML and create a Web page, you must create an HTML document. An ***HTML document*** is a file that contains HTML tags and the information you want to appear on your Web page. So, a Web page is simply an HTML document visually displayed in a Web browser. In Figure B.1 we've provided a Web page concerning astronomy facts. In Figure B.2 on the opposite page is the HTML document that creates that Web page.

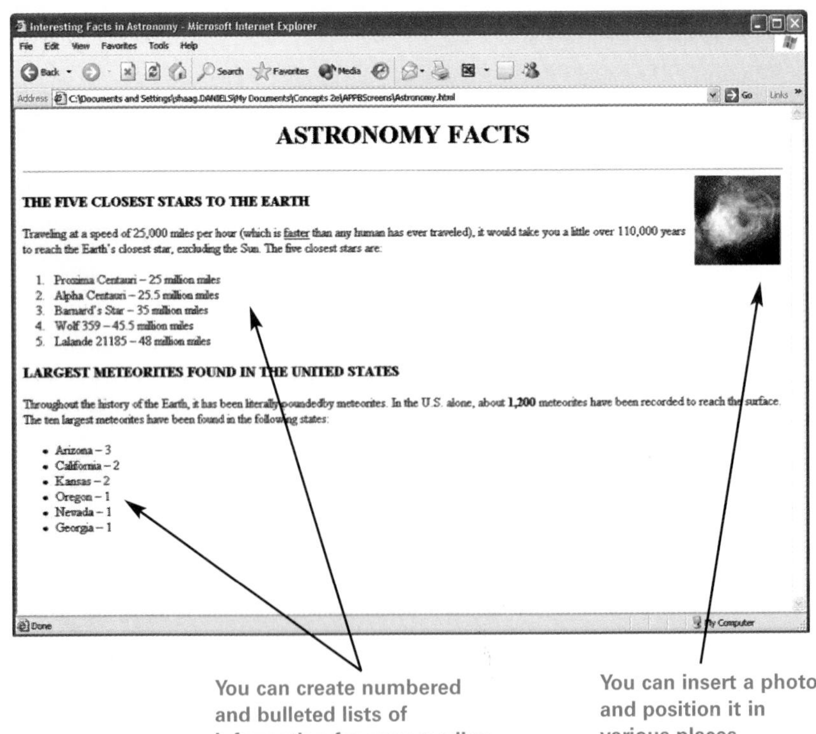

FIGURE B.1

This is a sample Web page that is created by the HTML document in Figure B.2.

The first set of HTML tags you need to use are called structure tags. ***Structure tags*** are HTML tags that set up the necessary sections and specify that the document is indeed an HTML document. Structure tags include: **<html>** and **</html>** that signify the beginning and ending of your HTML document; **<head>** and **</head>** that define the header section of your HTML document; and **<body>** and **</body>** that define the body section of your HTML document.

As you can see in Figure B.2, most HTML tags have a starting tag (such as **<body>**) and a corresponding ending tag (**</body>**). Typically, the ending tag is the starting tag with a slash **/** inserted after the first angle bracket and before the tag name.

Within the header section of your HTML document, you specify a number of important items. One of them is your Web page title, which you place between the **<title>** and **</title>** tags. This is not the logical title that appears within your Web page but rather the title that appears in the upper left title bar area of a Web browser. In this case, our title is **Interesting Facts in Astronomy.** This is also the title that will be displayed by a search engine if your Web page ever appears in a list.

You can also specify a description for your Web page in the header section. This description will also be displayed by a search engine. And you can specify in the header area key words by which a search engine will categorize your site.

Within the body section of your HTML document, you provide the content for your Web page and formatting. This, obviously, is the longest section in your HTML document.

WORKING WITH AND VIEWING YOUR WEB PAGE LOCALLY

Do I Need to Post My Web Page to My Web Space?

For other people to access and see your Web page, you eventually need to post it to your *Web space*. However, while creating your Web page, we recommend that you work with it and view it locally on your computer. In our

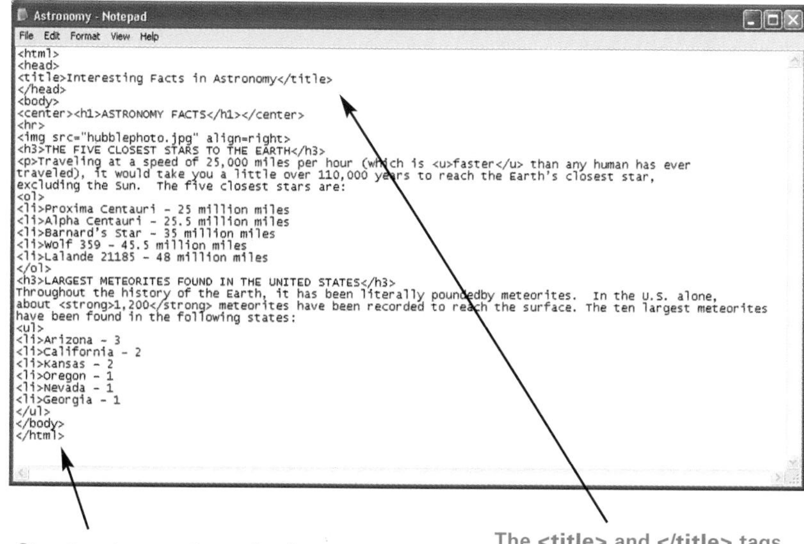


```
<html>
<head>
<title>Interesting Facts in Astronomy</title>
</head>
<body>
<center><h1>ASTRONOMY FACTS</h1></center>
<hr>
<img src="hubblephoto.jpg" align=right>
<h3>THE FIVE CLOSEST STARS TO THE EARTH</h3>
<p>Traveling at a speed of 25,000 miles per hour (which is <u>faster</u> than any human has ever
traveled), it would take you a little over 110,000 years to reach the Earth's closest star,
excluding the Sun.  The five closest stars are:
<ol>
<li>Proxima Centauri - 25 million miles
<li>Alpha Centauri - 25.5 million miles
<li>Barnard's Star - 35 million miles
<li>Wolf 359 - 45.5 million miles
<li>Lalande 21185 - 48 million miles
</ol>
<h3>LARGEST METEORITES FOUND IN THE UNITED STATES</h3>
Throughout the history of the Earth, it has been literally poundedby meteorites.  In the U.S. alone,
about <strong>1,200</strong> meteorites have been recorded to reach the surface. The ten largest meteorites
have been found in the following states:
<ul>
<li>Arizona - 3
<li>California - 2
<li>Kansas - 2
<li>Oregon - 1
<li>Nevada - 1
<li>Georgia - 1
</ul>
</body>
</html>
```

Structure tags such as **<body>**, **</body>**, and **</html>** set up the necessary sections and specify that the document is an HTML document.

The **<title>** and **</title>** tags help identify the content of your Web page.

FIGURE B.2

This is the HTML document that creates the Web page in Figure B.1.

demonstration, we'll be creating a number of small Web pages using Notepad, a simple text editor in all Windows environments.

When we first create a Web page, we'll save it to our hard disk with an extension of either **html** or **htm**. Then, we'll start Internet Explorer and perform the following steps to view our Web page:

1. Click on **File** and **Open**.
2. Click on the **Browse** button.
3. Choose the appropriate folder and HTML document name.
4. Click on **Open** and then **OK**.

We can then view our Web page within Internet Explorer. To make any changes and view the result of those changes, we'll move back to Notepad, make the changes, and save the file again. Then, we'll go back to Internet Explorer and click on the **Refresh** button to view the result of our changes. This is a good example of *multitasking* because we're working with two different pieces of software at the same time.

B.2 BASIC TEXT FORMATTING

Basic formatting tags are HTML tags that tell a Web browser how to display text. The common basic formatting tags include:

- strong (**<strong>** and **</strong>)** for bolding text
- emphasis (**<em>** and **</em>**) for italicizing text
- underline (**<u>** and **</u>**) for underlining text

In Figure B.3, you can see a sample HTML document that illustrates the use of these three tags. In Figure B.4 on the opposite page you can see how the content of the Web page is displayed. Notice that we combined the tags

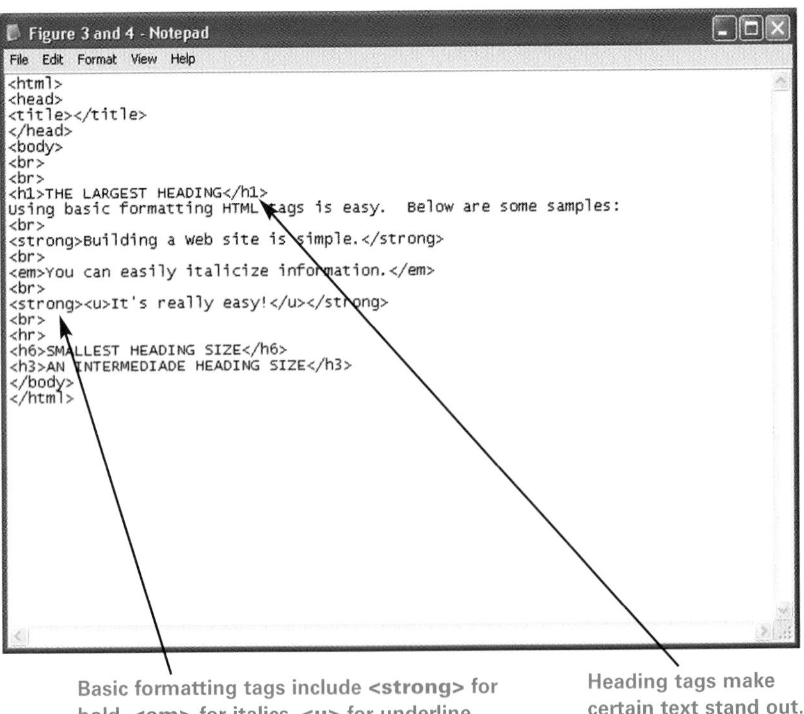

FIGURE B.3

This HTML document includes the use of basic formatting and heading tags.

in one instance. That is, we bolded and underlined the phrase "It's really easy!" by placing in the HTML document **<strong><u>It's really easy!</u></strong>**.

We also included two other basic formatting tags in Figure B.3—**
** and **<hr>**. The **
** tag is a carriage return in cyberspace and is necessary to get text to move to a new line. When interpreting an HTML document, Web browsers ignore carriage returns. So, you force a line break by inserting the **
** tag. We also included the **<hr>** tag which creates a solid line (or horizontal rule) in our Web page. Neither the **
** tag nor the **<hr>** tag has a corresponding ending tag.

B.3 CREATING HEADINGS

Heading tags are HTML tags that make certain information, such as titles, stand out on your Web page. Heading tags range from **<h1>** and **</h1>** to **<h6>** and **</h6>**, with **<h1>** being the largest. In Figure B.3 we included the use of several heading tags in the HTML document. Figure B.4 shows how the heading information is then displayed in a Web browser.

When you use heading tags, your Web browser assumes that the heading information is to appear on its own line. So, your Web browser, when encountering a heading tag, will move the heading information to a new line and place a blank line after the heading information (when it encounters the heading ending tag).

It's very important that you remember to end each heading tag you use. If you start a heading tag with **<h1>**, for example, and then don't ever provide an ending **</h1>** tag, your entire Web page content will be very large and bolded.

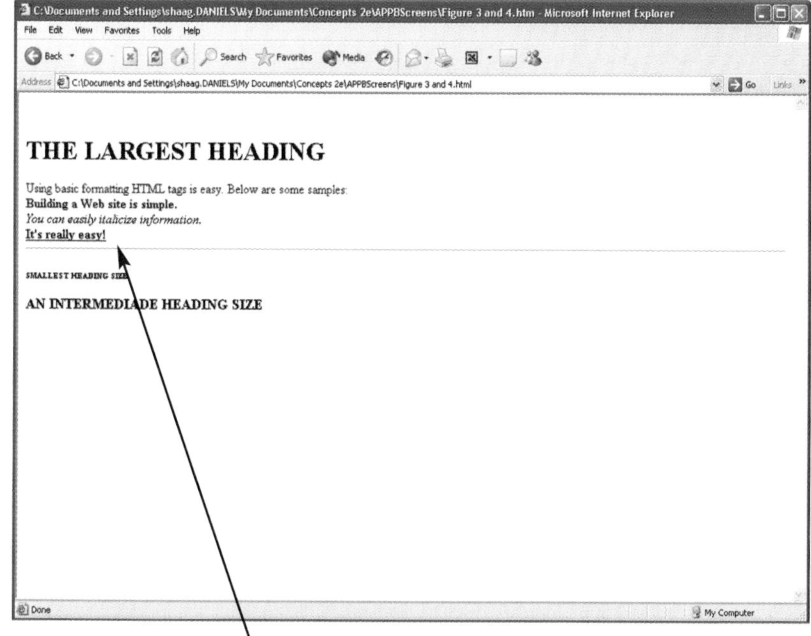

FIGURE B.4

This is the Web page created by the HTML document in Figure B.3.

B.4 ADJUSTING TEXT SIZE

You can make certain text stand out on your Web page by adjusting its size (called the *font size*). The default size of text is usually 3, with larger numbers creating larger text.

To adjust the size of your text, use the **<font size>** tag whose format is **<font size="number">**, where *number* is a positive integer, followed by the **</font>** tag to return the remaining text to the default size of 3. Consider the following statement in an HTML document:

<font size="10">A</font>stronomy is interesting.

When your Web browser displays that statement, the "A" in the word *Astronomy* will be very large and appear to be bold, a typical presentation format many books and magazines use to start a paragraph, while the remaining text will be the default size of 3.

You can also adjust the size of all your text on your Web page. To change the size of all your text to 8, you would include **<font size="8">** in your HTML document right after the **<body>** tag. You would then include the **</font>** tag in your HTML document right before the ending **</body>** tag.

In Figure B.5, we've illustrated the use of text sizing in an HTML document. Figure B.6 on the opposite page shows how that HTML document is displayed by a Web browser.

We would encourage you to consider not changing the size of your Web page text too often. Every time you change text sizes, the person viewing your Web page must stop reading for a split second and make a mental adjustment. If that happens too often, your content will seem fragmented and lose some of its value.

FIGURE B.5

This HTML document changes the text size and color.

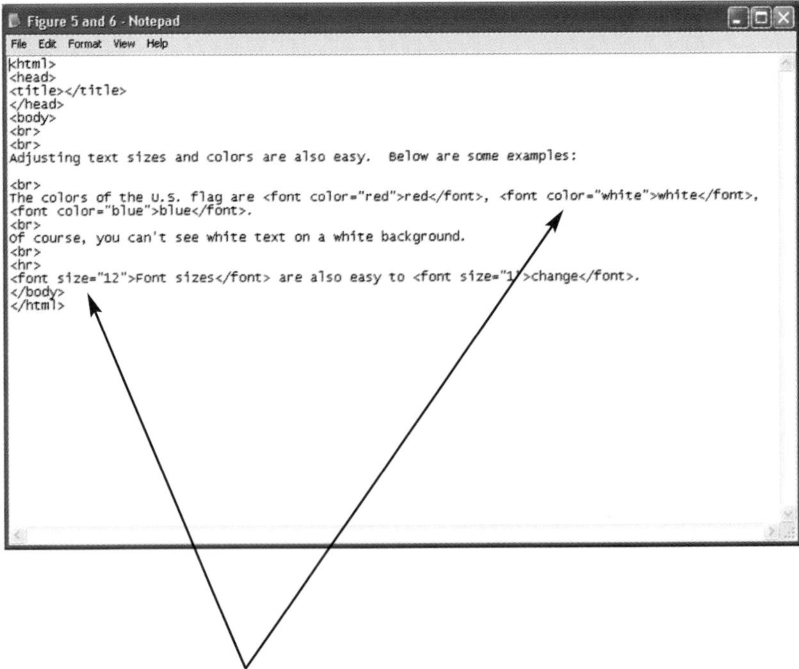

```
Figure 5 and 6 - Notepad
File Edit Format View Help
<html>
<head>
<title></title>
</head>
<body>
<br>
<br>
Adjusting text sizes and colors are also easy.  Below are some examples:

<br>
The colors of the U.S. flag are <font color="red">red</font>, <font color="white">white</font>,
<font color="blue">blue</font>.
<br>
Of course, you can't see white text on a white background.
<br>
<hr>
<font size="12">Font sizes</font> are also easy to <font size="1">change</font>.
</body>
</html>
```

You adjust text size and color with the
<font size> and <font color> tags.

B.5 ADJUSTING TEXT COLOR

Another way to make certain text stand out on your Web page is to adjust its color (called *font color*). The default color for text on a Web page is black.

To adjust the color of your text, you use the **<font color>** tag whose format is **<font color="color name">**, where *color name* is a color word such as blue or magenta, followed by the **</font>** tag to return the remaining text color to the default of black. Consider the following statement in an HTML document:

I like the color<font color="blue"> blue</font>.

When your Web browser displays "I like the color" that statement, along with the ending period, will appear in the default color of black. The word *blue* will in fact appear in the color blue.

In Figure B.5, we've illustrated the use of adjusting text color in an HTML document. Figure B.6 shows how that HTML document is displayed by a Web browser.

Let's stop and talk for a moment about Web design guidelines. When building your Web page, you must create a visually appealing presentation of information. Although adjusting the text color can certainly help, it can also be harmful. If you use too many different colors, the text can become hard to read. And if you use light colors such as yellow against a white background, the text can be equally difficult to read. In short—don't add text color to your Web page just because you know how.

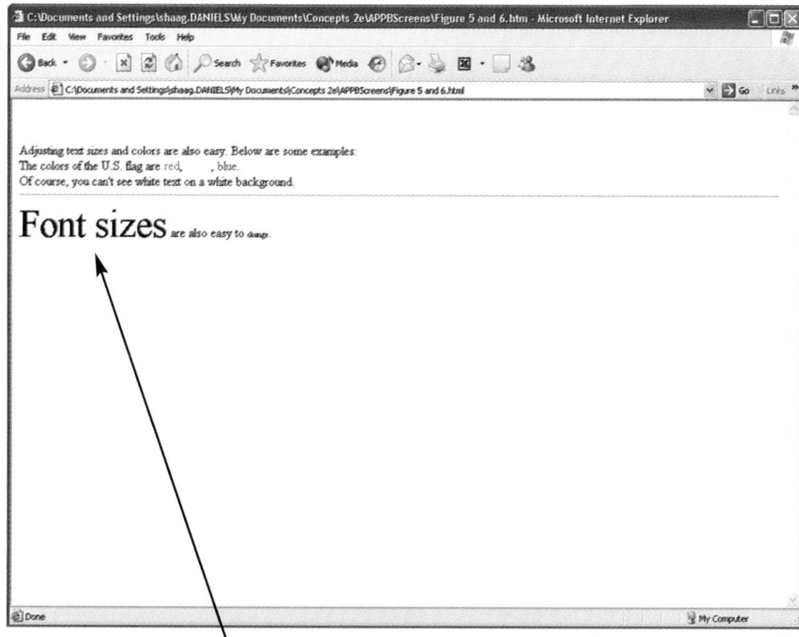

Adjusting the font size and font color are other ways to make certain text stand out. Be careful—if you make text the same color as the background, it will disappear.

FIGURE B.6

This is the Web page created by the HTML document in Figure B.5.

B.6 CHANGING THE BACKGROUND COLOR

The default background color of a Web page is white. To change the background color to a color other than white, you use the **<body bgcolor>** tag whose format is **<body bgcolor="color name">**, where *color name* is a color word such as orange or brown. So, to change the background color to green in your Web page, you would insert the following line in your HTML document immediately after the **<body>** tag:

<body bgcolor="green">

What you need to keep in mind is that the above tag will change the background color for your entire Web page. You cannot use the command again halfway through your HTML document to change the bottom half of your Web page to a different background color.

As always, we would stress to you that you should carefully consider why you need to change the background color before doing so. Some of the most well-known and successful e-commerce sites such as eBay, Amazon, and eBags all use a white background. There's obviously a good reason for this. Don't change the background color of your Web page just because you know how.

You also need to consider the overall theme of your Web page when selecting a background color. In Figure B.7 we changed the background color to green. However, if this page was to be patriotic in nature, we wouldn't recommend that you use green as the background color.

FIGURE B.7

You change the background color of a Web page by using the **<body bgcolor>** tag.

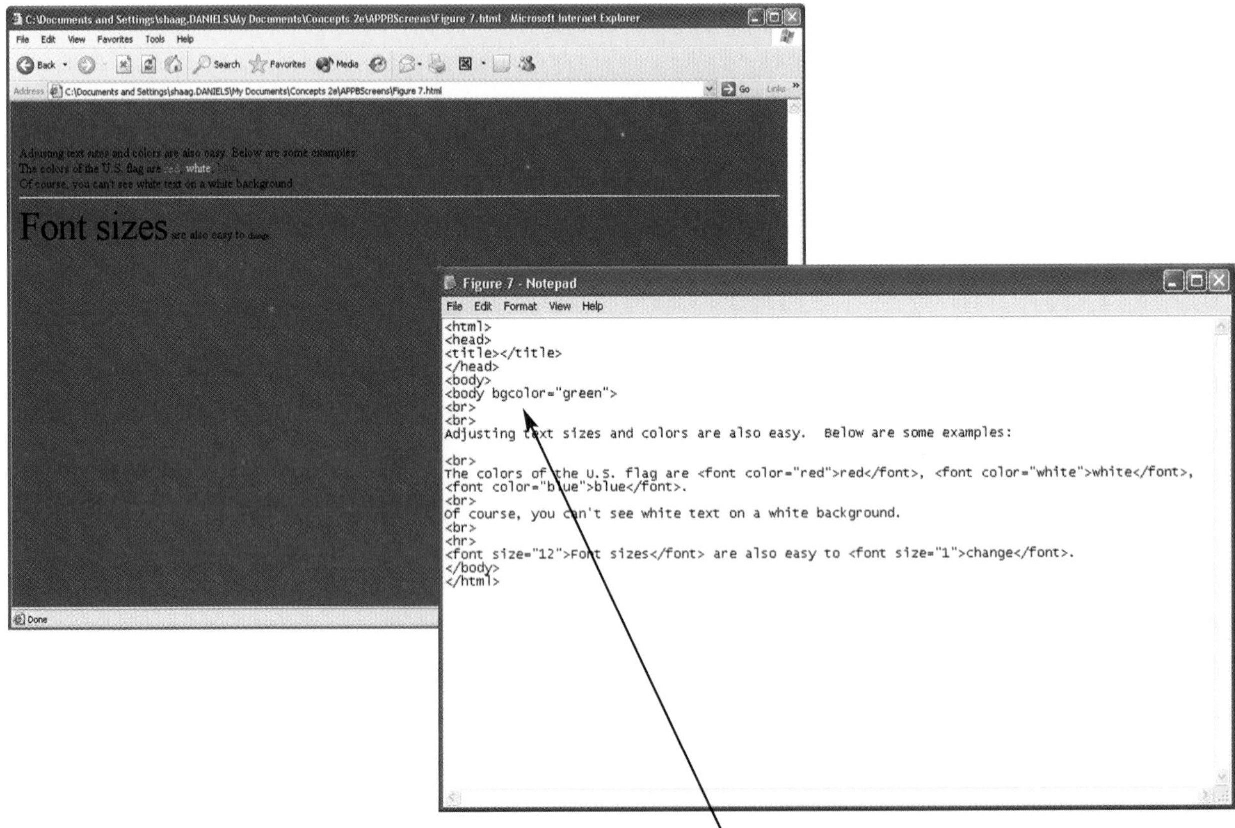

B.7 CHANGING THE BACKGROUND TEXTURE

An alternative to changing the background color of your Web page is to use a textured background. Textured backgrounds make use of an image (e.g., a jpg or gif file). But the image doesn't have to be big enough to cover the entire background of your Web page. Instead, when you include an image as a background, a Web browser will replicate the image as many times as it needs to both across and down.

To use an image and create a textured background, you use the **<body background>** tag whose format is **<body background="filename.extension">**, where *filename.extension* represents the name of the file containing your image. This statement should appear immediately after the **<body>** tag in your HTML document. For example, suppose you had stored a wavy blue image in a file called **wavyblue.jpg**. To use it as the background, you would use the statement **<body background="wavyblue.jpg">**. Don't forget, you must eventually store the image in your Web space.

Another word of caution concerning Web page design. Textured backgrounds can often be distracting to the person viewing your Web page. And textured backgrounds with dark colors will often hinder the person viewing your Web page from being able to easily read your content. As always, use textured backgrounds with caution and don't use them if your intended audience doesn't like them. Figure B.8 illustrates the use of a textured background.

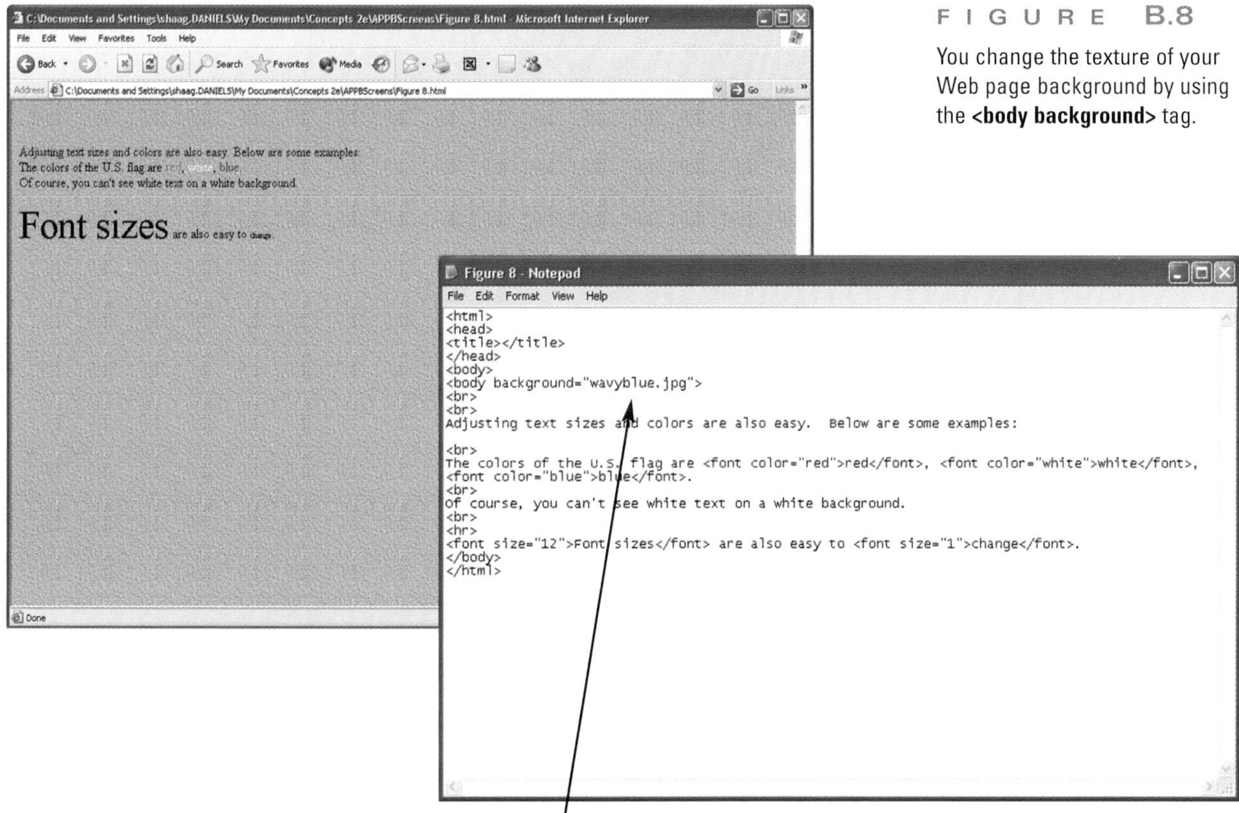

FIGURE B.8

You change the texture of your Web page background by using the **<body background>** tag.

To create a background texture, you use the <body background> tag. You must also have the image file stored in your Web space.

B.8 ADDING LINKS TO A WEB SITE

One of the great benefits of the Web is the ability to link logically related sites, pages, and documents. You do this in an HTML document with link tags. ***Link tags*** are HTML tags you use to create links on your Web page to (1) other sites and pages, (2) downloadable files such as audio and video, and (3) e-mail. The general format of the link tag is:

<a href="address or file name">text to appear on the screen</a>

Links to other Web sites or pages are the most common types of links. In Figure B.10 on the opposite page, you can see several different links to other sites (including the words *here* and *Visit MTV*). In Figure B.9 on this page, you can see the HTML document that creates those links.

For example, the link tag for providing a link to MTV's site is **<a href="www.mtv.com">Visit MTV</a>**. As you can see, the Web site address (in this case) appears within the quote marks and after the equal sign (**=**). The text that will appear as a link on the Web page appears after the greater than sign (**>**) and before the ending tag of **</a>**.

If you wanted to create another Web page in an HTML document called **SecondPage.html** and have the HTML document below link to it, you would use the tag **<a href="SecondPage.html">Here is my second page</a>**. Of course, you would need to store **SecondPage.html** in your Web space.

To create a link to a downloadable file, you use the filename and extension for the file in place of an address. For example, we included a link to a downloadable file called **Sample.xls**, an Excel workbook. The link tag to achieve that is:

<a href="Sample.xls">You can click here to download an Excel workbook</a>

If you do provide links to downloadable files, we recommend that you provide the size of the file as well. That way, viewers of your Web page can determine approximately how long it will take to download the file. Again, you must store the downloadable file in your Web space.

FIGURE B.9

This HTML document with links creates the Web page in Figure B.10.

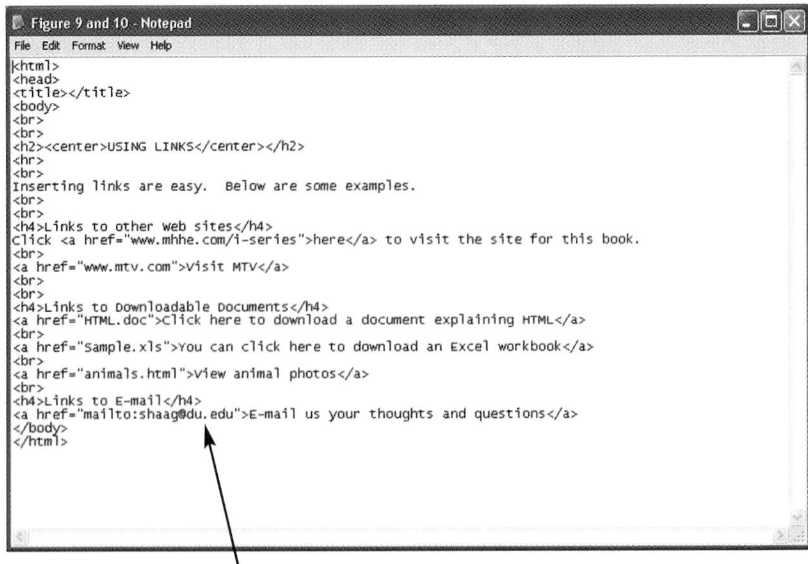


```
<html>
<head>
<title></title>
<body>
<br>
<br>
<h2><center>USING LINKS</center></h2>
<hr>
<br>
Inserting links are easy.  Below are some examples.
<br>
<br>
<h4>Links to other Web sites</h4>
Click <a href="www.mhhe.com/i-series">here</a> to visit the site for this book.
<br>
<a href="www.mtv.com">Visit MTV</a>
<br>
<br>
<h4>Links to Downloadable Documents</h4>
<a href="HTML.doc">Click here to download a document explaining HTML</a>
<br>
<a href="Sample.xls">You can click here to download an Excel workbook</a>
<br>
<a href="animals.html">View animal photos</a>
<br>
<h4>Links to E-mail</h4>
<a href="mailto:shaag@du.edu">E-mail us your thoughts and questions</a>
</body>
</html>
```

With the link tag (**<a href>**), you can add links to other sites or pages, downloadable files, and e-mail.

You may also want to add a link in your Web page that allows people to send you an e-mail. In this case, you would use the following statement:

<a href="mailto:your e-mail address">text to appear on screen</a>

As you can see in Figure B.9, we included an e-mail link to one of the authors to this text. That HTML statement is:

<a href="mailto:shaag@du.edu">E-mail us with your thoughts and questions</a>

Other words of caution are appropriate here again. First, if you do include links to other sites or pages, periodically check them to ensure that they are still active. No one likes to click on a dead link. Second, if you do include a link to your e-mail, expect to receive a lot of e-mail.

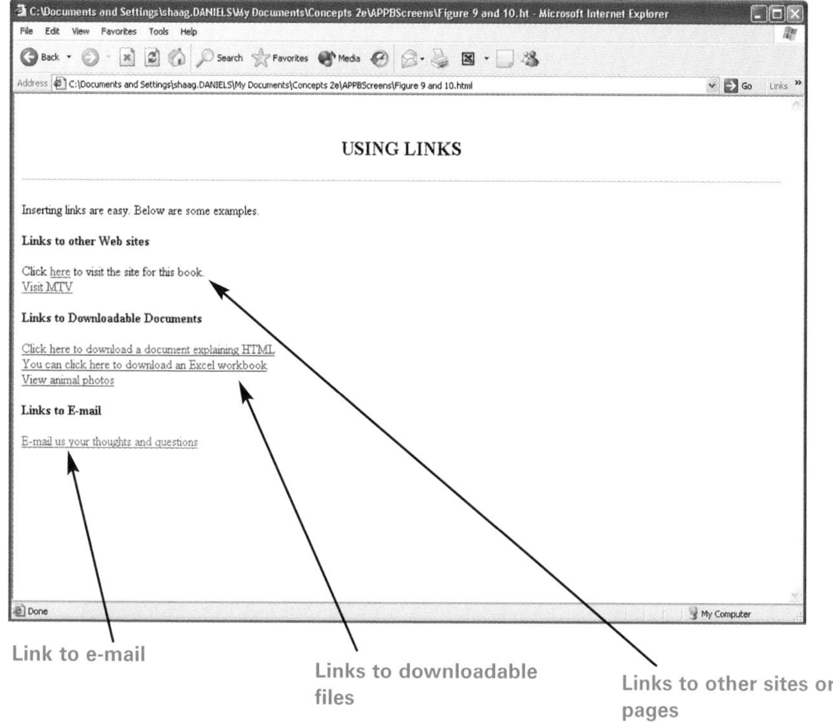

FIGURE B.10

This Web page with links is created by the HTML document in Figure B.9.

FIGURE B.11

This HTML document includes images.

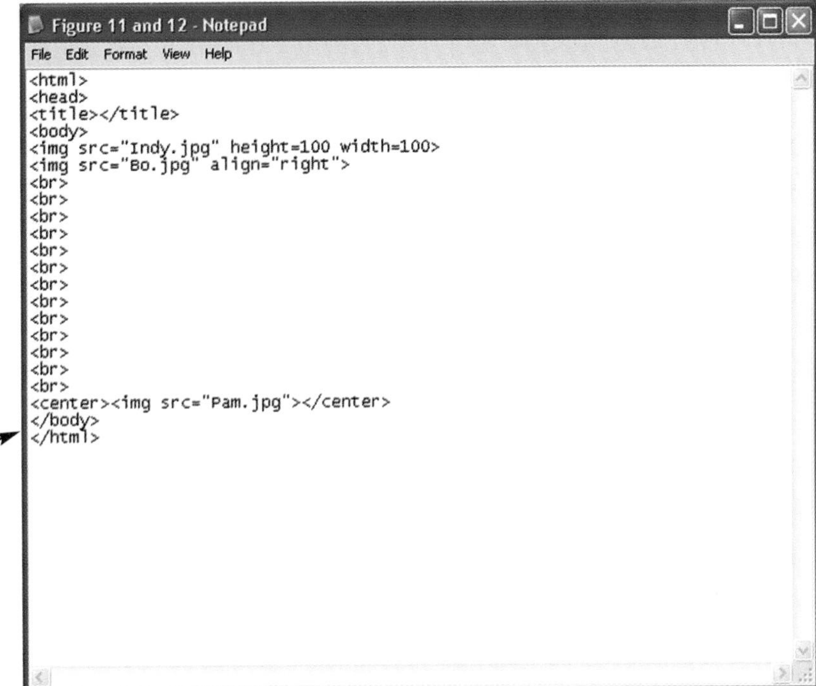
Figure 11 and 12 - Notepad

File Edit Format View Help

```
<html>
<head>
<title></title>
<body>
<img src="Indy.jpg" height=100 width=100>
<img src="Bo.jpg" align="right">
<br>
<br>
<br>
<br>
<br>
<br>
<br>
<br>
<br>
<br>
<br>
<br>
<br>
<center><img src="Pam.jpg"></center>
</body>
</html>
```

You add images to your Web page with the **<img src>** tag. You can also position and size images by adding the appropriate parameters.

B.9 ADDING IMAGES

Another nice feature of the Web is the ability to add images (photos and the like) to your Web page. If you refer back to Figure B.2 on page 505, you'll notice that we added a nice image that the Hubble telescope captured of a distant galaxy. ***Image tags*** are HTML tags you use to insert images onto your Web page. The basic tag format for inserting an image is:

<img src="filename.extension">

Wherever that statement appears in your HTML document is where the image will appear on your Web page. As with all other files, you must store your image files in your Web space.

In Figure B.11 you can see we've created an HTML document that includes several images. In Figure B.12 on the opposite page, you can see how those images are displayed within a Web browser. Notice that they are different sizes and that one appears centered within the Web page, one appears on the left side of the Web page, and one appears on the right side of the Web page. Where you place them and how you size them is completely up to you.

The default placement for an image is left justified. You can right justify an image by adding the **align** parameter in the image tag. We did so with the image tag **<img src="Bo.jpg" align="right">**.

If you want to center an image, you must surround the image tag with **<center>** and **</center>**. (There is no **align="center"** option.) That's what we did with the third image in Figure B.11; you can see the result in Figure B.12.

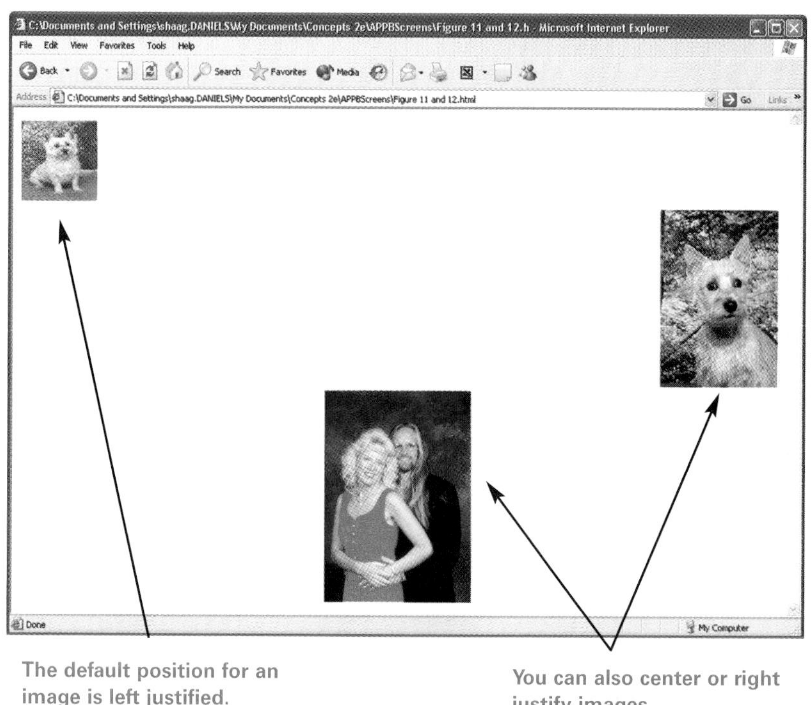

The default position for an image is left justified.
You can also center or right justify images.

FIGURE B.12

This is the Web page with images created by the HTML document in Figure B.11.

To size an image, you add the **height** and **width** parameters to the image tag. The general format for this is:

<img src="filename.extension" height=pixel count width=pixel count>

As you can see, you size an image according to the number of pixels. *Pixels* are the smallest display elements on a screen. In Figure B.11, we sized the first image for 100 pixels in height and 100 pixels in width. Depending on the size of the viewable screen, the first image is approximately 1.5 inches by 1.5 inches square.

Of course, you can provide different values for the **height** and **width** parameters, but that might skew the image one way or another.

Once again, let's talk about good design guidelines. Images are nice to have in your Web page *if* they add value. However, images can take a long time to transfer from a Web server to the person viewing your Web page. If you have large images or numerous smaller images, your Web page will take a long time to load, and the person viewing your Web page may become impatient and move on to another. Exercise caution when adding images.

FIGURE B.13

This HTML document includes the necessary tags for creating lists.

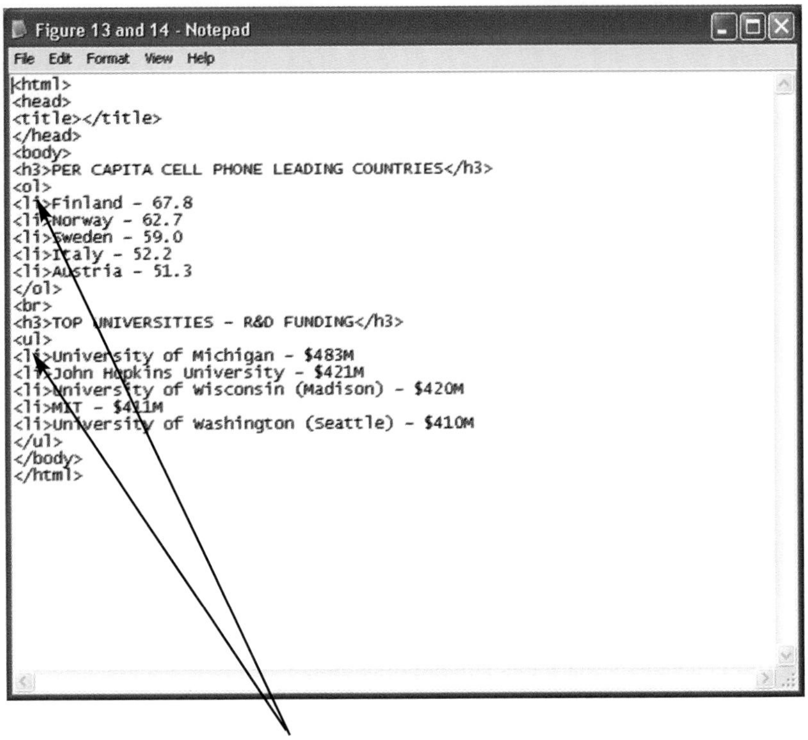

Figure 13 and 14 - Notepad

File Edit Format View Help

```
<html>
<head>
<title></title>
</head>
<body>
<h3>PER CAPITA CELL PHONE LEADING COUNTRIES</h3>
<ol>
<li>Finland - 67.8
<li>Norway - 62.7
<li>Sweden - 59.0
<li>Italy - 52.2
<li>Austria - 51.3
</ol>
<br>
<h3>TOP UNIVERSITIES - R&D FUNDING</h3>
<ul>
<li>University of Michigan - $483M
<li>John Hopkins University - $421M
<li>University of Wisconsin (Madison) - $420M
<li>MIT - $411M
<li>University of Washington (Seattle) - $410M
</ul>
</body>
</html>
```

You can create two types of lists—numbered with the <ol> tag or unnumbered with the <ul> tag.

B.10 CREATING AND USING LISTS

There are two types of lists: numbered lists and unnumbered or bulleted lists. If you refer back to Figure B.2 on page 505, you'll find an example of each. ***List tags*** are HTML tags that allow you to present information in the form of a list, either numbered (using **<ol>** and **</ol>**) or unnumbered (using **<ul>** and **</ul>**). Most Web surfers today won't read long, lengthy paragraphs. So, it's a good idea to break up your content into lists if possible.

To create a numbered list in an HTML document, you start the list with the tag **<ol>** and end the list with the tag **</ol>**. In between, you start each list item with the **<li>** tag (*li* stands for *list item*). Figure B.13 includes an HTML document that creates a numbered list—the five leading countries with the highest per capita cell phone use. Figure B.14 on the opposite page shows how that list is presented in a Web browser.

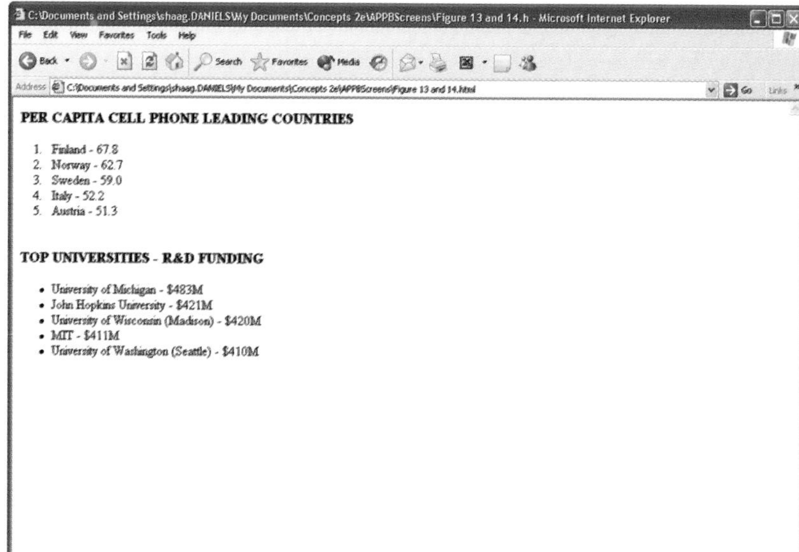

FIGURE B.14

This Web page presents both numbered and unnumbered lists.

Notice that the list begins with the **<ol>** tag and ends with the **</ol>** tag. And notice that each item in the list is preceded by the **<li>** tag (you don't need to use a corresponding **</li>** tag for each **<li>** tag).

The default numbering for a numbered list is Arabic. You can change that by adding the **type** parameter to the **<ol>** tag. Examples include:

- **<ol type=a>**—lowercase letters
- **<ol type=A>**—uppercase letters
- **<ol type=i>**—lowercase Roman numerals
- **<ol type=I>**—uppercase Roman numerals

To create an unnumbered list, all you have to do is use the **<ul>** and **</ul>** tags instead of the tags **<ol>** and **</ol>**. Figure B.13 includes these tags to create a list of the top universities in the country according to endowment assets. Figure B.14 shows how that list is displayed in a Web browser.

That ends our very brief introduction to creating a Web page with HTML. There's much, much more for you to learn if you're interested. We would encourage you to visit the following sites:

- W3C HTML home page—www.w3.org/MarkUp
- HTML Compendium—www.htmlcompendium.org/Menus index-e.htm
- Index dot HTML—www.blooberry.com/indexdot/html
- HTML Writer's Guild—www.hwg.org
- HTML Station—www.december.com/html
- HTML Goodies—www.htmlgoodies.com
- Dave's HTML Guide—www.davesite.com/webstation/html
- Rex Swain's HTML Sampler—www.rexswain.com/sampler.html
- HotSource HTML Help—www.sbrady.com/hotsource

You can also visit the Web site for this text at www.mhhe.com/i-series for more helpful tips, suggestions, and resources. You can also complete the "Web Pages" and "HTML—The Language of the Internet" tutorials on your SimNet Concepts Support CD.

making the grade answers

CHAPTER ONE

SECTION 1.1

1. button
2. icon
3. graphical user interface (GUI)

SECTION 1.2

1. hardware, software
2. storage
3. output device
4. notebook computer (laptop)
5. Supercomputers

SECTION 1.3

1. tablet PC
2. Web site
3. Instant messaging
4. Bluetooth
5. Ethics

CHAPTER TWO

SECTION 2.1

1. Electronic commerce (e-commerce)
2. Brick-and-mortar
3. pureplays, e-tailers
4. individuals
5. Consumer to consumer (C2C)

SECTION 2.2

1. plug-in
2. player
3. Web audio
4. Streaming media
5. VRML (Virtual Reality Modeling Language)

SECTION 2.3

1. Internet backbone
2. Internet service provider (ISP)
3. FTP server
4. TCP/IP
5. Http (hypertext transfer protocol)

SECTION 2.4

1. Commercial
2. DSL (Digital Subscriber Line)
3. cable modem
4. satellite modem
5. Connectivity

CHAPTER THREE

SECTION 3.1

1. System software
2. Application software
3. Personal productivity
4. version
5. suites

SECTION 3.2

1. word processing
2. Graphics
3. Presentation
4. Online banking
5. Internet Explorer, Netscape Communicator

SECTION 3.3

1. vector graphic
2. color palette
3. wireframe
4. Waveform audio
5. Video frame rate

CHAPTER FOUR

SECTION 4.1

1. personal operating system (personal OS)
2. multi-user operating system (multi-user OS)
3. network operating system (network OS, NOS)
4. Multitasking

SECTION 4.2

1. Windows 2000 Pro
2. Windows XP Home
3. Mac OS
4. Pocket PC OS
5. Palm Operating System (Palm OS)

SECTION 4.3

1. device driver
2. plug and play
3. Hot swap
4. utility software suite
5. Anti-virus software

SECTION 4.4

1. device letter
2. directory
3. FAT (file allocation table)
4. Fragmentation
5. zipped

CHAPTER FIVE

SECTION 5.1

1. wireless
2. joystick
3. pointing stick
4. scanner
5. Force feedback

SECTION 5.2

1. flat-panel
2. refresh rate
3. laser
4. photo inkjet printer
5. multifunction printer (MFP)

SECTION 5.3

1. hard disk drive
2. -R
3. DVD burner
4. flash memory
5. flash memory drive

CHAPTER SIX

SECTION 6.1

1. connector
2. port
3. central processing unit (CPU or processor)
4. expansion slot
5. expansion bus

SECTION 6.2

1. bit
2. byte
3. ASCII
4. Unicode
5. binary

SECTION 6.3

1. machine (CPU) cycle
2. random access memory (RAM)
3. system bus
4. virtual memory
5. CPU clock

SECTION 6.4

1. Firewire
2. infrared (IrDA)
3. PCI bus
4. expansion bus
5. parallel

SECTION 6.5

1. mobile CPU
2. PC Card
3. notebook
4. smaller
5. power

CHAPTER SEVEN

SECTION 7.1

1. network
2. network interface card (NIC or network card)
3. hub (switch or router)
4. local area network (LAN)
5. network operating system (network OS, NOS)

SECTION 7.2

1. peer-to-peer
2. network interface card (NIC or network card)
3. RJ-45 (Ethernet) connector
4. home router
5. antenna

SECTION 7.3

1. client/server
2. intranet
3. collaborative system
4. global positioning system (GPS)
5. radio

SECTION 7.4

1. communications media
2. Bandwidth
3. optical fiber
4. wired communications media
5. Wireless

CHAPTER EIGHT

SECTION 8.1

1. electronic catalog
2. pop-up ad
3. Opting in
4. conversion rate

SECTION 8.2

1. Financial cybermediaries
2. Secure Sockets Layer (SSL)
3. Encryption
4. Secure Electronic Transaction (SET)

SECTION 8.3

1. HTML (Hypertext Markup Language)
2. basic formatting tags
3. Meta tags
4. WYSIWYG (What You See Is What You Get)
5. FTP program

SECTION 8.4

1. CSS (Cascading Style Sheets)
2. XML (Extensible Markup Language)
3. XHTML (Extensible HTML)
4. WAP gateway
5. CGI (Common Gateway Interface)

CHAPTER NINE

SECTION 9.1

1. ethics
2. Fair Use Doctrine
3. license (right)
4. Pirated software

SECTION 9.2

1. Identity
2. hacker
3. virus
4. denial-of-service

SECTION 9.3

1. Privacy
2. sniffer
3. Spam
4. Spoofing

SECTION 9.4

1. firewall
2. Anonymous Web browsing (AWB)
3. Federal Trade Commission (FTC)
4. Social security number

CHAPTER TEN

SECTION 10.1

1. data
2. field
3. fields
4. file
5. database

SECTION 10.2

1. relational database model
2. field property
3. compound primary key
4. E-R (entity-relationship)
5. one-to-many

SECTION 10.3

1. data dictionary
2. database form
3. SQL (Structured Query Language)
4. Database administrators (DBAs)
5. application generation

SECTION 10.4

1. Web database
2. hypertext database
3. Middleware
4. personal portal

SECTION 10.5

1. OLTP (online transaction processing)
2. data warehouse
3. Data mining
4. Query-and-reporting tools
5. data mart

CHAPTER ELEVEN

SECTION 11.1

1. pattern classification
2. walkers
3. biometrics
4. two
5. thought-control

SECTION 11.2

1. E-cash (electronic cash, digital cash)
2. application service provider (ASP)
3. global positioning system (GPS)
4. intelligent home appliance

SECTION 11.3

1. CAVE
2. living tissue cells
3. Nanotechnology
4. implant chip

CHAPTER TWELVE

SECTION 12.1

1. efficient
2. reactive
3. competitive advantage

SECTION 12.2

1. time
2. systems analyst
3. Data flow diagramming (DFD)
4. plunge

SECTION 12.3

1. End user development
2. prototype
3. basic requirements
4. 3, 4

SECTION 12.4

1. Outsourcing
2. Horizontal
3. Vertical
4. request for proposal (RFP)

CHAPTER THIRTEEN

SECTION 13.1

1. Business logic
2. pseudocode
3. algorithm
4. logic error
5. Output

SECTION 13.2

1. programming language
2. Reserved words
3. comments
4. sequence control structure
5. if-then-else statement

SECTION 13.3

1. Debugging
2. Syntax errors
3. CVS (Concurrent Versions System)
4. program manual
5. software patch

SECTION 13.4

1. Portability
2. Assembly
3. compiler
4. macro
5. event-driven

SECTION 13.5

1. programming framework
2. programming object
3. object instance
4. Visual Studio .NET

CHAPTER FOURTEEN

SECTION 14.1

1. Tactical
2. Decentralized computing
3. granularity
4. External
5. downward

SECTION 14.2

1. customer-integrated system (CIS)
2. transaction processing system (TPS)
3. decentralize
4. customer-integrated systems (CISs)

SECTION 14.3

1. management information system (MIS)
2. summarized report
3. exception report
4. comparative report
5. drill down

SECTION 14.4

1. intranet
2. extranet
3. Groupware
4. Group scheduling
5. group document database

SECTION 14.5

1. Telecommuting
2. transnational firm
3. Culture
4. Transborder data flows

CHAPTER FIFTEEN

SECTION 15.1

1. decision support system (DSS)
2. model
3. geographic information system (GIS)
4. global positioning system (GPS)

SECTION 15.2

1. neural network
2. genetic algorithm
3. fuzzy logic
4. expert system (knowledge-based system)

SECTION 15.3

1. data mining
2. shopping bots (buyer agents)
3. user (personal) agent
4. intelligent agent
5. monitoring-and-surveillance (predictive)

glossary

.aif (Audio Interchange Format) Filename extension for audio that stores good quality sound that can be listened to within a browser without a plug-in but in a large, uncompressed format. (84)

.bmp Filename extension of the native bitmap graphic file format for Windows environments. (82)

.gif (Graphics Image Format) Filename extension for the graphics file format used primarily for Web sites and pages and downloadable images on the Web. (82)

.jpeg (.jpg) Filename extension for the graphics file format used for Web sites, pages, and downloadable images on the Web as well as in digital photography. (82)

.mp3 (MP3) Filename extension for audio that stores good quality sound in a compressed file format but requires the use of a player or a plug-in within a browser. (84)

.png (Portable Network Graphic) Filename extension used as a public domain alternative to .gif that provides good compression capabilities. (82)

.ra (RealAudio) Filename extension for audio that stores good quality sound (although not as good as MP3) in a compressed file format but requires the use of a player or a plug-in within a browser. (84)

.tiff (.tif) Filename extension for high-resolution bitmap graphics file format used in print publishing. (82)

.wav (Wave) Filename extension for audio that stores good quality sound that can be listened to within a browser without a plug-in but in a large, uncompressed format. (84)

24-bit color palette (true color palette) Takes advantage of 16.7 million different colors. (81)

3-D graphics Instructions including the length, width, locations, and drawing parameters for creating a wireframe of a 3-D image. (82)

32-bit bitmap color palette Takes advantage of 16.7 million colors as well as special effects such as transparency and dithering. (82)

Abacus Device consisting of rows of beads mounted within a rectangular hand-held device. (496)

Acceptance testing Formal, documented process in which users use the new system, verify that it works correctly under operational conditions, and note any errors that need to be fixed. (369)

Access speed Time between when you ask for a file and when the computer delivers it to you. (114)

Adaptive filtering Asks you to rate products or situations and also monitors your actions over time to find out what you like and dislike. (233)

Affiliate program (associate program) Allows an e-commerce business to sell goods and services via another Web site. (230)

AGP bus Used by an AGP video card, it's part of the expansion bus and ends in the AGP slot. (180)

AGP slot Expansion slot reserved exclusively for an AGP video card. (179)

Algorithm Set of specific steps that solves a problem or carries out a task. (392)

Analytical Engine Device developed in 1834 by Charles Babbage which was a general-purpose calculating device that embodied such concepts as memory, programming capabilities, and stored data on punched cards. (497)

Anonymous Web browsing (AWB) Prevents you from being tracked as you surf the Web. (280)

Anti-virus software Utility software that continually scans your RAM, storage devices, and incoming files for viruses and removes the viruses. (108)

Application generation subsystem Contains tools for generating transaction-intensive software. (303)

Application programmer Programmer who writes application software. (363)

Application service provider (ASP) Company that provides software, storage, and other services for other businesses and individuals to use. (336)

Application software Software that allows you to perform specific information-processing tasks such as managing inventory, paying accounts payable, handling payroll, writing a term paper, or creating slides for a presentation. (9, 68)

Arithmetic logic unit (ALU) Component of the CPU that performs arithmetic, as well as comparison and logic operations. (170)

Artificial intelligence (AI) Science of making machines imitate human thinking and behavior. (464, 500)

ASCII (American Standard Code for Information Interchange) pronounced *ASK-ee;* Eight-bit coding system that most personal computers use. (168)

ASP (Active Server Page) Uses a combination of HTML, VBScript, and specific commands to build interactive Web pages. (248)

Assembler Utility program that converts assembly language into machine language that a computer can then use to run software. (406)

Assembly language Machine-dependent, low-level language that uses words instead of binary numbers to program a specific computer system. (406)

Atanasoff-Berry Computer (ABC) Electronic computer developed by John Atanasoff and Clifford Berry (a graduate student) at Iowa State University during the late 1930s. (498)

Automatic speech recognition (ASR) Captures your speech and can distinguish your words and word groupings to form sentences. (325)

Backdoor Undocumented method a programmer uses to gain access to a program or a computer. (401)

Bandwidth Capacity of the communications medium, which is the amount of information that a communications medium can transfer in a given amount of time. (211)

Banner ad Graphical advertisement (often including movement and animation) that will take you to another site if you click on it. (229)

Basic formatting tag HTML tag that tells a Web browser how to display text. (238, 506)

Biochip Technology chip that can perform a variety of physiological functions when inserted into the human body. (344)

Biometrics Use of physical characteristics—such as your fingerprint, the blood vessels in the retina of your eye, or perhaps the sound of your voice—to provide identification. (328)

Bit 1 or 0 in binary. (167)

Bitmap graphic (raster graphic or bitmap) Grid of dots with each dot representing a specific color, which makes up the entire image or photo. (81)

Black-hat hacker Hacker with malicious intent—a cyber vandal. (270)

Bluetooth Standard for transmitting information in the form of short-range radio waves over distances of up to 30 feet, used for purposes such as wirelessly connecting a cell phone to a computer. (20, 178)

Brick-and-mortar business Exists only in the physical world and performs no e-commerce functions. (36)

Bug Common name for software error. (401)

Bus (data bus) Carries information in the form of bits around the motherboard in your computer. (179)

Business intelligence Knowledge about your customers, competitors, and internal operations that can help you make more informed and effective decisions. (309)

Business logic Set of rules used to govern a business process. (390)

Business to business electronic commerce (B2B e-commerce) Occurs when a business sells products and services through e-commerce to customers who are primarily other businesses. (37, 226)

Business to consumer electronic commerce (B2C e-commerce) Occurs when a business sells products and services through e-commerce to customers who are primarily individuals. (37, 226)

Button Graphic representation of something that you click on once with the left mouse button. (5)

Buyer agent (shopping bot) Intelligent agent on a Web site that helps you, the customer, find products and services you want. (470)

Byte Group of 8 bits. (167)

Cable modem Telecommunications device that uses your TV cable to produce an Internet connection. (52)

CASE, or **computer aided software engineering, tools** Software applications that help prepare reports, draw program flowcharts, and generate software code for prototypes. (403)

Case control statement (or **switch statement)** Tests a condition that can result in more than a true or false answer. (399)

Cat 5 (Category 5) cable More robust version of ordinary phone cable. (199)

CAVE (cave automatic virtual environment) Special 3-D virtual reality room that can display images of other people and objects located in other places and CAVEs all over the world. (341)

CD burner Drive that lets you read from and write information to a CD. (147)

CD-R (compact disc—recordable) Optical disc to which you can write one time only. (146)

CD-ROM (compact disc read-only memory) Optical or laser disc whose information cannot be changed. (145)

CD-ROM drive Device that lets you read (or play) a CD. (145)

CD-RW (compact disc—rewritable) Optical or laser disc on which you can save, change, and delete files as often as you like. (147)

Central processing unit (CPU or processor) Chip that carries out instructions it receives from your software. (12, 165)

CGI (Common Gateway Interface) specification that enables all Web clients to interact with all Web servers. (248)

Chat room Virtual meeting place on the Web in which you can communicate live with other people who happen to be on the Web and in the same chat room at the same time. (18)

Chief information officer (CIO) Person within your organization who oversees the use of information as a resource. (363)

Click-and-mortar business Has both a presence in the physical world (such as a store in a shopping mall) and a Web site that supports some type of e-commerce. (36)

Click-and-order business (pure play, e-tailer) Exists solely on the Web with no physical presence that you can visit to buy products and services. (37)

Click-through Information that is captured when you click on an ad to go from one Web site to another. (230)

Client/server network Network in which one or more computers are servers and provide services to the other computers, which are called clients. (203)

Client-side Web programming language Employs the computing power of users' Web browsers to add functionality to Web pages. (246)

Cluster Collection of sectors on a storage device. (113)

Codec (compressor/decompressor) Software that enables you to compress a video file as you create and edit it and then decompress the file when the video is displayed. (85)

Coding When you translate your algorithm into a programming language. (396)

Collaboration system Software that allows people to work together. (206)

Collaborative filtering Method of placing you into an affinity group of people with the same characteristics. (232)

Color palette Selection of colors that will be used for each dot in a bitmap graphic grid. (81)

COLOSSUS Electronic device developed in World War II by the allied forces which could decipher the codes of the German ENIGMA machine. (498)

Comment Explanation that tells other programmers what's happening in software code. (397)

Communications media Paths, or physical channels, in a network over which information travels. (210)

Communications protocol (protocol) Set of rules that computers follow to transfer information. (48)

Communications satellite Microwave repeater in space. (213)

CompactFlash (CF) card Flash memory card slightly larger than a half-dollar and about as thick as two quarters. (148)

Comparative report Report that shows two or more sets of similar information in an attempt to illustrate a relationship. (434)

Compiler Simultaneously translates high-level programming languages into machine language. (407)

Compound primary key Occurs in a database table when two or more fields together uniquely identify each record. (295)

Compressed file File that has been compressed. (115)

Computer (computer system) Set of tools that helps you perform information-processing tasks. (8)

Computer network (network) Collection of computers that supports the sharing of information, software, and hardware devices. (47, 194)

Computer virus (virus) Software that is designed intentionally to cause annoyance or damage. (23, 108, 267)

Condition Existing situation. (397)

Connectivity software Allows you to use your computer to connect to another computer or a network. (53)

Connector Plug on the end of a wire from a device, like a printer, hard disk, or scanner, that you use to connect the device to the computer. (165)

Consumer to consumer electronic commerce (C2C e-commerce) Occurs when a person sells products and services to another person through e-commerce. (38)

Control structure Specifies the order in which a computer will execute each line of software code. (397)

Control unit Component of the CPU that directs what happens in your computer. (170)

Conversion rate Percentage of potential customers who visit a site and then become actual customers by making a purchase. (233)

Cookie Small text file containing specific information about you that a Web site stores on your computer's hard disk. (118, 275)

Copyright Type of legal protection accorded to intellectual property. (261)

Counter Numerical value that tracks the number of iterations in a software code. (399)

CPU cache Type of memory on the CPU where instructions called up by the CPU wait until the CPU is ready to use them. (170)

CPU clock Sliver of quartz that beats at regular intervals in response to an electrical charge. (171)

Cracker Hacker who hacks for profit. (271)

CSS (Cascading Style Sheets) Allows you to format an HTML document's elements separately from its content. (241)

Culture Collective personality of a nation or society that encompasses language, traditions, currency, religion, history, music, and acceptable behavior. (444)

Customer-integrated system (CIS) Extension of a transaction processing system that places technology in the hands of an organization's customers and allows them to process their own transactions. (431)

CVS (Concurrent Versions System) Open source software tool that tracks all changes to a project's code. (404)

Cyberterrorist Hacker who seeks to cause harm to a lot of people or to destroy critical systems or information. (271)

Data Distinct items providing descriptions of people, places, and/or things that may not have much meaning to you, depending on their context. (292)

Data administration subsystem Contains tools for managing the overall database environment. (304)

Database Logical collection of files. (293)

Database administrator Designs, implements, and maintains solutions to business challenges using databases. (303)

Database form Graphical interface that makes it easy to add, change, and delete information. (301)

Database management system (DBMS) software Application software that allows you to arrange, modify, and extract information from a database. (78, 299)

Data broker Company that searches many databases and returns information to you. (308)

Data definition subsystem Helps you define the tables in a database and the relationships among them. (299)

Data dictionary Defines the structure and properties of a database table. (299)

Data file Group of logically related records. (293)

Data flow diagramming (DFD) Modeling technique for illustrating how information moves through various processes and how people outside the system provide and receive information. (364)

Data manipulation subsystem Helps you enter information into a database, query it to find information, and generate reports. (300)

Data mart Miniature data warehouse with a special focus. (312)

Data mining Process of extracting information from a data warehouse for decision-making purposes. (310)

Data-mining agent Helps you discover new information, trends, and relationships within a data warehouse without necessarily applying a specific mathematical model. (311, 472)

Data-mining tool Tool you use in a data warehouse environment to perform data mining. (310)

Data warehouse Collection of information from internal and/or external sources (mostly databases) organized specifically for generating business intelligence to support decision making. (293, 309)

Debugging Process of finding errors in software code. (401)

Decentralized computing Placement of technology into the hands of those people in an organization who need it in order to do their jobs effectively and efficiently. (426)

Decision support system (DSS) Software that uses models, information, and an interactive user interface to help you make decisions. (459)

deColmar's Arithmometer Developed in 1820, the first mass-produced mechanical calculator. (497)

Decompress "Unshrink" a file back to its original size. (115)

Defragmentation utility Utility software that reallocates file clusters and decreases fragmentation. (114)

Denial-of-service (DoS) attack Causes thousands of access attempts to a Web site over a very short period of time, overloading the target site and shutting it down. (269)

Desktop computer Most popular choice for personal computing needs, with prices ranging from about $500 to several thousand dollars. (13)

Desktop publishing software Application software that extends word processing software by including design and formatting techniques to enhance the layout and appearance of a document. (71)

Device driver Software and information that enables your operating system to establish the communications between your existing hardware and your new device. (105)

Device letter Unique identifier for each different storage device on your computer. (111)

Difference Engine Device invented by Charles Babbage in 1822 which used steam power to crunch numbers. (497)

Digital media Any type of media or information that is represented and stored discretely as a series of 0s and 1s. (80)

Directional microphone Input device that consists of a box or boxes, each containing one or more microphones. (136)

Directory List of the files (and folders) on a particular storage device. (112)

Directory search engine Organizes listings of Web sites into hierarchical lists. (41)

Disk compression utility Utility software that (1) automatically compresses your files of information when you save them to your hard disk and (2) automatically decompresses your files when you access and use them with your application software. (116)

Dithering Process of composing two or more colors to produce the illusion of additional colors and shading. (82)

Documentation Collection of instructions and explanations relevant to a piece of software. (404)

Domain name Unique name for an entire Web site. (39)

Dot pitch Distance between the centers of a pair of like-colored pixels. (139)

Do-until statement Repeats a portion of software code as long as a certain condition doesn't exist (it's false). (399)

Do-while statement Repeats a portion of software code as long as a certain condition exists. (399)

Downward flow of information Strategies, goals, and directives that originate at one level and are passed to lower levels. (429)

DSL (Digital Subscriber Line) modem High-speed telecommunications device using a phone line, which allows you to use your phone line for voice communication at the same time. (52)

DVD burner Drive that lets you read from and write information to a DVD. (147)

DVD-R or **DVD+R (DVD—recordable)** High-capacity optical or laser disc to which you can write one time only. (146)

DVD-ROM High-capacity optical or laser disc whose information can't be changed. (145)

DVD-ROM drive Device that lets you read (or play) a DVD. (145)

DVD-RW (or **DVD+RW** or **DVD-RAM)** Called different names depending on the manufacturer; very high-capacity optical or laser disc on which you can save, change, and delete files. (147)

EBCDIC Coding system, or set of patterns, that large IBM computers use. (168)

E-cash (electronic cash, digital cash) Electronic representation of cash. (334)

Electronic bulletin board Shared message space where you can post inquiries and schedules for events, and participate in discussion threads and chat rooms. (439)

Electronic catalog Electronic product or service presentation in which you enjoy a rich combination of media. (228)

Electronic commerce (e-commerce) Really just commerce—but it's commerce that technology facilitates and enhances. (36, 226)

Electronic job market Makes use of the Internet to recruit employees and is growing by leaps and bounds. (21)

Electronic meeting software Lets a team have a "virtual" meeting. (439)

Electronic Recording Machine Accounting (ERMA) Device developed in 1959 by General Electric. ERMA was the first technology that could read special characters. (499)

E-mail (electronic mail) Software you use to electronically communicate with other people. (18)

Embedded CSS Changes the appearance of a *single type* of HTML tag in *one* HTML document. (242)

Encryption Scrambles information so that it cannot be read without the right decryption key. (236)

End user development Development and support of computer systems by users (such as yourself) with little or no help from technology specialists. (372)

ENIAC Device developed by a team of U.S. scientists in 1943, headed by John Mauchly and J. Prespert Eckert, to calculate trajectory tables for the U.S. Army (498)

ENIGMA Encoded messages for transmission in such a way that the allied forces could not, by hand, decipher them. (498)

Entity-relationship (E-R) diagram Graphical representation of the tables in a database and the relationships among the tables. (296)

E-portfolio Personal Web site that contains your e-resume and a gallery of important projects you've completed, papers you've written, presentations you've made, references, and other types of valuable information. (22)

Ethernet card Most common type of network interface card. (198)

Ethics Set of principles and standards we use in deciding what to do in situations that affect other people. (23, 261)

Event-driven language Responds to actions users perform on the program. (408)

Exception report Report that shows only a subset of available information based on some selection criteria. (433)

Executive information system (EIS) Highly interactive MIS that helps managers solve problems and take advantage of opportunities. (434)

Expansion bus Highway system on the motherboard that moves information coming from and going to devices outside the motherboard. (165, 179)

Expansion card (board) Circuit board that you insert into the expansion slot on the motherboard and to which you connect a peripheral device. (166)

Expansion slot Long skinny socket on the motherboard into which you insert an expansion card. (166)

Expert system (knowledge-based system) Artificial intelligence system that applies reasoning capabilities to reach a conclusion. (465)

External CSS Uses a stylesheet file to change a *single* type of HTML tag in an *entire* Web site. (242)

External information Describes the environment surrounding an organization. (428)

External magnetic hard disk Portable storage unit that you can connect to your computer as necessary. (143)

Extranet Extension of an intranet that allows other organizations and people access to information and application software on an internal intranet. (205, 437)

Fair Use Doctrine Defines the situations in which copyrighted material may be used. (262)

Feature analysis In ASR captures your words as you speak, converting the digital signals of your speech into phonemes. (325)

Field Smallest piece of data, which may be information in a given context. (293)

Field property Type of information in a field (for example, numeric, date, and currency). (294)

File Collection of information you need to use your computer effectively. (110)

File allocation table (FAT) File that stores information about the physical location of every file on your computer's hard disk. (113)

File compression Shrinking of a file into a smaller file. (115)

File compression ratio Determines how small you want a compressed file to be. (115)

File compression software Utility software that allows you to compress and/or decompress a file or files. (115)

File manager utility software (file management system software) Utility software that helps you manage, organize, find, copy, move, rename, and delete files on your computer. (111)

Filename Unique name that you give to a file of information. (110)

Filename extension (extension) Further identifies the contents of your file usually by specifying the file type. (110)

File security software Utility software that contains security features (mainly encryption) to protect your files and folders of information as well as to enable you to send secure e-mail messages. (106)

File sharing Ability to share the files on your computer with others who are part of your network. (202)

File transfer protocol (FTP) Communications protocol that allows you to transfer files of information from one computer to another. (50)

Financial cybermediary Web-based company that makes it easy for one person to pay another person or Web-based business over the Internet. (235)

Firewall Hardware and/or software that protects a computer or network from intruders. (109, 281)

Firewire (IEEE 1394 or **I-Link) connector** Type of connector that allows you to connect hot-swap, plug and play devices to your computer. (177)

Firewire port Where you connect a Firewire device. You can connect up to 63 devices using a single port. (177)

Fiscal feasibility assessment Determines if your organization has sufficient resources to develop the proposed system and if the total cost of those resources falls within an allocated budget. (362)

Flash Software that helps you create animated and interactive Web pages. (45)

Flash memory card High-capacity storage laminated inside a small piece of plastic. (147)

Flash memory drive Flash memory storage device for a computer that is small enough to fit in your pocket and usually plugs directly into your USB port. (149)

Flash plug-in Enables you to view and interact with Flash-based Web pages. (45)

Flat-panel display Thin, lightweight monitor that is used in a notebook computer, tablet PC, PDA, or cellular phone, and increasingly with a desktop computer too. (137)

Floppy disk Removable magnetic storage medium that holds about 1.44 megabytes of information. (144)

Folder Special portion of your root directory into which you can place files that have similar information. (112)

Force feedback Technology that sends electrical signals from a game to the game controller that cause it to shake and move. (134)

Foreign key Primary key field of one database table that also appears in another database table. (295)

For-next statement Repeats a portion of software code a precise number of times. (399)

Fourth generation language (4GL) Machine-independent, high-level nonprocedural language that uses human words and symbols to program diverse computer systems. (406)

Fragmentation Occurs when your computer places parts of files over many disk areas or clusters. (114)

Freeware Public domain software, meaning that you can use it any way you wish free of charge. (86)

FTP program Moves files between computers. (240)

FTP server Maintains a collection of files you can download. (48)

Fuzzy logic Mathematical method of handling imprecise or subjective information. (468)

Gamepad Multifunction input device that includes programmable buttons, thumb sticks, and a directional pad. (133)

Gaming wheel Input device that uses a steering wheel and a separate set of foot pedals to imitate real-world driving. (134)

Gas plasma display monitor Shines light through gas to make an image. (138)

Genetic algorithm Artificial intelligence system that mimics the evolutionary, survival-of-the-fittest process to generate increasingly better solutions to a problem. (467)

Geographic information system (GIS) Software that allows you to see information in map form. (463)

Gigabyte (GB, Gig) Roughly 1 billion bytes of memory or storage. (142)

Gigahertz (GHz) for a CPU Number of billions of CPU cycles per second. (171)

Global positioning system (GPS) Navigational system that uses satellites to tell you where you are, how fast you're going, and what direction you're headed in. (208, 338)

Glove Input device that captures the movements of your hand and fingers. (327)

Graphical user interface (GUI) Graphic or icon-driven interface on which you use your mouse (or some other input device) to start software, use that software, and initiate various other functions. (5)

Graphics software Application software that helps you create and edit photos and images. (72)

Grayscale palette Color palette which is used to produce images and photos in a black-and-white style using shades of gray. (81)

Group document database Powerful storage facility for organizing and managing all documents related to specific teams. (440)

Group scheduling software Provides facilities for maintaining the day-to-day electronic calendars of team members. (439)

Groupware Popular term for the software component that supports team efforts. (438)

Hacker Very knowledgeable computer user who uses his or her knowledge to invade other people's computers. (23, 270)

Hacktivist Hacker who uses the Internet to send a political message of some kind. (271)

Handspring Type of personal digital assistant that uses the Palm Operating System (Palm OS). (104)

Hard disk drive Magnetic storage device with one or more thin metal platters (or disks) that store information sealed inside the disk drive. (142)

Hardware Consists of the physical devices that make up your computer system. (8)

Hardware key logger Hardware device that captures keystrokes on their journey from the keyboard to the motherboard. (177)

Heading tag HTML tag that makes certain information, such as titles, stand out on your Web page. (238, 507)

Headset (head-mounted display, HMD) Combined input and output device that (1) captures the movement of your head from side to side and up and down and (2) includes a special screen that covers your entire field of vision. (327)

Hertz Measure of cycles per second. For monitors it means the number of times per second the screen is refreshed. (139)

Hierarchical database model Creates a hierarchy of relationships among records in a database such that a child record can have only one parent record, but a parent record can have many child records. (297)

High-level language Allows programmers to use words and symbols closer to human language to code software. (406)

Hollerith Tabluating Machine Device that recorded census information for the U.S. government by punching holes into punched cards which could then be read and tabulated by a device consisting of long rods with needles on the end. (497)

Holographic storage device Stores information on a storage medium that is composed of 3-D crystal-like objects with many sides or faces. (331)

Home router Device that connects computers into a network, and also connects dissimilar networks together (like a home network and the Internet), separating the network traffic and keeping local traffic inside its own network. (199)

Horizontal flow of information Information that passes among various departments. (429)

Horizontal market software General business software that has application in many industries. (375)

Hot swap Operating system feature that allows you—while your computer is running—to unplug a given device and plug in a new one without first shutting down your computer. (106, 176)

HTML document File that contains HTML tags and the information you want to appear on your Web page. (238, 504)

HTML tag Specifies the layout and presentation of information on a Web page. (237, 504)

Hyperlink (link) Clickable text or an image that allows you to move from one Web site to another or move to a different place within the same Web site. (17)

Hypertext database Stores each Web address as an object linked to its respective Web page. (306)

Hypertext markup language (HTML) Basic language used to create Web pages. (237, 504)

Hypertext transfer protocol (http) Communications protocol that supports the movement of information over the Web, essentially from a Web server to you. (49)

Icon Graphic representation of something that you click on twice or double-click. (5)

Identity theft Impersonation by a thief of someone with good credit. (24, 265)

If-then-else statement Tests a condition in software code that results in a true or a false. (398)

Image resolution Density of the grid used for an image. (81)

Image tag HTML tag you use to insert images onto your Web page. (514)

Implant chip Technology-based microchip—containing at a minimum personal information but also perhaps GPS-tracking capabilities—implanted into the human body. (344)

Information Organized data whose meaning is clear and useful to you in a given context. (293)

Information granularity Degree of detail information contains. (427)

Inheritance Passing on of properties and methods from a class to an object. (411)

Inkjet printer Printer that makes images by forcing ink droplets through nozzles. (140)

Inline CSS Changes the appearance of a *single* HTML tag in *one* HTML document. (242)

Input Information that comes from an external source and enters the software. (394)

Input device Captures information and translates it into a form that can be processed and used by other parts of your computer. (11, 131)

Instant messaging Private version of a chat room in which you communicate only with people you choose. (19, 131)

Integrated circuit Incorporates many transistors and electronic circuits on a single wafer or chip. (499)

Integrated development environment (IDE) Another name for a software development environment. (402)

Integrity constraint Rule that helps ensure the quality of information in a database. (295)

Intelligent agent (bot) Software that assists you, or acts on your behalf, in performing repetitive computer-related tasks. (469)

Intelligent home appliance Contains embedded computer technology that controls numerous functions and is capable of making some decisions. (341)

Interface hardware Hardware that connects external devices to the motherboard. (179)

Internal information Describes specific operational aspects of an organization. (428)

Internal magnetic hard disk Magnetic hard disk that is contained in your system unit and is your primary storage device for both information and the software you use (including your operating system and application software). (142)

Internet Vast network of networked computers (hardware and software) that connects millions of people all over the world. (39)

Internet backbone Major set of connections for computers on the Internet. (47)

Internet server computer (Internet host computer) Computer on the Internet that provides information and services to other computers and Internet users such as you. (47)

Internet service provider (ISP) Company that provides individuals, organizations, and businesses access to the Internet. (47)

Interpreter Translates one line of source code into object code at a time. (407)

Intranet Internal organizational Internet that is guarded against outside access by special security hardware and/or software called a firewall. (204, 437)

IPO (input-process-output) table Shows what information a piece of software takes in, how it processes the information, and what information it produces. (395)

IRC (Internet relay chat) server Supports your use of discussion groups and chat rooms. (48)

IrDA (infrared data association), also known as **IR** or **infrared, port** Uses infrared light to send and receive information. (178)

Iteration control Another word for repetition control structure. (399)

Java Object-oriented 3GL programming language developed by Sun Microsystems. (411)

JavaScript Scripting language developed by Netscape that you can use to add interactivity and features to a Web page. (247)

Joystick Input device that controls movement on the screen with a vertical handle and programmable buttons. (134)

Key logger (key trapper) software Records keystrokes and mouse clicks. (273)

Kilobyte (KB, K) Exactly 1,024 bytes of memory or storage, but we round to 1,000 for the sake of simplicity. (142)

Language processing In ASR attempts to make sense of what you're saying by comparing the possible word phonemes to rules in a language model database. (326)

Laser printer Forms images using an electrostatic process, the same way a photocopier works. (140)

LCD (liquid crystal display) monitor Shines light through a layer of crystalline liquid to make an image. (138)

Link (hyperlink) Clickable text or an image that allows you to move from one Web site to another or move to a different place within the same Web site. (17)

Link tag HTML tag you use to create links on your Web page to (1) other sites and pages, (2) downloadable files such as audio and video, and (3) e-mail. (238, 512)

Linux Open-source operating system that provides a rich operating environment for mostly high-end workstations and network servers. (103)

List tag HTML tag that allows you to present information in the form of a list, either numbered (using **<ol>** and **</ol>**) or unnumbered (using **<ul>** and **</ul>**). (238, 516)

Local area network (LAN) Network in the same building, complex, or small geographic area. The term is used to describe a small network. (196)

Logic error Mistake in the way an algorithm solves a problem. (394)

Loop Another word for a repetition control structure. (399)

Low-level language Requires programmers to code at a basic level that a computer can understand. (405)

Machine cycle (CPU cycle) Consists of retrieving, decoding, and executing the instruction, then returning the result to RAM, if necessary. (170)

Machine-dependent language Programming language that works only on a specific computer system and its components. (405)

Machine-independent language Programming language that works on different computer systems regardless of their components. (406)

Machine language Machine-dependent, low-level language that uses binary code to interact with a specific computer system. (405)

Mac OS Operating system for today's Apple computers. (103)

Macro Scripting language program that executes a task or set of tasks within a software application. (407)

Macro virus Virus that spreads by binding itself to software such as Word or Excel. (267)

Mail server Provides e-mail services and accounts. (48)

Mainframe computer (mainframe) Designed to meet the computing needs of hundreds of people in a large business environment. (14)

Malware Malicious software that is designed by people to attack some part of a computer system. (267)

Management information system (MIS) System that provides periodic and predetermined reports that summarize information. (432)

Many-to-many relationship *Many* records in a database table can be related to *many* records in another database table. (297)

Mark I First electromechanical computer. (498)

M-commerce (mobile e-commerce) Allows you to use wireless devices such as smart phones or PDAs to buy and sell products and services through Web e-commerce. (56, 228)

Mechanical calculator Device that could autonomously calculate algorithms once you enter the appropriate information. (496)

Mechanical mouse Pointing device that has a ball on the bottom that causes the cursor on the screen to move as the ball rolls. (132)

Megabyte (MB, M, Meg) Roughly 1 million bytes of memory or storage. (142)

Megahertz (MHz) for a CPU Number of millions of CPU cycles per second. (171)

Megapixels Number of millions of pixels in a graphic (number of dots across by the number of dots down). (81, 136)

Membrane-based technology Stores and manipulates information within living tissue cells. (342, 500)

Memory Stick Media Elongated flash memory card about the width of a penny developed by Sony. (148)

Meta tag Provides information for search engines about your Web page. (239)

Microsoft Windows 2000 Millennium (Windows 2000 ME, Windows ME) Personal operating system designed for a home computer user with utilities for setting up a small home network. (102)

Microsoft Windows 2000 Professional (Windows 2000 Pro) Personal operating system for people who have a personal computer connected to a network of other computers at work or at school. (103)

Microsoft Windows XP Home (Windows XP Home) Personal operating system designed for a home computer user with utilities for setting up a small home network. It is the upgrade to Windows 2000 ME. (102)

Microsoft Windows XP Professional (Windows XP Pro) Personal operating system for people who have a personal computer connected to a network of other computers at work or at school. It is the upgrade to Windows 2000 Pro. (103)

Microsoft Windows XP Tablet PC Edition Primary choice of an operating system for a tablet PC. (105)

Microwave communications media Line-of-sight information transmission media. (212)

Middleware Software application that works between two or more different software applications and allows them to talk to each other. (305)

MIDI (Musical Instrument Digital Interface) Standard for storing audio information for computers, electronic MIDI instruments, and synthesizers. (84)

Minicomputer (mid-range computer) Designed to meet the computing needs of several people simultaneously in a small to medium-size business environment. (14)

Mobile CPU Special type of CPU for a notebook computer that changes speed, and therefore power consumption, in response to fluctuations in demand. (181)

Mobile telephone switching office (MTSO) Stores your cell phone's identification and location in its database so that it can find you when calls come in for you. (207)

Monitoring-and-surveillance (predictive) agent Intelligent agent that observes and reports on equipment. (472)

Motherboard Major circuit board inside the system unit connecting all computer components together so that information and instructions can move between them. (164)

Mouse Pointing device that you use to click on icons or buttons; select menu options; highlight text or images; and drag and drop images, text, files, and folders. (132)

MP3 (.mp3) Filename extension for audio that stores good quality sound in a compressed file format but requires the use of a player or a plug-in within a browser. (84)

Multidimensional analysis (MDA) tool Slice-and-dice technique that allows you to view multidimensional information from different perspectives. (310)

Multifunction printer (MFP) Printer that will scan, copy, and fax, as well as print. (140)

MultiMediaCard (MMC) Flash memory card that looks identical to a SecureDigital card (but SD cards have copy protection built-in) and is a little larger than a quarter and slightly thicker than a credit card. (148)

Multimedia Messaging Service (MMS) Technology upgrade to SMS, giving you the ability to send messages containing not only text but also sounds, images, and video, usually from your cell phone to the cell phone of another person. (19)

Multi-state CPU Works with information represented in more than just two states, probably ten states with each state representing a digit between 0 and 9. (331)

Multitasking Allows you to work with more than one piece of software at a time. (101)

Multi-user operating system (multi-user OS) Enables many people simultaneously to use the resources of a central computer, which is usually a minicomputer, a mainframe computer, or a supercomputer. (99)

Nanotechnology Study of controlling individual atoms and molecules to (1) create computer chips that are hundreds of times smaller than current chips and (2) encourage those atoms and molecules to "self-assemble" into new forms. (343)

Napier's Bones Device partially constructed of animal bones that automated multiplication tables by sequencing a series of strips of bones on several different rods. (496)

Natural language Human language that can program a computer. (406)

NCIC (National Crime Information Center) Huge database with information on the criminal records of more than 20 million people. (278)

Network Collection of computers that support the sharing of information, software, and hardware devices. (47, 194)

Network access point (NAP) Point on the Internet where several connections converge. (47)

Network database model Similar in structure to the hierarchical database model except that each child can have more than one parent. (297)

Network hub (hub) Device that connects computers into a network, broadcasting all messages it gets to every computer on the network, although only the intended recipient computer takes the message. (198)

Network interface card (NIC or network card) Expansion card or a PC Card (for a notebook computer) that connects your computer to a network and provides the doorway for information to flow in and out. (195)

Network operating system (network OS, NOS) Runs a network, steering information between computers, managing security and users, and enabling many people to work together across the network. (99, 195)

Neural network Artificial intelligence system that is capable of learning how to differentiate patterns. (466)

Nonprocedural language Requires that a programmer write code to tell the software only what it should accomplish. (406)

Notebook computer (laptop computer) Small, portable, fully functional battery-powered computer designed for you to carry around with you. (13)

Object class Object that contains all of the properties and methods a programming object can possess. (410)

Object code Machine language the computer uses to run your program. (407)

Object instance Exact copy of an object class. (410)

Objective information Quantifiably describes something that is known. (428)

Object method Allows you to manipulate the properties. (410)

Object-oriented database model Uses objects to represent people, places, and things. (297)

Object-oriented programming (OOP) Allows you to interact with objects when you code software. (409)

Object property Identifying characteristic of an object. (410)

One-to-many relationship *One* record in a database table can be related to *many* records in another database table. (296)

One-to-one relationship *One* record in a database table can only be related to at most *one* record in another database table. (296)

Online analytical processing (OLAP) Manipulation of information to generate business intelligence and support decision-making tasks. (309)

Online banking Use of your computer system to interact electronically with your bank, including writing checks, transferring funds, and obtaining a list of your account transactions. (77)

Online transaction processing (OLTP) Processing of information to support some sort of transaction such as the purchase of a product. (309)

Operating system software System software that controls your application software and manages how your hardware devices work together. (99)

Operational management Manages and directs the day-to-day operations and implementation of the goals and strategies. (425)

Optical fiber cable Fastest and most efficient medium for wired communication, using a very thin glass or plastic fiber through which pulses of light travel. (212)

Optical mouse Pointing device that senses movement with red light and moves the cursor accordingly. (132)

Opting in When you give permission for alternative uses of your personal information. (231)

Opting out When you say no to alternative uses of your personal information. (231)

Output Information software produces after it has processed input. (394)

Output device Takes information within your computer and presents it to you in a form that you can understand. (11, 137)

Outsourcing Delegation of work to a group outside your organization for (1) a specified length of time, (2) a specific cost, and (3) a specified level of service. (375)

Palm Type of personal digital assistant that uses the Palm Operating System (Palm OS). (104)

Palm Operating System (Palm OS) Operating system for Palm and Handspring personal digital assistants. (104)

Parallel connector Connector that plugs into a parallel port. It has 25 pins, which fit into the holes in the port. (369)

Parallel conversion Conversion method in which you run both the old and new systems until you're sure the new system works correctly. (177)

Parallel port Where you plug a parallel connector into your computer. (177)

Pascaline Device invented in 1642 which could perform addition, subtraction, multiplication, and division. (497)

Pathname Device letter, folder, subfolder (if present), filename, and extension that together describe a particular file and its location. (113)

Pattern classification In ASR attempts to recognize your spoken phonemes by locating a matching phoneme (or phoneme sequence) among words stored in an acoustic model database. (326)

PC Card Updated version of the traditional PCMCIA card; it's the expansion card you use to add devices to your notebook computer. (181)

PC Card slot Opening on the side or front of a notebook where you connect an external device with a PC Card. (181)

PCI (peripheral component interconnect) bus One part of the expansion bus. It ends in the PCI slots. (180)

PCI slot Type of expansion slot which you'd use to plug in video cards, sound cards, or network cards. (179)

Peer-to-peer collaboration system Software that enables people to communicate and share documents between peers without going through a central server. (206)

Peer-to-peer network Network in which all computers are equal, and each can have access to devices and files on the others. (197)

Periodic report Report that is produced at a predetermined time interval—daily, weekly, monthly, yearly, and so on. (433)

Personal digital assistant (PDA) Small hand-held computer that helps you perform simple tasks such as note taking, maintaining a calendar and appointment book, maintaining an address book, and perhaps even surfing the Web. (13)

Personal finance software Application software that offers you capabilities for maintaining your checkbook, preparing a budget, tracking investments, monitoring your credit card balances, and even paying bills electronically. (77)

Personal information management (PIM) software Application software that helps you create and maintain (1) to-do lists, (2) appointments and calendars, and (3) points of contact. (77)

Personal operating system (personal OS) Enables a single user to use a personal technology such as a PDA, smart phone, tablet PC, notebook computer, or desktop computer. (99)

Personal portal Web page for which you define the content you want to see. (306)

Personal productivity software Application software that is designed to help you be more productive in performing personal tasks such as writing letters, managing your checkbook, and creating electronic slides. (68)

Photo inkjet printer Inkjet printer that can produce good quality photos as well as other documents. (140)

PHP (Hypertext Preprocessor) Server-side scripting language Web developers use to create dynamic Web pages. (248)

Piecemeal conversion Conversion method in which you target only a portion of the new system for conversion, ensure that it works correctly, and then convert the remaining system. (369)

Pilot conversion Conversion method in which you target a select group of users to convert to the new system before converting everyone. (369)

Pirated software Copyrighted software that is copied and distributed without permission of the owner. (262)

Pixel (picture element) One of the dots that make up the image on your screen. (138)

Player Software that works outside your Web browser to play all forms of multimedia (not just Web-based). (44)

Plug and play Ability to add devices to your computer so that your operating system will find and install the appropriate device driver without your having to go through a manual installation. (105, 176)

Plug-in Software that works within your Web browser to play Web multimedia. (43)

Plunge conversion Conversion method in which you unplug the old system and use the new system exclusively. (369)

PocketPC Type of personal digital assistant that uses the Pocket PC OS. (104)

PocketPC OS Operating system for PocketPC personal digital assistants. (104)

Pointing stick Pointing device that consists of a tiny rod that looks like a pencil-top eraser in the middle of a keyboard, and as you move the stick, the cursor on the screen moves correspondingly. (133)

Pop-under ad Form of a pop-up ad that you do not see until you close your current browser window. (230)

Pop-up ad Small Web page containing an advertisement that appears on your computer screen outside the current Web site loaded into your browser. (229)

Port Place on your system unit, monitor, or keyboard through which information and instructions flow to your computer system. (165)

Portability A programming language has the ability to work on a variety of computer hardware and operating systems. (405)

Presentation software Application software that helps you create and edit information that will appear in electronic slides. (76)

Primary key Field in a database table that uniquely identifies a record in that table. (295)

Privacy Right to be left alone when you want to be, to have control over your own personal information, and not to be observed without your consent. (272)

Problem/opportunity statement Concise document that describes the exact nature of the problem or opportunity and provides broad statements concerning how the proposed system will benefit the organization. (362)

Procedural language Requires that a programmer write code to tell software what to accomplish and how to accomplish it. (406)

Processing Manages information according to the software's logic. (394)

Profile filtering Requires that you choose terms or keywords, providing a personal picture of you and your preferences. (233)

Program flowchart Graphical depiction of the detailed steps that software will perform. (363, 393)

Program manual Technical manual for programmers. (404)

Programmer Technology specialist whose expertise lies in taking user requirements and writing software to match those requirements. (363)

Programming framework Collection of software tools you use to create a complete business solution. (409)

Programming language Contains specific rules and words that express the logical steps of an algorithm. (396)

Programming object Item that contains properties and methods to manipulate that information. (409)

Project manager Person who oversees the project from beginning through implementation and support. (363)

Prototype Model of a proposed product (which can be a computer system). (372)

Prototyping Process of building a model that demonstrates the features of a proposed product, service, or system. (372)

PS/2 connector Connector with pins that fit into a small round port in your computer, which is used for keyboards and pointing devices like mice. (177)

PS/2 port Small round port that a PS/2 connector fits into. (177)

Pseudocode Uses English statements to create an outline of the necessary steps for a piece of software to operate. (392)

Psychographic filtering Anticipates your preferences based on the answers you give to a questionnaire. (232)

Query-and-reporting tool Similar to QBE tools, SQL, and report generators in the typical database environment. (310)

Query-by-example (QBE) tool Allows you to graphically represent what information you'd like to see from a database. (302)

RAM (random access memory) Temporary memory that holds software instructions and information for the CPU. (12, 165)

Rapid application development (RAD) Uses prototypes to test software components until they meet specifications. (403)

Raster graphic (bitmap graphic or bitmap) Grid of dots with each dot representing a specific color, which makes up the entire image or photo. (81)

Ray tracing Technique for adding shades and shadows to a 3-D graphic based on the location of a light source. (83)

Record Group of logically related fields. (293)

Refresh rate or vertical scan rate Speed with which a monitor redraws the image on the screen. It's measured in hertz. (139)

Relational database model Stores information in files or tables that have rows and columns. (294)

Rendering Process of covering a wireframe with colors and textures. (83)

Repeater Device that receives a radio signal, strengthens it, and sends it on. (212)

Repetition control structure Instructs a piece of software to repeat a series of instructions until it fulfills a condition or while a condition exists. (399)

Report generator Creates a report in a database environment. (302)

Request for proposal (RFP) Formal document that outlines your logical requirements for the proposed system and invites outsourcing vendors to bid on its development. (377)

Reserved word Command that a programming language has set aside for its own use. (397)

Resolution of a printer Number of dots per inch (dpi) that it produces. (139)

Resolution of a screen Number of pixels it has. (81, 138)

RJ-45 connector (Ethernet connector) Connector that is the same shape as the phone connectors on the ends of your telephone wire, but is wider. (198)

Robot Artificial intelligence device with simulated human senses capable of taking action on its own. (464)

Run-time error Mistake that occurs when you run the software code. (401)

Sampling rate Number of times per second that a sound is captured during the recording process. (84)

Satellite modem Telecommunications device that allows you to get Internet access using a satellite dish. (53)

Scanner Input device that creates an electronic image that your computer can use of text, images, maps, and so on. (135)

Schickard's Calculator Device that used a series of interlocking gears each with ten spokes representing a digit. (497)

Script bunny (script kiddie) Person who would like to be a hacker, but who doesn't have much technical expertise. (271)

Scripting language Interpreted programming language that works within another application to perform tasks. (407)

Search engine Facility on the Web that allows you to find Web sites by providing key words or questions. (40)

Sector Single area on a storage device that can hold a certain number of bytes of a file. (113)

SecureDigital (SD) card Flash memory card that looks identical to a MultiMediaCard (but has copy protection built-in) and is a little larger than a quarter and slightly thicker than a credit card. (148)

Secure Electronic Transaction (SET) Transmission security method that ensures transactions are legitimate as well as secure. (236)

Secure Sockets Layer (SSL) Creates a secure and private connection between a Web client and Web server, encrypts the information, and then sends the information over the Internet. (236)

Selection control structure Tests a condition to decide how a computer will execute software code. (397)

Sequence control structure Makes sure that a computer executes software code from top to bottom, left to right. (397)

Sequential execution When a computer performs each line of software code in the order it appears. (397)

Serial connector Plugs into a serial port and usually has 9 holes but may have 25, which fit the corresponding number of pins in the port. (177)

Serial port Where you connect a serial connector to your computer. (177)

Server-side Web programming language Uses Web server resources to retrieve information, process information, and customize Web pages for users. (247)

Shared information Concept that employees should have access to whatever information they need when they need it. (427)

Shareware Software that you can "test drive" or "try before you buy." (86)

Shockwave Software, published by Macromedia, that helps you create Web pages with significant interactivity through Web multimedia. (45)

Shockwave player Enables you to view and interact with Shockwave-based Web pages (these are often called *shocked pages*). (45)

Shopping cart Software that stores information about your e-commerce purchases. (227)

Short Messaging Service (SMS) Technology that enables you to send a text message, usually from your cell phone to the cell phone of another person. (19)

Shrink-wrap license Document that is shrink-wrapped to the outside of a software box. (86)

Slide rule Helps people work with logarithms and perform mathematical operations by "sliding" an interior strip of wood between two stationary strips of wood. (496)

SmartMedia (SM) card Flash memory card that is a little longer than a CF card with the thickness of a credit card. (148)

Smart phone Cell phone that includes such capabilities as surfing the Web and sending and receiving e-mail. (16)

Sniffer Software that sits on the Internet analyzing traffic. (276)

Software Set of instructions that your computer hardware executes to process information for you. (8)

Software development environment Application that provides programming tools to debug and manage software programs. (402)

Software license Defines the way in which you can use software. (86)

Software patch Small fix to a problem using a piece of software code. (404)

Software suites "Bundles" of related software packages that are sold together. (70)

Software upgrade Substantial revision of existing software to improve its usefulness. (404)

Software version (version) Tells you which iteration of the software you're using. (69)

Source code Contains all the commands and comments a programmer used to code the software. (407)

Spam Electronic junk mail or unsolicited mail, usually from commercial businesses, attempting to sell you products and services. (277)

Speaker Device that produces computer output as sound. (141)

Spoofing Forging the return address on an e-mail so that the e-mail message appears to come from someone other than the sender. (277)

Spreadsheet software Application software that helps you work with numbers, performing calculations and creating graphs. (73)

Statistical tool Helps you apply various mathematical models to the information stored in a data warehouse to discover new information. (311)

Storage device Stores information so you can recall and use that information at a later time. (12, 142)

Storage drive Writes information to the storage medium and reads information from it. (142)

Storage medium Surface where information is stored. Examples are CDs and floppy disks. (142)

Strategic management Provides an organization with overall direction and guidance. (425)

Streaming media Continually sends small parts of a large file to your Web browser as you watch and listen to what you've already downloaded. (45)

Structured decision Decision you can make by applying a formula. (457)

Structured Query Language (SQL) Standardized query language for most DBMSs. (302)

Structure tag HTML tag that sets up the necessary sections and specifies that the document is indeed an HTML document. (505)

Stylus Input device consisting of a thin stick that uses pressure to enter information or to click and point. (135)

Subjective information Attempts to describe something that is currently unknown. (428)

Summarized report Report that aggregates information in some way. (433)

Supercomputer Fastest, most powerful, and most expensive type of computer. (15)

Switch Device that connects computers into a network, sending messages only to the computer that is the intended recipient. (198)

Syntax error Mistake in a software code's grammar. (401)

System bus Electrical pathways that move information between basic components of the motherboard, including between RAM and the CPU. (170)

System champion Management person within your organization who (1) believes in the worth of the system and (2) has the "organizational muscle" to pull together the necessary resources. (363)

System identification code (SID) Unique number that the Federal Communications Commission (FCC) assigned your cell phone carrier. (207)

System programmer Programmer who writes operating system and utility software. (363)

System software Software that determines how your computer carries out technology-specific and essential tasks such as writing to a disk, starting your Web browser software so you can surf the Web, and sending a document to your printer. (9, 68, 98)

System unit What many people refer to as "the computer," that is, the case or box with the motherboard, internal storage units, and power supply. (162)

Systems analysis phase Second phase of the SDLC, which involves modeling how the current system works from a logical (not physical) point of view, identifying its weaknesses and the opportunity to improve, creating a logical model of the new system, and reviewing the project plan. (364)

Systems analyst Technology specialist who understands both technology and business processes. (363)

Systems construction phase Fourth phase of the SDLC that involves actually creating the new system. (367)

Systems design phase Third phase of the SDLC, which involves generating several alternative technical solutions for the new logical model, selecting the best technical alternative, developing detailed software specifications, and—once again—reviewing the project plan. (366)

Systems development project plan Document that includes a list of the project team, the problem/opportunity statement, the project budget, the feasibility assessments, and project timetable. (363)

Systems implementation phase Fifth phase of the SDLC that involves training users, converting existing information to the new system, converting users, acceptance testing, and reviewing the project plan. (368)

Systems investigation First phase of the SDLC in which you seek to lay the foundation for the systems development process by performing four tasks—defining the problem/opportunity, assessing initial feasibility, building the project team, and creating a systems development project plan. (362)

Tablet PC Pen-based computer that provides the screen capabilities of a PDA with the functional capabilities of a notebook or desktop computer. (15)

Tactical management Develops the goals and strategies outlined by strategic management. (425)

TCP/IP (Transport Control Protocol/Internet Protocol) Basic communications protocol that makes the Internet work. (49)

Technical feasibility assessment Determines if your organization has access to or can acquire the necessary hardware and software for the proposed system. (362)

Technical writer Explains concepts and procedures to nontechnical software users. (404)

Telecommunications device Helps you communicate information to people in other locations. (12)

Telecommuter Person who works outside the central office some of the time while connected to the central office through technology. (441)

Telecommuting Use of various technologies (especially telecommunications technologies) to allow employees to work in a place other than a central location. (441)

Telephone modem Telecommunications device that connects your computer through a phone line to a network of other computers. (52)

TFT (thin film transistor) display monitor LCD displays that provide a high-quality, crisp image. (138)

Third generation language (3GL) Machine-independent, high-level procedural language that uses human words and symbols to program diverse computer systems. (406)

Three-dimensional (3-D) technology Presents information to you in such a way that you have the illusion that the object you're viewing is actually in the room with you. (327)

Thrill-seeker hacker Hacker without evil intentions, who may even follow a "hacker's code," so that he or she often reports the security leaks to their victims. (270)

Time feasibility assessment Determines if your organization can develop the proposed system while meeting certain deadlines. (362)

Top-level domain Three-character extension of a Web site address. (40)

Touchpad Pointing device that consists of a little dark gray rectangle—as you move your finger around on it, the cursor on the screen moves accordingly. (133)

Trackball Pointing device that has a ball on the top, which you activate with a finger or thumb to move the cursor on the screen. (133)

Traditional systems development life cycle (SDLC) Structured step-by-step approach to developing systems that creates a separation of duties among technology specialists and users. (360)

Transaction processing system (TPS) System that processes transactions that occur within an organization. (430)

Transnational firm Produces and sells products and services in countries all over the world, so much so that it's difficult to know which country is the firm's home country. (443)

True color palette (24-bit color palette) Takes advantage of 16.7 million different colors. (81)

True search engine Organizes Web sites in such a way that it can provide you with a list of Web sites based on a question you ask. (41)

Unicode Coding system that uses 16 bits instead of 8, allowing for approximately 65,000 (2^{16}) different patterns. (168)

UNIVAC Considered the first commercially available electronic computer. (498)

Unstructured decision Decision for which there is no guaranteed way to get a precise answer. (457)

Unzipping Decompressing a file. (116)

Upward flow of information Describes the current state of the organization based on its daily transactions (such as sales). (429)

URL (uniform resource locator) Unique name for a Web page within a Web site. (39)

Usability How easy it is to use a Web page or site. (228)

USB (universal serial bus) connector Allows you to connect hot-swappable, plug and play devices to your computer. (176)

USB port Where you connect a USB device to your computer. You can even connect multiple USB devices (up to 127) using a single USB port on your computer. (176)

User agent (personal agent) Intelligent agent that takes action on your behalf. (471)

User interface Manner in which you communicate with the software package. (460)

User manual Tells users how to use a software program. (404)

Utility software Provides additional functionality to your computer's operating system. (106)

Utility software suite "Bundle" of utility software tools sold by the same manufacturer. (107)

Vacuum tube Electronic basis for the first-generation computers. (497)

Valid XML document XML document that adheres to a specific DTD. (244)

Variable Word or symbol programmers use to store values in a software program. (401)

VBScript Client-side scripting language based on Visual Basic. (248)

Vector graphic Creates and stores a set of instructions for recreating an image or photo. (81)

Vertical market software Software that is unique to a particular industry. (376)

Videoconferencing software Allows a team to have a face-to-face meeting when members are geographically dispersed. (439)

Video frame rate Number of frames per second (fps) used for a video. (85)

Viral marketing Set of techniques that e-commerce businesses use to gather personal information about you, use that information in their own promotional campaigns, and sell that information to other e-commerce businesses. (232)

Virtual memory Space on your hard disk that holds software instructions for a program currently in use. (174)

Virtual reality (VR) Three-dimensional computer simulation in which you actively and physically participate using special input and output devices such as gloves, headsets, and walkers. (327)

Virus (computer virus) Software designed intentionally to cause annoyance or damage. (23, 108, 267)

Virus hoax E-mail distributed with the intention of frightening people about a nonexistent virus. (268)

VIS (visible image size) Size of the image on a screen. For a CRT it's smaller than the screen measurement, but for LCDs it is identical with screen measurement. (138)

Visual Basic for Applications (VBA) Interpreted scripting language that works within Microsoft Office applications. (408)

Visual Studio .NET Software development environment that allows programmers to write code in Visual Basic, C++, or C# for the .NET framework. (412)

VRML (Virtual Reality Modeling Language) Creates a virtual world in which you have the illusion that you are physically participating in the presentation of Web multimedia. (46)

Walker Captures the movement of your feet and body as you walk or turn in different directions. (327)

WAP (Wireless Application Protocol) Collection of communications protocols that allows wireless devices to access the Web. (246)

WAP-enabled device Any technology that uses WAP. (246)

WAP gateway Server that translates Web pages into a language that WAP-enabled devices can read. (246)

Waveform audio Digital representation of sounds, in which samples of a sound are captured at periodic intervals (called a sampling rate) and stored as unique sequences of 0s and 1s. (83)

Wearable computer Fully equipped computer that you wear as a piece of clothing or attached to a piece of clothing similar to the way you would carry around your cell phone on your belt. (330)

Web audio All of the sounds and music on the Web. (45)

Web authoring software Application software that helps you design and develop Web sites and pages that you can publish on the Web. (71)

Web browser software (Web browser) Software that allows you to surf the Web. (39)

Web cam Video camera that you use to take images for uploading to the Web. (136)

Web client Computer you use to move around the Internet and access the information and services on a server computer. (48)

Web database Supports the access to, modification of, and presentation of information through a Web browser. (305)

Web developer Technical professional who creates Web sites. (237)

Web page Specific portion of a Web that deals with a certain topic. (39)

Web page address Unique name for a Web page within a Web site. (39)

Web personalization Process of customizing a Web page or series of Web pages according to a customer's preferences. (227)

Web server Provides information and services to Web surfers. (48)

Web site Specific location on the Web that you can visit electronically to gather information and perhaps order products and request services. (17, 39)

Web site address Unique name for an entire Web site. (39)

Web site management software Allows you to create, update, and manage all of your Web pages quickly and efficiently. (240)

Web space Storage area where you keep your Web site. (51)

Web video All of the video footage (full-length movies, video clips, trailers, and the like) on the Web. (45)

Well-formed XML document XML document that meets all syntax requirements. (244)

Whiteboard software Lets team members meet, view a presentation, and record electronic notes on a large board called a whiteboard. (439)

White-hat or **ethical hacker** Computer security professional who is hired by the company to find and fix the parts of a network that might be vulnerable to hackers. (271)

WiFi Standard for transmitting information in the form of radio waves over distances of up to 300 feet, often used for wireless access to networks. (20, 200)

Wired communications media Transmit information over a closed, connected path. (211)

Wireframe Complete skeletal structure of a 3-D graphic image, including its internal aspects that you cannot see once the surface colors, textures, and shades have been rendered. (83)

Wireless communications media Transmit information through the air. (211)

Wireless mouse Pointing device that sends signals about its movement to your computer by means of waves. (132)

Wireless network access point (wireless access point or **WAP)** Device that allows computers to access a network using radio waves. (200)

WML (Wireless Markup Language) Markup language based on XML that organizes content so WAP devices can read it. (246)

Word processing software Application software that helps you create papers, letters, memos, and other basic documents. (71)

Workgroup support system (WSS) System that is designed to improve the performance of teams by supporting the sharing and flow of information. (438)

World Wide Web (Web) Multimedia-based collection of information, services, and Web sites supported by the Internet. (39)

Worm Computer virus that spreads itself, not only from file to file, but from computer to computer via e-mail and other Internet traffic. (268)

WYSIWYG HTML editor Displays how your Web page will look in a Web browser as you write the HTML document. (239)

xD-Picture Card (xD) Flash memory card that looks like a rectangular piece of plastic slightly larger than a penny and about as thick, with one edge slightly curved. (148)

XHTML (Extensible HTML) Combines the strict syntax of XML to organize content with the presentation power of HTML to display information on almost any Internet device. (244)

XML (Extensible Markup Language) Markup language that uses customized tags to describe how to organize and exchange information between applications. (243)

XML declaration Tells Web browsers what XML version you're using. (243)

XML DTD (XML Document Type Definition) Contains a list of all valid XML elements and their required order. (244)

XML element One set of XML tags. (244)

XML syntax Set of rules and standards used to organize information for XML use. (243)

Zip disk High capacity removable magnetic storage medium. (144)

Zipping Compressing a file. (116)

did you know? credits

CHAPTER TWO

1. ElectricNews.net; www.enn.ie/news.html?code=8094651
2. The Media Audit; www.themediaaudit.com/
3. eMarketer.com; www.emarketer.com/news/article.php?1001876&c=newsltr&n=lead&t=ad#article
4. Nielsen NetRatings; www.nielsen-netratings.com/
5. Girl Scout Research Institute; www.girlscouts.org/news/net_effect.html
6. Datamonitor; www.datamonitor.com/~a77f1913312e41189c81c91a8bbda805~/all/home/index.asp
7. Pew Internet & American Life; www.pewinternet.org/releases/release.asp?id=46
8. Jupiter Research; www.jmm.com/xp/jmm/press/2002/pr_060302.xml

CHAPTER THREE

1. "Dawn of a New Definition," *Working Woman*, April 2001, p. 14.
2. American Society of Industrial Security, 1999 survey.
3. Jenn Shreve, "Tech Overload," *Working Woman*, April 2001, p. 30.
4. Federal Communications Commission, 2000 survey.

CHAPTER FOUR

1. Symantec Corporation, 2002 survey.
2. Privacy Foundation, 2002 survey.
3. ICSA Labs, published report.
4. Iomega Corporation.
5. Iomega Corporation.
6. American Management Association, 2001 survey.
7. Ibid.

CHAPTER FIVE

1. Federal Communications Commission at www.fcc.gov.
2. Federal Communications Commission at www.fcc.gov.
3. London *Times*, 1987.
4. EMarketer at www.Emarketer.com.
5. EMarketer at www.Emarketer.com.
6. Make-A-Wish-Foundation at www.wish.org.

CHAPTER SIX

1. Bureau of Transportation Statistics at www.bts.gov.
2. Cray at www.cray.com.
3. Cornell University at curious.astro.cornell.edu/question.php?number=31.
4. Useless Facts at www.facts.330.ca/statistics.
5. AngelFire at www.angelfire.com.

CHAPTER SEVEN

1. *NBC Nightly News*, February 1, 2003.
2. Claudia Kalb and Karen Springen, "Is Your Cell Really Safe?" *Newsweek*, August 7, 2000, p. 63C.
3. *USA Today*, June 5, 2002, p. 3B.
4. Ibid.
5. Ibid.
6. CyberAtlas, cyberatlas.internet.com.
7. Server Watch, serverwatch.com.

CHAPTER EIGHT

1. *Information Week*, January 15, 2003.
2. *E-Commerce Times*, August 22, 2000; and Forbes.com, August 16, 2002.
3. *E-Commerce Times*, November 5, 2002.
4. *Information Week*, June 17, 2002.
5. *E-Commerce Times*, August 22, 2000.

CHAPTER NINE

1. Erin Strout, "Spy Games," *Sales and Marketing Management*, February 2002, pp. 30–37.
2. ID Theft Center, www.idtheftcenter.org/html/facts_and_statistics.htm.
3. Sabastian Rupley, "Slammer: The Fastest Spreading Worm Ever," *PC Magazine*, www.pcmag.com/print_article/0,3048,a=36635,00asp.
4. *The Economist*, February 15, 2003, p. 28.
5. ACM's News Wise, www.newswise/com/articles/2003/SAPPHIRE.SSC.htm.
6. Angel Fire, www.angelfire.com/on3/mylastdefense.
7. Useless Facts, facts.330ca/statistics.
8. *Wall Street Journal*, May 7, 2002.

CHAPTER TEN

1. Christina Wood, "Privacy in the Ranks," *Working Woman,* April 2001, p. 13.

CHAPTER ELEVEN

1. Michael, Crichton, "Could Tiny Machines Rule the World?" *Parade,* November 24, 2002, pp. 6–8.
2. Andy Vuong, "New Data-Storage Technology Unveiled," *Denver Post,* April 8, 2002, p. C-1.
3. http://homepage.mac.com/laborcoach.
4. *The Federal Reserve,* 2001.
5. Brightmail, www.brightmail.com.

CHAPTER TWELVE

1. www.mastercard.com

CHAPTER THIRTEEN

1. http://icpc.baylor.edu/icpc/ (retrieved February 4, 2003).
2. http://www.geocities.com/connorbd/varaq/ (retrieved February 4, 2003).
3. Canada.com (February 15, 2003).
4. CNET News.com (January 7, 2003).
5. Sidney (Australia) *Morning Herald,* January 16, 2003.
6. *Associated Press,* January 29, 2003.
7. Sidney (Australia) *Morning Herald,* January 29, 2003.

CHAPTER FOURTEEN

1. Brian Dumaine, "What Michael Dell Knows That You Don't," *Fortune Small Business,* June 3, 2002, pp. 12–14.
2. www.schwab.com.
3. Larry Greenemeier, "Web Services Help MetLife Get Closer to Its Customers," *InformationWeek,* May 27, 2002, www.informationweek.com/story/IWK20020524S0005.
4. www.gartnergroup.com.
5. James Sheats, "Information Technology, Sustainable Development, and Developing Nations," *Greener Management International,* Winter 2001, p. 33.

CHAPTER FIFTEEN

1. Steven Kauderer and Amy Kuehl, "Adding Value with Technology," *Best's Review,* October 2001, p. 130.
2. C. L. Patrick, S. F. Frency, Keith Ng, and C. C. Chan, "A Study of the Roll Planning of Fabric Spreading Using Genetic Algorithms," *International Journal of Clothing Science and Technology* 2 (2000), pp. 50–62.
3. Rick Whiting, "Companies Boost Sales Efforts with Predictive Analysis," *InformationWeek,* February 25, 2002.
4. General Music Collection FAQs, members.tripod.com/~Vinylville/faq-3.html.
5. Angel Fire, www.angelfire.com/on3/mylastdefense.
6. Useless Facts, facts.330.ca/statistics.

photo credits

Fig. 1.6a, p. 11, Courtesy of Kinesis Corporation, www.kinesis-ergo.com

Fig. 1.6b, p. 11, Photo courtesy of IBM

Fig. 1.6c, p. 11, Photo courtesy of Intel Corporation

Fig. 1.6d, p. 11, © RF / Corbis

Fig. 1.6e, p. 11, © Spencer Grant / PhotoEdit

Fig. 1.6f, p. 11, Courtesy of Belkin Corporation

Fig. 1.7, p. 11, © Squared Studios / Getty Images

Fig. 1.8, p. 12, PhotoDisc / Getty Images

Fig. 1.9, p. 12, Photo courtesy of Intel Corporation

Fig. 10, p. 12, Craig Brewer / Getty Images

Fig. 1.11a, p. 13, Courtesy of Belkin Corporation

Fig. 1.11b, p. 13, © Nance S. Trueworthy

Fig. 1.12a, p. 13, Hewlett-Packard Company

Fig. 1.12b, p. 13, Gateway Profile 4

Fig. 1.12c, p. 13, Hewlett-Packard Company

Fig. 1.13a, p. 14, Hewlett-Packard Company

Fig. 1.13b, p. 14, © Steve Chenn / Corbis

Fig. 1.13c, p. 14, © Roger Ressmeyer / Corbis

Fig. 1.14a, p. 16, Source: Fujitsu Siemens Computers

Fig. 1.14b, p. 16, Reproduced with Permission From Motorola, Inc. © 2003, Motorola, Inc.

Fig. 1.14c, p. 16, FOSSIL

Fig. 1.17, p. 20, 3Com Bluetooth PC Card with XJACK antenna

Cut 1.1, p. 23, © Nance S. Trueworthy

Fig. 3.4a, p. 73, © Ronnen Eshel / Corbis

Fig. 3.4b, p. 73, © RF / Corbis

Fig. 3.4c, p. 73, AutoCAD 2002, Autodesk, Inc.

Fig. 3.11a, p. 80, James Martin / Getty Images

Fig. 3.11b, p. 80, © Danny Lehman / Corbis

Fig. 3.11c, p. 80, B. Busco / Getty Images

Fig. 3.12a, p. 81, Gate Bridge Justin Sullivan / Getty Images

Fig. 3.13a, p. 82, Eyewire Collection / Getty Images

Fig. 3.13b, p. 82, Eyewire Collection / Getty Images

Fig. 4.2, p. 99, Courtesy of the Microsoft Corporation

Fig. 4.7, p. 104, Image courtesy of Psion PLC

Cut 4.1, p. 109, McAfee Firewall 4.0 McAfee Security, Network Associates; www.mcafee.com

Fig. 5.1a, p. 130, Photo of Logitech MX700; Courtesy of Logitech International S.A.

Fig. 5.1b, p. 130, Courtesy of Eastman Kodak Company

Fig. 5.1c, p. 130, Image courtesy of KDS USA

Fig. 5.1d, p. 130, Courtesy of Hewlett-Packard Company

Fig. 5.1e, p. 130, Photo courtesy of Iomega Corporation

Fig. 5.1f, p. 130, Photo courtesy of Iomega Corporation

Fig. 5.2a, p. 131, Courtesy of Think Outside, Inc.

Fig. 5.2b, p. 131, Targus Stowaway Keyboard; Courtesy of Targus

Fig. 5.3a, p. 132, Photo courtesy of Microsoft® Corp.

Fig. 5.3b, p. 132, Kensington Technology Group

Fig. 5.4, p. 133, Photo courtesy of Toshiba America Information Systems, Inc.

Fig. 5.5a, p. 134, Photo courtesy of Essential Reality

Fig. 5.5b, p. 134, Photo of Logitech Freedom 2.4; Courtesy of Logitech International S.A.

Fig. 5.5c, p. 134, Kensington Technology Group

Fig. 5.6, p. 135, Epson Perfection 1660 Photo Scanner

Fig. 5.7, p. 135, Source: Fujitsu Siemens Computers

Fig. 5.8a, p. 136, Matsushita Electric Corporation of America

Fig. 5.8b, p. 136, Matsushita Electric Corporation of America

Fig. 5.9a, p. 137, Photos provided by Samsung Electronics America, Inc.

Fig. 5.9b, p. 137, Photos provided by Samsung Electronics America, Inc.

Fig. 5.9c, p. 137, Courtesy of Hewlett-Packard Company

Fig. 5.11a, p. 139, GCC Elite 21 N Laser Printer, Courtesy of GCC Printers

Fig. 5.11b, p. 139, Courtesy of Hewlett-Packard Company

Fig. 5.12, p. 140, Sony DPP-EX7 Digital Photo Printer; Courtesy of Sony Electronics Inc.

Fig. 5.14, p. 143, Courtesy of www.pocketec.net

Fig. 5.15, p. 144, Photo courtesy of Iomega Corporation

Fig. 5.19, p. 146, © Nance S. Trueworthy

Fig. 5.20a, p. 147, Photo courtesy of SanDisk Corporation

Fig. 5.20b, p. 147, © 2003 Olympus America Inc.

Fig. 5.20ca and P5.20cb, p. 147, Memory Stick ® Media with Memory Select Function™ and Memory Stick Duo™; Courtesy of Sony Electronics Inc.

Fig. 5.21a, p. 148, Viking InterWorks, A Sanmina-SCI Company, copyright 2003

Fig. 5.21b, p. 148, Photo courtesy of SanDisk Corporation

Fig. 5.21c, p. 148, Trekstor USA

Fig. 5.22, p. 149, Image courtesy of Palm, Inc.

Cut P5.C, p. 149, © AFP / Corbis

Cut P5.F, p. 159, Image courtesy of Contour A/V Solutions, Inc.

Fig. 6.1a, p. 162, Source: Fujitsu Siemens Computers

Fig. 6.1b, p. 162, Acer America Corporation

Fig. 6.1c, p. 162, Photo courtesy ViewSonic Corporation. Copyright 2003

Fig. 6.2, p. 163, Courtesy, Archos Technology

Fig. 6.3, p. 164, Photo by R.D. Cummings, Pittsburg State University

Fig. 6.4, p. 165, Courtesy, Archos Technology; Photo by R.D. Cummings, Pittsburg State University

Fig. 6.5, p. 166, Photo by R.D. Cummings, Pittsburg State University

Fig. 6.8, p. 169, Photo courtesy of Intel Corporation

Fig. 6.11, p. 172, Photo courtesy of Themaltake Technology, Inc.

Fig. 6.13, p. 173, Kingston Technology Company, Inc.

Fig. 6.15a, p. 175, Photo by R.D. Cummings, Pittsburg State University

Fig. 6.15b, p. 175, Photo by R.D. Cummings, Pittsburg State University

Fig. 6.15c, p. 175, Courtesy of Belkin Corporation

Fig. 6.15d, p. 175, Courtesy of Belkin Corporation

Fig. 6.15e, p. 175, Photo by R.D. Cummings, Pittsburg State University

Fig. 6.15f, p. 175, Photo by R.D. Cummings, Pittsburg State University

Fig. 6.15g, p. 175, Photo by R.D. Cummings, Pittsburg State University

Cut P6.B, p. 177, Allen Concepts, Inc. (www.keykatcher.com)

Fig. 6.17, p. 178, Gyration Mouse, Courtesy of Gyration, Inc.; Photo by R.D. Cummings, Pittsburg State University

Fig. 6.18, p. 179, Copyright ATI Technologies, Inc.

Fig. 6.20, p. 181, Photo courtesy of SimpleTech, Inc.

Fig. 6.21, p. 181, Kingston Technology Company, Inc.

Cut P6.C, p. 187, Photo by R.D. Cummings, Pittsburg State University

Fig. 7.2, p. 195, Box shot copyright © 2002 Red Hat, Inc. All rights reserved. Reprinted with permission from Red Hat, Inc.

Fig. 7.5, p. 199, © Copyright 2003 Linksys Group Inc. All rights reserved.

Fig. 7.6, p. 200, Courtesy of the Microsoft Corporation

Fig. 7.15, p. 211, Spencer Grant / PhotoEdit

Fig. 9.1, p. 261, © Nance S. Trueworthy

Fig. 11.4, p. 327, Science Photo Library / Photo Researchers

Fig. 11.5, p. 329, Courtesy Identix

Fig. 11.6a, p. 329, Euan Myles / Getty Images

Fig. 11.6b, p. 329, Andersen Ross / Getty Images

Fig. 11.6c, p. 329, © Stockbyte

Fig. 11.7a, p. 330, © Forestier Yves / Corbis Sygma

Fig. 11.7b, p. 330, Courtesy of Alex Lightman, Charmed Technology

Fig. 11.7c, p. 330, Photo Courtesy Xybernaut Corporation

Fig. 12.3a, p. 361, Bill Bachmann / Photo Researchers

Fig. 12.3b, p. 361, © A. Ramey / PhotoEdit

Fig. 12.3c, p. 361, RF / Corbis

Fig. 12.3d, p. 361, Blair Seitz / Photo Researchers

Fig. 13.18a, p. 412, Photo courtesy View Sonic Corporation. Copyright 2003

Fig. 14.7a, p. 431, © Charles Gupton / Corbis

Fig. 14.7b, p. 431, © Bonnie Kamin / PhotoEdit

Fig. 14.7c, p. 431, © David Young-Wolff / PhotoEdit

Fig. 14.15, p. 439, © Lisette Le Bon / SuperStock

Fig. A.1, p. 496, RF / Corbis

Fig. A.2a, p. 496, IBM Corporate Archives

Fig. A.2b, p. 496, Andrew Ward / Life File / Getty Images

Fig. A.3, p. 497, © Bettmann / Corbis

Fig. A.4, p. 497, Tony Freeman / PhotoEdit

Fig. A.5, p. 498, © TimePix

Fig. A.6, p. 499, Credit of the Computer History Museum

Fig. A.7, p. 500, Photo courtesy of Intel Corporation

Fig. A.8, p. 501, IBM Corporate Archives

index

d

e

h

i

n

o

p

q

r

s

x

y

z